Few people understand God's ways of handling money better than Ron Blue in his book *Faith-Based Family Finances*. If you want to get out of debt and help fund the great commission, read this book and do what it says.

Dave Ramsey
New York Times best-selling author and nationally syndicated radio talk show host

Worldview matters. Ron Blue and Jeremy White give us a wonderful antidote to the era of conspicuous consumption in which we live. This is a very valuable resource if you're interested in a solidly biblical view of financial planning.

Chuck Colson
Founder, Prison Fellowship

Ron Blue has been making sense out of cents for a long time. This new volume is a much-needed contribution to his library of work. You can count on him for sound, solid financial advice. I'm hoping that every family heeds the good counsel of this good man and this great volume.

Max Lucado
Best-selling author and minister

If you are looking for life-changing financial solutions that really work, search no more! Ron Blue and Jeremy White's masterful application of God's timeless financial truths makes this book a must-have resource for everyone!

Janice A. Thompson, CFP
President, Strategic Financial Solutions, Inc.

Ron Blue understands people, families, and money. If you are looking for practical, biblical financial help, then you've found it. This is a comprehensive book about your family finances.

Dr. Dennis Rainey
President, FamilyLife

In this day of overwhelming expectations, demanding schedules, family pressures, and an unpredictable economy, I want reliable and comprehensive resources at hand that I *know* I can trust. I've just added *Faith-Based Family Finances* to my "essentials" list for this critically important arena of life.

Bob Reccord
Founder and CEO, Total Life Impact Ministries

Barb and I believe that Ron Blue and Jeremy White have penned the gold standard resource of biblical and financial principles for the body of Christ. God has drilled down into Ron's heart for over 30 years the insights, practices, and biblical truths you are holding in this book. Read it. Practice it. Pass it on. And let God be glorified.

Dr. Gary and Barb Rosberg
Cofounders, America's Family Coaches and The Great Marriage Experience; authors of *6 Secrets to a Lasting Love*

Ron offers families a blueprint that, if followed, will lead to financial freedom and contentment. Full of biblical counsel and practical tools, *Faith-Based Family Finances* is a resource your family will turn to again and again.

Andy Stanley
Founding and senior pastor, North Point Ministries

Focus on the Family®
Faith-Based Family Finances

FOCUS ON THE FAMILY®

FAITH-BASED FAMILY FINANCES

Let go of worry and grow in confidence

AUTHORS

RON BLUE WITH JEREMY L. WHITE, CPA

A Focus on the Family Resource Published
by Tyndale House Publishers, Inc.
FocusOnTheFamily.com

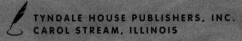
TYNDALE HOUSE PUBLISHERS, INC.
CAROL STREAM, ILLINOIS

TYNDALE and Tyndale's quill logo are registered trademarks of Tyndale House Publishers, Inc.

Focus on the Family and the accompanying logo and design are trademarks of Focus on the Family, Colorado Springs, Colorado 80995.

Faith-Based Family Finances: Let Go of Worry and Grow in Confidence

Copyright © 2008 by Ron Blue. All rights reserved.

Cover photo copyright © by JohnLund/Sarto Harrison/Getty Images. All rights reserved.

Photos of woman and couple on the spine of the cover and back cover photo of boy copyright © by Veer. All rights reserved.

Cover photo of calculator copyright © by iStockphoto. All rights reserved.

Author photo of Ron Blue copyright © by Bern-Art Studios, Atlanta, Georgia. All rights reserved.

Author photo of Jeremy White copyright © by Brad Gholson. All rights reserved.

Designed by Erik Peterson

Published in association with the literary agency of Wolgemuth & Associates, Inc.

Material on inflation myths on pages 94–99, much of the information in chapters 24, 25, and 28, as well as the glossary on pages 547–555 first appeared in *The New Master Your Money* (Chicago: Moody Publishers, 2004) by Ron Blue with Jeremy White. Used with permission.

Material on wealth transfer and estate planning in chapters 20 and 21, as well as guidelines for giving to children in chapter 17 first appeared in *Splitting Heirs* (Chicago: Moody Publishers, 2004) by Ron Blue with Jeremy White. Used with permission.

Much of the material on debt in chapters 10 through 14 first appeared in *Taming the Money Monster* (Colorado Springs: Focus on the Family, 1993). Used with permission.

Material on teaching your children about money in chapter 16 first appeared in *Your Kids Can Master Their Money* (Colorado Springs: Focus on the Family, 2006) by Ron and Judy Blue and Jeremy White. Used with permission.

All Scripture quotations, unless otherwise indicated, are taken from the HOLY BIBLE, NEW INTERNATIONAL VERSION®. NIV®. Copyright © 1973, 1978, 1984 by International Bible Society. Used by permission of Zondervan. All rights reserved.

Scripture quotations marked *The Message* are taken from *The Message* by Eugene H. Peterson, copyright © 1993, 1994, 1995, 1996, 2000, 2001, 2002. Used by permission of NavPress Publishing Group. All rights reserved.

Scripture quotations marked NASB are taken from the *New American Standard Bible*®, copyright © 1960, 1962, 1963, 1968, 1971, 1972, 1973, 1975, 1977, 1995 by The Lockman Foundation. Used by permission.

Scripture quotations marked NKJV are taken from the New King James Version®. Copyright © 1982 by Thomas Nelson, Inc. Used by permission. All rights reserved. *NKJV* is a trademark of Thomas Nelson, Inc.

Scripture quotations marked AMP are taken from the *Amplified Bible*®, copyright © 1954, 1958, 1962, 1964, 1965, 1987 by The Lockman Foundation. Used by permission.

ISBN-13: 978-1-4143-1576-8

Printed in the United States of America

I would like to dedicate this
book to all of those families
who desire to honor God
with the financial resources
entrusted to them.

They are legion, and I am
humbled to be able to assist
in their journey.

Contents

Acknowledgments

I first of all want to acknowledge Jeremy White as one of the most incredibly gifted people that I have ever had the privilege of working with. He has taken my life work, developed over the last 25 years, and compiled it into a very useable and practical form. I also want to acknowledge all of those at Focus on the Family and Tyndale House Publishers who had the vision for this book and gave me the privilege of writing it.

—Ron Blue

F. Scott Fitzgerald once said, "The reason one writes isn't the fact he wants to say something. He writes because he has something to say." I'm far more of a financial nerd than a novelist or acclaimed writer. But I've had "something to say" with Ron Blue's outstanding insights and perspective on managing money wisely. Working with Ron on this project, our fifth book together, is a blessing. Ron has mentored me in my career with his wisdom and content.

I'd like to thank my colleagues and staff at Blythe, White & Associates, PLLC, for their support during my research and writing endeavors. I gratefully acknowledge the encouragement and confidence-boosting from Sharon White, my wife and life partner. I'd also like to thank my daughters, Jaclyn and Jenaye, for their eager support along another writing journey.

—Jeremy White

Many others were involved in the creation of this book, and we have attempted to list them all below:

Focus on the Family

Larry Weeden, Director of Book Development, Curriculum, and Acquisitions

Tyndale House Publishers

Douglas R. Knox, Publisher
Jeff Rustemeyer, Senior Director, Focus on the Family Alliance
Linda Howard, Acquisitions Editor, Focus on the Family Alliance
Kimberly Miller, Editor
Elizabeth Kletzing, Copy Editor

Production

Amanda Haring, Project Manager
Joseph Sapulich, Art Director
Erik M. Peterson, Designer
Sandra Jurca, Typesetter
Keith Johnson, Print Buyer

Introduction

How did this book come about? Its roots can be traced back to a conversation I had in 1979 with my wife, Judy, over a hot-fudge sundae. During that fattening conversation in an ice cream parlor, we wrote a vision on the back of a napkin: to help individuals apply God's principles of stewardship in order to free up financial resources for the fulfillment of the great commission.

This book is more than just a reference book; it's really the result of a lifelong journey. Let me briefly explain my journey, and you may find some parallels in your own journey.

As I was growing up, my family was neither rich nor poor. My parents didn't go to college. My dad worked in a factory to provide for us. We weren't able to buy new clothes or toys but lived with hand-me-downs. I'll never forget the many broken baseball bats and worn-out gloves we taped together. I was motivated—by many wrong motives—to succeed.

At the age of 24, I had every appearance of success—a master's degree in business, my certified public accountant (CPA) license, a well-paying job in the New York City office of the world's largest CPA firm, ambition, and a pretty and supportive wife.

I didn't have a personal relationship with God at that time. I thought too much religion would get in the way of my focused effort to succeed. Oh, I went to church when it was raining—when it was sunny I was working on my golf game and networking for clients.

By the age of 32, I had achieved the financial goals I had set:

- I had moved rapidly up the corporate ladder.
- I had founded the fastest-growing CPA firm in Indiana, and it became one of the 50 largest accounting firms in the United States.
- Two partners and I owned two small banks in Indiana.
- I had the outward signs of success: new cars, country club memberships, and a new home.

Then our family experienced its first significant crisis. My wife, Judy, nearly died in 1972 through a series of medical problems. From that experience, she began seeking answers to the eternal questions of life. That search led her to a personal relationship with Jesus Christ. I didn't mind her pursuing some answers for comfort after her illness. What did bother me, though, was her asking what I thought about the Bible and about Jesus Christ.

Her question threatened the safe, socially conscious world I had created. Ever the sensitive husband, I turned on Judy and nearly exploded. "I know more about the Bible than you do," I said. Then I pointed out that I'd gone to a Christian elementary school and attended church all my life.

I now know that my anger back then stemmed from the conviction I felt because of my wife's gentle question. I had been pursuing an agenda leading to what I thought was success. Just as my efforts were paying off, Judy began asking me about my thoughts on Christianity.

Judy didn't argue with me. In fact, she said little about her faith for two years. The Bible instructs wives in this situation to win their husbands over without words but by their behavior (1 Peter 3:1-2). That's what Judy did. She continued to study her Bible, and she radiated vitality and a constant joy. Reluctant as I was to admit it, I could not help but notice the change in her life.

I attended church enough to hear a teacher manage to work something called "The Four Spiritual Laws" into his lesson: *God loves you and offers a wonderful plan for your life; Man is sinful and separated from God; Jesus Christ is God's only provision for man's sin; and We must individually receive Jesus Christ as Savior and Lord.*[1]

One day I found an evangelism tract with these four spiritual laws lying on my dresser. (To this day, Judy insists she did *not* put it there!) I put it in my pocket as I was headed out to play golf. Alone in the car en route to the golf course, I read through the four laws again. I knew they were true, and I made a conditional commitment to the Lord: "I believe in Jesus and I accept Him as my Savior," I said. "But I'm not going to change my life!"

Actually, I was not trying to be flippant. I reasoned that if what the Bible said about Jesus was really true and I accepted it, then my life would change on its own, without my forcing the issue. I was right, but I wasn't prepared for how quickly the change would take place. After playing the few first holes of golf that afternoon, I suddenly realized I had stopped swearing. Likewise, my desire for alcohol disappeared.

My whole way of looking at life, in fact, took a dramatic turn. I began to value my time with my family more and more—to the point where I almost resented my business contacts and commitments on the golf course. This represented a major change in my thinking, since I had once been consumed with the pursuit of wealth, power, and social recognition. And although I didn't immediately tell Judy about my decision on the way to the golf course, she spotted the difference.

Meanwhile, the business I had started continued to thrive. I sat behind my expensive mahogany desk each day and enjoyed calling the shots on all manner of financial decisions. But when Judy and I got involved in a citywide evangelistic campaign, I realized that my daytime activities could not compare to the work we pursued each evening during the crusade. I was in charge of the telephone center located in a warehouse that took calls from people who saw the campaign on television. Each night, sitting behind my stark metal desk in the barren warehouse, I tallied the results as our evangelism team ministered on the telephones to callers from all over the city. I knew that humble as it appeared, my ugly metal desk saw far more significant "profits" than its daytime mahogany counterpart.

My wife and I began to pray about a career change. Eventually, we sensed God calling us to move to Atlanta to work full-time in ministry. We knew the change would be dramatic. When we arrived in Georgia, we had four children; a smaller, 20-year-old house; and only 20 percent of the income to which we had grown accustomed in Indiana.

In my new role as an employee of a ministry, I was regularly traveling to Africa. I made 11 trips to Africa in a two-year period. When I was back in the United States, I was preparing for and leading seminars.

You can imagine how difficult it was for Judy—a mother with four kids and one on the way in a new town without family nearby and a husband gone 70 percent of the time. She called me at the office one day and asked, "How do you get 'un-Christianed'?"

Somewhat surprised, I asked, "What do you mean?"

She stated rather strongly, "If this is the abundant life I'm supposed to have, then I have all the abundance that I can take!"

I realized we needed some date time. So we went to our favorite ice cream shop, talked about a different job option, and jotted on a napkin the vision of helping individuals apply God's principles of stewardship in order to free up financial resources for the fulfillment of the great commission.

Our conversations and prayers led to starting a financial planning firm to achieve that vision and then to writing books to help others who may never be clients of my firm.

This book is by far the most comprehensive financial book I've ever written. In it, I explore the various financial stages of life and common financial concerns. As I do, you will learn to arm yourself with the truth and fortify yourself in a position of uncompromised freedom from fear—even amid the most uncertain or unstable financial conditions. Armed with such a proactive approach to financial planning, you can maximize your potential for posterity and prosperity while looking forward to a secure and stable future.

Certain financial strategies and topics covered in parts 2 and 3 of this book are based on U.S. tax code and legislation. But no matter where you live, I believe you will benefit from this book because the principles are rooted in biblical guidelines on the use of money, which, when followed, inevitably lead to a contented and meaningful life.

Perhaps you picked up this book because your family is struggling with specific financial questions or concerns, some of which may even keep you up at night. If so, you may be surprised—maybe even a little frustrated—that I don't address these questions right away (though I suspect you will find the answers you're looking for later in this book). The reason is simple: Unless the proper spiritual foundation is laid first, you'll never experience real financial freedom. You might apply a surface solution to the problem, but until the fundamentals are in place, you're likely to experience the same difficulty again, though perhaps in a different form.

To illustrate the importance of one's spiritual outlook in the area of finances, I often ask people to picture an iceberg. The entire iceberg represents all the wealth and resources for which you are responsible. It includes both financial and spiritual capital.

Your financial capital includes money and material assets such as land, stock, and jewelry and is represented by the ice you see emerging from the water.

Spiritual capital is knowing the Bible and being able to apply it. Spiritual capital manifests itself in understanding biblical absolutes, having a relationship with Jesus Christ, walking by faith, trusting God, knowing biblical principles of money management, developing child-rearing skills, and improving your relationship with your spouse. It is represented by the portion of ice below the surface. (By the way, scientists estimate that about 90 percent of an iceberg is below the ocean's surface.)

The visible or more obvious part of the iceberg deals with the "How?" questions of the financial tools, methods, and strategies. The more substantial portion of the iceberg, which provides its girth, volume, and support, is below the surface. It represents the less obvious spiritual capital, dealing with the "Why?" questions that drive financial decisions.

After being asked many different financial questions—whether by small groups of clients or in large seminars or by *Time* magazine reporters—I've learned that the answers all trace back to biblical wisdom. All good advice has roots in Scripture, but Wall Street and Main Street don't know it.

Because of my passion to spread God's truth concerning finances to as many people as possible, several years ago I transitioned from heading a financial planning firm to leading Kingdom Advisors. This organization equips other financial advisors to convey a biblical outlook on finances to their clients. Even this current project—the book you are holding—is designed to show that biblical wisdom is relevant to all good financial decisions. More than just a reference book, *Faith-Based Family Finances* is the result of the journey the Lord has brought me through. I've tried to bring together in one book all the learning, advising, counseling, and teaching I've done for over 40 years.

To help you navigate, I've divided the book into four major parts:

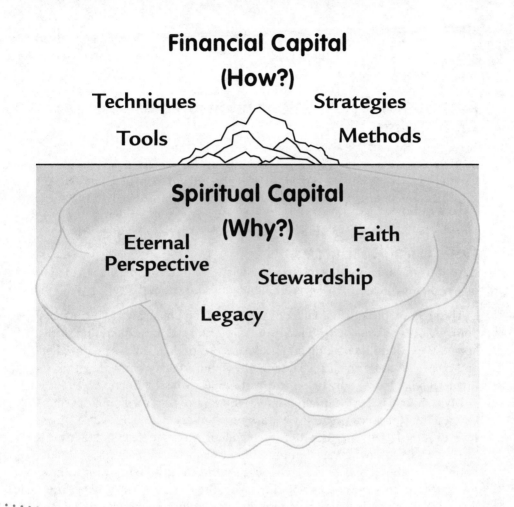

Financial Capital (How?)

Techniques Strategies

Tools Methods

Spiritual Capital (Why?)

Eternal Perspective Faith

Stewardship

Legacy

Part 1—The Big Picture: A Biblical Approach to Financial Decision Making

My approach in the first part is to explore topics applying to everyone, whether young or old, lower-middle class or upper class, financial novice or financial professional. This part lays the foundation and—by providing a biblical perspective—is different from secular money-management guides. All good financial advice has its roots in biblical wisdom.

Part 2—Managing Money through the Stages of Life

This part covers various topics from budgeting and credit card management to choosing pension options. For your ease as a reader, we group these topics among typical stages of a family's life cycle. For example, young married couples likely face the challenges of setting up a household, managing debt, and teaching kids about money. A 63-year-old will be more interested in wealth transfer and retirement issues.

Part 3—Financial Topics and Strategies: An In-Depth View

Because this section is divided into specific financial topics, you can find more in-depth information on specific subjects of interest. These topics generally apply to various stages of life and are not limited by age. Find out more about investment strategies or what insurance to avoid or how to choose a financial advisor.

Part 4—Bringing It Home: Final Thoughts and Additional Resources

Here you will find information on laws affecting your credit, more information on saving for college, a list of recommended resources, and a glossary.

Throughout the book I've included worksheets for you to use as you evaluate your finances and make decisions. You'll also find sidebars containing stories about several families making financial decisions of their own. And question-and-answer sections in each chapter address topics such as how long to keep financial records and how to make Christmas less stressful financially.

My writing partner is Jeremy White, who is also a certified public accountant and author. Because he's still working regularly with clients at his firm, he brings fresh, current insight on the challenges readers face. Neither of us intends this book to serve as an investment or financial planning textbook. Rather, it's written as a book of encouragement to those who want to have the proper perspective and plan for managing the resources entrusted to them by God. You *can* experience more contentment, reduce your stress about your financial future, and leave a meaningful financial and spiritual legacy. More important, you can look forward to standing before the Lord and hearing Him say, as He said to the faithful steward:

> Well done, good and faithful servant! You have been faithful with a few things; I will put you in charge of many things. Come and share your master's happiness! (Matthew 25:23)

PART 1

The Big Picture: A Biblical Approach to Financial Decision Making

IT'S A LITTLE OVERWHELMING to have to decide where to begin a book that weighs as much as the weights I work out with. I'm an avid reader, but committing to reading a book as large as this one causes me to pause. So how do I go about writing something so voluminous that it would scare me as a reader?

Here's the approach that Jeremy White and I came up with. We decided to delve into the key principles of a biblical approach to financial decision making first. That's the content of part 1. Then we'll drill down into more and more detail.

As I've transitioned away from working with clients to equipping financial advisors, I've spent more time researching and focusing on God's big-picture principles—such as acknowledging that God owns it all, defining the finish lines, and having an eternal perspective when making decisions. This runs counter to the worldly wisdom of "get rich quick" and accumulate perpetually in case something happens. It's no wonder people are stressed, because they never know if they have enough and they have no security if the stock market tanks. I'm convinced that focusing on God's principles as explained in His Word is where we need to start this book and where everyone needs to begin when trying to understand how to master their money without their money mastering them.

As I said previously, I've worked professionally in accounting, financial planning, and investing for over forty years. I've seen God's principles on managing money work in my own life, in the lives of hundreds of clients, and in the lives of thousands of others. I've seen the financial successes and failures of people from the vantage points of both before I was a Christian and after. I can confidently say that I've seen God's principles work. As my late friend Larry Burkett often said, "These principles don't work because I say they do; they work because God says they do."

Here's how I've organized part 1:

CHAPTER 1

Money: A Tool, a Test, and a Testimony

Perhaps, like me, you have briefly daydreamed about having a dependable butler. The portrayal of butlers in the movies—perpetually proper with their British accents and black suits—interested me as I was growing up. Though I never knew anyone with a butler, who wouldn't want someone to carry out the errands of the household efficiently and amicably?

Another common English word for a butler is *steward*. Some of the general definitions of *steward* follow:[1]

- one employed in a large household or estate to manage domestic concerns (as the supervision of servants, collection of rents, and keeping of accounts)
- shop steward
- a fiscal agent
- one who actively directs affairs: manager

In Christian circles, we use the terms *steward* and *stewardship* quite often. We usually apply them to someone who handles money wisely and gives regularly to the church. Actually, the Bible doesn't use the exact word *steward* for this meaning. If you look in a Bible concordance for the New International Version, you will find only a few uses of the word *steward*. All of those uses are in the typical context of an employee working for his employer or serving food or drink.

Throughout the Bible, however, the concept of stewardship is pervasive. The recurring idea is that God owns it all and that we are managers for a temporary period. All we have is from God's hand. He entrusts us with it. Throughout this book, here's our working definition of stewardship from a biblical perspective:

Biblical stewardship: The use of God-given gifts and resources (time, talent, treasure, truth, relationships) for the accomplishment of God-given goals and objectives.

As His steward, I use whatever He's given me for His goals and objectives. I'm trying to accomplish what He's asked me to do by using what He's given me. You could use the above definition of *biblical stewardship* to define *success* also. Someday I want to hear Him say, "Well done, good and faithful servant."

Let me illustrate what stewardship is by telling a story about a man who goes off on an extended trip:

> He called his servants together and delegated responsibilities. To one he gave five thousand dollars, to another two thousand, to a third one thousand, depending on their abilities. Then he left. Right off, the first servant went to work and doubled his master's investment. The second did the same. But the man with the single thousand dug a hole and carefully buried his master's money.
>
> After a long absence, the master of those three servants came back and settled up with them. The one given five thousand dollars showed him how he had doubled his investment. His master commended him: "Good work! You did your job well. From now on be my partner."
>
> The servant with the two thousand showed how he also had doubled his master's investment. His master commended him: "Good work! You did your job well. From now on be my partner."
>
> The servant given one thousand said, "Master, I know you have high standards and hate careless ways, that you demand the best and make no allowances for error. I was afraid I might disappoint you, so I found a good hiding place and secured your money. Here it is, safe and sound down to the last cent."
>
> The master was furious. "That's a terrible way to live! It's criminal to live cautiously like that! If you knew I was after the best, why did you do less than the least? The least you could have done would have been to invest the sum with the bankers, where at least I would have gotten a little interest.
>
> "Take the thousand and give it to the one who risked the most. And get rid of this 'play-it-safe' who won't go out on a limb. Throw him out into utter darkness." (Matthew 25:14-30, *The Message*)

God owns it all; we are managers for a temporary period.

I borrowed this story from Jesus, the genius storyteller. He told it primarily to give us a picture of His ultimate return, but it also gives us a picture of what it means to be a steward. I've read and taught from this passage many times, but God continues to provide new lessons from this insightful parable.

Let me comment on four biblical principles of money management, or biblical stewardship, in this story.

1. **God owns it all.** It's evident the master owns the money and gives it to the servants. Few Christians would argue that God owns it all, and yet if we follow that principle to its natural conclusion, there are three revolutionary implications. First of all, God has the right to whatever He wants, whenever He wants it. It's all His, because an owner has *rights*, and I, as a steward, have only *responsibilities*. I may receive some benefits while meeting my responsibilities, but the owner retains ownership.[2]

One of the reasons my hair turned gray early in life is because I taught five teenagers to drive. When my oldest child reached driving age, she was very eager to use my car, and as her father, I entrusted my car to her. There was never any question that I could take back my car at any time for any reason. She had responsibilities. I maintained all the rights. I, as the owner, gave her a great benefit by entrusting her with the car's use, and she returned that benefit with responsible use and care of the car. In the same way, every single possession that I have comes from someone else—God. I literally possess much but own nothing. God benefits me by sharing His property with me. I have a responsibility to Him to use it in a way that glorifies Him.

> It's all God's, because an owner has *rights*, and I, as a steward, have only *responsibilities*.

Try this exercise for me. If you own your own home, take a walk around your property to get a feel for the reality of this principle. Go barefoot if weather permits. Reflect on how long that dirt has been there and how long it will continue to be there. Then ask yourself if you really own it or whether you merely possess it. You may have the title to it in your fireproof file cabinet, but that title reflects your right to possess it temporarily, not forever. Only God literally owns it forever.

The ultimate truth about God's ownership of financial resources is found in Haggai 2:8. When encouraging the Israelites, recently back from their exile, to finish rebuilding the Temple, God reminded them of an important truth: "The silver is mine and the gold is mine, declares the LORD Almighty." Not only does God own it all, He has given written instructions regarding the proper attitudes and decisions about money and its management. We'll discuss these shortly.

If you really believe that God owns all your resources, two things will happen. First, you will treat each financial decision as something important to God because you are handling His resources. Second, you will have less anxiety regarding money because, rather than being an owner of financial resources, you are a manager, trustee, or steward of someone else's resources—and He has promised to meet all your needs.

Therefore, whether you have a little or a lot becomes unimportant to you. That's true contentment.

If you really believe that God owns it all, then when you lose any possession, for whatever reason, your emotions may cry out, but your mind and spirit have not the slightest question as to the right of God to take whatever He wants, whenever He wants it. Really believing this also frees you to give generously of God's resources to God's purposes and His people.

Every spending decision is a spiritual decision.

The second implication of God owning it all is that not only is your giving decision a spiritual decision, but *every spending decision is a spiritual decision*. Notice in the story how much leeway the master gave the stewards. He didn't set any limits or state any restrictions. There is nothing more spiritual than buying a car, taking a vacation, buying food, paying off debt, paying taxes, and so on. These are all responsible uses of His resources. He owns all that you have. He doesn't say you must use it all in one way, say as an offering. He doesn't say you must use it all the same way each time. He gives us resources to provide for us, benefit us, and reach the world for Christ. Many God-glorifying responsible uses fit into these broad categories.

FAMILY FINANCE

Brian and Tanya Park sat together at the back of the church, holding hands as people slowly filed out of the sanctuary.

Tanya wiped her eyes. "It was a beautiful funeral, wasn't it? So many people came. I still can't believe Grandpa's gone, though."

Brian put his arm around her. "I know you'll miss him, honey. Man, I just hope people have such great things to say about me when I'm gone."

"I know what you mean, Brian. He really was one of a kind," Tanya said. "I have so many wonderful memories of him playing catch and Candyland with me when I was little." She laughed. "Grandpa even took me clothes shopping once when I was a teenager and needed a new dress for Homecoming. I can still see the embarrassed look on his face when I made him sit down outside the dressing rooms and tell me what he thought about everything I tried on."

"Do you know what surprised me most about what I heard today?" Brian asked. "He can't have made much money working as a maintenance man at that factory, and he lived very simply. Yet he still gave a lot away. He definitely trusted God to meet his needs."

"I know. He told me that when he and Grandma were first married, they couldn't make ends meet. One time the only solution they could see was to take money out of the tithe envelope and use that to pay for groceries. They prayed about it and decided they just couldn't

Think about the freedom of knowing that if God owns it all—and He does—He must have some thoughts about how He wants you to use His property. The Bible reveals many specific guidelines as to how the Owner wants His property used. As a steward, you have a great deal of latitude, but you are still responsible to the Owner. Someday you will give an accounting of how you used His property.

The third implication of the truth that God owns it all is that *wise stewardship is an indicator of spiritual health.* Your checkbook reveals all that you really believe about stewardship. Your life story could be written from your checkbook. It reflects your goals, priorities, convictions, relationships, and even the use of your time. A person who has been a Christian for even a short while can fake prayer, Bible study, evangelism, and going to church, but he can't fake what his checkbook reveals. Maybe that is why so many of us are so secretive about our personal finances. Even within accountability groups, where people share many intimate struggles, it's rare that anyone shares about how much (or how little) he or she gives.

2. **We are in a growth process.** In reading the Scriptures, we can't escape the truth that our time on earth is temporary and is to be used for our Lord. I believe that God uses money and material possessions in our

take what they knew was God's money, even though they weren't sure how they would pay all their bills. The very next day, a neighbor told Grandpa he'd pay him to help him reroof his house! God was faithful to him when he was faithful in his giving."

"You know, Tanya," Brian said, "maybe we should think a little more about how to imitate your grandpa. We haven't been very deliberate about our finances since we got married last year. We haven't set a budget, and we sure haven't been tithing. We worry about money a lot more than we pray about it."

"Well, we did have to put down a lot for our apartment deposit, not to mention the furniture," said Tanya. "And then there are all those student loans."

"I'd hate to see us dig ourselves into a hole like my brother and his wife did," said Brian. He paused. "Remember my friend Rob at work? He told me that he and Kathy met with a financial planner a few weeks ago. Sounds like they learned a lot about how to budget and begin building their retirement fund."

Tanya was quiet for a minute. "A financial planner? Isn't that a bit premature? I mean, it's not like we have a lot of money or assets to worry about."

"Actually, Tanya, maybe now is the best time to talk to someone about our finances—before we have enough to really mess up," Brian said. "Life is a bit more complicated than it was when Grandpa started out."

earthly lives as *a tool*, *a test*, and *a testimony*. The apostle Paul seems to have mastered this growth process. As he says in Philippians 4:11-12:

> I am not saying this because I am in need, for I have learned to be content whatever the circumstances. I know what it is to be in need, and I know what it is to have plenty. I have learned the secret of being content in any and every situation, whether well fed or hungry, whether living in plenty or in want.

Money and material possessions are effective tools that God uses to help you grow. Therefore, you always need to ask, *God, what do You want me to learn?* You should not focus on the question (really a whine) *God, why are You doing this to me?* My role as a counselor has been to help people discover what God is teaching them, whether from their abundance or from their apparent lack of financial resources. God is not trying to frustrate us. He is trying to get our attention, and money is a great attention-getter.

Money is not only a tool; it is also a test.

FAITH & FINANCE

> So if you have not been trustworthy in handling worldly wealth, who will trust you with true riches? And if you have not been trustworthy with someone else's property, who will give you property of your own? (Luke 16:11-12)

I don't understand it, but I do know that somehow our eternal position and reward are determined irrevocably by our faithfulness in handling property that has been entrusted to us by God. And not only that, but this verse and others indicate that God trusts the true riches of knowing and understanding Him more to those who show their resolute commitment to Him in tangible ways, such as letting go of money or relationships. Remember our story earlier in this chapter about the faithful servants? Two were rewarded with even more, and the other had some taken away.

In Matthew 5:13-16, Jesus tells His followers that we are called to be salt and light. I believe we can say God can utilize our use of His resources as a testimony to the world. Our attitudes toward wealth as Christians become a testimony. Our attitudes when He withholds anything we desire are also a testimony. Our verbal praise when He arranges and allows financial blessings—or prevents our undoing—is also a testimony. Has He worked a financial miracle for you? Don't discount it as coincidence. Don't forget it years down the road when you have more affluence.

Remember, rest, and revel in His answered prayer over financial matters; just don't let resentment creep in when things don't go your way in human terms. This is teaching time. This is testimony time. Have you failed in your use of God's money? What was your response to His "no"? What is your verbal witness of His involvement in your life? Don't let your first failure keep you so defeated that you talk yourself into failing again. Confess it, receive His mercy, and move on. You'll have another chance tomorrow. Remember, growth is a process, not a once-for-all event. Jesus wants children who rely on Him and students who listen to Him, not grown-up graduates who don't need Him anymore.

3. **The amount is not important.** When you look back at the story of the three servants, notice that the commendation for the first two servants is exactly the same. Both are reminded that they have been faithful with a few things and both are promised something as a reward. You can draw the conclusion that the amount you have is unimportant but how you handle what you have been entrusted with is very important.

Yet as I was meditating on this story again for this book, I paused when reading the tongue-lashing that the master gives the unfaithful servant. Before this third servant is cast out into the darkness, his portion is given to the one who already has the most. Why is it not given to or shared with the other commended servant? They both doubled their shares. They both received the same commendation.

Perhaps the master feels the first servant can manage more and wants to bless him for the risk undertaken. It occurred to me that I have no idea why the master does what he does, but that it doesn't

> ## God uses money and material possessions as *a tool, a test,* and *a testimony.*

matter. It's his money. He can do what he wants to do with it. I don't need to know, and I don't have a right to know. It was his to begin with and his to decide what to do with. That's a life-changing thought.

How much energy and time do we waste trying to figure God out when He just wants us to be faithful? Why do some people in this world have more than I do? I don't know. I'm only accountable for what He's given me. I'm not the auditor; it's not my job to determine if everyone's received what I think is fair. Most of us don't ask, "Why do some have less than me?" We should be thankful for what we have.

There is much controversy today about whether an American Christian is more spiritual by accumulating much (God's "blessing") or by giving it all away (God's "martyr"). I believe that both are extremes and not reflective of what God desires. He neither condemns wealth nor commends poverty, or vice versa. The principle found in Scripture is that He owns it all. Therefore, hold with an open hand whatever He chooses to give you, allowing Him to entrust you with more if He so chooses, or allowing Him to take whatever He wants. It is all His. That is the attitude He wants you to develop, and whatever you have—little or much—your attitude should remain the same.

4. **Faith requires action.** Simply knowing God owns it all isn't enough. The lazy and wicked servant knows he has his master's money, but he does nothing. Many of us know what we ought to do, but we disobey or delay. We have emotional faith and/or intellectual faith, but not volitional faith. We know, *but* . . .

We know deep down what God would have us do, but we take no action because of the fear of making a mistake biblically or financially. Or we are frustrated and confused. We do only what we feel good about. Living by our feelings rather than the truth can be very dangerous. Jesus said, "I am the way and the truth and the life. No one comes to the Father except through me" (John 14:6).

Also, we are constantly bombarded with worldly input, which tells us to acquire and consume. This mind-set is so pervasive that it has affected many people's worldview—and consequently their beliefs and actions—without them realizing it.

Unfortunately, when you ask people about their worldview, most give you a blank stare. They likely have no idea what the word even means. Yet it colors every one of their perceptions and actions. A worldview epitomizes a person's ultimate core belief. It is the sum total of our convictions about ourselves and the world we live in.

The dictionary defines *worldview* as: (1) the overall perspective from which one sees and interprets the world; and (2) a collection of beliefs about life and the universe held by an individual or a group.[3] Your belief system, or worldview, comes from somewhere, whether television shows, friends, old wives' tales and superstitions, advertising, or family. Perhaps the most common worldview today—one that is evident in consumer advertising—is "it's all about me."

Yet my aim, and I suggest the same for you, is to have a biblical worldview that drives you to take the right actions. Unfortunately, the polls and research conducted by George Barna indicate that only 4 percent of adults have a biblical worldview and only 9 percent of born-again Christians have a biblical worldview.[4] These findings are startling, since a biblical worldview should be the basis for all decision making by believers. How can we act like Jesus if we don't think like Jesus?[5]

If you have a biblical worldview, then your behavior is dictated by what the Bible says. It follows, then, that your financial decision making is based on the biblical understanding that God owns it all and you're a steward. You're not driven by what advertisers tell you about how you need the newest car, beauty products, or other creature comforts financed by expensive debt.

But if your worldview is "grab the gusto" and "he with the most toys wins," then you may make the wrong decisions and choose the wrong products. The underlying worldview is a potent part of lifestyle decisions: living in a certain neighborhood, dressing a certain way, or driving a particular car. You may come to the erroneous conclusion that these lifestyle decisions will make you attain more importance, appear more attractive, experience less pain, and escape from challenges.

You may be thinking, *Now, wait a minute, what does worldview have to do with personal finances? I just want to manage debt, learn to budget, invest more wisely, or understand insurance.* Later in this book we'll cover the technical aspects of these financial basics. But your worldview has everything to do with *why* and *how* you make decisions. Ultimately, it determines whether you'll be a good steward of God's resources.

What Does a Good Steward Look Like?

The leader of a large evangelical organization once asked me what a major donor would look like. I answered that if a person *looks* as if he can give large sums of money by the home in which he lives, the car he drives, and so on, chances are good that he is actually *unable* to give significantly. Outward looks can be deceiving.

From my experience and observations, I can generally tell whether someone is a good steward or not. But until recently I hadn't developed a succinct list describing what a good steward looks like. When preparing to speak at a philanthropy conference of generous donors not long ago, I put together the following list of characteristics:

Indicators of stewardship

1. Proportionate giving
2. Controlled, debt-free lifestyle
3. Taxes paid with integrity and thanksgiving
4. Financial goals set as a family
5. Accountability

1. Proportionate giving

I can't tell you how many people have wanted to ask (really, debate) the biblical requirements of giving. Must Christians still give a tithe, or 10 percent, of their income? Is that the minimum or the maximum? Is it based on gross pay or net pay? Must the tithe go only to the church, or can it include other parachurch ministries? How do I tithe from increases of net worth and not just income? If the tithe is required, why doesn't Jesus specifically command it?

I believe there are answers to these questions (see part 3, chapter 27 for more discussion), but sometimes we miss the overall point. Your giving should be based on your income and should increase as your income increases. Proportionate giving is measurable. If you showed me your last five years of income tax returns, I could tell whether or not you are giving within your proportionate income. There is objective data.

Most people deduct everything they can for charitable giving—and, though it's not legal, perhaps a bit more. This is how the conversation between a client and tax preparer usually goes: "How much charitable giving did you do this year?"

The client often responds, "Well, how much did I do last year?"

"Exactly one thousand dollars," the tax preparer says.

"Oh, I did more than that this year; increase it by $500."

This is not the approach we recommend.

So based on the giving and income data on your tax return, how do you measure up? Test yourself over the past few years. What's the trend of your giving? Are you showing this indicator of good stewardship?

2. Controlled, debt-free lifestyle

A second indicator is your lifestyle. I've known athletes and doctors and businessmen who had very high incomes but lived beyond their means. If something unexpected occurred or they missed a few paychecks, financial ruin was near. I'm not suggesting you must be debt free to be a good steward. But you should at least be moving toward a debt-free lifestyle if you're not there yet. We'll drill down into the details of the types of debt, debt management, and getting out of debt in chapters 10–12.

Here's the lifestyle test: If God called you into full-time ministry tomorrow, could you go? Or are you in bondage to your lifestyle?

As a board member of a not-for-profit organization, I was involved in the hiring for a senior leadership position. Our committee had identified a talented professional who was passionate about serving the Lord. He was in the latter years of his career. He really wanted to get out of the rat race of his profession and work in a life-changing organization. As we tried to finalize the job arrangements, he finally declined the position. Despite his desire to work for our organization, he was making $450,000 a year as an attorney and couldn't live on less. Because of his present commitments—a couple of homes, expensive hobbies, memberships, etc.—he felt he couldn't accept our offer of a lower salary.

Debt is often symptomatic of maintaining a lifestyle beyond our means.

Please understand: I'm not saying it's wrong to have nice things, a vacation home, or a high salary. I'm also not saying it's preferable to work in a Christian ministry rather than the marketplace. I'm simply suggesting a litmus test: With

Q: To prepare for marriage, what should young couples do or talk about in regard to money and personal finances?

ANSWER: Everything! One of the greatest areas of conflict in a marriage is money. The reasons are easy to understand—when you put two people together with one checkbook who have different value systems, different personalities, different training, different goals, and different priorities, you're bound to have conflict. Determining how you are going to make financial decisions and who pays what bills, who determines the budget, etc., are absolutely essential in preparing for marriage. As I started answering this question, many other issues came to mind. Here are a few:

- What is your belief about credit cards?
- Are you bringing any credit card debt into the marriage?
- How soon do you expect to buy a house?
- What is your belief relative to financial assistance from parents and grandparents in the marriage? How are you going to handle that situation?
- What are your lifestyle expectations?
- Do you have student loan debt?
- What are your beliefs relative to private and public schools or Christian and non-Christian schools for your children? If you agree you want private education, how are you going to pay for that?

The list could be endless in terms of questions that need to be answered before couples ultimately get married. I go so far as to recommend that young couples prepare a combined budget before they get married, and if they are fortunate enough to know a good Christian advisor, have a financial plan prepared ahead of time. Most of the financial conflict that occurs in marriage can be avoided if couples spend any amount of time prior to their marriage talking through all of these issues.

An even bigger issue is when second marriages occur between divorced or widowed couples. My mother died, and my father remarried later in life to a widow. Both of them had some financial resources. They were able to decide ahead of time how their finances were going to be handled so there was no conflict when my father ultimately died before his second wife.

It's been my experience that many problems are, in reality, communication problems. If a couple can't discuss money, which will affect their lives on a daily basis, they are bound to have issues that show up in other areas of their lives. Values, goals, priorities, philosophies, training—all of these things are important for couples to understand about themselves and their intended spouse before they get married. This is a critical area that unfortunately most young couples never address until they are in conflict after they are married. Then, many other complicated dynamics can come into play.

some minor adjustments, would your lifestyle allow you to go full time into Christian work? We need to be unencumbered by the things of this world. Debt is not the only encumbrance, but it's often symptomatic of maintaining a lifestyle beyond our means.

3. Taxes paid with integrity and thanksgiving

Generally, most citizens dislike paying taxes. Oh, we may try to muster up some patriotic feelings to ease the displeasure. As Arthur Godfrey said, "I'm proud to be paying taxes in the United States. The only thing is—I could be just as proud for half the money."

It's quite a shift to pay the correct amount of taxes with thanksgiving. After all, any of us can find disagreement with spending decisions by a large and complex government. But I'm not suggesting we say thanks to the government as much as I'm suggesting we say thanks to God.

If you're paying more income taxes, most of the increase is due to making more money. No one pays 100 percent of their income in income taxes. You're taxed on a percentage far less than 100 percent. So if you have been blessed with property or income and have planned for your taxes well, the taxes you pay are evidence of God's provision. Because all we have comes from Him, I should utter thanks rather than curses when paying that property tax bill in the fall, the income tax amount on April 15, or the quarterly estimated income tax payment. I'm attempting to practice it myself in writing the tax check by saying, "Thank you, Lord, thank you for blessing me in this particular way, so that I can even do this."

I believe that you should not render unto Caesar any more than he requires. Avoiding taxes can be wise stewardship as well. (We'll discuss the tax system and tax strategies more in part 3, chapters 24–25.) The Bible commands us to pay taxes to those in authority. The availability of money to pay the tax *and* the attitude of gratitude are indicators of stewardship.

4. Financial goals set as a family

I've seen the power of goal setting work to my advantage and the advantage of many clients. God can use the process of goal setting. Working and praying through setting goals is where the benefit lies, not just the end goals.

Some people don't set any goals at all, and they suffer for it. Others go to the opposite extreme and set ambitious financial goals with little regard to family goals. Let's say the husband wants to have a certain amount of income per year or a target amount in his retirement plan. It's good to have a goal. But if he has to work a lot of overtime to earn the income or puts too much in a retirement plan instead of giving, then he may be sacrificing in other important areas, such as family time, health, or his wife working less outside the home. Set family goals first, then let the financial goals be a subset of the family goals.

Husbands and wives should be talking together, thinking together, planning together. Single parents can work with older generations or close friends or older teenagers to set family and financial goals. Remember that financial goals should be a subset of your family goals, not the driver of them. We've devoted an entire chapter later in this part on goal setting.

5. Accountability

I believe that the concept of accountability is scriptural—iron sharpens iron (Proverbs 27:17); we are to carry one another's burdens (Galatians 6:2), seek wise counsel (Proverbs 15:22), and so on. When it comes to financial matters, are you accountable to anybody?

You may be surprised to know that I've used a financial advisor for years. When I was involved with my financial planning firm, we required every staff member to have a financial advisor. I still have one. It's not because I don't understand how to plan—in fact, my advisor uses my material and the programs I developed to give me advice.

The reason I use an advisor is because I need somebody in my life to ask me questions such as "Why are you doing that?" "Why are you buying a vacation property?" "Why are you getting another car now?"

Here's a recent example of how accountability works. I bought a really nice car in 2001. It now has 100,000 miles on it and doesn't smell like a new car anymore. As it approached 100,000 miles, I thought maybe it was time to get a new car. But while researching and writing several financial books in the 1980s, I had concluded that the cheapest car is the one that you already have. No exceptions. Yet that was 20 years ago. Surely things had changed, I thought, as I considered replacing my 2001 model.

I called Layne, my advisor, who incidentally is five "generations" down from me in terms of training. That is, I trained an advisor in the firm who later trained an advisor and so on. I said, "Layne, I'm sure the rules have changed. Judy has her own business now. Perhaps it'd be better to buy a new car and use it in the business. Would you look at it?"

He called me back a couple of days later and said, "Ron, the rules still apply. The cheapest car you will ever have is the one you presently have." My own words hit me in the head like a boomerang. So now I understand—if I'm going to get a new car, it's strictly an ego decision. I can't justify it as a wise financial decision. But I needed him to challenge me on that.

(As a "P.S." to this car story: Only a few days after my discussion with Layne, a car pulled out in front of me. I hit him broadside—very hard. After realizing that nobody was hurt, my first thought was *Yes! God's provision.* I could smell that new car now! The wrecker towing my car stated the obvious: "It's totaled." The response from the collision center and the auto insurance, however, was that they never "total" that type of car. So they spent thousands of dollars repairing my car, and I am still driving this older, repaired car. God does have a sense of humor!)

We all need accountability. Whether or not I know the rules, I needed someone to say no and tell me why.

Having a financial advisor also enables spouses to get objective advice on issues that they may see differently and ensures that neither spouse will be left in the dark when it comes to their finances. In my family's case, I realize that chances are my wife will outlive me. Judy and I were talking recently one afternoon, and she said she wanted to meet with our financial advisor. We were getting ready to make a couple of major financial decisions. I knew what the financial consequences were, but she wanted somebody to talk to and wanted to make sure that we had thought through them well.

We can all seek to become better stewards by growing in these five areas. As citizens of one of the world's richer countries, we are blessed to have more wealth at our disposal than most people on this planet. As we've seen, with that privilege comes great responsibility. How do we make good decisions about the wealth over which we are stewards and managers? No, we don't need to be math whizzes, understand foreign currency exchange fluctuations, or budget every nickel to be wise stewards.

Summary View about Money

Earlier in this chapter, I described what money is.

- Money is a *tool* (Philippians 4:11-13).
- Money is a *test* (Luke 16:11-13).
- Money is a *testimony* (Matthew 5:13-16).

Money is simply something I use in my life to reach God-given objectives. God uses it as well as a "tool" to "test" me so that I may someday bring a "testimony" to Him.

It's also important to understand what money is not.

- Money is not a measure of self-worth (Deuteronomy 8:16-18; Proverbs 22:2; Ephesians 2:10).
- Money is not the reward for godly living (1 Corinthians 3:13-15; Hebrews 11).
- Money is not a guarantee of contentment (Ecclesiastes 5:10; Philippians 4:11-13).
- Money is not a measure of success (Joshua 1:8).

Throughout the book, I'm hoping to provide practical help in meeting a goal I assume you have: to become a good steward. Biblical stewardship can be defined as the use of God-given resources for the accomplishment of God-given goals or objectives. It's a lifelong process of growth in spiritual character and implies that spending decisions are spiritual decisions. But the lifelong process is worth it so that we can someday hear, "Well done."

God's Big Idea about Finances

For years I've said that "financial freedom" should be our goal. I published a pamphlet called the "Keys to Financial Freedom." I've written articles on how to experience financial freedom. In summary, I've taught that the pinnacle of doing well financially, giving cheerfully, managing debt, and so on is financial freedom.

My thought process was this: If a person is not a "slave to the lender" but has the right view of money and recognizes that God owns it all, then he is free. He isn't caught up in the bondage of materialism.

I don't believe any of this teaching was wrong. But I believe the Lord has been showing me that contentment is the ultimate aim and result.

Many people misunderstand the idea of financial freedom. They see it as meaning financial independence, applying it to people who have built up enough assets or income stream to work when they want, vacation where they want, and buy what they want. I've observed, however, that a person can be financially independent without being content. Conversely, a person can be content without being financially independent.

Besides avoiding the potential confusion between financial freedom and financial independence, I prefer focusing on contentment because that is the word the Bible uses. Here are a few notable examples:

> But godliness with contentment is great gain. For we brought
> nothing into the world, and we can take nothing out of it.
> But if we have food and clothing, we will be content with that.
> (1 Timothy 6:6-8)

> Keep your lives free from the love of money and be content with
> what you have, because God has said,
>> "Never will I leave you;
>> never will I forsake you." (Hebrews 13:5)

FAITH &
FINANCE

How to Be Financially Content

Is financial contentment really possible in today's society? A society where we are constantly bombarded with limitless options? A society where we are constantly told we will never be happy unless we have the latest innovation, the newest technology, the biggest-screen TV?

Before we consider those questions, let's define the term. *Contentment* is being satisfied with one's circumstances, not complaining, not craving something else, and having a mind at peace. I was teaching about contentment in a training session of financial advisors. One of the participants quoted to me what he remembered from David Jeremiah's (pastor of Shadow Mountain Community Church in San Diego, California) definition of contentment. I like what I heard. He said that it has three aspects: looking back without regret, looking at the present without envy, and looking to the future without fear.

I am convinced that this definition of contentment has nothing to do with money. A person may have a lot of money or a little money and still miss the whole point of contentment. We can complain whether we have a little or a lot. We can be covetous just as easily with a lot of money as with a little. We can have regret, envy, and fear.

Wise King Solomon writes, "Whoever loves money never has money enough; whoever loves wealth is never satisfied with his income. This too is meaningless" (Ecclesiastes 5:10). Contentment has nothing to do with money. It's a learned response. The apostle Paul states this very clearly: "I am not saying this because I am in need, for I have learned to be content whatever the circumstances. I know what it is to be in need, and I know what it is to have plenty. I have learned the secret of being content in any and every situation, whether well fed or hungry, whether living in plenty or in want" (Philippians 4:11-12).

The secret to which Paul alludes is the result of learning to think correctly about money and God. Contentment is learning to see money as God sees it, and nothing more. Money is a vehicle for providing for our needs and those of others, and funding can help advance God's Kingdom. Contentment also results from learning to see God for who He is. He is the bedrock of our contentment. I like what Major Ian Thomas, founder and director of the Torchbearers ministry, says: "All you need is what you have; what you have is what He is; you cannot have more; and you do not need to have less."[1]

Only when I realize that the Creator God of the universe loves me and has my best interests at heart can I be content. Only when I realize He is sovereign and providentially in control of my earthly lot (my vocation and income) can I truly be content. Only when I learn to trust Him can I have contentment.

Contentment really is a spiritual issue; it's not an amount-of-money issue. God is always there and never changes. He is consistent and stable. You can trust Him. But can you say the same about money? Proverbs 23:4-5 speaks to this when it says, "Do not wear yourself out to get rich; have the wisdom to show restraint. Cast but a glance at riches, and they are gone, for they will surely sprout wings and fly off to the sky like an eagle." How content can I be in something that flies away?

No financial principle can have a greater impact on you or free you up more than this truth: *Money is not the key to contentment!* Contentment has everything to do with your relationship with God and nothing to do with your money. Once you are free from the love of money and the pursuit of it, you can have a lot or a little and be content all the same. At that point you have learned the secret to contentment. It's not just the families struggling to make ends meet who wrestle with this. Many families with high incomes struggle with contentment as well.

What Does Financial Contentment Look Like?

The starting point for financial contentment is simply living within one's income. How we handle what God has given us will indicate whether we have financial contentment or not. As I've spoken in various venues I've met many families who are content to live in modest houses, drive older cars, and enjoy entertainment at home. Perhaps the breadwinner is a teacher, a church staff member, or in the early stages of a career. Many times they've chosen a simple lifestyle to stay within their means.

I remember one family who told me they'd chosen to give up some of the materialistic items they could have enjoyed. Why would they give that up when the wife had a master of business administration degree? She desired to be at home with their young children rather than traveling at her former job and working 50 hours a week. The husband desired to work—and worked hard—but his occupation didn't pay as much as others. They could have followed the American Dream—and charged everything. But they chose to live within their means to reduce their stress.

On the other extreme, I remember returning from a trip where I met a man who earned in excess of $600,000 a year. Instead of being content and at peace, he was miserable. He had financial pressures because he was spending $100,000 more each year than he was making. The key to contentment in one's finances is not the amount one makes, but rather a willingness to live within that amount.

Recently when I spoke to a group of men, I asked them how many of them were making twice what they were making 10 years ago. Every hand in the audience went up. I then asked them another question. If 10 years before they had been asked, "Would you be content if you were making twice what you're making now?" would they have answered yes? Here again they all answered positively.

But when I asked them if they were in fact content now, they said no. The

Q: Christmas is often the most stressful time for our finances. How can we survive and even enjoy the holidays?

ANSWER: The Christmas season can be a family's most memorable time of the year—but those memories can be either good or bad! Decisions we make in preparation for Christmas have an impact far beyond Christmas Day itself. Some of those decisions are economic, some involve the busyness of our schedules, others have to do with emotional pressure—but all of them build memories of the holiday season.

Here are some suggestions to make next Christmas a different and better one:

1. *Don't spend more money on Christmas than you can afford.* December 25 comes every single year. It's not a surprise, so plan for it. If you don't have the money saved for that special gift for your spouse, your kids, or your parents, it's easy to pull out a charge card, buy something you know they want, and not worry about paying for it until January. But January comes every year too. January and the months that follow are full of financial stress because of the extra Christmas debt on top of the other first-of-the-year expenses.

2. *Give something of lasting value.* If you have small kids, it's easy to buy something you think they will enjoy, only to find that by the end of Christmas Day the toy is broken, worn out, or boring to them. We've made it a point to let our kids know the kinds of gifts we would consider giving them as well as those we have absolutely no intention of giving to them. As you talk with your kids about these issues, try to reinforce a long-range perspective. Let them know you would rather pay the same money or more for something they will enjoy for a longer period of time.

3. *Do something meaningful for someone else.* You may be able to give presents of lasting value that have no cost at all. For instance, you could make a family project of doing a good deed for a neighbor, shut-in, or relative. The favor could be something as easy as fixing a meal, raking leaves, or cleaning out the gutters. It could be volunteering to babysit for a young mother or giving a "coupon" book that the recipients fill in themselves and redeem whenever they want to.

4. *Focus on spiritual, not material, issues at Christmastime.* I don't think there is a Christian alive who doesn't feel that Christmas is too commercial. And yet how many of us are willing to do something about it? We should be willing to take the focus of Christmas off the gifts, the decorations, the parties, and the clothes and try to do something creative with our families that reinforces the spiritual emphasis of Christmas. A few suggestions: Read aloud books about Christmas. Discuss with your family what it must have been like for Mary and Joseph and Jesus two thousand years ago. Talk about why you want to have a different Christmas than the one the world wants you to have. Research and discuss what Christmas is like in other countries and celebrate it in their typical custom.

5. *Give something to yourself at Christmas.* Not an impulse gift—I am talking about making a commitment to do some things right in the following year. For instance: (1) pay off debt; (2) start building an emergency fund; (3) begin a saving plan for long-term investments; (4) live within your means. Determine how much you can afford to spend in the various budget categories and make a Christmas gift to yourself to stay within those guidelines. If you get a bonus check from your employer, why not apply that money to one of these "gifts" to yourself?

6. *Here is the cheapest recommendation of all: Build memories.* If your house is like mine was with teenage kids, you have opportunities to do something every night of the week during the weeks before Christmas. The rush overtakes everyone, even the calmest of persons. Frankly, I have a harder time keeping a positive attitude at Christmas than at any other time of the year. But by changing your focus to functions that build family memories, Christmas can become a highlight.

point is, their income had doubled, but they had not learned to live within that income. Therefore, they were not content. I have found in my counseling that living within one's income is an indicator of contentment.

Some people look for a great financial secret—the magic pill, the black box, the cure-all financial step. If you've bought this book, you're looking for some helpful financial information. You might think, *Enough of this touchy-feely contentment stuff. Give me the solution to why there's more month than money or why my increased wealth doesn't satisfy.* Be patient. We'll have plenty of detailed information in the remainder of the book.

Financial contentment has less to do with money and more to do with our attitudes, belief systems, and decisions. Financial contentment brings peace of mind. Despite the claims in commercials for financial service companies, financial security is not the same as financial peace of mind. Both may help you move further along toward financial contentment. But it's possible to have financial security without financial peace of mind. Peace of mind comes from having

- Eternal perspective
- Faith-based decisions
- Biblically wise counsel
- Financially wise counsel

> **Financial security is not the same as financial peace of mind.**

Eternal perspective

Having an eternal perspective helps us deal with the earthly ups and downs, stock market highs and lows, and acquiring and losing of stuff. As author Beth Moore says, "All that will matter in eternity is the glory that came to God as a result of my life. I will be most blessed when God is most glorified." If I'm concerned about God being glorified, then I'm less concerned about hoarding, giving my kids the best stuff, being comfortable, seeking a life of leisure, or keeping up with my neighbor.

The Bible reminds us of the brevity of our lives:

> Now listen, you who say, "Today or tomorrow we will go to this or that city, spend a year there, carry on business and make money." Why, you do not even know what will happen tomorrow. What is your life? You are a mist that appears for a little while and then vanishes. Instead, you ought to say, "If it is the Lord's will, we will live and do this or that." (James 4:13-15)

FAITH & FINANCE

Faith-based decisions

I've been reminded in my recent daily devotionals of how faith is so vital to our relationship with God. If I'm exhibiting faith, then I'm pleasing God. If I'm pleasing my God, then it's easier to be content with my physical and financial position. As the Bible reminds us, "Without faith it is impossible to please God, because anyone who comes to him must believe that he exists and that he rewards those who earnestly seek him" (Hebrews 11:6). It takes faith to give a substantial amount to your church or a ministry. Faith is involved in launching a new career or business. It takes faith to give up immediate gratification now and invest for later.

Biblically wise and financially wise counsel

If you rely on movies, advertising, fashion trends, Hollywood celebrities, or the gang at work for your guidance and counsel, then you'll not be content. You'll be anxious and feeling as if you don't have what it takes to be successful. But seek first God's Kingdom and His counsel. The Bible compares the result of earthly wisdom and heavenly wisdom:

FAITH & FINANCE

> For where you have envy and selfish ambition, there you find disorder and every evil practice. But the wisdom that comes from heaven is first of all pure; then peace-loving, considerate, submissive, full of mercy and good fruit, impartial and sincere. (James 3:16-17)

> All Scripture is God-breathed and is useful for teaching, rebuking, correcting and training in righteousness, so that the man of God may be thoroughly equipped for every good work. (2 Timothy 3:16-17)

How to Experience True Financial Freedom . . . er, I Mean . . . Financial Contentment

We've all heard the saying, "He slept like a baby." Many things cause adults to be worried or anxious. But a baby is motivated by a few basic needs. After those needs are met, he has nothing to worry about. He can rest in total peace.

In my mind, contentment comes when money and financial decisions do not dominate my thought life. In other words, I am content when my attitude about money is totally free from worry and anxiety caused by any possible use or misuse of money; therefore, I can sleep like a baby.

As I previously mentioned, a common misconception about contentment is *If only I have more money, I will ultimately be financially free.* That money may come from a pay raise, an investment that goes up in value, or a business success, but the person assumes that at some point he or she will have enough to avoid day-to-day concerns about money, and therefore he or she will be financially free.

The truth is, however, that no amount of money is ever enough to provide contentment. In fact, just the opposite may be the case. Perhaps the most famous illustration in the past century of money not giving contentment is that of the recluse Howard Hughes. Hughes was one of the world's wealthiest men at the time of his death, and yet he lived a fearful and anxiety-ridden life for the last many years of his life. He was certainly not a picture of one who was financially free.

I believe that to be truly free from the love of money—as well as from money worries—four things are required: First, you must have a proper belief system regarding money. (See chapter 1.) Second, you need a money management system that works for your family. (We'll cover this in chapter 8 of part 2.) Third, you need a decision-making process for money decisions. (See chapter 6 to learn about this process.) And fourth, the ultimate key to contentment is giving the resources God has entrusted to us back to Him. (Giving is covered in chapters 26–27.)

> **Contentment comes when money and financial decisions do not dominate my thought life.**

The world's perspective:

- Our culture encourages us to spend all that we make. (It says, "Keep the economy going!")
- Our culture aggressively teaches us to be discontent. (It says, "You deserve a break.") This is the opposite of what God wants. We need to realize we're in a battle.
- Our culture attaches our self-worth to our net worth. (It says, "I'm winning the game because of what I own.")

Will Rogers is attributed to making the keen observation, "Too many people spend money they haven't earned to buy things they don't need to impress people they don't like."

Financial Idols

As we consider contentment, I have to ask the question: Are we drawn to try to find contentment in the stuff of this world because we are discontented with God?

One of the Ten Commandments is not to have any idols in your life before God. We're not to worship any other form of god. This seems like one of the easier commandments to obey—compared to not lying, not coveting, or honoring our parents. After all, we don't have wooden carved images or poles on a mountain like the cultures in the Old Testament.

But when I meditate on 2 Kings 17:15, I see parallels with today: "They rejected his decrees and the covenant he had made with their fathers and the warnings he had given them. They followed worthless idols and themselves became worthless."

The Lord reminded me that we are drawn to what we worship. A similar Scripture in Matthew 6 says, "Where your treasure is, there your heart will be also" (verse 21). That really is the same thought. What I treasure will ultimately capture my heart and will be what I think about, worry about, plan around, and spend time on.

Interestingly, the verse in Matthew doesn't say, "Don't have any treasures." In fact, it says to store up treasures in heaven. We are commanded to treasure, to value, and to worship. The issue, then, is not that we have treasure but what the treasure is. Whatever we treasure, worship, and value will determine the focus of our hearts and lives. If we want to become more Christlike, we must treasure, worship, and value Him.

Today, however, we're tempted to think about and spend time on financial idols. Here are examples of financial idols:

- Your house and its fair market value
- Income stream from your career
- Your retirement plan account value
- Certificates of deposit
- Pension plan and health insurance coverage
- Cars, trucks, and boats
- Value of your business or farm

FAMILY FINANCE

When the phone rang, Victoria Reyes jumped up to answer it. She had been waiting for this call all afternoon.

"Hello?"

"Hello, Mrs. Reyes? It's Stephen Alcaster from the antique shop. We spoke this morning when you brought in your porcelain vase for appraisal."

"Yes! Have you had a chance to look at it?"

"I did, but I wanted to let you know that I'm going to have a colleague of mine look at it tomorrow. He's an expert in this area. Just between you and me, though, I'll tell you that my preliminary estimate is more than $5,000. Why don't you stop by tomorrow and we'll make you a firm offer."

Victoria stood stock-still for a moment, then pulled herself together and said good-bye. *Five thousand dollars* for an old vase she had received from an aunt! With that amount, she and Luis could buy the new washer and dryer, redecorate the kids' rooms, and still have money left over to put in their savings account. Almost giddy with excitement, she called her husband at work and shared the good news.

That evening, she and Luis spent time looking at appliances online. After they had agreed to splurge on a high-capacity washer, Victoria gushed, "Won't it be great to buy these without worrying about how we're going to pay for them?"

"Yeah, this is the first time I can remember that happening! I just wish we didn't have to worry about finances all the time," Luis said. "I'm glad you only have to work part-time—but sometimes I wish we could just get to a point

So the challenge becomes focusing our hearts, thoughts, and intentions—our whole being—on treasuring and worshiping our Lord and Savior. By doing so, our lives have value, purpose, meaning, and more importantly, eternal significance. My challenge to you is to think about what you're worshiping: Is it a worthless financial idol or a treasure of eternal significance?

What's Your Goal—Prosperity or Posterity?

Except for two letters, the words *prosperity* and *posterity* are exactly the same. They sound so much alike, yet their definitions are so different. Though most of us have probably not stopped to think about the meaning of these two words, each of us is in pursuit of one or the other. The way we live clearly demonstrates which of these two we are pursuing.

Each of us places hope in something—something of value, profit, gain, or reward to us. Our hope keeps our motivation alive. It incites us to action. A person will never be motivated and thus disciplined to do anything unless he or she has hope. The key, then, is *what we place our hope in.*

where we're not so dependent on every paycheck."

In the morning, Victoria dropped off Manuel at preschool and drove to the antique store. Putting two-year-old Cristina in the stroller and handing her a sippy cup, Victoria walked in and approached the front desk. "Hello, Mr. Alcaster. I've come to get your offer on the vase."

He looked up and smiled nervously. "Oh, hi, Mrs. Reyes. Er . . . I'm afraid I have some bad news for you. I thought your vase was rare, but I was wrong about the imprint. My colleague informs me it's fairly common and worth about $25. I'm sorry."

There go the washer and dryer, Victoria thought glumly. When she got home, she called Luis at work.

"Sorry, Victoria," he said consolingly.

"I was excited about it too. But you know what? This morning on my way to work I started thinking about Pastor Richmond's sermon on Sunday. Remember how he talked about financial contentment?"

"Oh, yeah," Victoria said slowly. "He said we are content when we're free from the love of money—and when we see money the way God sees it."

"Money can't bring us freedom, even though sometimes it feels as if we would be free if we could make a big purchase without checking the bank balance first. But we're really free because we know that God will take care of us."

"Okay, I feel a bit better," said Victoria. "I'll remember that and keep watching the newspaper ads. Who knows, maybe washers and dryers will go on sale this week!"

When counseling couples, I've observed a great difference between people motivated by *prosperity* and those motivated by *posterity*. However, those motivated by prosperity are usually driven by a mistaken concept of posterity! Most Americans (Christians included) have defined *prosperity* as health, wealth, and materialism. As a result, they miss the true meaning. They subtly order their lives in the pursuit of things that God's Word tells us will not last. If I misplace my hope in material things and then apply all my motivation to attaining those things, I will find at the end of my life that I have missed what really matters.

This is vividly expressed in Psalm 49, which points out the plight of so many of us who have placed our hope in prosperity rather than in what God says is important. Psalm 49:11-12, 17-20, NASB, tells us that man's

> inner thought is that their houses are forever and their dwelling places to all generations; they have called their lands [and buildings!] after their own names. But man in his pomp will not endure. . . . When he dies he will carry nothing away; his glory will not descend after him. Though while he lives he congratulates himself—and though men praise you when you do well for yourself—he shall go to the generations of his fathers. . . . Man in his pomp, yet without understanding, is like the beasts that perish.

The Bible makes it plain, then, that prosperity—defined by material goods, houses, buildings, etc.—will not last. Stop and think about that for a minute. The high-rise office building you are in, the mighty fortress you have built as a house, the estates you have amassed . . . none of it will last.

It is interesting, however, that you can be prosperous and successful if you pursue the right thing. Prosperity is simply the state of being prosperous, or succeeding in advancing in wealth or any good. It is making good progress in anything desirable. In evaluating this definition of prosperity, one finds that having wealth, material goods, houses, and boats is really not the essence of the definition. Prosperity occurs when someone is making progress in the pursuit and accomplishment of a desired end.

Prosperity occurs when someone is making progress in the pursuit and accomplishment of a desired end.

Joshua 1:8 is so true when it says, "Do not let this Book of the Law depart from your mouth; meditate on it day and night, so that you may be careful to do everything written in it. Then you will be prosperous and successful." Therefore, one can only be truly prosperous and successful if one is doing what God says is important. That then brings us to the second word—*posterity*.

Your posterity is simply the descendants that come after you. This, of course, includes your children, but I think it also implies other people whom you impact for eternity. Psalm 37 says the righteous man will have posterity, but the posterity of the wicked will be cut off. In other words, if our focus is not on developing a godly posterity, then we will leave nothing of significance to mark the generations that come after us.

Clearly, one is prosperous and successful as one makes progress in developing and enhancing a godly posterity. What a travesty to pursue worldly prosperity at the exclusion of our posterity. After all, prosperity is not true wealth.

At a touching family reunion of one of my former clients, over 120 people of four generations were present. One of the 60 great-grandchildren, who was 21, was excitedly telling a story of how she had shared with some friends the person and reality of Jesus Christ. Interestingly back in 1882 one of her relatives had made this comment:

> Now if you wish these principles [to be] established and carried out by your descendants, inculcate into the minds and hearts of your children the principles of religious instruction. It is absolutely necessary to train the rising generation in the principles of Christ. It is the great work of the country. The Christian situations, friends, we have reason this day to thank God for, and what I ask of you who are now in the stage of action is that you should be true to the principles of Christ and humanity.

What will it be for you? Will you be motivated to spend your time pursuing prosperity as defined by materialism—which will not last—or will you pursue a godly posterity . . . and thus be truly prosperous?

How "Poor" or "Rich" Are You?

One day the father of a wealthy family took his son on a trip to the country to show his son how poor people can be. They spent a couple of days and nights on the farm of what would be considered a very poor family. On their return from the trip, the father asked his son, "How was the trip?"

"It was great, Dad."

"Did you see how poor people can be?" the father asked.

"Oh yeah," said the son.

"So what did you learn from the trip?" asked the father.

The son answered: "I saw that we have one dog, and they have four. We have a pool that reaches to the middle of our garden, and they have a creek that has no end. We have imported lanterns in our garden, and they have stars at night. Our patio reaches to the front yard, and they have the whole horizon.

"We have a small piece of land to live on, and they have fields that go beyond sight. We buy our food, but they grow theirs. We have walls around our property to protect us, but they have their friends to protect them."

With this, the boy's father was speechless.

Then his son added, "Thanks, Dad, for showing me how poor we are."

Too many times we forget what we have and concentrate on what we don't have. One person's worthless object is another's prize possession. It's all based on one's perspective. Give thanks to God for all the bounty you have been provided with, instead of worrying about wanting more. Take joy in all He has given—and be content with that.

Commonsense Financial Principles That Can Change Your Life

We've spent the first few chapters talking about the essential building blocks of wealth management and financial contentment. Now we'll begin to look at some of the practicalities of financial planning.

Just the term *financial planning* may make you nervous. Perhaps you're confused by the alphabet soup of credentials affixed to the names of those in the financial services industry—from personal financial specialists (PFS) to certified financial planners (CFP) to chartered financial consultants (ChFC).

We'll discuss the different types of professional advisors in chapter 33, but for now we simply need a working definition of financial planning:

> Financial planning: The continuing allocation of limited financial resources to changing and unlimited alternatives.

Let's translate this definition into everyday words. You only have so much income, so many built-up assets, and so much time. But there's an unlimited amount of items to buy and services to use. In this chapter, I want to explain the key points of financial planning by telling you about "4-5-6." I'm not trying to use sophisticated financial analyses, complicated jargon, or 50-cent consultant words.

Every field or discipline has basic, fundamental keys to success. In golf, tennis, or baseball, you must keep your eye on the ball, get set properly, follow through on your swing, and so on. Most of the time, you can trace errors—whether by professionals or amateurs—to the root cause of not completing the basic steps properly. The same is true with personal financial planning. Personal financial planning really is as easy as 4-5-6:

- The four transcendent planning principles of financial success
- The five uses of money
- The six common long-term financial goals

The Four Transcendent Planning Principles of Financial Success

On several occasions, I was honored to speak at Promise Keepers, a gathering of over 50,000 men learning to keep promises to God, families, and church. The following true story seemed to capture their attention more than just about any illustration I offered.

Several years ago, I was invited to Washington DC to testify before a Senate subcommittee that was holding hearings on "Solutions for the New Era: Jobs and Families." I was one of several "experts" from various economic and social fields. While others on the panel pressed for more social programs, I said I believed the American family could benefit from following a four-part financial plan:

- Spend less than they earn
- Avoid the use of debt
- Maintain liquidity (or emergency savings)
- Set long-term goals

The committee chairman, Christopher Dodd, listened carefully and recited the points back to me. He paused a moment, then said, "It seems like this plan is not just for the family. It seems it would work at any level."

"Yes," I said, laughing, "including the government."

I was smiling, but I did not miss the opportunity to exhort the senators to exercise strong leadership through wise financial planning. These four financial principles are so simple that they may easily be overlooked. Yet they have stood the test of time, having been developed and outlined thousands of years ago in the Old and New Testaments.[1] For Christian audiences, I've added a fifth principle: Believe that God owns it all.

I've had other professionals as clients, such as doctors and engineers, who at first think this is too simplistic. They want to make succeeding financially as technically challenging and sophisticated as their fields. But you can't go wrong if you follow these steps. What kind of financial trouble would you ever get in if you spent less than you earned, minimized debt, kept savings available and liquid (in other words, in a form that could easily be converted to cash for emergency needs), and thought about the long term?

The Five Uses of Money

For years, I've been teaching and explaining to clients that there are really only five uses of money in the short term. It seems to help them focus better when they are making plans and setting budgets. These five uses are

- Giving
- Taxes
- Debt repayment

Q: Help! I am spending more than I am earning every month and my credit card debt gets deeper and deeper. Some of your content doesn't apply to me because I am in too much trouble. My situation seems hopeless. What can I do?

ANSWER: First, in over 40 years of financial experience, I've not seen a hopeless situation. Granted, some problems are solved more easily than others, but the worst thing is to allow the momentum of the world's misguided financial principles and your own personal situation to carry you deeper into financial bondage. What do you do to get out? Whatever it takes.

You probably have to attack the income side and the expense side of your financial equation. Take extra jobs, sell stuff, and cut spending to the bone.

In desperate situations, you may have to sell an asset you prize dearly, such as a car that gives you some satisfaction to drive but at the expense of high car payments, insurance rates, and operating costs you cannot afford. Or it may mean that the first checks you write are for the credit card bills each month. It may mean increasing your monthly payment while at the same time destroying your credit cards. If you make the reduction of a debt a priority, write the checks first each month for that purpose, and commit to no further debt, then your remaining expenses will have to fall within your remaining monthly funds. You will have a "de facto" budget.

Decide what your highest spending priority is—savings, debt reduction, lifestyle, etc.—and then write those checks first in order to accomplish *at least one* financial goal each month.

No matter how hopeless your situation appears, it can be improved—often with very simple and small initial steps. A poor personal financial situation makes a person feel bad about everything. It is extremely important to take a step, however small, in order to get a feeling of accomplishment and self-worth. Then you can build on that by following my advice in chapter 8 to begin spending less than you earn—over a long period of time.

- Saving/investing
- Lifestyle choices

In the short term, every spending decision fits into one of these five uses, or categories. (See diagram on page 37.) How much of your money should go into each category? I can't give you exact amounts, and the Bible doesn't give a direct commandment—although it gives us many principles and guidelines about each one of these five areas. This is where our definition of financial planning comes into play—allocating those limited financial resources.

To determine what God would have you do to balance these priorities requires you to spend time with Him. No other person, including your financial planner, can tell you how to prioritize your spending. Why? God has not entrusted the resources you possess (but do not own) to someone else; only you are accountable for how you manage the use of God's resources in your hands.

How your money is allocated among the five categories is a function of two factors: the commitments you already have and your priorities. While raising our five children, for example, my wife and I had certain lifestyle commitments that others didn't have. Ultimately, our priorities dictated the use of our remaining resources. Was it a priority to give? How important was saving?

How you allocate your money is determined by your commitments and your priorities.

Because our lifestyles are funded with after-tax dollars, it takes an incredible income to fund some of the lifestyles that Christians—along with the world—have adopted. To have $10,000 to spend, you must earn $14,285 if you're in a 30 percent combined tax rate (federal, state, and local).

I don't believe the Bible calls us to live on a poverty level. Nor does it call us to live in luxury. However, it can help each of us determine an appropriate lifestyle for our families.

When determining how much of our resources should be devoted to lifestyle, the first principle to grasp is that God provides for our needs—we don't.

FAMILY FINANCE

Alysha Freeman sighed as she looked over the spreadsheet again. It showed all too clearly her main financial problem: She spent more than she earned.

The divorce four years ago had really thrown her for a loop, and she still wasn't back on her feet. After 12 years of marriage and two children, she had been shocked when her husband told her he was leaving her for a coworker. When Todd left, Alysha had gone back to work for the first time in years. He paid some child support, which helped with food and clothes for Donovan and Ellie, but she had had to get a job fast to be able to keep the house. She'd learned the hard way that staying home with two children wasn't considered good training for many jobs. And

not having a college degree didn't help either.

She'd finally found a job as an administrative assistant in a real estate office. The pay was okay, but after Alysha wrote the mortgage check every month, the family was still stretched. And now, after four years of using her credit cards every time money got tight, Alysha knew she was in trouble. It was time to get a grip on her spending and figure out some basics of financial planning. *I have to start paying down this debt and saving for an emergency fund,* she thought. *I guess the place to start is figuring out how to spend less.*

She took a sip of tea and looked down each column of her spreadsheet, considering how she could reduce spending. By the end of an hour she had this:

In fact, there's no correlation between how hard we work and how much we make. Scripture makes it clear that we are to work, but the income we make is in God's hands, and He will meet our needs. Psalm 127:2 tells us, "In vain you rise early and stay up late, toiling for food to eat—for he grants sleep to those he loves."

The apostle Paul writes, "Whatever you do, work at it with all your heart, as working for the Lord, not for men" (Colossians 3:23). Tremendous freedom results when we accept that it's our responsibility to work heartily and to trust God for our income, and then to live within that God-given income.

The Bible offers four basic commandments for the use of the income God provides to the individual or family. *First, we are commanded to give.* "Honor the LORD with your wealth, with the firstfruits of all your crops" (Proverbs 3:9). Paul adds, "On the first day of every week, each one of you should set aside a sum of money in keeping with his income, saving it up so that when I come no collections will have to be made" (1 Corinthians 16:2).

Second, we are commanded to pay taxes. Romans 13:7, NASB, says, "Render to all what is due them: tax to whom tax is due; custom to whom custom; fear to whom fear; honor to whom honor." Jesus Himself also gave us insight on this command when He said, "Render to Caesar the things that are Caesar's; and to God the things that are God's" (Matthew 22:21, NASB).

Third, we are commanded to pay our debts. Psalm 37:21 says, "The wicked borrow

· Pack a lunch instead of buying it every day. (Savings: $25/week, $100/month)
· Go out to eat or get takeout no more than once a week. (Savings: $40/week, $160/month)
· Rent movies or see them at the dollar theater instead of the full-price theater (Savings: $25/month)
· Clip coupons and drive a few minutes farther to shop at a discount grocery store (Savings: $60/month)

Wow, I had no idea how much money we were spending on food and movies, she thought. *We have been eating out a lot. If we can make all these changes, that's almost $350 a month we can save! I can put that money toward the credit card debt.*

Alysha sat back, relieved. She knew she still had some big decisions to make—such as whether to keep the house or sell it and buy something smaller, and whether to expend the time, money, and energy to get her real estate license. She needed to set some long-term financial goals, but as she heard her son come through the front door, she knew that would have to wait for another day.

"Hey, Mom! What's for dinner?" Donovan called as he entered the kitchen.

Pushing aside her first thought—to order a pizza—she stood up, hugged her son, and said, "Why don't you set the table while I whip together one of my world-famous omelets?"

and do not repay, but the righteous give generously." Not paying our debts responsibly makes us no better than the wicked.

Fourth, we are commanded to provide for our family's needs. "If anyone does not provide for his relatives, and especially for his immediate family, he has denied the faith and is worse than an unbeliever" (1 Timothy 5:8).

These commandments clearly indicate that God provides my income and He has determined what is the appropriate income for me. But I am then responsible to prioritize the use of this income to obey His commands to give, pay taxes, repay debt, and provide for my family's needs. The balance that is left is the amount available to be saved and set aside for the future, or to be spent to fund the lifestyle I believe God would have me live.

What has happened, however, is that Christians have adopted lifestyle as their top priority, letting their giving fall to fourth or fifth priority. The reasoning goes like this: "I'd like to give, but by the time I pay my taxes, repay my debts, and provide for my family, there's just not enough left over to give."

I believe God can be fully trusted to give us the income we need in order to obey His commands for the use of our money. My challenge to you is that you reprioritize the way you use your money in line with the Scriptures, and see how amazingly God will work in your finances.

Controlling Lifestyle Expenses

Of the five short-term uses, three are consumptive in nature and two are productive. Lifestyle expenditures, debt repayment, and taxes are all consumptive in nature; when the money is spent, it is gone forever. Both saving and giving are productive uses of money.

God can be fully trusted to give us the income we need to obey His commands for the use of our money.

The lifestyle use is the sum total of all financial spending not related to the other four uses of money. It's typically the most significant use of money for families, but it shouldn't absorb so much of the available dollars that too little is left for other more productive uses. The lifestyle use typically drives debt decisions; in other words, it's what causes the decision to incur debt. Also, it's always an "after tax" amount. The chart on page 38 shows what much of the world does and what it encourages us to do.

As we reviewed in the last chapter, financial contentment is a choice, not a function of lifestyle. Yes, you are commanded to provide for your family, but you can never accumulate enough to protect your family's lifestyle against all contingencies. So you can learn to be content, and your chosen lifestyle should be lived with joy.

The Bible does not define a Christian lifestyle. But the principles in the

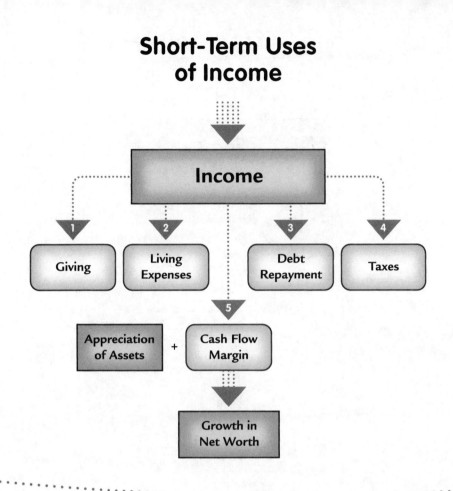

Short-Term Uses of Income

Income

1. Giving
2. Living Expenses
3. Debt Repayment
4. Taxes

5. Appreciation of Assets + Cash Flow Margin

Growth in Net Worth

Bible and commonsense financial wisdom can be summed up in the guidelines presented in the chart on page 41.

It's possible to reduce and eventually eliminate, as one becomes financially independent, the investing and debt repayment categories. (Perhaps it sounds hard to believe that a person would ever eliminate the investment step. You'll see this in the next chapter, about defining your finish lines and determining how much is enough.) Then, a person can give more. As you've met more of your goals, there are fewer commitments to meet and less debt to pay.

We'll look more closely at ways to control spending later in the book, but here's a summary of the steps:

- Estimate living expenses
- Record actual spending
- Refine your spending plan
- Control your spending plan
- Evaluate and revise, revise, and revise

Typical Use of Income

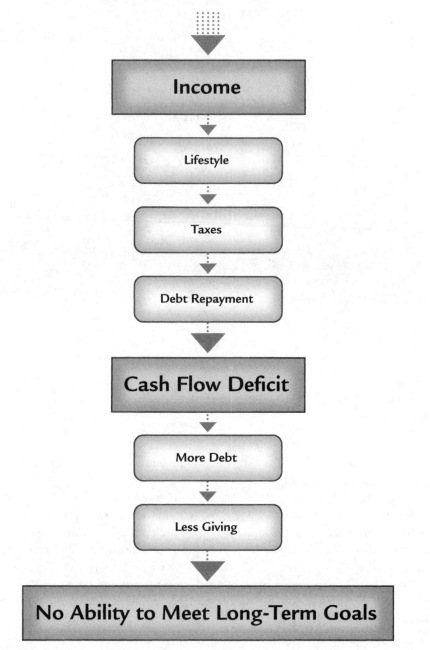

Income

Lifestyle

Taxes

Debt Repayment

Cash Flow Deficit

More Debt

Less Giving

No Ability to Meet Long-Term Goals

Along with these detailed steps, I want to provide you with principles regarding lifestyle and at least one Bible verse supporting each:

1. Prayerfully seek God's direction regarding your lifestyle

> Trust in the Lord with all your heart and lean not on your own understanding; in all your ways acknowledge him, and he will make your paths straight. (Proverbs 3:5-6)

2. Learn to be content

> I have learned to be content whatever the circumstances. (Philippians 4:11)

3. Learn to avoid coveting

> You shall not covet your neighbor's house. You shall not covet your neighbor's wife, or his manservant or maidservant, his ox or donkey, or anything that belongs to your neighbor. (Exodus 20:17)

4. Do not determine your lifestyle by comparing it to others'

> Do not love the world or anything in the world. If anyone loves the world, the love of the Father is not in him. For everything in the world—the cravings of sinful man, the lust of his eyes and the boasting of what he has and does—comes not from the Father, but from the world. The world and its desires pass away, but the man who does the will of God lives forever. (1 John 2:15-17)

FAITH & FINANCE

5. Freely enjoy whatever you spend in the "Spirit"

> For everything God created is good, and nothing is to be rejected if it is received with thanksgiving. (1 Timothy 4:4)

If you have inherited wealth, you don't have to feel undue guilt. God chose you to be born here. Or, if you're living a life as God desires and have saved for items, don't feel guilty about buying a new couch or going on a vacation.

6. Make an effort to live more simply

> Make it your ambition to lead a quiet life, to mind your own business and to work with your hands, just as we told you, so that your daily life may win the respect of outsiders and so that you will not be dependent on anybody. (1 Thessalonians 4:11-12)

7. Do not be conformed to this world

> Do not conform any longer to the pattern of this world, but be transformed by the renewing of your mind. Then you will be able to test and approve what God's will is—his good, pleasing and perfect will. (Romans 12:2)

The Six Common Long-Term Financial Goals

We've looked at the five uses of money in the short term. When there is a surplus, or margin, your net worth grows. As your net worth grows, you can use the accumulated assets to meet your long-term goals. (See chart on page 42.) While everyone's goals are somewhat unique, most long-term goals tend to fall under one of the following categories:

- Financial independence
- Maximized giving
- Debt elimination
- Lifestyle choices (second homes, cars, travel)
- Family needs (college education, dependent care)
- Starting a business

Integrating Your Short- and Long-Term Planning

As you consider the five short-term uses and six long-term goals, I'd like to encourage you to integrate these goals and begin an ongoing process. This process is the "plan" part of financial planning. Here's an outline of this four-step process:

Step 1: Summarize your present situation.

Step 2: Establish your financial goals.

Step 3: Plan to increase your cash flow margin.

Step 4: Control your cash flow.

I will take you through each step to develop your own financial plan in various chapters in part 1 and part 2. Once you know where you are, where you are going, and the steps to get there, you have made a major step toward being a planner rather than a responder, proactive rather than reactive.

> **Once you know where you are, where you are going, and the steps to get there, you have made a major step toward being a planner rather than a responder.**

Wise Use of Income

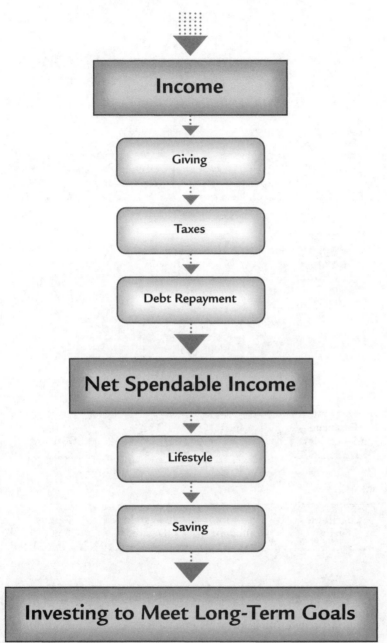

Income

Giving

Taxes

Debt Repayment

Net Spendable Income

Lifestyle

Saving

Investing to Meet Long-Term Goals

5 Uses and 6 Goals for Income

The diagram above illustrates three very important implications. The first is that there are no independent financial decisions. If you make a decision to use financial resources in any one area, by definition, you have chosen not to use those same resources in the other areas. This means that if you choose to set aside money for college education or financial independence, you no longer have that money available to spend on giving, lifestyle desires, debt repayment, and the like. By the same token, if you decide to spend money on lifestyle desires, you no longer have those same resources available for any other short-term or long-term goals.

The second implication, when looking at the diagram, is that the longer-term perspective you have, the better the possibility of your making a good financial decision now. The most dramatic example I can think of is the person who chooses a husband or wife. Taking a long-term perspective in that decision makes for a better choice than simply satisfying a short-term need. The same principle holds true in financial decisions.

The third implication of this diagram is the lifetime nature of financial decisions. I mentioned earlier that three of the uses of money in the short term are consumptive and two are productive. Whenever money is used consumptively, it is gone forever and can never be used for anything in the future. I like to remind those with whom I counsel that *decisions determine destiny*. Once I make a decision either to save or to spend, I have determined, to some extent, my financial destiny.

Why Have a Financial Plan?

As we've said, financial planning can be defined as allocating limited financial resources among various unlimited alternatives. When we know what financial resources we have, or will have, and have planned to use them to accomplish specific goals and objectives, our lives become much more orderly, and we sense greater contentment. Most of us, however, are responders rather than planners. We respond to friends, advertising, and emotions rather than planning when we make financial decisions.

A responder is like the person who starts on a trip yet has no idea how long he has to take the trip, let alone where he is going. The likely result is that he gets nowhere. The same happens with the person who manages his finances with no discernible plan. He is paralyzed with indecision and almost certainly will not be financially independent at retirement. (He has a lot of company. According to the Social Security Administration, the vast majority of Americans do not achieve financial independence by age 65.)

Whenever money is used consumptively, it is gone forever and can never be used for anything in the future.

Another significant reason for developing a personal financial plan is that it offers a basis for family communication, as the family is required to establish and prioritize goals. Once they are committed to a plan, the basis of disagreement—which in most cases is uncertainty—has been eliminated.

In addition, a financial plan serves as a guide for making financial decisions.

Financial Planning Diagram

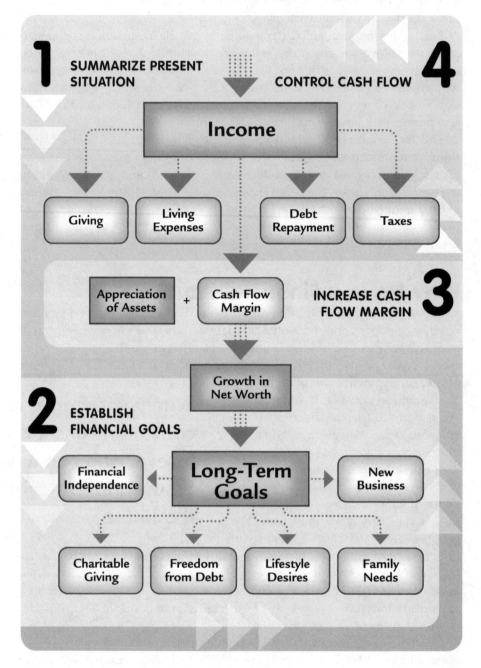

1 SUMMARIZE PRESENT SITUATION

4 CONTROL CASH FLOW

Income

- Giving
- Living Expenses
- Debt Repayment
- Taxes

Appreciation of Assets + Cash Flow Margin

3 INCREASE CASH FLOW MARGIN

Growth in Net Worth

2 ESTABLISH FINANCIAL GOALS

Financial Independence ← **Long-Term Goals** → New Business

- Charitable Giving
- Freedom from Debt
- Lifestyle Desires
- Family Needs

Because of it, many financial decisions are made in advance. For example, if the plan calls for the establishment of an IRA for a working spouse, then $5,000 has been committed to that objective and is not available for any other use, regardless of how attractive the alternative use might appear to be. Or if the money has been allocated for home remodeling or college education, these decisions have already been made; therefore, the alternative uses for those funds need not even be considered. In other words, a financial plan brings order rather than confusion.

In developing a personal financial plan, realize that you are *beginning a process* rather than *concluding a project*. Financial planning should be continuous because circumstances, goals, priorities, and commitments change over time. By using a financial plan to make good financial decisions, you bring balance into your life and have time for relationships—which really matter more in life than your net worth.

How Much Is Enough?

Pause and consider the penetrating question in the chapter title before
reading on.

In fact, this question is so central that I could entitle the book *The Most
Challenging Question for the Western World*. It would need only one page with one
question: How much is enough?

If you seriously considered this and allowed God to reveal over time the
answer to that question, you would get your money's worth from the purchase
of this book. (Jeremy White and I would have a much easier job of writing it too!
But I don't think our publishers would go for the abbreviated book idea.)

I may not know the answer for you, but I know the central question upon
which so much of financial planning is based: How much is enough? How
much is enough for retirement? for lifestyle? for giving? for financial independence? to earn? to give to kids? Keep in mind that the answer is not strictly
financial. More important than a dollar amount is attitude: For someone who
desires more and more, no amount of money will ever satisfy.

Why Answer a Hard Question?

In training financial advisors at Kingdom Advisors, I refer to the process of
determining enough as "knowing your finish lines." There are two good reasons for defining how much is enough:
to give hope and to avoid hoarding.
For those who are still accumulating
because they have not yet achieved
their goal of "enough," answering that
question with a dollar amount will
give them hope. Then, accumulating
"enough" will enable them to avoid the
temptation to hoard by knowing when they have enough.

> **There are two ways to attain enough: One is to accumulate more and the other is to desire less.**

The question "How much is enough?" implies that there is a definite answer in dollar terms. However, the exact amount depends on the needs and goals of the individual or couple answering the question. And by the way, there are two ways to attain enough: One is to *accumulate more* and the other is to *desire less*.

Everyone can answer the question as to how much is enough. The amount will differ for every family and is a number they should determine prayerfully. The answer will change periodically over time as circumstances change—after significant life events (marriage, divorce, death, additional children, children leaving the nest, retirement), significant changes in income, or significant changes in net worth. As an aid to those who prefer to analyze with a graph instead of words, the graph on page 50 illustrates the process of answering the "enough" question. If you can define your long-term goals, then you can determine how much is enough.

Your wealth is only a measurement of God's provision; not a measurement of your significance to God.

By the way, when I use the term *wealth* or *net worth*, I'm referring to how much you have in assets after subtracting any liabilities. As shown on the Financial Planning Diagram on page 44, net worth should grow over time from your cash flow margin and the appreciation of assets.

FAMILY FINANCE

"Wow, that first session with the financial planner gave us a lot to think about," said Tanya, setting down her iced latte and pulling a chair up to the table. "Coming to the coffee shop now to talk some things through was a good idea. My head is still spinning."

Brian sat down next to her, took a bite of his cookie, and spread out some papers on the table. "Okay, here are my notes. Sam gave us material on budgeting, investing, and retirement savings, and we can take time to read through that later. But I thought we should start with what he said was the most important question: How much is enough?"

Tanya stirred her drink thoughtfully. "Believe it or not, it's never occurred to

me that we could have 'enough.' I've always thought that the way to do things is just to accumulate as much money as you can. Then if you can buy what you want and still have some left over in the bank, I guess you have enough."

"I think that way too," admitted Brian. "That's why this idea of having a finish line is so strange. But you know, it's freeing, too. If we figure out how much we need for different things—like paying off our debts, making a down payment on a house, building up an emergency fund, and saving for retirement—then we can make a plan to get there. We don't have to keep worrying about it."

"That's true. And if we end up with more than we need, we can give it away

Is it wrong to have a long-term goal of increasing your net worth to the point of achieving financial independence? I believe not—unless financial independence is defined as having enough to be independent from God.

How do you increase your wealth over time in order to meet your "enough" goals? The beginning step is simple: Spend less than you earn and do it for a long time. As the Bible says, "He who gathers money little by little makes it grow" (Proverbs 13:11).

We discussed the lifestyle category as one of the uses of money in the last chapter. The level of lifestyle is one of the primary determinants of "How much is enough?"

If a couple knows their ongoing short-range objectives, they can calculate how large an investment fund they need to become financially independent. A family is financially independent when its fund is sufficient to meet the short- and long-term objectives. Once a family defines and quantifies their long-term goals, therefore, they will have answered the question, "How much is enough?" They then know where their finish lines are. The process is simple:

1. Quantify each long-term goal as of today.
2. Determine how much has been accumulated to date toward the accomplishment of each goal.

without fear." Tanya stole a bite of Brian's cookie. "Do you remember the two ways he said we can get enough money?"

"Yeah, that struck me too. He said we could accumulate more—or desire less."

"I'll be honest here," Tanya said. "Desiring less might be pretty hard for me. I love our apartment, and I've had fun decorating it. But I think a lot about a day when we can buy a big house with enough space that we can host parties and have guests stay with us."

"And it should have a big yard and at least four bedrooms so we have room for the kids we'll have someday," Brian added. He stopped suddenly and looked at Tanya. They grinned. "Okay,

so maybe we're getting carried away. When we do buy a home, we'd better be sure it fits our budget—even if it means no finished basement for that big-screen plasma TV that would be perfect for Super Bowl parties."

"I think asking 'How much is enough?' might be a great thing to do before we make any large financial decision," Tanya mused.

Brian stretched. "True. It's all a part of being content with what we have and trusting God to take care of us." He extended a hand to Tanya. "Ready to go back to our humble abode?" he asked teasingly.

"It's enough for me—at least for right now," Tanya answered, smiling.

How Much Is Enough?

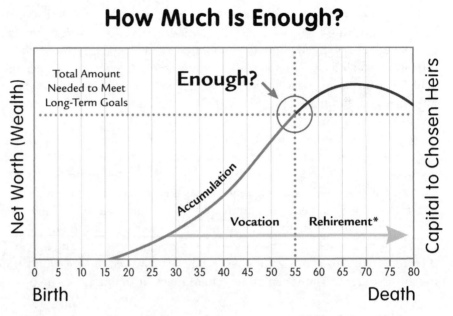

*For more on rehirement versus retirement, see page 266 in chapter 18.

3. Determine the difference between the amount accumulated and the amount needed to accomplish each goal; this is either the overaccumulation or the shortfall.
4. The shortfall divided by the number of years until the need must be met will give the average amount per year that must be accumulated to accomplish that specific goal.

Say you started supporting yourself at age 20 and for the next 40 years you always spent $1,000 less than you earned and put that $1,000 each year in an investment earning at least 12.5 percent interest. At age 60 you would have an investment fund of $1 million (ignoring the tax implications).

The 12.5 percent and $1 million are not magical nor necessarily even desirable, but they do illustrate what has been called the eighth wonder of the world—the "magic of compounding." The magic of compounding results because interest earns interest, which earns interest, *ad infinitum.* In other words, the amount is not nearly so important as the interest rate and the time period. The earlier you start and the more you earn in interest, the less you need to start with.

Here are two things to consider after you answer this question for yourself. First, if you have not yet accumulated enough, develop a plan to get there, outlining the specific steps you need to take now to start you on the path to your goal. Second, if you have accumulated more than your goal, consider giving the excess away. This decision may be difficult to make because of the uncertainty of the future, but remember that for the Christian, the future is eternally secure. As the Bible says, you will be storing lasting treasures in heaven, rather than on earth. Earthly treasures will not last eternally—although they could last longer than you do.

I strongly believe that you can't accumulate enough to feel financially secure, significant, or successful. Your wealth is only a measurement of God's provision, not of your significance to God.

Two More Hard Questions

After the question that I've repeated about a dozen times in this chapter ("How much is enough?"—just in case you missed it), two follow-up questions are legitimate:

- Will I ever have enough?
- Will it continue to be enough?

I believe that everyone, rich and poor, asks these underlying questions more frequently than he or she would like to admit. These questions are constantly in our subconscious, and therefore we all deal with them somehow in our decision making. Either we tend to hoard our resources or we tend to live out the philosophy of "get all the *gusto* you can—you only go around once."

The reason these questions are important is because there are uncertainties in the world. What kinds of threats are out there? Terrorist attacks? Health problems? Inflation? Real estate downturn? Stock market downturn? Changing interest rates? Medical care costs?

> "Enough" is when your finances no longer interfere with your thoughts and enjoyment of God.

Here's a summary of the worldly perspective on wealth and accumulation:

- Wealth is necessary for protection.
- Wealth produces anxiety. (What if my wealth, or protection, wanes?)
- Hoarding is acceptable.
- Time is an enemy.
- There's no limit on accumulation.
- It's all mine.

A quick sound-bite answer to the question "How much is enough?" would be that "enough" is when my finances no longer interfere with my thoughts and enjoyment of God. Sometimes "How much is enough?" has to be considered in the context of "If God owns it all, then how much do we keep?"

An important verse illustrating the concept of "How much is enough to

Q: Should Christians bring lawsuits?

ANSWER: This is a very difficult question because what's left unsaid is who is bringing a lawsuit against whom. I think it's clear in Scripture that a lawsuit between Christians is unbiblical. There certainly are better ways to handle disputes among believers, as Jesus and Paul both described. Mediation or arbitration through the church or a professional mediation or arbitration group is the much preferred way to handle conflict among Christians.

I had a situation in my previous organization where a group of Christians felt that my firm, which was a Christian firm, had wronged them, and they filed a lawsuit against my firm. We were then, of course, in a position of having to defend ourselves. In the midst of working on our defense, I picked up the telephone and called the leader of the other group and asked to sit down and talk about this—against the advice of my attorney. We met, and in a period of about two hours worked out an acceptable agreement between us. We were able to leave the meeting after having prayed together, with both of us in agreement that this was the best solution to our conflict. The attorneys were then able to draft the documents that were necessary to bring it to resolution, and I felt it was a fair resolution to a very difficult and complex matter. I think many lawsuits could be settled before reaching court if brothers and sisters who desire only to seek God's will and God's best get together and talk. I believe that God was honored by our resolution.

What my response has not yet answered, however, is lawsuits between Christians and non-Christians. The easiest answer is if you are the one being sued—by either a Christian or a non-Christian—you certainly have the right and probably the obligation to defend yourself using the legal system. Obviously, if a Christian is suing you, the preferable result is as I described in the previous paragraph. When you are being sued, however, by a non-Christian, you don't always have the opportunity for reconciliation and resolution except through the legal system. I don't see anything in Scripture that would prohibit me from using the legal system to defend myself.

The harder question is if you as a Christian want to bring a lawsuit against a non-Christian. First of all, from a practical standpoint, it's rare for any winners to emerge from any type of lawsuit. The expense and time taken offset much of any financial results in most cases, so just as a practical matter, avoiding lawsuits makes good sense. If the issue is significant enough, I do believe that the use of the legal system is justified, especially in commercial situations. In commercial transactions, people are used to dealing with contracts. A lawsuit is typically brought when a contract is in dispute, and in many cases the legal system can sort out the facts and come to the proper resolution. I believe that the proper approach is, first of all, to seek resolution through mediation or arbitration and then, if a lawsuit is warranted, to seek counsel from a Christian attorney who can give biblical advice. There is an organization called Peacemaker Ministries that is a tremendous resource for wisdom and help in these situations.

give?" is Luke 6:38: "Give, and it will be given to you. A good measure, pressed down, shaken together and running over, will be poured into your lap. For with the measure you use, it will be measured to you."

Jesus never defines what "it" is, whether it's your time, your love, or your money, but He says, "the quantity of what God will pour into your lap is generous." Yet giving costs you something—and you get to see the standard of how much is given back for you to steward. This is not a "name it and claim it" verse; it's about moving your treasure to heaven, like Jesus speaks of in Matthew 6:19-20. The key is asking yourself the questions "Am I in the act of regular giving now?" and "Am I limiting how much I will give in my lifetime?"

As the following true story illustrates, the question of "How much is enough?" doesn't mean you must sell everything and join a monastery.

A ministry invited me to speak on a cruise. (I like to say with a fake, suffering look that God called me to the "cruise ministry.") During my seminar, I focused on this question, "How much is enough?" A prosperous owner of a demolition business from California attended the seminar. Afterward, he told me that God had used that question to reveal to him that he had more than enough. The businessman then concluded that he should sell his business.

I asked him, "Well, then what are you going to do?"

He replied, "I may go full time into Christian ministry."

As we visited further and I learned more about him, I ventured, "You know, I think God has given you the gift of making money. Why don't you develop a giving plan?"

He and his wife developed a goal to give away $1 billion in their lifetime. That's right—no misprint. That number had a *b*. This was in the 1980s, when a billion was even more than today.

During this time, California was booming, his business was growing, many competitors were entering his market, and he was making a lot of money. He felt he had more than enough cash. I suggested that he take the available cash flow generated by the business and pay off all his debt. As was common in the demolition and excavation industry, he had borrowed to buy his heavy equipment. He paid off his debt even though this went against the conventional wisdom of using debt for leverage to buy more equipment.

Soon after, California went through a severe recession—more severe than in the rest of the country. The state had been through a boom and was going through a bust. The businessman's competitors all went out of business when they couldn't make the payments on their debt. He bought the competitors out and picked up their equipment for pennies on the dollar. He essentially had a monopoly in the western part of the United States.

You may remember the San Francisco earthquake in 1988 that occurred during the Oakland–San Francisco World Series baseball game. I happened to be in this gentleman's home in California when the earthquake hit. His equipment showed up quickly to the damaged area—he was the only demolition and cleanup company in town. He made millions from that earthquake.

A few years later, when a major earthquake hit Southern California, he still owned the main demolition company in the area. I told him, somewhat tongue-in-cheek, "God sends an earthquake every time He wants you to earn money to give to ministries."

This man gave away millions when he owned the company. He later sold it for a significant sum and gave away most of it. He and his wife are still working toward their billion-dollar giving goal.

No one could see these results, but they started with the question "How much is enough?" Although this example has more zeroes at the end of the numbers than most of us ever deal with, the approach is similar for those with less money. Let me give you an example at the other end of the financial spectrum.

Consider Oseola McCarty, an uneducated washerwoman in Mississippi. Day after day, year after year, McCarty earned her living washing and ironing clothes for others in Hattiesburg, Mississippi. She worked six days a week, often until midnight, for nearly 80 years.

Her highest earnings in a year as a laundress were $9,000. She tithed regularly to her church, lived frugally, and saved consistently. She shared a wild idea with friends at the local bank where she had always deposited her weekly savings. She wanted to give some of her savings to her church and some to family, but most to the University of Southern Mississippi.

Her ironing clients, her community, and the whole nation was shocked to learn that Miss McCarty had given $150,000 to a university she never attended. All the reporters, morning show hosts, and radio talk show hosts wanted to know how she did it. She said her secret was simple: regular saving and compounded interest. I'd add to her stated secret the fact that she had determined how much was enough. She determined her maximum lifestyle and stayed within that.

In her biography, *Simple Wisdom for Rich Living*, she said, "I'd go to the bank once a month, hold out just enough to cover my expenses, and put the rest into my savings account. Every month, I'd save the same amount and put it away. I was consistent."[1]

She multiplied her gift by giving while she was living. The ensuing media attention on her sacrifice created much excitement around the nation and inspired many others to give over $380,000 to her scholarship fund.[2]

"I try to be a good steward," said Miss McCarty. "I start each day on my knees, saying the Lord's Prayer. Then I get busy about my work. I get to cleaning or washing."

If she had waited to give until her death, she would not have been able to inspire others with her simplicity, work ethic, and faith.

Even in the last years of her life, she continued to challenge and inspire. "When I leave this world, I can't take nothing away from here. I'm old and I won't live always—that's why I gave the money to the school and put my affairs in order. My only regret is that I didn't have more to give."[3]

To Know, to Do, and to Meditate

I was interviewed by ABC News not too long ago. I asked the reporter, "Why are you talking to me? What perspective do I have that many other financial advisors wouldn't have?"

She responded, "Anything Christian is hot now." Of course, she was more interested in the latest trends than in searching out truth, but God is working in the world. Christians really do have the answer, and I want to be one of those who delivers it.

As baby boomers begin to retire, they are asking, "How much is enough for retirement?" But I think we can ask a similar question with a deeper meaning and application: How much is enough for me in light of God's desire to reach the world?

What are my finish lines? As I close this chapter on net worth and how much is enough, I want to summarize the key points by reminding you what's important to know with conviction, and what's important to do.

To know with conviction

- The question "How much is enough?" should be answered.
- "Enough" can be determined.
- "How much is enough?" will change over time.
- "How much is enough *for me*?" is the real question.
- Every financial decision ultimately impacts net worth.
- Your net worth is the sum total of every financial decision that you have ever made.
- You'll never be able to accumulate enough to feel financially
    secure,
    significant, or
    successful.
- Net worth is always and only a measurement of God's provision and never a measurement of success or significance.

To do

- Pray about your long-term goals.
- Quantify your personal finish lines.
- Answer the question "How much is enough?" for your family. (Use the graphics and steps on pages 49–50 to determine this figure.)

Life Planning Balance Sheet

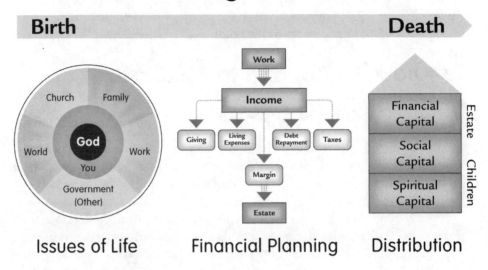

Birth ➤ **Death**

Work → Income → Giving, Living Expenses, Debt Repayment, Taxes → Margin → Estate

God / You — Church, Family, World, Work, Government (Other)

Estate / Children — Financial Capital, Social Capital, Spiritual Capital

Issues of Life   Financial Planning   Distribution

To read in God's Word

FAITH & FINANCE

If anyone does not provide for his relatives, and especially for his immediate family, he has denied the faith and is worse than an unbeliever. (1 Timothy 5:8)

Unless the LORD builds the house, its builders labor in vain. Unless the LORD watches over the city, the watchmen stand guard in vain. In vain you rise early and stay up late, toiling for food to eat—for he grants sleep to those he loves. (Psalm 127:1-2)

Do not wear yourself out to get rich; have the wisdom to show restraint. Cast but a glance at riches, and they are gone, for they will surely sprout wings and fly off to the sky like an eagle. (Proverbs 23:4-5)

From everyone who has been given much, much will be demanded; and from the one who has been entrusted with much, much more will be asked. (Luke 12:48)

Moreover, when God gives any man wealth and possessions, and enables him to enjoy them, to accept his lot and be happy in his work—this is a gift of God. (Ecclesiastes 5:19)

Do not store up for yourselves treasures on earth, where moth and rust destroy, and where thieves break in and steal. But store up for yourselves treasures in heaven, where moth and rust do not destroy, and where thieves do not break in and steal. For where your treasure is, there your heart will be also. (Matthew 6:19-21)

As a visual aid to summarize what I've been emphasizing so far in this part, please refer to the Life Planning Balance Sheet on the previous page. This will help you encapsulate the issues we've discussed as applied to the issues of life most of us face. As we go through life, we work, earn, and plan. We then build up various forms of capital—from financial capital to spiritual capital to social capital (our interpersonal support network, which includes family, friends, and other contacts). All of this will be passed on someday. So how much is enough for you now?

CHAPTER 5

Setting Goals for Financial Fitness

As this is being written, it's January. Resolution time. Despite much talk at this time of year of losing weight, getting out of debt, and organizing closets, most people don't set meaningful, written goals.

I remember reading about a study of Harvard students working toward their master of business administration (MBA) degrees. At the 10-year reunion of the graduating class, researchers found that about 3 percent of these Harvard MBAs had accomplished far more than the other 97 percent. In fact, they were earning, on average, 10 times more than the other 97 percent put together! The primary distinguishing characteristic was that the 3 percent had left Harvard as twentysomethings with written goals.[1] That is rather profound. Anecdotally, I've observed the same relationship between goal setting and accomplishment as I've worked with many people through the years.

Most people have good intentions or a vague idea of wanting to do something such as develop and keep New Year's resolutions. Most, however, do not intentionally and prayerfully set written goals. Why don't we set goals? I believe that the answers can include fear of failure, concern for the time it might take, no knowledge of how to set goals, belief that setting goals contradicts living by faith, or uncertainty of what goals to set.

> **Most people have good intentions or a vague idea of wanting to do something but do not intentionally and prayerfully set written goals.**

What Is a Faith Financial Goal?

In chapter 1, we defined biblical stewardship as the use of God-given gifts and resources (time, talent, treasure, truth, relationships) for the accomplishment of God-given goals and objectives. Focus on that final part of the definition: *God-given goals and objectives.*

If I believe the goals are "God-given," then there is an element of faith. So I like to refer to such goals as faith goals. Faith is acting on the basis that this is what God wants me to do. A faith goal is an objective toward which I believe God wants me to move.

When one of our daughters was very young and had no regular source of income except a small allowance, her heart was moved to pledge two dollars per week to our church's building campaign. As a wise, reasonable parent, my first intention was to step in and stop her. I didn't want her to make an impulsive commitment that was impossible to maintain. Her allowance was only one dollar per week!

After talking with our daughter further and seeing she had a serious desire to give and make her pledge, Judy and I shrugged our shoulders and agreed to see what would happen.

Somehow—and I'm still astounded by it—she met her pledge. Over the course of that year, she took on extra jobs around the house that we made available for our kids to do for pay. She seemed to receive more cash gifts that year from relatives. She saved more of her gifts, earnings, and allowances rather than spending them impulsively. What a lesson—for her and us doubting parents—about setting faith financial goals! She did her part and God did His part to meet a goal.

In chapter 4, we discussed the question "How much is enough?" Determining the answer—your finish line—is the result of faith-based goal setting. How much you want to give or what you'll do after your career is a faith process. God has a right to change that goal. As we see in the passage below, faith goals include God's part and our part:

FAITH & FINANCE

> To man belong the plans of the heart, but from the LORD comes the reply of the tongue. All a man's ways seem innocent to him, but motives are weighed by the LORD. Commit to the LORD whatever you do, and your plans will succeed. (Proverbs 16:1-3)

We have plans, and we can commit our plans to the Lord. He answers, weighs motives, and establishes plans. God is more interested in developing our faith than anything else—even getting to the how-much-is-enough level. He can use financial planning to build our faith. The process is more important than the end result. A faith financial goal is always a statement of trust and is one of the primary ways that I can see the hand of God in my financial affairs. Measurable goals need to be made, documented, and reviewed at least annually.

Setting Faith Financial Goals

Goal setting is dynamic. Write your goals in sand, not concrete. I've heard Dr. Howard Hendricks say God is interested in getting me moving. He gets me moving by setting goals. If I set a faith goal and I move in that direction,

God can intervene and change the goal in time and amount. Goal setting is a faith process. Decision making is by faith. Remember that "without faith, it is impossible to please God" (Hebrews 11:6).

I'd suggest writing your goals along these lines:

I believe God would have me _____.

How do you know what God would have you do? Spend time with God, write down your impressions, make those impressions measurable, and take action. Setting goals is not a process of ignoring God and relying on self. You should focus on what God directs you to do.

Write your goals in sand, not concrete.

The left-brained accountant part of me wants to say, "Set reasonable financial goals, considering your financial circumstances." But such rational, human-based logic limits our view of God. On the other hand, if you're a schoolteacher and you set a goal to have a seaside mansion, that does seem unrealistic. Keep in mind my earlier suggestion, however. Write your goals along the lines of what you believe God would have you to do.

I've prayed before, "God, I want your goal, and don't let me be limited by my own thinking or past experiences or what the world tells me I can or can't do." You should not focus on the past:

> Forget the former things; do not dwell on the past. See, I am doing a new thing! Now it springs up; do you not perceive it? I am making a way in the desert and streams in the wasteland. (Isaiah 43:18-19)

When setting faith financial goals, don't focus only on the present resources. Do you remember the story of Abraham and Sarah in the Bible? God was going to bless them with a child, but they looked only at their present situation:

> Then the LORD said to Abraham, "Why did Sarah laugh and say, 'Will I really have a child, now that I am old?' Is anything too hard for the LORD? I will return to you at the appointed time next year and Sarah will have a son." (Genesis 18:13-14)

God can do far more than we know and is not limited by our present resources. The idea of God doing His part of the goal is emphasized in the book of Ephesians:

> Now to him who is able to do immeasurably more than all we ask or imagine, according to his power that is at work within us . . . (Ephesians 3:20)

But then in the same book of Ephesians, the Bible tells us that we are to do our part:

Look carefully then how you walk! Live purposefully and worthily and accurately, not as the unwise and witless, but as wise (sensible, intelligent people), making the very most of the time [buying up each opportunity], because the days are evil. Therefore do not be vague and thoughtless and foolish, but understanding and firmly grasping what the will of the Lord is. (Ephesians 5:15-17, AMP)

These appear to be contradictory at first, but faith and practicality can co-exist. We may assume they are opposite ideas, but they actually work together. Understand what God can do—and then make it work with sensible plans. God is not an impractical God. He wants you to understand who He is and what He can do, and then work that out in your life. The consequence is that He gets the glory.

Gut Check—Diagnostic Questions for Your Goals

After you set your faith financial goals, here are three overall checkup and accountability questions:

1. If you're married, what does your spouse think about this goal?
2. What is the motive behind your goal—your glory or God's glory?
3. What would God think about your goal?

In chapter 3, we summarized the many short-term uses of money into five categories:

- Giving
- Taxes
- Debt repayment
- Saving/investing
- Lifestyle choices

Then we simplified the notion of financial planning by observing that most longer-term goals or uses of money tend to fall under the following categories:

- Financial independence
- Debt elimination
- Starting a business
- Family needs (college education, dependent care)
- Lifestyle choices (second homes, cars, travel)
- Maximized giving

I'd like to suggest more specific diagnostic questions by breaking down your faith financial goals into short-term and long-term goals. Using these five short-term uses of money, the six common long-term financial goals, and the

Financial Planning Diagram on page 44, review your faith financial goals with the following diagnostic questions. (If you're married, you may each want to complete this exercise separately.)

Short-term goals

What am I most concerned about in the next six to twelve months?

What am I most concerned about in the next one to five years?

Am I comfortable with my level of charitable giving?

Am I paying too much in taxes?

Are my living expenses too high or too low?

Are most of my goals focused on lifestyle rather than other short-term uses of money?

Do I have peace of mind with my short-term financial decision making?

Long-term goals

Are there some potential financial events that cause me fear?

Am I comfortable with my debt level?

Am I making progress toward my goals?

Should I reposition my investment portfolio?

What am I most concerned about in the long term?

Have I addressed my spouse's spoken or unspoken concerns?

Do I have peace of mind with my long-term financial decision making?

Goal-Setting Mistakes to Avoid

I once spent a day with a successful businessman who had a significant million-dollar business. We talked for five hours—yet he could not tell me what he really wanted to do with his money. In other words, he did not know where he was going. He was committing the serious financial mistake of having no goals. He likely had goals at the beginning of his business, but he didn't have any now.

I lost contact with this gentleman, but I was reminded of him as I worked on this chapter. Even for someone who was already experiencing some degree of success, he could incur problems in the future by not knowing where he was headed. He could waste opportunities; he could keep the business longer than needed; he could hire staff he didn't need or borrow and expand unwisely.

The first mistake, then, is not setting goals at all. If you don't know where you're going, you'll never know when you have arrived, nor will you know how to get there. So it's important to know where you are going. For mental health alone, goals help you have a better self-image because you know where you are going; then when you get there, you have a sense of achievement.

A second major mistake is what I call goal incongruity. Suppose a husband

Q: Do you feel it's the parents' responsibility to pay for a wedding? My husband and I have limited financial resources after putting our children through college. Our daughter and her fiancée have good, professional jobs and earn more than we do. They expect us to pay for the wedding, but we feel like we're done paying for our adult children's expenses.

ANSWER: It's been my experience that great abuses and many poor financial decisions are made when it comes to weddings. Weddings tend to happen with no real plan. Parents and children often begin the planning before thinking through what they want to accomplish, the cost, and whether or not they can afford the preparations.

In the best situations, the parents decided years ahead of time what they were going to do for their children financially as they went through the various stages of life. In other words, they agreed on what type of college they would pay for and what types of expenses they would cover both during and after college, including wedding expenses and first-home expenses. If parents haven't thought through those questions, they are apt to have emotional battles later, either between themselves or with the children.

The principle here is to avoid creating a "coping gap." A coping gap exists when there is a difference between expectations and reality. If parents can establish the right expectations for their children early, they're better able to reduce conflict during emotional times, such as after an engagement.

The approach Judy and I took with our children (we've had three daughters and two sons marry) is to decide before they ever went to college what we would do relative to weddings. We set a budget that outlined what we would be willing to spend for a wedding and communicated that clearly to our children. We let our children know they could spend the budget any way they wanted—on a reception, a wedding gown, invitations, flowers, etc. Also, if any money was left in the budget, they could use it as a nest egg to start their married life. The reality was that all of them spent the budget, but they spent it in varying ways—to one the wedding dress was more important than the reception, for example.

There's no right or a wrong answer on who pays for a wedding and how much to spend, but it's clearly better to have that question decided ahead of time.

says, "Our goal is to build a new home with three bedrooms on a wooded lot," while the wife says, "Oh, no, it's going to have five bedrooms and be within walking distance of our kids' schools." They both want to build a new home—they agree on that. But the specifics on how to accomplish the goal vary widely.

Unfortunately, few husbands and wives communicate specifically. And if you start a marriage with the attitude "Whatever my spouse wants he/she can have" that's fine and honorable. But how long does that attitude last? Few people keep it through the honeymoon! For a sustainable, harmonious relationship, seek unity with your goals. The prophet Amos asks rhetorically, "Do two walk together unless they have agreed to do so?" (Amos 3:3). Later in this chapter, I'll describe a goal-setting weekend. Chapter 30 is devoted completely to helping you learn to communicate with your spouse about financial matters.

> **A financial goal is not truly a goal until you can write it down in a specific, measurable way.**

A third mistake involves setting goals that are not quantified. That kind of goal is a purpose statement. It's fuzzy. Suppose your spouse asks you, "How would you like to take a ride Sunday afternoon?" and you answer, "Okay, that's fine." But before long you realize your spouse has in mind driving to the next major city, and you had assumed you were just going around the block. You both agreed to take a ride, but you had not quantified specifically where you wanted to go. You see, a financial goal is not truly a goal until you can write it down in a specific, measurable way. If you cannot state it in terms of dollar amount and time period, it is at best a broad statement of intention.

The fourth mistake involving goals is establishing them on the basis of fear rather than faith. So often we set our goals after listening to what others have to say rather than listening to God. If God has entrusted certain resources to you, do you think He is concerned about how they are allocated? Of course He is. That is why He has given us the Bible, as well as wise counsel from mature believers, for direction. He gives us the Holy Spirit to guide and direct us. A faith goal comes from God. I can truthfully say, "This is what God would have me to do with His resources." Knowing that can remove all fear.

As a financial counselor, I have found that people wrestle with two primary fears: the fear of failure and the fear of the future. I think psychologists would equate the fear of failure with our search for *significance*, while the fear of the future represents our search for *security*. In terms of financial planning, our thinking often runs along these lines: "If I have enough wealth, I will be secure (or significant or both)."

The danger is that money and possessions become our primary measures of success and significance. Anything that threatens our ability to accumulate wealth becomes a driving force in our goal-setting process. Ultimately, this mind-set leads to unwise decisions and wrong financial moves.

For example, many people fear an economic collapse. If that's your fear, what type of goals do you set to avoid an economic collapse? Perhaps you invest in gold, buy a farm in the country, or stock up on food. Before proceeding, however, your question should be "God, what would You have me to do with those resources?" The goals might be entirely different, or they might be the same. However, the basis for setting them is the critical issue. If the goal comes from God and God's Word, then it's a faith goal. If it comes from your fear or panic and you just assume it's the right thing to do, then it's a mistake.

FAMILY FINANCE

"This is perfect," said Victoria, looking around the small cabin. "No kids, no TV, and a quiet place to brainstorm and talk about our goals for the next few years."

"So you don't think we could have had our goal-setting weekend at home?" Luis teased.

"With Manuel chasing Cristina around the room every five minutes? No thanks. They're having a great time with your parents anyway."

After they unpacked the car and settled down in the living room, Luis said, "I think the best way to begin is for both of us to write down our thoughts about short-term and long-term goals for our family. Then we can discuss what we've written."

An hour later, Luis and Victoria made some coffee and sat down to compare notes.

"I'll start," said Luis. "I have some other ideas, but this one is the most important: Since before we got married we've talked about adopting internationally, and I know that's on both of our hearts. But right now it's a pipe

dream. We know we want to do it, but we don't know how to get there."

"I'm glad you brought this up, because it's at the top of my list too," said Victoria. "I've been seeing articles on international adoption everywhere recently! I'm so drawn to Guatemala. But we need some specifics. When are we going to pursue adoption, and how much money do we need to save to make it possible? How can we get there financially?"

"We've talked about wanting Manuel and Cristina to be older before we adopt, so they can understand what's going on. I would love to have them travel with us when we go to pick up the new baby. And waiting a few years would give us more time to save money," Luis said thoughtfully. "At the same time, it's going to be a long process, so I don't want to wait too long to get started."

"Hmm. Do we let our finances dictate the pace, or do we begin when we feel the time is right and trust that the finances will work out?" Victoria wondered.

"One significant question is whether we're willing to go into debt to pay the

Goal-Setting Weekend: A Tool for Husbands and Wives

Judy and I made it a goal to get away together at least one weekend a year. This has helped us preserve a good marriage—remember, we raised five kids and needed some time alone. Besides some relaxation and romance, we spent time discussing our goals. (I guess we made it our goal to have a weekend away and set some goals. Reminds me of a committee on committees!)

I would strongly urge you to make the same commitment with your spouse. Many people have shared with me how much my recommendation to do so has helped them. Here's an outline of an agenda. This is not a hard-and-fast

adoption fees. I read some information online and saw that an adoption from Guatemala could run more than $25,000."

"I know, and that amount terrifies me," Victoria admitted. "We're so careful with our money, and we've managed to avoid most debt besides our mortgage, but we don't have much in the way of savings. Sometimes I'm afraid we'll never be able to accumulate that amount."

"I know what you mean," Luis said. "But I remind myself that we both feel God calling us to do this. So we can have faith that this is a wise way to spend our money, and He will help us get there."

"You're right," Victoria said. "So how are we going to do this? What goals should we set?"

After more discussion that weekend, they came up with the following:

· Within the next two weeks, Victoria will ask her supervisor at the hospital about picking up another two evening shifts a month. Since Luis will be home with the kids, no child care will be needed, and this money will go straight into savings.
· Within the next month, they will request information from two different agencies that facilitate adoption from Guatemala, including all fees and travel costs.
· Within two months, they will set up an automatic $200 monthly deduction from the checking account to a mutual fund.
· Within three months, they will meet with a certified public accountant about the tax benefits of adoption.

Their list ended with a final statement: "We believe God is calling us to adopt from Guatemala. We will have a financial plan in place within six months. We will initiate the process with an adoption agency within two years."

On their drive home, Luis turned to Victoria. "I feel great about what we accomplished this weekend," he said. "We have a plan in place, and we're trusting God to help us. We're well on the way to the family God is calling us to."

schedule. It's simply a plan that has stood the test of time and experience in our lives. Feel free to make revisions to suit your individual needs, but remember to allow plenty of time for quality communication.

Although I'm describing married couples, a goal-setting time to think and pray is just as necessary for singles. It would not need to last an entire weekend. If you're a single parent, I'd suggest finding another single parent interested in the same idea. Perhaps you could watch her kids one Saturday afternoon so she could get away. Then she could return the favor by watching yours one afternoon. Hold each other accountable by sharing your goals with one another.

Goal-setting weekend agenda

Friday Evening

Start your weekend with an unstructured evening. Make no attempt to start setting goals; instead, just enjoy talking with your spouse over a relaxing dinner, a leisurely walk, or some other communication-fostering activity.

Establish your goals on the basis of faith, not fear.

Take time to pray together, even if praying with your husband or wife is a new or unfamiliar activity. The goal-setting process must be grounded in prayer; otherwise it becomes merely an exercise in wishful thinking or selfish dreaming. Make this focus on prayer the backbone of the entire weekend.

Saturday Morning

Take time apart from one another to set goals as outlined in the how-to section of this chapter. Use the lists on pages 69–70 if you need help or direction. Do it all—from listing your hopes and dreams to categorizing and quantifying your goals. The only step you should omit is selecting your five top-priority goals; this is a step you and your spouse will work on together.

Long Lunch Break

Saturday Afternoon

With your lists in hand, get together and compare notes. This can be a real eye-opening time. Judy and I usually agree on 70 to 80 percent of our goals; we tend to spend most of our time in this session discussing the other 20 to 30 percent. Remember, there are no right and wrong answers. Use this time as an opportunity to recognize and appreciate one another's priorities.

Saturday Evening

Relax. You have done a lot of work, and you may feel mentally or emotionally drained. Saturday evening should be a chance for the information you have garnered to simmer while you take time simply to enjoy one another.

Sunday

This is the fun—and challenging—part. Remember that a goal-setting weekend is not a time to establish "my" or "your" goals but to come up with a list of "our" goals. Pick no more than 10 objectives.

Next, be sure that these goals are well defined, and try to quantify them. Wherever possible, set times, dates, or amounts that will let you know when you've accomplished each goal.

Armed with a list of 5 to 10 goals you have agreed to pursue together, you are now ready to establish a strategy for accomplishing them. Congratulations: You have already done the hardest part!

GOAL-SETTING TOPICS
A Catalog of Ideas to Get You Started

Saving Goals	How much do we need? How often should we save? Weekly? Monthly? Annual bonus? Why? What are we saving for?
Debt Goals	How much is okay? Should we avoid it altogether? Should we get out of it?
Lifestyle Goals	What should we allocate for entertainment? How often will we eat out? How much will we spend on clothing?
Education Goals for Children or Self	Public, private, or homeschooling? College? University? Trade school?
Vacation Goals	How many this year? Where to go? With kids? Without?
Insurance Goals	Life, home, health, auto, other? How much do we need? What kind of policy suits our needs?
Giving Goals	How much to give? Where to give? When to give? Weekly? Biweekly? Monthly?
Tax Goals	Can we reduce our taxes? How can we manage them? Do we underwithhold? overwithhold?

continued on page 70

GOAL-SETTING TOPICS
A Catalog of Ideas to Get You Started

Family Goals	Special needs for aging parents? family members with disabilities? a gifted child? Family time: When? What? How? Where? Why? One-on-one time with children?
Marriage Goals	Date nights? Intimacy? Communication needs?
Career Goals	Starting a business? Advancement? Job satisfaction? Location?
Children	How many? Spacing? When to start a family?
Household Goals	When, where, and what kind of home to buy/rent? Furniture needed? Special needs: Room for guests? Home office? Other?
Investment Goals	Where to invest? Why invest? How much to invest?

The Benefits of Faith Goal Setting

I recently read an analysis of the presidency of George W. Bush and his approach to focusing on goals:

> A second broad and important lesson the President learned at Harvard Business School is to embrace a finite number of strategic goals, and to make each one of those goals serve as many desirable ends as possible. The truism of this lesson is that if everything is a priority, then nothing is a priority. If you can't focus on everything, then you need to be able to focus on those few goals which will have the broadest impact, leading to a future capacity to attain other desirable ends. No exact number of goals is the limit, but three is an awfully good number to aim at. Those goals should be mutually consistent, so that the step-by-step accomplishment of each one aids in the achievement of the others.[2]

Setting fewer but more far-reaching goals can have a big impact in your life. As you set goals for your life, you will see that they provide the following benefits:

- They provide direction and purpose.
- They help crystallize your thinking.
- They provide personal motivation.
- They are a statement of God's will for you.

Meaningful life planning begins with goals. As goals always concern the future, they are a statement of faith. Goal setting is one of the primary ways that I can see God at work in my financial affairs. As Proverbs 16:9 points out, "In his heart a man plans his course, but the LORD determines his steps." So set goals, write them in sand, and see God at work.

| **FAITH-BASED FAMILY FINANCES**

CHAPTER 6

Making Smart Financial Choices

My mom appointed herself to carry the worrying responsibilities for our family. If worrying needed to be done, she was the one to do it. I once told her that psychologists estimated 90 percent of the things a person worries about never happen. Her response? "See, that proves that worrying works."

I often called her when I was traveling out of the country. I forgot to do that once when traveling to Africa. Upon returning to the United States, I called her. After hearing I had been in Africa, she gave a classic line: "You should have called me, because I could have worried!"

Not surprisingly, my mom often worried about and second-guessed decisions she made and decisions my dad made. We teased her that she had the gift of hindsight because she frequently said, "You should have known."

The ability to make sound, confident decisions without regret and anxiety is an important skill. Notice I didn't say *gift* or *genetic trait*. I think wise decision making is a skill that is best developed through a process. In this chapter, we'll look at the barriers and key principles to good decision making, as well as a practical matrix for you to use when making financial decisions. To tie these ideas together, we'll work through a case study later in this chapter about a couple deciding how to handle an inheritance the husband received.

The Decision-Making Process— a Key Part of Financial Success

I've observed from working with many individuals, families, and businesses that there are four key skills to master to be a wise steward:

1. Goal setting
2. Decision making
3. Cash flow management
4. Wealth transfer

To master these skills, you need a process, or a sequence of steps to follow. Just like planting a garden or baking a pie, you need to follow certain steps in a certain order.

We'll be examining each of the four above skills throughout this book. We looked at goal setting in the last chapter. Although we covered the big-picture view of cash flow management in chapter 3, we'll look at it in more detail in chapter 8. Wealth transfer is our topic in chapters 20–21.

This chapter's focus is on decision making. I have had the privilege of working with Pat MacMillan, chief executive officer of Triaxia Partners (formerly Team Resources, Inc.). Pat's seasoned expertise in decision-making processes, leadership development, and team-building practices has benefited many organizations for over 30 years. Some of this material we worked together on many years ago, but Pat became the expert. We collaborated just recently on the case study in the latter part of this chapter.

Decision making often leads to fear. Decisions always involve the future; therefore, you are dealing with unknown events and consequences, so you're always at risk of making a mistake. Furthermore, because decisions are always future-oriented, you never have all the information you need. The unknown variables may cause fear.

As a result, people tend to make three mistakes when making decisions: (1) They make decisions intuitively; that is, they decide strictly on the basis of how they feel about a decision. (2) When not trusting their own feelings, they gather the opinions of others and therefore fall prey to the devices and feelings of those who are not at risk in making the decision. (3) There is almost always the possibility of falling into the "binary trap." That means that you only contemplate two alternatives—to do or not to do whatever it is you are considering. Because you see only two alternatives, your decision can never be any better than those two, though, in fact, there may be other better alternatives.

The late Peter Drucker, famed management consultant, stated astutely:

> A decision is a judgment . . . a choice among alternatives. It is rarely a choice between right or wrong. It is at best a choice between "almost right" and "probably wrong."[1]

In order to avoid falling into the "probably wrong" choice, you must have a process for making decisions. This is particularly important for those decisions that determine other aspects of your life—such as buying a home, choosing a school for your children, accepting a job, selecting a college, or deciding what car to buy. Those decisions are obviously of greater consequence than deciding what to order at a restaurant or what outfit to purchase. An established process can make decision making less overwhelming because you'll have

Decision making often leads to fear because decisions always deal with the future, so you never have all the information you need.

worked through certain steps to determine objectives and consider alternatives. This process gives you a chance at a much better, and certainly a much better-informed, decision.

Barriers to Good Decision Making

Think back to a poor financial decision you've made. Leasing an expensive car? Not starting your retirement savings earlier? Buying consumer electronics on credit? Changing jobs too soon or too late? Investing in a company based on a "hot tip"?

Whatever your bad financial decisions have been—and we've all made them—see if the following list of barriers to good decision making includes the culprit in your decision:

- **Time.** When your time is limited, when you face a deadline, when someone else involved is rushed, your decisions are rarely the best ones. On some occasions, we simply perceive we have little time when, in fact, we have more time available. For example, the pressure of a salesman at the car lot, the time period of a sale, or the urgent schedule of your life leads you to think something must be done now for later convenience.

- **Raw data versus relevant information.** Information is important in making decisions, but we can be overwhelmed by it. Too much information can cause "paralysis by analysis." Especially with the vast information available through the Internet, we can have lots of data but no relevant information.

- **Poor process.** Throwing darts, rolling dice, or mindlessly doing something just because your parents did—these are processes, but poor ones, when making decisions. Some people gather recommendations from friends before deciding. Or they make a decision and then go ask friends or counselors for affirmation. Often when asking for affirmation, they color the decision, or the factors in the decision, to tilt the listener to their decision.

- **Lack of experience and skill.** If you've let your spouse or your parents make decisions for you, then your lack of experience and skill is also a barrier.

- **Answering the wrong question.** At times, poor decisions are the result of addressing the wrong issue or answering the wrong question. In making a decision about purchasing a vehicle, the question to be answered should be "What is the best way to meet my transportation need?" Sometimes, though, we make our decision based on the wrong criteria, such as "How can I give the best impression that I'm successful?" or "What's the highest monthly payment I can afford?"

   The chart on page 77 shows two approaches: The one on the left is very action oriented and tends to be a more Western-world approach. The size of the blocks represents the amount of time spent on each category. The approach on the right is more common in the Eastern world—discussing first and spending more time deciding and implementing later.

- **Making *your* decisions in *God's* name.** Just because we tack on the phrase "this is God's will" doesn't mean our decisions are proper. God's ways of doing things are not our usual ways. I'm reminded of a few verses in Isaiah:

   > "Woe to the obstinate children," declares the LORD, "to those who carry out plans that are not mine, forming an alliance, but not by my Spirit." (Isaiah 30:1)

   > "For my thoughts are not your thoughts, neither are your ways my ways," declares the LORD. (Isaiah 55:8)

- **Falling into emotional traps.** Our emotions can sometimes get the better of our logic and rationale. Here are five common emotional traps:

   ➤ *Flying by the seat of your pants.* This trap is doing something that just feels right. Fortunately trained pilots go by instruments. It's easy to be disoriented in the air, so pilots learn to fly by

Decision Making:
Wrong and Right Approaches

```
        Implement                        Implement

          Decide                           Decide

         Discuss                          Discuss
```

Wrong "Try-angle"   Right "Try-angle"

instruments, not by gut or intuition or by the seat of their pants. We're to follow and rely on our "instrument"—God's Word.

➤ *Underestimating the influence of personality . . . yours!* Personality tests and surveys are helpful in understanding your particular bent. Overall, no personality bent is better than another. All types have uniqueness and usefulness. With that disclaimer being made, some personality types are not naturally conducive to good decision making, and people with those personalities may have to work harder. For example, I've used the four personality types from a common personality inventory called DISC to illustrate people's tendency toward decision making:

D—Decisive/Fast
FIRE, READY, AIM

I—Spontaneous
FIRE, FIRE, FIRE

S—Conferring/Methodical
READY, AIM, FIRE

C—Deliberate/Detailed/Cautious
READY, READY, READY

➤ *Moving too fast, jumping to conclusions.* It's natural for first impressions to last. Too often, though, we rely too much on initial impressions. We may jump to a conclusion that this situation will be like the last somewhat similar situation, or that this person will be like the last person we encountered.

➤ *Overconfidence.* After some success in an area or after several good decisions, it's tempting to think you'll always have similar success. Overconfidence can trick you into thinking you don't need to analyze, pray, or work through a process.

➤ *Groupthink.* Groupthink is the momentum a group can build that stymies critical thinking or the vocalizing of dissenting voices. If all or most of the people in a group vote in favor of a particular decision, the members conclude it must be the right one. When the 12 spies from Israel went to check out the land promised to them by God, 10 were in agreement that they couldn't overcome those in the land. Caleb and Joshua were the two who said God had promised the Israelites this land. But they were outvoted. The other 10 and the entire nation of Israel regretted that decision for the next 40 years.

Too often we rely too much on initial impressions when making decisions.

Key Principles of Decision Making

As I review the important principles, I'll make reference to the barriers just discussed. The principles are the reminders and ways you can overcome the barriers.

Generally, we have so many distractions in our Western culture that it's hard to clear the clutter from our schedules. When's the last time you had 10 minutes in solitude to think hard about a decision? Turn off the radio, TV, iPod, cell phone, and Internet connection. Schedule a time slot between soccer practice, Wal-Mart errands, and piano lessons. As to lack of *time*—you have time for everything God wants you to do. Notice I didn't say you have time for "everything"—but for everything God desires. Jesus died after only three years of public ministry. There were still people who weren't healed, people who hadn't heard Him teach, and people who hadn't believed. But Jesus was able to say that He had finished the work God had for Him to do. Learn how to sift the *relevant information* from large quantities of *raw data*. Apply an effective and *robust process* that will help you avoid the barriers. (Stay tuned for my suggested process later in this chapter.)

Practice the process and develop the needed *skills* to become a consummate decision maker (Proverbs 22:29). Focus on the *question*, not the answer. While you're at it, focus on the right question.

God wants to be involved in your decision making. Seek *God's* will on any given decision, not just yours. See decision making as a team sport between you and God. God can guide your decision making as you read Scripture, pray, respond to the Holy Spirit's promptings, and listen to counselors. Beware of the *emotional/psychological traps* in decision making. Don't make key decisions at weak emotional moments.

Here are the right financial questions to ask with regard to decision making:

- What do you think God would have you do? If you ask the question in this way, how many alternatives do you have? Perhaps far more than you could have originally imagined. Some alternatives with moral implications will have a black-and-white answer from biblical commands. For example, should you cheat in a situation? Others, such as choosing a college to attend or another career to pursue, involve a number of alternatives that may not be black and white. If you just ask "What should I do?" then you're limited to your alternatives.

> **Learn to sift relevant information from large quantities of raw data.**

- What is the best use of this money?

My Recommended Decision-Making Process

As I've said, to become an effective decision maker, you need a process. Such a systemized process has certain elements in sequential steps. I'd like to suggest the Criteria-Based Decision Model laid out on page 80.

One common but ineffective approach to decision making is simply comparing alternatives. Perhaps we note the pros and cons of each alternative. The problem with this is that our decision is only as good as the best alternatives. We trap ourselves into option versus option versus option, or alternative versus alternative. For example, you want to buy a house. So you view houses for sale on the Internet or work with a real estate agent. You have an idea of what you want, but you make your decision after just comparing and selecting one of the houses you find available for sale. Having a process such as I'm describing in this chapter can help you avoid just comparing a few choices.

Our family has used this matrix for various decisions. Our kids have used it when evaluating college or career options. As an example, our younger son faced a difficult decision about college. He had the fortunate distinction of receiving scholarship offers from various colleges to play tennis. Having been

CRITERIA-BASED DECISION MODEL

Step 1	Pray
Step 2	Define your decision—What's the question? Many times, your decision statement will have the words *choose/select* and *best* in it.
Step 3	Clarify your objectives—What are you attempting to achieve? What are the decision criteria?
Step 4	Prioritize your objectives—What are the non-negotiables? What are the trade-offs?
Step 5	Identify your alternatives
Step 6	Evaluate your alternatives—What are the facts?
Step 7	Make a preliminary decision
Step 8	Assess the risk—What could go wrong here?
Step 9	Make the final decision
Step 10	Test the decision

raised with this decision-making process, he created a matrix that included five colleges and fifteen criteria including the school's academic reputation, the strength of the tennis coach, and even how pretty the girls on campus were. We were glad he gave the school's academic strength a higher value than the number of pretty girls he saw. Nevertheless, his objectives, not ours, counted!

After he developed the matrix, the choice was very obvious to him. He chose to attend the University of Texas. Now that he has graduated, we all know he made a great choice.

In his first year, however, he began to doubt his decision. His experience provides another reason for writing down the factors involved in a decision.

One common but ineffective approach to decision making is simply comparing alternatives.

After attending his chosen college for six months, he was ready to leave. He retrieved his decision-making matrix to look back at why he had gone to Texas in the first place and realized it still was the best choice. He was able to remember why he had made the decision. He ended up with a successful college career, making All-American in tennis, graduating with honors, being accepted into law school, and meeting the wonderful woman who agreed to become his wife.

This multistep matrix using the Criteria-Based Decision Model has these benefits:

- Maximizes objectivity and minimizes bias
- Effectively sifts relevant data from the trivial
- Directs thinking
- Makes thinking visible
- Facilitates the participation of others
- Increases confidence for implementation

Case Study: The Inheritance—Windfall or Whirlpool?

To show how you can use this matrix for financial challenges you may face, I'd like to use a case study. After presenting the story and the options, you can see how the decision-making model works and how the matrix can be put to use.

10:20 p.m., Thursday, April 22

Bob sat pensively, chewing on his pencil. Sheets from a yellow pad were scattered across his desk. He had been working for over an hour. Actually, *working* was not a good term for what he had been doing: thinking, fretting, doubting, scheming . . . all were better descriptions of his late-night endeavors than working.

Bob had attempted to spend some time in the Word when he first entered his study earlier that evening. But he found himself too unsettled and distracted from his dinner interaction with Laura to focus his attention on Scripture. Prayer proved even more difficult. He remembered reading somewhere in the Bible that if you were crossways in the chute with your wife, your prayers would be hindered. That certainly seemed to be the case tonight.

The week had started off so great. Receiving a $40,000 inheritance check from the estate of his dad's sister was a total surprise to both him and Laura. They had met his aunt only once nearly 15 years ago, on a vacation trip through upper New York. She had passed away over a year ago and had never been close to Bob's side of the family. For all practical purposes, aside from that 45-minute visit for coffee, Bob and Laura had had no contact with this woman. They had no idea she was even wealthy enough to have an estate.

Despite the pleasant surprise, what appeared at first to be a windfall seemed to be turning into a whirlpool of problems. And if tonight was any indication, by tomorrow they would be sinking even deeper.

Over dinner, their 18-year-old daughter, Elizabeth, challenged Bob and Laura's commitment to good parenting with all the force her melodramatic mind could muster. Bob was so angry with Elizabeth's outburst that he could hardly remember the points of her message, but something along the lines of "You are ruining my life" seemed to summarize it.

Alternative 1: College

Liz had received an unexpected note from Mathom University that afternoon concerning her application. Over the past 12 years Mathom had become recognized as the ninth Ivy League school because of its academic excellence. Although Liz had been accepted to Mathom the previous fall, the entire family had agreed that they could not afford the cost, which was about $40,000 per year. So Liz had decided to attend Georgia on the Hope Scholarship and attempt to go to Mathom later as a grad student on a fellowship. Her school counselors had agreed that this was a viable strategy, and one had observed that it might even be preferable: A graduate degree would carry a lot more weight than an undergraduate degree.

Liz had reluctantly agreed, but on her own she made a long-shot application for a scholarship to Mathom. Most had already been awarded at this late time, but she had been placed on the alternate list for a Nightengale Scholarship. It had a unique structure in that it did not kick in until year two. Students paid full tuition in year one, and if they achieved a certain academic threshold, they received a 50 percent reduction in tuition for the second year. Those students who again achieved the required GPA got an additional 50 percent reduction in year three and another in year four. However, if the threshold was not achieved, they forfeited the scholarship and regular tuition costs applied during their remaining college years.

Even if they invested Aunt Sara's money in the tuition, Bob was not convinced that Liz could sustain the academic rigor necessary to earn the scholarship for three years. She was extremely bright, but she was also patchy in her performance. Laura was also doubtful but seldom took Liz on in head-to-head conflict, particularly when tempers were flaring. She generally left that to Bob, as she did tonight. As a consequence, Bob had taken the brunt of Liz's wrath.

Alternative 2: Stock investment

Liz's outburst began as a result of Bob and Laura's conversation over dinner. Bob had excitedly shared news of another opportunity: Gary Garfield's offer concerning the initial public offering (IPO) of a promising stock. "It's a sure bet," Bob explained. "You know Gary. He is one of the brightest and most successful brokers on Wall Street. We will get at least a 500 percent return within 18 months. This could really help us build up our retirement account."

"It's a bet all right," Laura responded. "It's a big gamble. And you are right, I do know Gary. He is the poster child for the eat, drink, and be merry club. With his lifestyle he has to be successful. Alimony to two ex-wives is no small matter."

Laura had never thought highly of Gary. Gary and Bob had been fraternity brothers in college and remained close friends for years afterwards. However, because of distance, the relationship had cooled a bit over the past few years, due in part to Bob's newfound faith in Christ and a change in priorities and directions. Going out for a couple of beers just wasn't an enjoyable night's entertainment anymore.

"Honey, he's not a saint. That's for sure. But he is a genius when it comes to money. Remember in grad school when I invested $1,000 with him? I had $3,500 by the end of summer. That paid my tuition for fall quarter."

"Speaking of tuition," Liz interrupted, "I got a very big surprise from Mathom today." The evening went downhill from there.

After Liz had stomped out of the dining room, Laura stared into her coffee and Bob toyed with a piece of cheesecake for which he had lost his appetite. Laura gathered her thoughts first. "Bob, I know she is upset, but she will get over it. The strategy for Georgia is solid. We both know that Liz doesn't demonstrate the discipline to achieve those academic marks consistently, and if she misses a beat with this scholarship, the overall cost would place us under tremendous financial strain. Once we make the commitment to Mathom, she needs to stay regardless of whether she is on scholarship or not. Even if she does, the total cost is still $55,000 more than Georgia on the Hope Scholarship." Bob, still playing with his cheesecake, nodded absently.

Laura continued. "I am sorry if I hurt your feelings with what I said about Gary, but he has not demonstrated mature behavior since I first met him over 20 years ago. I believe risking the entire amount on that investment idea is foolhardy." Bob shook his head, thinking, *She is so predictable*. Laura was, by Bob's standards, very conservative and looked at risk from a much different vantage point. Bob was a risk taker: decisive, optimistic, and spontaneous (or in Laura's words, "impulsive").

Laura, on the other hand, was risk averse, conservative, and in control of things. If she had to come up with a T-shirt slogan it would be something like "Better Safe than Sorry" or "Caution Is the Better Part of Valor." In this respect, Bob and Laura could not be more different. When they were able to gain a little altitude and laugh at themselves, they would often remind each other that opposites attract.

Alternative 3: Pay off loan

Again, Laura ventured into the conversation. "Bob, we need to look at this gift as an opportunity to make an investment that will bring longer-term benefits. This last week you reminded me of the importance of paying off our home equity loan. When Bill Oliver gave us our financial plan, he explained to us that paying off debt was the same thing as saving."

Bob nodded but interjected, "Using the money that way is like minimizing the loss versus maximizing the profit. If we invest this money with Gary, we'll have the potential to make a tremendous impact on our financial goals. We need to have an investment mind-set. We need to use this money to make more money."

Alternative 4: Kitchen remodeling

"If you want to invest, let's consider using the money for the kitchen," Laura said. "Remodeling the kitchen gives us the possibility of staying in this house or, if we elect to move, selling at a premium greater than the investment because of the improvements.

"Remember how I had Kitchens Extraordinaire come out last month to give us a bid? They came in at a little over $46,000." Noticing Bob's stricken look, Laura quickly continued, "But that was for a complete overhaul, right down to the studs, and we could have it done in phases. Phase 1 would give our kitchen a completely new look and updated plumbing and would be just $22,000."

Though it was obvious from his look that Bob wasn't convinced, Laura continued anyway. "Our real estate agent said that for every dollar we invest in that kitchen, we will get four dollars in return on the selling price. What could be a better investment than that? That's a sure thing in contrast to that IPA thing of Gary's."

"It's an IPO," responded Bob, "and it is not such a long shot. It certainly would have a higher return than a kitchen!"

"Well, it's clear that we are not of like mind on this," said Laura. "We need to pray about this. We have learned too many times the hard way that if we are not in agreement on a major decision, it inevitably doesn't work." She paused, thinking for a moment: "How do we know what God wants us to do with this money?"

Alternative 5: Build reserve for parents' long-term care

Bob stared back, perplexed and very much up in the air about how to answer that question. "I need to go call Mom and Dad," Laura said as she began to gather the dishes. "I talked to Mom yesterday, and although Dad is getting stronger after his heart attack, she can sense he is growing frailer. I know that we have talked about needing the resources to support one of our two sets of parents as time goes on, but I never guessed that it might be mine and that the possibility would be so imminent. That is one more issue we need to work through."

Alternative 6: Church building fund

At that point Bob had retired to his study and begun noodling the issues. He had collected a number of papers that argued for one direction or another for this newfound wealth. He shook his head, musing about how calm life had been prior to the arrival of Aunt Sara's attorneys. On top of the stack of papers

Evaluating the Alternatives, Steps 2–7

Decision to Make: Bob and Laura want to choose the best use for their inheritance money.

MUST-HAVES · **WANT-TO-HAVES**

Decision-Making Criteria	Priorities	OPTIONS					
		Retirement Account	Mathom University	Kitchen	Reserve for Parent Care	Equity Debt	Church
Do not violate biblical principles	Must have	Saving for future (yes)	Providing for family (yes)	God gives all things richly to enjoy (yes)	Providing for family (yes)	Repaying debt (yes)	Giving (yes)
Bill Oliver (FP) will agree	Must have	In plan (yes)	Uncertain	In plan (yes)	In plan (yes)	In plan (yes)	Uncertain
Honor God as good stewards	10	Appears to in every respect CV = 10 P × CV = 100	Appears to in every respect CV = 10 P × CV = 100	Appears to in every respect CV = 10 P × CV = 100	Appears to in every respect CV = 10 P × CV = 100	Appears to in every respect CV = 10 P × CV = 100	Appears to in every respect CV = 10 P × CV = 100
Maximize flexibility and future options	6	Basically unavailable in short term CV = 5 P × CV = 30	No liquidity CV = 0 P × CV = 0	No liquidity CV = 0 P × CV = 0	Liquidity committed until CV = 7 P × CV = 42	Future borrowing ability CV = 10 P × CV = 60	None CV = 0 P × CV = 0
Maximize contribution to financial objectives (financial freedom)	8	Meets financial plan objectives CV = 8 P × CV = 64	Not an objective in current plan CV = 2 P × CV = 16	Meets financial plan objectives CV = 5 P × CV = 40	Meets financial plan objectives CV = 6 P × CV = 48	Meets financial plan objectives CV = 7 P × CV = 56	Not in current plan; outside giving plan CV = 1 P × CV = 8
Reach unity on the decision as a couple	8	In agreement CV = 7 P × CV = 56	Uncertain CV = 2 P × CV = 16	In agreement CV = 6 P × CV = 42	In agreement CV = 8 P × CV = 56	In agreement CV = 7 P × CV = 56	Uncertain CV = 2 P × CV = 16
Maximize ROI	7	Good ROI but not max CV = 8 P × CV = 56	No financial ROI for Laura and Bob CV = 2 P × CV = 14	Good ROI but not max CV = 6 P × CV = 48	Minimal ROI CV = 2 P × CV = 14	ROI = 6% CV = 8 P × CV = 56	No earthly ROI CV = 0 P × CV = 0
COLUMN TOTALS:		306	146	230	268	328	124

CV = Criteria value   P = Priority rank   ROI = Return on investment

was one more unsettling issue in this decision. Saturday morning Bob had mentioned the windfall to Pastor McElrath after the men's fellowship. Bob and Laura had attended First Church for nearly 12 years and really felt a part of the body this past year. Bob had made a serious personal commitment to get more involved in church life, and as a result, he and Laura had begun hosting a small group in their home Tuesday evenings. Bob had become a faithful member of the Saturday morning men's fellowship and prayer group, and this past summer he was elected an elder. He felt that God had truly blessed him as he took that faith step toward more involvement.

However, when the letter from Pastor McElrath arrived that morning, Bob felt a bit like Hezekiah after he shared the wealth of the Temple with the Babylonian ministers. *Loose lips sink good intentions about a surprise inheritance*, mused Bob. In his letter, First Church's pastor had asked Bob and Laura to consider making a generous gift toward the church's Christian Education Center, which was to be built on property adjacent to the church. Pastor McElrath said he was approaching 15 key couples in the church, asking each to consider making a gift of $25,000 to jump-start the project.

Bob had wrestled with the alternatives and wanted to resolve the use of this inheritance tonight because he and Laura had their quarterly update meeting with Bill Oliver, their financial planner, Saturday morning. Although Bill was aware they had received the check, Bob had not had an opportunity to share with him the growing conflicts over its use. As Bob began to straighten his desk, he wondered if he should delay the meeting with Bill until he and Laura could find some middle ground and resolve the differences between them.

Here, our reader, is your assignment. After learning about decision making in this chapter, how would you counsel Bob? If you were he, how would you go about making this decision? Another way to think of this exercise is to put on the hat of a financial planner. As Bill Oliver, Bob and Laura's financial planner, what would be your counsel to them regarding the best disposition of this surprise inheritance?

Stop and think about this before you go further.

Let's go through the Criteria-Based Decision Model mentioned earlier in this chapter and apply them to this situation.

Step 1: Pray. This is the first step for a reason. It's vital. It's not a token acknowledgment of God but a source of wisdom. Remember:

> If any of you lacks wisdom, he should ask God, who gives generously to all without finding fault, and it will be given to him. But when he asks, he must believe and not doubt, because he who doubts is like a wave of the sea, blown and tossed by the wind. That man should not think he will receive anything from the Lord; he is a double-minded man, unstable in all he does. (James 1:5-8)

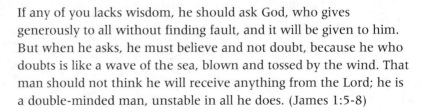

FAITH &
FINANCE

5 Biblical Tests for Decision Making

BIBLICAL TEST	SCRIPTURE	HOW-TO
PROMISE TEST	*"If any of you lacks wisdom, he should ask God, who gives generously to all."* **James 1:5** *"I will instruct you and teach you in the way you should go."* **Psalm 32:8**	1. Ask God for His wisdom. 2. Ask yourself, "Do I believe that by faith, He heard my prayer and has given me the wisdom I need?" 3. Develop a biblical basis for your decision.
PARTNER TEST	*"A man of understanding will acquire wise counsel."* **Proverbs 1:5, NASB**	1. Identify two people who could give you wise counsel concerning your decision. 2. Review your decision-making process with them.
PURPOSE TEST	*"Everyone who is called by my name, whom I created for my glory."* **Isaiah 43:7** *"Whatever you do, do it all for the glory of God."* **1 Corinthians 10:31**	1. Ask yourself, "Is my purpose for living to bring glory to God?" 2. Identify specific ways in which your decision will glorify God.
PREFERENCE TEST	*"Delight yourself in the LORD and he will give you the desires of your heart."* **Psalm 37:4** *"For it is God who is at work in you, both to will and to work for His good pleasure."* **Philippians 2:13, NASB**	1. Spend time with God in prayer and in His Word, letting him give you His desires. 2. Ask yourself, "What is the desire of my heart (which God has given me)?"
PEACE TEST	*"Let the peace of Christ rule in your hearts."* **Colossians 3:15** *"And the peace of God, which transcends all understanding, will guard your hearts and your minds in Christ Jesus."* **Philippians 4:7**	1. Wait at least 24–48 hours on major decisions. 2. As you pray, picture yourself implementing the best alternative. 3. Do you experience an inner peace concerning the implementation of the chosen alternative?

Step 2: Define your decision. What should Bob and Laura's decision statement be? A decision statement should usually start with *Choose* or *Select*. Often, you should use the word *best* as well. In their case, the statement may be as straightforward as "Choose the best use for the inheritance."

Step 3: Clarify your objectives. If you were Bob or Laura, what objectives would you attempt to achieve with this decision? In other words, what are the decision criteria?

Bob and Laura's Decision Objectives/Criteria:
- Maximize flexibility and future options
- Honor God as good stewards
- Do not violate biblical principles
- Maximize contribution to financial objectives (financial freedom)
- Reach unity on the decision as a couple
- Maximize return on investment
- Bill Oliver, financial planner, will agree

Step 4: Prioritize your objectives. It's not enough to list objectives. You need to assign a value to them. Not all objectives are equally important.

Bob and Laura's Must-Haves:
- Do not violate biblical principles
- Bill Oliver, financial planner, will agree

Bob and Laura's Want-to-Haves (Priority Value with 10 being the highest):
- Maximize flexibility and future options (6)
- Honor God as good stewards (10)
- Maximize contribution to financial objectives/financial freedom (8)
- Reach unity on the decision as a couple (8)
- Maximize return on investment (7)

Step 5: Identify your alternatives. When these alternatives are identified, they can become the columns across the top of the decision-making matrix. The objectives can be listed down the side. Refer to the example for Bob's inheritance.

Step 6: Evaluate your alternatives. Analyze each alternative, noting key points in the matrix with summary comments. For example, see the matrix on page 85, with comments under each alternative.

This step is an analysis of the facts. You use a bit of math in this step. Value each option against the criteria on a scale of 1–10 (with 10 being the highest). Then multiply the value times the priority rating. Write the total in each matrix block.

Step 7: Make a preliminary decision. You continue the math to continue the objectivity. The highest total of each column is your initial choice.

Step 8: Assess the risk. I suggest asking these questions:

- What is the worst thing that could go wrong?
- How bad would that be?
- What is the probability this would happen?

Step 9: Make the final decision.

Step 10: Test the decision. After making your decision, I think it's helpful to test it and challenge it. Here are five biblical tests to consider. (See the chart on page 87).

- Promise test: Does your decision line up with the promises contained in God's Word? Or does it contradict any biblical principles or promises?
- Partner test: Two heads are better than one. If you're married, then you should ask your spouse about your decision. If you made the decision together with your spouse or if you're not married, find another friend, person you respect, or family member to review your decision-making process.
- Purpose test: Is your decision aligned with God's purpose for your life? for the lives of others?
- Preference test: Perhaps your decision isn't specifically addressed in Scripture. If so, does it align with your desires? Are those desires or preferences God-inspired?
- Peace test: Do you experience the peace of God with this decision?

Using a process like the one that I've outlined in this chapter will help you make better and wiser decisions. Wise decisions lead to better stewardship.

Does What Happens in China Stay in China?

In the movie *It's a Wonderful Life*, the main character, George Bailey, is about to realize his dream of travel and adventure and leave Bedford Falls by taking a trip abroad on his honeymoon. Though he's planned to leave the town for college or travel several times, some event or dutiful obligation always prevented him from doing so.

After leaving their wedding, George and his bride ride away in a taxi. They are giddy with excitement. Their joy fades as they see the beginning of the run on the town's banks and his family's Building and Loan. George and his bride, Mary, spend their honeymoon savings to keep the business's doors open and the depositers happy. The Great Depression has begun—and ruined their honeymoon plans.

In the real world, the Great Depression in the United States ruined many people's plans and savings. Even though very little may have changed in their local town or economy from one day to the next, the national changes had a drastic effect on many individuals. It was a classic case of how an uncertain and changing national economy affected the local economy of regions and individuals. Today, the situation has gotten even more complex as countries coexist in a global economy. In other words, what happens in China no longer stays in China.

How the Global Economy Affects You

You've seen headlines in the newspapers or heard the lead-in to the economic news stories on TV or radio:

- Oil Consumption on the Rise in China and India
- The Fed Raises Interest Rates
- The Dollar Hits Record Low against the Yen and Euro
- Technology Changes Harm Workers, Help Corporate Earnings
- The Dow Hits Record High, NASDAQ Closes Higher Too
- Internet Increasing Productivity Statistics

- Government Deficit Is Higher, but a Smaller Portion of GNP
- Trade Imbalance Increases
- OPEC Lowers Production; Oil Prices Likely to Increase
- Lower Unemployment Rattles Bond Market

After perusing these types of headlines, it's easy to want to skip to the comics quickly. Are any of these matters vital to your everyday financial concerns? Well, the answer is yes and no. These can drastically affect your personal financial situation, yet you could also do well financially without even paying attention to them. In this chapter, I'll explain how this is true.

Having Serenity about an Uncertain Economy

When considering the overall economy and how it affects you, it's important to consider what you can control and what you can't. No one individual can affect the long-term stock market changes or the unemployment rate or inflation. I'm not saying those items are unimportant or useless to track. But you can't do much to influence them. Some argue that the global economy is too big and powerful even for the presidents of nations to impact.

I'm reminded of the "serenity prayer" so often seen on plaques or cards. (It's not a Bible verse, by the way.)

God grant us the serenity
to accept the things we cannot change,
courage to change the things we can,
and wisdom to know the difference.

I think the idea of this prayer can apply to the economy. We have to accept the overall economic conditions in which we find ourselves. But we must have the courage to change what we can about our personal financial situation. To better prepare for uncertain changes in the economy, you should spend less than you earn, maintain liquidity, avoid debt, set goals, and invest long term. We'll explore these topics in greater detail in part 2.

Doomsayers: "It's Déjà Vu All Over Again!"

As I was building a financial planning firm in the early 1980s, interest rates were nearing 20 percent, inflation was raging, and the stock market had been flat for several years. Those predicting gloom and doom were everywhere. *Ruff Times* was one of the most popular financial newsletters, and it told people inflation would always be high.

After the October 1987 stock market crash, various doomsayers were back in vogue and in demand. They urged people to take action and take cover.

Many predicted the world would slow to a crawl on January 1, 2000, due to the uncertainty of whether the millions of internal clocks in computers could make the change to a new century. In advance of Y2K, some people stored up years' worth of food and bought land in rural areas to prepare for the worst.

After the terrorist attacks on the United States in 2001 and the three-year downturn in the stock market, some doomsayers predicted the global economy would be in shambles.

When considering the overall economy and how it affects you, recognize what you can control and what you can't.

Frankly, I remember getting depressed by hearing about everything supposedly going wrong. Perhaps the fundamental problem with doomsayers is that, although they have a depression mentality, they are unwilling to take "depression actions." If they really believed that a depression was coming, they would get out of debt, convert all their investments to government securities, buy a one-year supply of food, and otherwise prepare for the worst. The problem is, although people like to talk about and believe that an extreme situation will happen, very few are willing to take extreme steps to plan for it.

During my years as a financial planner, I did not believe in emphasizing planning for extremes. Planning for extremes usually dictates radical action. Radical actions can have radical consequences. Radical steps, whatever they may be, usually put one in a high-risk position. One example of planning for extremes is to avoid diversifying and instead put all your investment dollars (or even your margin) into the precious metals on the theory that that market will continue to outperform all other investments. If the extreme happens and you are right, you have won a great reward. But if you are wrong, you have been damaged severely. Not only would you lose the money you put in gold or silver, but you are left without an investment base to cushion the loss.

Well, if I don't plan for doomsday or extremes, what should I think? I tend to like balanced practicality.

I remember reading a column years ago by Caroline Donnelly, the former executive editor of *Money* magazine, in which she outlined some common-sense thoughts on money that she had learned over 15 years. I agreed with her views then—and still do today. Several of her comments related directly to the idea of maintaining a balanced view of finances.

First, Donnelly pointed out that no one else, despite their financial ability and good intentions, cares about your money as much as you do. She's right: You have the final responsibility for stewardship. When making an investment, make sure you understand it totally, both from an upside and a downside perspective. What is your real risk? What are your alternatives? Do you have a peace about it?

ANSWER: You can do nothing to avoid the risk entirely. If a doomsday economic scenario comes along, even the most prudent person will be swept away with the tide. The key word in your question is *avoid*.

Every few years, there seems to be an increase in fears about a depression. Recessions are normal; depressions are not normal, nor are they guaranteed to happen. Several people have asked me for the perfect investment in order to profit during any upcoming depression. There is no such animal. Nor is there a painless solution. While you can't avoid a major economic downturn, you can certainly *minimize* its effects. How? The good old-fashioned way—reduce your debt and build personal liquidity through savings and investments.

FAITH & FINANCE

Donnelly reminded readers there is no "best investment." That's why diversification is critical. This fundamental investment principle is even in the Bible.

> Divide your portion to seven, or even to eight, for you do not know what misfortune may occur on the earth.
>
> (Ecclesiastes 11:2, NASB)

The wise and rich King Solomon wrote this thousands of years ago. He's essentially advising diversification. My grandmother would have said, "Don't put all your eggs in one basket."

We can't count on anything lasting forever—whether investments, jobs, tax breaks, or shortages, Donnelly said. Life moves in cycles. Her comment reminded me that we brought nothing into this world; we will take nothing out (see Job 1:21). God is sovereign. Some investments will work—others won't.

So in the end, what are the best kinds of investments? Donnelly recommended "plain vanilla investments," which she said offer the best returns. Again, I agree with her perspective. Even with the benefit of 20/20 hindsight over a large client base, I've yet to find a client who can consistently make money by using options, margin, futures, contracts, or commodities.

Planning for extremes can be risky, depressing, and perhaps futile. Common sense is the best way to approach investing and spending. Amazing, isn't it, how closely these commonsense insights agree with biblical truths!

Inflated Myths about Inflation

Inflation was very tame throughout most of the 1990s and 2000s, partially due to the effects of globalization, which allowed companies to access cheaper labor in China, India, and developing countries. As these economies improve and a middle class emerges in this part of the world, demand for oil, food, and other commodities will continue to increase. The resulting inflationary pressures are likely to affect everyone.

In addition, though I am not a prophet nor an economic forecaster, I believe the very basic greed nature of man will force inflation on our society.

Inflation: The rate at which prices for goods and services is rising.

The effects of inflation can be found in Haggai 1:6: "You have planted much, but have harvested little. You eat, but never have enough. You drink, but never have your fill. You put on clothes, but are not warm. You earn wages, only to put them in a purse with holes in it."

The problem with inflation is twofold, and both problems cause fear. First of all, inflation destroys the purchasing power of the money already accumulated, and second, it requires that you continually earn more just to stay even with the increasing costs for the goods and services you need to live on. This is true because inflation has a compounding effect that makes the magic of compounding work against us.

The problem is not so much inflation as it is the fear of inflation. A leftover effect of prior periods of inflation is that we have become a "now" society. Too many of us adopt the philosophy that goods will never be any cheaper than they are now, and besides, we only go around once.

Planning for extremes usually dictates radical action. If the extreme happens and you are right, you have won a great reward. But if you are wrong, you have been damaged severely.

Out of this fear and emphasis on the now have evolved four basic myths regarding inflation. They are (1) Buy now because it will cost more later. (2) You should always borrow to buy (the use of OPM—"other people's money"). (3) You can never accumulate enough. (4) The rate of inflation is standard for everyone.

These myths have just enough truth in them to make them believable, and many people govern their economic lives by them.

Myth 1: Buy now because it will cost more later

This statement appears to make good financial sense at first reading, but it presupposes that in the future you absolutely will need the item you are buying.[1] The real question, then, is not what it costs or what it will cost, but rather do you need it? The myth encourages us to delude ourselves into funding our *greeds* rather than our *needs*. Advertisers really play on this myth by advertising that next year the cost is going to go up. So what? God has obligated Himself to meet my needs always (see Philippians 4:19), and He didn't qualify that by saying "except for times of inflation."

The second thing that this myth presupposes, of course, is an increasing price; but there is example after example of the fallacy of sure increases, even during times of inflation. In the 1980s "everyone"

The problem is not so much inflation as it is the fear of inflation.

knew that the price of farmland would always go up because there is a limited supply of it. Yet prices were stagnant throughout the 1990s. Most of us pay far less per minute in long-distance telephone charges now than 20 or 30 years ago. Or what about the price of computers and electronic equipment? Or how about the price of clothes? I'm paying the same or less now as many years ago. Or what about mortgage rates? Those who purchased and mortgaged homes in 1983 at a 14 percent or 15 percent fixed rate because the rates would never go down have probably refinanced at least once or twice in the recent years.

Be wary of the trap of buying anything because the price is going up in the future. Ask

FAMILY FINANCE

Bob Zikowski groaned as he looked at the credit card statement. They had spent $300 on gas in the past month. "These high gas prices are going to bankrupt us!" he growled at Laura, who was sitting nearby. "This price gouging is getting out of hand. Why can't the government do something about these oil companies?"

Laura nodded sympathetically. "I filled up yesterday, and it cost me $50! Prices have been high for the last six months, and who knows when they'll go back down—if ever. It's scary."

Bob took another look at the statement. "Wait. You just said that prices have been high for the last six months, and that's true, although they've fluc-

tuated a bit. But we spent $150 more on gas this month than last month. Why? We can't blame all of that on rising prices."

Laura looked thoughtful. "Well, I've been driving to job interviews. And we did take that trip to Philadelphia and another long drive to the city for the baseball game last week. And of course Liz has been driving a lot more now that school is out for the summer and she's working. She's also gone to visit her friend Bethanne a few times, and that's 50 miles away."

Bob nodded. "That explains a lot. Well, it's clear that we can't control gas prices, as much as I would like to. Grumbling about them or worrying about them isn't going to change any-

yourself, first of all, *Do I really need this?* The second question is *If I do but can't afford it, has God promised to meet my needs?* Of course He has, but not necessarily until you *really have a need* and not for the finest, most costly merchandise when something more affordable will do. He never seems to meet my needs in advance, but always right on time. Larry Burkett often said, "God is seldom early, but never late."

If you decide to fund your *greeds* now because of the possibility of future price increases, my advice is to do so with cash and never with borrowed money. Paying cash will cause you to make a better decision, and at least you will not have compounding working against you.

Myth 2: Always borrow to buy

Two elements of truth support this myth: First of all, in times of inflation, the loan is paid back in cheaper dollars than those borrowed (because of the decline in purchasing power); and second, the tax deduction for interest expense reduces the cost of interest on some loans (though not most consumer debt, such as credit cards).

However, the myth has two presuppositions:

1. It presupposes a rate of interest that is less than the inflation rate, and a purchase that appreciates or earns more than the after-tax cost. In other words, it makes economic sense.

thing. What we can do is be deliberate about how much gas we buy."

"What do you mean?" Laura asked.

"Basically, we need to stick with our budget, which means being a little more careful about how much gas we use. We have to go to work—and I'm not letting go of baseball games—but we can be more careful about long drives. And of course we can keep an eye on our spending in other areas."

"That makes sense," Laura affirmed. "We can also ask Liz to contribute a certain amount each month for the privilege of using the family car. I don't think she ever buys gas—"

"No, she doesn't!" Bob jumped in. "This morning I got in the car to drive to work, and the gas light was on. Liz drove the car last night, and she had to have seen that the tank was almost empty, but she left it for me."

"Well, she needs to understand that there's cost associated with driving. What if we ask her to log the miles she drives this week? Then we can figure out how much gas she's using and how much she should pay each month."

"Sounds reasonable to me," Bob agreed. "Even better, we could all log the miles we drive, and note whether they're for work, errands, or entertainment. When we look at that, we'll have a better idea how much we can cut back. Then maybe next month I won't get so upset over the Visa bill!"

"I won't hold my breath," Laura teased.

2. The cash or investment that could be used for the purchase is earning more than the cost of borrowing. Again, borrowing in that case makes economic sense.

These presuppositions are generally either ignored or not known. The guiding principle now seems to be: Always borrow because you need the interest expense for a tax deduction, and you will always be paying back with cheaper dollars.

To borrow money for the tax deduction is foolish. If you are in the 25 percent tax bracket, for every $100 spent on interest, you reduce your taxes by $25, *but* it cost you $100 to do so; therefore, you are out of pocket $75 ($100 - $25). Spending more than what you save is hardly the way to achieve financial success, and yet this advice is given regularly, even by professionals who should know better.

It is true that in times of inflation you will be paying back borrowed dollars that are worth less than when you borrowed them. However, if you used the borrowed dollars to buy anything that depreciates in value, you have gained nothing financially by doing so and may have even lost in the whole transaction.

Be wary of the trap of buying anything because the price is going up in the future.

In recent years with lower inflation, I hear less of these arguments for debt financing during inflationary times. But these myths die hard. My point is that always borrowing to buy just because of inflation ignores the presuppositions mentioned previously on pages 97–98. Using debt during times of inflation for leverage purposes can make sense, *but* only if these presuppositions are not ignored. In the next chapter we will take a close look at the leverage issue and the way leveraging has been distorted to justify funding whatever we want.

Myth 3: You can never accumulate enough

In times of inflation, people may feel like they can never get ahead. Health care costs, gas prices, movie prices, and college tuition seem to go up faster than income. Extending this fear, people may throw up their hands and conclude, "Why save for the future? Why bother thinking about retirement? Prices are increasing faster than I can earn interest on my savings."

First of all, this myth raises the question of what is "enough"? (See chapter 4.) In my opinion, to accumulate enough means that I must have enough in an investment fund at retirement to generate enough income to live, give, and pay taxes. In other words, that investment fund must have sufficient earning power to provide for your lifetime.

In times of inflation, the earning power of investment funds will, over time, always be greater than the inflation rate, unless the investor ties his or her money up at a fixed rate of interest for a long term—which is foolish in times of inflation.

A wise and knowledgeable person can beat inflation by spending less than is earned. When doing so, the power of compounding is unleashed. If the excess money is put to use in investments such as mutual funds, the earning power of the excess money will likely, over a long period of time, be greater than the inflation rate. That earning power will even offset the required increase in income needed just to maintain a standard of living. I'll discuss investment options more in the next part. To bust this myth, you'll just need to remember that spending less than you earn and investing the excess may provide a higher return than the inflation rate.

Myth 4: The rate of inflation is standard for everyone

In personal financial planning, we figure for the impact of inflation by using the reported inflation rate. However, the reported national rate of inflation is an average and assumes that one makes significant purchases, such as a home, monthly. Such things just don't happen.

It has been my experience that when couples who plan to have a cash flow margin do so by living on some type of workable and simple budget, their personal rate of inflation is substantially less than the reported rate. They know what they spend and become price sensitive so that they are not victimized by inflation. On the other hand, if they have expenses over which they have no control, at the very least, they know how to pray specifically for God's intervention in the sure faith that God can supply their needs.

> A wise person can beat inflation by spending less than is earned because the earning power of money will, over time, always be greater than the inflation rate.

My friend the late Larry Burkett wrote the best-selling book *The Coming Economic Earthquake* in the early 1990s. At that time, our country was coming off a recession, the first Gulf War was just ending, and deficits were increasing. Larry projected ahead and described how bad our economy could get. Despite the gloom-and-doom outlook, he said to prepare your own financial house by reducing debt, building savings, living within your means, and diversifying. Whether his dire predictions were right or wrong, you would be better off. That's the serenity prayer—change what you can and accept what you can't change.

The overall global economy is nothing to be feared either. God is ultimately in control of governments and economies. Keep reading the next units to prepare for uncertain economic changes—while continuing to walk in faith with the One who's in charge and knows the future.

DOES WHAT HAPPENS IN CHINA STAY IN CHINA?

·· . . . . ·

PART 2

Managing Money through the Stages of Life

·· . . . . ··

MIKE, A HUSBAND AND FATHER of three young children, feels frustrated about his financial progress. He has the financial brains in the marriage and has a hard time getting his wife interested in financial matters. He heard somewhere that he "should be" saving 15 percent of his pay for retirement. After reading and watching ads from financial companies, he's gotten the impression that he should also be saving a lot of money for his kids' college education.

Yet Mike also has a number of short-term goals. He knows he still has student loan debt to pay off, he would like to move out of their starter home to a larger home, and he needs to increase his life insurance after the birth of the last two children. Mike could easily be depressed if he thought he was the only one facing these challenges and if he thought there were no solutions.

Perhaps that's your experience too. Whether you're most concerned right now about funding college education for your children, planning for a near-term retirement, buying a home, managing your debt, or determining how much life insurance you should have, I can assure you that you're not alone. In fact, these financial challenges are so common, particularly during certain stages of life, that collectively they can be called Family Life Cycle Planning.

Family Life Cycle Planning recognizes that although circumstances and needs change over time, there are three primary financial planning time periods for every family:

- Accumulation
- Preservation
- Distribution

The beginning point and the length of time spent in any one of the three time periods will vary from family to family.

The primary variables that determine the financial planning needs during any of the above time periods are your choices regarding

- Your location (where you live)
- Your vocation
- Number of children you have (or plan to have)
- Your level of lifestyle

Why are these so critical? Living in New York City costs two to three times as much as living in a small town in the southern part of the United States. Living on the coast or in sought-after mountain areas costs more than living in the Midwest.

Vocation can dramatically affect the challenges and opportunities that you will face. For example, a Harvard law graduate can make a starting salary of $70,000 to $90,000 and earn perhaps as much as a million dollars a year in middle age, whereas a minister of the gospel or a teacher may never earn more than $30,000 to $45,000.

You may have to spend as much as $250,000 to raise a child to age 18. College may cost another $30,000 to $100,000 per child.

Your choices about house size, cars, boats, entertainment, vacations, or clothes affect your lifestyle expenses. These household expenses are much like a business's overhead costs, the ongoing expenses necessary just to keep the organization running. These costs dramatically impact your planning during any of these time periods.

The Unique Challenges of Each Time Period

The accumulation period of life is the first and longest time period. It typically stretches from age 20 to as late as age 55 or 60. During this time, a family establishes its lifestyle. If the family includes children, this period continues until the kids leave the proverbial nest. Household income tends to go up fairly rapidly, but unfortunately, not quite as rapidly as the cost of living does. The primary financial challenges during this time period are establishing a career and income stream, purchasing a home and furnishing it, managing cash flow and debt, obtaining life insurance, and beginning an investment plan for retirement and education costs. Almost no one is able to go through this time period without some amount of debt.

The biggest tension in the accumulation period is the trade-off between the short term and the long term. The short-term needs and desires of providing a house, furniture, cars, or education take away from the long-term goals of financial independence, getting out of debt, providing for retirement, and even major giving. Every dollar spent to fund short-term needs takes multiple dollars out of the ability to meet long-term needs.

During the preservation time period of life, which typically lasts from a person's midfifties to midseventies, a person or couple focuses on building and maintaining retirement funds. They're trying to preserve and build upon what they saved from the accumulation phase. Trying to save is more of a challenge when people are "sandwiched" between family responsibilities—looking after the older generation while helping the younger one get established.

Another challenge confronting people during this time period is that they have much less time to meet their long-term goals. As they earn more during the prime of their careers, they try to save more to fund their retirement years. Investments become very important to them, and panic can set in when they realize how little time they have to meet their longer-term goals. They may be tempted to make riskier investments than appropriate to try to make up for a late start in their earlier years.

During the distribution phase of life, we disperse the assets we've accumulated over our lifetime. This phase can happen, of course, at any time because we do not know when death will occur. For most folks, however, the distribution phase occurs after age 65. The primary challenge in the distribution phase is to make sure that a surviving spouse is taken care of financially. The next challenge is distributing the estate. There are really only four alternatives in leaving an estate. It can go to (1) the chosen heirs, (2) charitable organizations, (3) professionals who are in charge of administering the estate, and (4) the government, in the form of taxes.

Why Does Knowing about Family Life Cycle Planning Matter?

A strange aspect of our inquisitive human nature is that we want to know how we are doing compared to others. Understanding where you are in the typical financial life cycle may help encourage you—you're not alone. It can also help you to concentrate on the financial planning areas critical to you now. The truth is that none of us have unlimited resources. So we are always faced with financial challenges and decisions, and unless we can look at them knowledgeably, we will certainly experience frustration.

I've organized the topics in this part to correspond generally to the three stages of Family Life Cycle Planning. I say "generally" because some topics, such as financial wisdom for car purchases, may interest you even though you are in the middle of the preservation period. Everyone, in order to exercise good stewardship and wise planning, would benefit from a budget, or spending plan.

Here are the chapters in this part and their primary life-cycle periods:

To help you look further ahead, let me remind you that part 3 covers in greater depth targeted topics that apply to all periods of life, such as giving, investing, taxes, and insurance.

Let's begin in the next chapter with the most important step throughout all periods: maintaining a budget or spending plan. Beginning this habit will help you spend less than you make. If you continue it regularly, you will do well financially.

How to Spend Less Than You Make

I was a junior at Indiana University when several buddies and I decided to spend the coming summer on Waikiki Beach. As none of us came from wealthy families, we had to scrounge our way to Hawaii. I hitchhiked to California and found a "nonscheduled" (read: cheap) flight to the islands.

I'll never forget our first moments near the ocean. How many surfboards should we buy? Would we need two motor scooters or four? As my friends and I stood in the warm island sunshine, the possibilities seemed unlimited.

Just one week later, we were forced to rethink our perspective. We couldn't find any jobs. With no work and no money, we resorted to combing the beach for spare change dropped by sunbathers. Our sand sifting netted enough nickels and dimes to buy groceries. We survived, but there were no surfboards or motor scooters.

Poking around in the sand to find extra money is one way to survive financially. A much quicker way, however, is simply to reduce living expenses. It may take less mental effort or discipline to sift along a beach, but as one who has tried both methods, I can safely say that curtailing your spending is a far more effective means of retaining the cash you need.

The truth is that most of us spend as much or more money than we earn. The key to a smart and successful spending plan, however, is to spend less than you earn. This provides more financial freedom and flexibility. It doesn't matter whether you make $40,000 a year or $140,000. A disciplined spending strategy is critical to achieving and maintaining fiscal fitness.

The key to a smart and successful spending plan is to spend less than you earn. This provides more financial freedom and flexibility. A disciplined spending strategy is critical to achieving and maintaining fiscal fitness.

By echoing this refrain throughout this book, I'm challenging you to develop a proactive approach and take control of your finances. You have already taken your financial physical and set some specific goals in part 1. Now you must evaluate your income, develop a budget, and come up with a plan that will enable you to reach your financial finish lines. This process will probably involve hard work, careful planning, and a good deal of self-discipline, but smart spending is not an impossible task.

The Rewards of Smart Spending

Mark and his wife, Rachel, have come to dread the end of the month. Now that their older daughter is in college, they not only have to pay the mortgage, a car payment, and other bills, they also help pay some of her monthly tuition. On top of that, their younger daughter is scheduled to begin orthodontic treatment in a few weeks. As they sit down to pay bills together this month, they worry that they just won't have enough cash available to meet all these demands.

Spending less than you earn is the commonsense key to living within your income. Mark and Rachel didn't intentionally set out to assume greater obligations than they could afford. Nobody intentionally plans to overspend. On the contrary, most of us aim to make room in the budget for the things we know are important, such as saving and giving. What generally happens, though, is that we fail to budget or plan properly, and we come up short when it's time to pay the bills.

As common as they are, the financial problems associated with unforeseen or unbudgeted expenses are actually fairly simple to prevent.

Saving and giving are often the first casualties. Next, we use credit cards when we face a cash shortfall, reasoning that we can make it up in a month or so. Then, as we slip further and further behind, we give in to the temptation to make only the minimum payment required on the cards.

In this precarious position, our wallets are no match for an unexpected calamity when it comes along. And it will come along. A major car repair, a medical emergency, a leaking roof, a broken water pipe—any one of a hundred sudden needs can catapult us into debt with astonishing force. Peering into our 10- or 15-thousand-dollar hole of debt, we teeter on the edge of disaster and wonder, *How in the world did I get here?*

As common as they are, the financial problems associated with unforeseen or unbudgeted expenses are actually fairly simple to prevent. The strategy is to make sure that your income exceeds your outflow—even in the face of unexpected expenses. Following this rule opens the door to several significant benefits:

Q: Can a person reach a point where he or she no longer needs to budget? Ron, do you still maintain a budget for your family? If so, why?

ANSWER: Yes, we still use a budget—even though we've found our spending habits are pretty well set. We don't really budget from the standpoint of having to control every dollar. But we use our budget to be aware of where, over time, we might be tempted to overspend. Typically, we are well within our budget every year just because we budget conservatively.

Another benefit of budgeting for us is that Judy and I are able to sit down periodically and ask ourselves the question, Are we spending money where we want to spend money? That's a very good exercise for everyone to go through.

1. **Spending less than you earn decreases the likelihood of debt.** A person who spends less than he or she earns creates margin. Job losses, investment downturns, and even relatively minor mishaps such as broken appliances or car repairs can drive the best-intentioned money manager into debt if no savings margin exists.

2. **Spending less than you earn makes saving money possible.** The standard pecking order for most budgets looks something like this:

Lifestyle Spending — Taxes — Debt — Savings — Giving

Typically, many people tend to divvy up their paychecks so they cover everything from clothing to entertainment. Then, they try to squeeze out enough to cover taxes and make the payments on their debts—not because they want to but because they have to. Finally, the leftovers—if there are any—are begrudgingly parceled out to savings, and finally to giving.

Margin: The cash reserve that provides protection from the storms of economic uncertainty.

By flipping this order around, however, we achieve a biblical—and successful—spending plan:

Setting the right priorities is an integral part of controlling your spending. By following this giving-and-saving-first spending plan, chances are much better that you'll avoid financial trouble. In addition, you'll be able to rack up significant savings to help you meet an unpredictable future.

3. **Spending less than you earn decreases the possibility of future financial problems.** Because smart spending eliminates the debt option and creates a legitimate savings plan, the longer you follow this practice, the less likely it is that you will encounter severe financial hardship in the future.

Jim was laid off from his six-figure management position and remained jobless for more than a year. With two children to put through college, the family's future might have been grim. But Jim had long practiced frugality—from clipping coupons to buying a modest home to setting aside money in an education fund. With little or no debt and a carefully tended nest egg, Jim countered the blow of unemployment and survived far better than most.

Reducing debt, saving money, and establishing a secure financial position for the future may sound like an ideal—but impractical or impossible—objective. Yet it's actually a relatively straightforward task, provided you follow a sound financial plan. Spending money is easy; knowing how to spend wisely takes common sense, discipline, and occasionally a few tricks from the files of folks who have taken control of their finances and learned how to stretch a dollar in both good times and bad. The following sections describe some of those tricks.

The How-Tos of Smart Spending

Anyone who has ever tried to live on a budget knows that the process requires both dedication and discipline. Before you can begin to control your spending, however, you must recognize exactly how much money you have available. You must accurately evaluate your spendable income.

Evaluating your spendable income

Only about 50 or 60 percent of your total paycheck can be considered discretionary income. A family making $50,000 per year does not have $50,000 to spend. Assuming they tithe 10 percent and about 20 percent of their income is withheld for taxes, the family is left with no more than $35,000 to cover everything from housing, food, and clothing to entertainment, car repairs, medical expenses, and more. And that does not include putting anything aside in savings! Add outstanding debt to the list, and the belt gets even tighter.

> **Only about 50 or 60 percent of your total paycheck can be considered discretionary income.**

To gain an accurate picture of your individual spending resources, begin by completing the Projected Annual Income worksheet on the following page. Before you begin, a few notes may help:

- The chart is meant to be comprehensive; it is unlikely that all categories will apply to your situation.
- The Amount Received Monthly column is for regular monthly cash inflow. Use the Amount Received Annually column to record money you receive less regularly, such as tax refunds or cash gifts.

Gross income: The total before any money is deducted, whether for taxes, health insurance premiums, or other expenses.

- When calculating your estimated interest and dividends, refer to your prior year's tax return and bank statements. For example, if you have $2,000 in a money market fund that will earn approximately 4 percent annually, you should record $80 in estimated interest from that fund. If you have rental property, estimate your annual rental income, and then subtract your annual expenses (including your mortgage payment) to arrive at a net cash-flow amount.
- To calculate the Annual Amount column, multiply the number in the Amount Received Monthly column by 12 and add it to the number in the Amount Received Annually column.

PROJECTED ANNUAL INCOME

Year: _____

Income Sources	Amount Rcvd. Monthly	Amount Rcvd. Annually	Annual Amount
Gross wages (husband)			
Gross wages (wife)			
Business income			
Bonus or overtime income			
Pension income			
Miscellaneous income			
Rental property, net			
Interest			
Dividends			
Gifts received			
		Total Gross Income	

Having calculated your total gross income, you can figure out how much money you actually have available for spending, using the Annual Spendable Income worksheet on the next page. Following the biblical spending model described earlier, make allowance first for annual giving totals, then savings, then debt repayment, and finally taxes.

Developing a spending plan

Having evaluated your spendable income, the next step in developing a successful spending plan is to determine how much you actually have been spending in the past. Then, decide how much you would like to spend on a monthly basis in the future. This process, known as living on a budget, takes self-discipline, realism, and a long-term commitment.

George once worked in my financial planning firm. He used to play professional football, and while he would never have been considered fat, he did have some leftover weight lifter's bulk he wanted to shed. He changed his eating habits, and at six-foot-four, he ultimately cut a rather dashing figure.

Meanwhile, I continued to struggle to deflate the spare tire that circled my waistline. "Why don't you look like George?" Judy teased me one day.

"I would," I hastily assured her, "if only I were seven inches taller!"

Like many people, I have no problem dropping five pounds in a couple of

ANNUAL SPENDABLE INCOME

1. Total gross income	
2. Charitable giving	
3. Savings	
Via payroll deduction	
Personal	
4. Debt repayment	
Credit card payments per month x 12	
Car payments per month x 12	
Other	
5. Taxes	
Federal withholdings	
State withholdings	
FICA/Medicare withholdings	
Current year federal estimates	
Current year state estimates	
Prior year taxes	
6. **Total** (add lines 2–5)	
7. **Total spendable income** (line 1 minus line 6)	

days—only to gain it back again the moment I let down my guard. But I realized I didn't need to lose just five pounds; I needed to take off about 15 pounds. Recognizing the importance of setting a "big" goal and allowing myself ample time to achieve it, I decided to lose 25 pounds and gave myself 6 months to get the job done. I'm happy to report that I accomplished my goal. To do it, I had to change my eating habits and adopt a long-term attitude about the task.

The same principles hold true in establishing and maintaining a budget. You need to set a worthy goal (that is, a big goal). Then you must be realistic about what you are trying to do and give yourself enough time to finish the job. Like the weight loss that results from a change in eating habits, the only permanent solution to spending woes must be fueled by a long-term shift in spending patterns.

To create a realistic spending plan, begin by answering two questions: What are you spending? And what would you like to spend? Getting the correct information can take as long as two years, but if you discipline yourself to stick with the process, your eventual budget will be better equipped to withstand the ups and downs of family life and uncertain economic conditions.

1. **What are you spending?** Go back over the last 12 to 24 months and gather data from checkbook registers, credit card receipts, and other records. Include ATM withdrawals and checks written for cash. If you can't remember what the money was used for, record the amounts as miscellaneous.

   If you don't have past records, then consider keeping a spending diary for at least one month. Write down each check, cash expenditure, or automatic draft. As you write a transaction in your spending diary, try to put it in a category for easier review at the end of the month.

2. **What would you like to spend?** This question reflects your first attempt to develop a budget. Ask yourself, "Given my spending history, what would I like the future to look like?" All of us would like to spend more on items like entertainment and clothes, but we need to live within the boundaries

FAMILY FINANCE

"Shannon, I don't know where I'm going wrong!" Alysha exclaimed to her friend as they sat in Alysha's living room. "I'm trying so hard not to spend extra money. I'm packing my lunch each morning. I've been better about saying no to the kids when they want something they don't really need. I'm going to the discount grocery store at least some of the time. But I'm still coming up short every month. I need to be paying down my credit card debt, but last month I added to it."

"You sound pretty discouraged," Shannon said sympathetically. She handed Alysha a wrapped package. "But I have a surprise for you that might help."

"Really?" Alysha opened it curiously and pulled out a financial software package. "Shannon, thank you! How did you know I needed this?"

Shannon smiled. "I bought it last week after you told me you were going to work on a spending plan. I know how much you love your laptop, and I figured having your finances on the computer might work better for you than doing everything on paper."

"You're right! I can't wait to try it out."

Two weeks later, they met at the coffee shop. "How is it going?" Shannon asked. "Have you had a chance to use the software yet?"

"Yes," Alysha said. "It took a while to input all the information, but now that it's all set up, I love it! I sat down last night and finished my Projected Annual Income worksheet. It tracks all my income—from work, from Todd's child support payments, and from interest on investments—not that I have too many of those. Then I can put in how much I want to give and how much

Q: How do I account for ATM withdrawals in my budget?

ANSWER: One approach is to consider what the ATM withdrawals are for—are they for lunch money, spending money or gasoline? Then record those in your budget accordingly. Or if the amounts are small and miscellaneous in nature, you may lump the withdrawals into one category in the budget called "ATM withdrawals."

Here's another practical approach if you maintain a checkbook. When you make an ATM withdrawal or a credit card charge, you enter that charge in the checkbook just as if it were a check written. Then, reduce the balance in the checkbook register accordingly. Effectively, at the end of the month, you have set aside whatever you need to pay for the ATM withdrawals and your credit card charges. In so doing, you shouldn't overdraft your checking account.

I want to save, and it shows me how much money I actually have to spend each month."

"So at least you're not in the dark about where your money is going," said Shannon.

Alysha took a sip of her coffee. "Yeah, and I figured out one of my problems. When I put together my budget a few months ago, I based my income on my June paychecks. But yesterday I realized that June was when our office sold 23 houses. It was the biggest month all year, and I worked about 20 hours of overtime."

Shannon leaned forward. "So those checks had extra overtime pay."

"Right." Alysha sighed. "I'd been assuming my regular paychecks would be that high, and of course they're not. The real estate market is in a bit of a slump right now, so I'm lucky to be working full-time, let alone getting any extra hours. No wonder I'd been coming up short every month. I thought I had an extra $300 to spend!"

"Wow! Well, it looks like you're happy that you figured out the problem, but frustrated that your income is lower than you thought. What's the next step?"

"Now I have to do the second half of the worksheet and track my spending in detail. Then I have to figure out how to cut back." Alysha tapped her fingers on the table. "You know, Shannon, it's not much fun to confront my money issues. It would be easier to close my eyes to it and keep using my credit card like I have been for the past four years."

"That's what a lot of people do, unfortunately," Shannon said. "But I've got a feeling that's one bad habit you're beginning to break."

YOUR LIVING EXPENSES

Year: _____

	Actual Prior Month	Monthly Expenses	Nonmonthly Expenses	Total Amount
Housing:				
Mortgage/rent				
Insurance				
Property taxes				
Utilities				
Telephone				
Repairs/maintenance				
Furnishings				
Total Housing				
Food				
Clothing				
Transportation:				
Car payment				
Insurance				
Gas and oil				
Maintenance and repairs				
Total Transportation				
Entertainment				
Medical Insurance/ Expenses				
Other Insurance				
Children				
Gifts				
Miscellaneous				

of our income. (Note: Most people underestimate how much they spend by at least 5 percent. After you determine how much you want to spend, add 5 percent to each budget category to give yourself a more realistic picture.)

The answers to these two questions provide the basis for your spending plan, which you can develop by using the worksheet on page 114. Record the amounts you spent last month in the Actual Prior Month column and use them to help you determine the amounts for the next two columns. In the Monthly Expenses column, record the amounts you plan to spend each month. Expenses paid less regularly go in the Nonmonthly Expenses column. Multiply the amount in the Monthly Expenses column by 12 and add it to the amount in the Nonmonthly Expenses column to get the Total Amount.

Analyzing and adjusting your plan

Your Living Expenses worksheet represents your budget. Once you have attempted to live according to this spending plan for a period of time (at least several months, but preferably an entire year to get an accurate picture of total spending), you will probably need to make some adjustments.

Obviously, your goal is to live within your budget so that more money comes in than goes out. By analyzing your cash flow, you can determine how much margin your budget includes. Remember, margin is essentially extra cash; it's the amount of income received over and above your outflow.

If you currently have a negative margin (meaning that expenses are greater than income), then focus on the discretionary expenses, such as entertainment, going out to restaurants, or gifts. It's hard to adjust nondiscretionary items such as housing, taxes, and insurance very quickly.

Use the simple Cash Flow Analysis worksheet that follows to figure your margin, both on your initial budget and then on your adjusted plan.

CASH FLOW ANALYSIS

	Initial Budget	Adjusted Plan
Total spendable income (see Annual Spendable Income worksheet total)		
Total living expenses (see Your Living Expenses worksheet total)		
Cash flow margin (Line 1 minus line 2)		

If you exceed your budget, your margin is reduced. The only way to live on a negative margin is to borrow money—which only increases your debt commitments, further reducing your future margin.

Again, your goal is to live within your budget. As your income increases through salary raises or other means, your margin will increase—provided your living expenses do not change. Your margin (extra cash) will enable you to take advantage of the investment strategies and options outlined later in part 3.

Checkbook Basics

While visiting with a couple regarding their financial situation, I was surprised when the wife explained why keeping a checking account was so simple. She faithfully recorded her checks as she wrote them, and whenever she ran out of money she used a "neat" column she had discovered in her check register called Deposit. If she ran low on money, she merely added another $1000 to the Deposit column. However, that didn't mean she actually deposited anything in the account. Upon hearing this, her husband was shocked, to say the least. But at least he learned why they were continually overdrawn at the bank even though both of them had positive balances on their check registers.

Many adults simply don't know how to maintain a checking account. I'm always surprised to discover how many people *never* reconcile their checkbook with their bank statement; some don't know that it is even possible to balance it with the bank statement.

Balancing and maintaining a checkbook are skills that children absolutely must have by the time they leave home. Because children typically cannot cash checks until they have a driver's license, it's impractical for them to open a checking account until age 16. At that time we opened checking accounts for each of our children and spent some time teaching them how to balance their account every month.

> **Balancing and maintaining a checkbook are skills that children absolutely must have by the time they leave home.**

If you're not balancing your checkbook monthly, you must start doing it before you can teach your children. Please do not allow them to leave your home and strike out on their own without knowing how to maintain a checkbook properly.

If you don't know how to balance your checkbook, then the first step is to learn how. Balancing your checkbook requires that you maintain a correct running balance in your check register. When you receive your monthly bank statement, the amount *you* say you have must match the amount the bank says you have.

The process of reconciliation involves (1) *adding* to *the bank's* balance any deposits you have made that the bank has not yet recorded; (2) *subtracting* from *your* balance any services or fees the bank has charged you that are not recorded in your check register. If the bank's balance and your balance do not agree, one of you has made an error that must be found and corrected.

If you need specific instructions on how to balance your checkbook and reconcile it to the bank statement, ask your banker to explain how it is done. Helpful instructions about how to reconcile your accounts can usually be found on the back of your monthly bank statement.

Using Computer Software with Your Spending Plan

You may use a computer regularly for work or entertainment. It's just as valuable a tool when it comes to helping you track your family's budget. Computer software lends itself easily not only to helping you create your spending plan but also to maintaining your overall personal financial management. It takes the tediousness out of manually tracking, recording, and adding and subtracting. You can use it to allocate planned income and expenses in various categories and then monitor the actual income and expense compared to your plan. This enables you to know where you stand at any point during the month.

Several good software packages, ranging in price from about $30 to $70, are designed specifically for home money management. The dominant players are Intuit's Quicken software and Microsoft's Money software. You can also find excellent specialty choices such as Crown Financial Ministries' Crown Money Map Financial Software (see Recommended Resources on page 537). A creative personal computer user who already makes use of a spreadsheet program can develop his or her own personalized budgeting system using one of these templates.

Let me describe certain features to consider when setting up and choosing your computerized home money management system:

Budgeting. A personal management system must be able to create budget categories and assign income and expenses to them. Without a budget (the plan), you have nothing against which to measure your actual expenses.

Check writing. You want to be able to enter your expenses as if you're working directly from your checkbook. Include the date of the expense (or income), the payee (or the income source), the amount of the expense (or deposit), and the budget category.

Reporting. You need to see how your actual numbers compare to your budget. The computer-generated reports should clearly tell you whether you are under or over budget by category. Besides the standard reports included in the software, you can customize your own report to track information in a unique way.

Standard monthly entries. In households, many checks are written to the same payee each month, often for the same amount. Our paychecks are usually the same each pay period. A good system should be able to remember and record standard entries so you don't have to reenter every item over and over.

Bank reconciliation. You'll want to balance your checkbook with your bank statement regularly. Personal finance software makes this dreaded chore fun (okay, perhaps it's only fun for financial nerds like me—but at least it's not as painful for most folks as manual reconciliation).

In addition to these important functions, financial computer software should offer the following:

Stability and enhancements. If you're buying commercial software, look for a company with a proven track record of providing quality service to their customers and upgrading their product. Is their Web site helpful? How do other consumer-reporting and financial publications rate them? If you needed to talk to a live person, how much is the charge, if any, for product support?

Flexibility. You need the ability to tailor budget categories and reports to meet your personal needs. Your software should be able to handle multiple banking and credit card accounts.

Easy to learn and use. Ideally, after entering your income and expenses the very first time, your software will produce a set of reports. Some systems are easy to pick up; others are more difficult.

Internet compatibility. Most commercial software products offer many financial updates regularly through the Internet. Also, you want to be able to download your credit card transactions or banking account transactions. You might even want to be able to update the market value of your investments daily. Some of this setup involves more sophistication and isn't as necessary as the basic checkbook and budgeting features.

Affordability. You certainly don't want to blow your budget buying a computer to set up a budgeting system, but it may be the best expenditure you make all year. Having a personal budgeting system for a home computer may not be the only valid reason to buy one, but combined with a few other tools, it may help you become a much better steward of your resources.

All these criteria relate mainly to budgeting and monitoring capabilities. Some software systems offer special enhancements. For instance, some have word processing and contact management software for names and addresses. Other features available are income tax estimates, portfolio management, life insurance needs analysis, home inventory tracking, personal calendars, and to-do list systems. I rarely use all these bells and whistles, but even after all these years I still track our checkbook balance, set up our budget, and print checks using software.

As you apply the techniques in this chapter, you will be able to begin building a margin, or emergency savings. In the next chapter, I'll tell you more about the importance of emergency savings and where to put them.

"Oh No!
How Will I Pay for That?"

Despite the importance of emergency savings, few families have them. It's startling to consider how many would go bankrupt after missing just a few paychecks.

In a recent radio interview, Elizabeth Warren, a Harvard University professor who has spent years studying personal debt, explained the dilemma many families face today. "Consumers, to the extent that they've stayed afloat, have managed to stay afloat by using their credit cards and taking out home equity lines of credit," she said.

Contrary to what many believe, Warren argued that this is not because they're spending money on lattes and exotic vacations. "Americans are in a lot of debt not because they're overconsuming, but because of big fixed expenses that they really can't wiggle out of . . . the things over which they have little or no control."[1]

I believe this professor has summarized well the problem facing many people today, particularly young married couples. Most have three priorities—a home, children, and financial security—but can afford only one of them—or two at most. As they've stretched themselves trying to attain all three, many have made serious financial mistakes. Cars, houses, and furnishings are the big-ticket items that get many people into trouble. I'd like to offer a bit more hope than the professor implies when she says such expenditures are "things over which they have little control." In the short term, this is true. It's hard to immediately unwind out of the house or car. But in the longer term, you can make adjustments and changes. You do have control; no one forced you into those decisions.

The first common mistake is for a second wage earner (usually the wife) to work to provide the income necessary either to purchase consumer items or to pay off debt they assumed when buying their first home. (According to the U.S. Census Bureau, 53.5 percent of American families headed by a married couple included two wage earners in 2006.[2]) As we'll discuss in chapter 31, the benefit of a working mother is generally overvalued; often it costs the family more than she makes in the long run.

ANSWER: If you are being charged 18 to 21 percent in credit card interest and have the savings to pay it off, do so. But this advice is contingent on two factors. First, if an emergency arises you must be able to borrow at an interest rate equal to or less than the current debt you have. Second, you must determine to replenish your savings with the monthly payments you would have made toward credit card debt.

Second, many families fall into a debt mentality and assume it is unavoidable. I recently counseled a young couple unable to make ends meet. It was quickly obvious why: Their $450 monthly car payment sapped their resources. I suggested they trade that car for a less expensive one, but they both said that was impossible because the car was a gift from her father. The father had made the down payment and then given them the payment book! I thought to myself, *What a terrible gift!*

The Federal Reserve estimates that 19 percent of disposable income goes toward the repayment of debt.[3] That means if a couple or single person tithes, pays taxes, and has this debt burden, then about 50 percent of their gross income is available for living expenses and saving for the future. It's no wonder that debt causes such problems for many families!

The third significant financial mistake many families (particularly young couples) make is thinking they need to own a home. In the past a home was generally a good investment because high inflation and fixed interest rates were guaranteed. In many areas of our country, neither of those two benefits now exists. Today, the dream of home ownership may have to be given up if it does not make good economic sense.

Couples who make any or all of these financial mistakes generally are stretched so thin that they make a fourth: They do not build any savings for emergencies. People often ask me questions such as "Should I pay off my credit cards first or put some money in savings?" and "Should I start giving or saving?" My usual response, somewhat tongue-in-cheek, is simply, "Yes, of course." Preparing for financial emergencies is another thing so many families know they "should" do but never achieve, often with very painful consequences.

In chapter 3, I mentioned the four transcendent planning principles of financial success. They apply all the time to all levels of income and all organizations: spend less than you earn, avoid debt, set long-term goals, and maintain liquidity. In this chapter, we'll focus on liquidity.

Liquidity: The ease and speed with which an asset can be turned into cash.

Think of liquidity as available savings. It includes cash and bank accounts or other holdings that can be converted to cash quickly. Certificates of deposit and savings bonds, for example, are liquid assets. Real estate lots or rental properties are not liquid assets.

Insight into Liquidity

Have you ever wondered why liquidity is so important? It's simply because the future is so uncertain—companies downsize, cars break down, medical emergencies occur, and so on. A recent survey shows that one in ten Americans fears losing his or her job. Fifty-four percent of Americans worry that they wouldn't be able to pay their medical costs if they had a serious injury.[4]

Liquidity—or having readily available cash (such as an emergency fund)—is a key aspect of financial flexibility. In many cases it makes the difference between going into debt and remaining debt free when you encounter unexpected expenses or major purchases. It gives you the choice of how you will pay and where you will buy, and allows you to pay without incurring interest costs.

One reason that families without liquid assets feel so much pressure is that our society is structured so that the less money you have, the more things cost, and the more money you have available, the less things cost. If, for example,

About 19 percent of disposable income goes toward the repayment of installment and credit card debt.

you have cash to buy consumer items like clothes and furniture, you do not need to use a credit card, which will charge up to 22 percent interest—not to mention other charges, such as late fees or annual fees just to carry the card.

Also, if you need to borrow money for items such as cars or furniture, you not only pay interest, but you are likely to have bank fees, loan insurance, and late payment penalties. The same applies for purchasing a home, where, in addition to the debt cost, you have such expenses as credit report fees and settlement charges, which can amount to thousands of dollars. The same is true if you are late on a utility payment because of low cash. You are charged additional fees and may even suffer the loss of service.

As you can see, liquidity is important because the Western monetary system requires people to have money in order to function (to pay for utilities, clothes, mortgage, etc.). A person who does not have the money available will pay a premium for anything he or she wants to purchase.

Think about that as you decide how much money to keep on hand. Cash can work wonders. When you have it available, you can take advantage of sales and often even negotiate lower prices. For example, Rick is a new homeowner. A company approaches him offering to install replacement windows in his home. Rick agrees to a quote. The quoted price is $9,500 to replace all his windows. The company offers a special deal, telling Rick he won't have to pay for one year. Rick offers to pay in full upon completion rather than accept the one-year payment deferral. After a call to the sales manager, the salesperson says the company can lower its price to $8,700. The company is willing to do that in order to receive payment now.

If you can pay your car insurance or term life insurance annually or semi-annually, you'll pay less than if you pay monthly.

So how much should you put in an emergency savings fund? Once again, there are no absolutes. It depends on your job security, level of living expenses, debt situation, plans for major purchases, and your own comfort level. Beginning this fund may seem daunting; however, you can begin to build it simply. Some families begin by setting aside any extra income above normal salary (overtime, tax refund, bonus, or garage sales). Others arrange an automatic transfer from their payroll check or checking account to a savings account each month. Even saving their daily pocket change separately is a start.

> **Our society is structured so that the less money you have, the more things cost, and the more money you have (liquidity, that is) the less things cost.**

For example, two months' living expenses would be adequate for someone with job stability. If your job is susceptible to strikes and layoffs, saving three or four months of living expenses would be better. A person working on a 100 percent commission basis may need six months' expenses (especially if the commissions come in random intervals).

An initial target would be one month's living expenses in checking and two months' living expenses in savings.

Investing for the Short Term

Liquidity enables you to easily access funds needed for daily living expenses. Remember that *liquid* means the funds are either in cash or can be readily converted to cash at the fair market value. They will not lose value at sale because of the lack of a ready market. Because you need to be able to get to this money immediately, these assets cannot be placed in long-term investment vehicles. Yet even liquid assets have the potential of producing some return.

Remember that while the purpose of an *investment* is to enhance one's income and/or asset growth, an emergency fund has a different purpose. It is used to provide *liquidity*. Your emergency fund should be kept in a place that offers a market rate of return (interest) but without any risk, e.g., a bank money market savings account or a money market fund. The intention is to have these funds readily available as cash without the risk of losing principal. *Availability*, not *return*, is the chief criterion.

Listed below are several options for parking your margin or savings until they are needed, while at the same time maintaining a high degree of liquidity and safety and maximizing your investment returns:

1. **Passbook savings accounts.** These savings accounts, offered through any bank or savings and loan, offer low interest rates. Consumers may qualify for higher rates if their account reaches a certain balance.

2. **Checking accounts.** Many banks offer interest-paying checking accounts at passbook savings rates (NOW accounts), provided a minimum balance is maintained. In some cases, free checks may also be included. If you keep one month's living expenses in checking, you will probably qualify for these interest-bearing accounts. But beware: In some geographic areas, monthly service charges can be significant!

3. **Money market funds.** (Also called money market mutual funds or daily money funds.) Most mutual fund companies, such as American Funds, Fidelity Investments, or Vanguard, offer these accounts. Money market funds pay higher rates of interest than the bank. The rates vary daily according to the prevailing market interest rates. If prevailing rates increase, the money market funds will reflect this rise. If rates fall, the funds will track downward. The funds are as liquid as banks or credit unions, and most offer check-writing privileges. Although they are not insured by the government through the Federal Deposit Insurance Corporation (FDIC) like bank deposits, they have not had defaults or losses historically. Money market funds are excellent parking places for short-term funds or funds being accumulated for investment. They offer liquidity, flexibility, and check writing all rolled into one package.

> **The purpose of an *investment* is to enhance one's income; the purpose of an *emergency fund* is to provide liquidity.**

4. **Market investment accounts.** These savings accounts offered by local banks pay interest at money market rates. Your bank may call it something else, but simply ask about their "money market account." They may require a minimum balance (e.g., $1,000) and limit you to writing three checks against your account each month.

5. **Credit unions.** Credit unions usually offer slightly higher interest rates than banks on both checking and savings accounts. Depending on the point in the cycle of interest rates, they may even beat the money market funds.

6. **Certificates of deposit (CDs).** CDs can be a good place to park money as long as you don't need the money immediately. CD terms may vary from 90 days to six months to five years. Again, according to geographic location, some banks or credit unions may offer a percentage point or two premium compared to savings accounts if a depositor is willing to tie up his or her money for a guaranteed period of time. If an emergency arises, you can either make a premature withdrawal or borrow from the bank using the CD as collateral. In this case, you are risking the probability of an emergency occurring before your CD matures against the increased yield you can get from a CD. CDs carry a surrender penalty—usually six months of interest—for an early withdrawal.

We Had an Emergency Savings Fund . . . but We Used It Up in an Emergency

An emergency fund enables you to withstand life's uncertainties, such as repairs, medical expenses, job layoffs, and so on. When these crises happen, emergency

FAMILY FINANCE

Luis stared at Victoria. "You're sure that's what the mechanic said? Almost $730 to replace the fuel pump?"

Victoria nodded glumly. "Yep. And he said the rear brakes are about ready to go out, so that will be another $550."

Luis leaned back on the couch. "I guess we'll have to put it on the credit card," he said. "I don't know what else to do."

Victoria groaned. "I hate doing that! But we both knew taking the trip last month was a financial risk. I guess now it's clear that it wasn't a wise idea."

The previous month, Luis's sister had suggested a weekend getaway for all six of the Reyes siblings and their families.

Luis hadn't seen two of his brothers in over two years, and Victoria had longed to see her kids get closer to their cousins. Going on vacation together over the Labor Day weekend would bring them all together for the first time in years. And the hotel with an indoor water park and spa had initially sounded fantastic. But Luis's sister Sophia, who had organized the trip, hadn't planned on a budget. And by the time Luis and Victoria had realized how much the whole weekend would cost, all the other siblings were on board and Victoria would have felt bad backing out.

"We had a great time," Luis said, smiling. "Manuel loved the water slides, and Cristina enjoyed splashing in the

savings help you deal with the financial consequences. After the crisis passes, you should try to replenish the emergency savings fund over the next several months. (People often ask whether building this fund or paying off their debt should take higher priority. See page 350 in chapter 23 for my recommendation.)

Unfortunately, some people think this extra savings can be available for other needs—not emergencies. After not using the emergency savings for six months or a year, it may be tempting to tap into it to fund gifts, impulse purchases, and vacations. These are items that should be planned for in your family's budget, as we discussed in chapter 8.

Occasionally, I meet someone who suggests that building an emergency savings fund indicates a lack of faith. If that's your perspective, consider Proverbs 6:6-8:

> Go to the ant, you sluggard;
>   consider its ways and be wise!
> It has no commander,
>   no overseer or ruler,
> yet it stores its provisions in summer
>   and gathers its food at harvest.

Matthew 25:3-4 says, "The foolish ones took their lamps but did not take any oil with them. The wise, however, took oil in jars along with their lamps."

kiddie pool. I got in a round of golf with Juan and Pedro . . . "

"And I did some shopping with Sophia," Victoria added. "Then there was the evening we asked your niece and nephew to babysit so we could go out for a romantic dinner—at a place that cost twice as much as any restaurant we'd ever been to!"

"All told, that weekend cost us more than $900," Luis said. "It was fun, but it almost wiped out our savings account."

"Next time, maybe we should stay home and just get together with our friends at the local pool," Victoria added. "We could do that, get a babysitter, and go out to dinner for less than $100."

"You know what I think?" Luis asked. "We shouldn't think of that savings account as a place to turn when we want to splurge. We really need to think of it as our emergency fund."

Victoria nodded. "You're right. If we agree that fund is for emergencies only, we'll be much less likely to use the money for something trivial that's not in our budget."

"Agreed," Luis said. "We learned the hard way this time, and now we need to set up a payment plan. Let's get this car repair paid off as soon as we can and start building up that emergency fund again. I'd love to get it even higher, so we can cover a few months of living expenses if we have to."

Finally, Proverbs 21:20 states: "In the house of the wise are stores of choice food and oil, but a foolish man devours all he has."

The key to prudent savings is following a plan. Ask yourself, for example, what you are saving for and how much is needed. If cash is being accumulated simply because it gives you a good feeling or a sense of security, then you're probably following a hoarding plan rather than a savings plan. If your faith increases only as your bank account increases (or vice versa), then you don't have a money problem, you have a spiritual problem.

Yet creating an emergency savings fund is an important part of any balanced financial plan that will help you avoid debt—the subject of our next three chapters. When parking money for emergency living expenses or short-term major purchases, look beyond the yield (which may sometimes be low) and determine how this sequential step can help you achieve your overall financial goals.

Don't Drown in Debt, Part 1: The Ins and Outs of Debt

Seventy-two-year-old Ed Carlson, a retired insurance executive, looks around his dining room table with satisfaction. His two children have come home to their parents' home in Ohio for Thanksgiving. Ed's son, Jeff, and Jeff's wife, Kathy, sit on one side of the table with their teenage son. Jeff and Kathy's two daughters sit on the opposite side, next to Ed's daughter, Robin, a single professional who owns a small marketing firm.

Ed smiles as Kathy jumps up to help his wife, Shirley, clear away the leftover pumpkin pie and stack the dirty dessert plates. "We've got a lot to be grateful for, don't we? Jeff, your wife is still as pretty as the day you first brought her home to meet us. Remember? That was the night you hit a three-pointer and sent your team to the conference finals. I think I remember you bragging that someday you were going to play for the New York Knicks!"

"Ah, yeah, Dad. The best part is I really did get to marry the woman of my dreams," he says, winking at Kathy. "I didn't quite make the majors, but I'm having fun coaching other would-be superstars at Fenton High." *Though the million-dollar salary of a pro sure would come in handy right now,* he thinks. *Kathy and I would never have taken our family on that cruise last Christmas if we'd known our pipes would freeze and burst while we were gone. Can't believe we're still trying to pay for new drywall, wallpaper, carpeting, and furniture. Man, I wish I'd listened to Dad when he told me I should look over the contingencies on our home-owner's policy carefully. . . .*

"And Robin," Ed says, looking fondly at his daughter. "Look at you. You always said you wanted to own your own business, just like me, and here you are getting rave reviews from your clients!"

"Well, I still go to you first when I have a question about operating my business," Robin says. *Of course, I've been too ashamed to tell you how far I'm falling behind on my accounts payable,* she thinks. *Why don't clients pay on time? Why are the costs of doing business going up so high so fast? And what was I thinking the first time I used my Visa card to cover my office rent?*

Unaware of the financial pressure his kids feel, Ed assumes both are doing well. Jeff and Robin are not alone, of course. While it may not be a common topic at the dinner table, many people's minds churn with anxiety as they try to figure out how to handle their debt. That's why no reference book on money would be complete without an in-depth view of handling debt, whether from credit cards, student loans, or mortgages. Almost everyone has debt, has had debt, or will have debt.

In this initial chapter, we'll focus on what the Bible says—and doesn't say—about debt. We'll also examine the attitudes that lead a person down the road of debt. But first, I want to give you a summary snapshot—like that offered in the CliffsNotes literature summaries that help so many get through school—of debt issues. This may be enough for some people. Or if you are concerned about your debt situation, it can serve as an introductory overview.

The Summary Version of Handling Debt

My key beliefs concerning borrowing are as follows:

- Borrowing is not a sin.
- Borrowing may deny God an opportunity to work.
- Borrowing always presumes upon the future.
- Excessive borrowing may lead to financial bondage.
- Debt may be symptomatic of spiritual problems.
- Consumptive borrowing will sentence one to a reduced lifestyle in the future and will also limit financial flexibility and future financial independence.
- A husband and wife should be in agreement with debt decisions.

Here are some evaluation questions to ask when contemplating debt:

- Does assuming this debt make economic sense? In other words, will the economic return be greater than the economic cost?
- Do I have a guaranteed way of repayment?
- Do my spouse and I have unity in this decision?
- Do I have peace of mind when I consider making this borrowing decision?
- Do I have peace of mind when I pray through this borrowing decision?
- What personal goals and values am I meeting that can be met in no other way?
- What are my motives for assuming this debt?

The Bible contains great insights into how we should view debt and advises caution before falling into it:

> The rich rule over the poor, and the borrower is servant to the lender. (Proverbs 22:7)

> Now listen, you who say, "Today or tomorrow we will go to this or that city, spend a year there, carry on business and make money."

Why, you do not even know what will happen tomorrow. What is your life? You are a mist that appears for a little while and then vanishes. Instead, you ought to say, "If it is the Lord's will, we will live and do this or that." (James 4:13-15)

Suppose one of you wants to build a tower. Will he not first sit down and estimate the cost to see if he has enough money to complete it? (Luke 14:28)

Borrowing always presumes upon the future.

Do not be a man who strikes hands in pledge or puts up security for debts; if you lack the means to pay, your very bed will be snatched from under you. (Proverbs 22:26-27)

Borrowing is dangerous on several fronts:

- Economic
  - ➤ Compounding works against you. You need to be on the other side of compounding. Compounding works exponentially over time. Think of it this way: Simple interest is like addition. (2 + 2 + 2 + 2 + 2 = 10); compounded interest is like multiplication (2 x 2 x 2 x 2 x 2 = 32).

Compounding: The process of earning interest on the interest already applied to the principal. As an investor, this works to your advantage. As a borrower, it is detrimental, since you pay interest not only on the principal amount you borrowed but on the total amount you now owe.

  - ➤ Getting in debt is easier than getting out.
  - ➤ You pay back debt with after-tax dollars. So, to repay a debt of $4,000, you have to earn $5,333 of income.
  - ➤ Debt mortgages the future.

- Spiritual
  - ➤ Debt presumes upon the future.
  - ➤ It may deny God an opportunity to provide.
  - ➤ Debt may limit opportunities to serve God.

- Psychological
  - ➤ A family's stress level increases with debt. Even if you have a plan to repay, something in the back of your mind always wonders, *How will I repay?*

- Testimony (witness)
  - ➤ Your testimony suffers if you are unable to repay or are forced into bankruptcy.

That's the quick view. I have more good information to share on the debt topic, which is more complicated than "never borrow." As we should when considering all aspects of life, let's begin with the biblical perspective.

A Biblical Perspective

When I was practicing as a CPA in Indiana, my firm did a lot of bank auditing and consulting work. As a result, I got to know many small-town bankers. I remember meeting one young banker who had worked in all his company's departments, assuming increasing responsibilities. His bank had recently been sold to a much larger bank.[1]

The new bank wanted to expand the retail side of its business—that is, consumer lending. Over the next several years, it planned to greatly increase its credit card and installment loan portfolios.

But that raised a serious question for my friend, a committed Christian. On the one hand, he was an excellent banker, and his bank's expansion offered him the chance to become a top executive in the near future. On the other hand, he wondered if encouraging individuals to take on personal debt was consistent with biblical principles. He wrote me a letter and asked, "Can a Christian be a banker?"

Trying to discern if he could be true to his spiritual convictions and still promote a business he had serious questions about, my friend asked many respected Christians for their counsel. To his frustration, he discovered that there's not much clear understanding of or consensus on the biblical teaching about debt.

As my friend's experience shows, the biblical perspective on borrowing and related issues is not well understood—and there is often a great deal of inconsistency in how Christians talk about debt and how they use it. For example, many Christian organizations have lines of credit to operate parts of their ministries. Those that sell materials, such as books and tapes, often accept credit cards for payment.

Churches spend lots of money employing professional fund-raisers to help them set up programs for the members to fund new facilities and building improvements. These programs may involve selling church bonds (a debt assumed by the church) to fund the improvements. And recently we've seen the advent of "Christian" banks or credit unions that promote borrowing by individual believers and Christian institutions. Yet there is little teaching and training from our Christian leaders on this vital topic.

When pastors and teachers do address this issue, they are frequently misunderstood. I myself feel I've often been misinterpreted. To address the biblical perspective on debt, the remainder of this chapter will

1. Outline what the Bible does not say about debt

2. Explain what the Bible does say
3. Examine Scripture to see why people enter into debt
4. Summarize the biblical perspective on debt

What the Bible Does Not Say about Debt

Many misunderstandings about debt occur because people assume the Bible takes certain positions that it does not. The following list is not all-inclusive, but it's a good starting point, since most misunderstandings come from one of these faulty assumptions.

It doesn't say . . . it's a sin to borrow

The Bible does not say it's a sin to borrow money—though it gives many warnings about being in debt. However, it doesn't say you are out of God's will or have violated a commandment when you borrow. You may have violated a biblical principle and therefore must bear the consequences, but there's no indication you need forgiveness for having violated one of God's commandments. That's the difference between an unwise decision and a decision that disobeys God's orders. And in some cases, debt may simply be unavoidable—medical emergencies, job layoffs, or bankruptcy due to a lawsuit.

Romans 13:8 is the verse generally used to "prove" it's a sin to borrow money: "Let no debt remain outstanding, except the continuing debt to love one another, for he who loves his fellowman has fulfilled the law." That verse, however, deals not with money issues but with relationships. Having a debtor-creditor relationship does require us to honor our obligations to both Christian and non-Christian creditors. However, the verse doesn't say you've committed a sin when you borrow money. (On the other hand, Scripture is clear that when you borrow, you may not experience God's best for you. We'll cover this issue in the section on what the Bible does say.)

It doesn't say . . . it's wise to borrow

A second thing the Bible does not say about borrowing money is that it's wise; in other words, leverage is not biblically condoned as "the way" to prosperity. Many Christians have fallen prey to the misuse of leverage. I've seen leverage—using borrowed money to buy assets for appreciation—misused in every real estate boom cycle. People borrow to buy more real estate because they assume real estate will continue to go up. They assume they will pay off the debt after the real estate is sold. But sometimes real estate slows down in appreciation or declines. Many also use leverage when borrowing to buy stocks (referred to as buying on "margin"). This works well when the stocks go up but can be disastrous when they fall. Some people believe leverage is the wise way to conduct business and personal affairs. But absolutely nowhere in the Scriptures are we advised or commanded to use debt to accomplish God-given economic goals. On the contrary, the Bible contains many warnings against the use of debt.

> Leverage: Using borrowed money in an attempt to increase profits or assets.

Early in my practice as a financial planner, I met with a young real estate developer who was preparing to declare bankruptcy. He had earned a significant income every year, yet he was planning to declare bankruptcy the next week. When I asked how that could be, he made a comment I'll never forget: "Anyone can make money during times of inflation if he's willing to take the risk of high leverage." Unfortunately for him, the economy in his area had become very weak when he was the most highly leveraged, and he was unable to sell the properties he had developed. His cash flow dried up, he couldn't continue making the payments on his properties, and the lenders began calling his loans. Despite a college education and access to the best financial advisors money could buy, his only alternative at that point was to declare bankruptcy. After 15 years of business, he had nothing. The obvious question is, how could such a thing happen to an intelligent businessman with a lot of good financial advisors?

While most people can't envision trying to leverage on such a large scale, those who assume the only way to financial security is through home ownership (financed principally by a mortgage) are putting their confidence in a form of leverage. The subtle implication, again, is that borrowing for a home is the way to prosperity. Therefore, it must be the wise thing to do. Please do not hear me say it's wrong to have a home mortgage. (We discuss mortgages in chapter 13 and will discuss rules for borrowing in the next chapter.) However, the Bible does not say that leverage is the way to prosperity for the home owner, the real estate developer, or anyone else.

It doesn't say . . . God will bail you out of debt

Nowhere in the Bible do I find evidence that God is obligated to bail us out of debt. Many people who are heavily indebted have the impression that God has promised to get them out of their problems. The verse quoted most often is Philippians 4:19: "And my God will meet all your needs according to his glorious riches in Christ Jesus." That promise is true, of course, and God will meet our needs. But He doesn't promise to cancel the consequences of our unwise behavior.

The most vivid illustration I can think of is this: If you jump off the top of a 25-story building and then claim Philippians 4:19 for deliverance, God is not obligated to rescue you. He doesn't usually interfere with the natural laws He established. He made them for our good, so He allows us to live with the consequences when we violate them.

It doesn't say . . . debt is an exercise in faith

The Bible talks a lot about faith, but it doesn't say that the use of debt is an exercise of faith. Pastors whose churches are launching bond programs to raise money for new church buildings often tell me they're taking a tremendous step of faith by obligating themselves to pay back the debt. They seem to assume that since their churches will have to pay debt from resources they don't already possess, they are taking a bold step of faith. I have never seen a scriptural basis for this belief, however. I personally think it's a direct contradiction of Scripture. Rather than being a mark of faith, it's testing God, which we're warned not to do: "We should not test the Lord, as some of [the Israelites] did—and were killed by snakes" (1 Corinthians 10:9) and "Do not test the LORD your God" (Deuteronomy 6:16), which Jesus quoted when tempted by Satan.

My strong conviction, therefore, is that to say we're exercising faith by borrowing money is wrong. It's the same as saying God needs to use a lender to meet our needs. In fact, in many cases we put the lender in the place of God and allow him to meet the desires of our hearts as opposed to our true needs.

It doesn't say . . . it's a sin to loan money

Just as the Bible doesn't say it's a sin to borrow money, it also doesn't say it's a sin to loan money. Without question, however, a debtor-creditor agreement changes the relationship between two parties. Anyone who has borrowed money knows the feelings of dread it brings. It's no fun. Thus, when you loan someone money, you inevitably change your relationship with that person, even if that person is your own child.

For this reason, I suggest you do two things if you're considering loaning money. First, determine if the borrower has a legitimate need (as opposed to a desire or an opportunity). If there's a legitimate need, such as for shelter, food, or clothing, *give* the money with no thought of repayment. If you can't afford to give it, think seriously before you loan it, because it will change the relationship between the two of you, and you may never get it back. Second, before loaning any funds, ask if doing so may cause you or the borrower to miss out on God's provision. Seeing how God can work in a situation may increase the borrower's faith more than your loaning the money.

What the Bible Does Say about Debt

This section may be the most important part of the book because it establishes a biblical framework for evaluating borrowing decisions. In addition to financial principles from the Bible, we'll consider many noneconomic or nonfinancial principles that have a bearing on debt.

The apostle Paul says, "If anyone does not provide for his relatives, and especially for his immediate family, he has denied the faith and is worse than an unbeliever" (1 Timothy 5:8). The implied command to care for family members may outweigh any financial consideration when it comes to making a borrowing decision. Sometimes we must borrow to adequately care for a family member.

For example, on occasion I have recommended that a family with a handicapped child borrow to buy a van in which to transport the child. To me, that is a noneconomic decision that overrides the "foolishness" of borrowing to buy a depreciating asset. Some may argue (justifiably) that if the church were doing its job, this family would not need to borrow. Instead, the money would be provided by the church body. But the simple fact is that churches don't often provide such assistance.

A father may be forced into borrowing on a short-term basis to provide for his family because of illness, a layoff, or some other economic hardship. Or consider a single mother who is unable to meet all her obligations because the father is behind in child support. Borrowing to pay for school supplies or tutoring makes no economic sense, but it may make sense from a priority

FAMILY FINANCE

Alysha looked across the table toward her mom, Nancy Hedrick. Every Sunday after church they got together for lunch—sometimes at a restaurant, but now more often at Nancy's house. It had been a tradition for years, ever since Todd and Alysha had moved within a few miles of Alysha's parents. These days, the gatherings were much smaller than they used to be. Todd had stopped coming even before the divorce, and Alysha's dad had died of a heart attack two years ago.

Ellie and Donovan had already eaten and asked to be excused. Ellie was playing with her dolls in the living room and Donovan was on the porch swing, leafing through a *Sports Illustrated* Todd had given him. "It's just you and me now, Mom," Alysha said, sighing. "When the kids were younger I thought I'd never make it to the point when I wouldn't have to watch them every minute. Now that they're so independent, I actually

miss those times. I never thought I could be lonely with two kids in the house!"

Nancy nodded. "I know. They're great kids, though, even after all they've been through. Affectionate, polite, and bright."

"Not that you're biased," Alysha responded, chuckling.

They got up and began to clear the table. After loading the dishwasher and putting away leftovers, Alysha rolled up her sleeves to wash the remaining dishes. Nancy grabbed a towel to dry. "Alysha," she began hesitantly, "I have an idea, and I want you to think it over before you answer."

Alysha looked surprised. "Okay, Mom. What's going on?"

"You just mentioned feeling lonely. Since your dad died, I've really struggled with loneliness too. I have my job, and a few times a week I see my friends from church. But the ordinary evenings are tough for me. There's no one to cook

standpoint. She may have determined that helping her children succeed in school is much more important than the financial priority of avoiding debt. I don't think any of us would or could argue with her reasoning.

In these two cases, the breadwinner is providing for his or her family as God commanded. But there's a big difference between meeting the family's needs (food, shelter, clothing, medical care) and meeting its desires (vacations, entertainment, houses, cars). The problem is not with borrowing to meet needs, but with borrowing unwisely and contrary to scriptural warnings.

The Bible does say three things that have a direct bearing on borrowing decisions:

1. It's wrong not to repay debts.
2. It's foolish to be in a surety situation.
3. Debt may violate two biblical principles that are paramount in our relationship with the Lord.

for, so too often I just eat canned soup or frozen entrées. I end up with the TV on so I don't have to listen to silence."

"Mom, I had no idea it was so hard for you!" Alysha glanced at Nancy and went back to scrubbing the saucepan. "I guess I've been absorbed in my own problems, but I thought you were coping so well."

Nancy shook her head. "Here's the thing: I know you're struggling financially, and a big part of that is your mortgage payments. I have a big house that's already paid for, and I would love to have more people around. What would you think about moving in with me?"

Alysha looked shocked. "Sell my house and move here?"

"There's plenty of space. You and the kids could have the bedrooms upstairs. I'd stay in my bedroom down here, where I have my own bath. We could work out a cooking rotation and assign some chores to everyone. You could pay me a little rent. Ellie and Donovan would be in the same school district they are now." She looked at Alysha almost shyly. "What do you think? Could you stand me as a roommate?"

Alysha smiled. "Of course, Mom. We get along well." She continued slowly. "Not having a mortgage payment would be huge. We don't have a lot of equity in the house, but still, by selling it, I could pay off my debt and have a little left over." She looked at her mom, surprised. "This might be a huge answer to prayer. Maybe God is providing this solution for both of us!"

Nancy smiled. "I'm glad you think it's possible. I won't hold you to a decision now, of course. You'll need to talk to Ellie and Donovan, and I suppose you might need to talk to your lawyer about how the house assets would be divided with Todd. But think about it, okay? I'd love to have you here."

It's wrong not to repay debts

All borrowing must be repaid. Psalm 37:21 states, "The wicked borrow and do not repay." The conclusion from this verse is obvious: If you borrow money, you have no alternative but to repay all amounts borrowed. If you don't, by definition you're what the Bible calls "wicked."

An obvious question arises at this point: Is it wrong for a Christian to declare personal bankruptcy? To answer, we need to separate the moral from the ethical (i.e., the biblical from the legal). Our legal system allows individuals and businesses to have some protection from creditors through the various bankruptcy laws. However, I believe a Christian has a moral duty to repay the money he or she has borrowed. Failing to repay violates the principle in Psalm 37:21.

On the other hand, in some situations the legal system can be used for protection until debts can be repaid. But even though the law would allow you to pay less than what is owed, or to pay back with no interest accruing while the legal process works itself out, morally you are obligated to repay 100 percent of the money borrowed according to the interest terms originally agreed upon.

A notable example of a Christian businessman who declared bankruptcy is Walt Meloon, the founder of Correct Craft Boats. Through a series of circumstances following World War II, Walt and his brother were forced to declare bankruptcy for their company. Then they were able to reorganize their company under the protection of bankruptcy. And even though they weren't obligated to repay anything to their creditors, they spent the next 25 years searching out and repaying every creditor every penny that was owed. Walt's story is featured in a book called *Saved from Bankruptcy* that's a testimony to his commitment to follow through on his Christian responsibility. (For more on the topic of bankruptcy, see pages 522–524.)

Surety is foolish

The book of Proverbs may not go so far as to call surety a sin, but it explicitly warns against it.

Surety: Guaranteeing another person's loan.

Look at these strong, vivid words in Proverbs 6:1-5:

> *My son, if you have put up security for your neighbor,*
> *if you have struck hands in pledge for another,*
> *if you have been trapped by what you said,*
> *ensnared by the words of your mouth,*
> *then do this, my son, to free yourself,*
> *since you have fallen into your neighbor's hands:*
> *Go and humble yourself;*
> *press your plea with your neighbor!*

FAITH &
FINANCE

Q: Do you think it is wise to have loans among family members, i.e., brother to brother, adult to child, parent to child, etc.?

ANSWER: Whenever a financial transaction ends up in a loan, you've changed the relationship between the parties to a borrower-lender relationship. The Bible says the borrower becomes a slave to the lender. That is, in fact, reality, so when you lend money to a family member, you have created another level of complexity to the relationship, that of borrower-lender.

My counsel is that if there is a family member in need, the first thing to consider is whether to give them the money. The Bible says that a man who does not provide for his family is worse than an infidel. If the need is a legitimate one, I would suggest thinking about giving the money first. If that is impractical or unwise, then there should be a clearly designated borrower-lender relationship established with repayment terms and interest rates defined. It shouldn't be left to uncertainty in any way. Both the borrower and the lender need to clearly understand the terms. Those terms should be documented so the expectations for repayment are very clear.

Lending to or borrowing from family members is an extraordinarily dangerous thing to do because of that change in relationship. Paul writes in Romans 13:8 that we are to owe no man anything except love. Borrowing and lending between family members can certainly get in the way of the love relationship. It's not necessarily wrong biblically to lend or borrow between family members, but it may not be a wise thing to do. That also applies to becoming a cosigner for family members. In other words, guaranteeing the debt of a family member is no different than lending that family member the money. You're lending them your credit availability. The Bible has strong admonitions against becoming a cosigner (surety).

Allow no sleep to your eyes,
  no slumber to your eyelids.
Free yourself, like a gazelle from the hand of the hunter,
  like a bird from the snare of the fowler.

Proverbs 11:15 makes a prediction that I've found usually happens: "He who puts up security for another will surely suffer, but whoever refuses to strike hands in pledge is safe."

The Bible advises that if you find yourself in a surety situation, waste no time getting yourself out of it. Even if it isn't a sin, it makes absolutely no sense to be in a surety agreement when we are warned so strongly against it in Scripture.

My counsel about guaranteeing another's loan, therefore, is that if you do it, set aside the money in a separate account and absolutely expect to have to repay that debt. If you're unwilling to go that far, you certainly should not guarantee the loan because that's equivalent to entering into the debt yourself.

Thus, not to ensure repayment is a violation of Psalm 37:21, which we discussed in the last section.

A particularly difficult question regarding surety is whether to guarantee a loan for a relative, especially a child. My counsel is still the same: You should put the money aside and be willing to repay the lender with no thought of repayment by the relative. And remember that becoming a surety for someone changes the relationship just as if you had loaned the money yourself. Thus, you need to decide how much you want that relationship to remain as it is, because guaranteeing a loan will change the relationship.

Martha, a widow, is trying to stretch her deceased husband's retirement accounts to cover her bills. Particularly challenging are her prescription drug costs. Martha's daughter, Ann, regularly seems to be in financial difficulties. Martha thinks that Ann could live more frugally, but she's very concerned about her grandchildren (Ann's children). So in the spirit of helping Ann, Martha cosigns for a new credit card. This new card will allow Ann to consolidate her existing credit card debts at a lower rate.

After a couple of years, Ann files for bankruptcy. The collection agency pressures Martha to pay. Martha pays the entire credit card debt because she's on the hook as the cosigner. This outlay of funds puts even more strain on Martha's already weak finances. Every time Martha sacrifices an item to help make ends meet, she feels resentment toward her daughter. Sitting down for meals at holidays is a bit more uneasy than before. Ann feels the resentment, along with a bit of guilt, so she doesn't come around as often.

Debt may violate two biblical principles that affect our relationship with God

Debt always presumes upon the future. If you borrow money and believe borrowed money should always be repaid, then you're implicitly presuming upon the future unless you have a guaranteed way to repay the loan. Many loans are based upon optimistic forecasts of the future that don't pan out. Here's an example of a guaranteed way to repay a loan. Harold, age 65, has no debt. His home, valued at $200,000 is paid for. He's found a rural cabin he'd like to buy for $50,000. Rather than taking money out of his retirement plan all at once and being pushed into a higher tax bracket, he's planning on borrowing the money. He has a guaranteed way to repay through retirement plan withdrawals. Another guaranteed way is the fact that his home is worth far more than the home equity line against it.

If you think you may have the ability to repay but in fact you don't because your circumstances change, you will have presumed incorrectly upon the future. James 4:13-15 says, "Now listen, you who say, 'Today or tomorrow we will go to this or that city, spend a year there, carry on business and make money.' Why, you do not even know what will happen tomorrow. What is your life? You are a mist that appears for a little while and then vanishes. Instead, you ought to say, 'If it is the Lord's will, we will live and do this or that.'"

When borrowing, you need to ask yourself what assumptions and presumptions you're making about the future. If you assume, for example, that your health will remain good, that your job will continue to provide income, that the asset borrowed against will continue to go up in value, or that the business you own will continue to generate profit, you may very well find yourself in bondage if these assumptions do not work out. Again, a distinction needs to be made: The Bible does not say it's wrong to borrow money, but it does say it's wrong to presume upon the future. Thus, presuming upon the future to repay borrowed money violates not only a caution, but also a command.

So are there any circumstances under which you can borrow money and not presume upon the future? The answer is yes—when there is a guaranteed way to repay. We'll talk about those situations later.

Borrowing may deny God an opportunity to provide. God is interested in increasing our faith, and He has promised to meet all our needs. Therefore, I believe that in many cases, borrowing money denies God the opportunity either to meet our needs or to show Himself faithful, thereby increasing our faith.

It's easy, however, to get confused about the difference between a need and a desire. Desires are driven by our emotions and are very strong. Because of their intensity, they're easily misinterpreted as needs. So if we have a lack of money to meet what we have misinterpreted as a need (e.g., a large-screen TV), it's not hard to justify borrowing.

Several years ago, my family made a giving commitment that was above and beyond our tithe. When we did our budget planning for the year, however, we realized we would not be able to take our desired vacation at a ranch in Colorado and meet the giving commitment. So we canceled our vacation plans and gave the money as we had said we would.

Some time after canceling our reservations, the owner of the ranch we had planned to visit called to ask if we would consider coming to the ranch all expenses paid, including airfare for our family of seven. In return, he asked if I would give a financial seminar to his staff. So our whole family was invited to vacation there without charge in exchange for my speaking. We, of course, agreed to go. Subsequently, without making our desires known to anyone, we received four more vacation opportunities that year—all expenses paid!

That's a great illustration, but please do not hear me say that God will always work in this way. According to Isaiah 55:8-9, God's ways are not our ways. How He chooses to work in our individual lives is up to Him. He knows what each of us needs in order to grow our faith. I'm convinced, however, that if we had not given the money and had instead taken the vacation, or if we had given the money and borrowed for the vacation, God would not have provided as abundantly as He did.

Dan needed to replace an old, worn-out car. But he had read my first book and become convinced that he should not borrow to buy another. (See chapter 14 to find out why he felt this way.) By the time he needed to replace his vehicle, he had not been able to save nearly enough to buy a new model. What happened next is a wonderful story of God's provision for someone committed to following biblical principles.

Dan could find nothing suitable in his price range. Then the starter on his car went out, just when he was scheduled to go out of town on a business trip. That meant he would have to use the family's second car, stranding his wife. He started his trip on a Thursday.

On Friday, his wife, Jo, found a ride to work with a friend named Connie. During the day, Jo told Connie what was happening, and Connie said she and her husband had an extra car that Jo could drive while her car was being repaired. So Jo had the transportation she needed while Dan was gone.

Jo liked the car, a used model with only 34,000 miles on it. After driving it for one day, she decided to call Connie to ask if they would consider selling it. Connie replied that the car was indeed for sale. They just hadn't gotten around to putting an ad in the paper.

When Dan returned from his trip, Jo told him about the car and asked if he would be interested. He checked it out and concluded that it was in good shape and ought to be safe and reliable. When he asked Connie and her husband how much they wanted for the car, he was pleasantly surprised to hear that their asking price was just half of the amount he had saved. And when Dan looked at the service records, he found the sellers had spent nearly $1,500 on new tires and brakes for the car in the preceding 16 months.

Dan wrote me a letter to tell me his story. He concluded it this way: "You must know by now that I am the proud owner of that car. I almost felt guilty about the deal that I had just gotten, but I had to remember that we do have a powerful God and that He had just shown me a miracle. Thank You, God."

The Road to Debt: Common Human Tendencies

These four deceptions play right into fallen human nature, which strives to advance self and often attempts to use illegitimate means to meet some very legitimate needs. Let's consider four tendencies that are common to people in various cultures, socioeconomic levels, races, and economies. In a culture like ours, which encourages people to put themselves first, these also contribute to the problem of debt. These four tendencies are

1. Lack of discipline
2. Lack of contentment
3. Search for security
4. Search for significance

Lack of discipline

Based on my professional experience, I've concluded that most people who find themselves drowning in consumer debt lack self-discipline.

To illustrate the consequences, assume the following: A hypothetical husband and wife have a first-year salary of $40,000 that increases by $1,000 per year. They overspend their income by $2,000 per year, and they pay only the interest on their growing debt, or 13.9 percent of their total debt at the end of the year. (Note: To keep the figures simple, we are assuming one interest rate on what could be a variety of credit card and installment loans and that only the interest is due to be repaid each year.) The chart below shows what happens to them over a period of time.

Year	Income	Amount Spent	Difference	Total Debt	Total Payment	Payment as % of Income
1	40,000	42,000	2,000	2,000	278	0.69%
2	41,000	43,000	2,000	4,000	556	1.35%
3	42,000	44,000	2,000	6,000	834	1.98%
4	43,000	45,000	2,000	8,000	1,112	2.58%
5	44,000	46,000	2,000	10,000	1,390	3.16%
6	45,000	47,000	2,000	12,000	1,668	3.70%
7	46,000	48,000	2,000	14,000	1,946	4.23%
8	47,000	49,000	2,000	16,000	2,224	4.73%
9	48,000	50,000	2,000	18,000	2,502	5.21%
10	49,000	51,000	2,000	20,000	2,780	5.67%
11	50,000	52,000	2,000	22,000	3,058	6.11%
12	51,000	53,000	2,000	24,000	3,336	6.54%
13	52,000	54,000	2,000	26,000	3,614	6.95%
14	53,000	55,000	2,000	28,000	3,892	7.34%
15	54,000	56,000	2,000	30,000	4,170	7.72%
16	55,000	57,000	2,000	32,000	4,448	8.08%
17	56,000	58,000	2,000	34,000	4,726	8.43%
18	57,000	59,000	2,000	36,000	5,004	8.77%
19	58,000	60,000	2,000	38,000	5,282	9.10%
20	59,000	61,000	2,000	40,000	5,560	9.42%
					$58,380	

Notice that what begins as a small burden compounds over time. While in the first year this couple has to allocate only $278 to debt repayment on their income of $40,000, over time they have to commit $5,554 per year to debt repayment. That means 9.41 percent of their total income can't be used for any other purpose.

Second, because it takes 20 years to reach this point, they may be unaware of their compounding debt problem. Without understanding why, they've probably experienced increasing financial frustration as debt repayment takes an ever-increasing percentage of their income.

Third, after 20 years of marriage, this man and woman probably have one or more children at or near college age. But just as they're approaching the highest financial-need years, they have a decreasing amount of money available to meet those needs. It's easy to see why their lack of self-discipline over a long period might now cause frustration, confusion, conflict, and anger. A small problem has grown into a huge headache.

If this couple decides they want to begin repaying their debt over 10 years, they will experience in years 21 to 30 what the following chart outlines. To make the needed payment in year 21, their total expenses must go down by $10,800 from the previous year, more than 16 percent, even though they will receive a $1,000 raise. That lifestyle reduction will be painful! Debt repayment as a percentage of their total income must increase.

Year	Income	Expense	Difference	Total Debt	Total Payment	Payment as % of Income
21	60,000	50,200	9,800	35,760	9,800	16.33%
22	61,000	51,700	9,300	31,431	9,300	15.25%
23	62,000	53,600	8,300	27,399	8,400	13.55%
24	63,000	55,200	7,800	23,408	7,800	12.38%
25	64,000	56,800	7,200	19,462	7,200	11.25%
26	65,000	58,300	6,700	15,467	6,700	10.31%
27	66,000	59,900	5,900	11,517	6,100	9.24%
28	67,000	61,500	5,500	7,618	5,500	8.21%
29	68,000	63,100	4,900	3,777	4,900	7.21%
30	69,000	64,700	4,300	1	4,300	6.23%
					$70,000	

Note that it will be eight years before they reach the same level of spending they had prior to choosing to get out of debt. In other words, the choice to start repaying debt means reducing their spending to the level at which they had been at year 20. It's no wonder many people throw in the towel at this point and say, "It's not worth the cost to get out of debt!"

As bad as this couple's situation looks, it's actually unusual to find people with a self-discipline problem who overspend by only $2,000 per year. My hypothetical case also understates the problem in that most consumer debt costs a lot more than 13.9 percent interest—it's more likely to be 18 or even 21 percent.

The example ignores the consequences of taxes and charitable giving, too. If the couple receives a $1,000 raise per year and allocates 30 percent of their income to giving and taxes, that raise amounts to only $700 per year in additional spendable income. When receiving a raise, however, most people assume they have the full amount to spend. If they therefore increase their spending by $1,000 per year, they're going into an even deeper hole than what's illustrated.

> **Being self-disciplined means making the right decisions consistently.**

My experience is that most people who lack discipline don't even realize they're overspending. There's one tool that will point out the overspending problem and help overcome it—a budget.

Being self-disciplined means making the right decisions consistently. Some people are just naturally more self-disciplined than others because of their personalities, and some have learned self-discipline over time. Because of what self-discipline is, how it's learned, and how it's applied on a daily basis, there are many ways to acquire it. This book may aid you in the process, but the ultimate decision is up to you.

Lack of contentment

A lack of discipline may be caused by a lack of contentment. People often think this way: *If I lived someplace else, had something else, or did something else, I would be content.* But, as we discussed in part 1, contentment is really a choice.

Many things cause discontentment. Reading and believing ads is a common cause. Another is browsing in shopping malls, which can raise your level of discontentment so that it becomes almost impossible not to yield to the temptation to buy. It's no coincidence that the level of personal debt and the amount of time people spend in front of television and in shopping malls have both increased dramatically in the last 30 years.

Contentment is found by understanding and accepting a few important truths: There is much more lasting joy to be had by nurturing relationships with friends and loved ones than by buying things. It's much healthier to focus on what we have than on what we don't. Contentment is also a spiritual issue. Replacing an "I want" attitude with an "I'm grateful for what I have" attitude begins in the heart.

Search for security

A couple in the Northeast inherited a large sum of money several years ago. The wife spent almost the entire inheritance buying and then decorating a new home. Once they'd almost depleted their small fortune, the couple assumed borrowing was the only way they could maintain their lifestyle in this new home—which the woman hoped would give her the security she'd never experienced as a child.

Another way people's search for security often shows up is in the desire to participate in get-rich-quick schemes. I've seen many people compromise their standards and good judgment to try to quickly achieve the financial independence they think will make them secure.

Search for significance

The drive for significance is another reason people make foolish financial decisions. In my observation, this is more of a male problem than a female problem.

As a man myself, I can readily identify with the drive for significance. Unfortunately, men often attempt to achieve significance through investments, businesses, and possessions. They also try to meet this need through heavy borrowing, which threatens the security of their wives. As has been said, "The only difference between men and boys is the price of their toys."

Both security and significance are legitimate needs—and drive people in all cultures and generations. Likewise, lack of discipline, contentment, security, and significance transcend time and culture. However, the debt symptoms of these problems are more pervasive in Western cultures because of the ease of borrowing and obtaining debt.

Don't End Up on a Debt-End Street

Sometimes it's difficult to make the hard decisions, especially when our desires or the demands of our families are so strong. But choosing to trust God is always the best decision. Hebrews 11:6, NKJV, says, "Without faith it is impossible to please Him, for he who comes to God must believe that He is, and that He is a rewarder of those who diligently seek Him." Many times we borrow before seeing how God might provide, or asking Him to take away our desire for something that isn't really a need, or even watching to see how He might come up with a creative alternative to what we think we need.

Debt is more pervasive in our culture because of the ease of borrowing and obtaining debt.

The bottom line is this: (1) Don't ever put a lender in the place of God by depending on a lender to meet your needs; (2) don't ever play God by determining that the only way to meet your needs is to borrow. That denies God the opportunity to be who He is. The One who created the universe by a spoken word can certainly meet all our financial needs.

From a biblical perspective, we are free to borrow money, but there are consequences we must bear when we do. In other words, God isn't obligated to bail us out of difficulties resulting from foolish decisions. The nonrepayment of money borrowed is not an option for a Christian. Personal bankruptcy may be warranted in some cases, but never to avoid repayment.

Finally, remember that debt often violates two biblical principles by presuming upon the future and denying God an opportunity to do what He really wants to do in our lives. However, as I said earlier, borrowing isn't always wrong or foolish. How do you know when it makes sense? That's what we'll consider in chapter 11.

CHAPTER 11

Don't Drown in Debt, Part 2: Good Debt/Bad Debt

I remember my daughter Cynthia calling once from college to tell me she had received an unsolicited application for an American Express card. The accompanying promotional material said that as a college student, she already had a good credit rating. Her question to me was, "Dad, how can I already have a good credit rating when I haven't borrowed or had a credit card?"

I was amazed when credit card companies began offering credit cards to college seniors before they had a job. Now, freshmen are inundated with credit card offers. I've known of high schoolers who, once they turned 18, received credit card flyers in the mail announcing they'd been "preapproved." In 2004, 83 percent of undergraduate college students had at least one credit card in their name with an average outstanding balance of $2,300.[1] The aggressive tactics of lenders are similar to what a drug pusher does in terms of trying to get people hooked on something addictive.

The number of Americans who have absolutely zero debt throughout their lives is extremely small. Almost everyone has, or will have at some point, a home mortgage. In addition, every day we're confronted with borrowing opportunities. Something as simple as cashing a check usually requires two forms of identification, one of which needs to be a credit card. We live in a society that forces us to use credit or to have good credit to transact the daily business of living.

Having a credit card does not force someone to go into debt. It's essential, therefore, that you understand the different types of debt, the assumptions underlying them, and your own convictions regarding them to be able to respond wisely to the many offers to use debt.

I also feel strongly that parents and grandparents have the responsibility to train their children and grandchildren in the proper use of credit and debt. Children won't receive this training from anyone outside the home. It's not taught in most schools or churches, and certainly not by peer groups. The home is the place where kids must get sound, consistent teaching in this area.

Not only do most of us have some debt and live in a society that compels us to have at least a working knowledge of credit and debt, but all of us establish a credit record in the daily affairs of life. Most of us seem to fear our credit rating, but it's really nothing to worry about when credit and debt are managed properly. (See appendix A for more information on credit reports.)

The Difference between Credit and Debt

So what's the difference between credit and debt? Credit is having the ability to borrow. Credit reflects the potential borrower's integrity—his or her faithfulness and timeliness in paying bills. Based on that integrity, a potential lender extends credit. A person who believes that having credit cards is wrong should understand that having credit cards does not cause one to go into debt. It only means that credit has been made available to someone. An individual's use—or misuse—of those credit cards causes him or her to go into debt.[2]

Credit is not the same thing as debt, but it's used to go into debt. Debt results when the credit extended is used for the purchase of some product or service. That credit may require either the personal guarantee of the potential borrower, as with a signature loan, or collateral—some type of security interest in something of value, either the item purchased, such as a house or vehicle, or another asset of the potential borrower.

It used to be that "being able to afford it" meant you could pay cash for whatever you were purchasing. If you didn't have the cash on hand, by definition you couldn't afford it. Unfortunately credit allows us to live in the short term, as if there were no limit to our spending.

Credit is not the same thing as debt, but it's used to go into debt.

Deficit spending, at every level, has made any budgeting plan almost irrelevant because financing always seems available to spend more than planned. A crisis surfaces only when all sources of credit have dried up and a family's lifestyle has led them to borrow more than they can repay. At this point, the options are so devastating that many couples end up in severe conflict. This results in stress and division, sometimes even divorce or personal bankruptcy.

I have counseled many godly families who were in desperate financial conditions because they never established a spending plan. The opportunity to fund needs and greeds by using credit cards enabled them to overspend year after year.

When they ran out of credit, they had to make some tough decisions. Houses and cars had to be sold, children had to be taken out of private schools, clothing budgets had to be readjusted, and standards of living had to undergo a dramatic reduction in order for them to survive.

Though such scenarios are difficult, they shouldn't be surprising in an age when "being able to afford it" has nothing to do with whether you have the resources to pay for an item but strictly that you're able to afford the monthly payments.

In fact, every borrowing decision can be manipulated simply by extending the length of time of repayment in order to make it "affordable." Prior to World War II home mortgages rarely went beyond 10 years. Today, 30 years is standard, and in some cases it's possible to get a 40-year or 50-year mortgage. Fifty years is probably longer than the buyer will live. But by extending the terms over half a century, the payments come down to the "affordable" level.

This change in the way we view debt is one of its major deceptions. Debt-related deceptions are so effective because they make borrowing appear to be the wise and logical thing to do. For example, if you believe that "being able to afford it" means being able to afford the payments rather than being able to pay cash, you're certainly not equipped to resist the advertising that offers "easy payments." Nor will you consistently resist the advertising slogan offering "no interest for one year."

Deceptions come from advertising, from salespeople, from financial counselors, and even from respected periodicals. Major portions of every weekly newsmagazine are devoted to money and money management— and many of them generally perpetuate these borrowing deceptions. That's why it's critical to understand the falsehoods so we won't be taken in by them.

Four Rules for Making Borrowing Decisions

We considered the biblical perspective on debt in the previous chapter. Let's now consider how and when borrowing is appropriate.

I use the following four rules in making my own borrowing decisions, and I recommend them to you as you make yours:

Rule 1: Common sense
Rule 2: A guaranteed way to repay
Rule 3: Peace of heart and mind
Rule 4: Unity

These rules don't necessarily make it easy to decide whether to take on debt. The reason we consider going into debt is to meet a need or desire that has become a high priority to us. In many cases, however, the temptation to use credit to meet the perceived need overwhelms both common sense and spiritual convictions. That's why having objective rules to follow is so important. Weighing today's desires against future benefits is a classic psychological definition of maturity. These rules, then, will help you act maturely.

Rule 1: Common sense

This rule can be stated as follows: For borrowing to make sense, the economic return must be greater than the economic cost. To state it another way, when money is borrowed, the thing it was borrowed to purchase should either grow in value or pay an economic return greater than the cost of borrowing.

Looking at this rule in reverse, it makes no sense at all to borrow money if it's going to cost you more to borrow than what you're going to get in the way of an economic return. That return can be twofold. Your purchase could grow in value, such as a home, or it could pay a return, such as a stock that pays dividends.

I call this a commonsense rule because it makes no sense whatsoever to break it. To ignore this rule is to say, in effect, that you're willing to borrow money and pay 12 percent interest in order to deposit it in a savings account earning 5 percent interest. Yet every day many people agree to do just that—to "rent" money at a much higher cost than they can ever expect to receive in the way of an economic return. (Items like clothes and restaurant meals, of course, provide no financial return at all.) You may not have thought about paying interest as the privilege of "renting" money, but that is what it is.

> **For borrowing to make sense, the economic return must be greater than the economic cost.**

Rule 2: A guaranteed way to repay

If you borrow money to buy a home and owe less than the home would go for if it had to be sold quickly in the event you were unable to pay, you have a guaranteed way to repay the debt. You're not presuming the continuation of favorable economic conditions.

Paying with a credit card merely for convenience is another example of this rule at work. A few weeks ago I used my credit card to pay for gasoline. I did this knowing the money was already in the bank to pay for that service. I was not presuming upon the future.

There are three guaranteed (not presumed) sources from which to repay borrowed money:

1. Income earned from sources other than that for which the money was borrowed
2. The sale of whatever the money was borrowed for
3. The sale or liquidation of some other asset, such as a certificate of deposit or savings account

The reliability of these sources of repayment depends on many factors. Only you, as the potential borrower, can make that evaluation.

Rule 3: Peace of heart and mind

To determine whether you satisfy rule 3, you must ask yourself

1. Why am I doing what I'm doing?
2. Does what I'm doing violate any ethical or spiritual principle?
3. Do I have peace in my heart, or spirit, about this purchase?

The first question gets at motives. Is the reason for borrowing to get rich quick, to avoid working, to satisfy a want, to give an appearance other than the truth, to meet a need, or to attain some other desire?

This is a penetrating question to ask yourself. If you can become disciplined enough to ask and answer it honestly before every borrowing decision, at the very least you'll delay making impulsive decisions. In most cases, you won't borrow for the wrong reasons. If you're unwilling even to ask yourself the question, chances are pretty good that your motives aren't right.

Another way to check your motives is to explain to your spouse or a good friend why you're doing what you're doing. Most of us are masters at deceiving ourselves so we can justify what we want to do. But when we have to explain our motives to someone else and it's unpleasant or uncomfortable, or if the borrowing "just doesn't sound right" to that person, our motives are most likely wrong.

After answering the first question, you almost always know the answer to the second. If the motive is wrong—greed, lack of discipline, lack of contentment—you know you're violating a spiritual principle.

To illustrate the application of this rule, suppose a man could afford to pay $25,000 cash for a car, enough to buy a moderately priced new car or a nice used one. On the other hand, if he adds $15,000 of debt to this amount, he could drive a new luxury car. He may even be able to "afford" the payments on this luxury car. By asking himself, *Why am I considering going into debt to buy the luxury car?* he's challenging himself to examine his motives.

Closely related to peace of heart is peace of mind. I would separate the two this way: The mind is the intellectual evaluation, whereas the heart is the spiritual and emotional evaluation. Applying this to a borrowing decision, you should ask yourself, *Am I free from confusion about this? Do I have clear thinking and a solid conviction that this is the right decision?*

The questions related to this rule are not all-inclusive. They're meant to get you to examine your motives.

Rule 4: Unity

I don't understand it, but I know women have an intuitive sense about financial decisions that men usually don't. I also don't know why my wife can see things clearly that I can't seem to see at all. But I do know that when I've listened to her out of respect for her insight—and even gone against what I felt to be right—I have avoided problem situations.

The rule of unity applies to all of a family's financial decisions, investments as well as borrowing. Specifically regarding investing, I have two rules for husbands: (1) If you can't explain it to your wife, don't do it, and (2) even if she understands your explanation, don't do it if she doesn't feel good about it.

A commitment to unity between marriage partners (or, in the case of a single person, with an accountability partner) will help avoid most debt problems. But because accountability and unity go against our natures, it is the rule most often violated. Many men even consider it unreasonable. Their comment to me is, "You don't know my wife" or "You don't live with my wife." And of course they're right: I don't understand their wives. I don't understand my own wife many times!

Yet I've seen many come to harm by not following the unity rule. One example I recall is when I spoke at a conference for current and former football players. A woman toward the back of the room was noticeably weeping as I talked about the wisdom of this rule. As I spoke with her and her husband afterward, I learned that he had played on three Super Bowl teams. He earned a lot of money during his career. After he retired from football, he borrowed money—against her wishes and counsel—to start various businesses. The businesses failed, and they lost all their savings.

When I married Judy, I implicitly agreed that it was no longer "her way" or "my way" but "our way." And making a debt decision on my own could have tremendous impact, not only on her sense of security, but also on her real security. Thus, I am morally and ethically obligated to make her a part of that decision.

I don't borrow or invest money without talking to Judy. I don't even travel apart from her approval or commitment to what I am doing. She's saved me numerous times from overcommitting our time and financial resources. I've not been burdened with obtaining her input; I've benefited from her wisdom.

I encourage you to reread these four rules until they become so ingrained that you aren't even tempted to make a foolish debt decision. Let me say again, however, that I'm not suggesting that borrowing money is always wrong. Only the failure to repay is wrong. Following these rules will help you to live with a great deal of inner peace, as well as maintain peace within your family.

Understanding the Types of Debt

I can think of almost nothing that credit can't be used to fund. Giving to some ministries can be done using credit cards. Groceries, furniture, and all forms of entertainment can be bought with them. Cars can be bought on time. Homes can be purchased—and almost always are—using debt. Even funerals can be paid for using some type of loan.

The difficulty with discussing these types of debt is that most of them generate a high degree of emotion because of what they mean to the individual or group involved. In examining each type of borrowing, I'll use the four basic rules we just discussed. They provide some objectivity in evaluating these emotionally charged areas, such as college borrowing or church debt.

Here are the types of debt we'll review, so you'll be better equipped to make good debt decisions:

- Credit card debt
- Installment debt
- Home mortgage debt
- Investment debt
- Business debt
- College debt

The chart below provides a quick comparison of the typical interest rate, term, and collateral for each type of debt.

DEBT CATEGORIES

Category	Interest Rate (in percents)	Term	Collateral
Credit card	12–24	30 days	Personal guarantee
Installment	7–15	6–60 months	Item purchased
Mortgage	5–10	15–50 years	Real estate
Investment	8–16	Varies, usually <3 years	Investments
Business	8–16	Varies, usually <10 years	Assets of business
College	5–12	5–20 years	None but future earnings

Credit Card Debt

Most likely, your grandparents didn't use credit cards. The first widely accepted plastic charge card was issued in 1958 by American Express. The first general use credit card that allowed balances to be paid over time was the BankAmericard (which changed its name to Visa in 1977), issued in 1959. Consider the following statistics—and see what drastic changes have occurred in a generation or two:

- There were 1.3 billion credit cards in circulation in the United States in 2004, including about 574 million Visa and MasterCard accounts in the United States in 2004. Keep in mind there are approximately 300 million people in the United States including children. The average American had over seven payment cards in his or her wallet including credit cards, retail store cards, and bank debit cards in 2004.

- Total credit card debt reached $805 billion, or more than $7,000 per household, in 2005.
- Average household credit card debt has increased 167 percent between 1990 and 2004.
- The average balance *per open credit card* was $4,617 in 2004.
- The average interest rate paid on credit cards was approximately 14.54 percent in 2005.

Negative personal savings rate: Spending is greater than earnings, meaning a person is either dipping into his or her savings or borrowing to pay for purchases.

- Over 45 percent of American cardholders were only making minimum payments in 2004, up from 42 percent who did so in 2003.
- The average credit card balance in 2005 would require over 13 years to pay off if a consumer made only a minimum payment of 4 percent at an average interest rate of 14 percent.
- Among middle-class households, the average amount of credit card debt paid off with home equity loans in 2005 was $12,000.
- According to a national survey, the most significant predictor of financial stress is if households rely on using credit cards to cover nondiscretionary living expenses like rent, groceries, and medical expenses.[3]

I certainly don't want to bore you with statistics, but I find these both fascinating and alarming. Even after years of working with people and knowing

FAMILY FINANCE

Victoria Reyes sorted through the day's mail. Ads, a political flier, a thank-you note from her niece, who'd just turned seven, and the Visa bill. She threw the ads and flier into the recycling bin, read the thank-you note and left it out for Luis to see, and ripped open the bill. *How much will it be this month?* she wondered. *We had the car repair, so definitely higher than our usual $500.*

She pulled the paper out of the envelope and stopped in shock as *$3,400* caught her eye. *More than $3,000? This has to be a mistake!* Horrified, she looked down the list of charges, line by line.

West Emerson Urgent Care. Oh yes—that was when Cristina had woken up screaming in the middle of the night with what turned out to be a perforated eardrum. *MidAmerica Plumbing.* She sighed. That was a stressful Sunday afternoon when Luis had heard water dripping in the basement and realized the water heater was leaking rusty water all over the carpet. The plumber charged time-and-a-half on weekends. *Town & Country Appliances.* When the dryer had started taking three or four hours to dry each load, Victoria had put her foot down. They had been talking for months about

the extent of people's credit card debt problems, I'm still surprised by the enormity of the credit card debt problem. Beyond statistics, the burden ultimately falls on families, marriages, and children. It becomes very personal and human.

How do you determine whether you have a problem with credit card debt? Answering the following questions should be quite revealing.[4]

- Do you take cash advances on one credit card to make payments on another?
- Do you generally make only minimum payments rather than paying the entire balance on your credit card bill?
- Do you spend at least 20 percent of your income on credit card bills?
- Do you regularly use credit cards to buy groceries or pay restaurant tabs, knowing you won't pay off the balance that month?
- Do you pay your monthly credit card bills but miss payment on other bills, such as utility or medical bills?
- Do you hide credit card purchases from your family?

Misconceptions about credit card debt

People typically get into trouble with credit card debt because they fall victim to one or more popular misconceptions about credit. Their slide is hastened by the way these misconceptions appeal to our natural desires or fears, and by the fact that lenders aggressively promote this form of borrowing because they find it so profitable.

getting a new washer and dryer, and she had found a decent sale, so she convinced Luis they should go ahead. *In retrospect, not a good decision,* Victoria thought.

She sighed and kept looking down the list of charges. *What are all of these?* With a pit in her stomach, she realized that she and Luis had charged most of the Christmas gifts for the kids and their extended families. That, plus the several hundred dollars they still owed on their car repair, brought them to the horrible amount of $3,400.

How are we ever going to pay for this? She sat down at the kitchen table and stared blankly out the window. She and Luis had always been so careful about paying down their credit card balance every month. They tried to stay out of debt, and they'd been chipping away at the Labor Day getaway for a few months now. But so many things had happened at the end of the year, and they had spent more money than they thought. They hadn't realized how quickly it would all add up.

Well, I know what Luis and I are going to do for our date this weekend, Victoria thought wryly. *Cancel our dinner reservations and sit down together to figure out how to pay this off.*

Misconception 1: You can't live without it. This easily accepted notion accounts for a lot of credit card purchases. It helps explain why people who already have credit cards will apply for another they see advertised using that pitch. Credit cards are used almost exclusively, however, to buy temporal and depreciating items—nothing of any permanence. They're often used to pay for entertainment, which is certainly important to living a well-rounded life. But it's not the reason for our existence.

One way to avoid the unnecessary use of credit cards is never to make an impulse purchase. Always wait at least 24 hours to buy something you want after you first see it. That means you never buy anything the first time you go to a store unless it was already on your shopping list.

Following this procedure helps you think through what you want to buy and why. It allows the emotion of the impulse to fade and gives you a chance to consider how much you need the item and whether you really want to spend your limited dollars that way. If, after 24 hours and careful reflection, you still want the item enough to make a second trip back for it, you're more likely to be making a good decision.

Misconception 2: Having a credit card means you're creditworthy. A second misconception is that because you're able to get a credit card, you must be creditworthy. As pointed out earlier in this chapter, while credit card companies are concerned about creditworthiness, they're much more concerned about their profits. They're willing to take some significant losses while earning almost 20 percent in interest plus the fees they charge. Don't assume that just because you have a credit card, you can afford to take on debt. The questions you answered on page 155 should have highlighted for you whether you have a problem with credit cards. When you think about it, it's really scary how easy it is to get approved on a credit card application. In some cases, it requires little more than your name, address, and telephone number.

Misconception 3: All interest is equal. Another misconception is that there's no difference between an interest rate and an interest charge, when in fact there's a big difference. For example, suppose you borrow $1,000 at 12 percent interest for one year, with the full amount due at the end of 12 months. At that point you would owe $1,120. The interest rate and the interest charge would be one and the same, 12 percent.

Interest charge: The percentage of annual interest charged on a loan.

Interest rate: The actual interest rate paid on a loan, based on the fact that the borrower continues to pay the interest charge on the original borrowed amount, even though the principal decreases each time he or she makes a payment.

However, suppose you borrow the same $1,000 at 12 percent, but instead of paying it back with one payment at the end of the year, you pay it back at the rate of $93.33 per month ($1,120 divided by 12 months). The stated interest charge is 12 percent, but the *actual* interest rate paid is now approximately 21 percent, even though the total of interest dollars paid remains the same in both cases ($120).

The reason for this is that as you pay the $93.33 each month, you reduce the amount of principal you still owe by about $83. Yet you're still paying 12 percent interest on the full $1,000 throughout the year, even though the principal shrinks steadily from month to month.

If you borrowed the $1,000 to buy a flat-screen television, the salesperson would most likely congratulate you on paying for it the "easy" way. At only $93.33 per month, you could well "afford" it. But the fact is that while you could afford to take $93.33 out of your income each month, it was an extremely costly decision. Twenty-one percent interest, not many years ago, was considered usurious. Now it's considered normal for that type of purchase. This illustration graphically points out the deception of easy payments and the deception of interest.

Years ago, the government began requiring all lenders to disclose to the borrower what is known as the APR, a uniformly calculated "annual percentage rate of interest." The proper way to evaluate what it costs to rent money is to know the APR—the real interest rate the lender has charged and you have paid. If you undertake a car loan, home equity line of credit, or buy furniture on credit, the lender is required to disclose this to you. On your credit card statement, you can see the interest rate used to compute the finance charge. On the back of the credit card statement, in the "squint print," you can learn the details of how late charges work and how the interest rate can be adjusted.

There are many superficial differences between credit cards. Companies charge different fees and interest rates and have various ways of calculating the interest rate. They have different repayment terms, and many offer attractive "come-ons." For instance, I recently received a signed $500 check in the mail from a credit card company; I could cash the check, and the amount would be added to my credit card balance. I could then "repay the $500 conveniently over many months." Other incentives are free hotel rooms, frequent flier points, merchandise, and so forth offered to induce you to either accept or use the credit card. Just remember, however, that credit grantors are not benevolent. The enticement will cost you something.

Recommendations for Battling Credit Card Debt

Most of us must use credit cards at least occasionally to function within our credit card society. However, we *don't* have to use them to go into debt. There are three ways to get the benefits of using credit cards without going into debt:

1. Begin with a spending plan.
2. Use a debit card rather than a charge card.
3. Always pay the full balance at the end of the month.

Begin with a spending plan

My first recommendation is to begin with a spending plan. Unless you're operating according to that hated word, *budget*, you'll never have any real reason to control your spending. To use credit cards to fund your living expenses is to invite temptation into spending decisions. Researchers have shown that you'll spend 34 percent more using a credit card than if you don't. At first, I didn't believe this statistic. So I did a comparison by closely monitoring what I spent on credit cards for a month compared to cash for a month. I learned that I spent 33 percent more! It's easier to buy on impulse with a credit card. There's something about laying down cash for a purchase that causes a person to stop and think.

Researchers have shown that you'll spend 34 percent more using a credit card than if you use cash.

The way to use credit cards legitimately is for convenience only, staying within your spending plan and paying the balance in full when the bill comes. If you haven't already done so, set up an annual spending plan using the forms from chapter 8.

Use a debit card

My second recommendation is to use a debit card rather than a normal credit card. An amount charged to a debit card is immediately deducted from your bank or brokerage account balance. It's really no different from writing a check. When we use the debit card, we enter the item in our checkbook just as if we had written a check. Then we deduct it from our available balance. In place of the check number in the check register, we write "Visa."

Using a debit card allows you all the conveniences of a credit card, but you never have a credit card bill to pay because, in effect, it's paid the moment you use it. The only economic cost is the opportunity cost of not being able to "float" your purchases (i.e., earn interest on your money) for 30 days until the

Q: I firmly agree with you that a budget is crucial. However, my husband doesn't. He says it won't work and that we have more bills than paycheck, so why even try? How can I convince him that a budget is critical for us?

ANSWER: The challenge of living with expenses that exceed income unfortunately is quite common. Having a husband who feels a budget won't work only makes it more frustrating. It appears, however, that your bottom line question is not simply, "Is a budget required?" but "How can my husband and I work together with our personal finances?" A financial plan is built upon goals, which must be mutually agreed upon. It appears that the goals you and your husband have are incongruous—you do not see eye-to-eye on financial goals or spending patterns. I suggest that you consider some reading assignments that deal with the areas of marital communication and goal setting. (Chapter 30 might be a good place to start.) You may even consider taking a planning weekend during which the primary agenda is to discuss your financial situation and set some financial goals. (See page 67.) As a basis for all of this, I would certainly encourage you to pray that the two of you would see your finances from the same perspective.

statement is received. But that's a small price for the freedom of never having a credit card statement to pay.

Always pay the full balance

My third recommendation is that you never allow a month to go by without paying off the full balance on regular credit card accounts. If you're tempted not to pay the full amount because it will make a big dent in your available cash, you're not using the credit card properly. A credit card can be a great convenience, but it should never be used to go into debt. Credit card debt violates the first rule in borrowing earlier in this chapter. The cost of credit card debt—12 to 21 percent interest—is always greater than the economic return of whatever the card was used to buy.

Do plastic surgery—eliminate your credit cards

If you can't follow the preceding suggestions, or if you know you have a problem with credit cards, get out the scissors and perform plastic surgery by cutting up those cards. Then, don't even open the numerous unsolicited offers from credit card companies sent to you in the mail. (To protect your identity, shred them rather than just throwing them away.)

Installment Debt

Many times people tell me they don't have any debt. Yet when I ask if they owe on their car, they say, "Oh, yes." The point is that most people don't even think of installment debt as debt. And those who pay cash for cars, trucks, boats, furniture, and other expensive items are rare. When you do pay cash for a car, as I recently did, the price may go up because the dealership doesn't get to earn interest from lending you the money (or a commission from referring you to a bank).

Installment debt is usually incurred for consumer items purchased where the borrower pays back in "installment payments." The lender reserves the right to repossess whatever is financed should repayment fall behind schedule. The repayment itself is typically made on a monthly basis over a period of time no longer than four or five years. This type of borrowing is promoted by the advertising phrase "easy repayment terms." Installment debt is most commonly used to purchase a vehicle. Because I cover car financing in depth in chapter 14, I will not review it further here.

Home Mortgage Debt

The number of Americans who have absolutely zero debt throughout their lives is extremely small. Almost everyone has, or will have at some point, a home mortgage. A mortgage simply means a type of debt where the collateral is the real estate, usually a home. I cover this type of loan in greater detail in chapter 13. Let's look here at our rules of borrowing to evaluate whether to rent or take out a mortgage to buy a house.

Rule 1 says that the economic return from borrowing must be greater than the economic cost. That's just common sense. And because a home provides no economic return other than appreciation, the application of this rule comes down to determining whether the appreciation will be greater than the debt cost.

When money is borrowed for a home mortgage, the true cost of the interest must first be determined. Mortgage interest is deductible on federal and most state income tax returns, and it therefore costs the borrower less than the amount actually paid. The first chart on page 161 illustrates the true cost of interest at different tax rates. In most cases, adding your state's income tax rate to the federal rate gives you the overall rate that should be used. For illustration purposes, I have used increments of 10 percent in the tax rates and increments of 2 percent in the interest rate charged.

If you're in a total tax bracket of 30 percent and are considering a home mortgage with a 10 percent interest rate, your true cost of interest is 7 percent. To say it another way, the government, in effect, pays 30 percent of your interest cost by allowing you to deduct it from your taxable income. However, there's no way to recover the other 70 percent of interest paid.

TRUE COST OF INTEREST AFTER TAX CONSIDERATION

Tax Rate (in percents)	Mortgage Interest Rate (in percents)					
	6.0	8.0	10.0	12.0	14.0	16.0
10.0	5.4	7.2	9.0	10.8	12.6	14.4
20.0	4.8	6.4	8.0	9.6	11.2	12.8
30.0	4.2	5.6	7.0	8.4	9.8	11.2
40.0	3.6	4.8	6.0	7.2	8.4	9.6
50.0	3.0	4.0	5.0	6.0	7.0	8.0

The next chart takes the illustration further and shows the appreciation that's required to break even on a home mortgage at different down payment levels and interest rates. The left-hand column lists the loan value. (If you put 10 percent down on a home, you have a loan value of 90 percent.) Listed across the top are interest rates that might be charged by the lending institution, and below them are the true costs, assuming a 30 percent tax rate. Your true cost of mortgage interest will vary depending on your particular total state and federal tax rate.

APPRECIATION REQUIRED TO BREAK EVEN: TRUE INTEREST COST AT 30 PERCENT TAX RATE

Loan % to Cost of Home	Loan Interest Rate (in percents)					
	6.0	8.0	10.0	12.0	14.0	16.0
100.0	4.2	5.6	7.0	8.4	9.8	11.2
90.0	3.7	5.0	6.3	7.5	8.8	10.0
80.0	3.3	4.4	5.6	6.7	7.8	8.9
70.0	2.9	3.9	4.9	5.8	6.8	7.8
60.0	2.5	3.3	4.2	5.0	5.8	6.7
50.0	2.1	2.8	3.5	4.2	4.9	5.6
40.0	1.6	2.2	2.8	3.3	3.9	4.4
30.0	1.2	1.6	2.1	2.5	2.9	3.3
20.0	0.8	1.1	1.4	1.6	1.9	2.2
10.0	0.4	0.5	0.7	0.8	0.9	1.1
0.0	0.0	0.0	0.0	0.0	0.0	0.0

The next chart illustrates how to determine and apply the break-even computation. The chart assumes that a 30 percent taxpayer buys a home for $200,000 with a down payment of 20 percent. The borrower must experience an appreciation of at least 3.92 percent in the first year in order to break even. Thus, a 3.92 percent or greater appreciation would be required to provide an economic return greater than the economic cost. (Interestingly enough, many planners assume a 4 percent historical increase in residential real estate. In the United States, the appreciation rate was greater than 4 percent in the early 2000s. However, the appreciation rate slowed significantly, and even declined, a few years later.)

BREAK-EVEN ANALYSIS

Assumptions

	Tax rate	30%
	Home cost (or value)	$200,000
	Down payment (or equity)	40,000
	Loan balance	160,000
	Loan interest rate	8%
	Appreciation required to break even (second chart on page 161)	4.4%

Proof

	Interest cost	8% x $160,000 = $12,800
	Tax reduction	$12,800 x 30% = -$3,840
	True annual cost	$12,800 - $3,840 = $8,960
	Appreciation required to break even ($8,960/$200,000)	4.48%

Conclusion

This house must be worth $208,960 ($200,000 + $8,960) at the end of the year for the appreciation to have offset the true interest cost of the mortgage. This does not include any closing cost that may have been incurred when the home was purchased. If two points were charged for closing cost, an additional $4,000 appreciation must occur in the first year for you to break even. In other words, the house must sell for $211,840 to break even.

The implications for applying rule 1 to the borrowing decision for a home are as follows:

1. The greater the down payment and the lower the interest rate paid, the less the appreciation needed to break even.

2. The lower the tax rate, the less advantageous it is to borrow on a home mortgage.

It's interesting that while these conclusions make clear, logical sense, "conventional wisdom" over the last several years contradicts them. The worldly view encourages home buyers to put down as little money as possible in order to get the full benefit of leverage and inflation.

This analysis is applicable whatever the level of equity you have in your home. For example, if you've been paying on your mortgage for a number of years so that your loan now only equals 40 percent of the value of your home, just go down to the seventh line from the top in the left-hand column of the second chart on page 161, then read across to the column showing your interest rate, and you'll find the appreciation you need to continue to break even on your mortgage. Obviously, it's far less than someone who has only 10 percent equity in his or her home. The illustration will also work if you have an adjustable rate mortgage, where interest rates can change periodically. The assumptions still apply, and you can calculate for yourself, using the chart on page 161, the appreciation you must have next year in order not to violate rule 1 (economic return should be greater than economic cost).

Rule 2 (guaranteed way to repay) says that in borrowing, we should not presume upon the future, and thus there must be a guaranteed way to repay the loan. A home mortgage seemingly offers two guaranteed ways to repay. One is that the income being earned by the owner, or owners, provides the necessary money for the monthly payments. The second is for the house itself to act as the collateral on the loan through an exculpatory clause.

Exculpatory clause: A provision in a mortgage that prevents the lender from going after the borrower's personal assets— other than the property itself—should that person be unable to keep up with mortgage payments or abandon the property.

Another way to repay using the home as collateral, but without an exculpatory clause, is to have so much equity in the house that there's almost no way the house could not be sold for the mortgage amount or more. If, for example, you had 60 percent equity in your home and you had to sell it as the only way to repay the mortgage, you could lower your price by more than 50 percent if necessary and still be able to pay off the loan. That's an extreme example, and I hope you never have to sell a house for half its value, but it shows the degree of loan protection provided by a high level of equity.

Without significant equity in a home, your ability to make the monthly payments will depend on your stream of income, and there's almost no way to guarantee that income will continue. Illness, economic downturns, changes in family situation, and many other things make an income tenuous. If you have a good job with a good company, you may think your income is guaranteed, but it's not. Even if you live off investment income, that's not guaranteed either.

I stress this so strongly because many young couples borrow money for a home mortgage implicitly assuming that their income will, at the worst, remain constant. They generally don't even realize the risk they're taking.

The only way to determine the margin for error in taking on a home mortgage is to make a budget and live according to it. The risk won't go away entirely. However, the greater the margin for error in the budget, the more you have minimized the risk. And once again, the higher the down payment, the less the risk of losing the home because of a loss of income or a deflation in the home's value. Likewise, the lower the interest rate, the lower the risk.

Rule 3 (peace of heart and mind) challenges you to examine your motives. The first questions that need to be addressed in making any major decision, and especially the decision to purchase a house, are, Why do you want that particular house? What criteria are you using to evaluate the house? What motive is driving you? Is it to satisfy a need or a desire?

If you're buying a house to meet a need for security or significance, the house has become your god. As pointed out earlier, only God can meet your real needs. If you try to use a house to meet those needs, you're dishonoring and disobeying God. Do not buy until your motives are pure.

The only way to discern whether you're violating any spiritual principles in deciding to borrow for a house is to spend time alone with the Lord, asking for His wisdom and guidance, which He has promised to provide.

The greater the margin for error in your budget, the more you have minimized the risk of taking on a home mortgage.

Many people are afraid to put their decisions before God because they assume He's a heavenly killjoy who doesn't want them to have anything good or desirable. That is not the God revealed in the Bible, however, and such an attitude is almost blasphemous. The proper attitude is to trust God to give you direction and to provide for you. God is the only One you can trust fully to provide for your unique and personal needs. There's risk associated with trusting Him (you may not always like His answers), but that's what faith is all about. Hebrews 11:8 praises Abraham's faith: "By faith Abraham, when called to go to a place he would later receive as his inheritance, obeyed and went, even though he did not know where he was going." Risk depends on the object of your faith, and with God there is no risk, even though it feels like risk. If you're contemplating buying a house, I recommend you read Hebrews 11 several times until you are convinced in your mind and heart that God can be trusted to guide you in this decision.

God can certainly use friends and honest professionals to help you. But in the end, God is the most trustworthy. Trying not to be too cynical, I suggest you ask yourself these questions:

1. Will my peer group give me the wisdom, discernment, and guidance I need?
2. Will the lender make sure I don't borrow more than I can afford?
3. Will the real estate agent guide me unerringly to buy no more house than I can afford?

In the book *Money and Your Marriage*, Russ Crosson suggests a question couples should ask themselves in evaluating Rule 4 (unity). I paraphrase it as follows:

> Which would make us more anxious: living in a smaller house and seeing our income go up enough to support a larger house, or living in a larger house where, if our income went down, we might not be able to afford the mortgage payments and so would run the risk of losing the house?[5]

Asking yourselves that question is an excellent way to evaluate whether you're potentially making a foolish financial decision and risking your financial future.

One other point regarding unity for husbands and wives on this decision is that women typically have a lower tolerance for mortgage debt than men do. A woman's home is the center of her influence and her environment, and she knows instinctively that debt puts it at risk. A man views a home much differently. To him it's more a signal to the world of how well he's doing financially. For this reason, and because men are greater risk takers by nature anyway, he has a much higher debt tolerance than his wife. The partners should blend their needs to come to the right decision regarding a mortgage. No house is a home when the debt on it is a source of conflict.

If you are a single person desiring to buy a house, I advise you to follow these same rules, putting yourself in an accountability relationship with an older, wiser person to help you think through your decision. It will still be your decision, and you—not the other person—will live with the consequences. However, seeking the counsel of an elder is biblical and, consequently, wise.

Investment Debt

Investment debt is used to buy something with which you hope to make a profit. An example is when a broker allows you to borrow to buy more stocks and bonds. This is called buying "on margin."

One point I need to emphasize. No investment looks bad initially—investments "just happen" to go bad. And because all investments are "good deals," there's a tremendous temptation to assume it makes economic sense to borrow money to enter into an investment.

With every investment looking like a good deal initially, the decision maker is easily lured into a binary trap. A binary trap sets one up to ask, "Should I do this or not?" It assumes those are the only two options, thus begging the real question, which is, "What's the best use for the money I have?"

A decision can never be better than the alternatives considered. When making an investment decision, if you consider only whether or not to make that particular investment, you're ignoring all the other alternative uses for that money, which may very well have a higher priority and be of greater value to you. The best way to avoid the binary trap is to ask yourself, *Are there any other possible uses for this money?*

> **Repaying existing debt gives you a guaranteed investment return.**

A strong caution regarding investment borrowing: Most people should never consider borrowing for investments—or even make investments, for that matter—until they're totally out of debt, including mortgage debt. Whenever extra cash flow is available that could be used for an investment debt payment, it should be used to pay off all other forms of existing debt. Repaying existing debt gives you a *guaranteed* investment return. (One clarification here: I mean investing outside of employer-sponsored retirement plans. I think it's beneficial to participate in retirement plans at work, especially if a company match is involved, while you still have mortgage debt. See chapter 15.)

Business Debt

Business debt is borrowing done by a business rather than an individual. For example, a business may borrow to buy furniture, fixtures, and equipment; to expand its facilities; to buy a building; or to provide working capital. (There may be some overlap in these categories. For example, a business may buy real estate with a mortgage or a business may use a credit card.)

Business debt looks a lot like investment debt and should be evaluated similarly. Business borrowing usually *appears* to be a good deal. Most new businesses don't have enough capital with which to start, so they quickly run into the need to borrow. Such debt certainly seems to meet at least the first rule of borrowing, and the other rules seem to be of less consequence when the first is so overwhelmingly met. The return on the money borrowed seems to be so significant that there's no question about repayment. The spiritual convictions, along with the unity rule, are ignored because the deal appears to be so right.

The way to avoid the undercapitalization problem in a new business is to make sure there's a well-prepared and well-reviewed business plan in place before beginning a business. My general counsel is to calculate the amount of start-up money needed and then double it. Using that figure, you might come close to the amount of capital you will actually use.

In my own business, we have needed almost six times the original capital projection, which fortunately we have been able to fund without borrowing. We needed so much money for a common reason of new businesses: success. The additional capital is required to fund a buildup in receivables, inventory, marketing costs, and so on. In fact, working capital is the greatest need of a prospering business, and the strong temptation will be to borrow that capital instead of saving it ahead of time or bringing in other investors.

One question I'm frequently asked regarding business debt is related to rule 2: a guaranteed way to repay. Because a corporate form of organization limits the liability of the shareholders to their invested dollars, many times a businessperson will assume that business debt is okay. The businessman himself takes on no personal legal liability for the firm's debts.

My belief, however, is that in a closely held business, the lenders are looking to the owner to be responsible for the debt, even though they don't require personal liability. And I believe the Christian has a moral obligation to repay every amount owed whether or not he is personally liable for it.

I recently had the unpleasant experience of observing a Christian business-man borrow his way into bankruptcy. Because he had organized his company as a corporation, he was able to walk away from the debts he had generated. But by doing that, he acquired a terrible reputation, not only for himself, but for the local Christian community. A legitimate question was asked by the town's non-Christians: "Is this the way Christians do business?" I cannot say it any more plainly than to quote Psalm 37:21: "The wicked borrow and do not repay." You can't hide behind legalities when borrowing money. It is the responsibility of the one who entered into the debt to repay it *regardless of his legal protection.*

Student (College) Loans

It seems that every year the cost of college tuition and related fees rises faster than the inflation rate. A major financial problem facing parents and students alike is how to pay for their children's college costs.

The prognosis for college costs is so bad that if there are two children in a family and both of them go to private schools, the parents are likely to spend as much for four-year college educations as they did to purchase their home. That expense is especially burdensome because it's compressed into four years as opposed to a 30-year mortgage for the purchase of a home.

The problem of funding a college education may not fall only on the parents, however. Maybe the child has chosen to pay his own way through college or chooses not to go because his parents can't afford to send him. But that doesn't mean an education is out of the question.

Many years ago, I counseled with a prospective seminary student who felt God was calling him to full-time ministry, but he didn't have the money. He asked me if I thought he should borrow the money. A problem with borrowing to go to seminary, however, is that the salary earned after graduation may never be sufficient to repay the loan. I advised him that if he was sure God had called him to go to seminary, he should forget borrowing. Instead, he should take one semester at a time, trusting that God would meet his needs, because it didn't look as if this man would ever have a guaranteed way to repay a loan.

Later, I received the following letter from that young man. It makes the point better than I can that God is faithful to meet the needs of those who depend on Him.

> *Dear Mr. Blue:*
>
> *I am sure you may not remember me as I have only met you via the telephone on the WM——— radio program. My question to you went something like this . . . "I'm single, age 36, no outstanding debts (which you said was un-American!), and I have a small savings account (around $600). I dislike going into debt. I'm feeling called to the ministry. Should I borrow money to enroll in seminary?" Your response to me was something to the effect that I should not limit God, but to step out and trust Him to supply the money.*
>
> *I did just that, and the blessings have been phenomenal. May I share with you what has happened?*
>
> *On my first day of summer Greek class, I received a note in my mailbox saying an anonymous donor had sent a check to my account for $325; four weeks later, another note, and another $325. My thoughts were that someone had just wanted me to get a good start in seminary, so I thought nothing of it until a third check arrived in early September for $375. I was then notified by the Financial Aid Office that the checks would apparently be coming each month for the foreseeable future. They did—ranging from $325 to $475.*
>
> *This is not the end, however. In late August, following the summer session, I went to visit a friend and helped paint a house for a week. I never expected to be paid, but he insisted. I received a check for $180.*
>
> *The church where I was raised (I am no longer a member there) sent me a letter and a check for $300, saying they had decided to give me part of the mission budget. In October I knew I was to be the recipient of the Sunday school mission offering; I expected $30 to $40. They decided to open it up to anyone in the church who wanted to give, and I received a check for $376.50.*
>
> *In November I was able to preach at that church. During the service, the pastor announced that an offering plate would be placed at the back door for anyone wanting to assist me financially; the offering was $406.*
>
> *My work-study position here at the seminary is in the Advancement and Development Office, and because of a shortage of help in January, I was given*

the opportunity to work extra hours. And then last week I was asked to work additional hours during a minister's conference on campus.

The Lord knows I came here on faith, and He has supplied "above and beyond all that I could ask or think." My goal is to be a hospital chaplain, and I am excited about what God has in store for me. May God continue to bless your work.

Please understand I'm not suggesting that borrowing to go to college is wrong per se—no more than I've suggested getting a home mortgage is wrong. But the proper way to evaluate a college loan is the same way we've evaluated every other borrowing decision, using the four basic rules. Most of the time, a college education will enhance a person's earning ability over time. Thus, such loans often are justifiable. But I would question whether a master's degree in Renaissance art or classical clarinet would really add much earning power and violate rule 1 of common sense. I've also observed that student loans are used to finance more than tuition: They also allow the purchase of pizza, clothes, and gas. It doesn't make sense to finance such items over a 20-year student loan.

If you determine that borrowing to pay for a college education meets the rules and you are not denying God an opportunity to work, here's my challenge to you: Immediately upon graduation, make repaying the debt your top financial priority. The federal government has found that because it makes or subsidizes most student loans, many students don't feel a moral obligation to repay their loans, even though they have well-paying jobs. The Christian, however, has no option to ignore his obligations.

In the next chapter, we'll explore how you can get back on solid financial footing if you're currently sinking in debt—because of student loans or any other type of debt.

CHAPTER 12

Don't Drown in Debt, Part 3: Debt Busters

I saw a television commercial recently that made my eyes water—first from laughter and then from weeping.

The camera shows a 40-something, confident male with a big smile. He says pleasantly, "I'm Stanley Johnson."

Soothing piano music plays in the background as you see Stanley embracing his attractive wife as they stand with their three kids in the front yard of their two-story house in suburbia. "I've got a great family," he says.

Then you see Stanley leaning casually against a fireplace mantel in his large, tastefully decorated living room.

"I've got a four-bedroom house in a great community," he adds as the camera pans to a perfectly manicured lawn with a neighbor pushing a stroller and a young boy riding his bike along a wide sidewalk.

We then see Stanley driving down the tree-lined neighborhood street in a shiny SUV. "Like my vehicle? It's new."

Stanley's pleasant tone and the lively piano music keep you from hating him for his boasting. You simply think this is another commercial showing a family with the perfect life.

We then see him golfing with other men and saying, "I even belong to the local golf club." The *thwack* sound of a golfer teeing off is heard in the background.

Then we see Stanley sitting on his lawn as he pets his golden retriever and his family enjoys a picnic with a water fountain behind them. He asks, "How do I do it?"

The camera cuts to Stanley, who is shown cleaning his in-ground pool while the kids play and his wife suntans in the background. He breaks into a larger smile and says, while practically laughing, "I'm in debt up to my eyeballs!"

This surprise answer—in contrast to his grin and almost proud look—is what creates the first jolt of laughter. The next scene shows him grilling on a large patio while his smiling family eats hamburgers in the background. Looking up from the sizzling burgers, he glances back at his family and then confides to the audience with another bright smile, "I can barely even pay my finance charges!"

You can't help but laugh at Stanley's candor in explaining how he has obtained the so-called idyllic American Dream. The narrator then intones, "Need a smart way to handle your debt?" and goes on to discuss the virtues of the company's consolidated loan services.

After chuckling a bit, I couldn't help but feel burdened. The very reason an advertiser broadcasts such an ad on national television is because many people will relate. The advertiser knows many people are in the same situation and will need the company's services.

Then, on further reflection, I was saddened by the fact that many people are stressed out by debt. Excessive debt incurred trying to reach a lifestyle beyond one's means has broken many marriages, derailed careers, siphoned money away from Kingdom work in the form of interest, worsened health, distracted ministry volunteers, and brought shame behind a facade of material success.

The commercial ends with a final shot of Stanley on a riding lawn mower with a double-bagger in back. As he crisscrosses his perfectly manicured, green lawn, he's still smiling as he says, "Somebody help me."

In this chapter, I hope to offer you the help Stanley so desperately needs. Unlike the advertiser who promised to help you with your debt problems by offering more debt through a consolidation loan, I will give you an outline to manage and eliminate debt. Notice I didn't say, "five easy steps," because it's not easy. But it is possible. . . .

How Do You Get Out of Debt? Very Diligently

To put it simply: You get out of debt little by little over time, and the major requirement is discipline. The challenging part of eliminating debt is that it usually requires a change in lifestyle and a reordering of priorities. That's painful. Our natural human tendency is to avoid such pain or change. You may wish there were some easy, painless way to get out of debt. But it doesn't exist. If you want to be free of debt problems, you've got to make up your mind, with your family's cooperation, that you'll pay the price now to enjoy financial freedom later.

If you think about it in broad, simple terms, the only alternatives to gradual repayment of debt are selling assets, increasing your income, or reducing spending. Selling assets may mean selling a car, a boat, a house, an investment, or something else that's part of your lifestyle now. Generating more income may mean working longer, having both parents work outside the home (which I don't recommend as a way to maintain a standard of living, as you'll see later), obtaining a second job for the breadwinner, or asking adolescent children to work part-time. Obviously, reducing spending means trimming your budget

Q: My credit cards are eating me alive. What should I do? Some people say to get rid of them, but I can't because I travel a lot.

ANSWER: Get rid of all your credit cards except one and make a plan for paying off all your credit card debt. Set a target date for when you would like to be able to pay off the entire balance of your one remaining credit card so that you will not be charged the usurious rate of 18 to 25 percent interest. As a businessperson who travels, it may not be practical to go without a credit card. However, debit cards are accepted at most places now and may be a better alternative.

Credit cards are not evil; the abuse of credit cards is the problem. Credit cards and debit cards are just as much a form of money as cash; in fact, they are the only way to perform certain transactions such as renting an automobile. We live in a modern society, and we need modern tools.

By having only one credit card, however, you will always know the balance on that card and always know whether you are able to pay that card off within the normal 30-day billing cycle. Unfortunately, it's very easy, and common, to have a dozen credit cards, lose track of the balances on each one, and overspend a little bit here and a little bit there. My advice is to have only one credit card. If you shop at Sears, write a check or use a debit card. If you buy gas, pay cash. Most of the excuses for having multiple credit cards are invalid.

and cutting spending. Each of these alternatives requires a change in lifestyle, as something must be given up—namely, time or possessions. Reducing spending and applying the new cash flow to debt repayment is very helpful but may not go far enough.

Keeping these three general alternatives in mind, let me break them down into five specific steps to take in getting out of debt. They're easy to list, hard to do. But there's no other moral way.

1. Determine where you are financially.
2. Stop going further into debt.
3. Develop a repayment plan.
4. Establish accountability.
5. Reward yourself.[1]

Step 1: Determine where you are financially

It's interesting to hear people talk about their debts, because most do not consider either a home mortgage or a car loan as debt. Those two kinds of debt have become such a normal part of most of our lives and economy that we think of them differently.

The first step to getting out of debt, however, is knowing the total amount of your debt. You'd be surprised at how few people know their total indebtedness. You can use any type of listing. I've included an example below.

DEBT SCHEDULE			
Lender	Amount Owed (in dollars)	Due Date	Payment Schedule (dollars per month)

In addition to your credit card balances, include your installment loan balances (e.g., car payments), student loan balances, mortgage balances, and any other term note balances you owe. Then you'll have a realistic and honest appraisal of your total debt. In listing the amounts owed, do not include such regular monthly expenses as utilities, school tuition, food, and clothing, as those are normal monthly bills and not debts.

Now that you've listed all amounts owed and you're certain of your commitments regarding debt repayments, we'll look at the next step to overcome debt.

Step 2: Stop going further into debt

This step is extraordinarily difficult to take, I know. It requires a decision that there will be no additional borrowing for any purpose. Before you even consider taking on more debt, you should at least go through the process described for evaluating the borrowing decision. (See "Four Rules for Making Borrowing Decisions" on page 149 for more on this subject.)

If you're an overspender and in debt, however, then even the latter sections will not be justification for avoiding this step. You absolutely must decide to use debt no longer. If that requires destroying your credit cards, cut them up. My friend Dave Ramsey refers to this cutting procedure as a "plasectomy." (For those who can't relate, think of it as performing "plastic surgery" on your credit cards.)

This commitment to stop using debt in any form needs to be made to another person or couple who will hold you accountable (see step 4 for more about this).

Step 3: Develop a repayment plan

In addition to knowing your current debt level, you need to learn what your annual cash flow and living expenses are (see chapter 8). As the Financial Planning Diagram on page 44 illustrates, you must have more "margin" to generate more toward debt repayment. To repay, you must spend less than you make.

After tracking your expenses and developing a spending plan, you should now know where you are from a debt, cash flow, and living expense standpoint. Having also made the commitment to stop going into debt, you can develop a strategy for repaying those debts. There is no one right way of repaying your obligations. Several suggestions of sources for repayment follow. Using a combination of them will provide you with even more momentum in repaying debt.

> **The only alternatives to gradual repayment of debt are selling assets, increasing your income, or reducing spending.**

Sell assets

The first idea for repaying your debts is to determine if there are any assets that can be sold. Even small things that could be sold through a garage sale—clothes that aren't worn anymore, sports equipment that's no longer used, books already read—can help you get out of smaller debts.

The sale of bigger items such as cars, investments, and perhaps even homes should also be considered—but only after you have sold the more accessible, less drastic items lying around. As I said earlier, selling the big items may require a change in lifestyle. You have to stop and consider—how badly do you want to be free from the bondage of debt?

Use savings accounts

You should consider using "excess" savings in passbook accounts or surplus cash balances in checking accounts to pay off debts. Using a low-yielding savings account to pay off high-cost debt is a guaranteed high-yield investment. If you have a savings account and are still carrying credit card or installment debt, consider using the funds from your savings account to reduce debt. As we discussed in chapter 9, emergency savings are important and necessary—but can you pare down slightly your emergency savings temporarily? I think the minimum emergency savings is one month of living expenses. Not one month of income, but one month's worth of the expenses, such as to keep a roof over your head, utilities on, food on the table, and transportation to work.

If you take this approach, replenish your savings accounts as soon as the debt is paid off. Just keep paying the same amount you had been putting toward credit cards and installment debt—only now put it into your savings.

Make double payments

A third strategy for getting out of debt is to double up on your payments. I recently received a letter from someone who indicated he paid $60 per month on one credit card, thinking he was reducing the debt. In fact, however, he was paying only a few dollars on principal each month and making no real dent in the total owed. But by doubling up on the payments and cutting expenses in another area of the budget, he could pay off debt much more quickly. One extra payment—all going toward principal—can make a huge difference.

> **Pay off your smallest debt first. When that debt is gone, apply the extra funds toward the next smallest debt.**

Pay off smaller debts first

A fourth strategy is relatively painless but nonetheless essential: Keep constant the total amount of payments you're making each month. Concentrate on paying off your smallest debt first. That's the quickest way to be rid of one debt,

---

Victoria ran her hands through her hair—again. "I can't believe I got so carried away with Christmas presents! And got so impatient about the washer and dryer! Why didn't we realize December wasn't the month to buy them?"

Luis shifted in his chair and gave Victoria a slight smile. "Vic, I think we've beaten ourselves up enough. We can't go back and change anything, right?"

Victoria sighed. "You're right. Okay. So now let's move on to something constructive. We have $3,400 in credit card debt. What are we going to do about it?"

"Well, we have a few options," Luis started. "We can repay it gradually by allocating as much as we think we can afford each month. We could also sell something, or we could cash in part of our retirement."

Victoria bit her lip. "I think selling something is out. What would we sell?

Our so-called antique vase was a bust when we tried that a few months ago. Trying to sell the new washer and dryer doesn't make sense because we already got rid of the old ones. We don't have much else of monetary value, besides maybe the piano. But that was a gift from my parents, and I'd hate to give it up. Besides, I want Manuel to start lessons in a few years."

"I think gradual repayment is the way to go," Luis suggested. "What if we set aside $500 each month toward the bill? We'd have the whole thing paid off in . . . well, I guess probably not for eight or nine months, once you think about interest."

"That sounds awful," said Victoria. "And besides, what if we have another horrible month like this one? Some of the expenses were our own fault, like the gifts. But a lot of them were pretty unavoidable—like the car repair and

and it will encourage you to keep going. When that debt is gone, rather than spending the amount freed up by no longer having that payment, apply it to the next-smallest debt (in addition to what you were already paying on that debt). It's like making a huge snowball—start small and increase.

For example, let's say you have three credit card balances and two installment debts totaling $20,000. Your minimum monthly payments total $300 per month, but you're currently paying $500. I'm suggesting you keep all debts current by making the minimum payments. Then, apply all of the additional payments beyond the minimum (or $200, in this case) to the smallest debt balance. After you pay off the smallest debt, apply what was going to the smallest debt (the minimum plus the excess $200) to the smallest remaining debt. So, instead of reducing the amount repaid each month as the smaller debts are eliminated, continue to pay at least what you were paying before toward other debt. The idea is that you can begin to feel momentum and additional motivation as you see the progress you're making. If your budget could afford $500 per month with all debts, you should be able to keep paying at least $500 toward fewer debts.

Cristina's urgent care visit. We can't guarantee that's not going to happen again. If we add new debt to the old debt, we'll end up even more in the hole."

Luis tapped his fingers on the table. "I guess our other option is to cash in part of our 401(k)."

Victoria looked serious. "Getting the money from our retirement fund sounds drastic. But on the other hand, thinking about paying off this debt so slowly, and even possibly getting into more debt, ties my stomach in knots."

They looked at each other. "How can we reach agreement on this?" Luis asked. "Maybe we need to brainstorm more options." After a moment, he said, "We could increase our income. My boss talked to me last week about some extra projects he has. I could get some overtime if I want it. Normally I'd rather be home with you and the kids,

but in this case maybe it's more important to pay off the debt quickly."

Victoria nodded. "Sylvia asked me about watching her kids after school on Mondays and Wednesdays. That would bring in a little money each week. And Monica asked if I wanted to go in on a garage sale."

Luis took his wife's hand. "Let's do it. We'll work extra hard for the next month or two, knowing that it's a small sacrifice for getting out of debt. If we don't come up with enough additional income to pay off the credit card in two months, we'll have another brainstorming session."

Just then the phone rang. Victoria jumped up to answer it. "Hello?" She gave a thumbs-up to Luis when she realized who had called.

"Sylvia, yes, I've been meaning to call you back. I'd be happy to watch Mike and Megan. Do you want me to start this Monday?"

DEBT SCHEDULE

Lender	Amount Owed (in dollars)	Due Date	Payment Schedule (dollars per month)
Visa	3,700	Monthly	115/month
MasterCard	1,900	Monthly	85/month
Sears	1,000	Monthly	55/month
Discover	300	Monthly	15/month
Amoco	100	Monthly	10/month

In the example shown on the chart above, the person is now paying a total of $280 per month on her credit card bills. Using this strategy, she might make minimum payments on the larger balances such as those for Visa, MasterCard, and Sears. Then she could take the rest of what she had been paying to those accounts and apply it, first of all, to her Amoco credit card bill, which would probably be paid off in one month.

Next, by keeping her payments constant at $280, still maintaining minimum payments to the larger account balances, she could apply all the excess to Discover until it's paid off. Then she could tackle the Sears bill with the same strategy.

Within six months, three of the five credit cards would be paid off. Within 12 months, four of the five would be clear. By the second year, she would be paying off only one card balance; $280 a month to Visa. She may still need 12 to 24 months to eliminate that debt because of the accumulating interest, but it's easier emotionally to have just one credit card to deal with rather than five bills every month.

Reduce living expenses

A fifth strategy is to review your living expense summary and as a family decide where you can cut expenses. Apply the amount cut to specific debts. You might decide to cut down on your entertainment, clothing, food, or home maintenance budgets—whatever fits your family situation. The fact is that in almost every family budget, as much as 10 to 20 percent could be used to repay debt. Again, it will require a change in lifestyle, but that cost will be more than offset by the sense of satisfaction in seeing yourself gradually free of payments.

Reduce tax withholdings

A sixth strategy is available if you're now receiving a federal income tax refund each year: Reduce your tax withholdings, and apply the increase in take-home pay to your debt repayment. The IRS doesn't require you to pay in withholdings (or estimated payments) any more than what you will actually owe. It's a simple matter to decrease your withholding to the amount of the actual projected liability.

Here's how to reduce your withholdings. First, determine your tax liability for the year. Begin by looking at last year's federal income tax return to see how much you paid. Then calculate the effect of any relevant changes this year (a raise, the birth of a child, having an older child become self-supporting, etc.). Your tax preparer or accountant may help you with this. Or if you prepare your taxes yourself, check on the Web site of your tax software program. Also, see the many resources at the IRS Web site at http://www.irs.gov.

After you have determined what you're likely to owe in federal taxes, you can have your withholdings decreased to no more than that amount. Simply go to your company's personnel office and fill out a new W-4 form.

A regular significant tax refund is a sign of poor financial management. You're allowing the government to use your money interest-free, whereas you could be using that same money to pay off high-interest debt.

There may be other strategies you could use, and the ones offered here are only suggestions. The important thing is that you develop your own strategy and then implement it. In making your plans for debt reduction, however, there are certain things you absolutely should not do.

Do not decrease giving

You may be tempted to lower the amount you give. Don't do it. If you are actively giving to a place of worship or ministry, you shouldn't decrease your giving. For people of faith, giving should be the first-priority use of money. Giving recognizes God's ownership of everything one has.

In almost every family budget, as much as 10 to 20 percent could be used to repay debt.

The only time when a reduction in giving to repay debt might be acceptable is if the debt situation is extremely severe, you have prepared a budget that cuts out all surplus uses of money, and you were already giving a relatively high percentage of income (say, more than 10 percent).

Do not use tax money

Don't reduce your tax payments below your projected liability. If you do, you're just borrowing from the government to pay someone else. You aren't really reducing your debt at all. The day of reckoning is merely postponed to the following April 15. The IRS is not a pleasant creditor.

Do not use a debt consolidation loan

In most cases you should not take out a debt consolidation loan. The typical reason for such a loan is that it "feels good" to have just one payment to worry about, but it doesn't solve the basic problem. Many people who go for debt consolidation find they later need another consolidation loan because the first loan didn't really solve their spending problems.

If you're seeing a debt counselor, however, and the counselor recommends a debt consolidation loan as your only alternative—and if the counselor will work with you to set up a realistic budget—then it may be appropriate. But it should be a one-time step to relieve symptoms—it never cures the underlying problem.

Do not seek a second full-time income

The last recommendation regarding what not to do is the one violated most often by couples. Namely, if the wife is currently a stay-at-home mom, she should not get a job to increase the family's income. When you consider the additional expenses of giving, taxes, child care, transportation, wardrobe, and so on associated with the second job, the economic benefit of most second income jobs is very small.

> **Find ways to motivate yourself to maintain the disciplines required to get out of debt.**

Besides, most debt problems are spending problems, not income problems. If a homemaker goes to work to fund a consumptive lifestyle, the root problems have not been identified and dealt with.

I realize there are exceptions to this general rule: A family may face unexpected medical bills or desire to send their children to a private school for good reasons. But given human nature, extra income tends only to raise the level of discontentment, increasing the desire for more and more "things" that won't meet real needs.

Consider counseling

In severe debt situations, the repayment plan may require professional assistance. There's nothing disgraceful about asking for help. You might be a single mother with several children to support, for example, and increasing your income, selling assets, and decreasing expenses may not be viable alternatives. (If you live in the United States, you can visit Crown Financial Ministries' Web site, http://www.crown.org, to find a trained financial counselor by zip code. Crown has global contacts serving in many other countries throughout North and South America, Europe, Africa, and Australia as well.)

Step 4: Establish accountability

One helpful business axiom is this: "Don't expect what you don't inspect." Anyone who has raised children understands the wisdom in this saying. And I've found that even as adults, we benefit from accountability. If you must report to someone you respect on a commitment you've made voluntarily, such as getting out of debt, you're more likely to follow through. If you're unwilling, however, to verbalize to another person your commitment to get out of debt, the likelihood of your sticking to your payoff plan is reduced dramatically.

Ask someone to hold you accountable, not in a general sense, but to make specific payments on designated dates. Set up a schedule of reporting times. Establish the length of the accountability period. In other words, neither the commitment nor the time should be open ended.

When you ask that person or couple to hold you accountable, be honest about why you're doing it. Most people who care about you would be honored to help.

Step 5: Reward yourself

When we have something positive to look forward to, we're encouraged to maintain the disciplines required to get there. Many people who have trouble losing weight, for example, develop a reward system that motivates them to maintain a diet. In the same manner, it's a good idea to reward yourself as you pay off debt.

When you pay off your first debt, for instance, you might treat yourself to a special lunch. When the second debt is paid off, you could enjoy a nice dinner. When the third debt is paid off, it might be time for a more expensive treat like a weekend away. Paying off the fourth or final debt could result in a reward such as clothes or furniture.

Obviously, you don't want to get yourself into more debt through your reward system. The idea is to find ways to motivate yourself to maintain the disciplines required to get out of debt. They don't have to cost much money— or any at all. You might look forward, for example, to a coupon-book-burning ceremony or to hanging a homemade "Graduation from Debt" certificate on the family-room wall. Whatever the rewards you choose, they need to be personally motivational. The most significant reward will be the financial freedom that comes from getting out of debt.

The steps I've outlined are all that's required to be relieved of the bondage of debt. The key is to take the first step. Someone once asked, "How do you eat an elephant?" The answer: "One bite at a time." Getting out of debt likewise is done one step at a time. It may appear to be an impossible task at this point, but I'm convinced that you can do it, just as many have before you.

Since getting started is usually the most difficult part of any task, I've provided the Action Plan for Getting Out of Debt form for you to use to begin the process of diligently eating your elephant (see page 182).

How to Keep from Going Back into Debt

If you could continue to live debt free, wouldn't you want to do so? You might think that's an obvious question. Then why do so many go back into debt? Why do wealthy people still incur debt?

At the end of chapter 10, we looked at the reason people get into debt.

ACTION PLAN FOR GETTING OUT OF DEBT

Step	Action	Date to Be Completed
1. Determine where you are financially.	1.	1.
	2.	2.
	3.	3.
	4.	4.
2. Stop going further into debt.	1.	1.
	2.	2.
	3.	3.
	4.	4.
3. Develop a repayment plan.	1.	1.
	2.	2.
	3.	3.
	4.	4.
4. Establish accountability.	1.	1.
	2.	2.
	3.	3.
	4.	4.
5. Reward yourself.	1.	1.
	2.	2.
	3.	3.
	4.	4.

Complete the chart prayerfully and promptly. Now is the best time to begin.

The truth is, these are the very same reasons people go back into debt. Our consumer culture will always try to entice you back into debt with empty enticements like these:

Get cash instantly!
Reward yourself!
Why wait?

Don't miss out!
You deserve the best!

Staying out of debt means recognizing these lies and refusing to succumb to them. As we close this three-chapter section on debt, perhaps it would be wise for you (and your spouse, if you're married) to consider which of these are most likely to lead you into debt:

- Lacking self-discipline when it comes to spending or saving for an emergency fund
- Searching for contentment by purchasing items that aren't in your budget or that you can't afford
- Seeking security in possessions, even if it means borrowing to get them
- Seeking significance by buying items that will impress others
- Falling prey to the lie that borrowing is smart because you can pay back what you owe with cheaper dollars
- Assuming the money saved from the tax deductibility of interest is equivalent to the interest you're paying
- Charging because you're afraid it will cost more later
- Assuming that borrowing is just a smart way of using other people's money—rather than realizing it's just a way other people make money off you

You may recall that a smart spending plan includes four priorities: (1) spending less than you earn, (2) maintaining liquidity, (3) avoiding debt, and (4) setting long-term goals. Now that we've covered the first three, let's move on to long-term goals. For many, this immediately brings to mind the dream of owning their own home.

CHAPTER 13

Rent or Own? Read This First

Perhaps I'm showing my age, but I remember a time when hearing about a "home worth a quarter of a million dollars," made me picture a mansion. In today's real estate market, that figure is a bit below the average price of a home! In 2006, the average price for a new home in the United States was $299,500, while the average price of an existing home was $273,300.[1] Some readers, particularly on either coast of the United States, would say those prices sound like a bargain compared to the market they face.

Because home prices are far higher than average family incomes, the purchase of a home is a major financial commitment. A house is probably the single biggest purchase you'll ever make. And though housing prices historically have increased, that doesn't mean a home purchase is a no-brainer. Thousands and thousands of houses are foreclosed upon every year. These foreclosures indicate that many house-purchase decisions were bad decisions.

Judy and I used to teach a young marrieds' Sunday school class at our church.[2] On one of the first Sundays we taught, we asked the group to name some of their personal goals and objectives. We had a spirited conversation that was finally summarized by one young man who said that most of them expected to start financially where their parents had left off after 25 to 40 years of hard work. They wanted to have two cars and a three- to four-bedroom home in a nice area that was close to work. They also wanted the home to be fully furnished when they moved in.

Judy and I had to laugh in private afterward. We had been married 28 years at the time, and our home still wasn't as well furnished as we would have liked. It had taken us a long time to get where we were. (I expect that about the time we finally finish decorating, we'll want to move into another home.)

As I talk with many young couples, I discover they have unrealistic expectations. This is typified by the house-purchase decision, probably the most significant financial decision any married couple will ever make. To make it wisely, I believe they must align their expectations with four realities.

First, unless they have financial help from relatives, a house purchase right after marriage may very well be out of reach. With the run-up in real estate prices in the past decade, the average price of a house is so high that it's difficult for any couple, especially a young couple, to afford one unless they both work or are willing to overextend themselves financially.

Home ownership is part of the American Dream, but it certainly isn't a right. When and if God chooses to provide a house, that's a privilege. I'm disturbed by the often selfish, short-term attitude expressed by many young Christian couples. One of my desires in writing this book is to help young couples face reality so they won't try to borrow themselves into the illusion of prosperity. Going into debt to buy cars or to furnish a gargantuan house should generally be avoided.

> **Owning a house is not a right but a privilege.**

Second, owning a house is not a right, but a privilege. When it's viewed as a privilege, the appreciation of ownership is much greater when it's finally achieved. When something is perceived as a right, however, couples feel very frustrated if that "right" remains out of reach.

Third, purchasing a home will require financial sacrifices in some other part of the budget. Many ancillary costs of home ownership—such as repairs, insurance, taxes, replacement of appliances, and decorating—aren't usually taken into account because they're unknown or not anticipated. But the money for these expenses has to come from somewhere.

Fourth, God can be trusted to meet our needs. He won't necessarily meet our wants, but without question He will meet our every legitimate need. And while everyone has a need for shelter, that doesn't necessarily mean a house, and certainly not a dream house. Many times God will withhold a blessing until it can be provided in such a way as to demonstrate His faithfulness, goodness, and trustworthiness.

In this chapter, we'll first look at some of the common misconceptions concerning buying and owning a house. Next we'll examine some common issues: how to select an affordable house, selecting a real estate agent, the best type of mortgage, refinancing, and paying off a mortgage early. Then we'll go over some helpful hints that appear to provide a "free lunch."

Common Misconceptions

Believe me, I understand the pull many couples feel to own their own home; in fact, I confess I haven't always followed the principles I now know should govern the house-buying decision. When Judy and I bought our first home in 1968, we paid $25,000 for a four-bedroom, two-bath brick home in the northern suburbs of Dallas, Texas. We borrowed the 5 percent down payment from my parents and financed the other 95 percent with a 30-year, 7 percent fixed-rate mortgage. That home is now, most likely, worth substantially more than $25,000.

In retrospect, our decision to borrow to buy looks wise because of the home's subsequent appreciation. But the financial risks to a young couple are greater today: Jobs aren't as secure as they used to be, and appreciation is by no means guaranteed, as Texans know well from previous busts in the real estate market. To put it simply, I would never finance a home today the way I did it back in 1968, and I wouldn't have done it then if I'd known the facts I'm giving you in this chapter.

A second misconception is that conventional wisdom is always right and never changes. Owning one's own home is viewed as superior to renting, which is often equated with "throwing money down the drain." This conventional wisdom has generally been true since World War II because of three things: fixed-rate, long-term mortgages; appreciation (inflation); and the tax deductibility of mortgage interest. But we'll look more closely at the numbers later in this chapter. Renting provides more flexibility—and may sometimes make more financial sense.

One other common misconception is the belief that a home is a good investment. I have a strong reaction against that notion, because to those of us in the financial business, an investment is something you make for one of two purposes. You expect it to generate income, which a home does not do, or to appreciate enough in value that at some point you can sell it for a profit. But a home is rarely purchased with the idea of selling it when the value reaches a particular point. Even if it increases in value, you're no better off if you must buy another house to replace it in the same area that has also realized appreciation.

Renting provides more flexibility than buying a home—and sometimes makes more financial sense.

A better way to state what most people mean is that a home may be a good purchase, but it's seldom bought as a true investment. I can assure you that most wives would be pretty upset if their husbands advised them that as soon as their home had appreciated 20 percent in value, it was going to be sold. This would be especially true if the wife had expended any time or emotional energy in decorating and furnishing the home. A house may be an investment, but a home is not. At best, it's a good purchase.

Renting or Buying: Which Is Smarter?

Most Americans want to experience the pride of ownership. And the personal residence is probably the most sought-after asset. Although owning a home means mowing the grass, fixing leaky roofs, and replacing worn-out furnaces, nearly all Americans desire their own homes. No matter the cost, most attempt to buy homes as soon as they can. Creative financing, longer terms, equity-sharing arrangements, and the like have made home ownership possible for most Americans.

But there are several issues to consider before rushing into the purchase of a home. Depending on your own economic condition and vocational situation, renting is sometimes a smarter option.

Benefits of Home Ownership	Benefits of Renting
A portion of mortgage payments go toward building equity	Flexibility in moving later—no waiting on a house to sell
Owner keeps any price appreciation	No maintenance worries
Pride of ownership—it belongs to you	Low amount of initial savings needed to begin renting
May make home improvements and keep the benefit of those	Rent payments may be lower than mortgage payments with interest, taxes, and home insurance

FAMILY FINANCE

"Can you believe that kitchen?" Tanya whirled around in the parking lot, unable to contain her enthusiasm. "Stainless steel appliances, double the counter space we have now, and an adorable breakfast nook!"

Brian joined in the litany. "The living room was incredible too. A fireplace, hardwood floors, beautiful view of the pond out back . . ."

Tanya continued, "Two bedrooms, two bathrooms, and a separate dining room. Beautifully decorated. I love the mossy green they used in the master bedroom." She stopped and looked up at Brian. "I love it. You love it. It seems like it's in our price range. I know we just started looking, but why wait? Shouldn't we go talk to the real estate agent?"

That afternoon, they sat in Jessica's office as she ran the numbers on the computer. "Okay, here's the monthly payment, given a 30-year, fixed-rate mortgage." She jotted down a number on a memo pad and slid it across the desk.

Tanya and Brian looked at it in shock. "How can it be that much? We tried one of those monthly payment calculators online, and it gave us a payment $400 lower than that!" Brian said.

Jessica raised her eyebrows. "Well, that number includes more than just your mortgage payment. It also includes your property taxes, which are high in this suburb; your private mortgage insurance, since you're only planning to put down 5 percent; and your association dues. And, of course, you'll have to count on paying a little extra for your home insurance premiums."

The agent quickly snapped back into sales mode. "The monthly payment may be larger than you expected, but based on your income, you can definitely afford it. And with such beautiful decor and in such good condition, that townhouse is a bargain that's going to be snatched up soon."

Tanya bit her lip. "I'm sure we can still swing it. It's perfect."

Brian remembered something. "Speaking of perfect—or not quite perfect—I noticed what looked like a water mark around the light fixture in the kitchen. I'm wondering whether there's water leaking from the bathroom right above it."

My advice to young people is this: As you enter the workforce and begin accumulating cash, resist the urge to jump immediately into a house before having an emergency fund and a significant down payment. Otherwise you will soon be using credit cards to buy many things needed to operate the house and keep it going. This can start an unending cycle of credit. A good goal is to pay at least 20 percent of the purchase price as a down payment on a house, since that will eliminate additional costs such as mortgage insurance. From a practical standpoint, this means you should save a little longer to buy that first house than you expected—or than is even typical.

Generally, rent should not exceed 25 percent of your gross pay. However, this rule of thumb is not as important as a mortgage payment guideline because rent is usually short term. If you've overcommitted to a rent

"Oh, you'll have a chance to have that inspected later," Jessica said lightly. "But several other couples have been looking at this property. I think at least one is seriously thinking about making an offer. So what do you think? Are you ready to make one too?"

Brian and Tanya looked at each other. "I think we need to discuss this a bit more in private," Brian offered.

"Of course," Jessica said. "Why don't you keep talking while I go out and make some copies? Sure I can't get either of you some coffee or bottled water while I'm at it?"

As they shook their heads, Jessica walked out, shutting the door behind her. Tanya spoke up. "Don't tell me you're having second thoughts, Brian! This is everything we want."

Brian spoke slowly. "I love it too, Tanya. But it's a lot more money per month than we'd planned, and that water mark makes me nervous. I'm not sure I want to wait to see if the seller explains it on the disclosure form. Besides, I guess when it comes down to it, I just think it's more than we need right now."

"What do you mean?"

"We're newlyweds who live close to our families. No one stays overnight with us except for old college friends who don't mind sleeping on the couch. We're not planning to have children for several years. Why do we need a second bedroom?"

Tanya looked horrified. "We'd never be able to resell a house without a second bedroom!"

Brian chuckled. "I think you're missing my point. I agree that when we do buy a house, it should have at least two bedrooms. I'm just not sure this house is the one."

Tanya sighed. "I suppose you're right. We would have to buy a lot of furniture for an extra bedroom and the dining room. And I suppose hardwood floors and a fireplace aren't exactly necessities. So I guess it's back to square one."

As they heard their real estate agent's voice just outside her office, Brian asked teasingly, "So which one of us gets to tell Jessica she won't be getting that commission right away after all?"

payment, then you can usually change your circumstances fairly quickly. Even with a lease as long as one year, you're not as financially constrained by renting as you are by owning a house with buying and selling fees, possible maintenance and repair expenses, and the threat of having to sell to recoup equity.

Even if you have an emergency fund and a significant down payment, it may still not be economically wise to buy a home. On the chart on page 191, note that, once taxes and repairs are taken into account, renting a home for $700 a month costs less than it would to purchase it for $100,000 with a $10,000 down payment.

In most cases, a home buyer counts on the appreciation of the house to make it a "good" purchase. In the first year, the $100,000 house would have had a net cash outflow (not counting the down payment) of $10,085 for the owner, whereas if he had rented it, it would have cost $8,975 ($9,350 minus interest income earned). If that house were to be sold at the end of the year and the 6 percent real estate commission paid, the net cost of that house would be $12,325 ($3,350 more than renting) due to the sales commission. (Over 90 percent of all houses are sold through a realtor; therefore it's realistic to assume your home would be.) Of course, if you get a great deal in selling your house, your home purchase would be a better deal. But that does not usually happen.

If you hold on to the $100,000 house for two years, its appreciation will be about $8,000 ($4,000 a year). However, you'll also pay about $1,100 a year more in net expenses ($10,085 - $8,975) than renting. If you sell the house after two years, paying the real estate commission, you'd be very close to breaking even ($8,000 - $1,100 - $6,085). Therefore, *in most cases you are better off to buy only if you can live in a house for at least two years.* This assumes a sale through a realtor and no special appreciation factors such as buying below market (a foreclosure) or selling above inflation appreciation. *The higher the price of your house, the longer you must live in it to make it more cost-effective than renting.*

In most cases you are better off to buy only if you can live in a house for at least two years.

When deciding whether to buy or rent, you should take into account the nature of your occupation, the location, and your needs and goals. It may be that your vocation requires you to move every two to five years. If so, renting would probably be just as wise as purchasing. However, if your family wants to establish roots in a neighborhood and minister to others through your home, owning a house may be more appropriate than renting.

RENT VERSUS BUY: EFFECT ON NET WORTH

	Rent	Purchase Price		
	700/month	100,000	150,000	200,000
Annual Expenses				
Mortgage or rent	8,400	7,185	10,778	14,370
Private mortgage insurance	0	468	702	936
Utilities	600	1,200	1,500	1,800
Taxes	0	1,000	1,500	2,000
Home or renter's insurance	350	800	900	1,000
Repairs/maintenance (1% of purchase price)	0	1,000	1,500	2,000
Tax savings	0	-1,568	-2,352	-3,136
Total annual outflow	-9,350	-10,085	-14,528	-18,970
Gain				
Appreciation (4%)	0	4,000	6,000	8,000
Interest income (net of tax)	375	0	0	0
Effect on net worth	-8,975	-6,085	-8,528	-10,970
6% sales commission expense	0	-6,240	-9,360	-12,480
Effect on net worth after sale with 6% commission	-8,975	-12,325	-17,888	-23,450

Based on 10% down, 7% interest on mortgage, 25% tax bracket.
Appreciation is calculated at 4% of sales price.
Interest income assumes renter invests $10,000 down payment at 5% less taxes.
Private mortgage insurance calculated at .052% of loan amount (the rate used for a 90% loan-to-value ratio).
Sales commission is calculated on the appreciated value of home, assuming house is sold in one year.
Tax saving will decrease every year due to interest decreasing.

Remember, these calculations do not take into consideration buying costs such as loan origination fees, appraisal fees, tax service fees, attorney fees, points, and selling costs such as title insurance, which amount to about 3 percent of the original loan balance, and which must also be recovered in the appreciation of the residence. (In our illustration, these costs would range from $3,000 to $6,000.) This is another reason why you need to live in the house more than two years to make it pay compared to renting.

In this illustration, you can see that a home is not always a good investment in the short term. In summary, evaluate the purchase of a house with a long-range perspective and also in light of your vocation and lifestyle desires.

Buying a home may be the American Dream, but use wisdom in deciding whether it's best for you.

Buying a House

While it's prudent to proceed cautiously before buying a home, there are obvious benefits to owning a home and establishing roots in a community. Home buying can be an intimidating and exhilarating experience, especially the first time. It involves so many decisions! But the following guidelines will help you avoid most of the pitfalls of finding and purchasing a home.

Once you have made the decision to buy, your first consideration is money: How much do you have, and how much can you borrow? The answers to these two questions will control the location and price range of your home.

Borrowing for a house

The best way to buy a home is to pay cash, but most home buyers must arrange financing. Although borrowing money is not prohibited in Scripture, Proverbs 22:7 tells us that the borrower becomes "servant to the lender." So use restraint and proceed cautiously when borrowing money.

Many types of loans are available. Most are arranged through banks and lending institutions, but it is possible to finance a home through its owner or other private individuals. In either case, the terms of the loan will specify the minimum down payment, interest rate, length of loan, repayment terms, and qualifying criteria.

Down payments. A down payment is the difference between the purchase price and the loan amount. It is an up-front payment toward the purchase price of the house. Historically, lenders have required a down payment of at least 20 percent of the purchase price. In recent years, as home prices increased and lenders became more aggressive, many lenders began accepting a down payment of as little as 3 percent or 5 percent. Mortgages with minimal down payments will end up costing the borrower more (whether in mortgage insurance premiums or other costs) in order to protect the lender's additional risk.

Closing costs and prepaid items. These fees are paid in addition to the down payment. Closing costs include the attorney's fees, loan processing fees, and a property appraisal. Prepaid items include prorated property tax and homeowner's insurance escrows. These costs can be estimated as a percentage of the loan amount, with closing costs generally running about 3 percent and prepaid items about 1 percent. On any loans in which the purchaser pays less than 20 percent down (except some veterans' loans), lenders also usually require the purchaser to pay for private mortgage insurance (PMI). The PMI—which doesn't help you at all and only protects the lender in case of foreclosure—is often added to the total of the loan borrowed or added to the house payments.

Q: Should I withdraw money from my IRA for a down payment on a new home? The stock market's been flat, but real estate has been rising.

ANSWER: Economically, withdrawing money from an IRA for a down payment on a new home has several negative consequences. First, you lose the benefit of the magic of compounding on a tax-deferred basis. Second, there may be onerous tax consequences that would offset the benefit of borrowing from yourself for that down payment. The issue of whether the stock market's been flat but real estate has been rising assumes that you are buying the real estate or the home for investment purposes. It's been my experience that most people purchase a home as a place to live and not as an investment. I think it would be best to leave the money in the IRA and save for the down payment.

Private mortgage insurance (PMI): A home buyer who makes a down payment that is less than 20 percent of the purchase price may have to purchase this insurance, which will reimburse the lender should the borrower default on the loan and the foreclosure price is less than the amount still owed on the property.

As you can see, there are many costs associated with borrowing money and purchasing a home. Obviously, the less money you borrow, the more you save on financing costs. Because first-time buyers' down payment money and monthly income is usually limited, some home builders and sellers offer to pay some of the closing costs. Depending on the loan, lenders place some restrictions on the percentages a seller can pay. Check with a loan officer or real estate agent about these.

Interest rates. The interest rate is the percentage rate charged for the use of the money. It can be a fixed rate, meaning it remains the same during the entire loan period, or an adjustable or variable rate, meaning it can change during the loan period. Adjustable interest rates are generally tied to some standard interest rate index, such as the current rate on U.S. treasury bills, and can adjust up or down. Adjustable rates are initially lower than fixed rates. Since the interest rate on a loan directly affects the principal and interest payments, adjustable rate mortgages attract buyers who expect their incomes to increase in future years, but who initially need lower house payments than current fixed loans allow.

Loan term. The length, repayment terms, and qualifying criteria of a loan can vary. Most are set up for 15 or 30 years with monthly payments. The length and repayment terms affect the repayment amounts and the total amount paid for interest over the term of the loan. Some loans are repaid with bimonthly payments and others are repaid in full at the end of a certain period (i.e., a balloon note).

A new phenomenon in recent years is the interest-only loan, where the regular mortgage payment covers only interest and no principal. These loans allow the borrower to pay interest only for a specified period, usually 5 to 10 years. These loans result in a lower monthly payment initially but result in more interest being paid over the life of the loan.

How much can you afford to borrow?

To determine how much a person is "qualified" to borrow, a lender compares the gross monthly income of the applicant(s) to the monthly debt payments. If the ratio of income to debt falls within the qualifying ratios, the lender generally grants the loan. Lenders will, however, also consider credit history and employment stability before approving the loan.

Freddie Mac, the common name for the Federal Home Loan Mortgage Corporation, which is a private corporation chartered by Congress to increase the supply of mortgage funds available to home buyers, provides some helpful information about affordability. To get a rough estimate of what you can afford for a home, they advise consumers to multiply their gross annual income (i.e., before taxes) by 2.5. So a family with an annual household income of $50,000 may be able to qualify for a $125,000 home. Applicants' debt and credit history generally also affect whether they are offered a loan and how much they can borrow.

In addition, mortgage lenders consider two other factors when determining whether to offer applicants a mortgage:

- **Housing expense ratio.** A monthly mortgage payment should be less than or equal to a quarter of a family's gross income, though this percentage may change depending on the type of mortgage and the area in which an applicant is buying. (For example, because of the high cost of housing in California, lenders realize it is likely to take a higher percentage of an applicant's gross income.)
- **Debt-to-income ratio.** Other debt is a factor in determining what is considered an affordable monthly mortgage payment. If your total debt payment is more than 30 to 40 percent of gross monthly income, it is a red flag. Such debt may include credit cards, student loans, car loans, housing expenses, alimony, or child support.[3]

To illustrate how qualifying ratios are used, let's assume a young couple with a combined yearly income of $60,000 are looking for a home. Dividing $60,000 by 12 gives a gross monthly income of $5,000. Let's assume they apply for a loan that requires a 10 percent down payment and has qualifying ratios of 28 percent and 36 percent. Their monthly house payment (principal, interest, taxes, and insurance) cannot exceed 28 percent of their gross income ($1,400), and their house payment plus all debt payments, such as car loans, student loans, credit cards, etc., cannot exceed 36 percent of their gross income ($1,800).

Note that I used typical qualifying ratios in my illustrations, but I'm not recommending you get a house costing that much. You're better off if you can find a home meeting your needs—maybe not all your wants—at a lower price so that your ratios are lower. This will reduce your financial pressures and debt load. In the booming U.S. real estate market of the last decade, some bankers and real estate agents advocated even higher ratios (meaning higher debt loads compared to income) based on the assumption that real estate prices are rapidly moving higher each year. I think this is a dangerous assumption for families. (Because this book has been a two-year project, I wrote the last sentence before the softening and decline in some areas of the U.S. residential real estate market and mortgage concerns in 2007. As the end of this decade approaches, many banks, financial institutions, and families are having financial indigestion from the excesses earlier in the decade.)

Another way to determine one's price range is to speak directly with a loan officer. Most lenders offer a prequalifying interview at no charge, which is an excellent way to learn about loans, closing costs, and prepaid items involved in purchasing a home.

Solving the Mortgage Mystery

For most families, the single biggest loan decision of their lives will be how to finance their home purchase. Ten years ago that was a "plain vanilla" decision: everyone got a 30-year fixed rate mortgage and made this payment faithfully each month. Times have changed, however, and people are looking at a variety of options for paying off mortgages early.

Type and term of mortgage

In trying to evaluate what type of mortgage to get, you'll have to learn many terms: ARMs, PLAMs, Fannie Maes, Freddie Macs, VA loans, buy downs, and so on (the variety in terminology is limited only by lenders' creativity). Mortgage loans can be entered into for almost any number of years up to at least 30, and in some cases 50, years.

I've concluded that anything other than a fixed-rate, fixed-term loan is an attempt to make it "easy" on the buyer and to protect the lender in the event of changed circumstances (i.e., rising interest rates). Therefore, ARMs (adjustable

ANSWER: Mortgage insurance is purchased for the exclusive purpose of paying off the debt on the home in the event of the death of the home owner. It is actually a decreasing term type of insurance because as the debt is decreased, the insurance company's liability is decreased. Most mortgage insurance is very expensive, especially if it is purchased through a mortgage company or bank. In my opinion, a better alternative is to increase your existing life insurance to provide this coverage (if it is not already provided through a previous needs analysis) or to purchase a separate decreasing term life insurance policy for this purpose and cancel it when the mortgage is paid.

rate mortgages) and PLAMs (price level adjusted mortgages) are not wrong, just much riskier. The lender in each case is protected, and you, the buyer, are the one taking all the chances. You're implicitly assuming either deflation (which is a rare economic occurrence) or your income rising faster than interest rate and payment increases.

If you're considering taking any type of adjustable mortgage, make sure it includes two things. First, there should be absolutely no possibility of negative amortization (where the amount you owe actually goes up rather than down) on the loan. Second, there should be caps on possible increases in the interest rate charged. For ARMs, that cap has typically been 5 or 6 percent over the life of the loan (1 to 2 percent per year), and I see no reason to ever agree to a higher total cap.

Amortization: Gradual repayment of debt through regular payments that include principal and interest.

If you're considering a mortgage that doesn't include a fixed rate for a fixed term, you should assume your income will be constant and your mortgage payments will go up as much as possible each period. Then ask yourself, *Can I afford it?* Not only is this the safest course, it also will give you a much better understanding of the risks associated with an adjustable mortgage.

The term of the loan is relatively easy to evaluate. The chart on the next page indicates how many times you will pay back the original amount borrowed, assuming various interest rates and terms in years. For example, if you borrow money at an 8 percent rate on a 30-year mortgage, you will pay back 2.64 times the original amount borrowed. So the true cost of the home, ignoring the time value of money and the tax impact of the interest payments, is over two-and-a-half times what you thought you paid for it.

TIMES A HOME WILL BE PAID FOR USING A MORTGAGE TO PURCHASE

Mortgage Term (in years)	Loan Interest Rate (in percents)						
	6.0	7.0	8.0	9.0	10.0	11.0	12.0
5	1.16	1.18	1.22	1.25	1.28	1.30	1.33
10	1.33	1.40	1.46	1.52	1.60	1.65	1.72
15	1.52	1.62	1.72	1.83	1.93	2.05	2.18
20	1.72	1.86	2.01	2.16	2.32	2.48	2.64
25	1.93	2.12	2.32	2.52	2.73	2.94	3.16
30	2.16	2.40	2.64	2.90	3.16	3.43	3.70

Notice what happens when you cut the term of the mortgage in half, to 15 years, and leave the interest rate at 8 percent. Even though you borrow the same amount, you pay back only 1.72 times the original amount borrowed, rather than the 2.64 percent you would pay with a 30-year term. The conclusion is clear: the shorter the term of the mortgage, the less you pay in interest.

With these facts in mind, my recommendations regarding the type and term of the mortgage are simple:

1. You're better off in the long run to use a fixed-rate mortgage rather than any type of adjustable loan. The latter almost always forces you to assume favorable economic circumstances in the future, which may not in fact occur.

2. You should put down at least 20 percent when buying a house, even though it's possible to put down as little as 5 percent. Once again, the reason is to reduce the danger of presumption about the future.

3. If at all possible, choose a 15-year loan instead of a 30-year loan. The payments are typically only 20 to 25 percent more per month, but the total amount paid over the life of the mortgage is significantly less.

I've been asked whether the fact that home mortgages are typically paid off in eight years (because the house is sold again) affects my recommendations, which seem to assume a home buyer will be in the house long term. But whether you're in a house 3 years, 15 years, or 30 years makes no difference. The shortest-term loan at the lowest rate with the largest down payment is always the most prudent approach in mortgaging a house.

There's a significant risk in accepting an adjustable rate mortgage because you think you're only going to be in the home a few years. Such a loan is essentially a bet that the future will bring favorable economic conditions, and if those conditions don't come about, the borrower pays the price. Even with a 2 percent yearly cap on the interest rate, the monthly payment can go up dramatically. Unless income goes up just as dramatically, you may find yourself unable to make the payments.

> **The shortest-term loan at the lowest rate with the largest down payment is always the most prudent approach in mortgaging a house.**

You need not understand all the buzzwords if you understand the principles underlying mortgages. The fact of the matter is that the best mortgage is no mortgage. The second-best alternative is a fixed-rate, short-term mortgage (10 to 15 years). The third-best option is a fixed-rate, 30-year mortgage.

Equity Sharing

With the increase in housing prices, young families can be priced right out of the housing market even though their income is rising. This is especially true in heavily populated areas with a scarcity of land.

As a result, some young couples have explored equity sharing arrangements—someone else, often an investor, makes the down payment on the home in exchange for a share in the home's appreciation. There are many variations on how equity-sharing deals are structured. Who gets the tax deductions, how the appreciation is to be split, and who is liable for the mortgage can all be negotiated.

Because of the complexity of this type of arrangement and its applicability to such a small number of people, I'm not going to cover in detail how to structure such a deal. My recommendation, however, is that if equity sharing seems to make sense in your case, the terms need to be well understood by all parties concerned. And without exception, the terms should be written down and signed by all concerned, even if the arrangement is with a parent.

The terms of the equity-sharing relationship must give either party an opportunity to get out of the deal. This may require the sale of the home or a buyout of the other party. Such a sale may not be desirable to the people living in the home, but it's more desirable than continuing in a relationship that becomes antagonistic.

Shopping for a House

Now that you have a general understanding of financing and your price range, you can realistically begin listing and prioritizing your housing needs and wants. The wants and needs of people in different stages of life will differ greatly. But whether you are interested in single-family housing or a condominium, you can venture out on your own or contact a real estate agent. Using the Internet may reduce the time you spend looking for homes that match your criteria (number of bedrooms, price, etc.), and you can view pictures of homes.

Freddie Mac offers some helpful tips on how to make the house-hunting process easier. Their Web site includes articles to help you determine what you want in a house, choose the best neighborhood for your family, find a real estate agent, and make an offer. See http://www.freddiemac.com/corporate/buyown/english/purchasing/hunting/. Their site also includes helpful information on securing a mortgage.

After You've Signed on the Dotted Line . . . Other Mortgage Questions

Mortgages have become big business over the past few decades, which means home owners often have questions regarding their mortgage long after they've moved into their own home. Most commonly, home owners have questions about home equity loans, refinancing, and the advantages of paying off their mortgage early.

Home equity loans

Forget the fancy label—home equity loans are simply second mortgages. They may be useful in certain circumstances when you're in need of cash or if they can convert what would typically be nondeductible interest expense into deductible mortgage interest expense. They can also be useful in meeting short-term needs, such as for a college education. However, like any other form of debt, they're easy to enter into but deceptively difficult to pay off. The greatest danger with a home equity loan is that it risks a valuable asset, your home equity, for something less secure, such as an automobile, a vacation, or a boat.

In addition, home equity loans typically have variable rates of interest, with no cap on how high the interest rate can go. Thus, when interest rates rise, these loans can be tremendously expensive to repay. Be extremely careful about entering into a home equity form of debt, as it may become a real burden and put your house in jeopardy.

Refinancing

After the attacks on the World Trade Center and the Pentagon, and the launch of the war on terror in 2001, U.S. and global interest rates dropped in an attempt by central bankers to stimulate the economy. With the resulting decline in mortgage interest rates, the refinancing stampede was on. For many people, refinancing their mortgage was an easy decision. As rates have stabilized and slowly moved up in recent years, deciding whether to refinance requires more analysis.

Remember that refinancing involves some costs. What are the costs? To the lender, refinancing a mortgage is just like starting all over again. The lender charges the borrower for a credit report, origination fees, closing costs, legal fees, fees for title search, a new survey, an appraisal, deed recording expenses, discount points, and possibly private mortgage insurance.

A widely quoted rule of thumb for refinancing is that the new interest rate should be at least 2 percentage points below your present rate. The question is, does this rule fit your situation? How long will it take to recover the costs of refinancing, and how much can you save? The answer may depend on the financing fees, the time you intend to remain in your house, and your tax bracket. The less difference between the existing and new mortgage rates, the more time will be required to recover your refinancing costs.

When deciding whether to refinance, determine how much you would save and how long it would take to recover your costs.

When interest rates fall, people ask whether they should refinance their mortgages to lock in a lower interest rate. Generally, that's a wise move. However, the attorneys' fees, appraisal fees, points charged, and so on make it costly to refinance. Because the closing costs can be a total of 3 to 5 percent of the loan amount, it usually takes about two years to recoup those expenses with a 2 percent differential in rates. Again, that means you should be planning on staying in the home for at least two more years.

Another consideration in refinancing is whether you can do so without paying a prepayment penalty on your original mortgage. By checking the loan document or calling the lender, you can determine your cost to refinance. It may very well be that you can negotiate those costs with the lender, even though the lender will be taking a lower interest rate (better that than have you borrow from someone else).

Paying your mortgage off early

Over the past 40 years having a home mortgage has become as American as apple pie. These days, living in a home without a mortgage is the exception rather than the norm.

Today many financial experts have offered conflicting advice about whether or not one should pay off one's home mortgage. I recently read a newspaper headline that said, "Don't Use Windfall to Pay Off Mortgage." And yet others would contend that the first thing you should do with excess cash is to pay off your mortgage. Which advice is right? It's difficult to answer that question with finality; however, let's consider some issues so you can draw your own conclusion.

First, consider your *marriage relationship*. The wife's security orientation generally causes her to be more adverse to risk; as a result, she typically wants to avoid debt—particularly when it involves the home. Therefore, for marital harmony, it may be a good idea to pay off the mortgage to remove the house from any economic risk.

Second, consider your *investment return*. If a person maintains a home mortgage and yet has available cash to make other investments, that person is implying that he or she can earn "risk free" with other investments more than he or she is paying on the home mortgage. I say "risk free" because paying off the home mortgage is not a risky investment. Let me illustrate: If I owe $100,000 on a 10 percent mortgage, then I pay $10,000 a year in interest; I'm out of pocket $10,000. If I pay off my mortgage, then I don't have the outflow of $10,000 and so in essence have earned $10,000 on my $100,000 investment. I earned the $10,000 without any risk; I simply paid off my mortgage. If I elect not to pay off my home mortgage and invest $100,000, I must earn more than 10 percent on my investment to have the same net worth at the end of the year. From my own experience, I know it's very difficult to consistently earn more each year than the interest rate you'd pay on your home mortgage on a risk-free basis. Therefore, the repayment of the home mortgage as the first use of excess funds is a good investment move.

Third, consider the *liquidity*. It wouldn't be wise to pay off or even pay down the mortgage using all your liquid funds. Liquidity gives you flexibility to meet changing circumstances and emergencies. *A person should have at least three to six months of living expenses in an emergency fund before considering using excess funds to pay off a home mortgage.* Otherwise, if I had an emergency but no longer could tap into liquid funds, I would have to borrow the money at a higher interest rate than my home mortgage.

Fourth, consider why you would *not* want to pay off your home mortgage. The answer is typically a feeling that you can earn a higher investment return with the money somewhere else. You need to weigh your motives and make sure greed is not driving you. Paying off your home mortgage gives you not only a decent investment return but peace of mind, a strengthened marriage

> **A person should have at least three to six months of living expenses in an emergency fund before considering using excess funds to pay off a home mortgage.**

relationship, and other benefits. I typically ask couples to close their eyes and think about not having a home mortgage. Do they feel better about that alternative or having the money in the bank? Almost always the answer is, "We have a greater sense of security when the mortgage is paid off." If so, I always recommend they go ahead and pay off the mortgage. In such instances, it may not be as much an economic question as it is a peace-of-mind question.

Let's turn the question around: Why should someone prepay a mortgage? Besides being the best risk-free investment you can make, prepaying the mortgage is a type of forced savings. By keeping my extra cash in the bank, I might be tempted to use it to buy unneeded consumer goods. By sending some of my cash margin to the mortgage company each month, I have made the money more difficult to get to. In fact, if I want to get that money back I have to get a home equity loan, which requires effort, paperwork, and time. We're all human, and the more barriers we can place between ourselves and our money, the less likely we will be to spend it frivolously.

If you don't have a windfall of money to pay off your mortgage, you could do it gradually. You might even find that there is indeed such thing as a free lunch.

Maybe There Is Such a Thing as a Free Lunch. . . .

Earlier we did a comparison of mortgage terms, tax benefits, and interest rates to determine the true cost of a loan. We concluded that a shorter-term loan at a lower interest rate is the most advantageous way to purchase a home. We also determined that the lower the tax rate, the more this is true. Although the payments for a 15-year mortgage will be 20 to 25 percent more than those for a 30-year loan, they'll last only half as long.

In effect, the shorter mortgage is like a free lunch, because you're borrowing the same amount of money at the same interest rate but having to pay far less in total payments. Also, the interest rate is usually lower on shorter-term mortgages compared to longer-term ones. Thus, the true cost of the home is significantly less than what it would be if you financed over a longer time period.

An alternative way to accomplish the same effect is to make one extra payment per year. The chart on the next page shows the incredible impact of this strategy. Just one extra annual payment can reduce the total term of the mortgage by almost a third.

There are several other ways to make early payments as well. You can pay one-half your usual monthly payment every two weeks and reduce your interest costs. Then, you end up making 13 payments per year instead of 12. Or, you can add one-twelfth of a payment to each payment and thereby end up with one extra payment per year. You can also make periodic lump sum payments of principal.

EFFECT OF ONE EXTRA PAYMENT PER YEAR ON A 30-YEAR FIXED INTEREST RATE

Mortgage Interest Rate (in percents)	Original No. of Payments	Actual No. of Payments	Difference	Payment (in dollars)	Amount Saved (in dollars)	Actual No. of Years Paid
8	360	279	81	440.26	35,661.06	21.5
10	360	257	103	526.54	54,233.62	19.8
12	360	235	125	617.17	77,146.25	18.1
14	360	213	147	710.92	104,505.24	16.4

Before doing any of these things, however, you need to check with the lender to determine that prepayments will be accepted. Ask also about rules regarding those prepayments. Some mortgage companies, for example, will use them to reduce the principal amount owed but not to reduce the payments; and if you're in default one payment in the future, you're in default on the mortgage. This is true even if you've prepaid a significant part of the principal amount borrowed.

The best alternative when prepaying the mortgage is to have the mortgage company commit to you that it will accept that prepayment in lieu of future payments. This will be critical should you ever find it necessary, because of extenuating circumstances, not to make a payment when it's due. Determining the lender's prepayment policy is best done before the mortgage is entered into, as there's no real incentive for the lender to change the terms of the loan once the documents are signed with terms in its favor.

A radical option, but certainly not out of the question, is doubling your monthly mortgage payment. Doing so will repay a 30-year mortgage in 7.5 years. A strong commitment and setting a faith goal can result in a young married couple being debt-free by age 35. The discipline of prepaying these extra dollars per month on the mortgage payment will allow a couple to increase net worth faster than investing the money into an alternative investment. Why? Because the mortgage prepayment is more of a forced savings, and it can become more of a discipline than alternative types of investment.

All of us are stewards or managers of our spending decisions. Even the traditionally mundane mortgage payment should be proactively managed from a stewardship perspective. After all, it's probably the one area that takes most of your cash flow. Your car or other vehicle probably comes in a close second, and we'll consider how to make wise purchasing decisions on those in the next chapter.

CHAPTER 14

A Car Won't Make You, but It Might Break You

I once heard a female comedian ask, "Why do women wear perfume that smells like flowers to attract men? If they want men to pursue them, they should wear the scent of the inside of a new car!" I agree. Such a perfume would appeal to me and many other men I know.

Americans are notorious for their love affair with the automobile. In the days when having an automobile was more of a luxury, Will Rogers said, "We're the only nation in the world to go to the poorhouse in an automobile." That wisecrack still has some truth to it. Many people barely have a positive net worth, yet they drive cars with every known option. We use our cars for far more than basic transportation. We eat and get dressed in them—watch what happens on the highways of major cities during the morning commute. With their DVD players, TV screens, satellite radios, and stereos, many vehicles are mobile entertainment compartments. From heated car seats to GPS systems to cars that automatically parallel park, they do it all—for a price.

In this chapter we'll review the financial principles for purchasing vehicles. We'll examine the ways to finance their purchase from leasing to borrowing to using cash. You'll learn the common deceptions in the financing of cars. I'll also tell you where you can find the cheapest car you'll ever own.[1]

Your Car's Reason for Being: Transportation or Significance?

Often I am asked, "Should I buy a new car?" My response is always, "That's the wrong question."

Over the years, I've learned that, when deciding what car to buy, the ego satisfaction of driving a new car often outweighs the economic criteria. It's amazing how our egos can justify a new car when in fact it never makes economic sense to purchase one! A quality car may have a better resale value than another car, but I have never yet seen a car (other than a rare antique model) that appreciates in value. Instead, cars depreciate and are never a good "investment." At best, it's a wise purchase. (And when you pay cash, you typically make a better purchase than when you finance—but more on that later in this chapter.)

The real question is "How can I best provide transportation?" The answer depends on your objectives and the priority of those objectives. For example, some of your objectives may be (1) to minimize your annual costs; (2) to provide comfort; (3) to provide safety; (4) to minimize the down payment; (5) to minimize the annual financing cost; (6) to achieve a dream (owning a Jaguar or BMW).

The cheapest car you will ever own is the one you are presently driving. The cost of financing, depreciation, and the lost opportunities for the down payment funds when buying a new car will always more than offset the annual maintenance and upkeep of an older car (even though the newer car might get better gas mileage). The higher the price of the car, the higher the actual cost to drive that car, and therefore the more desirable it becomes to drive the older car. A new car will also cost more in insurance and tag fees than an older car.

While economically it never makes sense to get a new car, obviously there comes a time when one must get a *different* car. I think there are three times to consider getting a different car: first, when the cost of repairs becomes greater than the value of the car; second, when for safety reasons a different car is needed; and third, when the cost of your time to continually take a car in for repairs outweighs the economic cost of a different car. For example, if you need your car for your business or occupation, time spent in a repair shop prevents you from realizing your full income potential.

> **The cheapest car you will ever own is the one you are presently driving.**

Three topics need to be addressed whenever a car purchase is being considered: (1) Why buy a particular car? (2) When should a vehicle be replaced? (3) How should its replacement be paid for?

Why Buy a Particular Car?

It's rare to find a family that doesn't have at least one car. And some families have three, four, or even five vehicles. The need for cars is obvious. Our family lives in Atlanta, where it takes at least 30 minutes to get anyplace. All the roads and interstate highways seem to be under continual repair or construction.

As a consequence, getting around is extremely time consuming. It's not uncommon for a mother with school-age children to spend several hours a day in her car getting them to and from school and extracurricular activities. Commuters going to and from work can easily spend an hour a day in their cars.

When our oldest daughter was about to turn 16, I realized I could save my wife many hours per week if I bought our daughter a car and allowed her to do a portion of the carpooling to and from school. The question was not "Should a 16-year-old have a car?" but "How can I best meet the transportation needs of my family?" My daughter is a responsible young lady, but I purchased the car and loaned it to her for my wife's and my convenience.

There's only one reason people should buy cars, and that's to provide transportation. Our daughter, like many teenagers, was delighted by the opportunity to drive. Even though we provided her with an older, inexpensive "tank," she was more than happy to drive it for several years because it took her safely where she wanted to go.

The point is that all the "bells and whistles" that go along with cars are nice but certainly not necessary. They're luxuries. Whether you're willing to pay for them comes back to what you're really trying to do in buying a particular car. If you're searching for significance or contentment by driving a luxury car, then you may make foolish economic decisions.

When to Replace?

In 1972, I was a fairly successful businessman. Not yet a Christian, I was seeking all the trappings of success. Because I was only 30 years old, I chose to buy an Oldsmobile 98 rather than a Cadillac as my first new car. My reasoning was that it would be a few years before I was old enough and "mature enough" to look right driving an expensive luxury car. The Olds 98 actually had all the luxury features of the more expensive car, but it didn't have the Cadillac aura.

Two years after I bought the car, I became a Christian. Many things about my life changed, particularly my value system. As I mentioned earlier in this book, I moved my family to Atlanta to enter full-time ministry work. By the early 1980s, the Olds 98 had over 100,000 miles on it and was still running fine. It looked terrible, however. It was a vintage rusted color. The vinyl top peeled. The power seats and windows didn't work all the time. The seat fabric was worn. The car generally just did not give a favorable impression. Therefore, I began looking around to replace what had become known affectionately as "Old Blue."

Being an accountant, I assumed I would be able to analyze a new car purchase and come up with a most economical replacement. Smaller foreign cars had become quite popular, often getting 30 to 50 miles per gallon; Old Blue got only 8 or 9 miles per gallon. The cost of repairs and maintenance had also gone up on Old Blue.

I spent months evaluating the car alternatives. And the conclusion I finally reached amazed me: The unhappy and unwanted fact was that the cheapest car I could own was the car I already had. I extended my evaluation using all types of purchase scenarios, and in every case the cheapest car I could own was Old Blue. Over the years, I've also evaluated other people's car-buying options, exploring all the opportunities, and in every case I had to conclude that the cheapest car they could own was the car they presently had.

Your current car is the cheapest because even though some costs go up the longer you own a car, many others go down. Interestingly, drivers are taking advantage of this truth by hanging on to their cars longer than ever before. According to the vehicle population report released recently by R. L. Polk & Co., the median age of passenger cars in operation increased to 9.2 years in 2006, a record high. Also, the scrap rate is near historic lows.[2]

Years ago, I read an article in *Money* magazine titled "The Case for Hanging On to Your Aging Family Car for 100,000 Miles." It was based on extensive research by Runzheimer International, an independent transportation consultant, which demonstrated the considerable financial advantages of keeping a car for at least eight years. Runzheimer compared the costs of operating a debt-free four-year-old car for another four years versus buying and operating a new one for that period. When considering loan payments, gas and oil, insurance, repairs, and maintenance, along with the trade-in value, Runzheimer determined an owner would save over $5,000 by keeping the older car—and that was about 20 years ago!

FAMILY FINANCE

As they sped down the highway on the way to the used-car dealership, Elizabeth said, "This is so cool, Dad! I can't believe I'm going to drive myself to school tomorrow in my own car."

Bob smiled. "Did I ever tell you about my first car?" he asked. "A gold 1969 Mustang, two doors, manual transmission, a powerful engine . . ." A dreamy look came over his face. Glancing at his daughter, he quickly cleared his throat and took on a more businesslike tone. "Remember, Liz, your mom and I think you need a car so you can drive back and forth to work—not to mention driving to college in the fall."

"That's the practical side of it, Dad," Elizabeth said, "but I'm looking forward to picking it out. Maybe we'll find something red and sporty."

Bob slowed the car down and turned into the dealership parking lot. "Okay, here we are," he said. "Remember the parameters we talked about?"

Liz nodded. "You and Mom are putting in $15,000 for something *safe and reliable with good gas mileage*," she recited teasingly in a singsong voice.

"You got it," Bob said, opening the door. "Let's go."

As they walked through the lot, they were greeted by a young salesman, who asked what they were looking for. Before Bob could get out "safe and reliable," Liz blurted, "We're looking for my first car! Do you have anything red and sporty?"

Within minutes, the salesman had shown them five cars that made Liz giddy with anticipation. "Dad!" she hissed when the salesman turned away for a minute. "That one over there is perfect!"

"The lost value, together with financing costs, is what knocks the new car out of contention," according to the *Money* report. "Those two items would be expected to account for nearly 55 percent of the total costs of keeping a new model on the road during its first four years of life. On the debt-free older model, depreciation would total just 35 percent of expenses. And in this regard, a Chevy is no different from a Ford, Cadillac or Mercedes."[3]

We don't often give depreciation and financing costs enough weight when we consider buying a new car. How often have you heard (or used) these reasons for trading in a car:

"My car is now approaching 100,000 miles, and that's a good time to trade because the car loses value so quickly after that point."

"The best time to trade is when a car is three or four years old."

"Because gas prices are higher, I should get a more fuel-efficient car to save money."

"Things will surely break soon now that it's not covered by a warranty."

All these reasons are really justifications; they are not borne out by any economic study. There are, however, three legitimate reasons for replacing a car, and they have to do with time, repairs, and safety.

She pointed to a cherry red Mazda Miata at the front of the lot. "Only 30,000 miles. It's sporty, it's cute, and it has a multi-CD stereo system! Oh, and it has air bags and gets decent mileage too, so it fits the criteria, right?"

Bob tilted his head. "It's cute all right. But it also has a price tag of $19,500."

"I know your limit is $15,000. But I could pay the extra. I could get financing and pay off the $4,500 over a couple of years."

Bob shook his head. "Liz, remember that you're going to be fully responsible for gas and insurance too. That's easily $200 a month. You're only working part-time now, and you don't know what kind of job you'll be able to find once you start school. How can you afford car payments?"

Liz bit her lip. "Well . . . "

"Listen," Bob continued, "what I didn't tell you about that 1969 Mustang was that it took me five years to pay for it. By the time I did, I'd also had to repair the engine three times and I was ready to get a different car. I don't want you to start out burdened with that kind of debt." He put a hand on his daughter's shoulder. "Let's keep looking and see if we can find something that makes us both happy. After all, the most important thing is that the car can get you where you need to go."

Three hours and a trip to the mechanic later, Liz drove off the lot in a Honda Civic. At 50,000 miles and five years old, it was still going strong. With its price tag of $13,200, it fit all of Bob and Laura's requirements. And with a red exterior and good stereo system, it fit Liz's too.

Time. When a car requires so much of your time to keep it repaired that the cost of your time is greater than the cost of replacing the car, it should be replaced. If my wife is spending two or three days a week with her car in the shop and is therefore using my car or going without transportation, at some point the cost of our time is such that it becomes wise to replace the vehicle. From a straight dollars-and-cents standpoint, it may still be more economical to keep and repair the old car, but the cost in time is too great.

People who depend on their cars for their livelihood (salespeople, real estate agents) also have to consider the cost of time. If their cars are unavailable one or two days a week because of repairs or maintenance, it makes sense to replace them and get back that one or two days of productive time.

Only you can put a value on your time and determine if keeping your old car is costing too much. Obviously, time spent in the repair shop is time you can't spend on other activities, including those that generate income. But valuing your time can be a highly subjective exercise. I would encourage you, therefore, if you think your cost in time validates a decision to buy a new car, to talk it over with an accountability partner.

Cost of repairs. The second reason for replacing a car is excessive repair costs. Determine if the cost of needed repairs is greater than what the car will be worth after it's fixed. This typically doesn't happen until well over 100,000 miles or 10 to 12 years of driving the vehicle.

Safety. The third legitimate reason to replace a car is that it has become unsafe and unreliable. For example, I would never want my wife or daughters to take the risk of becoming stranded at night along the road. Obviously, saving money is not the overriding consideration when you're concerned about your family's safety.

> **The three legitimate reasons for replacing a car have to do with time, repairs, and safety.**

When I speak to groups on this topic, someone usually asks what kind of cars I have. You might assume from my recommendations that I drive 15-year-old, 200,000-mile cars regardless of their appearance. And you might assume I force my wife and children to do the same. I jokingly answer that question by saying I have a Mercedes and two BMWs. Please be assured that's not the case, but neither is the first perception true. Over the years, our family cars have been decent vehicles, most of which were purchased used.

I, like you, want to drive a nice car. I can identify with those who love to drive a new car because "it smells so good." There are few things so satisfying, so appealing to your sense of pride and self-fulfillment, as to be able to drive a new car off the lot for the first time. Some relish it so much that they trade for a new car every year. Others never will experience the feeling because they have the discipline not to fall into that trap. My counsel to those who are particularly susceptible to the temptation to replace cars prematurely is to always pay cash. When I suggest that, people generally respond, "I can't afford that." And to me that answers the question of whether it's time for them to replace their cars.

How Should You Pay for the Replacement?

If you need to buy a car, there are three issues that must always be considered when it comes to funding the replacement:

1. New versus used
2. Lease versus buy
3. Cash versus borrow

New versus used

In almost every case, it will be less expensive to buy a used car rather than a new one, providing you make your choice carefully. Frequently people insist on purchasing a new car to avoid buying someone else's problems. But new cars break down too. What you're really looking for is a reliable car that will get you where you're going.

You can take a few steps to ensure you're buying a reliable used car. Never buy one without first taking it to a mechanic to have it checked. Also examine the service records of the previous owner to determine the kind of care the car has received.

Buying a new car can be a legitimate decision, however, if you follow two rules. First, you must plan to drive the new car for at least 8 to 10 years. That way the heavy early depreciation of the car is irrelevant, because you will spread out the total depreciation over a lengthy time period. The second rule is that you pay cash for the new car. As has been proven already, it's always more advantageous economically to pay cash rather than borrow. This is never truer than when buying a new car.

Paying cash generally causes you to make a better decision than you would if you borrowed. It's much easier to borrow $20,000 to $25,000 because you have "easy payments" of $350 per month than to write a check for $20,000. Somehow it's difficult to part with money that has been hard earned and hard saved. And that's exactly why I recommend paying cash for a car, especially a new one.

Every major purchase, in fact, should be made with cash. It's even helpful (though I've rarely seen it done) to go to the bank and draw out the money in large bills. That helps you focus on the reality that you've traded off a part of your life to earn that money so you can now have whatever it is you desire so strongly.

Q: I'm considering leasing my next car. I like the idea of just taking it back to the dealer several years from now and avoiding the hassle of reselling it. What do you think about leasing?

ANSWER: Two arguments are given for leasing, even when it's clear you pay a premium to do so. You've mentioned the first: It's more convenient to replace the car because you don't have to sell it at the end of the lease. The other is that it's easier to take a tax deduction for a business car by leasing rather than buying.

It's true that with a lease you can replace your car at the end of three, four, or five years merely by turning it in for another leased car. However, there's a cost associated with doing so. The lessor will require you to guarantee his back-end value on that car. When you turn it in, if the actual value is less than the originally estimated value (because of depreciation, high mileage, or the condition of the car), you pay the difference in cash.

Additionally, you're paying the lessor a premium to do something you can do yourself: sell the car or trade it in. If you've followed the "new versus used" rules above, you'll be driving it for at least 8 to 10 years anyway. To say that it's more convenient to lease because of the trade-in or replacement aspect is shortsighted. Leasing is a very profitable activity for auto dealers. It's best for them, but not for you, the consumer.

The second argument for leasing doesn't hold up either. If you can meet IRS requirements for deducting a lease payment, you can certainly qualify to deduct the costs of owning a car. Those costs are depreciation, repairs and maintenance, parking, tolls, and so on. The determining factor for the deductibility of a car is not whether it's leased or purchased, but whether it's used for business purposes. Leasing has nothing to do with tax deductibility.

If you gather that I feel strongly about the deception of leasing versus buying, you are right. Leasing may be convenient, but it's almost never prudent.

Leasing versus buying

Recently I heard a commercial from a luxury auto dealership here in Atlanta that basically said, "You can probably drive much more car than you think you can." The salesman promised that through their leasing program, he could put the listener in a foreign-made luxury car he didn't think he could afford (with good reason). The deception of "easy payments" was being used to appeal to consumers. The lease-versus-buy decision, which is becoming more and more common, preys on this deception. Absolutely the only economic benefit to leasing is that in most cases the payments are lower than comparable financing payments.

The leasing decision, however, will never be more advantageous than financing, let alone paying cash. A lease is set up strictly for convenience. The lessor (car dealer) allows the lessee (customer), within limits, to set up his own convenient lease plan. All the lessor does to make it work for the lessee is to adjust the time period of the lease and/or the back-end replacement cost the lessee must guarantee (more on this below).

In calculating how much to charge on a lease, the lessor does the same calculations you should do when buying a car. He determines what his actual cost is going to be depending on the terms you want; he adds to it the financing cost he's going to bear (dealers buy their inventory on credit); and then he adds on his profit margin. All he's really doing is giving you the ease of making one payment rather than taking the multiple responsibilities of ownership. You can put the license plates and insurance in the lessor's name. Repairs and maintenance can be handled by the lessor. But for that convenience, the lessor charges you all those costs plus his profit margin. It is never economically advantageous to lease. At best, it is only more convenient.

Paying cash versus borrowing

Without question, the best way to purchase a different car is to pay cash for it rather than finance it. Then, instead of making car payments, make payments into an auto purchase savings account, so that every time it becomes desirable or necessary to get a different car, the cash is available.

When you pay with cash rather than borrow, you think differently. Somehow, the outflow of cash hurts more. But while it may not hurt now to borrow, it can hurt in the future. I recall a conversation with a businessman who was trying to justify buying a luxury car for his business by financing it. I suggested to him that he consider paying for the car with cash instead of borrowing. He replied, "Well, I can't afford that." He made my point for me. If he couldn't afford to pay cash, then he couldn't afford to borrow.

Car-Buying Deceptions

Cars are commonly financed with installment debt. So, we're going to look briefly at the deceptions related to this type of borrowing and discuss an important principle called the opportunity cost of consumption. Then, we'll discuss tips on purchasing used cars and auto insurance.

Deception 1: It makes more sense to borrow than to pay cash

One argument I sometimes hear is that a consumer who is able to pay cash for a car would do better by investing that money and taking out a loan for the car. If you begin to do the math, this argument appears to be valid. In fact, the first chart on page 214 seems to show that if someone has the cash to pay for a car, they're better off keeping the cash and financing the purchase.

PAY CASH OR FINANCE?

Cost of car	$15,000
Cash in bank	$15,000
Payments on car loan	$311.38 per month for 60 months
Interest rate	9.0%
CD saving rate	5.0%
Dealer's Analysis	
$15,000 invested at 5% for 60 months grows to:	$19,144
Original investment	$15,000
Interest income	$4,144
Total payments on car loan ($311.38/month x 60 months)	$18,683
Original amount borrowed	-$15,000
Interest expense	$3,683
Advantage of financing	$461

The scenario seems to work so well because the 9 percent interest rate is charged against a declining balance while the 5 percent is paid on a growing balance.

Those who advocate this view imply that assuming installment debt can be advantageous. But a better alternative would be to use the cash to pay for the car. Then, instead of making a monthly loan payment, make the monthly payment to yourself and deposit it in an interest-bearing account. The next chart shows the result.

ADVANTAGE OF PAYING CASH

Investment value of a monthly savings of $311.38 that earns 5% for 60 months	$21,176
Taxes paid on interest earned (15%)*	-$396
Net investment	$20,780
True value of investment in dealer's analysis from the chart above	
Future value of CD	$19,144
Taxes paid on interest earned*	-$674
Net investment	$18,470
Advantage of paying cash	$ 2,310

*The difference in taxes is due to the difference in interest income from the average principal actually invested. One begins with a large principal—producing more interest income—while the other amount grows over time.

The gain is $2,310 if cash is paid for the car and a monthly payment of $311.38 is invested at 5 percent, as opposed to keeping the cash and financing the car. It's always financially advantageous to pay cash for a car and save the monthly payment, literally as well as figuratively.

The only time this wouldn't be true is if the interest rate charged by the lender dropped to about half the rate that could be earned through investment. If the lending rate ever drops that low, however, the dealer is assuredly making up the lost interest by charging a higher price for the car. In that case, you'd still be better off paying cash for the car and negotiating the price down accordingly.

I've never found a better alternative than paying cash for a car. A vehicle is a depreciating item; borrowing to buy it doesn't make sense. Many times someone will say to me, "Well, I can't afford to pay cash." In that event, the answer is simple: "You can't afford that car."

A money maxim summarizes the situation well: "If you can't afford to save in order to pay cash, you can't afford to buy it on credit." For example, if you can find room in your budget for a $400 truck payment, then you should be able to save $400 per month. Don't kid yourself.

Deception 2: Easy payments

The second common deception with installment debt is the idea of "easy payments." There's no such thing. Again, if you can't afford to save, you can't afford to make payments. Payments appear to be easy only when you extend the term of repayment. Car loans used to be made for 24 months. Now they're commonly extended to 60 or even 72 months. According to the *Wall Street Journal*, the average maturity of a car loan today has exceeded five years, and the average vehicle price is at an all-time high of $29,316![4] As prices go up, the length of repayment becomes longer. And you will usually pay a higher interest rate on a longer-term loan.

The Opportunity Cost of Consumption

Assume that you borrow $10,000 to buy a used car and pay off the loan over four years. During those four years, you have an average amount borrowed of approximately $5,000 (the principal balance owed declines as you make payments). Further assume that you continue to borrow $10,000 every four years in order to replace your car throughout a working life of 40 years. You have thus borrowed an average of $5,000 for 40 years.

Now assume that the average interest rate you pay is 12 percent. Looking at the chart on page 216, come down the left-hand column to 40 years, then find the 12 percent column across the top. At the point where the two columns intersect, you see a factor of 93.1. That factor multiplied times $5,000, the average amount borrowed, computes to $465,500. This is the amount the lender has earned by collecting your interest and reloaning those funds to someone else at 12 percent.

To state it conversely, if you made a $5,000 deposit in an account earning 12 percent compounded interest and left it untouched for 40 years, you'd have the $465,500 the lender has earned at the end of that same period.[5]

OPPORTUNITY COST OF CONSUMPTION

Years with Auto Loan	Loan Interest Rate (in percents)						
	8.0	10.0	12.0	14.0	16.0	18.0	21.0
5	1.5	1.6	1.7	1.9	2.1	2.3	2.6
10	2.2	2.6	3.1	3.7	4.4	5.2	6.7
15	3.2	4.2	5.5	7.1	9.3	12.1	17.5
20	4.7	6.7	9.6	13.7	19.5	27.4	45.3
25	6.9	10.8	17.1	26.5	40.9	62.7	117.4
30	10.1	17.5	30.1	50.6	85.9	143.4	304.5
35	14.8	28.1	52.7	98.1	180.3	328.1	789.8
40	21.7	45.3	93.1	188.9	378.7	750	2048

Thus when you choose to borrow rather than save, you're giving up the opportunity to earn. That forfeited opportunity is what I call the opportunity cost of consumption.

Opportunity cost: The cost of giving up one alternative to get something else.

You can do your own calculations using the chart to see what you're likely to give up (or maybe have already given up) when you borrow. Think about it. Would you rather be a borrower or a saver (lender)? I'm reminded of the golden rule: "He who has the gold, rules."

By now you know my recommendation on the cash-versus-financing alternative. But if you're feeling a need to replace a car now and you don't think you can afford to pay cash, let me show you a way to be able to pay cash for your cars.

Let's assume you have a $1,000 repair bill facing you on your car, which is why you think you should trade. If you spend that $1,000 now and then save $100, $200, or $300 per month in a savings account earning 6 percent, you'll have one of the amounts shown in the chart on the next page at the end of whatever time period you choose.

If, instead of spending $300 per month on car payments, you put that amount in savings and wait one year, you can have a $3,698 car (less taxes on the $98 interest) for which you could pay cash. It's true you won't be driving the same luxury car that $300 per month could buy. But it's also true that you won't have the installment debt. If you continue to save the $300 per month, three more years later you'll have another $11,773 (less taxes on the interest), and then you can upgrade to a car costing that amount. If you keep that car for just four years, you'll have saved $16,177 (less tax) more to buy the next new car.

SAVE TO BUY

Amount in Fund at the End of Year (Before Taxes)
If Given Amount Saved per Month:

Year	$100/Month	$200/Month	$300/Month
1	1,233	2,465	3,698
2	2,539	5,079	7,618
3	3,924	7,849	11,773
4	5,392	10,785	16,177

You can see from this chart that the longer you save to buy the car, or the longer you drive the car you now have and make the payments to yourself, the more car you'll be able to afford later. This again illustrates the value of delaying gratification of your desires, as well as the truth of our maxim "If you can't afford to save for it, you can't afford to borrow for it." If the money is available to make payments, the money is also available to be saved. All you have to do is delay making the decision to buy until later.

It's easy to justify making a poor decision—often on the advice of an advertiser, a salesperson, or a friend who points out some great-sounding deal. But as I've told my children on more than one occasion, "If it sounds too good to be true, it probably is."

All this counsel is really a call to return to the way our parents and grandparents lived. We would benefit greatly from getting back to their definition of "being able to afford it," which is that you can afford to pay cash. Old-fashioned? Yes. Revolutionary? That would be great.

How to Buy a Used Car

The primary motivation for purchasing a used car is affordability. With new car and truck prices easily approaching $40,000, a used car looks more attractive in terms of price. When you buy a used car, even if it is only several months old, you avoid paying for the privilege of driving it off the showroom floor. Most new cars are now sold with lengthy (and transferrable) 36- to 60-month warranties (though if the warranty is still in effect when you buy a used car, you may pay more for the vehicle).

Yet many people begin shopping for a used car with much trepidation, fearing they'll wind up with a "lemon." Perhaps it is all summed up by the adage, "No one ever sold a car because it ran too well!" Still, despite all the used car salesman jokes, most people in the market for a used car believe if they buy it from a dealer, the vehicle will run better than if they buy it from someone off the street. They take a degree of comfort in seeing a dealer's nameplate on the back of the car, presuming that the dealer will "back up" the deal with appropriate service and repairs. However, there's a price for that degree of comfort. In addition, most people I know trade in their problem cars to dealers because they do not want to be individually hassled by an unhappy buyer. So the problem cars can end up on the dealer's lot—which is where most people buy used vehicles.

Another fallacy that leads a person to the dealer's showroom is the feeling that only the dealer can get financing. As I mentioned earlier, I would encourage you to purchase your vehicles with cash if at all possible. If this is not possible, however, realize that when the dealer finances the car, or even when he arranges the financing with a local bank, he receives a commission for it. So who, in reality, pays that commission? You do. Rather than accepting dealer financing, check with your local banks to determine who offers the most attractive rates. Take the time to do your homework, and it will save you in the long run. Incidentally, you can finance a used car bought from an individual. If you need to finance, check with your local bank before you start looking to determine the procedure.

> **When buying a used car, determine in advance how much you can spend, research what's on the market, and once you've selected a vehicle, have it checked by a reputable mechanic.**

There are three basic steps to buying a used car. If you violate any of them, you will pay a price. The first step is to determine in advance how much you can spend. Look at cars in that price range only—another reason to avoid dealers' lots, where you're likely to be tempted to buy up. In America, cars are a status symbol—the more status, the higher the cost. By following this step you won't get caught in the trap of paying more than you should.

Second, do your homework by researching what is on the market. Give yourself four to six weeks to do this. Keep your eyes open for "For Sale" signs, particularly around your neighborhood. Check the newspapers or used car guidebooks available at convenience stores. The Internet offers a productive way to compare prices and availability—from eBay to superstore dealers to pricing reference services, such as Kelley Blue Book (http://www.kbb.com) or edmunds.com. You can also use the Internet to trace the history of a car (using its vehicle identification number, or VIN), which will alert you if a car is under a recall or has been involved in a wreck. Select several potential vehicles and then begin interviewing the sellers. Ask for the following:

1. Correct mileage (generally, you can assume about 15,000 miles per year times the age of the car)
2. Number of owners
3. If the car has been in an accident or damaged
4. If the car has been used to tow a boat or a trailer
5. The reason the car is being sold
6. Availability of the car's service records
7. The asking price and whether they're willing to negotiate

From your interview list, select the cars you want to see and test drive. Then allow yourself plenty of time to look over your options and make a decision. Consider taking a friend with you who can objectively look at the car and not fall prey to "car-buying fever."

Finally, once you've found the car you want, you must arrange to have the car checked by a reputable mechanic. Plan to pay up to $100 or $200 for this inspection, which should include a complete check of the car from top to bottom, especially the engine, including compression, transmission, electrical system, and fuel and brake systems. Do not buy the car without this examination. If the seller hesitates to let you get the car checked, the car is not for you. Once the mechanic okays the car, then you can make the purchase.

Don't buy the car without getting the title. If you don't have the title, you don't own the car. Also obtain a written bill of sale signed by both parties.

To the extent you follow these steps, you will end up with a better car for your money. Remember: There is no such thing as a perfect car; whether it's a BMW or a Kia, it will give you problems. The goal is to minimize your problems in advance by not buying the wrong car.

Shopping for Auto Insurance

Nobody enjoys paying for automobile insurance. Rates seem to rise continually. As a matter of fact, in 10 years they have risen at twice the rate of inflation—but not without cause. New car prices, repairs, personal injury lawsuits, and health care costs have all jumped dramatically. The auto insurers have passed these costs on to the buyer.

Yet after years of advising clients, I've learned you can keep your rates down by following these tips:

1. **Choose the right car.** Make insurance costs a part of your criteria in selecting a car. You may be able to afford the car, but can you afford to insure it? The cost of insurance is influenced by the driver of the car, and

the make, model, and year of the car. High-performance cars cost the most to purchase, replace, and repair, and they're stolen more often than "family cars." They also tend to be driven by people who are higher risks. One study found that the most likely time for a Camaro to be totaled was between 1 and 3 a.m. on weekend nights. I doubt it was the Camaros' fault!

2. **Find ways to pay lower rates for youthful drivers.** The industry recognizes that accidents happen more among those ages 16 to 25. Therefore, they charge them higher rates. A young person often qualifies for a lower rate by

   - Keeping a grade point average of at least a B, which may provide a 5 to 25 percent discount.
   - Taking driver's training, for an additional 5 to 10 percent discount. This, and a child's GPA, must be documented by your insurance carrier.
   - Being insured as an "occasional driver" on a family car rather than a "principal driver" on his or her own car. If the insurance company sees more drivers than cars, they may allow the young driver to qualify as an occasional driver. However, if the number of cars and drivers is equal, it is hard to avoid the principal driver classification and higher rate. Raise the deductible on insurance for the car driven by the younger person if he or she is the principal driver.
   - Getting married (if the insured is female). Youthful drivers are those under 25 (sometimes 30). But young women who marry by age 25 are rated as adults.

3. **Maintain a safe driving record.** Most insurance companies give discounts after three to six years of driving without a chargeable accident or a moving violation. If either is on your driving record, you may pay additional premiums for three years.

4. **Recognize that when you replace a car, the new car inherits the insurance record of the old car.** For instance, if you total your car and your insurance pays the claim, the new car carries the insurance record of the one that was totaled.

5. **Remember that your location will impact your rates.** Where you live definitely affects your insurance rates, though it hardly makes sense to move into the country from the city to reduce your insurance rates!

6. **Understand liability insurance.** Never be underinsured. Each state has minimum requirements for liability insurance. These amounts, however, may be very impractical. Remember, you can't choose what kind of car you may hit or driver you may injure. If you hit a Ferrari and have only $100,000 in property damage insurance, you may be responsible for

an additional $150,000 of repair costs! If you injure or kill a professional such as a medical doctor, the courts may assess a large "loss of earnings" claim against you. Your $50,000 of minimum liability won't go very far. Spend more insurance dollars on liability coverage rather than on comprehensive and collision coverage. Consider an umbrella policy in addition to your automobile insurance. Most agents would recommend at least $100,000 per person and $300,000 per accident for personal liability coverage and $300,000 for property damage. Even higher coverage may be wise if you regularly carry others (ball teams, Girl Scouts, etc.) or if you have a significant net worth or income and may be the "deep pocket" target of a lawsuit.

Umbrella policy: A supplement to the liability coverage on your auto or home insurance policy that kicks in only after other policies have run out.

7. **Raise the deductible on collision and comprehensive.** If you can save a *guaranteed* $100 on your premium versus the *possibility* of paying an additional $100 on deductible, it's an even trade. If you are a safe driver, the odds are that you will come out ahead. If you raise your deductible from $100 to $1,000, be sure you bank the premium savings, which will probably *not* be $900, so you can pay the deductible in case you are involved in an accident.

8. **Shop the market.** Rates are competitive, but make certain you compare "apples to apples." Great differences exist between companies in their service, products, ability to do on-site claims, etc. You may save money dealing with a less expensive company, but be sure you know what you are giving up. It often pays to develop a long-term relationship with an insurance agent and a company. In the event you get into a bad situation, they can help you consider all your options.

9. **Check with the state insurance commission on questions involving carriers.** A simple search on the Internet will provide your state's insurance commission Web site and contact information. Also, ask friends for references on companies you are considering.

Some of these options may not apply to your situation; others may require some thought or research. A little of your time could save you a lot of money.

Hidden Compensation: Don't Leave Anything on the Table

ate's palms sweat as she walks through the double glass doors of the suburban office building. She's reentering the workforce—not exactly by choice—as she puts her life together after a divorce. She's run in the rat race before, so she knows what it's like to dress up in business attire every workday, rush out the door, and commute a long distance.

After a few hours of introductions and orientation, she meets with a human resources representative to review the company benefits. Kate feels a bit over-whelmed by the choices in the glossy company brochure touting benefits designed to "attract and retain quality employees." By tomorrow, Kate's home-work assignment is to sign a stack of papers related to a pretax dependent care account, cafeteria plans, and cash balance retirement plan.

Whether you're reentering the workforce like Kate or you've worked for the same company for 20 years, it's important for you to understand how you're paid. Your financial compensation package is not just made up of your salary; it also includes the employee benefits. Employee benefits are also referred to as "fringe benefits." But the word *fringe* is not the best choice. *Fringe* implies that these benefits are very minor compared to the entire overall compensation pack-age. The whole point of this chapter is that they are not minor!

Whether you work for a large or small organization, employer-provided benefits may be a significant part of your overall financial package. They can

Employer-provided fringe benefits are often worth many thousands of dollars annually.

often be worth many thousands of dollars annually. Depending on the sector (private vs. government, type of industry, etc.), the benefits may be up to 30 percent of the total compensation. The United States Department of Labor esti-mates that the composition of compensation for the average private industry worker is 73 percent wages and salaries and 27 percent fringe benefits.[1]

This ratio of benefits to total compensation is very different today than at the turn of the 20th century. According to the U.S. Department of Labor, employer costs for employee benefits as a percent of compensation rose from 3 percent in 1929 to 27 percent in 1999. An aging workforce, competitive labor market, desire for more choice, and customization by employees due to changing family circumstances, changing tax code, and employers trying to control costs have resulted in the compensation changes. Consider the following developments over time:

DEVELOPMENTS IN COMPENSATION PACKAGES

	1900	1925	1950	1975	2000
Wages	Wages	Wages	Wages	Wages and annual bonuses	Wages and supplements that tie pay to performance
Time Off and Reimbursement Account	—	Paid holidays	Paid holidays and vacations	Paid holidays, vacations, and personal leave	Consolidated leave plan giving employee choice of days off; unpaid family leave
Health Care and Life Insurance Benefits	—	Company doctor; benevolent association death and disability benefits	Basic medical plan through Blue Cross and Blue Shield; fixed amount life insurance and weekly disability benefit	Basic medical plan plus major medical through commercial insurer; dental plan; Medicare; life insurance varying with earnings; paid sick leave	Choice of dental, vision, and prescription drug plans; Medicare and retiree health insurance; choice of life insurance amounts; paid sick leave
Retirement and Savings Plans	—	—	Social Security benefits available at age 65	Social Security benefits available at age 65, with reduced benefits at age 62; defined benefit pension	Social Security full benefits available at age 67, for workers born in 1960 or later; combination of pensions and 401(k) savings plans

Source: U.S. Department of Labor, Bureau of Labor Statistics, "Report on the American Workforce" (2001).

When people ask my advice on personal investments, I automatically ask them if their employer offers a pension, profit sharing plan, or 401(k) plan into which they can make voluntary contributions. I am amazed by how many people don't know. So I give them a homework assignment: to bring their employee manual or a description of the company retirement plan to our next meeting. They usually discover that the first place they should invest is through their own company.

Let's consider some common employee benefits . . . and how to take advantage of them.

Retirement plans. Company-sponsored retirement plans come in all forms. They may be called a thrift plan, profit sharing plan, defined contribution plan, 401(k) plan, money purchase plan, or a SIMPLE IRA plan. A common characteristic is that they allow the participant—the employee—to contribute pretax dollars (dollars that are deducted from your pay before taxes are calculated) that will grow tax deferred until retirement. Many employers also contribute and/or match funds to the employee's retirement plan. (If you do not have access to an employer-sponsored retirement plan, see pages 271–274 for more information on self-directed retirement plans.)

> Tax deferred: Taxes on income or investment earnings are postponed until some later time, often retirement, when they are withdrawn.

Contributing pretax dollars enables you to receive a tax benefit for contributing your money. Let's consider an example. If your gross weekly pay is $1,000, then you are usually taxed on $1,000. If you choose to contribute 3 percent to a retirement plan on a pretax basis, then your federal income taxes are calculated on $970 ($1,000 - $30) of your gross pay.

If the employer contributes money to the plan, then that contribution is not taxable to you, the employee, in the year it's contributed. Both the employer's and the employee's contributions are not taxed until later (thus the name "tax-deferred" plans), when money is received out of the plan at retirement.

The power of tax-free compounding can be illustrated in the chart below.

THE BENEFITS OF TAX-FREE COMPOUNDING

	Personal Investment (in dollars)	Tax-Deferred Retirement Plan (in dollars)	Tax-Deferred Retirement Plan with 50% Employer Contribution (in dollars)
Salary/Plan Contribution	5,000	5,000	5,000
Employer Contribution	0	0	2,500
Set Aside for Investing	5,000	5,000	7,500
Fed & State Taxes (30%)	-1,500	0	0
Net Available for Investing	3,500	5,000	7,500
Estimated Return on Account (10%)	350	500	750
Tax on Earnings (15%)	-53	0	0
Balance after One Year	3,797	5,500	8,250

Three examples are given for investing a $5,000 personal investment. The first is a $5,000 personal investment; the second is a $5,000 contribution to a tax-deferred retirement plan where the employer does not contribute any funds; and the third illustrates a tax-deferred plan in which the employer contributes 50 cents for every dollar the employee contributes.

As you can see, not having taxes withheld from an investment can dramatically increase the return. Although taxes must be paid upon withdrawal at retirement, the fund will usually have grown to the point that even the after-tax distributions far exceed what the person would have accumulated in an after-tax investment. Any employer contributions to the plan are free money. You can't beat a return like the employer match, although you should become familiar with your company's vesting policy, since it determines how long employees must serve before they are entitled to, or vested in, the employer contributions in their accounts.

FAMILY FINANCE

Brian walked through the door of their apartment and set down his briefcase. "How did the interviews go?" Tanya asked eagerly, looking up from her laptop.

He grinned and sat down next to her on the couch. "You're looking at a guy who has received not one, but two job offers!"

Tanya squealed and hugged him. "That's fantastic! How are you going to decide? When do you have to let them know?"

"I told them I needed a few days to think it over," Brian said. "And as for how to make the decision, I think we'll need to pray about it—and lay out the pros and cons really clearly."

"I've got my computer right here," Tanya said. "How about this: You talk about the jobs, and I type. Then we'll compare the details."

"Okay," Brian said. "Both positions have the same title—associate programmer. At both companies, I liked the guy who would be my supervisor, and I think I'd find both jobs rewarding. The

position at GJ Enterprises involves Web applications, so I'd be able to use more cutting-edge technology. The other company, Serval, has been around longer and might be more stable. The data integration project I'd be working on there sounds pretty interesting.

"The commutes are about the same, since both jobs are in the city. I'd take the train and then walk just a few blocks," he continued. "The salary at GJ Enterprises is $5,000 higher than the one at Serval."

"Five thousand?" Tanya said, looking up from her typing. "That's significant."

"Yes, but Serval might have stronger benefits," Brian said. "Let me list them."

After several minutes of more specifics, Tanya had put together a chart (see page 227).

"Hmm," Brian said, looking over Tanya's chart. "It looks like Serval is coming out ahead on several fronts. Dental insurance, 401(k) matching, and matching charitable grant."

"And medical insurance, at least for

Fully vested: The point at which employees are entitled to all the contributions an employer has made to their retirement plan.

At one time, many employers offered their workers a defined benefit plan, in which the employer provided a fixed benefit at retirement. Though far less common than they once were, such plans still exist. See pages 271–272 for more details.

Insurance. The next broad category of employee-sponsored benefits is insurance—medical, group term life, and disability insurance.

- *Medical insurance.* Many employers provide group medical insurance. It may cover an employee and his or her family at no cost to the employee, or the employee may be asked to pay a portion of the insurance.

now," Tanya pointed out. "Right now I have insurance through my job, and the cost is pretty minimal. So you could get individual coverage through Serval for no out-of-pocket costs."

"That's true," Brian said, nodding.

He looked at her teasingly. "But GJ Enterprises has a health club right in the building! With Serval I'd have to walk a whole two blocks!"

Tanya rolled her eyes and laughed. "Poor, poor you."

	GJ Enterprises	Serval
Vacation	Two weeks per year after a three-month probationary period	Two weeks per year after a three-month probationary period
Health Insurance	$150/month employee cost for individual coverage $300/month employee cost for family coverage	No employee cost for individual coverage $200/month employee cost for family coverage
401(k)	Match $.25 on the dollar up to 5 percent of employee's salary	Match dollar-for-dollar up to 5 percent of employee's salary
Dental and Vision Insurance	Not available	Available
Matching Charitable Grant	No	Yes
Tuition Assistance	Yes	Yes
On-site Athletic Facilities	Yes	No

ANSWER: Sometimes in two-income families, both husband and wife will purchase employee-sponsored medical insurance coverage for themselves and their dependents, thinking that they have twice the coverage and therefore have gained some type of advantage. That is not the case. Medical insurance has what is called "coordination of benefits." For example, consider a two-earner family with both spouses covered by insurance. If a child breaks his arm, only one insurance company will pay—not both. If one spouse has a good health insurance policy covering dependents through their company, my advice would be for the other spouse to save the money he or she is paying for dependent coverage.

From a tax standpoint, medical insurance is an outstanding benefit. The premium that your employer pays for medical, dental, and vision coverage for you and your family is not considered taxable income. Medical insurance is called an "excludable fringe benefit." It's not taxed to you—so it's better than more salary from a tax viewpoint. In addition, any portion of the health care insurance premium that you pay can be taken from pretax dollars.

Being part of a large group—your fellow employees—allows you to purchase a better medical insurance policy at cheaper rates than you could purchase on your own. With medical expenses at all-time highs, the risk of even intermediate-term illness is too great for any individual to bear. Even though you may pay for a portion of your own insurance, which seems tremendously expensive, your employer is probably doing the best job it can to provide you the best coverage at a reasonable cost. Also note that if you leave your current employer, you can continue with your current insurance company for up to 18 months (but you're responsible for the entire premium) until you find employment at another company that offers medical insurance, as part of the COBRA provisions.

- *Group term life insurance.* Optional group term life insurance is also offered as a payroll deduction option for employees of large corporations. The advantage of group term life insurance is that anybody who applies must be insured. If you are not a very high insurance risk, buy the group term life. But if you are healthy, you can often buy an individual policy cheaper by shopping around.

In group insurance there is a phenomenon known as "adverse selection." This means difficult-to-insure people tend to wind up in the groups; healthy people tend to get individual policies. Therefore, these not-so-healthy groups experience more claims and rates go up. The annual cost per $1,000 of group coverage can often exceed the coverage of comparable individual term coverage. Sometimes the premium is disguised as a few pennies per month payroll deduction and it doesn't seem to cost much. My advice: Shop around and compare annual costs. (For more information on life insurance, see chapter 28.)

> **"Excludable" fringe benefits are not taxed to you—so they're better than more salary from a tax viewpoint.**

- *Disability insurance*. Disability insurance ensures you'll keep getting a paycheck if you are unable to work. Long-term disability is the type of disability insurance needed by most people. Absences from short-term disabilities, from 8 days to 13 weeks, can often be met by your emergency savings. (See pages 433–435 for more on disability insurance.)

Cafeteria plans. Having nothing to do with food, a cafeteria plan allows employees to choose from a "menu" of taxable and nontaxable benefits that best suit their individual needs, preferences, or lifestyles. For working couples, a cafeteria plan means that if one spouse has health insurance, the other may forgo health coverage and choose another benefit in its place.

Flexible spending plans. These plans allow you to contribute part of your paycheck (before taxes) to child care, medical or dental insurance premiums, health care copayments, deductibles, etc. Be careful not to put too much money in during the year, because you may lose any unspent money at the end of the year. Your contributions to these plans are exempt from federal income taxes.

Other fringe benefits. Many companies offer other employee benefits such as adoption assistance, tuition assistance, charitable matching grants, on-premise athletic facilities, and retirement planning services. Check with your company's human resource department to see which apply to you. Also, be sure to check with your tax professional to determine whether any of these perks are taxable.

Common Mistakes with Employee Benefits

From my experience, the most common mistakes people make when working with and implementing fringe benefits are:

- *Failing to review beneficiary choices.* Your choices of a beneficiary for your retirement plan or group life insurance don't automatically change just because you have remarried or have had other family circumstances change. You must request the change. After a death occurs, many spouses are surprised to learn they were not named as beneficiary—because of negligence on their spouse's part.
- *Assuming the HR department will take care of everything for you.* The trend is for more and more choice (and the burden of making the choice) to fall upon the employee. Be proactive.
- *Failing to take advantage of available employee benefits.* Make sure you know all the available benefits. Then, as the name implies, use them to your "benefit."
- *Holding too much company stock in stock option plans or retirement plans.* Talk to those who suffered great misfortune at Enron. Stay diversified. Hold other stocks or mutual funds when possible.
- *Failing to review your benefit choices annually.* Your family circumstances change, and new options are frequently added to your company's plans. Stay informed.
- *Contributing too much to flexible spending plans.* Although it's great to receive a tax deduction, if you don't use the money in these plans, you lose it. Estimate conservatively what you will spend for medical expenses or child care. Otherwise, you may be buying three pairs of glasses in December to spend excess contributions you would otherwise lose.
- *Failing to obtain professional consultation outside the company.* You should seek professional counsel for some of the decisions you make, such as choosing a pension payout option. Many decisions made regarding employee benefits have lifetime implications.

The Bible doesn't provide direct guidance on dental insurance plans or dependent care plans. Many of your decisions with your employee benefits fall under the category of being wise and a good steward as you live in this fallen world.

CHAPTER 16

Teaching Your Children about Money

Emily wastes more money on cheap accessories at the mall's costume jewelry store than you made in an entire summer mowing yards when you were her age.

Jacob begs and manipulates you for every new electronic gadget for the computer and game console. You're not even sure what some of them do! Resourceful but unwise, Jacob simply advises you to whip out the plastic.

Nichole saves her best tantrums and pouting lips for the checkout lane when she doesn't get her sweet tooth satisfied.

Michael just added a few more gray hairs and wrinkles to your collection when he told you he intends to quit college after one year. He has to work to pay off his credit card debts. He didn't handle wisely the numerous credit card offers and opportunities for late-night pizza on campus.

In a world bent on enticing kids with the trendiest fashions, newest gadgets, and tastiest treats, how will you ever equip your children to survive financially? Where and how do your children learn about money? How can you get your children interested in saving and giving rather than only spending?

To help parents answer these questions, my wife, Judy, and I, along with Jeremy White, coauthored *Your Kids Can Master Their Money: Fun Ways to Help Them Learn How* (2006, Tyndale and Focus on the Family). Aimed at equipping parents, this resource explains the "why" of teaching and offers parents detailed information to teach their kids about money. Since most family calendars don't have room for a dissertation about money management, we included many fun and engaging learning activities to encourage the win-win situation of having fun with your kids while teaching them something too. We've adapted some of the material from that book, including some sample activities, to help you begin passing on your financial knowledge and experience to your kids.

Whether you like it or not, as a parent you have some role in teaching your kids financial principles. Somehow, somewhere, in some way, you've probably sensed that raising money-smart kids is important. Well, you're exactly right.

Five powerful trends support your notion that you are vital to your child's financial education:

Trend 1: Most youths are financially illiterate.

- A Visa survey found that 49 percent of youth think they are more likely to become millionaires by starring in a reality TV series than by learning how to budget and save wisely.
- According to a *Consumer Reports* survey, 28 percent of students did not know credit cards are a form of borrowing and 40 percent did not know that banks charge interest on loans.

Trend 2: Advertisers and credit card companies are targeting our kids and teens, who they know have money and significant spending influence.

- Marketers target children as young as 18 months old.[1]
- One study estimates that by the time your kids reach 21, they will have seen or heard 23 million "advertising impressions."[2]
- One consumer-marketing group reported that today's kids will have seen 360,000 thirty-second TV commercials by the time they are 20 years old.

Trend 3: Most parents believe someone else is teaching kids about money and finances.

- Eighty percent of parents believe that schools provide classes on money management and budgeting.
- Only seven states require students to complete a course that includes personal finance before graduating from high school.[3] As a comparison, sex education is taught in 90 percent of public schools starting in fifth grade; it's a required course for 69 percent of schools.[4]
- Pastors frequently say little about money and a stewardship lifestyle.
- Very few evangelical churches have active stewardship discipleship courses to teach young people God's perspective on how to handle money.

Trend 4: Whether or not parents like it—or even realize it—kids look to them for financial guidance.

- Sixty-three percent of older teenagers, notorious for knowing it all and not listening to parents, say they get *most* of their information on money matters from their parents.[5]
- The Financial Educational Survey by Capital One found that more than 70 percent of parents say they have spoken with their teens about credit and using credit cards wisely; less than 44 percent of the teenage children of those respondents say their parents have talked to them about credit cards.

- The Jump$tart Coalition survey found that only 26 percent of 13- to 21-year-olds reported that their parents actively taught them how to manage money.

Trend 5: Financial support to churches and ministries is dropping—and is likely to be even weaker in the future.
- According to one study, most church giving comes from people over age 55.
- Howard Dayton, CEO of Crown Financial Ministries, has stated that many pastors have told him most of their giving comes from members over 65. They estimate that it takes five people under age 35 to replace one senior's giving.

> **Whether or not parents like it—or even realize it—kids look to them for financial guidance.**

Kids learn about money mostly from their parents and their own experiences—not in the classroom. How ironic that they go to school to learn how to be successful in life but don't learn how to manage money wisely there! In fact, those who go for advanced schooling may end up with huge student loan debts.

When your kids learn from you, you're teaching either intentionally or inadvertently—the latter through the habits they observe. Teaching intentionally is better. You do that by sharing truths "as you go" or by creating experiences that help kids learn.

As You Go

Passing along financial wisdom to your children doesn't mean sitting down on a Saturday night to discuss the benefits of budgeting. Consider the teaching methods of the Bible.

God recognized that the Israelites taught their children best in daily life. The basis for this method is found in Deuteronomy 6:4-9:

> Hear, O Israel: The Lord our God, the Lord is one. Love the Lord your God with all your heart and with all your soul and with all your strength. These commandments that I give you today are to be upon your hearts. Impress them on your children. Talk about them when you sit at home and when you walk along the road, when you lie down and when you get up. Tie them as symbols on your hands and bind them on your foreheads. Write them on the doorframes of your houses and on your gates.

This instruction was to parents. Parents should impress upon their children the commandments and truths of God as they go along. If we were to reword these verses in a more modern translation, we might say:

FAITH & FINANCE

Q: What's an average allowance that children receive? My child says everyone else gets more than he does.

ANSWER: It's hard to answer generalities with specifics—or at least it gets me into trouble. Let me share some benchmarks to satisfy your curiosity about what others do. I think you should set the amount you think is appropriate for your family. Don't be manipulated by the "what everybody else does" reasoning of your child.

One rule of thumb used by some financial counselors is an allowance of one dollar per week multiplied by your child's age. Thus, an eight-year-old gets eight dollars per week. That may sound high, but, with this approach, your child should be paying some of his own expenses (school lunches, clothes, etc.).

For reference, here are the results of a survey published in the *Wall Street Journal*.[*]

Age Group	Percentage Receiving Allowance	Average Weekly Amount[**]
15–17	57%	$19.30
12–14	67%	$11.30
9–11	56%	$ 8.00
6–8	50%	$ 6.00

I suggest intentionally setting the allowance (or the funding of specific categories) to cover your children's needs. That's probably a better way to determine an allowance instead of some arbitrary amount times an age. See the envelope training system idea on page 235 for more information.

---

[*] Of those receiving an allowance.

[**] 2003 survey by Yankelovich Youth Monitor as published in Jonathan Clements, "Teach Your Children Wealth: Why I Decided to Close Down the Bank of Dad," *Wall Street Journal*, October 15, 2003.

Talk about them when you sit at the dinner table and at family devotions and when you drive along the highway, when you are tucking them in at night and when you are at the breakfast table and driving them to school. Write them on Post-it notes on the mirrors and pin them to the corkboards in your kitchen.

Jesus continually taught His disciples as they went along. Seeing a fig tree, walking through a field, attending a wedding, fishing, settling disputes among the disciples, talking with a beggar in the streets—all were everyday happenings He used to teach them.

As harried parents, we can fool ourselves into thinking we are teaching when we use clichés, such as "Money doesn't grow on trees" or "Don't spend it all in one place." These well-worn maxims likely confuse kids more than teach them. Instead, as you go along through life, explain why you are able to retrieve cash from an ATM, why you leave money on the restaurant table as a tip, or why you save money for emergencies.

> **As harried parents, we can fool ourselves into thinking we are teaching when we use clichés, such as "Money doesn't grow on trees."**

Let your older kids help you write checks for the monthly bills. While you drive down the road, explain how taxes pay for highways. While you're at Grandma's house, talk about Social Security. Show them your paycheck stub to see the taxes withheld to pay for Social Security and Medicare for older citizens. In the store, compare the prices and list of ingredients for a brand-name aspirin or vitamin to a generic version. Ask your children why they think stores put candy at the checkout lane instead of the back of the store.

Creating Teachable Times for Kids with Their Money

Besides modeling money management for your children and teaching principles "as you go," kids learn about money from their own experiences. Earning money from chores, receiving an allowance, or earning money through jobs outside the home are valuable teaching opportunities.

Learning experiences take a bit of effort to set up or prepare, but they're worth it. They may keep your kids from learning every lesson the hard way. If you can create experiences, mentor your kids through them, and evaluate the results, your children will be better prepared to handle real-life situations on their own.

When we look at how Jesus trained His disciples, we learn four principles regarding training children in all areas, including money management.

1. They must experience what is being taught.
2. They must have an opportunity to fail.
3. They must have feedback.
4. They must have rewards.

Through various speaking and writing opportunities, Judy and I have presented an envelope training system that we think provides kids with the best learning experiences with money. Over the years, we've received overwhelmingly positive feedback from parents—and even the children. We're thankful to have young adults approach us to tell how their "envelope" experience helped them as kids. (Quite a bittersweet feeling—we've been around long enough to help more than one generation!)

The concept is simple, but the results are powerful. We will go into detail during the next few pages, but here's the essence of the system.

First, you designate certain categories, such as clothes and entertainment, for which your kids need money. Give them the cash amount you've budgeted and have them put it in specific envelopes. Let them have the control and responsibility over spending the money. Over time, you may expand to school supplies, gifts for others, or music and athletic lessons.

Here's an example of the feedback I've received from a parent:

> *Ron,*
>
> *I had read about your idea of using a cash envelope system and decided to try it in our family. We saw instant, positive results with our two preteen daughters in the area of clothing.*
>
> *Previously, a battle ensued every time my daughters and I went shopping. Our kids never knew exactly how much we were planning to spend on their clothes. They had no incentive to find the best deal. They begged, pleaded, whined, compared to friends, complained, cajoled, manipulated, argued, and reasoned their way to our wallet and purse. They figured out what buttons to push to try to get what they wanted—or until they wore me down. It was a tug-of-war; they pulled and tugged, and I pulled back.*
>
> *Even though my husband is an accountant and is good at setting our family budget, we knew our approach for clothes wasn't working. So, we decided to take a different one based on your idea. After looking at our family budget and what we'd spent last year on clothes, we began funding the girls' "clothing" envelope. We simply put the amount we were planning to spend anyway in their envelopes. We let them decide what to spend (retaining the right to veto purchases based on modesty or appropriateness).*
>
> *In less than a year, our kids have became wiser shoppers and better planners. They made a list of their clothing needs at the beginning of the quarter. Then, with list in hand, they went shopping with me.*
>
> *When we praise our children for shopping wisely, it brings a smile to their face. We're smiling, too, because we're now on their team. They even ask for my advice instead of arguing like before! Thank you for sharing such a practical idea that's brought more peace to our household.*

Some may consider this system an allowance. In reality, you're turning over certain areas of the family budget—items you'd be paying for—to your children, to develop their financial skills.

This envelope system establishes boundaries, affirms the importance of giving and saving, empowers your child, and actually frees him or her. This system also opens the lines of communication so that you and your children are on the same team, rather than adversaries, with spending decisions.

I don't claim to have invented the idea of putting money in a container in order to control spending. The simplest, yet most effective approach to managing money may have been Grandma's cookie jar.

That's right! Grandma's system was simply to put income received into the jar and to take money out of the jar as needs occurred. When the jar was empty, that signaled the end of spending. No credit, no robbing Peter to pay Paul, no payday check advances.

Many parents used that system. As household management became more complex, many grandparents gave up the cookie jar and switched to envelopes.

Cookie jars and envelopes both demonstrate a basic, but profound, financial planning principle: The outgo can never be greater than the inflow. The cookie jar is not a bottomless pit; when the jar is empty, you're done spending.

In training our children, we've used multiple "cookie jars," which are merely letter-sized envelopes with a label on the outside indicating how the cash in the envelope is to be used. These envelopes are kept in a simple file box or recipe box. The beauty of the envelopes is that the spending can never be greater than the amount originally put in.

Two elements are necessary in any budget, whether it's for family, business, or government. Those elements are a *plan* for spending and a *system of controls* to ensure that the spending is never greater than the plan allows. That's the beauty of the envelope system. It's very simple and operates according to the basic budgeting principles.

The Mechanics of Our Envelope System

The system we used with our children was very simple. We gave each child, beginning when they were about eight, a recipe file box containing five letter-sized envelopes: a tithe envelope, a save envelope, a spend envelope, a gifts envelope, and a clothes envelope.

The spend envelope contained money that could be used in any way they chose. The gift envelope was the amount allocated for buying gifts at Christmas, birthdays, and other special occasions for friends and relatives. The clothes amount was used to purchase *all* their clothes.

They were given a monthly allowance, in cash, to place in each of the envelopes according to a preset plan. The amount set for each envelope came from an annual planning session that Judy and I had. We discussed the allowance amounts for each of the five categories, based on what our children were required to pay for; then we gave them $1/12$ of that amount each month in a lump sum.

As they earned money or received gift money during the year, our kids deposited it in at least three envelopes, and sometimes all five envelopes. When they were beginning to learn about the system, they were required to put 10 percent into the tithe envelope and 10 percent into the save envelope. The balance could go into the spend, gift, and clothes envelopes.

Your children's save envelope accumulates money that they may spend on a specific item or deposit periodically in a savings account in their name. For a larger purchase, such as a bicycle, a tennis racket, or a seasonal wardrobe, children may need several weeks or months before they accumulate enough to make the transaction. But when they've saved enough, they can take the envelope with them and pay for the item with cash.

We allowed our children to borrow from envelope to envelope, except for the

FAMILY FINANCE

Alysha sat at the table, chatting with her kids as they ate breakfast. They had been living with her mother for three months now, and it was going more smoothly than she could have imagined. She'd been surprised by how enthusiastic Ellie had been about moving in with Grandma. Donovan had been a bit more reluctant, especially since he had a close friend in their old neighborhood. But Alysha had promised to drive him back to visit Sean weekly, and once Donovan knew he wouldn't have to change schools and would be able to decorate his new room, he started getting excited.

Their old house had sold within seven weeks, and Alysha had immediately used her share of the proceeds to pay off her credit card debt. The relief was incredible. With no debt and no large mortgage payment, she was hoping to start building up an emergency fund and start saving for retirement.

"Well, guys," she said, "what do you want to do this Saturday? For once, we don't have anything planned. No games, no rehearsals."

Donovan and Ellie looked at each other. "Go to the mall!" they chorused.

"Go shopping? For what?" Alysha asked.

"A bean bag chair for my room!" Ellie chirped. "And I want to go to the toy store."

"I need new gym shoes, and I want a new CD," Donovan said. He saw Alysha's face and added hastily, "We have a lot more money now that we're living here, right?"

Alysha took a deep breath. In the past she would have taken the kids shopping, argued with them over what to buy, and then come home, frustrated that she had spent too much money. No more. She had just paid off that credit card debt, and she wasn't about to add to it.

"Okay," she told them. "We can go shopping—but we're going to handle things differently from now on."

"What do you mean?" asked Donovan.

"I've been learning a lot about money in the last few months, and it's time for me to start teaching you kids, too. You're right, Donovan—we do have more money now that we're living with Grandma. But I'm saving a lot of that money. I've learned the hard way that

tithe and the save categories. We tried to help them see the value and benefit of giving and saving. They needed to feel responsible for the management of the money, so we allowed them quite a bit of flexibility in how they spent it.

As they got older and understood the purpose of the system, our kids were given the freedom to divide the money as they saw fit. When they chose for themselves, they enjoyed the experience of decision making.

Each family has to decide what children will be responsible for in the various categories. If you want your kids to buy their own sports equipment, for instance, that's great. Allocate enough money to the clothes envelope so that they can cover those expenses, then require them to make the purchase.

sometimes I shouldn't buy something I want because it's more important to have money later for something I really *need*, like repairs on the car."

"You mean we can't ever buy things we want?" Ellie whined.

"I didn't say that. But we need to think more carefully about how we use our money. Here's what we're going to do: I'm going to give each of you a certain amount of money each month."

"Like an allowance?" Ellie asked.

"Right," Alysha said. "You'll each have four envelopes. You'll need to put a certain amount in the tithe envelope to give to church and in the save envelope to save for later. Then you'll divide the rest between a clothes envelope and a spend envelope. You can spend the money in that last envelope any way you want, but when it's gone, it's gone for the month."

Donovan took that in. "What if my money is all gone and then Sean and I want to go to the bowling alley? Will you give me $10 for that like you used to?"

Alysha smiled and shook her head. "Nope."

"What about if we want to buy something you think isn't a good idea?" Ellie asked. "Like if I want to buy that Barbie dollhouse you think is too expensive."

Alysha chuckled. "Well, you would have to save up for a while to have enough money for that dollhouse. But if you save up the money and still want the dollhouse, you can buy it. It's your decision." Ellie looked thrilled. Alysha glanced at Donovan. "I reserve the right to veto some purchases, though, like CDs with parental advisory labels."

Donovan nodded slowly. "So basically, you'll give us more money up front than you used to, but then we can't ask you for more until the next month. We're in charge of it."

"That's right," Alysha agreed. "I know it may be hard at first. We'll all make mistakes, but that's how we learn. And I think you kids are ready for the responsibility. I want you to learn good habits now so you don't make the same mistakes I did."

She got up and came back with her wallet and a stack of envelopes. "Okay, let's get started! Once we get set up, you can grab your spend envelopes and we'll head to the mall."

The most important thing is not *what* children are responsible for buying, but how they handle the responsibility of managing the money. They need to know what they are responsible to buy, and that when the money is gone, there is no more. They must learn to live within the designated amount.

Children may make the mistake of poor allocation. For example, if you've chosen to give your children a lump sum for an entire season of clothing, one child may spend all of his money in October for fall clothes and, consequently, have no money left to buy the desperately needed winter coat.

> **The most important thing is not what children are responsible for buying, but how they handle the responsibility of managing the money.**

There are several ways to deal with this challenge. First, you may decide not to make them responsible for what you consider to be the "necessities"—winter coats, snow boots, Sunday shoes, haircuts, school lunches, and so forth. *You* provide the money for those things. Or, second, you can let them do without. Third, they can live with the consequences of wearing last year's coat or boots. Fourth, you can have them earn the extra money needed for the purchase.

You can come up with other creative alternatives. The point is that children should have responsibility for certain budget items, and they must learn to allocate properly within those budget categories.

In our family, we used a special dinner activity to help us decide how much each child's allowance should be. Judy and I took each of our children out to dinner and discussed his or her goals for the next year as well as the goal accomplishments over the past year. To prepare for that conversation we kept a journal containing the goals. These might include meeting a new friend, making a significant purchase, or spending time daily reading God's Word.

Every year we sat down with each child to review what the allowance would be for the following year for each of the envelope categories. We also reviewed the chores he or she would be responsible for, both those that were expected and those that were optional for which he or she could earn compensation.

Principles and Practices

Children can begin to manage money at early ages. By age eight or nine, many kids can handle all five envelopes, planning for and buying all their clothes and all the gifts they need. The significant purchases—such as clothes and gifts—will require the greatest amount of discretion and provide the greatest value in training, right on through their college years.

When children reach adolescence, they may choose to have more envelopes, and that's okay. Still, we didn't encourage our children to have more than six or seven envelopes until they reached college age. The system needs to be simple to work most efficiently.

Every child is unique and will have different financial requirements. Some will spend more time participating in sports or taking music lessons than others. So the funding amounts should vary accordingly.

As children reach the teen years, they may have earnings they can use to meet some of the budget categories. Parents should decide about a child working while still in high school, based on the child's own unique circumstances and desires. Whatever the decision, it will affect the amount of the teen's allowance. We did not require our two oldest daughters to work while they were participating in athletics or in cheerleading, but once the season was over we strongly encouraged them to get a job.

Each budget category should be reviewed for each child regularly; circumstances and needs change. The budget categories we've presented are good recommendations, but they're only recommendations. Give yourself time to determine the amounts needed and recognize up front you'll need to make modifications.

If this is the first time you've used this type of system, it may take a couple of years before you're comfortable with determining the amounts per category and even with the number of categories. Remember that the purpose of the envelope system is not to have the perfect, inflation-adjusted, budgeted amount in each envelope, but to teach your children the basic tools of money management.

How frequently you give an allowance (or funding) will depend on the ages of the children and your available income. If you begin the system with very young children, it probably should be given weekly because kids can't fully comprehend how much time is in a month or a year. Most older children can be given the money monthly. For example, their clothes money for the year is divided by 12 and given to them monthly. They then have the responsibility for the money in the envelopes, the freedom of decision making, and the freedom to fail. We gave some of our teens the funds on a semiannual or even annual basis so that they could plan for and buy a wardrobe for a season.

Many parents are concerned that children will spend unwisely if they receive a large amount on a monthly basis. They may in the beginning, but that's how they're going to learn. After a series of mistakes, they'll plan much more wisely. They must have the freedom to make their own decisions and the freedom to fail.

Once the amount for each category has been determined and you're comfortable that it's a fair amount, you should not change it without a serious discussion. Be wary of being manipulated by your children. If they learn that they can constantly change the amount by resorting to the old argue-pout-scheme-whine method, the whole system of spending *limited* resources has been destroyed. In fact, there are no limits on the resources when you vary them according to the children's protests or desires.

Credit card companies and advertising firms are intent on teaching you and your children to get all you can *now*—no matter what the cost will be in the future. Your challenge is to try to teach your children delayed gratification through good money management and long-range planning. Don't add to the challenges they already face each day by allowing them to have unlimited resources to meet their wants and desires. Help them learn to be responsible, mature individuals by balancing today's desires with future needs.

You don't have to require your children to keep track of where they spend the money within each envelope. The remaining amount in the envelope is the record of how much they spent and how much is left. If they want to know why they're running out of money each month in a particular envelope and want to write down how they're spending it, that's fine. Don't be too rigid, though, in requiring them to keep track of every penny.

The amount given to children as an allowance should definitely not be used as a disciplinary tool. What happens if their grades go down? Do you take away their allowance? The answer is no; they still need clothes. You shouldn't use this envelope system to motivate them to get good grades. You can use other means for that.

Also, the allowance is not a payment for chores. As members of the family, children should perform certain chores, such as doing the dishes, cleaning their room, making the bed, or carrying out the trash. Children have to meet their responsibilities as members of the family, and one of those is helping with chores around the house. All members of the team must do their part.

Other chores, however, may be optional. These might include raking leaves, cleaning out the garage once a year, babysitting, or doing tasks above and beyond the normal expectations of the household. For these chores your children deserve extra compensation.

What the Kids' Envelope System Teaches

If the envelope system appeals to you, you should adapt it to your unique situation. We've found that this method is a useful tool for teaching our children the following truths:

FAITH & FINANCE

Tithing. In 1 Corinthians 16:2 we find the principles of giving, which are applicable for the New Testament church:

> On the first day of every week, each one of you should set aside a sum of money in keeping with his income, saving it up, so that when I come no collections will have to be made.

The book of Proverbs says,

> Honor the LORD with your wealth, with the firstfruits of all your crops; then your barns will be filled to overflowing, and your vats will brim over with new wine. (3:9-10)

Q: At what age do you recommend a child start a summer job?

ANSWER: When J. C. Penney was eight years old, his father took him aside and advised him that as of that moment he was on his own financially. He now had to provide enough income to purchase all his clothes and buy any necessities of life, with the exception of food and shelter. At the time, Jim Penney had a pair of old shoes. He asked his father if he could begin at least with a new pair of shoes so he wouldn't have to replace them. His father said no, that he was now on his own, and he would have to make do.

Because this seems rather harsh, you may wonder about the motivation of Jim Penney's father. I suspect it was to teach him the necessity of discipline, responsibility, and the rewards of work. It is for those reasons that I recommend children begin some type of summer job starting between ages 8 and 10.

Parents may provide a summer job of working around the home in the early ages. But by the time children are 16, they can find employment in other places. I recommend they be required by their parents to work for someone else as soon as they are able. The benefits are incalculable for the process of living in a responsible manner, being on time, taking instruction from other authorities, and so on. It's not a question of whether or not the parents can afford to support the child; rather it's the question of what the child needs in order to live responsibly.

Other legitimate reasons for having a summer job are to earn money to help pay for college education or major purchases such as a car, as well as to relieve the boredom that comes during the summer vacation months. In our society today, it's generally not as necessary for a child to work as it was when this was an agricultural society and work was accepted as a way of life from the moment a child was able to contribute.

The only reasons I can think of *not* to require your child to hold a job during the summertime is when other priorities are higher, such as a planned mission trip, summer school, planned family activities that would inhibit holding a regular job, participation in sports, and illness. In other words, I wouldn't recommend children work at all costs, but the benefits of holding a summer job far outweigh any negatives. And, frankly, I can think of no negatives.

The tithe is the recognition that God owns it all. If your children put money into a tithe envelope and then give that money away, they're learning the habit of tithing. This habit can become a meaningful way of acknowledging that ultimately God owns it all.

Rewards for work. With a limited supply of money, children must earn additional funds for the discretionary items they want. When they make such a purchase, they're receiving a significant reward for work.

Savings. Saving involves delayed gratification. Putting money into a save envelope regularly is an important discipline to ensure financial success.

Allowing some savings to be spent periodically for significant items will begin to teach your children the value of patience. Remember the definition of financial maturity—"giving up today's desires for future benefits."

Limited supply of money. The envelope system is built around the principle that there is only so much money to go around. When the cookie jar or the envelope is empty, the only way to get funds is to work.

Our society promises, with all the power of advertising, that you can have it all. The reality is that you can't; if you choose to consume today, that money is gone forever. That's true whether you are a child or an adult. God is the only One who's never exhausted, and never will exhaust, His resources.

Opportunity cost of consumption. When the money is gone, you can't buy anything else. There's no more dramatic way to teach the "opportunity cost" of consumption. The cost isn't dollar for dollar; multiple dollars have been taken out of the future that could have been available had the money not been spent. This envelope system makes that principle visible.

Decision making. Dealing with limited resources and unlimited possible expenditures requires that decisions be made. One time we took our boys to Disney World, although our major family vacation was planned for later in the summer. They took all the spending money they'd been saving for the main family vacation to Disney World. On our first day there, they saw lots of desirable stuffed animals and other gifts. But both realized that if they spent their money at Disney World, they wouldn't have money to spend later in the summer.

It was difficult for Judy and me not to offer advice as the boys discussed whether to buy a stuffed Mickey Mouse. But we both felt they needed to learn their lesson. They agonized over their decision. Ultimately, they made a good one—by spending some and saving some for later. It was *their* decision, and they were learning the principle that we tried to teach them. Had we given them extra money—outside the envelope system—to spend at Disney World, an important teachable moment would have been lost.

Budgeting. Budgeting is simply planning your spending. The envelope system requires thinking ahead to determine how much can be spent today.

Wise buying. Children don't have to be wise buyers for the system to work. But they'll learn quickly that by being smart shoppers, they'll have more money available to do other things.

Goal setting. Our boys began realizing at ages 9 and 11 that if they didn't spend the money they earned during the summers, they'd save enough money to buy a car at age 16. The system teaches the wisdom and value of setting long-term as well as short-term goals.

The most critical issue regarding the envelope system activity is that children must have goal ownership. In other words, it must be their system rather than something you impose on them. While most kids will welcome this system, you'll need to help them set it up and understand what they can learn from it. Then allow them to have control of the money and freedom to work within the system.

You may have to change the system to fit the needs of your children. One of our daughters, Karen, was having trouble with the system when she was 10 or 11; she prefers to live spontaneously. The five envelopes were too confining.

> **The most critical issue in the envelope system is that children have goal ownership—it must be their system rather than something you impose on them.**

Karen told Judy that she was fed up with the whole system. Talking with her, Judy discovered that Karen didn't feel free to spend. What she really wanted was to have some money to "flit" away if she chose.

Judy, with great wisdom, suggested to Karen that she add a sixth envelope and call it her "flit envelope." Money in the flit envelope could be used any way that Karen chose. She already had that freedom with her spend envelope, but she didn't feel it. Merely by setting up another envelope and labeling it the way she wanted, she experienced tremendous freedom to operate within the system.

Karen has become a very disciplined young lady who does an excellent job of managing her money. I believe some of her success resulted from the freedom she experienced when she was allowed to modify the system. The flit envelope taught me something I need to remember: Money is nothing more than a resource. Money management is nothing more than a tool to use that resource. Neither is an end in itself!

We continued the envelope system even while our kids were in college. We refigured the amount needed each year. Thus, we avoided the proverbial "send money" pleas from college students. They knew how much pizza money they had to spend.

You may only want to use a part of the envelope system activity. For example, you may want to use your allowance approach or pay for work as you've been doing. Perhaps you're already teaching your kids to save and give from those sources of income. You can adapt this envelope system by using it only for specific categories, such as clothes or gifts for friends and family.

To wrap it all up, here's our challenge to you for the envelope system:

1. Discuss the system with your children and make sure they understand the extent of their responsibility.

2. Review the budgets and set the allowance/funding amounts for each of your children.
3. Give your children the file box with the money already inserted in the envelopes for the first month.
4. Be flexible!
5. Watch your children take responsibility for this very important area of their lives.

Remember that your kids will learn about money from two primary sources: (1) watching you and listening to you and (2) having their own experiences with money. The book *Your Kids Can Master Their Money* includes more than 50 interactive activities you can use with your kids to help them become financially mature in the areas of giving, saving, shopping, investing, planning, and working.[6]

Why Does It Matter?

Is making the effort to teach your children about money worth it? Don't just look at the cost—look at the benefits. I can think of at least four rewards for training kids to be good stewards.

First, while your kids ultimately will be responsible for the choices they make as adults, the groundwork you lay now will increase the chances that they make wise financial decisions later.

Second, you can expect your children to be good stewards of the resources God has entrusted to them and to train their own kids to manage their financial resources in a godly, responsible manner.

Third, teaching your kids about money can eliminate most of the conflict with kids over money. That alone is sufficient reward for many parents. Shopping at Wal-Mart or stopping at the corner convenience store should not result in a battle with your kids.

Fourth, you can expect to see your children, even in their preteen years, begin to make sound financial decisions.

At no time are individuals more moldable than in childhood. Children generally want to learn what parents want to teach them. Sure, they may act stubborn or rebellious at times, but most are teachable. As they experience the rewards of self-discipline and wisdom, they'll make good decisions more often.

Commit by faith to pay the price to train your children in the way they should go. When they get old, they won't depart from it. And you will rejoice as you see them "live a life worthy of the Lord and . . . please him in every way" (Colossians 1:10).

Double Whammy: Taking Care of Your Parents While Your Kids Still Need You

After having several of our grandchildren over for a short stay recently, Judy and I were exhausted. We certainly enjoy our grandchildren, but we agreed that there's a reason why God gives you children while you're young—you have more energy to keep up with those youngsters!

Yes, we're all growing older. If we're not careful to keep the right spiritual perspective as we get closer to heaven, we can get depressed about that. However, someone recently sent me an e-mail that reminded me of the good things about aging:

- Your investment in health insurance is finally beginning to pay off.
- Your secrets are safe with your friends because they can't remember them either.
- Your supply of brain cells is finally down to a manageable size.
- Your eyes won't get much worse.
- People no longer view you as a hypochondriac.
- Things you buy now won't wear out.
- There's nothing left to learn the hard way.
- Your joints provide more accurate forecasts than the National Weather Service.
- In a hostage situation, you are likely to be released first.
- You are smarter, *much smarter*, at over 50 than you were at 25.

Getting older often hits middle-aged adults in two ways. Many people in their forties through sixties are not experiencing the freedom of the empty nest. Instead they are caring for their aging parents even as their children return home after a "failure to launch." Sociologists use the phrase "the sandwich generation" to describe this period of life.

Each of these situations may involve time and financial commitments. Many middle-aged adults have been planning or saving for retirement, but few have considered the not-so-pleasant thought of assisting a 25-year-old who works at a low-end job or subsidizing the prescription drug bill of an

DOUBLE WHAMMY: TAKING CARE OF YOUR PARENTS WHILE YOUR KIDS STILL NEED YOU 247

80-year-old mother-in-law. Not only do these situations involve financial commitments, the family relationship dynamics add complexity and stress. In this chapter, we'll discuss the family and financial implications of the following "sandwiching" forces:

- Suffering from maltuition: paying for college
- The not-so-empty nest: helping adult children
- Becoming a parent to your parents: helping the older generation

Suffering from Maltuition: Paying for College

I remember how expensive higher education was when our oldest daughter began attending college. But the current costs for college are even more staggering. Some private universities can cost up to $50,000 per year. That doesn't even include the pizza eaten on the weekends!

AVERAGE ANNUAL U.S. COLLEGE EDUCATION FIGURES 2007–2008

Type of Institution	Annual Tuition and Fees	Total (tuition, fees, room and board)
Four year, public	6,185	13,589
Four year, private	23,712	32,307
Two year, public	2,361	2,361

Source: College Board, "Trends in College Pricing 2007," http://www.collegeboard.com/prod_downloads/about/news_info/trends/trends_pricing_07.pdf.

Many adults have the long-term objective of assisting their children (or grandchildren) in paying some of their college education costs. I think it's a worthwhile objective. The motivation of paying for college is usually a loving one—such as not wanting young adults to be saddled with student loan debt or removing an excuse (not having the money) for enrolling in higher education.

Yet I've also observed that many feel a parental *obligation* to pay for their child's college costs. They have the notion that any decent parent always pays for all the education costs. Here's where I think that can get out of balance. I think you have a biblical obligation to provide for the needs of your children (1 Timothy 5:8). But receiving a college education or other advanced technical training is more of the child's obligation. He or she must desire it, be willing to work for it, and be willing to help finance it. Nearly grown children may contribute to the cost of college through their own work and savings.

However, the expensive higher education costs are beyond the savings of most young adults and most families' current income. Most people in America today resort to their usual fallback approach for all major purchases—borrowing. Borrowing for college education is more justifiable than borrowing money on a credit card to go out to eat or buy furniture.

Sallie Mae, the largest provider of student loans for education, states that college graduates earn substantially more—on average $1.5 million more over the course of their careers—and experience less unemployment than high school graduates. A college education can be valuable in the marketplace.

Receiving a college education or other advanced technical training is largely the student's obligation. He or she must desire it, be willing to work for it, and be willing to help finance it.

Before borrowing any money, however, you should ask, "Are there any alternatives?" In the case of funding a college education, there are some other options to consider. The absolute best alternative is to begin to save for it early.

For example, if you deposit $100 per month for 18 years in a mutual fund earning 12 percent per year, that fund will grow to $75,786. A one-time deposit of $5,000 when your child is a baby would grow to $42,893 over the same time period. Thus, starting early to save for a college education greatly reduces the burden on the family budget when Junior actually goes off to school.

Four major types of accounts can be used to save for college. (We're not talking about specific investments yet, but the type of account to hold the investments.) You can save in an account under your own name, a custodial account in the name of the child with a parent as custodian (sometimes called an UTMA or UGMA account), a Coverdell Education Savings Account, or a 529 plan account. Most of the differences among these accounts relate to their tax treatment.

For example, if college education costs are $9,000 per year and the parents are paying, they must earn the $9,000 plus the taxes on that $9,000 in order to have $9,000 left over to pay for the college education. If their tax bracket is 30 percent, then they must earn approximately $12,857 to have $9,000 left over with which to pay education costs. If, on the other hand, that money is put into a custodial account and the income earned is assigned to the child for tax purposes, the taxes due are likely to be much lower. If the child is in the 10 percent tax bracket, he or she can earn $10,000, pay the income taxes, and still have $9,000 left over. The parents, then, have paid for the college education for that year with substantially fewer dollars than if they had paid the taxes on their earnings and then funded the college education with after-tax earnings.

Recent tax law changes have brought better tax-advantaged ways of saving for education expenses than the classic shifting technique described in the previous paragraph. The Coverdell Education Savings Account (ESA) provides tax-free growth if the withdrawals are used to pay education expenses. Parents may invest up to $2,000 each year for each child/student. The ESA may be invested in various mutual funds. Let's say that a parent contributes $2,000 for one year only. Over time, the investments in this ESA increase so that the account is valued at $5,000. When the parents withdraw the $5,000 to help pay for education costs, no tax is due! The growth is not simply tax deferred, but tax free.

Start saving for college early. The method isn't nearly as important as the discipline to save.

If parents (or grandparents) want to contribute more than $2,000 per child per year, then another alternative is the 529 plan. Named after the Internal Revenue Code Section 529, the 529 plans offer tax-free growth similar to the ESA. However, a maximum of $60,000 may be contributed at once. Contributions to 529 plans are removed from the donor's estate and are no longer taxed if the withdrawals are used for education. Mutual fund companies have teamed up with states to offer these plans. The 529 legal landscape has been changing regularly since their recent introduction; therefore, I would recommend working with a financial advisor to select the best fund.

In addition, many states offer various prepaid tuition programs. Although the various options have resulted in more complexity, think of them as a blessing. When I was saving for and assisting my children with college costs, I didn't have these outstanding tax-advantaged plans available.

The shifting strategy and funding of tax-advantaged accounts typically works best within a family. The reason these strategies work best within families is that the ultimate objective is not to give money away, but to reduce taxes on income that is earned. You could, for example, give me $12,000 of income-producing assets (which, incidentally, I would gladly accept). However, you are out-of-pocket for the total gift, and even though your income taxes went down, this did not make good economic sense. But if you put mutual funds producing $12,000 in your child's name to pay for college or in an ESA or 529 plan, your family will pay significantly lower taxes.

Many stock mutual funds offer systematic investment programs to allow automatic withdrawals from your bank account each month. This amount can be as low as $50, depending on the fund. If you start early and have a 10- to 18-year time horizon (depending on your child's age), you'll be able to weather the ups and downs of different market cycles. Many funds have exceeded a 10 percent annual return over a long time period.

An alternative to those four accounts is the tuition prepayment program. The parents prepay a child's tuition at a particular school based on current costs. The school invests the money and guarantees the payment of tuition costs when the child reaches college age. Obviously, the earlier that prepayment is made, the less the initial cost to the parents.

The big disadvantage is that the child may not want to matriculate at the school the parents chose years earlier. Another risk is that college costs won't continue to escalate, since the purpose of the program is to protect against rising costs. If costs stay level or drop, paying into such a plan will prove to be an unwise decision. The better approach is to put a "prepayment" in your own savings program and allow that money to grow at compounded rates of return. If costs should drop, the excess in the fund is yours.

Still other vehicles, such as trusts, can be used to set aside money for college education. If you're interested in exploring this option, you'll want to work with a qualified financial advisor, CPA, and attorney.

In addition to your own savings, it might be helpful to have your children save a certain percentage of the money they earn and receive as gifts for birthdays and holidays. With a small amount here and there, some discipline, and a long-term perspective, significant amounts can be accumulated toward college expenses.

If your investments and a portion of the kids' savings still are not enough, you might require your children to earn all or part of their own way through school. They can take summer jobs, work for a couple of years prior to college, work while in school, and so on. Some teens may opt for a military stint to pay for a college education through the GI Bill.

Remember: While many parents think they owe their children a college education, it should be considered a luxury rather than a necessity. Just because your kids' peers are attending college on a full ride from their parents doesn't mean that's also your responsibility.

Perhaps God has a better plan for your children than sending them to college, or maybe they should work their way through. Perhaps a military stint first would be helpful. I would never recommend borrowing to fund a college education for a child who was unwilling to act responsibly toward the opportunity. That may mean providing a portion of the cost, and it certainly means maintaining good academic performance.

If you are committed to helping your children pay for their advanced education, start saving early. Your choice of method isn't nearly as important as the decision to be disciplined to save. For more tips on how to pay for college, see appendix B, "Saving for College."

The Not-So-Empty Nest: Helping Adult Children

I remember how parenting five young kids nearly wore Judy and me out. Changing diapers, disciplining, playing referee, teaching values, enduring puberty, and acting as chauffeur took a lot of energy and effort. Back then my wife and I were sure the toughest parenting challenge was when our kids were living under our roof, demanding our care and attention.

We recently shared a meal with our friends and mentors, noted author and teacher Dr. Howard Hendricks and his wife, Jeanne. They are about 20 years older than we are and have four kids. Judy and I had been dealing with some difficult situations with our adult children, so we asked the Hendricks, "Does parenting adult children soon get easier?"

To our surprise, they said, "No, it gets harder."

The more we thought about it, the more their statement made sense. The challenges and problems our adult children face are more significant than when they were younger, yet we have less control over them. No longer are we dealing with whether the kids buy designer shoes or not, who can sleep over, whether Johnny can go to camp this summer, or which prom dress Mary wants. Our adult children deal with life issues such as selecting a mate, choosing a career, buying a home, or going through sickness, death, or divorce.

Life as a parent may seem backwards at times. Just when your children's issues become more significant, you have less control and influence, but you may have more money to give them. So what do you do? It's probably better to avoid fixing things for adult children by "buying" solutions. It's so tempting

FAMILY FINANCE

Brian ran to the ball and hit a perfect crosscourt volley. Tanya's dad, Kevin, lunged for it but missed. "Nice shot," he said, grinning, "but it's not polite to make your father-in-law look bad."

Tanya stuck out her tongue playfully at Brian and tossed her dad the ball. "Come on, Dad. We're up 5–3, 40–30. One more point to get this set."

Kevin moved back to the service line and tossed the ball. His serve raced toward Tanya's mom, Louise, who hit a beautiful backhand down the line. Tanya ran toward it, but it fell just out of bounds. "Sorry, Mom. It was a bit wide."

Her mom shrugged and smiled. "You win. Let's take a break."

As they sat at a picnic table by the tennis court, Tanya passed out water bottles. "I'm glad you guys live close enough that we can keep up our monthly Saturday morning tennis match."

Her parents exchanged glances. Kevin reached into his bag and pulled out an envelope. "Today might be a slight deviation from our usual pattern," he said.

"You mean besides the fact that you happened to win today?" Brian said teasingly.

Kevin laughed. "We have a gift for you." He handed the envelope to Tanya, and she ripped it open curiously.

She and Brian stared at it in shock. "Twenty-four thousand dollars?!"

Louise smiled. "We thought you could use it for a down payment on a house."

Brian swallowed hard. "I don't know what to say! With that plus what we have saved, we'll be able to meet our goal of putting down 20 percent."

for parents with more wealth than their adult children to throw money at the problems life brings, but it can do more harm than good.

Judy and I didn't anticipate a divorce among our children, but it happened. We hurt for our kids, but there is little we can do to control or prevent these life issues. We can encourage, support, pray, and offer some assistance along the way, but grown children, particularly married children, need to run their own lives.

What effect does your lifestyle have on your children? A very big effect. It establishes their expectations—most kids want to start out where their parents are now. As parents, we sometimes implicitly give them that expectation. For example, we might make a down payment on a home that commits them to a lifestyle they can't afford.

Giving to your adult children . . . without giving in to them

You may remember the Holiday Inn commercials that ran a few years ago. They featured an early-thirty-something man who still lived at home expecting others to cook his meals, clean up after him, launder his clothes, and maintain

Kevin cleared his throat. "Louise and I want you to know that there are no strings attached to this gift. We've thought a lot about this, and we decided that we don't want to wait until we die to give away our money. This is probably the time in your life when you can most use extra money, so why not give it to you now?"

"Th-thank you!" Tanya said. "I'm thrilled, but shocked. We know it's important to you that we're independent, and we never expected money from you."

Louise glanced at Brian. "We know that both of you work hard, and we're pleased by the decisions you've been making with your money. Seeing a financial planner is an excellent way to start your marriage, and your decision not to pursue that townhouse because of the unexpected costs showed a lot of maturity. You're on the right track, and we know you will use this money responsibly."

"Thanks for your vote of confidence, Mom." Tanya took a drink of water. "Why did you decide to do this now?"

"Our financial planner started talking to us about giving some money away now so we reduce our estate taxes someday," Kevin said. "We knew you were thinking about buying a house, so the timing seemed right."

"We want you to know that we're giving the same amount to your sister," Louise added. "You know how hard she and Doug have been working to start their own law practice. This should finally allow them to do it."

"Of course," Tanya said. She reached over and took Brian's hand. "We're very grateful."

his room. With the increase in real estate prices, more young adults—sometimes called "adultescents" or the Boomerang Generation—have little incentive to check out of Hotel Mom & Dad.

> **Just when your adult children's issues become more significant, you have less control and influence, but you may have more money to give them.**

Certainly, when an adult child is sick, disabled, recently divorced, or experiencing temporary hard times, you may choose to help him or her, either by giving direct financial support or indirect support by providing shelter or a car. If that occurs, then it may be helpful to set some rules or time limits. I've known of some parents who charge rent or expect some heavy-duty maintenance chores to be completed by their adult children living at home.

Beyond the stereotypical basement-dwelling adultescents, I'd like to provide some guidelines on giving to your adult children.

Guidelines for giving to your children

If you have the financial ability and desire, I think it is more beneficial to give to your children while you are alive rather than leave them a large inheritance. These are the guidelines Judy and I follow.

Give with no manipulative strings attached. Gifts should be gifts, not behavioral modification tools. If you are trying to change adult children's behavior by what you do for them financially, you are being manipulative. For some parents and grandparents, this poses a challenge. Instead of giving money freely, we may be tempted to want something in return: phone calls, visits during the holidays, a license to "meddle" in our children's marriages, and so on. But those kinds of expectations run contrary to the spirit of generous giving. When you make a gift to your children, be sure it is exactly that: a gift.

Transfer wealth gradually without changing their lifestyle dramatically. Our youngest son recently moved into a new home in Texas. We bought him and his wife a new washer and dryer. A washer and dryer did not change their lifestyle, although the gift helped them financially. But a washer and dryer are not luxury items.

Another way my wife and I have helped our adult children is helping pay for their home. Our approach, however, has been different than the usual giving of money for a down payment. We waited until our adult children and spouses saved their own money for a down payment. They selected the home they wanted, chose the mortgage option they wanted, and settled on a monthly payment they could afford.

Then we surprised them with a monthly gift to help them pay down the principal on their mortgage. Our approach doesn't affect their lifestyle, doesn't help them live beyond their means, and doesn't involve surety on our part.

We give a certain amount each month to build equity in their home. It's a phenomenal financial help to them because it means they will probably pay their mortgage debt in 10 to 15 years instead of 30 years.

We enjoy helping them now—when they most need the help—but without keeping them dependent on us. It's our way of taking the wealth God has given us and transferring it to them, blessing them without changing their lifestyle. We can stop at any time if needed. They would continue making the required monthly mortgage payment, as they do now.

Respect the husband's need to provide. Whether it's your son or son-in-law, don't provide so much that he feels he is not needed or has his motivation to work dampened. If our adult children ever became dependent on us—when they could provide for themselves—then we would change the level of financial gifts or help that we give.

Respect the sanctity of marriage of your children. Our giving shouldn't cause conflict or give the impression that we are taking sides in a disagreement between a husband and wife.

Respect your children's parental wishes. Avoid coming between the parents and the grandchildren. Let's say your children respectfully ask you to reduce your Christmas giving. Perhaps they think too many gifts are making their children selfish. Respect their wishes. Don't get into a situation where your desire to give causes problems.

Stay out of the way of God dealing with your children. It's hard for more affluent parents to watch their kids struggle with problems that could be solved with a check. But it may not always be God's will for you to solve your children's problems. God may have a lesson for them to learn or may want them to seek another solution that He has in mind. The more you have, the more difficult it is to allow your children to be fiscally disciplined and suffer the consequences of their mistakes, since it is easier for you to take away the financial pain.

If you follow these guidelines, giving to your adult children now can be a joy and a blessing to you both.

> **It may be more beneficial to give to your children while you are alive rather than leave them a large inheritance.**

Inheritance training

You may have decided to transfer some of your wealth to your children. As I outline in my book *Splitting Heirs*, if you want to include your children in your will but are unsure about their ability to handle money, you might consider giving them "training" inheritances while you are alive.[1]

When each of their four children reached his or her 18th birthday, Sam and

Q: My parents give their grandchildren very expensive toys—sometimes items we prefer our kids not have or items similar to toys our kids already have. They also give them large amounts of "spending" money. They feel that they have a "right" to spoil their grandchildren, that this is how grandparents are "supposed" to behave. When I brought the topic up, they implied that I had no basis to interfere with this "right." What can we do?

ANSWER: Unfortunately, there's not an easy solution to this question. A child's relationship with his or her grandparents is certainly one to be treasured and cultivated. But when it keeps your children from learning the principles of a successful and godly life, you may need to stand firm.

My recommendation is to pick one or more of the following alternatives. The first and best alternative is to lovingly confront the grandparents with what they are doing. Do this after you have a teaching system, such as the envelope system mentioned in chapter 16, in place so that the *system* becomes the standard—not you, and certainly not them. Perhaps you can even ask them to participate with you in the system. By doing so you may be able to point out the behavior that is giving you a challenge.

A second idea is to present them with an alternative to the large gift. For example, you could ask them to set up savings accounts or a college fund for your children instead of giving gifts. You could also ask them to spend time, rather than money, with your children. A relationship with their grandparents is a blessing they can never purchase. Or perhaps you could set a limit on the amount of the gifts.

Third, your children could accept financial gifts but put them in their savings accounts. Then at some point they could share with their grandparents how they used the total of the gifts given to them.

You may wish to provide a list of needs (such as school supplies or clothes) to the grandparents. This may help them give more practical gifts instead of a 15th stuffed animal or 20th doll.

A last-resort alternative is to say on your children's behalf, "No, thank you" and return the gift. There is obviously great risk in choosing this alternative in terms of the relationship with the grandparents, but it may be the only one that meets your objective—teaching your children wisdom. You have to be careful not to put your children in an adversarial relationship with their grandparents. It's not your children's fault.

Becky gave them a portion of their inheritance. Their goal was to find out how the kids would handle a small amount of money—and, consequently, how they would likely handle more.

Sam and Becky's children may have had good intentions, but being young and relatively inexperienced in financial management, they wasted most of the money. But, like the Bible's wayward son who returned to his father, the children learned some valuable lessons from their mistakes. Today, Sam and Becky periodically give their children lump sums of money, and they do a masterful job of handling it wisely.

By demonstrating generosity toward their children, Sam and Becky are sowing and reaping the benefits of "lifetime giving." Sam and Becky are giving their kids hands-on experience and training in financial management. I have observed that experience is a good teacher; "coached" experience is a great teacher.

Sam and Becky's lifetime gifts have also provided blessings that reach beyond material values. Family vacations that otherwise would not have been possible have become an affordable reality, thanks to Sam and Becky's generosity. Likewise, their gifts have opened the door for a number of their grandchildren to attend private Christian schools—an education that Sam and Becky see as a valuable and practical investment in their family's spiritual, academic, and financial future.

I know of many others who have adopted a similar outlook on giving to their children. One couple offered to pay the life insurance premiums for their son-in-law until he could afford to make the payments out of his own salary. Another man gave his children money toward a Roth IRA.

While practical helps like these obviously involve a financial cost, the benefits they provide can make a significant difference in your children's lives and their ability to raise a family.

Another advantage of lifetime giving is the effect it can have on reducing your estate taxes. At the time of this writing, the tax law permits you to give away $12,000 per year (this figure is adjusted periodically according to the inflation index) to as many individuals as you like. In other words, a husband and wife together could give $24,000 a year to each of their four children—thereby reducing the size (and taxability) of their estate by $96,000 each year. By including sons- and daughters-in-law and grandchildren in the distribution plan, the size (and taxability) of the estate could shrink even further. When you're looking for creative ways to minimize estate taxes, taking advantage of the annual gift exclusion can make good economic sense.

> **It may not always be God's will for you to solve your children's problems. God may have a lesson for them to learn or may want them to seek another solution that He has in mind.**

One of the best things about giving money to your children (or grand-children) is the opportunity you get to watch them use it to enrich their lives—an opportunity you would miss if you waited to distribute your assets through your estate. Perhaps one of your children feels called to be a mis-sionary. Would a financial gift from you help him or her make the vision a reality? Likewise, your generosity toward your children, exercised with wisdom, can open doors and alleviate financial burdens when it comes to expenses like starting a business, buying a first home, or funding your grand-children's college education.

Unfortunately, lifetime giving also means you have to watch your children make mistakes. While you need to be ready to offer financial guidance and advice when your kids ask for it, you must also remember that they will learn from their failures.

There was a young businessman eager to learn from the founder of the company. He went to the wise old man and asked him, "Sir, could you tell me what it takes to become wise like you?"

The wise old businessman paused and said, "Certainly, my son—two words."

The young man then asked, "Please tell me, sir, what are those two words?"

The wise old man answered, "Good decisions."

The young man thought about this and then boldly inquired, "Sir, can you tell me how you learn to make good decisions?"

After thinking for a moment, the wise old businessman said, "Certainly, my son, one word—experience."

Persisting, the young man said, "Please, sir, permit me one more question. How do you get experience?"

The wise old businessman said, "Son, two words—bad decisions."

This story conveys much truth. You learn more from your failures than you do from your successes. I suspect that Peter was a better apostle after his denial of our Lord than he would have been had he not experienced that tremendous failure. He most certainly was more teachable and humble afterward.

Failure is a part of life. The issue is not whether children will fail, but how they will respond to failure. The best time for them to fail is while they are young and parents are available to counsel them. (Notice I said "counsel," not "criticize.") Probably the biggest mistake parents make in training children to manage money is not giving them the freedom to fail. Parents either make decisions for them or are so critical of their decisions that children quickly learn not to risk anything on their own.

Despite the benefits associated with lifetime giving, you may feel finan-cially unable or emotionally unwilling (for whatever reason) to begin passing on your wealth right now. In that case, providing for your heirs by a well-designed wealth transfer plan becomes all the more important. (See chapters 20 and 21.)

Becoming a Parent to Your Parents: Helping the Older Generation

Few Christians plan for the long-term care of their parents when they can no longer take care of themselves either physically or financially. Let's face it—it's awkward, maybe a bit embarrassing, and difficult to even know how to approach the subject with those who have raised you. It's almost like meddling in business that's not yours. You hope it will go away or take care of itself. But you know down deep that it won't, and eventually you will be faced with some tough decisions if your parents live long enough.

The fact is that most of us must either: (1) put our parents (one or both) in some sort of extended care facility or (2) have them live with us until they die. Depending on how our parents have managed their finances during their lifetime, we will have to assist them in making prudent expenditures for the aging care or assist them financially in their twilight years. A comprehensive book such as the *Complete Guide to Caring for Aging Loved Ones* (Colorado Springs: Focus on the Family, 2002) can help prepare you to you manage the practical, emotional, and spiritual aspects of caregiving when that time comes.

First Timothy 5:8 provides clear instructions regarding our responsibility to care for family members:

> If anyone does not provide for his relatives, and especially for his immediate family, he has denied the faith and is worse than an unbeliever.

And James 1:27 adds this insight:

> Religion that God our Father accepts as pure and faultless is this: to look after orphans and widows in their distress and to keep oneself from being polluted by the world.

These verses can serve as an incentive to sit down right now with your parents, express your desire to fulfill your responsibility in a prudent and orderly manner, and begin to develop a plan for practical decisions in the future. If one of your parents is already deceased, it should intensify your motivation to begin this process as soon as possible.

The two basic subjects you need to discuss with your parents are: (1) where to live, particularly after one parent has died, and (2) the financial aspects of long-term care.

Where to live

The decision either to put your parents in a nursing home or have them live with you is laden with emotion, anxiety, and a myriad of concerns. There are some practical advantages for having your parents live in a professional, well-run

FAITH &
FINANCE

Q: Can we use part of our tithe to help our aging parents financially?

ANSWER: In the book of 1 Timothy 5:8, Paul says that a man is "worse than an unbeliever" if he does not provide for his family. There's no question that we have a responsibility for our children, for our parents, and for others in our immediate family.

I'm reminded that Jesus spoke very harshly to the question of whether the tithe should go to church as opposed to the parents. The Pharisees taught that you should take care of the church first. Jesus seemed to imply in His response that there is a tremendous responsibility to take care of the family. With this in mind, I would be hesitant about not doing both—tithing and helping my aging parents financially. I think both are biblical commands and admonitions and both should be done. So it's not a question of either/or, but it may be a question of not doing something in another area of my life, such as taking a vacation or buying clothes or some other use of money. These other spending choices, in my estimation, should have a lower priority than either tithing or helping parents financially.

nursing home or extended care facility: (1) socialization with people of their own age and similar interests, (2) care by trained professionals, and (3) greater flexibility for you and your family.

However, extended care facilities are expensive. Many people also experience a great amount of guilt for putting their parents in a "home." And, in my opinion, you miss opportunities to develop some intimate relationships between your parents and any children who are still living at home.

Although the Bible does not specifically command that aging parents live with their adult children, the spirit of 1 Timothy 5:8 and James 1:27 suggests that we give serious consideration to this alternative. The benefits to your family can include:

- Opportunity for shared wisdom. Parents have a wealth of experience and wisdom to share with us if we will take the time to ask them about their life experiences, beliefs, fears, and joys.
- Opportunity for bonding. The only way deep, rich family bonds are developed is by communicating and spending time together frequently. Our "mobile society" has virtually destroyed the extended family relationships that God intended for us. Elderly parents can be true blessings to us and our children.
- Opportunity of service. There is no more worthy object of Christian service than caring for your parents, particularly if they are physically ill and require a great deal of care, attention, and sacrifice. This builds

the kind of character and servant spirit that Christ exhorted His disciples to have.

- Opportunity to love. No one can love and care for your parents like you. Caring for an aging parent is perhaps the greatest opportunity God gives us to express our love for them.

Financial considerations

Most people do not have long-term care insurance policies to help pay for the cost of prolonged nursing home stays or home care. (Note: We discuss these policies in more detail in chapter 29). Without substantial assets or some sort of insurance, many people in need of such care could be forced to turn to their children for help or to Medicaid, the government welfare program for the poor.

Whether you and your parents decide that they will live in an extended care facility or nursing home, financial considerations must be a candid part of your discussion. A long-term care (LTC) insurance policy makes sense only for people with incomes over $20,000 a year and assets over $50,000 at retirement (excluding your home).

The decision to have parents come live with you involves other financial considerations also. Your home may require an addition, transportation must be considered, and a myriad of other subjects should be discussed. The key is to have open, frank, and genuine discussions in which you express your concern for your parents' welfare. Now is the time to begin planning for this spiritual responsibility God has entrusted to you.

Adult children need to sit down with their parents and begin to develop a plan for practical decisions in the future.

CHAPTER 18

Retirement: Work's End or Second Wind?

Recently my wife and I spent several days in Florida for a getaway and some long-range planning. While there, we were often frustrated trying to find a place to eat—every restaurant was packed with people. Driving was also virtually impossible because of the number of cars on the roads. We observed that a large majority of the people there were much older than we are. By all appearances, they had retired to Florida.

The word *retirement* conjures up all sorts of pictures—many images put in our minds by commercials. We've all seen the advertisements of a tanned, gray-haired couple laughing as they walk the beach arm in arm. The travel industry, the financial services industry, and home builders in the Sun Belt states all dangle the retirement utopia to encourage sales of their products.

Some soon-to-be retirees think of buying an RV, traveling, fishing, shopping, golfing, or spoiling grandchildren. The water-cooler chatter at work and the social talk among those 50 and over frequently includes phrases about how they "can't wait until retirement."

In this chapter, I hope to challenge the typical notions about retirement and perhaps dispel a few myths. The first myth is that retirement is the beginning of the golden years. Retirement may not be as great as you imagine it to be in your thirties. Lady Astor, the first woman to serve as a member of the British House of Commons, said, "I used to dread getting older, because I thought I would not be able to do all the things I wanted to do, but now that I am older, I find that I don't want to do them." As Ann Landers once said, "Inside every 70-year-old is a 35-year-old asking, 'What happened?'"

As he got older, folksinger Pete Seeger liked to sing, "How do I know that my youth's all spent? Well, my get up and go has gone up and went." Speaking of "golden oldies," the wave of baby boomers nearing retirement may want to listen to their favorite songs—rereleased favorite songs, that is, for the new demographic graying boomers:

- "You're So Varicose Vein" by Carly Simon
- "How Can You Mend a Broken Hip?" by the Bee Gees
- "The First Time Ever I Forgot Your Face" by Roberta Flack
- "You Make Me Feel Like Napping" by Leo Sayer
- "Bald Thing" by the Troggs[1]

While the aging process offers plenty of material for comics, many older adults find it no laughing matter. Yet our later years can be a meaningful time of life, and I'd like to review the following topics to help you get the most from this time of life:

- The changing view of retirement
- Current retirement trends
- A biblical perspective on retirement
- Tools for retirement planning

The Changing View of Retirement

Though many people today expect to leave the workforce at some point in their later years, for most of our great-grandparents, there was no such thing as "retirement." They worked as long as they were able to. When they became unable to work, they often moved in with their adult children or extended family, who probably lived on the family farm or in the same town as they did.

Retirement is a relatively new idea, made possible in affluent societies over the last century. According to the Social Security Administration, four changes in the early twentieth century led to a populist movement that demanded government-provided pensions and paved the way for retirement for the masses:

1. **The Industrial Revolution.** As more workers moved from self-employment, either as farmers or tradesmen, to employment in factories and businesses, they gave up economic security, since their work could be threatened by recessions and layoffs.
2. **Urbanization.** Workers moved away from farms and extended family to cities.
3. **Few employer retirement plans.** Even in the United States, only 5 percent of workers received retirement pensions in the early 20th century. In 1900, only five American companies offered their industrial workers company-sponsored plans.
4. **Increased life expectancy.** The average life span increased by 10 years between 1900 and 1930, a more rapid rate than at any other time in recorded history.

In the United States, these trends, along with the lengthy Great Depression, led to the passage of the Social Security Act of 1935, which provided for benefits to be paid to workers beginning at age 65. This age was selected for a few reasons. First, most of the few private pensions, as well as about half of the various state old-age pensions, used this age. Also, the U.S. committee drafting the benefit rules for Social Security determined from actuarial studies that using age 65 would allow the government to fund expected benefit payments using revenues from modest payroll taxes. Since the average life expectancy at birth in 1930 was 58 for men and 62 for women, offering benefits at age 65 seemed sustainable.[2]

Through various amendments later made to the Social Security Act, Congress allowed seniors to begin collecting at age 62, began Medicare coverage for those aged 65 and over, and provided cost-of-living increases. Before long, Americans began viewing retirement as an entitlement. In fact, many people began planning to retire even earlier. This attitude mirrors that in other industrialized nations. In fact, a study by the University of Surrey in Great Britain found that Western European workers ages 50 to 69 overwhelmingly want more time with family and less at work. Furthermore, their perception of the importance of work has declined significantly in the past decade.[3]

New Retirement Realities

Even as more people retire earlier, the trends that generated the initial push to retirement are no longer predominantly true. The following factors are affecting retirement today.

From backbreaking labor to mind-stretching work. Most workers in the early twentieth century performed physically demanding work that was also often dangerous or monotonous. Today work is largely information based and requires far less physical stamina. The late Peter Drucker, the well-known management professor and author, noted:

> Today, a growing number of people expect to find . . . that they enjoy their work, that they become better as they become older, that they are not ready to retire even though they may have the means to do so. A large and growing number of people—I call them "knowledge workers"—not only do much better financially than anybody in history has ever done, they do infinitely better in terms of personal fulfillment.[4]

Longevity. Globally, the number of senior citizens is skyrocketing. The United Nations reported that about 10 percent of the world's population was 60 or older in 2002. By 2050, that percentage is expected to increase to 22 percent, larger than the percentage of children ages 0 to 14. These statistics underlie a sobering trend: The number of younger people available to support older citizens is declining rapidly—in developed and less developed countries alike.

"These dramatic demographic changes will affect social security schemes, particularly traditional systems in which current workers pay for the benefits of current retirees."[5]

Medical improvements enhancing active lives. Besides medical advancements increasing longevity, many medical and technological advancements have improved the mobility and activity of older people compared to previous generations. Why sit in a rocker if drug advances, scooters, cell phones, and better arthritis medicines help you move about more?

Changing needs of employers. Because of low unemployment for the past few decades, employers, particularly those in the services and retail industry, have scrambled to find enough workers. In addition, to save overhead and maximize flexibility, companies are using more part-time workers, consultants, and temporary workers. These positions often fit the needs of retirees who desire temporary positions, as well as the needs of employers, who realize that older workers offer valuable life experience and are often more dependable than younger workers.

Lower interest income and declining stock market. Low yields of 2 to 3 percent on certificates of deposit in the early 2000s made it difficult for seniors to live off the interest on their savings. Although interest rates have risen since then, they are still lower than rates in the 1970s and 1980s. In addition, the stock market decline in the early 2000s eroded the asset bases of many retirees. These economic trends have led many retirees to return to work to supplement their lower income.

A Biblical Perspective on Retirement

The Bible is virtually silent on the concept of retirement and never mentions ceasing work at age 60, 62, or 65. As you approach retirement, don't look at it as an end, but rather as a beginning. It's the start of the next phase in your service in God's Kingdom. With proper planning, you can have the financial freedom to use your talents and abilities to fulfill God's next purposes for your life, even after your primary career is completed. As the writer of Hebrews says, "Let us run with perseverance the race marked out for us" (Hebrews 12:1).

According to one dictionary's definition, retirement means "withdrawal from one's occupation, business, or office. Withdrawal into privacy or seclusion."[6] I don't believe that the Bible calls for "withdrawal." Instead of thinking of retirement, I encourage people to think of "re*hire*ment." You may stop working in one position in order to change jobs, change occupations, or begin volunteering. That's rehirement.

Only in wealthier countries, such as the United States, Western European countries, or Japan, is it possible for large numbers of persons to quit working

Q: I'm a widow in my midsixties. Should I pay off my home or invest the money my husband left me?

ANSWER: If you plan on staying in the house and if your income needs are met from other sources, then my counsel to you—and it'd be same to my own wife—would be to pay off the mortgage.

Although I don't know your specific risk tolerance, my experience is that a widow of your age tends to be very conservative with investments—as you likely should be. Anything can happen in our economy, and any investment can be lost. Regardless of what happens in the economy, a mortgage liability will survive because the lenders are protected by law. Take a portion of your assets to pay off and retire your home mortgage. Keep some funds available and liquid.

Many people never thought they would lose a large portion of their wealth, but they did when the economy turned down. Any investment, whether it is stocks, a farm, oil and gas, precious metals, art, or anything else, can decrease in value when the economy sours.

Do what the Bible says: "Listen to counsel and accept discipline, that you may be wise the rest of your days. Many plans are in a man's heart, but the counsel of the LORD will stand" (Proverbs 19:20-21, NASB). In other words, take your counsel from the Lord. As a widow, He is your primary counselor. If you have peace about paying off your home, do it. If you don't have peace about paying it off, don't do it.

at some age in order to retire. Retirement plans funded by companies, unions, and other groups, as well as Social Security and the general affluence, have made retirement or quitting work at a certain age an option to a majority of people in these countries. In most of world, quitting work is generally not an option. And if you reflect on the Bible, it's hard to think of anyone who retired. The real question is probably not "Can you retire?" because many can. The question rather becomes "Should you retire?"

To help us answer this question, let's look further at a story Jesus told in Luke 12:16-21:

FAITH & FINANCE

> And [Jesus] told them this parable: "The ground of a certain rich man produced a good crop. He thought to himself, 'What shall I do? I have no place to store my crops.'
>
> "Then he said, 'This is what I'll do. I will tear down my barns and build bigger ones, and there I will store all my grain and my goods. And I'll say to myself, "You have plenty of good things laid up for many years. Take life easy; eat, drink and be merry."'
>
> "But God said to him, 'You fool! This very night your life will be

demanded from you. Then who will get what you have prepared for yourself?'

"This is how it will be with anyone who stores up things for himself but is not rich toward God."

The man in this parable had a life purpose: to take life easy. Eat, drink, and be merry. But God said to him, "You fool." I personally don't believe that eating, drinking, and merrymaking is what we, as Christians, are called to. I believe instead that God has called us to a life of purpose, meaning, and accomplishment for the cause of Christ. Our perspective must be that we are here on earth as pilgrims and sojourners for a limited amount of time, and during that time all our energies and activities should be directed toward accomplishing God's plans and purposes for us.

Therefore, I may retire from a particular occupation or vocation, not so I

FAMILY FINANCE

Bob unlocked his car, deposited his briefcase into the passenger seat, and slipped behind the wheel. He leaned back in his seat and let out a deep breath, a small smile on his face.

Wow. A meeting with the financial planner that actually leaves me smiling? That's got to be a first! Bob had met with Bill Oliver that afternoon to review his and Laura's retirement accounts. With 10 years left until he turned 62 and Social Security could kick in, Bob was anxious to make sure he was on the right track with retirement savings. Selling medical equipment had been lucrative over the years, and he was good at it—but frankly, he didn't want to keep that job any longer than he had to.

But today's news had largely been positive. A few of the growth funds he had invested in years ago had done very well in the past decade. Bob had always contributed fairly substantially to his 401(k), but based on Bill's advice when they started seeing him five years ago, Bob had stepped up his automatic contribution to the maximum he was allowed. That, plus an employer match of 50 cents on the dollar, had helped boost their accounts.

Laura hadn't had a 401(k) while she had been home with Elizabeth, of course, but when Roth IRAs first became available, she had opened one. Every year they tried to put in the maximum contribution allowed. And now it looked like all of that was paying off. Now that Bob and Laura were in their fifties, Bill was recommending that they decrease the amount of risk in their portfolio. He had given Bob a number of less aggressive mutual funds to consider, but at the end of the meeting, he had said, "Basically, Bob, you're on the right track."

As Bob began driving home, he let his mind wander toward thoughts of retirement. What would it be like not to have to go to work? Not to have high-pressure sales quotas or multiple presentations a day? He smiled. *Aaah . . . I can imagine waking up late, making some coffee, reading the newspaper, maybe meeting a friend for lunch . . . and, uh . . .*

can live a life of ease for the rest of my days but because God has called me to another activity, ministry, or vocation. At age 62, I started my fifth career. I expect this career to last the rest of my life.

Equating financial independence and retirement confuses many people. They are not the same thing. Many people I know are financially independent but far from retired. For example, a good friend of mine sold his business a couple of years ago in order to devote himself full-time to a ministry to businessmen. He is so busy ministering now that he has little time even to manage the wealth with which God has entrusted him. He is certainly not retired.

The fundamental question we must answer is a basic question of life: Why am I here? At some point all of us will stand before our Lord in order to give Him an account of how we have used the time entrusted to us (2 Corinthians 5:10). I certainly would hate to have to stand there and say, "What have I done for

reading some books I've always wanted to read. His fantasy quickly dissolved as he tried to figure out what else he would do with his time. Yes, he had projects on the house he would like to finish, and he had a golf game to perfect. But would he really be happy with those things as the center of his life? Especially if Laura was still teaching, as she planned to be?

Maybe I should revisit Laura's idea of working with a nonprofit, Bob thought. *My background makes me a natural for fund-raising. What about Meadowview?*

Meadowview Resource Center was a local relief agency just a few miles away from their house. Bob and Laura had first heard of it through their church, which collected food for Meadowview's food pantry. One month Bob had been recruited to drive the collected food over to the center, and he had been amazed at what he saw. Who knew that in his community, which he had always considered fairly affluent, there were so many families who needed help? After he agreed to deliver food there

each month, he got to know some of the staff and learned more about their other programs—literacy training, job assistance, tutoring, and basic computer classes. When he'd come home and enthusiastically told Laura all about the center, she had suggested that he volunteer. He had brushed it off at first. But as he thought about it now, he realized that Meadowview could become a place of purpose for him once making more money—his perceived purpose for so long—was no longer critical.

What if he started volunteering now? He could teach a computer class or mentor someone trying to get a job. Not only would he be helping, but he would be learning about Meadowview from the inside out—which would make him more effective later if he ended up helping them with fund-raising.

As Bob pulled into the garage, he turned off the engine, pulled out his cell phone, and punched in Meadowview's number. "Hi, Chris," he said to the executive director. "Bob Zikowski here. I wondered if you could use some help."

you, Lord? Well, my handicap dropped 10 strokes after I retired." Or "My major accomplishment was to try 37 different restaurants offering a senior citizen's discount." Actually, neither of these activities is necessarily bad in itself. But these activities do become wrong if they become the overriding motivation for one's life. Our perspective should be that, in light of eternity, we have so little time and so much to do.

> **Instead of thinking of retirement, I encourage people to think of "rehirement."**

I believe one of the greatest natural resources available to the Christian community is older people who have so much to offer in the way of wisdom, knowledge, and perspective. But the younger generation often ignores that great resource.

Consider Moses, who didn't even begin his work for the cause of God until age 80—and then served as judge and leader until 120. His brother, Aaron, accompanied him as a spokesperson from ages 83 to 123. Think of Zacharias and Elizabeth in the New Testament. Anna the prophetess spent her time serving in the Temple and at age 84 prayed over the baby Jesus. Noah, Abraham, Joshua, and John the disciple served the Lord until the end of their lives. As the psalmist says, "Teach us to number our days aright, that we may gain a heart of wisdom" (Psalm 90:12). Let's make that our prayer as well.

We can find inspiration in modern-day heroes of faith as well. Billy Graham, unable to walk from Parkinson's disease and injuries sustained in a fall, held a crusade in New York City at age 86! During that crusade, he held an interview with broadcaster Katie Couric. Despite his age, his goal in life was obviously not retiring to leisure.

> *Katie Couric:* So, first of all, of course, everyone wants to know—I know you're 86 years old. How are you feeling?
>
> *Rev. Billy Graham:* I feel 86.
>
> Graham then acknowledged that he'd had to slow his pace because of a broken pelvic bone and other health issues.
>
> *Couric:* How do you manage to keep going? And to have a positive outlook?
>
> *Graham:* I think it's the power to live. I can barely walk, but it's a privilege to be able to move at all. And I'm thankful to the Lord for the strength. And to preach the gospel. That's the reason I'm in New York.
>
> *Couric:* What will be the message of this crusade?
>
> *Graham:* The love of God. The fact that he loves all of us, is willing to forgive all of us. But only through Christ.[7]

Many other examples of seniors contributing their experience and wisdom exist in our modern era, from Mother Teresa of Calcutta serving the forgotten in India until her death at age 87 to Pope John Paul II leading his church until age 84. Bill Bright, founder and president of Campus Crusade International, called this time of his life the most productive and prolific. Before he died at age 81, he spent most days writing books and preparing training materials—all the while hooked up to an oxygen tank due to his pulmonary fibrosis condition, an ailment affecting the lungs. These people exemplified Gen. Douglas MacArthur's point when he said, "Nobody grows old by merely living a number of years. People grow old only by deserting their ideals. . . . Years may wrinkle the skin, but to give up interest wrinkles the soul."

I urge you not to accept the "default" view of hanging it up and pursuing leisure at a certain age. Please understand that I'm not saying all retirement is wrong. Many people genuinely enjoy their retirement years. Many must retire from their jobs due to poor health, mandatory age retirement, or to take care of a family member. You may need to change the scenery of your job or your location. Many of us do need to slow down and deemphasize the importance of our career. I'm just suggesting that you be open to the idea that God may have more in mind for your retirement years than you imagined possible.

Tools for Retirement Planning

If you survey the personal financial sections in large bookstores, most of the books are written about retirement. They tend to focus on "how to retire rich and enjoy the life you've always wanted." I've written more than a dozen personal financial books before this one but have never written one entirely about retirement. In fact, my books scarcely mention retirement. I'd rather focus on managing money wisely as a good steward and keeping the right perspective on work and leisure. (Refer back to chapters 1 and 3 to learn more about that perspective.)

Although I have challenged our traditional view of retirement, I do think it's important to save for long-term goals such as a "rehirement" or slowing down later in life. U.S. tax policy has long encouraged people to save money for their retirement years by offering tax incentives. Generally, money is deposited into an investment account by an employer and/or employee and not taxed until the employee retires and begins to make withdrawals.

Traditionally, investors have had access to three primary types of retirement plans: Defined Contribution Pension Plans, Defined Benefit Pension Plans, and Individual Retirement Accounts (IRAs). These alternatives offer some significant advantages that should be considered in the financial planning process.

Defined Contribution Pension Plans

The popularity of this type of plan has grown in recent years. Several different types exist, all giving the contributor flexibility and control in directing a percentage of his or her employee benefit. Most employers will match a portion of the contributions based on overall company performance.

Some of the most familiar plans include: the 401(k), which is generally offered by corporations and businesses to their employees; the 403(b), which is similar to the 401(k) but offered to employees of not-for-profit organizations; and the SEP (Simplified Employee Pension) and SIMPLE IRA, both commonly used by the self-employed or companies with a small employee base.

The 401(k) plans in the workplace are designed for long-term savings, usually retirement. Generally, employees cannot access the money until retirement. If they do before age 59½, then there is a price to pay: a 10 percent penalty. In addition, they must pay income tax on the amount withdrawn.

Defined Benefit Pension Plans

Prior to the introduction of Defined Contribution Pension Plans, this was the type of plan predominately offered by corporations and not-for-profit organizations. These plans offer employees a regular stream of income upon retirement. The employer contributes an "actuarially determined amount" sufficient to pay each participant a fixed or defined benefit at his or her retirement. Methods of defining the benefit may be based on a flat percentage of compensation, a percentage that increases with years of service, or a percentage that changes at certain compensation levels.

Individual Retirement Accounts (IRAs)

Saving for retirement while deferring taxes can also be accomplished through a traditional IRA, although the IRS has certain limits on the deductibility of contributions. Traditional IRAs are also frequently used to receive tax-deferred rollovers from other retirement plans when an employee changes jobs or retires.

> **Unlike the traditional IRA, contributions to a Roth IRA are not tax deductible but their contributions grow tax free.**

A variation is the Roth IRA, which was introduced in 1998. Unlike the traditional IRA, contributions to a Roth IRA are not tax deductible. However, money invested in this type of IRA accumulates tax free and distributions are not taxable, provided IRS guidelines are followed.

Another benefit of the Roth IRA is that no minimum distributions are required at age 70½. Assets can grow inside a Roth IRA for the owner's lifetime and be passed on to adult children or grandchildren and continue growing with no tax ever to be paid. For this reason, Roth IRAs are much more useful as estate planning vehicles than traditional IRAs or 401(k)s.

To open a Roth IRA account, you must have earned income—in other words, employment. (A good motivation to take a part-time job during retirement.) Your adjusted gross income must be less than $150,000 for married couples filing jointly or $95,000 for single filers (based on 2006 tax rates). Roth IRAs should be used whenever possible to shield future income from taxes.

The majority of people's net worth is held in their retirement plan accounts. It's important, therefore, to monitor, estimate, plan, and invest the money in your retirement plan accounts wisely. Our perspective should be that, in light of eternity, we have so little time and so much to do.

A number of planning tools are available to you today. On the Internet, you can easily find retirement calculators. The Web sites of mutual fund companies, government agencies, and many accounting firms offer you the ability to estimate your future retirement plan balance or living expense requirements. For instance, Bloomberg.com, a publisher of financial data, offers a calculator to help you compute future numbers based on a variety of assumptions about investment return, inflation, contribution growth, and future expenses. (It also includes information to help you determine how Social Security benefits might influence how much you need to save.) You may find it interesting to compare how much faster your retirement fund will grow if you start contributing as early as possible, contribute just one percent more a year, or invest in funds that give you just a one percent higher return.

Doing some advance research and planning will make the following points about saving for retirement clear:

- Investing regularly and over a long period of time can result in significant amounts of savings.
- What sounds like a big amount in the future is not so much when inflation is considered. You must consider inflation. Having a number goal, such as $1 million, is useless if you haven't taken inflation into account.
- Starting sooner is much better than starting later.
- Your actual results may vary. Understand that the likelihood of this scenario unfolding exactly as portrayed is extremely remote. It's based on the assumption that fixed rates of return, which never vary from year to year, will apply to your entire retirement portfolio. In the real world, you'll never get a steady return each year.
- A small difference in return over a period of years makes a significant difference over time.
- Saving more rather than spending on consumable items will pay off in the future.

Only about half of Americans surveyed said they believed they had enough money to live comfortably when they retired.[8] (Keep in mind that this is a self-assessment; if done by independent professionals, the actual analysis could be worse.) In a robust economy, many investors mistakenly believe that strong investment returns will continue, and that there is no need to plan or save for a leaner future. On the other hand, some investors are so aggressive when it comes to retirement savings that they rob themselves (and their families) of opportunities to enjoy life and be generous toward others. Neither extreme is healthy—and neither reflects wise stewardship.

Investing regularly and over a long period of time can result in significant amounts of savings.

Questions for You to Consider about Retirement

If you are nearing retirement age, I encourage you to carefully consider the following questions.

1. Should I retire from my current occupation?
2. How would retiring from this occupation help me fulfill God's purpose in my life?
3. When should I retire?
4. How will I continue to provide for my family?
5. What will I do next?

Discuss these questions with your spouse and family. Stew on them for a while. Pray over them and seek counsel from others, such as a pastor or mentor several years older than you. Consider your spiritual gifts and passions. Taking the time to contemplate how you can use your gifts and experience as you grow older will give more meaning and purpose to your retirement years.

How to Keep the Income Flowing after the Paycheck Stops

Yogi Berra, the former New York Yankee catcher who is perhaps equally famous for his memorable quotes, once said, "You've got to be very careful if you don't know where you're going, because you might not get there." Yogi could have been describing the strategies for many people nearing or beginning retirement.

After many people retire, or otherwise "rehire" or transition as we advocated in the last chapter, they face the stark reality of not having their regular paycheck. This leads them to ask a series of questions: *Where will my income come from? How fast can I draw down from my IRA? When should I start Social Security?*

Creating a sustainable income stream is challenging in light of these current trends:

- Longer life expectancies
- More baby boomers being responsible for grandchildren
- Fewer defined benefit plans (pension plans) from employers
- Unknown future spending amounts after retirement
- Higher property taxes due to the increase in real estate values
- Increased health care costs
- Fewer companies providing retiree health care benefits
- Uncertainty of long-term stability of Social Security
- Debt carried into retirement

Barbara Roper, director of investor protection at the Consumer Federation of America in Washington, says, "In terms of an investor education message, I worry a little bit about the message that starts with: 'You need this level or you're going to be eating cat food.' On the other hand, there is no question in my mind that people at all income levels need to be saving and investing more."[1]

In deciding about various income streams from pension payouts to Social Security to annuities, life expectancy plays a very important role in the decisions. Longevity is increasing, yet many studies have shown that people underestimate their own longevity. You may be surprised at the following actuarial statistics:

FOR MARRIED COUPLE AT AGE 65, PROBABILITY OF ONE SPOUSE LIVING TO CERTAIN AGES	
Age	Probability (in percents)
70	99.5
75	97.5
80	90.6
85	75.9
90	50.3
95	22.1

Source: Milevsky and Abaimova, "Applied Risk Management During Retirement," June 19, 2005, Society of Actuaries RP-2000 table.

With these trends in mind, let's consider four types of retirement income:

- Social Security
- Pension
- Retirement account withdrawals
- Annuities

Social Security

Though you've probably never heard of her, Ida May Fuller, a legal secretary from Vermont, made history when she became the first person to receive monthly Social Security benefits. She retired at 65 in 1940 after working and paying in taxes for three years. She lived to be 100 years old, so she collected monthly checks for 35 years after paying in for only three years.[2] (Perhaps Fuller's situation should have been a warning to policy makers of the ultimate dangers of promising lifetime benefits without an initial funding.)

Since its establishment in 1935, Social Security has been the primary source of income for many U.S. senior citizens like Ida May Fuller. Almost 60 percent of beneficiaries derive more than half their income from Social Security; for 30 percent, these payments make up 90 percent of their income. In 2000, about 10 percent of America's elderly lived in poverty; without Social Security, that figure would have been about 48 percent.[3]

For the past several decades, economists and demographers have warned about the Social Security program's insolvency. The first baby boomers turned 62 in 2008, which is expected to trigger an unprecedented number of benefit applications. (Kathleen Casey-Kirschling recently made news for another Social Security first: Not only is she the first recorded baby boomer—she was born one second after midnight on January 1, 1946—she was the first baby boomer to apply for Social Security benefits, which she was eligible to start receiving in January 2008.)[4]

U.S. policy makers will continue to debate the best way to preserve Social Security's viability—whether by delaying retirement age further, decreasing benefits, and/or increasing taxes. Yet even if Social Security remains solvent, it is unwise to depend too heavily on Social Security benefits. That's clear from a statement by the top-ranking official of the Social Security Administration, which appears on the front page of every benefits statement that is sent to working Americans:

> ## Almost 60 percent of beneficiaries derive more than half their income from Social Security.

> Social Security can't do it all. Social Security was not intended to be the sole source of income when you retire. You'll also need a pension, savings, or investments. Think of Social Security as a foundation on which to build your financial future.[5]

Virtually all American workers qualify for some Social Security benefits. Workers who earn at least $1,050 per quarter (2008 rates) can earn up to four credits each year. If a person earns at least 40 credits during his or her lifetime, he or she is eligible to receive Social Security benefits. Total benefits are based on the total number of credits and earnings during a person's work history.

The Social Security Administration estimated the following average monthly benefits for 2008:[6]

All retired workers	$1,079
Retired couple, both receiving benefits	$1,761
Retired widow(er) alone	$1,041

Those who earned higher-than-average wages throughout their working career receive higher monthly benefits than those shown above. Yet in 2003 the maximum monthly benefit was only $1,404 for a person retiring at age 62 and $2,045 for a person retiring at age 70.[7] Only those who have earned very high incomes every year after age 21 receive the maximum benefits. Whether that person earned $150,000 or $1,000,000 every year, his or her monthly benefits are the same.

To help workers anticipate their eventual earnings, the Social Security

Administration sends "Your Social Security Statement" letters each year that show each worker's earnings record and estimated benefits. (You should always review this annual statement closely for any errors.)

The amount of benefits workers receive annually depends on when they begin receiving benefits. Those who begin drawing Social Security at age 62 will receive reduced benefits. Those who wait until "full retirement age" (as defined by law) will receive normal benefits. Full retirement age used to be age 65; however, because of the strains on the Social Security system, Congress raised the retirement age gradually for those born after 1938.

FULL RETIREMENT AGE FOR SOCIAL SECURITY BENEFITS

Year of Birth	Full Retirement Age
1937 (or earlier)	65
1938	65 and 2 months
1939	65 and 4 months
1940	65 and 6 months
1941	65 and 8 months
1942	65 and 10 months
1943–1954	66
1955	66 and 2 months
1956	66 and 4 months
1957	66 and 6 months
1958	66 and 8 months
1959	66 and 10 months
1960	67

Most analyses of Social Security use three key reference ages—62, full retirement age, and 70—to estimate benefits, but workers can begin receiving benefits at any point between these ages. For example, if you wait until age 63, then your monthly benefit is higher than if you began collecting at age 62. If your full retirement age is 66 and you begin drawing benefits early, your normal, full-retirement-age benefits will be reduced as follows:

- 25 percent reduction at age 62
- 20 percent reduction at age 63
- 13 percent reduction at age 64
- 6 percent reduction at age 65

Since the future problems of the Social Security system have been so well publicized, many people are nervous. As a result, those in their 60s often decide they must "get my benefits while I can." We don't advocate letting this anxiety drive your present decision making. If you are nearing retirement age, your Social Security benefits are fairly secure. Your children and grand-children are the ones who should not count on Social Security remaining in its present form.

If you decide to work beyond your full retirement age without receiving benefits, your benefit will be increased by a small percentage for each month you don't receive benefits between your full retirement age and age 70. The following table shows the rate benefits increase annually.

RATE INCREASE FOR DELAYING RETIREMENT

Year of Birth	Yearly Increase Rate
1929–1930	4.5%
1931–1932	5%
1933–1934	5.5%
1935–1936	6%
1937–1938	6.5%
1939–1940	7%
1941–1942	7.5%
1943–or later	8%

The Social Security Administration advises workers to apply for benefits three months before they want them to begin.[8] This decision should be made care-fully, and it's important to keep several facts in mind before determining when to apply for benefits:

- This decision is irrevocable. Once you begin receiving benefits, you cannot change your mind if your health, employment, or financial situation changes.

- Your monthly benefit will remain the same, other than minor cost-of-living adjustments. If you choose to begin receiving benefits at 62, your benefit will be permanently lower than if you had begun at the full retirement age.

- If you begin receiving benefits before reaching the full retirement age, you are limited as to how much additional income you can earn until you reach full retirement age. (No limits exist for unearned income, such as investment income, pension income, rental income, or IRA distributions.) See page 282 for more details.

- When you die, the benefits stop. You will continue receiving benefits no matter how long you live. On the other hand, if you don't begin collecting benefits until age 70 and die a year later, the government gets to keep all the money you paid in but never collected. (However, if you have a surviving spouse, he or she may begin receiving survivor's benefits depending on how long you've been married, their age, their earnings records, etc.)

So how should you determine when to begin collecting benefits? Consider the process that Ralph, a married 61-year-old man who's spent nearly 40 years

FAMILY FINANCE

Nancy Hedrick sat on a park bench watching Ellie and her friend Paige climb together on the playground. Paige was also the granddaughter of Nancy's friend Helen, a retired banker. She and Nancy had become friends years ago when they sat next to each other in the church choir's alto section. It wasn't long before they were chuckling their way through rehearsals and going out for lunch after church. Both proud grandmothers, they enjoyed meeting at the park occasionally so they could catch up while their grandkids played together.

"How is it working having Alysha and the kids living with you?" Helen asked.

"Really well," Nancy said, smiling. "I'm amazed at how quickly Ellie has adapted. Alysha works long hours sometimes, and I think Ellie was lonely. She's thrilled that I can take her to the park or the museum—or even just play dolls with her. Donovan is coming around too. He needs his private space, no question, but we've had some good conversations. And Alysha—" Nancy paused. "It's like she's free of a terrible

burden now that the debt is gone. I am so grateful to see her more relaxed and smiling again."

"Sounds perfect," Helen said.

Nancy laughed and waved at Ellie, who was swinging. "Well, almost. I'd forgotten how noisy kids can be when they're tearing through the house with their friends. Alysha and I have had to set down some guidelines about personal space and chores. But overall it's been good."

She paused and then began again. "Now I have another decision to make, and I could really use your perspective. My 62nd birthday is approaching in a few months, and I'm trying to decide if I should start drawing Social Security now or wait until later."

"Ah," Helen said, nodding. "That's a hard decision. Are you getting any Social Security survivor benefits now from Joe?"

"No. I was 59 when he died, and widow benefits don't start until age 60 unless there are minor children or disability involved."

"Right," said Helen. "Well, let's talk

working as a tool and die maker in a machine shop, went through before making his decision. First he considered how much he would receive in monthly retirement benefits at various ages:

Age 62: $1,054 a month
Age 65 years, 10 months (full retirement age): $1,433 a month
Age 70: $1,933 a month

Obviously, the decision would be much easier to make if Ralph knew when he would die. That isn't possible, of course, yet his accountant illustrated how he could compute the break-even point in months and years—in other words, if he chose the normal benefit, he could determine how long he must live to have received more benefits than if he had started receiving them early.

it through. What are the pros and cons? Of course, if you start drawing benefits early, your monthly payments will always be smaller. That's the biggest difference."

"Hmm," Nancy said. "The last benefit summary I received in the mail showed that my payments would be about 25 percent smaller if I started drawing early instead of waiting until full retirement age."

"How much will you rely on Social Security?" Helen asked. "Do you have other retirement savings?"

Nancy nodded. "Joe had several IRAs, and I started a 401(k) when I went back to work. The accounts aren't huge, but they exist."

"What about working?" Helen asked. "If you receive early benefits, you can't make more than a certain amount—I think it's $12,000 or $13,000 per year—without reducing the benefit even more. That's pretty part-time work. Are you ready to make that change?"

Nancy shook her head slowly. "I didn't realize that."

For the past 10 years Nancy had been working as an emergency room nurse, and she thrived on the fast pace.

"I've been thinking about retiring mainly because sometimes I would like more flexibility to travel or to do things with friends," she said. "And it's getting harder to do those overnight shifts! But overall, I enjoy my job. I've thought about working part-time, but I definitely need some job—not just for the money, but also for my own sense of purpose. I'm not sure I want to deal with those tight income limits."

Helen nodded. "I'm no expert in this area. Perhaps you should meet with a representative from the Social Security office. He or she could run the numbers for you. Then, you and your financial planner can figure out how many years your retirement savings will likely last when combined with different Social Security benefit amounts."

Nancy smiled at her friend. "Thanks, Helen. I'll run it by my financial planner, but I feel better having talked it out—especially with someone who has been through it herself."

Ralph's break-even point is approximately 10.7 years; in other words, he must live at least 10.7 years beyond his full retirement age of 65 years and 10 months (or until he is about 76 years and 6 months) to come out ahead with the full-retirement-age option instead of the early benefit option.

He used the following formula:

(T x E) / D = Number of monthly payments to break even, where
T = Time in months from start of early benefit to start of later benefit
E = Earlier benefit amount
L = Later benefit amount
D = Difference in waiting, or L - E

These are the numbers Ralph plugged into the formula:

T = 46 months (age 62 to age 65, 10 months)
E = $1,054
L = $1,433
D = $379 (1,433 - 1,054)
T x E = 46 x $1,054 = $48,484 (the amount of benefits between 62 and
    65 years, 10 months)
$48,484/$379 = approximately 128 payments
128 / 12 months = 10.7 years

Please note that this formula provides an approximation of the break-even point. To be even more accurate, it would need to factor in the time value, or present value, of the monthly stream of payments. Yet it's not necessary to be that precise to get a good estimation of the break-even point.

The break-even point will vary among individuals, depending upon an individual's specific circumstances and benefit amounts. When I have calculated this number for others, the time span usually ranges from 8 to 14 years.

With that in mind, it's important to consider whether it's likely you'll live 8 to 14 years beyond full retirement age. For example, are you trim and healthy? Do you have several immediate family members who are still alive in their 80s? If so, you would probably lean toward waiting until you reach full retirement age before receiving benefits—in fact, you might even delay your benefits. Yet if all the men in your family died in their early sixties of heart disease and you are taking medication for high blood pressure and cholesterol while battling obesity, your life expectancy is probably rather short. You might consider starting benefits before you reach full retirement age.

However, even then you should be aware of the catch to starting Social Security at 62. If you take the early benefits, you may be limiting your work options for several years because other income cannot exceed an annual limit without affecting your benefits. If your wages or self-employment income is higher than the annual limit ($12,960 in 2007, adjusted annually), then your Social Security benefits are reduced.

For every two dollars you earn above the annual limit, your benefits are cut by one dollar. Some call it the "two-for-one" rule, and it has led many to quit or limit their work for pay. If you begin receiving benefits early and your dream job comes along or your side business starts booming, your benefits will be reduced in two ways. They are already reduced for your lifetime by starting early. They are reduced even further because you earned more than the limit. After reaching full retirement age, however, you can earn an unlimited amount without any reduction in benefits.

Some who feel they have been penalized by this rule decide to cheat the system by working for cash and never reporting this income. We exhort you to reject this temptation to cheat. Although you may escape notice, we recommend doing what is right in God's eyes and honestly reporting income. "He who walks in integrity walks securely, but he who perverts his ways will be found out" (Proverbs 10:9, NASB).

If you are nearing retirement age, your Social Security benefits are fairly secure. Your children and grandchildren are the ones who should not count on Social Security remaining in its present form.

In general, we recommend waiting until full retirement age to begin Social Security because it provides a higher benefit for life and because longevity trends mean most people are living longer.

We say "in general," though, because in some situations starting Social Security early makes sense. Let's say you wish to volunteer at a charity or go on mission trips. Starting Social Security early may provide you with the liquidity you need to meet your expenses. The earned income limits will not likely be a problem because you will not have much earned income as a volunteer.

Although you should never be dishonest, you may be able to plan wisely (and legally) your sources of income. Self-employed people, in particular, may be able to start benefits early by reducing or delaying their earned income.

For example, a farmer who plans to continue farming well past age 65 may begin collecting Social Security early and realize a stable income, perhaps for the first time in his life. A farmer can delay his income (store crops or build a herd) and increase his expenses in the short term. If he purchases farm machinery, more acreage, or builds a needed barn, he will have greater depreciation expense that will lower his earned income. After several years of lower income, his farming operations will be set to realize greater earned income. Once he is past full retirement age, he is free from any income limits. He should, however, work with a certified public accountant to help you with the intricacies of this type of tax and Social Security planning.

Retirement Funds: When It's Payout Time

Employer-funded pensions

The days of walking to the mailbox to pick up the monthly pension check are numbered. Remember, a defined benefit pension plan means the company has defined the benefit—usually based on a formula of years worked and earnings—to be received by the employee. An employer sets aside company funds and assumes the investment risk to have enough money to pay the monthly pension. Once quite common, pensions may soon be extinct. Companies are offering them less and less.

Most large, well-established companies once offered defined benefit pension plans. During the last 15 to 20 years, as the expense and risk to these funds have increased, companies have moved away from them. Companies now structure more of their retirement plans as defined contribution plans, such as 401(k)s. These plans are still built using defined contributions; however, the employee assumes the investment risk and the future benefit is unknown.

Yet many people still have a pension benefit from one or more former employers. They must decide when and how to collect their benefits. As with the decision about Social Security, their decision is irrevocable and involves some unknown factors, such as longevity.

Because the benefit amounts vary for each person depending on their company's program, their age, spouse's age, salary, and years of service, no one-size-fits-all calculations are possible. Yet let's consider the situation of Charlotte, the beneficiary of such a pension plan, who plans to retire soon. She is married and has worked for 31 years as an executive assistant for an office machines manufacturer. A few months before retiring, she met with a human resources employee at her company to review her pension options. She was given these choices:

1. Monthly pension benefits at age 65 for Charlotte's life only: $1,935

2. 50% surviving spouse option:
   Monthly pension benefits at age 65 for Charlotte's life: $1,638
   50% of monthly benefit over surviving spouse's life: $819

3. 100% contingent annuitant option (a beneficiary named by Charlotte, such as spouse or other, receives same monthly benefit as Charlotte): $1,517

4. Lump-sum option (pension received at once, not monthly): $156,000

Remember that these calculations are specific to Charlotte and are different from those offered to anyone else—including those at her own company. Furthermore, some companies do not offer a lump-sum option.

Which option should Charlotte choose? The bottom line is this: Does she want a higher monthly income immediately or a lower monthly income, but one that would potentially be available for years? Furthermore, is it important that her spouse continues to receive benefits even after she dies?

The first option would provide Charlotte with the highest amount of current income. If she chooses this one, she takes a risk. If she dies within a few years, her surviving spouse (or heirs) receives nothing.

Generally, this "one life only" option isn't recommended for married workers since 1 Timothy 5:8 reminds us "if anyone does not provide for his own, and especially for those of his household, he has denied the faith and is worse than an unbeliever" (NASB).

Unfortunately, though, some people feel they must choose the higher monthly benefit because they have debt or a costly lifestyle. If the pension participant dies sooner than expected, the surviving spouse is left without a monthly income benefit. (By the way, most pension plans require the spouse to sign an acknowledgment before a married pension participant chooses an option without surviving spouse benefits.)

Charlotte should opt for the 100 percent contingent annuitant option if she wants her spouse to receive the same monthly benefit as she receives during her life (instead of a 50 percent reduction). This monthly benefit is lower than the 50 percent surviving spouse option ($1,517 versus $1,638) but would protect her husband if she is also contributing part-time income that would disappear at her death or if they believe he is likely to live longer than average.

Charlotte has yet another option. She can collect all her benefits up front. When offered, the lump sum option is often the most popular. According to one report, as many as 90 percent of departing employees choose the lump sum.[9] However, it is also the least valuable to the employee, since it's usually configured to be worth less than the monthly benefits. Charlotte is certainly tempted to take it.

The lump sum is so appealing to Charlotte initially because it is more money than she has ever had access to all at once. Given the choice of $156,000 or $1,517 a month, the lump sum is attractive—particularly because she knows it is impossible to say for sure how long she will live and any money remaining from a single payment could be passed on to her children. On the other hand, if she and her husband collect $1,517 per month as long as either of them live, their total payments could exceed $300,000 or even $400,000.

Does the lump-sum option ever make sense? It might if Charlotte's spouse also has a substantial pension or if both Charlotte and her husband are in poor health.

In most cases, however, you are generally better served by choosing pension options that pay a lifetime benefit for both you and at least 50 percent for your surviving spouse. Longevity trends and the danger of outliving your income need to be carefully considered when choosing how your benefits will be paid out, and lifetime benefits protect against losing this important income source.

Of course, individual circumstances will vary and may warrant another option, which is why we included chapter 3 about decision making.

Retirement accounts—401(k)s and IRAs

While the number of retirees who must decide how to structure their pension payouts is shrinking, more and more people must determine how to withdraw funds from their retirement accounts at a sustainable rate. For them, interest and dividend income—sometimes even the gradual use of "investment principal"—is a key source of income in their later years.

Accumulating assets in Individual Retirement Accounts (IRAs), company 401(k) accounts, or brokerage accounts is a wise move. As Proverbs 6:6-8 says, "Go to the ant, O sluggard, observe her ways and be wise, which, having no chief, officer or ruler, prepares her food in the summer and gathers her provision in the harvest" (NASB).

When you reach this stage of life, you are transitioning from the accumulation phase to the distribution phase, sometimes a difficult move psychologically. Why are withdrawals difficult?

First, withdrawing funds from retirement accounts is an admission of getting older. You are no longer in your prime earning years, socking away money for retirement. Also, finding ways to build your IRA or 401(k) can be fun in the accumulation phase; once the withdrawals begin, the balances begin to fall and the game is not so fun anymore. You might even feel uncertain about whether you will have enough income to sustain you during your retirement years.

But remember the ant: It knows why it is saving. The ant is not upset that it needs in the winter what it stored in the harvest of late summer.

While Americans are regularly encouraged to save using IRAs and 401(k) accounts, little is said about the withdrawal phase. First, it's important to understand the tax rules and limits on these tax-deferred savings, which include 401(k) accounts, traditional IRAs, Keogh and profit-sharing plans, fixed annuities, and variable annuities. (Remember that "tax-deferred" means that you never had to pay income tax on your assets as they increased.)

In exchange for allowing you to delay taxation on the earnings of these savings, Congress and the IRS created some rules governing these accounts. (As you may recall, the Roth IRA operates on slightly different rules. See page 272 for details.) First, you generally cannot withdraw money from these plans before age 59½ without a penalty. (An accountant can provide information about certain exceptions for withdrawals by people under that age.) You are free to withdraw all or a portion of your tax-deferred savings without penalty anytime after 59½.

Secondly, you must begin at least a minimum amount of withdrawals at age 70½ or face penalties. In other words, you cannot defer the income tax indefinitely. The minimum amount to withdraw at age 70½ is based on IRS mortality tables. If you have $100,000 in an IRA at age 70½, then your minimum required distribution would be $3,650 per year ($100,000 divided by the IRS table factor of 27.4). (You can check with your tax preparer for a list of these tables or go to http://www.irs.gov.)

While it's wise to defer income taxes for as long as possible, leaving your children or grandchildren a sizable 401(k) or traditional IRA means they will have to pay more taxes than you would have, assuming they are in a higher tax bracket than you.

Nonspousal beneficiaries, including adult children, must pay income taxes on the tax-deferred savings. Why? Because the original owner of the traditional IRA never paid income taxes on it. (The exception is the Roth IRA, which we introduced on page 272. Contributions are not tax deferred; however, all earnings grow tax free.)

Consider Doris, a 72-year-old widow, who received a traditional IRA worth $400,000 from her deceased husband. Doris has few sources of income and is in the lowest income tax bracket of 10 percent. When Doris passes away, she leaves the IRA to her two children, a doctor and a business executive. Her son and daughter are both in the higher 30 percent income tax bracket. They must begin recognizing income from the inherited traditional IRA either all at once or over their lifetimes. Then they must pay income tax at their tax rates. The family would have paid less tax overall if Doris had received more distributions from the IRA and paid income tax at her lower rate.

Seniors in a similar situation to Doris should talk with their accountant and advisors to begin traditional IRA or 401(k) distributions. If they do not need the money immediately, then they can continue to invest it outside of a traditional IRA or give it away.

Common Questions on Withdrawals from Retirement Investments

How do I figure out how much I'll need?

Your spending determines the amount of income you'll need to withdraw from your investments. And how do you determine that figure? First, retirees' expenses are generally lower than in their younger years. For years, in fact, planners have assumed that a retiree's expenses would be about 80 percent of preretirement income. (Some peg it at closer to 90 percent of preretirement income due to rising medical costs; others suggest only 70 percent is needed if one previously had a long commute or moves to lower-cost housing.) In reality, it depends on your personal situation.

The worksheet on page 288, which allows you to calculate essential versus discretionary retirement expenses, can help you determine that figure.

DETERMINE YOUR ANTICIPATED RETIREMENT EXPENSES

As you envision your life in retirement, think about the expenses you expect to incur. As you consider your lifestyle and goals, decide which projected expenses you must meet (essentials) and which would simply be nice to have (discretionary). Finally, write your estimated monthly retirement expense in the Essential or Discretionary column.

		Essential	Discretionary
Housing	Mortgage/rent/fees	$	$
	Property taxes and insurance	$	$
	Utilities	$	$
	Household improvement	$	$
	Household maintenance	$	$
Food	At home	$	$
	Dining out	$	$
Transportation	Vehicle purchases/payments	$	$
	Auto insurance and taxes	$	$
	Fuel and maintenance	$	$
	Public transportation	$	$
Health Care	Health insurance	$	$
	Medicare/Medigap	$	$
	Copays/uncovered medical services	$	$
	Drugs and medical supplies	$	$
Personal Insurance	Life/other	$	$
	Long-term care	$	$
Personal Care	Clothing	$	$
	Products and services	$	$
Entertainment		$	$
Travel		$	$
Hobbies		$	$
Family Care/Education		$	$
Income Taxes		$	$
Charitable Contributions		$	$
Other		$	$
Subtotal		$	$
Total Essential and Discretionary Monthly Expenses			$

Source: Fidelity Investments

Q: I recently retired, a few years after my husband. We have both been amateur artists for years and would like to convert a large garage on our property into a studio. We will need about $10,000 to do so. Would it be best to use funds from our CDs or tap into our 401(k)s?

ANSWER: You'll need to withdraw less money if you use your CDs, because you have already paid at least part of the tax on these taxable investment accounts. This money will go further than tax-deferred savings where you must pay income tax. If you withdraw money from a traditional 401(k), you will really have to withdraw almost $15,000 to end up with a net amount of $10,000 (assuming you are in the 28 percent tax bracket for federal and 5 percent for state). But if you use money from a taxable account, such as a mutual fund or CD, you will use up less principal by withdrawing only what you need.

How do I account for inflation in future years?

Though inflation rates have been fairly low in the United States during recent years, it remains your primary enemy during retirement. At an inflation rate of 3 percent per year, prices double every 24 years. That means if you retire at age 62, your cost of living will have doubled when you reach 86. With that in mind, try to structure your sources of income to increase along with inflation. This may be done by keeping some of your investment portfolio in equities (stocks) or selecting a cost-of-living rider on an annuity payout.

Is there a commonly accepted withdrawal rate?

This question has resulted in many studies in the financial planning field. One of the first and most commonly cited studies found that a withdrawal rate of 4 percent or less is likely to withstand any 30-year payout period. The researchers found that a withdrawal rate of more than 7 percent probably won't last beyond 30 years. The study found that a more sustainable payout is between 4 and 6 percent annually.[10]

Four percent may seem small. But you must remember the potential for a loss—even for a diversified, balanced portfolio. Even though such a portfolio may *average* a return of, say, 8 percent per year, it may incur losses in the early years. Losses plus withdrawals begin the death spiral of portfolio values. Look at the following chart showing the "arithmetic of loss."[11]

THE ARITHMETIC OF LOSS			
Stock Market Decline (in percents)*	Number of Occurrences in Past 40 Years	Percent Return Required to Break Even During Accumulation (no withdrawals)	Percent Return Required to Break Even During Distribution** (5% withdrawal at end of year)
-5	46	5.3	11.1
-10	12	11.1	17.6
-15	6	17.6	25.0
-20	5	25.0	33.3
-25	4	33.3	42.9
-30	3	42.9	53.8
-35	2	53.8	66.7
-40	2	66.7	81.8

* The unmanaged S&P 500, 1967–2006, with reinvestment of dividends.
** Assumes declines lasted 12 months or less.

Annuities: Income Set for Life

Investors wanting a regular stream of income after retirement often choose annuities, which are generally issued by insurance companies or charitable institutions coordinating planned giving for their donors. There are two types of annuities: fixed, which offer a fixed rate of interest similar to a CD, and variable, which offer a variable return depending on how the investments perform.

Annuity: Contract that provides regular payments to investor at specified intervals.

Both types of annuities have two phases: the accumulation phase (deferred) and the distribution (immediate) phase. Most attention is placed on the accumulation phase—the time period that you contribute and try to build the total assets within the annuity. Yet you may purchase an annuity at either time: the accumulation phase or the distribution phase. We will focus, however, on the distribution side because that is what yields income.

An immediate annuity is simply a contract guaranteeing a lifetime income. Immediate annuities are particularly beneficial if you do not have a pension from past employers. Let's assume that Arthur, age 65, purchases an immediate fixed annuity for $50,000. He is beginning the distribution phase immediately, so he will receive $353 per month for the rest of his life.[12] If Arthur waited until age 70, the same $50,000 would buy an annuity paying him $398 per month. It pays more because he will likely not live as long (or receive as many payments) as he would at 65.

Immediate annuities act as "longevity insurance."

And what if Arthur dies three years after beginning his immediate annuity? The payments end and, in essence, the insurance company wins. What if Arthur lives to be 97 years old? He continues to receive a payment every single month of his life; in other words, he wins and the insurance company loses. When contracting for his annuity, Arthur could select several options, such as a minimum 20-year payout. Under this contract, either Arthur or his beneficiaries would receive payments for a guaranteed period of time (in this case, 20 years); however, his monthly income would drop from $353 to $313 per month.

Immediate annuities act as "longevity insurance." Young fathers buy life insurance in case they die too soon. An immediate annuity offers protection in case a person lives so long their investment income dries up.

Obviously, to obtain all the benefits of an immediate annuity, you have to put up with a downside: irrevocably transferring some of your savings or capital to the policy. Let's say a 65-year-old man needed an income of $700 per month; he would have to pay about $100,000 for an immediate annuity.

Those interested in buying immediate annuities should

- Buy from high-rated, financially strong insurers
- Not use all of their savings to buy an annuity
- Buy as late as possible
- Buy for only as much income as they need (they can always buy another one later if needed)
- Spend no more than $100,000 per insurer
- Obtain a joint-and-survivor annuity if married, to pay income for as long as one spouse is living

As you consider creating lasting income streams, keep in mind another old-fashioned basic idea: that four-letter word spelled W-O-R-K. An enjoyable part-time job during retirement will keep you active and provide a base level of income without disturbing investments.

CHAPTER 20

Passing It On before You Pass On

Analysts project that $41 trillion (that's right, this number has a *t* on it) of wealth will transfer in the United States over the next 50 years.[1] A trillion is a million millions. Do you know how long it would take to count to a trillion? If you counted nonstop with no breaks, without eating or sleeping, it would take 31,710 years to count to one trillion. It would take 1.3 million years to count to 41 trillion. As big and unimaginable as the U.S. government debt is, it's only about one-fifth of the amount that will move out of the hands of one generation into another.

While you might think that your share of that $41 trillion is so insignificant that you don't need to worry about estate planning, you're wrong. Regardless of the amount of your assets, your family may have more hardship than necessary if you die without an estate plan. My dad never talked about or shared his plans or desires about distributing his wealth until he made a request on his deathbed. Judy's father, a doctor, died suddenly at a young age without providing adequate life insurance or enough savings for his family. In short, these are two examples from my own family of how not to go about wealth transfer. I see many more examples nearly every day. I have a burden to see such situations change—starting with you. You don't have to make these kinds of mistakes.

One would think that this issue of wealth transfer involving trillions and trillions of dollars would be big news. Surely people would be talking about this, acting upon it, seizing opportunities, making plans. Yet this startling projection has received little treatment in the popular press, and I find that most people have done nothing about it. That means some adult children are about to inherit a sum that has the capacity to change their lives—for better or worse. Some charities may—or may not—receive bequests that could help them make lasting spiritual, cultural, or medical changes.

Oh, people may have a will—but it's often out of date. And most have not had important conversations with children and family members that would prepare them for what they will face after parents die. Most of us feel quite unprepared for that type of family discussion. We are intimidated by the emotions it might bring out. That's why I wrote an entire book, *Splitting Heirs: Giving Your Money and Things to Your Children Without Ruining Their Lives*, to help people—rich and poor, men and women, young and old—successfully complete the difficult and complex process of transferring wealth.[2] I've summarized the process of wealth transfer and the underlying principles in this chapter.

Why Wealth Transfer Is Challenging

From a straightforward financial man, here are the straightforward realities:

1. We will all die.
2. We will take nothing with us.
3. We will probably die at a time other than when we would like.
4. Someone else will get our stuff.
5. We can decide only *before* we die who gets our stuff *after* we die.

I think we can all acknowledge the truth and certainty of these five statements. So why do so many people procrastinate when it comes to planning the transfer of their wealth? Ah, because it touches upon many other relational and spiritual life issues. Let me summarize some of the challenges:

- Helping your children and grandchildren without harming them
- Managing expectations of your spouse and children
- Dealing with sons-in-law, daughters-in-law, stepchildren, stepgrandchildren
- Providing for your spouse
- Providing for God's Kingdom purposes
- Deciding what charities or ministries to support
- Avoiding family conflict and sibling jealousy
- Dealing with the reality of your death
- Acknowledging that all of your hard-earned wealth will be left to someone else
- Talking about a difficult subject
- Reaching agreement with your spouse
- Desiring to control your prized assets or business beyond the grave
- Handling change in personal and family circumstances
- Experiencing significant changes in wealth
- Desiring to finish strong
- Learning about complex legal and financial matters, such as wills, trusts, and estate taxes

Whew! No wonder people (including myself) tend to procrastinate. We all gravitate toward the easy and routine actions rather than the difficult and important ones.

Wealth Transfer
Decision-Making Process

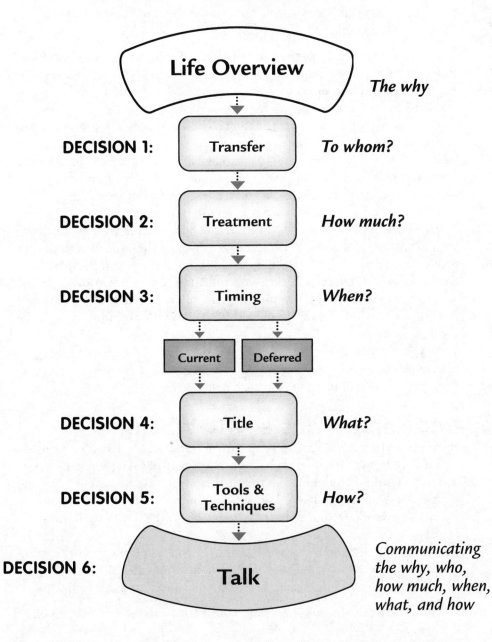

Life Overview — *The why*

DECISION 1: Transfer — *To whom?*

DECISION 2: Treatment — *How much?*

DECISION 3: Timing — *When?*

Current   Deferred

DECISION 4: Title — *What?*

DECISION 5: Tools & Techniques — *How?*

DECISION 6: Talk — *Communicating the why, who, how much, when, what, and how*

For challenges like these, we need wisdom. The Bible says,

> Wisdom, like an inheritance, is a good thing and benefits those
> who see the sun. Wisdom is a shelter as money is a shelter, but the
> advantage of knowledge is this: that wisdom preserves the life of
> its possessor. (Ecclesiastes 7:11-12)

In my counseling and planning sessions with clients over the years, I've found
it helpful to use a process to prepare them for "when"—not "if"—something
happens. Because wisdom is knowledge applied to life, I want to share my outline of the wealth transfer decision-making process.

Please note that I have described this chart as a "process." A process should
be followed in sequence. Do step 1 before step 2. Never do step 4 until you
have done step 3. If you were to try to make a lemon meringue pie and you
threw all the ingredients together, you would have a mess. Even if you used
the right ingredients in the right amounts, you would not have a good lemon
meringue pie unless you followed the steps in sequence.

When planning their estates, most people and professional advisors begin
with decision 5: Tools and Techniques. This part of the process includes the
technical aspects of drafting a will, avoiding estate taxes, or establishing a
trust. But you should first decide who is getting how much. How much do
you give to missions and how much to your children? When should you give
to either of them—now or at your death? Follow the suggested process for
the best outcome.

As I mentioned in chapter 9, your best decisions result from focusing on
principles. For each wealth-transfer decision in the chart on the previous page,
I will provide one or more principles to guide you.

Decision 1: Transfer—To Whom?

If we place His stuff in the hands of unworthy stewards, I suspect God will
find a way to take it away from them. Still, part of being a good steward
includes choosing and preparing the next steward of your assets. What are
your options? Looking at the big picture, you only have three choices for
the next steward: (1) your heirs, (2) charity, or (3) the government (through
taxes).

The transfer decision is the first and most important decision in the wealth-
transfer process. It drives the other decisions. To whom does the wealth go? To
help with your transfer decision, I recommend considering three principles:

- The treasure principle: You can't take it with you but you can send it
  on ahead.
- The unity principle: Your spouse completes you and doesn't compete
  with you.
- The wisdom principle: Transfer wisdom before wealth.

The treasure principle: You can't take it with you but you can send it on ahead

In his outstanding book *The Treasure Principle*, Randy Alcorn summarizes this principle: "You can't take it with you—but you can send it on ahead."[3]

Randy says it like this:

> Many have stored up their treasures on earth, not in heaven. Each day brings us closer to death. If your treasures are on earth, that means each day brings you closer to losing your treasures. . . . He who lays up treasures in heaven looks forward to eternity; he's moving daily toward his treasures. To him, death is gain. He who spends his life moving away from his treasures has reason to despair. He who spends his life moving toward his treasures has reason to rejoice.[4]

What I do on earth will be rewarded. Financially speaking, we can give some of our resources to churches, missions, charities, needy individuals—and be rewarded. Of course, we don't give in order to get. But we often fail to grasp the eternal significance of our actions.

From our discussion so far, you might think that I am implying you should leave all your money to mission work or a charity. I am not saying that. Please understand that I am simply recommending that you think through, pray over, and consider your decisions using this process. Remember, not deciding is a decision.

Giving to charity is one way, but not the only way, to gain treasures in heaven. Actually, God doesn't need the money. What God wants is the use of His money in productive ways. Maybe a productive way is buying that dresser for your wife, taking that vacation to build a memory, or paying off your debt to gain financial freedom.

You have three choices when deciding who will receive your assets after you're gone: your heirs, charity, or the government (through taxes).

Jesus said, "If you have not been trustworthy in handling worldly wealth, who will trust you with true riches? And if you have not been trustworthy with someone else's property, who will give you property of your own?" (Luke 16:11-12).

You may conclude that your children should get all of your wealth. That's fine. But you should then understand the implications of *choosing and preparing* them to be the next stewards of your wealth. In other words, you shouldn't leave everything to them by default or simply because that's what everyone else does. If you're married, God has given you an in-house consultant to help you make these decisions. This leads us to the next principle.

ANSWER: Absolutely! What Judy and I did first was figure out how much we are going to leave to each child. This is an absolute amount, not a percentage of our estate. Everything above that is going to charity.

We figured an absolute dollar amount because our estate value could vary according to the value of our businesses and other factors. We would not want to risk ruining our kids if we left all of the inheritance to them; we love them too much to take that risk. Our goal is to transfer wisdom as well as wealth.

And we feel God has called us to be concerned about building His Kingdom. Once you have adequately—or in many cases today, more than adequately—provided for children and grand-children, you can feel the freedom and joy of funding God's work. The ministries and charities that Judy and I support do work that we can't do after our deaths. I might also add that we're not just waiting until after death to give via our wills, but we're trying to do much of our "givin' while we're livin' so we're knowin' where it's goin'." (For information on charitable remainder trusts, one vehicle to pass on assets to Christian ministries and other nonprofits, see page 324.)

The unity principle: Your spouse completes you and doesn't compete with you

My friend and mentor, noted teacher and author Dr. Howard Hendricks, first told me the phrase behind the unity principle. In Howie's words, "God did not give you a spouse to frustrate you but to complete you." He helped me see that Judy and I can make better decisions together than either of us can alone. King Solomon, who had some experience with money and wives, said the following:

> *Two are better than one,*
> *because they have a good return for their work:*
> *If one falls down,*
> *his friend can help him up.*
> *But pity the man who falls*
> *and has no one to help him up!*
> *Also, if two lie down together, they will keep warm.*
> *But how can one keep warm alone?*
> *Though one may be overpowered,*
> *two can defend themselves. (Ecclesiastes 4:9-12)*

Husbands and wives have different strengths and weaknesses. Marriage brings about a challenging but complementary blend of emotions and logic, estrogen and testosterone.

How does a lack of unity raise its ugly head? Often it sounds something like this: A husband says something along the lines of "I don't want that worthless son-in-law to get one penny of our money." His wife responds, "Think about what this will do to our grandchildren."

Or the disagreement may not even be verbally expressed. The husband believes, *We have enough. Our kids have enough. Let's give more of our wealth to missions.* But his wife thinks, *I want to have enough to live on comfortably if you die before I do.*

When you are making these decisions related to wealth transfer, unity between husband and wife is necessary. If at first you don't succeed, keep talking, keep listening, keep compromising, and keep praying together. If you still don't agree, consider involving professional advisors (lawyers, financial planners) or trusted family members to help address the thorny issues. (See chapter 30 for more on communicating with your spouse about financial issues.)

Keep processing these decisions until you come to an answer. You may need a temporary plan in place while you work out a better plan. Frankly, Judy and I have found we even have to reprocess these decisions as circumstances change. Kids start careers, marriages occur, grandkids arrive, divorces may happen. All the while, Judy and I find ourselves reassessing whether our decisions are still the right ones. It's not always comfortable or easy, but it's necessary for us to agree.

The wisdom principle: Transfer wisdom before wealth

Wealth never creates wisdom. Wisdom may create wealth. If you pass on wisdom to your children, you probably can pass wealth to them. If they have enough wisdom, then they may not need your wealth.

Too often in our culture, the attitude of parents is "I'll take care of the money. You kids just stay in school or play the piano or play soccer." I strongly urge you to reconsider this philosophy. With each passing year, you can pass on more practical experience and needed knowledge about handling money. Don't make money mysterious or a factor in controlling your children and making yourself seem powerful in their lives. You'll actually have more influence (which is God's gentle version of power and control) over their behavior if you teach them how and why your family handles money as it does. The worst thing you can do is pass on wealth if you haven't also passed on wisdom.

The Bible says, "An inheritance quickly gained at the beginning will not be blessed at the end" (Proverbs 20:21). In biblical times, sons inherited their fathers' property and thus provided for the rest of their families. What is not so obvious is that, in most instances, the sons received their inheritances while their fathers were still living, enabling fathers to oversee their sons' stewardship.

In turn, the sons, particularly the oldest, inherited great responsibility for providing for the parents and extended family. Would you be more interested in training your children to handle money wisely if you knew that one day your estate would be in your children's hands and you would have to depend on them for your support?

Good stewardship includes not only providing for your family, but also being sure that every family member knows how to manage your resources. It's so easy to procrastinate. It's a "tyranny of the urgent" problem that keeps us from addressing the most important items.

Three questions to ask when making the transfer decision

We've discussed the three choices (heirs, charity, and government) and three principles (treasure, unity, and wisdom) in determining your wealth transfer

FAMILY FINANCE

Laura and Bob leafed through the pages of account summary statements their financial planner had handed to them when they walked into his office. He had just spent half an hour summarizing each one.

"So," Bill Oliver said as he leaned over the large desk, "your retirement is looking good, as Bob and I talked about last month. During the next 10 or so years, when you're both working, I encourage you to keep socking away as much as you can. Then once you reach 62, we'll talk about Social Security and starting to withdraw from some of your investments."

Laura nodded. "So it sounds like we're kind of in maintenance mode right now," she said.

Bill smiled. "In a manner of speaking, at least in terms of investments. But you also have an important question to consider: How, when, and to whom are you going to pass on your wealth?"

Bob glanced up quickly. "Like a will? We made one of those years ago, when Liz was little."

"Well, that's a start," said Bill. "You should review a will at least every time you experience a major life change—so you're probably overdue, especially since Liz is no longer a minor. But a will directs the distribution of your assets only after your deaths. You might want to consider giving some away before you die."

"Before?" Laura asked. "What are the benefits to that?"

"It depends on the scenario. Perhaps at age 25 your daughter would be able to use a legacy in a significant way, but the money wouldn't be nearly as important later on after you die—which of course we hope is decades from now. Or perhaps you see a current need in

plan. To help you further, I would recommend asking yourself three questions as you consider transferring wealth.

1. What is the worst thing that could happen if I transfer wealth to _____?
2. How serious is it?
3. How likely is it to occur?

You can then repeat these three questions in a more positive frame of mind, such as "What is the best thing that can happen if I transfer wealth to _____?"

Decision 2: Treatment—How Much?

How can children coming from the same two parents with the same gene pool living in the same environment with the same stimuli be so different? Probably every parent of more than one child has asked this question at one time or another. Judy and I are amazed at how our five children have such different personalities and approaches to life.

One of our children recently went through an unexpected divorce and became a single parent. We believe that we should be available to help her

your church or an organization you support. If you give money now, you can meet that need. Later on, that specific need might be gone."

"That's an interesting way to think about it," said Bob. "How would we give a large lump sum? I've heard about a charitable remainder trust; is that the way to do it?"

Bill shook his head. "Don't get ahead of yourself, Bob. I really encourage both of you to sit down and think through some big questions before you start figuring out the details. In other words, think about who you want to give money to, how much, and when you want to give it. After you've gotten that straight, then come back and we can talk through some techniques."

Bob gathered up the papers and reached out to shake Bill's hand. "Will do. I'm sure Laura and I have some talking to do before we reach a consensus."

He winked at Laura. "Especially since I'm dead set on giving a lot of money to my favorite baseball team. Maybe we can get a chair in the third-base section with my name engraved on it. The Bob Zikowski bleacher seat . . ."

"Sure, Bob—as soon as I get an endowed Laura Zikowski chair at the opera house," Laura answered wryly. "Seriously, though, Bill mentioned figuring out *who, how much, when,* and then finally *how.* I think we already know the *who*— the main people or groups we want to give our money to: Liz, our church, Meadowview Resource Center, and the local pregnancy resource center. It seems to me deciding on the *how much* and *when* will take some thought and prayer."

"You're right," Bob said more seriously. "It's really a matter of stewardship. We have to figure out how, even at the time of death, we can best use the money God has entrusted to us."

with babysitting and some financial assistance that we might not give another of our children in more stable circumstances. For example, if we give her $300 to help with expenses, we don't feel obligated to write a $300 check to each of our other children.

Is such treatment unfair? We don't think so. Our approach to the second decision, the treatment decision, in our wealth transfer process is based on the uniqueness principle: *Love your children equally and treat them uniquely.*

To do otherwise would dishonor them. Sons are different than daughters, sons-in-law are different from daughters-in-law, grandchildren are different from other grandchildren. You may have heard it said that the greatest inequality is treating unequal people equally.

As you contemplate choosing the next steward of God's wealth, you may realize that some of your children are much better equipped to handle wealth than others. You may reflect upon your family situation and realize that some have more genuine needs than others. Love them unconditionally, but treat them uniquely. They are unique in their character, values, and ability to deal with life; unique in their vocation, health, and immediate family situation.

I also believe that a parent should consider differences in children—differences due to age, gender, temperament, their demonstrated ability to handle money, their spiritual commitment, their spiritual maturity, their known or unknown marriage partners, and their children. It is a parent's and grandparent's responsibility to entrust God's resources to children only if they have demonstrated the ability to handle those resources in a manner that would please Him who is the Owner of all.

For example, if a parent entrusts God's resources to a slothful child, it's no different than giving those resources to any slothful stranger. Just because you have a child does not make the child the automatic beneficiary of your estate. The scriptural precedent is that the money should be left to those who have demonstrated sound stewardship. According to Ecclesiastes 7:11-12, if we leave money to someone to whom we have not left wisdom, it can be a devastating situation. I believe that much prayer, wisdom, and courage are needed in making the treatment decision. This is why ultimately you must talk with your family about your decisions. It's better to discuss unequal distributions to children while you are alive than to run the risk of bitterness toward you, or toward each other, after you are dead.

But treating our children differently doesn't feel right. . . .

I acknowledge that this is a hard decision to process. If you have more than one child, it can seem unfair at first. So let's examine this notion of fairness further.

As parents, we work hard to avoid favoritism. Rightfully so, as favoritism has caused much pain and divisiveness in families for thousands of years. Look at the story of Joseph in the Old Testament. The Bible says that his father, Jacob, "loved Joseph more than any of his other sons" (Genesis 37:3). Jacob later gave Joseph a richly ornamented coat of many colors.

Love your children equally and treat them uniquely.

Although Jacob gave Joseph unique treatment, Jacob violated the uniqueness principle. Jacob did not love his sons equally. Treat children uniquely, yes, but such treatment should be motivated by equal love for each one. Because Jacob showed favoritism (as his father, Isaac, had shown preference for his brother, Esau, over Jacob), the unique treatment of the coat became a symbol and lightning rod of conflict with Joseph's brothers.

To avoid a *perception* of unequal love, you must communicate with all of your adult children. That is why the talk decision (which I discuss later on in this chapter) is important. I have observed that distributing money usually generates some emotion. Money has a symptomatic power about it—it brings out in people and families symptoms of problems that lie underneath. Curiously, the more money being distributed, the more intense the symptoms. Money aggravates these family problems and is not the magic cure that people imagine it to be.

When parenting *young* children, you do have to be concerned with their perceptions of fairness. If you go away on a business trip and bring a gift for only one of your three children, the other two kids are likely to conclude that you love them less. That would be cruel. This is why most parents of young children go to great lengths to treat them equally. Our society takes this fairness so far that even when bringing a gift to a newborn baby most people will usually bring a gift to the three-year-old brother as well.

The problem comes when parents continue these legalistic notions of exact fairness to adult children. However, adult children can understand subtle distinctions of why an act of generosity to another adult child may be appropriate or convenient. They wouldn't necessarily expect the same treatment, but you may need to communicate the reasons behind your actions to help them understand how you came to your decision.

You are a steward of God's resources on His behalf. You are *not* a steward of your children's resources. You are not accountable to your children for how you transfer or spend His money. You *are* accountable to God.

That's why it's important to pray diligently for God's direction, work through this process of thinking and decision making, and seek professional counsel from a Christian perspective.

The first two decisions of "to whom?" (transfer) and "how much?" (treatment) pave the way for the next decision of "when?" (timing).

Decision 3: Timing—When?

Let's say you've decided to transfer some of your wealth to a mission organization. When should you give it?

How does a widow who, after prayerfully considering the wealth transfer process, has decided to give her wealth to her adult children equally, decide when to distribute it? Should she give it now—when they could use it the most—or give it later?

I recommend basing your timing decision on the following two principles:

- The kingdom principle: Time your wealth transfer to maximize its use by you, your heirs, and Kingdom servants.
- The givin' while livin' principle: Do your givin' while you're livin' so you're knowin' where it's goin'.

These principles often work together. They apply to timing decisions for wealth transferred to charities or to adult children or grandchildren. Let's say that you have been active in supporting a ministry through your volunteer efforts for many years. Let's further assume you have enough wealth to last your lifetime and you plan to give a substantial gift to the ministry upon your death as mentioned in your will.

> **Time your wealth transfer to maximize its use by you, your heirs, and Kingdom servants.**

The ministry has a current need to complete an obvious God-directed mission. By waiting to give (through your will) until after you die, you may outlive the usefulness of that ministry and your gift may not be needed as much later as it is now. By applying the kingdom principle and givin' while livin' principle, you may choose to make substantial gifts now instead of later.

The same principles may apply to your heirs. They may have more need for your inheritance now—to allow a young mother to stay at home, to pay off student loans, or to replace an aging car—instead of when they are 50 or 60. You can also receive the joy of giving now and seeing them benefit. You could train them further and be around to share wisdom as to how they might handle portions of wealth received now. Although these reasons may sound logical, many people choose to postpone their giving. Why? They are concerned about the "enough" questions discussed on page 51.

Another problem with giving out of your estate—instead of currently—is that you don't know the future. Let's say that Bob made a will in 1985 that directed half of his estate to go to free Christian prisoners in the USSR. In 1988, Bob experienced a debilitating stroke, causing him to lose mental capacity. When Bob died in 1996, several years after the Iron Curtain fell in the former

Soviet empire, the organizations he named no longer existed. That would complicate matters during the probate process after his death.

Presuming upon the future can be dangerous. How can you know what the most important needs to support years from now will be? If you limit your giving until after you die, then you may be giving to a cause that is not nearly as urgent or important.

Also, as you consider the long-term effects of inflation, you may decide to give more now rather than later to your kids or to your church or other ministries. If you have defined "How much is enough?" and reached that level, then prayerfully consider how your giving could help and bless your heirs and chosen charities now rather than later. After you have made your timing decision, you can address the next decision of titling your assets (land, bank accounts, beneficiary designations, etc.), as explained in the next section.

Decision 4: Title—What?

My wife recently laughed out loud when she came across the following: "The older you get, the tougher it is to lose weight . . . because by then your body and your fat have become really good friends."

I think the same can be said about your money or possessions. After controlling those assets for a long time, it's hard to shed them. You begin to think that those assets are yours. You feel ownership for that business or that stock or that land. You want it safeguarded in perpetuity for yourself and your line of descendants. However, all that is currently within your control belongs to God. This is the stewardship principle that should help with your titling decision: God owns it all.

After you have decided to whom you'll transfer wealth, how much you'll transfer, and when the transfer will happen, you should actually begin transferring ownership. Unfortunately, many people erroneously focus more of their efforts on these technical aspects of the title decision rather than thinking through the other decisions first. Yet you transfer title in order to accomplish the other decisions you have made. The title decision is when you take actual steps to change the deed, transfer the stock, set up the trust, or write the checks.

This is where the rubber meets the road. You may have agreed conceptually with me about givin' while you're livin', but actually writing the check takes faith that the Lord will provide enough for the rest of your life. The business owner may agree with the idea that he needs to set up succession planning for his business, but actually transferring the stock is difficult. Signing the wills to treat your children uniquely takes courage.

In traditional estate planning, much attention is paid to the titling of assets and attempts to control assets beyond the grave. I will talk more in the next section and the next chapter about various strategies, which may involve titling decisions. I also recommend obtaining competent legal and tax counsel when contemplating these significant titling changes of business succession, beneficiary designations, or establishing trusts.

Decision 5: Tools and Techniques—How?

As I've emphasized repeatedly, your wealth transfer planning is more effective and complete when you address the decisions such as *to whom* and *how much* before you address the *how*. Unfortunately, many people, particularly lawyers and accountants, make the tools and techniques the focus, rather than a tool of planning.

Only after you have considered the other decisions in the wealth transfer process should you begin drafting wills, trusts, or other legal instruments. The underlying principles of the tools and techniques decision are the following:

- The tools principle: Estate planning tools and techniques help you accomplish objectives, but are not *the* objective.
- The trust principle: Never use a trust because of a lack of trust.
- The KISS principle: Keep your estate matters as simple as possible.

Let's start with the basic tool in the wealth transfer process: *your will*. Your will is the foundational cornerstone of an estate plan. It's a written, witnessed document that defines your final wishes and desires regarding many things, including property distribution. A person who dies with a will is said to have died testate. A person who dies without a will dies intestate, and the laws of intestacy apply.

Intestacy: Dying without a valid will, meaning that distribution of assets will be overseen by a probate court.

The laws of intestacy differ from state to state, but in general, if one dies intestate, that person gives the state government the right to determine the following:

- The control of his or her assets
- The distribution of those assets
- The choice of executor
- The choice of a guardian for minor children
- The ability to waive fiduciary bonds
- The right to authorize a business continuation plan

On the other hand, a person who dies with a will retains the right to determine the following:

- The control and the use of their assets
- The distribution of those assets

- The bequeathing of specific personal possessions to loved ones
- The choice of executor
- The choice of a guardian for minor children
- The right to waive fiduciary bonds (such bonds can be expensive)
- The right to set up various trusts to reduce estate taxes and probate costs

Many Americans don't have a will. Survey after survey reveals that the number of procrastinators ranges from 50 to 60 percent. An important step for all good stewards is to implement the basic tool of a will. Your good intentions or your prayerful consideration of the wealth transfer process won't get the job done. In many states, the surviving spouse has no say in the distribution of assets if there is no will. For example, you may have wished all your financial assets be left to your surviving spouse. Many states have distribution rules that say without a will the surviving spouse receives only half and the surviving children receive the other half. Your estate becomes subject to the responsibility and function of the court system.

Only after you have considered the other decisions in the wealth transfer process should you begin drafting wills, trusts, or other legal instruments.

In the following chapter, I'll discuss more advanced tools and techniques involved in traditional estate planning.

Decision 6: Talk—Communicating the Why, Who, How Much, When, What, and How

Is it easier to share your wealth transfer plans with your children around the coffee table or from your coffin? Who can better share your motivations, hopes, desires, and blessings with your family: you or the lawyer reading your will?

If you have diligently worked through the wealth transfer process I've presented but fail to complete this last step, you will reduce the potential positive impact of your decision and may cause harm to your heirs. I know it is hard enough to talk about money—even harder to talk about money and death. You have to make a conscious decision to do so, and then *just do it*.

The underlying principle of the talk decision is the expectation principle: Communicate to align expectations with plans.

The aim of the expectation principle is to get everyone on the same page with no surprises. Try to avoid creating a "coping gap" for your heirs. Bruce Wilkinson, author of *The Prayer of Jabez*, first shared the coping gap

Q: I had planned to use a trust upon my death for my wife. My reasoning is that she doesn't like handling money. Also, I wouldn't want some scoundrel of a man to take advantage of her and live off of all I have earned. But your trust principle—"Never use a trust because of a lack of trust"—made me wonder if my planned approach was incorrect. Does my thinking violate the trust principle?

ANSWER: No, I don't think your concern violates the trust principle. It *validates* the trust principle. You are not using a trust for the wrong reasons. It appears that your motives are to preserve assets for your wife and to provide for her. You, knowing your wife best, seem to think she might be susceptible to losing those assets in some way.

I knew of a situation where a widow was left with $1 million. She moved to the warm climate of Arizona. She later married the golf pro at the senior community where she lived. He persuaded her to change the title of her assets so they were in his name only. You can see what's coming—he later left her. Of course, he didn't leave the assets. He took all of her wealth. She could do nothing legally to recover them. If her first husband had set up a trust with some protective provisions, then this might never have happened.

Trusts can be useful. My wife's grandfather died and left about $100,000 with a trust department at a local bank so they could invest the money and provide for his wife's needs. In 37 years—she lived to be over 100—she never ran out of money. In fact, when she died her estate was worth over $1 million. Because of her husband's wisdom, she was adequately provided for, and his wise investment resulted in a large inheritance for the heirs and charities.

Too often, however, people use the tool of the trust only because they never applied the wisdom principle—in other words, they never took the time to transfer the wisdom necessary to handle assets responsibly. Don't use the vehicle of a trust to transfer wealth to a participant who is untrustworthy or lacks wisdom. The best approach is to teach wisdom and develop trustworthy character in the recipient while you are living. You may still choose to use a trust for your recipient's convenience or for help when the recipient doesn't have investing expertise.

concept with me. It is simply this: If your expectations are at one level and you discover reality is at a much different level, then the difference between them is your coping gap. The bigger the gap, the more challenging it may be to cope.

Let's say you have an adult son who is expecting a $500,000 inheritance.

However, you plan on giving substantially to mission work in your state and leaving him only a $5,000 inheritance. When your child discovers this after your death, he is left with a $495,000 coping gap! He may have difficulty accepting a gift that is significantly different than his expectations. (Hopefully he hasn't spent that half million dollars yet!)

It can work the other way too. Let's say your children are expecting, according to their best guess, about $20,000 each. After you're gone, your lawyer contacts them and informs them they will receive $2,000,000 each because of some mutual funds tucked away that grew over the years. The surprise and resulting impact—although pleasant—may be difficult for them and their families to deal with.

I have regularly seen this coping gap at work. How can you help your adult children have the right expectations? How can they know your plans? Talk. Communicate. Have a family conference while you are alive. Of the ideas I have presented in this chapter, I think you and your heirs may receive the most benefit from this one.

You see, your family will have a conference. The only question is whether you will be alive to attend. Every family has a family conference in the attorney's office after a death occurs to read a will. Wouldn't it be far better to have this meeting prior to your death? Then you will have an opportunity to teach, share, and explain your reasoning to your heirs. A family conference can be an invaluable time of bringing a family closer together. Parents, children, and grandchildren can understand each other better. Parents can bless and affirm their children. The heirs can see the heart, the passion, and the love of their parents or grandparents. They also will have a proper expectation of their inheritance.

After my wife and I had completed the wealth transfer decision-making process, we set a dollar amount to leave to each child's family. Beyond that, we decided to give a significant amount through a donor-advised fund (a fund to be given to charities determined at a later date). The adult children will be involved in determining which charities receive gifts.

I still feel healthy and strong, but Judy and I have held a family conference with our adult children and their spouses. Our children and sons- and daughters-in-law appreciated being informed about our plans. We chose not to tell them the exact dollar amount they'll receive because that could change in the future. We shared with them how we don't want to see money come in the way of their relationships and our relationships with them. We prayed together and talked together about how the Lord had led our family through the years.

Their input during our meeting helped Judy and me improve our plans. We had initially planned on putting an amount in one donor-advised charity fund with all ten of them (five children and their spouses) deciding where it should go. Instead, they suggested five separate funds so each couple could direct the charitable donations to the ministries they are passionate about. That was a better idea than trying to get agreement (and endure fighting!) among all ten adults if we'd set up only one such fund.

The families who have a family conference, meeting, or retreat to discuss their wealth transfer plans rarely regret it. Communication is the final and very important step for implementing your wealth transfer plans.

CHAPTER 21

Estate Planning Tools and Techniques

Estate planning tools and techniques? I realize you may be tempted to flip ahead to the next chapter. But in the next several pages you'll learn a simple technique to save over $500,000 in federal estate taxes. You can also find out how to receive a stream of income for life while giving to charity. Sound interesting? Then stay with me.[1]

Charitable remainder annuity trusts, foundations, unified estate and gift tax credit, irrevocable trusts—the legal mumbo jumbo can be overwhelming. In my opinion, the perception and fear of complex legal and technical matters explains why so few people implement their wealth transfer plans. They meet with a lawyer or accountant or advisor. They hear technical terms that overwhelm them. So they end up letting the latest draft of their plans gather dust.

If, on the other hand, you turned to this chapter immediately after perusing the table of contents, I urge you to first read the preceding chapter. As I emphasized there, many people approach estate planning tools and techniques too early in the planning process. Your stewardship and financial planning is more competent and complete when you address the decisions such as *to whom* and *how much* you will give before you address the *how*.

Wealth Transfer Planning versus Estate Planning

You may notice that I will use the term *wealth transfer* instead of *estate planning*. My approach is not the norm in most popular media forms, so the use of *wealth transfer* is very intentional. Its aim is much different than estate planning.

I am discussing death in the context of helping you live life to the fullest. In the Bible, Paul tells Timothy of the goal to "take hold of the life that is truly life" (1 Timothy 6:19). I want you to be one of the few, the proud, one who finishes well. Don't let any of the following false perceptions keep you from that.

Objectives of Wealth Transfer	Objectives of Estate Planning
Consider impact on recipients as highest priority	Consider impact on the donor and estate
Implement plans that can (and should) begin now	Implement plans that begin at death
Involve family input now and professional advisors later	Involve professional advisors now and family later
Make stewardship decisions	Make tax-efficient decisions
Bring honor to God	Bring honor to oneself
Transfer ownership	Retain control as long as possible— even beyond the grave

Myths That Keep People from Using Tools and Techniques

"My estate is too small." An estate may be too small to have estate taxes due on it, but there is more to a wealth transfer plan than just the tax aspects. Appointing a guardian to care for minor children is far too important a matter to be left to a total stranger. In addition, a relatively simple will can avoid many of the administrative costs associated with death.

When considering the size of an estate, many people forget that life insurance can add significantly to the estate and may cause not only tax problems, but other problems as well.

One other reason for planning the wealth transfer rather than leaving it for the state court system to handle is that any particular personal effects you want to go to specific relatives or friends must be designated in a will. Otherwise, your intentions mean nothing, and the law of the land will determine who gets what.

"It's too expensive." Many people are "penny wise and pound foolish" and think that a will and other actions necessary for proper wealth transfer and end-of-life planning are too expensive. First of all, that thought may be an assumption and not a fact. You may easily save 10 to 100 times the cost of will preparation in taxes! My recommendation is to get an estimate from those professionals qualified to prepare the documents. Lawyers perhaps receive an unfair portion of jokes (some from me—especially now that I have a son in the profession!). But they provide valuable services by helping ensure your documents are drafted, signed, and witnessed properly. Probably no price is too great to pay for making it easier on friends and family who have never had to experience life without you.

"I don't have enough time." The underlying reason for this myth is probably a fear of death. Many people superstitiously believe that as long as they don't prepare a will, they won't die. Also, many just avoid talking about death. It is a very uncomfortable topic of discussion for them. Again, with certainty, everyone will die, and for the Christian to be superstitious about his or her death is to have a poor understanding of the promises God has made in the Bible.

"I'm not certain about what I want to do." Because estate planning can be a very complex and certainly unfamiliar topic, many do not know how to go about setting those objectives. This is a legitimate concern. However, God promises to provide us the wisdom that we need (see James 1:5). When we are planning for the future, we certainly need God's wisdom.

You can also draw on the wisdom and expertise of others. You may wish to involve a certified public accountant and financial advisor in your estate planning, particularly if it is complicated. As president of Kingdom Advisors, a not-for-profit network of Christian financial and legal professionals, I have worked with many outstanding advisors. For a referral to someone near you, go to the Web site http://www.kingdomadvisors.org.

Where There's a Will, There's a Way (to Protect Your Family)

The most common and basic type of will is known as the "I love you" or "simple" will. This type of will simply states that the first spouse to die leaves everything to the surviving spouse using the unlimited marital deduction. Since all assets are left to your spouse, no estate tax is due upon the death of the first spouse. This is a very attractive will for an estate that is smaller than the size at which estate taxes begin to apply. (For example, $2 million in 2008. See the chart on page 315 for the size in future years.) If the estate is worth over $2 million, a second type of will is commonly used. (See page 320 for details.)

Working with a lawyer to draft a simple will is relatively easy and inexpensive. A simple will allows people to

- Name guardians for their minor children
- Designate beneficiaries for meaningful family heirlooms and other valuables
- Outline their wishes for their funeral or memorial service
- Name executors to ensure the terms of the will are carried out

When simple won't do

Depending on the monetary value of your estate, the simple will may not adequately protect your assets. I will discuss an alternative, the A-B will, a bit later. First, however, let's consider the ramifications of estate taxes and other taxes on larger estates. Some estate planning books focus on the challenges of the super rich and their desire to reduce estate taxes. Such books are usually written on a technical level and focus on complicated trusts, foundations, and techniques. News articles and popular culture often focus on high-profile family feuds. Their typical case study is Dad the Entrepreneur and Control Freak who founded a successful company and is worth hundreds of millions.

Dad the Entrepreneur and Control Freak spends a modest fortune on complicated schemes with Good Ol' Boy Lawyer to keep the Old Wife and her New Husband from getting the riches. Sometimes the so-called estate planning gets messier when there is a remarriage. Dad the Control Freak doesn't want the Old Wife to take all the money away from his New Young Greedy Wife. The Old and Resentful Kids try to influence Dad the Control Freak to exclude the Young Spoiled Kids of New Young Greedy Wife from an equal inheritance. Some of the Old and Resentful Kids have worked for years in the company to get Dad's approval; others have led rebellious lifestyles.

On and on such disputes go, hurting family relations for generations, diminishing the personal drive and purpose of many of the children and grandchildren, and resulting in excessive legal fees and wasted energy.

For the most part, these situations make tantalizing headlines or entertaining movies. These plots do happen in real life, but they represent a small percentage of families and estates. I intentionally developed the previous chapter and this one to apply to middle-class American families as well as to the very wealthy. The typical family in America has more wealth than they realize—along with family relational challenges, bedeviling inertia, and periodic procrastination when it comes to matters related to death.

Will You Have to Pay Estate Taxes or the So-Called "Death" Taxes?

Since 1916, the federal government of the United States has levied taxes on estates. The original and continuing official rationale is that the estate tax prevents the concentration of wealth. In reality, the estate tax is another means of raising revenue for a government eager to spend it. If its aim were to prevent concentration of wealth, then the tax would be based on what each heir receives rather than what the deceased person owned. The estate tax is the same on the deceased person's wealth whether one person receives it or 30 people receive it.

In a technical sense, you do not pay the estate tax. You have to die before it applies. Your estate will pay the tax. That means, of course, that your heirs receive fewer assets than they might have. Here's the equation: Your total assets owned at death minus any estate taxes owed equals the amount available for your heirs. The irritating aspect of the estate tax is that much of your wealth was already taxed when you earned it. Let's say you worked as a teacher for

40 years and diligently saved and invested your earnings. You paid income tax throughout your working life on the wages and interest and dividends earned. If you did a great job of saving and investing to build an account of $3 million, then your estate may have to pay estate taxes too—at very high rates (a minimum of 18 percent rising very quickly to a top rate of 48 percent).

Notice in the last sentence that I said your estate "may" have to pay estate taxes. Despite the bad news that wealth may be taxed twice, the good news is that everyone receives a standard credit from estate and gift taxes. (I have added gift taxes because the estate and gift taxes are related to each other. You can't escape estate taxes simply by giving away everything—because gift taxes would then likely apply.) This standard credit is technically called the unified credit. The amount of the unified credit effective for 2008 is $780,800. This credit will offset the tax on an estate totaling $2 million. So, you can give away or transfer to individuals up to $2 million without triggering estate or gift taxes. Accountants and lawyers refer to this amount as the technical term *exemption equivalent*, but I will refer to it as the lifetime exemption.

> Unified credit: A federal tax credit that may be applied against any estate or gift tax due on any taxable transfers of property.

For many years, the lifetime exemption was $600,000. In response to their constituents, Congress began raising the lifetime exemption in 2000. The Tax Act of 2001 implemented a schedule to gradually phase in an increase in the amount of assets that can be excluded. (See chart below.) In 2009, it will reach $3.5 million. Effective for 2010, the estate tax is entirely repealed. Then, in a strange result of political compromise, the estate tax will be reinstated! In fact, it will revert back to the 2001 rate, or $1 million. (So now, apparently, you must choose a tax-effective year to die!)

UNIFIED CREDIT AGAINST ESTATE TAX

Year	Amount Excluded from Estate Taxes
2002	$1 million
2003	$1 million
2004	$1.5 million
2005	$1.5 million
2006	$2 million
2007	$2 million
2008	$2 million
2009	$3.5 million
2010	Estate tax repealed
2011	$1 million

I mention the future planned chaos in the federal estate tax code to point out that these rates and approaches to taxation are in constant change. The concepts and ideas presented in this chapter will likely continue to apply despite changes in the estate and gift tax rates and in the lifetime exemption. Congress and the president may radically change the nature and amount of the estate tax rules.

The typical family in America has more wealth than they realize.

That's one reason you should periodically review your wealth transfer plans with a competent tax professional.

Let's say Marge Smith, a widow, knows that the estimated assets available at her death total $1.3 million and include her house, CDs, investments, IRA, and life insurance benefits. She made no significant gifts to individuals during her lifetime, so she's not yet tapped into any of her lifetime exemption. The bottom line is this: Her estate will owe zero in estate taxes. (I am assuming a lifetime exemption amount of $2 million for illustrative purposes in her story and the other illustrations in this chapter.) Her heirs will not even have to file an estate tax return because the total value of her estate is less than the lifetime exemption.

FAMILY FINANCE

Luis sat forward on the couch as he emptied Manuel's preschool bag. "I can't believe how much paper comes out of this school!" he grumbled to Victoria. "I have to go through trip permission slips, information about soccer camp, an invitation to an open house at the local Christian school, and a snack list before I even get to the important stuff—Manuel's artwork!" He pulled out one last piece of paper, unfolded it, and started reading. Suddenly he froze.

"What's wrong?" Victoria asked, glancing at him.

Wordlessly, he handed her the paper. She smoothed it out and read:

Dear Parents: We want to inform you of a very sad event in our preschool family. Alex Lopez, father of Luci, a student in Mrs. Hamasoto's class, passed away suddenly on Monday evening. The visitation is this Friday morning at Eldridge Funeral Home. If you wish, you may send a card with your child and we will see that it gets to the Lopez family.

Victoria let the paper drop on her lap. "Alex Lopez? We met him at parents' night. Do you remember? His wife, Anita, was in charge of the refreshments, and he was helping out. I think they have two other young children. How horrible!"

Luis still looked shocked. "To die so unexpectedly . . . I hope he had things in order for his family."

They looked at each other. "We don't have everything in order, do we?" Victoria said slowly. She sighed. "I know I've been the bottleneck for some of it. Every time we talk about choosing a guardian for Manuel and Cristina, I freeze. It's so awful to think of someone else raising them, I have trouble getting past it."

Luis took her hand. "I know. There's

Do Estate Taxes Apply If I Leave Everything to My Spouse?

You can leave an unlimited amount of property to your spouse and your estate will not have to pay any estate taxes. This sounds too good to be true, right? It is true, but there may be a trap. Let me explain further using the concept of lifetime exemption we discussed in the last section.

A *marital deduction* means property that one spouse can transfer to the living spouse at his or her death without paying an estate tax. The amount is unlimited. This means a person avoids all estate tax at the death of his or her first spouse. The same idea applies to lifetime gifts made by one spouse to the other. The *marital gift exclusion* allows one spouse to transfer an unlimited amount to the other spouse before death without paying a gift transfer tax.

As an illustration, let's say Tom dies and leaves his land holdings worth $5 million to his wife, Arlene. Because of the unlimited marital deduction, no estate tax is due upon his death. Sounds good so far, but the trap comes at Arlene's death. Let's assume that she was grief stricken over Tom's death and dies the month after him. Her estate will be taxed. How much of Arlene's

no getting past the fact that someone else's raising our children would never be as ideal a situation as our raising them. But we have to accept that and make the best possible decision."

"You're right." Victoria bit her lip. "And the reality is that if we don't choose and something happens to both of us, we would be putting our children through a terrible ordeal." She shuddered. "I hate to think of the court picking their guardian. What else do we need to do?"

"We need a will," Luis said. "Something that will explain how, when, and to whom we want our assets dispersed. We also need to consider life insurance. I know it's an additional cost, but if something happened to one of us, a life insurance policy would give us enough cash to help us through the initial expenses and confusion and figure out what to do next."

Victoria nodded. "Basically we need

to make sure that the kids will be taken care of, and that if one of us dies, the other won't be in financial panic."

"Right. Do you remember my telling you about the estate planning attorney who came to talk at the men's group last year? I think I can find her materials. Why don't we make an appointment with her for next week?"

Victoria agreed. "Thinking about death is scary to me. But it's far better to plan for it than to be surprised by it."

"Also," Luis said, "it helps me to remember that God will never be surprised. I was reading Psalm 116:15 today, and it says, 'Precious in the sight of the LORD is the death of his saints.' He loves us and he loves our children. If something happens to us, he will still be there to help them and protect them."

"Amen," said Victoria. "That's the ultimate plan for the future."

estate will be taxable? The taxable portion will be $3 million ($5 million less her lifetime exemption of $2 million).

Remember that the lifetime exemption applies to *each* person. Tom has $2 million and Arlene has $2 million that they can exempt from estate taxes, but by transferring everything to Arlene, Tom forfeited his $2 million lifetime exemption. No estate taxes were owed because of the unlimited marital deduction. He didn't use the Lifetime Exemption, it died with him, and his family lost the benefit of it. We will look at how this situation could have been avoided in the following section.

How Do Gifts Affect Estate Taxes?

The estate and gift tax laws state that any gifts (greater than the annual gift exclusion limit, currently at $12,000 per year) made during the last three years of a person's life must be counted in the deceased person's estate. In other words, those gifts are considered, on paper at least, as part of a person's estate and will be taxed if given within the last three years of life. These laws effectively limit "deathbed" gifts or signing over of deeds to reduce estate taxes.

Another important concept with gifts is the *annual gift exclusion*. As of 2007, the annual gift exclusion amount was $12,000. For many years the amount was $10,000 per person.

> Annual gift exclusion: The dollar amount of assets that can be transferred annually from one person to another without incurring gift taxes or using up the giver's unified credit.

Remember that the estate and gift taxation system works together; it is unified. If John makes a single gift of $500,000 in stock to his son, then gift tax is due (because this is more than the $12,000 annual exclusion amount). John can pay the gift tax in the year the gift was made. Or John may choose not to pay gift tax now, but he will use up $488,000 of his lifetime exemption for estate taxes. If John's total estate is expected to be less than $2 million, he can safely use up some of his unified credit because his estate will not owe estate taxes.

How to Save Half a Million Dollars in Taxes

Now that you have some facts, let's see how they might apply.

Although the estate tax seems onerous, the good news is that it is the easiest tax to legally avoid. Minimizing your tax is a valid goal of a good steward, but it is not the most important aim. Remember the tools principle: Estate planning tools and techniques help you accomplish objectives, but are not *the* objective.

Q: Is it true that life insurance proceeds count as part of my estate and may be subject to estate taxes?

ANSWER: Yes—if you own the policy. I understand that it may seem odd that your estate will be taxed on something you never received. Life insurance proceeds made payable to your beneficiaries will be added back to your estate for purposes of calculating the estate taxes.

Let's use an extreme example to illustrate this fact. When Barbara died in 2007, she had $100,000 in a CD and a house worth $250,000. Therefore, her assets owned before death total $350,000. She also owned a life insurance policy for $2 million with her only daughter named as beneficiary. Upon Barbara's death, her estate was valued at $2,350,000. The taxable portion was $350,000 (the total estate value less the lifetime exemption).

Many people wisely use life insurance to provide liquidity at the time of death, to provide for survivors, and perhaps to pay estate taxes. However, keep in mind that unless the ownership is properly structured, the life insurance will be added back to your estate's value when computing the estate tax due. (See page 324 for a tip on how to structure your estate properly and avoid this situation.)

If your objective is to give generously to charity and to your adult children, then minimizing taxes supports your objective. Less to the government means more to charity and to your children.

If, after you complete the wealth transfer decisions presented so far, you recognize that the value of your estimated estate is likely to be more than $2 million, then consider the following ideas to save literally hundreds of thousands of dollars in estate taxes. These are simple steps. They are not the most advanced steps, but the KISS principle (of course, the acronym for this principle is from the saying "keep it simple, stupid") reminds us that we do not need to be more complex than necessary to reach our objectives and to minimize taxes.

Maximize the lifetime exemption

You can maximize the lifetime exemption by retitling property between the spouses and passing some property to eventual heirs upon the death of the first spouse. Because each person gets a lifetime exemption ($2 million in 2007), use that exemption. Instead of transferring all your assets to your spouse, transfer an amount equal to the lifetime exemption to your adult children or some organization upon your death. The benefit: Your eventual heirs will get assets earlier and there is less property in the estate of the second spouse. Less property means less tax.

Let's revisit the example of Tom and Arlene, the couple who died within one month of each another. Tom had a total of $5 million in land holdings. These properties were held jointly with his wife. If Tom had changed the title on a few of the properties that totaled $2 million in value so that he owned them individually, he could have mandated through his will that these properties be transferred to his children. The $2 million in transferred assets would have been offset by the $2 million lifetime exemption, resulting in no estate taxes. After his wife, Arlene, died, her estate would have totaled $3 million. After deducting the lifetime exemption of $2 million, only $1 million of her estate would have been taxed. In other words, each spouse would have been able to use the lifetime exemption. (In the earlier example, remember that estate taxes were due on $3 million of Arlene's estate.) Voila! Tom and Arlene's heirs will have saved more than $750,000 in taxes.

> If your objective is to give generously to charity and your adult children, minimizing taxes supports your objective.

While this idea may work in some cases, there may be practical problems. What if the assets are not easily divisible into a portion equaling the lifetime exemption? What if the surviving spouse needs the income from the assets to live on? Because of these practical challenges, you may wish to consider a second way to maximize the lifetime exemption.

Use a marital (or A-B) will

On page 313, we discussed the "simple" will, which is also the one most commonly used. The second type of will, the A-B will, is more appropriate for those who need to maximize their lifetime exemption because large amounts of estate taxes would be due when the surviving spouse dies. This type of will sets up one or two trusts. The objective is to keep a portion of the assets in the estate of the first spouse to die to utilize the lifetime exemption. (Sometimes the resulting trust is called a bypass trust because the principal bypasses the spouse.)

Rather than leaving all assets to the spouse, those above $2 million (or the current amount of assets excluded from estate taxes) are diverted to a trust. The will includes a statement like "I leave everything to my spouse (outright or in trust) except the maximum amount I can keep in my estate and not be subject to estate tax. The amount kept in my estate will go into trust for the benefit of my spouse."

Trust: A separate taxable entity set up during life or through a will to enable an individual to accomplish desired planning objectives.

If you bequeath everything under the estate tax exclusion amount to your spouse outright, the A-B will establishes only one trust—for the assets above that exclusion amount. If the exclusion amount is put in a trust, you end up with two trusts. Refer to the chart on page 322. (The legalese will be much different from what I have stated, but in essence that is what happens.)

If two trusts are included, the terms of the trust that will hold the assets left in the decedent's estate (the first to die) are written in such a way that the survivor has "virtual" ownership of the assets in the trust. In other words, he or she can get income and principal from the trust as needed. Another benefit of the trust is that it provides the surviving spouse with the assistance of a trustee in managing the assets.

By the way, the *trustee* is responsible for managing the estate left in trust in accordance with the terms of one's will. The trustee could be a corporation, such as a bank, or an individual. I typically recommend having an individual trustee because he or she is likely to be more responsive to the needs of the surviving spouse. This does not negate the fact that in many specific cases a bank trustee is preferred. Professional counsel should be sought in making this trustee selection.

The executor and the trustee can be one and the same. The trustee does not necessarily need to be knowledgeable in financial affairs, although that may help. Trustees usually seek outside expert financial advice from a trust department or financial planning firm. The key concerns in appointing both the executor and trustee are the following: Are they trustworthy? Will they be sensitive to the needs of your family? Do they have integrity? Do they have wisdom to avoid being taken advantage of?

The A-B will and marital trust are a common technique used to minimize estate taxes. Although they require a bit of setup work, such documents may save you well over $500,000 in taxes, while giving your spouse the benefits of the income and safeguarding your assets for your heirs.

Begin giving to individual heirs now to take advantage of the annual gift exclusion

As I mentioned on page 304, you may decide that giving to your adult children currently—rather than after your death—benefits them more. If your estate may be subject to taxes, an added reason to give now is the reduction in your estate and, consequently, the reduction in taxes. Every $12,000 gift saves between $4,000 and $5,000 in taxes. Everyone wins—except the IRS.

This exclusion provides an attractive way to remove assets from one's estate with no legal fees or complication—a great example of the KISS principle. For an illustration of how this can work, let's assume that Jay and Carol have plenty of income to live on through pensions and rental income and plan to transfer their wealth to their children and grandchildren. They have three

A-B Will
Example with Two Trusts

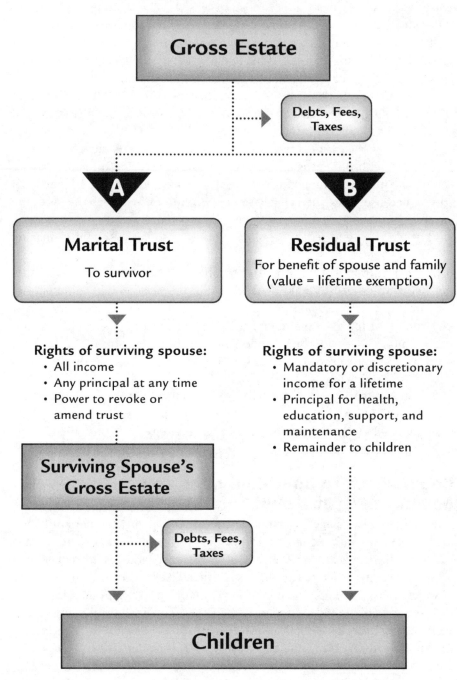

Gross Estate

Debts, Fees, Taxes

A

B

Marital Trust

To survivor

Residual Trust

For benefit of spouse and family (value = lifetime exemption)

Rights of surviving spouse:
- All income
- Any principal at any time
- Power to revoke or amend trust

Rights of surviving spouse:
- Mandatory or discretionary income for a lifetime
- Principal for health, education, support, and maintenance
- Remainder to children

Surviving Spouse's Gross Estate

Debts, Fees, Taxes

Children

children, all of whom are married and have two children. The three children plus three spouses plus six more children make a total of twelve family members. In this example, because both husband and wife can each give $12,000 to each family member annually, potentially they can each give $144,000 ($12,000 x 12 family members). Together they can give $288,000 to their family every year.

This technique—an application of the givin' while livin' principle—can save a very significant amount of estate taxes. I can't estimate specifically how much it would save for you because it depends on how long you live, how long you give, and the number of people you give to. There is one caveat to keep in mind, however: To prevent "deathbed" gifts designed to avoid taxes, U.S. tax code requires that any gifts you give three years or less before your death be applied to your estate.

Give away assets that will likely appreciate rapidly in value to reduce the future potential value of your estate

This idea is essentially a turbo-charged version of the gift exclusion. Instead of giving cash each year, you could give shares of stock or land that may increase in value in the future. By doing so, you eliminate future growth of your estate and limit estate taxes.

Let's say that in 1988 you bought 600 shares of a growing software company for $30,000. The stock began to increase in value, and you believed that one day this relatively small software company could dominate the technology world. You gave 150 shares to each of your four children at Christmas 1988. Each of those gifts was valued at $9,000—less than the annual gift exclusion. Therefore, no taxes were due at the time of the gift and you didn't have to draw on your unified credit.

Your children held on to the shares of that company, which later did dominate the technology world. If you had held on to the stock within your estate, then all of the increase would be subject to estate tax. But by giving away the stock before it appreciated, you were able to leverage a tax-free wealth transfer. The potential tax savings could range from a few thousand to theoretically a few million dollars given the right circumstances.

> **U.S. tax code requires that any gifts you give three years or less before your death be applied to your estate.**

If you own assets that have already appreciated substantially, it may be wise to hold on to them or use a more advanced technique described later in this chapter. My standard advice is to work with a certified public accountant and/or your lawyer to understand the potential income tax and estate tax impact of giving business or investment property.

Use an irrevocable life insurance trust (ILIT) to exclude life insurance proceeds from your estate

With a wee bit of legal work, setting up an ILIT can save a very significant amount of estate taxes. In simplified terms, here's how this idea works.

The ILIT, that is the trust, owns the insurance policy. You are the insured. When you set up the ILIT, you name the beneficiaries of it. You also name the trustee of the ILIT. You pay the premiums each year; this action is considered a contribution to the trust. The trustee makes sure the premiums are paid, receives notices, notifies the insurance company upon your death, and basically has the power to act on behalf of the trust.

In essence, you have given up ownership of the policy in exchange for getting proceeds to beneficiaries of your choice. Because life insurance proceeds are not taxable for income taxes, your beneficiaries receive the full value of the insurance death benefit. No estate taxes or income taxes are subtracted.

Explore advanced tools and techniques

If you have more significant wealth or special needs, then a whole alphabet soup of creative tools and techniques exist—including the CRT (charitable remainder trust), CRAT (charitable remainder annuity trust), CRUT (charitable remainder unitrust), and CLT (charitable lead trust). If you're interested in finding out more, contact a lawyer who specializes in estates and trusts.

Also, be sure to check with your professional legal and tax advisors to ensure compliance with current tax provisions and avoid any other problems or challenges with your situation. Kingdom Advisors (http://www.kingdomadvisors .org) is a network of Christian professional planners that can also assist you.

> **Your wealth transfer plans should be written in sand, not concrete.**

If you are charitably inclined, keep in mind that many charitable organizations have development and planning offices that work with donors. Many of them provide will and estate planning services at no charge. Although they do, of course, desire that you include them in your wealth transfer plans, their staff members are generally competent and helpful. Many provide annuity payments to you in exchange for your significant contributions.

As you develop your wealth transfer plans, remember that they should be written in sand, not concrete. Their design should always be flexible since your needs, desires, and circumstances may change over time. With that in mind, I urge you to begin making your will and related estate plans. Get your tools and techniques in place to accomplish your objectives. Then talk about these plans with your family.

Using the various tools described in this chapter, you can achieve, and perhaps leverage, a wise wealth transfer. So much more could be done for our churches, our communities, and our own families by using valid, legal, and effective tools and techniques. Don't waste this part of your legacy.

PART 3

Financial Topics and Strategies: An In-Depth View

IN PART 2, YOU CONSIDERED the common challenges in Family Life Cycle Planning. In this unit, you'll learn more about important financial topics applying to all ages and stages of life, such as investing, giving, or taxes. This section also includes information on topics that may be of particular interest to women, including the financial ramifications of widowhood, divorce, and working outside the home. Finally, you'll learn how to determine whether consulting a financial advisor is right for you—and if so, how to find the right one.

This added technical and reference information will enable you to consider your strategies in these key financial areas. In the investing chapters, you'll find a simple explanation of mutual funds as well as important investment strategies. For example, you'll see how to invest in your Roth IRA using a dollar cost averaging strategy.

In the insurance chapters, you'll learn the pros and cons of different types of life insurance. You'll see why you may need long-term care insurance more than life insurance in later life.

Here's how I've organized these topics within part 3:

CHAPTER 22

Investing 101

More people than ever before are investors—even though they may not have an account at a stockbroker's office. In the United States, for example, over 96 million are investing in mutual funds, the majority through a defined contribution retirement plan offered by their employer. As companies have moved away from offering pensions, employees have had to build their own investment funds for retirement. Many of these same people are using mutual funds to save for their children's future education as well.[1]

Contributing to a 401(k) or IRA is almost always a good strategy. However, before making other investments, I advise you to be sure you've (1) eliminated all credit card and consumer debt and (2) set aside three to six months' worth of living expenses. Whether you're currently able to invest into a retirement account or are ready to invest surplus funds, you need to become familiar with this part of your financial plan.

Investing is an activity undertaken with the hope of making a profit. In other words, an investment is something that is purchased with one or two expectations: growth in value and/or a yield or return. An investment is something that can and will be sold when it has accomplished its purpose, or when it can't and won't accomplish its purpose.

> Investment: The use of money for the purpose of making more money—to gain income, increase capital, save taxes, or a combination of the three.

With this definition in mind, we can see that the following do not qualify as investments: home, car, diamond ring, jewelry, or furnishings. Investments are not an end in themselves. Many things may have "investment value," but they are not in reality an investment. Jewelry has value but doesn't provide a yield or return on an on-going basis. It may grow in value, but if a man suggests to his wife that they sell her wedding ring, he's likely to face fierce resistance.

We see many biblical examples of investing, from the wise woman who invested in land and sold it for a higher price (Proverbs 31) to farmers planting seeds (Matthew 13) to the wise servants who increased the Master's resources through shrewd investing (Matthew 25). These are simply more primitive types of investments compared to the sophisticated financial instruments we use today.

In this chapter, we'll explain the basic concepts, terms, and available avenues of investing. In the next chapter, we'll examine strategies and approaches to investing.

Taking Stock of Stocks and Bonds

Every year *Forbes* magazine releases its list of the richest people in the world. It's usually their most popular issue of the year. I suppose we all wonder how much others have. (At worst, the popularity may be explained by a "lust" mentality, similar to the reason that the "swimsuit" issue of *Sports Illustrated* is so popular.)

Many items may have "investment value" without in reality being an investment.

At the top of the annual riches list are business owners like Bill Gates (Microsoft) and Warren Buffet (Berkshire Hathaway).[2] In capitalist countries, owning a successful business is one way of greatly increasing wealth. Owning a business is a challenge. Having an idea, meeting a need, executing a plan to deliver a product or service, making a profit, and staying ahead of competition are very difficult tasks with much uncertainty. In the financial world, we refer to uncertainty as risk. Owning a business involves a high potential for reward—and much risk, or uncertainty.

Not everyone has the opportunity or the willingness to own his or her own full-time business. Many of us do own tiny parts of businesses by owning stock. When I refer to stock, I simply mean a certificate showing ownership in a company. These certificates, or stocks, are traded between people at a stock market. The value of a stock goes up or down depending on the general demand of others wanting to own that stock.

Stock: A certificate signifying ownership in a company.

When you own stock of General Electric Company (GE), you own a tiny piece of the company. You're entitled to a share of the profits and appreciation potential if others are willing to pay a higher price for the stock than you paid. If you own 100 shares of GE, then you own .00000001 of the company.

A bond is a loan made to a corporation or a government agency. When you own a GE bond, you have loaned money to GE. As a bondholder, you're entitled to interest payments and a repayment of the principal.

Bond: A loan from you to a corporation, municipality, government, or church, which promises to pay you interest at a stated rate and repay the face value of the bond.

Stocks tend to go up and down more than bonds. Thus, stocks have a greater reward potential (the good news) and higher risk (the bad news) than bonds. Stocks are also referred to as equity securities and bonds as fixed-income securities.

Investing in stocks: Some basic rules

When asked to summarize their key investment philosophies, most investors—including professional money managers—would have a difficult time doing so. Why? Because the most used investment approach is the "seat-of-the-pants" method. Investment results from this approach are usually mediocre *at best*.

Over long periods of time, the overall U.S. stock market has increased significantly. Various studies have shown, however, that the average individual investor has not realized returns as high as the overall market. The bar graph on page 334 shows that market returns are three times greater than the return actually received by individual investors.

> **Stocks are also referred to as equity securities and bonds as fixed income securities.**

Not many investors have consistently produced returns close to, much less exceeding, market investment returns. With that in mind, here are eight commonsense maxims followed by some of history's most successful stock market investors:

1. **Set realistic, achievable investment goals.** Based on the stock market's past performance and returns achieved by successful money managers, a goal of a 7 to 10 percent annual total return, on *average*, is considered reasonable.

2. **Value wins out.** The most successful investors develop a method of measuring value. A stock is bought only when its price is significantly undervalued in relation to the company's earnings and assets. When a stock is overvalued, it is sold, without exception.

3. **Avoid financial torpedoes.** Don't buy stocks of companies with poor financial quality. These companies have a much higher probability of cutting dividends, declaring bankruptcy, or announcing some other negative surprise. Any one of these "torpedoes" could produce a 50 percent decline in a stock very quickly.

4. **Diversify.** To minimize risk, hold at least 10 stocks in your portfolio and have representation in at least five industries (e.g., oil, utilities, banks).

Q: What's the difference between gambling and investing in the stock market?

ANSWER: There's a huge difference between gambling and investing in the stock market. Even though in both cases you may win or you may lose, gambling is purely a matter of chance, whereas investing should be a matter of wisdom, planning, and professional counsel. People can make investing decisions that are biblically based with professional counsel coming from a Christian perspective—and they still may lose a portion of their investment. But that is a far cry from merely relying on chance in terms of making investments. The lottery is a classic case of gambling and makes no sense economically or biblically.

Proverbs 6:6-8 says, "Go to the ant, you sluggard; consider its ways and be wise! It has no commander, no overseer or ruler, yet it stores its provisions in summer and gathers its food at harvest." To me this is the principle of saving for the future, which is an investment principle. Second, Proverbs 11:14 says, "For lack of guidance a nation falls, but many advisers make victory sure." This, also, is a biblical principle relative to investing that says that professional counsel is a wise thing to do. Investing a little bit over a long time frame, using wise Christian counsel, is much different than gambling.

5. **Don't listen to rumors.** When someone tells you about a "hot tip," it's most likely false, and following it will cause you to lose money. The few times a rumor turns out to be true, you may actually be relying on inside information, which is illegal.

6. **Be patient.** Only buy a stock you are willing to hold for at least three years. Studies have shown that investors who buy and hold stocks for long periods realize better returns than those who trade often. Long-term investing is the right frame of mind. (Of course, the cynic wisecracks that a long-term investment is a short-term investment that failed.)

> **Not many investors have consistently produced returns close to, much less exceeding, market investment returns.**

7. **Exercise discipline.** Develop your own investment rules and *never* stray from them.

8. **Use common sense.** We have all been blessed with a measure of common sense. In evaluating an investment, consider whether it makes sense. If a stock sounds too good to be true, it probably is!

Applying all these rules will not guarantee investment success, but the chances of achieving attractive returns will be much higher. Perhaps as you read this list, you began thinking, *Whew! I don't know if selecting individual stocks is my cup of tea. I don't have the time or the expertise.* Such a sentiment is common. You can have the opportunity of investing in the stock market without having to select individual stocks—by investing in mutual funds. Let's explore the benefits of mutual funds.

Mutual funds: A reasonable alternative to individual stocks

Many small investors start their investing at the peak of the market cycle and find themselves in a prime position for the ride down. Very few individuals are able to accurately pick (or predict) the peaks and the valleys of a given stock or the stock market.

Those who make money investing in the market usually buy when public information concerning performance is at a minimum. With less information they take greater risks, but they also get greater rewards. When the information is the greatest, the investment has usually peaked. Without good sources for timely information and the time and ability to evaluate the data, the chance for reward diminishes for the individual investor.

What's an alternative for the small-to-moderate investor to get in on stock market performance? The answer is a mutual fund. As the name implies, the investments in stock mutual funds go to buy shares of company stock. Money market funds are invested in such assets as Treasury bills and commercial bank certificates of deposit. Their interest rates fluctuate with the prime interest rate. Stock mutual funds generally offer higher rates of return over the long term, while money market funds carry less risk to the investor. They are also a good choice for an investor's emergency savings.

> Mutual fund: A fund that allows people to pool their money into a single investment company, which invests in stocks or bonds to meet any of several investment goals.

One significant advantage of investing in either type of mutual fund is the professional management they offer. Fund managers have access to research sources and work full-time at selecting and analyzing the investments for the fund.

IRA, 401(k), and 529 plans are types of investment accounts that are often made up of mutual funds. Because these funds should be viewed as long-range investments, they are particularly well suited for retirement and college savings plans.

While professional management is never a guarantee for success, many mutual funds have shown consistent performance above market averages for many years. In a mutual fund you are really buying the professional management

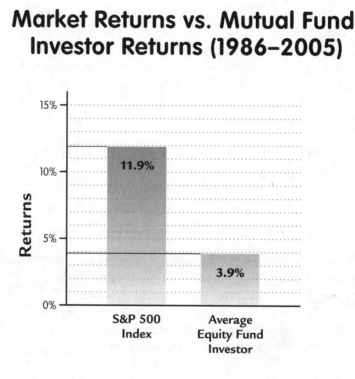

Market Returns vs. Mutual Fund Investor Returns (1986–2005)

Returns

- 15%
- 10%
- 5%
- 0%

S&P 500 Index — 11.9%

Average Equity Fund Investor — 3.9%

Source: Dalbar, Inc.

expertise so you don't need to master the technicalities of picking, tracking, and selling stocks.

Another major advantage of mutual funds is diversification. Typically, the small investor may own two to three stocks. The mutual fund may own anywhere from 100 to 500 stocks in many different industry categories. Diversification gives a measure of safety by reducing investors' risk of loss. Losses on a few stocks are not likely to have a serious impact on the fund's performance.

Mutual funds also provide liquidity. This means shares in the fund can be sold easily, allowing ready access to your money.

Another advantage of mutual funds is that the record keeping is done for you. When the stocks held by the mutual fund merge, split, or pay dividends, the mutual fund keeps track of these transactions. Mutual funds provide simplicity, summarized statements periodically, and regular reports of what is happening in the fund. And as with the stock

> **Studies have shown that investors who buy and hold stocks for long periods realize better returns than those who trade often.**

market, you can track a fund's daily performance on the Internet or, in some cases, in the newspaper.

Many funds offer different options on the use of dividends they earn. You can reinvest them automatically or take them in cash.

Do these glowing advantages mean one fund is pretty much like another? Do they always make money? In both cases, the answer is no.

Different funds invest with different objectives. Some may be growth funds. Professional managers of growth funds concentrate on stocks that may increase in value quickly as the companies grow. Some may be growth and income funds. They invest in stocks that produce income through dividends and have some potential for growth. Other mutual funds are referred to as income funds. These mutual funds may invest in bonds that provide mainly interest income. Your investment objectives will have a bearing on the type of fund you pick.

Funds go up—that is, their shares increase in value—and they also go down. That is why mutual funds should be purchased with long-range investment (five years or more) objectives in mind.

You should evaluate funds on the basis of their long-range performance. This month's winner may be next month's loser. Good funds to pick are those that exhibit consistency in performance in both up and down market periods. They may not always be the top funds, but they also are not consistently among the bottom funds.

Because funds are categorized according to their basic purpose, you need to know your investment goals. For example, long-term growth funds invest in the stocks of companies with rising earnings. Income funds invest in

Fund managers have access to research sources and work full-time at selecting and analyzing the investments for the fund.

companies or bonds that produce high dividends. Sector funds invest in a specific industry, such as health care or gold. (It's usually best to stay away from sector funds, because they tend to have more risk due to less diversification.)

Once you have picked a fund category, the starting point for evaluation is performance history. The performance over the past five to ten years is a good measure to use when comparing funds. Some fund-rating services also publish a risk rating. Beware of picking a fund simply because it is the top fund in a given year—it usually won't do as well the next year. Consistent performance is what counts. Another caution: Past performance does not guarantee future results. The old adage applies: You can never tell which way the train will go by looking at the track. Investing in stocks involves some market risk regardless of how you do it.

All mutual funds charge a fee for stock selection and record-keeping services. The fees for mutual funds are deducted from your investment balance in the mutual fund. These fees, published in the mutual fund's prospectus, are called expense ratios. The typical expense ratio for a growth mutual fund ranges from 1 to 2 percent.

Comparing the annual fees and the experience of the fund managers are two other factors to consider when selecting a fund. Is this fund's expense ratio among the lowest? Does the mutual fund have experienced managers? Have these managers worked for the fund when the historical performance was achieved?

Sometimes mutual funds are categorized by whether or not there is an up-front charge for investing in the fund. A fund that charges an up-front fee—typically anywhere from 3 percent to 6 percent of the amount invested—is called a load fund. Those without up-front charges are called no-load funds. Usually, the no-load funds have higher annual expense charges.

Investing in mutual funds brings two key benefits for the average investor: professional management expertise and diversification.

When you buy a mutual fund, you are actually purchasing shares of the fund (the same as you would shares of a stock). You can redeem these shares at any time. (You'll incur fairly substantial penalties, though, if you tap into an IRA, 401[k], or 529 before it reaches maturity.) By contacting the mutual fund company or your broker, you can receive a check for your proceeds in only a couple of days.

Because mutual funds actually involve buying and selling stocks or bonds, they make money from gains on sales and dividends and interest. Dividends and interest can be disbursed in cash or reinvested back into the fund at the option of the shareholder. Regardless of the option, the dividends and interest are taxed in the year they are distributed. Any gains from the sale of stocks are also taxable in the year disbursed, but at the more favorable capital gains rates.

Our discussion of mutual funds so far has assumed that the professional managers of the mutual fund are researching, analyzing, and selecting the best stock in which to invest. This is true for the majority of mutual funds that are actively managed. Another type of mutual fund is passively managed mutual funds called index funds.

A market index, such as the well-known S&P 500, tries to measure the movement of the overall U.S. stock market. It's made up of 500 of the largest stocks and is weighted according to market value. Thus, General Electric's stock makes up a greater proportion of the index's value than Target because GE is worth more in total market value. Index mutual funds invest in stocks in the same proportion as the underlying index. Their main advantage is a lower cost of professional management—actually there is no professional selection and analysis. A computer program is selecting the stocks, instead of people, strictly through a mechanical process. An index fund doesn't try to determine if Wal-Mart has any future growth potential; it simply buys some of every stock in the index.

Which type of fund is better: actively or passively managed mutual funds? That's quite a heated topic in the investment community—and it has been for years. There's no conclusive evidence. Both can be practical ways for average investors to achieve potential growth. In some time periods, actively managed funds outperform index funds (particularly in downward markets). In other time periods, index funds outperform actively managed funds.

Beware of picking a mutual fund simply because it is the top fund in a given year—it usually won't do as well the next year.

Each year, the fund will send you (and the IRS) a Form 1099 spelling out your tax obligation. If your option is to reinvest gains and dividends, you will still have to pay tax on the dividends and interest—even though you didn't receive the cash directly.

However, funds contained in IRAs, 401(k)s, or various college savings plans have special tax characteristics that allow the investor to postpone the annual income tax recognition until distribution of the accounts.

Understanding Fixed-Income Securities

Besides stock investments, a wise investor will diversify part of his or her portfolio into fixed-income securities. When interest rates drop and investment yields decline, many people begin to look around for a way to improve or enhance that yield. What most investors do not realize—and what many salesmen fail to tell them—is that there is no free lunch. If you chase yields, you are going to face increased risk. Investing in some fixed-income securities, however, lowers the risk to one's total portfolio.

What is a fixed-income security? It's usually a promise by the issuer to pay a stated amount of interest income (yield) either periodically or at a certain future date (maturity) in exchange for the use of the investor's money (principal).

The most common fixed-income securities are certificates of deposit (CDs) and money market funds. More complicated fixed-income investments include preferred stocks, corporate bonds, convertible bonds, municipal bonds and municipal bond mutual funds, taxable bonds, taxable bond mutual funds, United States Treasury issues, Government National Mortgage Association bonds, and savings bonds.

If you contact your local bank about a certificate of deposit, it may promise to pay 4.2 percent (the interest rate, which is sometimes referred to as the coupon) on a $1,000 deposit, the principal amount, on May 1, 2013, the date of maturity. As an alternative, you might consider investing in a money market fund with a current money rate of 4 percent, which is essentially a risk-free yield.

To search for a higher yield involves taking a higher risk. Where is the risk—on the interest rate earned or on the principal? On the principal. But aren't government securities mutual funds (GNMAs) backed by the full faith and credit of the United States government? Yes, but if someone is forced to liquidate his or her portfolio prior to maturity, any gain is contingent on the interest rates rising subsequent to their initial investment. If it hasn't risen high enough, the principal is at risk.

For example, consider $1,000 placed in a long-term bond fund or a government securities mutual fund on January 1, 1987. Soon after, interest rates began to rise. The Fed raised the discount rate, major New York banks raised their prime rate, inflation factors fueled interest rate increases, etc. As a result, many fixed-income mutual funds lost 5 to 12 percent in principal in the following nine months. This means if immediate liquidation was desired, the investor would only get $800 to $900 back on his $1,000 investment. The yield did not change on the original investment—only the principal amount.

FAMILY FINANCE

Nancy Hedrick sat in the nurse's lounge, eating her lunch and flipping through the business section of the newspaper. She paused to skim an article about the market's recent upswing, then turned to the daily stock listings.

"What are you doing, Nancy?" She looked up to see Isabel Yarmen, one of her coworkers, pulling out the chair across the table.

"Just thinking about investments," Nancy said. "Ever since my daughter moved in with me and started paying some rent, I've been building up extra money. It's sitting in my savings account right now, but I'd like to get a higher return."

"That's a great problem to have," Isabel said, smiling.

Nancy nodded. "I agree. It's not money I need for retirement, so I was thinking that I would give it to my grandchildren when they're a little older—maybe when they graduate from college."

"If dollars are still worth anything by then!" Isabel said. "My husband and I started investing in gold three years ago in addition to our other investments in mutual funds. We've heard that even if inflation soars and the dollar loses some of its strength, gold may hold its value."

"I've read a little bit about that," Nancy said, nodding. "I know I could buy coins, bars, or invest in mutual funds that specialize in gold. But I know that the transaction costs can be high

In this instance, the investor would have come out ahead if he had held on to his fund longer. Bond funds recovered some by the end of 1987. Bond funds generally lost a bit in 1994, but had positive years from 1994 to 2006. The weakness in the real estate markets in 2007 and 2008 increased the volatility and risk of mortgage-backed securities.

Are fixed-income investments bad for all people? Not at all. Usually the principal is at risk only if the investment is sold prematurely. If the current fixed-income investments being offered will accomplish the objectives of an investor, he or she should invest without worrying about future interest rate fluctuations.

For example, you might buy a zero coupon bond so that you'll have a predictable amount when your children reach college age. Though the principal value could rise and fall, you have relative certainty that the principal value at maturity will be there when your child enters college.

Buying a one-year CD in April of this year to mature in April of next year as a means of setting aside your income taxes is another good example of using a fixed-income investment to accomplish a purpose. By purchasing a one-year CD, you will get a slightly higher interest rate than you would from a money market fund, and you will have set the money aside so that you are not tempted to touch it. You could also defer taxes on the interest earned in this year until the maturity of the CD next year.

Again, diversification is the key. When making an investment selection,

and storage may be a problem. Hmm . . . I was actually thinking about trying some individual stocks, although I know that there are risks with them as well."

"If you're thinking about giving the money to your grandchildren, what about investing in a company they know about or one that produces something they enjoy?" Isabel asked.

"What do you mean?" Nancy asked, interested.

"Well, if they like soccer, you could buy stock in a sporting goods company, for example. Ellie likes collectible dolls, right? Maybe you could buy stock in a toy company."

"Hmm . . . I like that idea," Nancy said. "If I bought shares for both Dono-van and Ellie, we could make a kind of game of checking the stock price each month and tracking its growth on a chart. It might be a great learning tool for them."

Isabel laughed. "That sounds like fun."

"Yes—although fun isn't ultimately what I'm after. I worked with a financial planner for a while after Joe died. Might be time to call him up again to see what he recommends."

Nancy stood, crumpling up her empty lunch bag. "You're welcome to today's paper," she said to Isabel, smiling. "Maybe you'll find some hidden nugget about a high-flying stock that I overlooked!"

people often mistakenly let current market conditions influence their decision parameters. When they are negative, individuals desiring complete safety from market fluctuations generally buy CDs. Their overall returns, therefore, are lower than they might otherwise be.

Hard Assets, Hard Choices

"Choose my instruction instead of silver, knowledge rather than choice gold." (Proverbs 8:10)

When you listen to the business news, two indicators of our economy are frequently mentioned: what happened to the Dow Jones Industrial Average that day and the spot price of gold. One reason gold is quoted frequently is that it is used as a barometer to indicate the direction people think our economy is going. In addition it provides a tangible measure of wealth.

Although I don't think that gold and silver should comprise more than 5 percent of your total portfolio, two strategies come to mind when purchasing gold and silver. The first strategy is buying and trading it for investment purposes. My advice is to avoid this. I have several friends who lost money during the silver run-up of the late 1970s. With a tenfold increase, people became crazed with the excitement of potential profits. For the vast majority of readers, however, trading in gold and silver does not make sense. Novices are no match against professionals who control this volatile and active market.

The second strategy is to buy gold as a "wealth preserver." This is a valid approach. Gold will protect your purchasing power in times of runaway inflation. In the early 1900s you could have bought a man's dress suit for either a $20 gold coin or a $20 bill. Let's suppose you had that same $20 gold coin today and a $20 bill. The $20 gold coin will still allow you to buy the man's suit—probably the best one available—while the $20 bill may not even pay for a shirt. Gold has indeed preserved purchasing power through the years.

While the long-lasting purchasing power of gold is exciting, there's also a very unexciting side to gold and silver as an investment. It just sits there; it doesn't earn you any interest; you don't show it to your friends. You just hide it and then worry about it if it isn't in a safe deposit box.

Years ago I placed some of my hard-earned money in gold and silver. I then proceeded to watch the real estate market take off with inflation. After the real estate market cooled down, the stock market began its great bull surge in the early 1980s. Even the interest on my money market funds over the last few years outperformed gold and silver. Many times during that period I was tempted to switch into something that could earn more money, but I had to remind myself constantly that I originally purchased the gold and silver as a long-term investment and an inflation protector.

The most frequently asked question regarding investing in gold and silver is, "How do I begin?" The second most frequently asked question is, "Should I take possession?" It seems that many Christians are fearful that an economic collapse, political upheaval, or other form of judgment will hit our country. If you believe this, then the best way for you to invest is to take possession of your gold and silver and put it in a safe deposit box. You can even bury it in your backyard if you don't trust banks, but I don't recommend that.

If you purchase gold, I recommend gold coins such as the Canadian Maple Leaf, the South African Krugerrand, or the Chinese Panda. Before purchasing U.S. coins, compare coin shops in your area, or write to the U.S. Mint. These gold coins usually trade at a slight 3 percent to 5 percent premium above the meltdown bullion content of the gold itself. This premium represents some collectible value.

If you wish to invest in silver, I recommend buying either junk silver coins or silver bars. Junk silver coins are dimes, quarters, and half dollars minted prior to 1965, when the U.S. coins were real silver instead of today's alloys. There is a premium above the meltdown value of the coins, and it fluctuates according to demand.

Silver bars come in one-ounce, 10-ounce, and 100-ounce sizes. A 100-ounce bar at $8 per ounce should cost about $850 with shipping and handling. Only buy bars that have well-recognized mint marks such as Credit Suisse. If you own these types of bars, you can sell them readily without having them assayed (professionally appraised).

If you would like to invest in gold or silver but don't want to take possession and don't think that a monetary collapse is just around the corner, then consider a gold-oriented mutual fund. These funds tend to be volatile and can lose or gain as much as 50 percent in a year. That is fine if you invest with a long-term perspective. If you hold the funds long term, they should accomplish your objective of preserving wealth.

Buying gold as a "wealth preserver" is a valid approach, since it will protect your purchasing power in times of runaway inflation.

I bought each of my children a set of uncirculated or proof coins each year from the time they were born until they graduated from college, when I gave them their sets. I hoped that this would be a training tool for them and that they would continue collecting on their own. For very little initial investment, I was able to turn something of significant value over to them.

Please note that I am not an expert in precious metals, and these tips are based on my opinions. I have tried to present a balanced approach between the "gold bugs" who think that gold is the only investment a person should pursue and those who don't like gold and silver because of their unexciting nature and the discipline it takes to buy and hold them. With any investment, a balanced approach is best.

Tips for Tax-Advantaged Investing

The "perfect investment" has a high rate of return, low risk, and tax-free proceeds. But of course, to achieve all that is impossible! We've looked at some investment vehicles that offer varying rates of return and risk. Now let's focus on several tried-and-true methods of investing in a tax-advantaged manner. There are two types of tax-advantaged investments. One has *tax-free income*; the second has *tax-deferred characteristics*.

Tax-free income investments

Tax-free income from an investment is simply income that is not taxed at the federal, and in some cases the state, level. Why is tax-free income a good investment? A tax-free yield of 6 percent in the tax bracket of 35 percent equates to the yield on a 9.2 percent taxable investment. One approach for tax-free investing is to consider the tax equivalent yield or the before-tax return.

Tax-free investments usually come in four well-known forms:

Tax-free money market funds. The net asset value per share in these tax-free investment vehicles does not fluctuate with interest rates. If you put $1,000 into a tax-free money market fund, you'll get $1,000 upon redemption plus interest earned.

Recently tax-free money market funds were paying slightly in excess of 3 percent, while the taxable money market funds were slightly below 5 percent. Therefore, an investor would have been better off investing in the tax-exempt money market fund rather than the taxable fund. The monthly yields on these accounts change, and it takes active management to decide the best place to park money.

Municipal bonds. Municipal bonds are obligations usually issued by local, city, or state governments. For example, if a municipality needs to build an airport runway costing $10 million, it issues an equivalent amount of bonds, puts a market rate of interest (the coupon) on them, and assigns maturities of 5, 10, 15, 20, or 30 years. In general, the longer maturity one selects, the higher coupon rate one will receive. The investor takes a bigger risk because the longer the maturity of the bond, the greater the fluctuation in net asset value when the interest rates move up or down. Municipal bonds are somewhat liquid, but if you sell them before maturity, you may get more or less than what you paid, depending on the direction of interest rates since issue.

Municipal bond unit investment trusts. Usually the underwriter in this case is a major brokerage firm that, for example, will assemble a portfolio of $500 million of bonds whose maturities range from four to six years. The shares of this trust will rise and fall during the life of the trust as interest rates fluctuate. The shares are publicly traded. The bonds in the portfolio are not traded but are held for the life of the portfolio. The investor has the assurance that if he holds his shares for this entire period, he will get his full principal back and a stable coupon rate of interest.

Municipal bond mutual funds. These bonds are constantly traded and managed. As the bond portfolio manager anticipates moves in interest rates, he or she may buy or sell bonds for a profit. If the bond manager is astute and can correctly anticipate interest rate moves, shares in this fund have the ability to provide capital appreciation on top of tax-free income to its investors.

Although there is potential for profit, there is also potential for loss. Historically, municipal bond mutual funds have not been one of the better investments for those investors seeking a stable *total* return over a long period of time. However, those who are looking for a source of tax-free income and can afford to hold the shares should consider these funds.

When pursuing any type of tax-free investment, remember to consider the trade-offs. One might give you stability of net asset value, a second might offer predictability of performance, a third might provide greater potential for capital appreciation.

Tax-deferred investments

A tax-deferred investment, while not producing tax-free income, does defer the payment of taxes until some future point. The two most popular are tax-deferred annuities and some types of life insurance. You may be aware that traditional IRAs, 401(k)s, and 403(b)s are examples of tax-deferred vehicles. You hold investments inside of these vehicles. But a tax-deferred traditional IRA is not an investment itself; it just holds investments. These will be discussed in chapters 24 and 25.

Tax-deferred annuities. These are offered by insurance companies. Although they are not insured by the FDIC, they are guaranteed by the life insurance company that contracts with the annuity holder. Annuities have favorable tax characteristics because Congress has passed laws giving them certain advantages. Annuities can be useful when one has a need for tax deferral and has already funded other available retirement plans fully, wants to take very little risk, and has a fairly predictable financial situation in the future.

Fixed annuities pay a set rate of interest according to the terms of the contract. Contracts may allow for the interest rates to be changed by the issuer every six months; some only allow interest rate adjustments every year or two. The insurance company declares that during a certain period of time it will credit, for example, 6 percent on that contract. If interest rates go up, the insurance company may choose to increase the interest rate.

Variable annuities. These differ from fixed-rate annuities mainly because the investor chooses between varieties of investments. These funds have all the characteristics and are often "clones" of well-known mutual funds. Depending on the direction the annuity owner feels the market will take, he or she can move the principal amount between different types of funds, usually at different time periods, once or twice a year as outlined in the contract.

When a contract annuitizes and the annuitant begins to receive distributions, a portion is allocated to the principal and the balance is returned fully taxable. In the case of the tax-deferred annuity, an investor has not avoided taxes but merely deferred them while his or her investment grew at a greater rate than it could have in a fully taxable vehicle.

Life insurance. Although I do not advocate using life insurance as an investment (see more on this in chapter 28), proceeds inside of a permanent life insurance policy grow in a tax-deferred manner. Traditional whole life guarantees that the policyholder will have a certain amount of insurance in effect for a specified premium payment over the life of the contract.

Variable life insurance. This option offers different investment alternatives similar to those in a variable annuity. If the policyholder chooses to invest his entire insurance premium into a growth stock fund and the market goes down, then his future premiums could increase. On the other hand, if over the life of the contract he invests in funds that increase in value, he may build up a greater cash value or death benefit than with a fixed-rate contract.

Single premium whole life insurance. In a single premium whole life policy, the entire premium is paid at the starting date of the contract. One can allocate the premium between different investment opportunities. In certain situations (large potential estates are a good example), tax-advantaged life insurance contracts can be appropriate.

How to Evaluate a Specific Investment

I'm often asked, "How do you evaluate a specific investment?" I usually respond that there is no perfect investment. A perfect investment would have the following characteristics: (1) no risk of loss to the principal; (2) instantly convertible to cash; (3) maximum yield; (4) constant growth in value; and (5) morally responsible.

We live in an imperfect, fallen world. We are not perfect. Our situations or opportunities are tainted by imperfection all around us. Yet there are some questions every person should ask to evaluate his or her motivation and the soundness of his or her decision before making an investment:

- What are my reasons for making this investment? Three good reasons are to
  - ➤ become debt free (Proverbs 22:26-27)

- ➤ provide for my family by meeting future needs and establishing an inheritance (Proverbs 30:25)
- ➤ allow increased giving (Proverbs 22:9)

- Could I be investing unwisely due to an attitude of
  - ➤ greed? (1 Timothy 6:9)
  - ➤ pride? (Proverbs 16:5)
  - ➤ fear? (Proverbs 18:11)

- Am I presuming on the future and creating anxiety for myself or my family? (Matthew 6:25; Philippians 4:6-7)

You need to seek independent counsel in the initial stages of your investment analysis. Answering these questions will help ensure that you are investing for the right reasons and as a good steward. The following questions will help you determine how wise a potential investment is:

- Does the investment fit my long-range plan? How does it affect other areas of my portfolio? (Remember, there is no such thing as an independent financial decision.)
- What is my purpose for making this investment?
- What is the downside risk of the investment?
- Can I handle the risk?
- If the investment does what it says, is it worth the risk?
- What are the alternatives? Am I caught in a binary trap? (The binary trap is when you ask yourself whether or not you should buy a certain investment. The answer is either yes or no. It's best to avoid that situation. You should instead ask yourself: "What is the best use of these funds at this time? What am I trying to accomplish with this investment?" Questions like these will keep you from falling into the binary trap.)
- Will this investment make my portfolio balanced and diversified, or am I purchasing too much of one type of asset?
- Does the broker-dealer (salesman) have expertise in what he or she is recommending?
- Is the salesperson/founder/general partner/promoter a reputable individual? (Here we are not asking whether or not he or she is a Christian. We are asking if he or she is an honest, fair businessperson. When you evaluate investment opportunities, you need to look for honesty in the general partner as well as economic merit in the investment itself.)
- Look at the program's track record. What has it returned to investors in relation to what they have put into the deal?
- Do earlier track records provide legitimate insights, or has the structure of the program changed?

- What kind of a front-end load, or sales fee, will you be charged? (For example, most mutual funds with a front-end load start with 5.75 percent of the dollars invested, which gradually goes down as the amount of the investment increases.)
- What would happen to the investment if any of the key founders/partners died? Would the investment carry on and live up to the projections?
- How will future changes (technology, tax laws, new competition, new trends) affect this investment? Are the assumptions used in the investment proposal valid and realistic?
- How is the deal leveraged?
- Has an appropriate market analysis been prepared?
- What will the investment be worth in five years? Could it be given away then? What would the tax consequences of a subsequent gift be?
- When will I get my investment back? What is my expected return on the investment?
- Will the tax incentives withstand close scrutiny by the IRS?
- What will be the effect of inflation/deflation on my investment?
- What are the terms of the investment? How is it structured with regard to cash flow and income taxes?
- Am I personally liable for anything? (This question applies when considering a small business partnership.)
- Is the business involved in immoral activities that I would not want to be associated with?

If your investment advisor can't or won't answer these questions, get another advisor. By consulting with an advisor to carefully evaluate each investment opportunity in light of these questions, you will more likely make wise investments and maintain good stewardship of your assets. I encourage you to consider each question carefully as you evaluate a particular investment opportunity. If you don't know an answer, find out before investing. Finally, remember that there will always be plenty of investment opportunities, so don't make decisions in haste or with incomplete information.

Making Your Money Work for You

One of my earliest childhood memories is of my family's garden. The company my father worked for provided garden plots for employees, and I remember traveling with my parents to the plot, preparing the ground, sowing the seeds, tending the seedlings, and eventually harvesting the crop of tomatoes, beans, sweet corn, and cucumbers. I can still remember how good they tasted, even though I was no more than four or five years old at the time we had that garden. (I also know we only reaped what we had planted. Never did we have any surprises about what grew.)

The Bible has much to say about the principle of sowing and reaping. In 2 Corinthians 9:6 Paul said, "Whoever sows sparingly will also reap sparingly, and whoever sows generously will also reap generously." (See also John 4:35-38 and Galatians 6:8-9.) There is a lot to be learned from sowing and reaping, and I want to pull out one small part of that principle in talking about delayed gratification.

Delayed gratification means that I give up today's desire in order to save for a future benefit. This principle is critical to financial success because unless you receive an inheritance, strike it rich in an investment, or otherwise receive a windfall, you will not be able to have everything immediately. This can cause frustration if your perspective is totally short term. Delayed gratification requires a long-term perspective and is the key to financial maturity. (Giving up today's desires for future benefits is also a definition of financial maturity.)

To help you understand the importance of this principle, let me illustrate two key concepts: first, the difference between consumptive and productive uses of money, and second, the concept of financial maturity.

Remember the Overview of Financial Objectives chart (in chapter 3, page 41)? This illustrates that only one of the five short-term uses of money provides financially to meet the long-term goals we have. These long-term financial goals are attaining financial independence, paying off debt, providing for major acquisitions such as a home, starting a business, and giving significantly. Where does the money come from to meet these needs? The amount of money spent in the short term must be reduced so that funds can accumulate.

To say it another way, if all your money is consumed by lifestyle and debt in the short term, there is no way to provide for long-term goals unless you receive an inheritance, acquire more debt, receive a higher income later on, or succeed with a get-rich-quick scheme.

The best way to provide for the long term is to spend less in the short term; make saving a little bit over a long time a priority. Think of a tree used for firewood. Once it has been consumed, it is no longer available for building the house or perhaps making paper for a book, both of which continue to produce benefits for a long time.

Financial maturity involves giving up today's desires for future benefits. Without delayed gratification, you'll have no money to meet long-term goals.

The truth of financial maturity is also the truth of spiritual maturity. Christians are willing by the very act of becoming Christians to give up today's desires for future benefits. We live with the hope of eternal reward rather than succumbing to the materialistic philosophy of our society or any other vain short-term philosophy.

> **Financial maturity can be defined as giving up today's desires for future benefits.**

The basic philosophy that I've been attempting to communicate throughout this book is that accumulating a little bit over a long time period will allow you to accomplish your long-term goals. The alternative is to attempt to "get rich quick" and live with the high risk of losing it all. Most persons invest by responding rather than planning. I hope by this point you are convinced that planning your investments is a far more secure path to achieving your long-term financial goals than merely responding to the alternatives presented to you.

The accumulation strategy revolves around planning for a cash flow margin and then determining the best use of this margin. The "best" will depend on four things—your personal goals, the commitments you already have, your personal priorities, and all the other alternatives for spending this margin.

The Investing Hierarchy

Throughout my years as a financial planner, I've used a strategy called the Sequential Accumulation Strategy.[1] That was quite a mouthful, so I've changed the title to Investing Hierarchy. It's a chart, really a stair-step set of recommendations, for the sequential use of your cash flow margin. With this investment strategy, you use the first dollar of cash flow margin to accomplish level 1. After you complete level 1, you move to level 2, and so on. Following the chart is a description of each step.

Investment Hierarchy

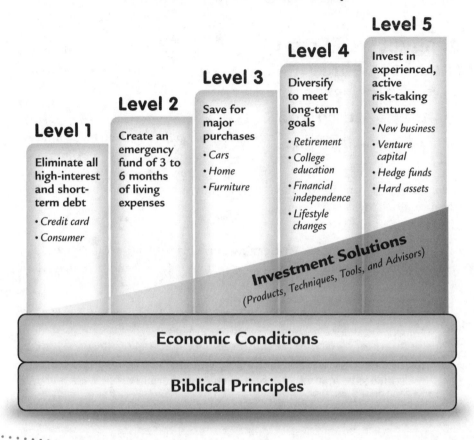

Level 1

Eliminate all high-interest and short-term debt
- Credit card
- Consumer

Level 2

Create an emergency fund of 3 to 6 months of living expenses

Level 3

Save for major purchases
- Cars
- Home
- Furniture

Level 4

Diversify to meet long-term goals
- Retirement
- College education
- Financial independence
- Lifestyle changes

Level 5

Invest in experienced, active risk-taking ventures
- New business
- Venture capital
- Hedge funds
- Hard assets

Investment Solutions
(Products, Techniques, Tools, and Advisors)

Economic Conditions

Biblical Principles

Level 1: Eliminate all credit card and consumer debt. As explained in chapter 11, this step provides an immediate "investment return" of 12 to 21 percent. Not having to pay that interest cost each year is, in effect, the same as achieving the same rate of return on any monies invested by you. This provides the surest and highest form of investment return you can make.

Level 2: Set aside three to six months' living expenses in an interest-bearing money market fund account. This emergency fund becomes, in effect, your own "bank." You can borrow from yourself out of this account rather than from a lending institution when you need to make a major purchase or when you face an emergency or unexpected expense. If you tap into this account for an emergency, replace it as soon as possible. If you have a very secure job and little debt, three months of living expenses may be adequate. If you have a less secure job, older cars, or a variable income (such as that of a commissioned salesperson), then six months of living expenses should be your target. Meeting this level will provide you with flexibility so that you will be prepared for emergencies that may tap your resources or cause further debt.

By the way, levels 1 and 2 should be done in sequence. In other words, you do not go to level 2 until you have paid at least the minimums you've established on your credit card and consumer debt. You should regularly ask yourself, *What's the best use of the next available dollars I receive?* By doing so, you eliminate the need to make a decision whenever an investment alternative comes to you. If you have not already accomplished the first levels, then you let the "investment opportunity" go by. This takes discipline, but it is the right thing to do.

> **Eliminating all credit card and consumer debt is the surest and highest form of investment return you can make.**

Level 3: Save in an interest-bearing account for major purchases. Plan for the purchase of major items such as automobiles, furniture, and even the down payment on a home, using this fund to save for these items.

Level 4: Accumulate to meet long-term goals. The long-term goals of financial independence, college education, giving beyond the tithe, owning your own business, paying off mortgage debt, and major lifestyle changes, as depicted in your financial planning diagram, can be funded through various investment alternatives. These investment alternatives provide a greater potential return to meet your long-term goals and involve more risk, such as investing in mutual funds through your employer's retirement plan. Yet if you have a cash flow margin, an emergency savings reserve, and little or no short-term debt, you're probably able to take more risk.

Level 5: Invest in more experienced and active opportunities. You might choose to provide capital for a start-up business, buy raw land for future subdivision developments, or buy bonds of a distressed company in hopes of a turnaround. Use investment dollars to speculate in higher risk investments. At this point, by definition, every short-term and long-term goal has already been met. I have seen few people reach this step of investing, and many who have completed the preceding levels don't like to speculate because they don't want to risk the loss. They prefer to adopt what I have called the preservation investment strategy.

Remember that achieving this Investing Hierarchy is totally dependent upon having a positive cash flow margin. As you have a positive cash flow, the first priority use of that cash is level 1, and so forth in sequence. This sequence obviously represents my opinion about what the priorities should be; your priorities may be different. If level 4 is a higher priority for you than level 3, that is perfectly acceptable. Just be sure to set your priorities prayerfully and have a strategy to meet them.

Also, you may decide to do your later levels of investing concurrently rather than sequentially. I believe levels 1 and 2 must be met first, but then levels 3, 4, and 5 could be met concurrently with the cash flow margin.

A Philosophy of Investing

When I was involved in our financial planning firm, we were often asked to help a person make an investment, only to discover that he or she had never created a personal philosophy of investing. This is not to suggest that every philosophy of investing should be the same. I've tried to base my philosophy of investing on biblical principles. As shown in the chart below, the biblical perspective is much different than the worldly perspective.

BIBLICAL VERSUS WORLDLY PERSPECTIVE	
Biblical Perspective	Worldly Perspective
Preservation and steady growth of capital (Proverbs 28:20)	Get rich quick
Long time horizon (Luke 14:28)	Short time horizon
Save/invest first (Proverbs 24:27; Ecclesiastes 5:13-14)	Spend/consume first
Time is a tool (Proverbs 6:6; 28:22)	Time is an enemy
Cycles are inevitable (2 Peter 3:4)	Upward trend hopeful
Diversification strategy (Ecclesiastes 11:2)	Timing strategy

I believe that the primary source of wealth or capital for most people comes from accumulation and multiplication of one's annual cash flow margin, or the difference between one's income and expenses. (Although some people receive an inheritance, life insurance proceeds, or a settlement, most must focus on their annual cash flow margin.) It's absolutely necessary that the cash flow margin be a positive number in order to accomplish one's long-term objectives.

I've observed that it's harder to *keep* wealth than it is to *earn* it. Many of my clients earned their income through sophisticated technical and vocational skills. However, very few of them had the professional expertise in investments to know how to build that wealth and make it grow over a period of time. Therefore, I placed capital preservation (not losing the accumulated investments) as a much higher priority than even yield or growth of capital.

I also believe that the most important strategy affecting the preservation of capital is a diversified portfolio. In other words, people must spread their investments among several alternatives so that if any of them suffer, the entire investment portfolio does not suffer. Obviously the trade-off is to give up the potential for hitting it big in a single investment for a modest return on the entire investment portfolio.

Neither a diversified portfolio nor delayed gratification fits the world's mind-set. That creates tension. It takes a regular renewed commitment to do things that are contrary to our natural impulses. The world teaches that happiness is found in a consumptive lifestyle and success in investing is found in achieving high yields. This appeals to our pride.

The world's orientation is toward present circumstances rather than long-term goals. However, investment history indicates that the probability of the loss of capital is greatly reduced, possibly even eliminated, when an investment strategy is implemented with a long-term horizon.

My desire has been to help people become financially and biblically mature. A mature individual is one who is willing to delay consumption, has a proper attitude toward giving, has limited use of (and certainly does not misuse) credit and debt, and has a long-term horizon with a desire to pass this mind-set to future generations. With that attitude, wealth becomes a tool to be used to accomplish God's purposes in one's life rather than to acquire toys to fill one's life. How a person handles the wealth that God has entrusted to him or her demonstrates a measure of maturity—emotionally, spiritually, and financially. This is biblical stewardship: managing the resources of another well.

Because a person's resources are always limited, certain things must be traded off. The classical trade-off is between risk and reward. It is impossible to consistently buy high quality at low prices. Therefore, one can't expect that the yield on high-quality investments will be equal to the yield on high-risk, low-quality investments. One gains safety in exchange for reduction in yield.

If you keep a long-term perspective, then you have plenty of time—not just your generation, but future generations—to compound modest yields. Then you take yourself out of the position of having to predict the future regarding tops and bottoms of market and economic cycles.

The short version of my philosophy: Develop a cash flow margin. Invest for the long term through a diversified portfolio. Keep a long-term, sustainable stewardship mind-set. God cares where and how you invest His resources.

The Most Common Investment Mistakes

Mark Twain once quipped, "October. This is one of the peculiarly dangerous months to speculate in stocks. The others are July, January, September, April, November, May, March, June, December, August, and February."

People make so many (and such creative) investment mistakes that it's difficult to boil down the most common. Many people are extremely ingenious when it comes to thinking of ways to lose money. Admittedly, the mistakes that follow are generalizations, but they should offer some wise warnings.

1. **Envying others who have more.** People often think if they can hit a "home run" with their investments, they can achieve a standard of living equal to their more affluent friends' standards. Do not try to keep up with the Joneses through high-risk investments.

2. **Thinking that this time is different.** Stock market historians can point to many memorable quotes illustrating this mistake. One such infamous statement was made by Irving Fisher, a professor of economics at Yale University, on October 15, 1929: "Stock prices have reached what looks like a permanent high plateau. . . . I expect to see the stock market a good deal higher than it is today within a few months." Soon after, the stock market crash of 1929 occurred.

> **The most important strategy affecting the preservation of capital is a diversified portfolio.**

In January 1987, the S&P 500 gained 13.5 percent in one month. Millions of investors invested a disproportionate amount of their assets and even borrowed money to place in the "surefire" stock market. The stock market crash in October 1987 not only destroyed those previous gains but put many people under financial bondage as they were forced to make payments on borrowings used to buy stock (margin calls).

After the run-up in the stock market, especially on Internet stocks, in the 1990s, many investors became too aggressive, claiming, "The market is different now because of the Internet revolution." The Internet was new and different, but stocks fell in the early 2000s anyway. The declines from 2000 to 2002 were a gut-wrenching experience for many.

What lessons can be learned? First, don't put all your assets in one place. Second, if emotionally you can't stand the risk associated with an investment, then don't make it.

3. **Having no goals.** Investments are tools to accomplish long-term objectives such as children's education or retirement. But investing often occurs just because an "irresistible" deal comes along, rather than because of a decision based on an integrated financial plan. Ask yourself, or your financial advisor, how each potential investment fits your long-term goals.

4. **Making tax-motivated investments.** Although this type of investing has been less common because of tax law changes, many investments have been made in items such as tax shelters simply because of the tax benefits. Think about it: If you saved $1,000 in income taxes but lost $10,000 of your original investment, did you make a wise decision?

5. **Trying to get rich quick.** People often have a "lottery" mentality as a means of reaching financial freedom quickly. Often I see people who think that, even though they have made 20 bad investments in the past, the next one will be the one that makes up for all the rest. The problem is simply greed.

6. **Ignoring the risk/reward relationship.** For some inexplicable reason, people forget the risk/reward relationship when deciding to plunk down their hard-earned dollars. The higher the expected reward from an investment, the higher the inherent risk with the investment. You may be trying to get rich quick, but you have a much higher probability of getting poor quick.

7. **Neglecting unity between husband and wife.** One of the best checkpoints one spouse can have when making investment decisions is determining whether the other spouse understands and agrees with the investment.

   If you and your spouse do not agree totally that an investment fits your family's goals and objectives, then don't do it. God gave spouses to each other in order for them to be complete. Usually, though not always, the husband is by nature more risk oriented and the wife more security oriented. God obviously gave us a good balance, because investments contain both risk and security.

8. **Borrowing for an investment.** Sometimes a deal seems too good to pass up, and people borrow in order to take advantage of such a wonderful opportunity. But as the saying goes, "If you can't afford to take the trip, don't buy the ticket." Nothing feels worse than making loan payments on a worthless investment.

9. **Investing before paying off credit cards.** Remember the risk/reward relationship mentioned in the previous chapter? If you want to get a high rate of return, you have to take high risk. If I could offer you an 18 to 21 percent guaranteed rate of return on an investment, would you take it? Most people would quickly answer yes. If someone pays off his credit card and no longer pays interest of 18 percent, it's the same as making an investment and receiving an 18 percent return on his investment. (As you likely know, I can't offer you a traditional investment offering such a high guaranteed rate of return—and you should be very skeptical if anyone offers you such a deal.)

10. **Investing over the telephone or Internet.** Oil wells, gold and silver mines, penny stocks, Florida land, you name it—all are being sold via e-mail, the Internet, or over the telephone now. And unbelievably, people are actually lured into buying such investments from someone they have

never seen, giving their money to a company they know nothing about. Somehow the promise of getting rich causes people to lose their normally rational thought processes. Would you buy furniture or a car sight unseen?

If you are serious about making investments, don't use the telephone as your resource; instead talk to your accountant or friends whose judgment you trust. If you want to establish a relationship with a stockbroker or investment advisor, interview two or three before choosing one.

11. **Not following the sequential order of investing.** Don't skip levels in the Investing Hierarchy. Instead pay off your debt, achieve some liquidity, and invest in lower-risk investments before you jump to the higher nonliquid investments.

12. **Failing to diversify.** "Don't put all your eggs in one basket" is one of the best investment maxims I have ever heard. Putting all your investment dollars into one investment exposes you to a tremendous amount of risk when the market turns against your investment—and it will.

13. **Accepting personal liability.** Often in oil and gas investments, an investor is asked to place $5,000 down and sign a recourse note or letter of credit for four times his original down payment. The general partner assures the investor that the letter of credit will never need to be paid, but guess what? Many find the investment doesn't quite work out, and guess who knocks at your door then? The bank, wanting payment. Therefore, avoid contingent liabilities.

14. **Failing to understand your competition.** When making an investment on your own, understand that your dollars are competing against investment dollars managed by full-time investment advisors. These advisors are very good at what they do. If you have a full-time job not related to investing, you probably do not have the time or expertise in investing that the advisors do. Logically who do you think will do better—you or the professional? That's why I recommend that most people buy professionally managed mutual fund shares rather than individual stocks.

Don't invest without fully understanding a venture. Investment sponsors are extremely creative in packaging products with bells and whistles that mean absolutely nothing if your investment goes bad. Bond insurance, general partner guarantees, purchase agreements, buy-back arrangements, liquidation provisions, hedging strategies—all of these can be used to give you a false sense of security that an investment is safer than it really is. Investments operate in an efficient market, and risk is directly related to reward. Don't think you can invest in real estate, for example, and avoid the risk of national and local real estate markets, occupancy rates, and competition.

Before making an investment, make sure you have asked all the right questions so that you understand the worst-case scenario. Then make sure you can live with that outcome. Unless it is a treasury bill or a CD, the worst case usually is that you could lose all your money. Yet few salesmen ever point out what could go wrong.

15. Investing so you can give more later. People often defer current giving with the rationale that they will invest the money they should have given, allowing it to "grow for the Lord" so they can give more at a future date. But ministries around the country need money now, and many times this rationale is used as a smokescreen for not giving God the firstfruits. Trust God for increases in the future, and let Him "invest" His money as He sees fit.

> **Before making an investment, make sure you understand the worst-case scenario and are sure you can live with that outcome.**

What should you do if you have made some of these investment mistakes? Learn from them. A $3,000 mistake can be considered a good investment if it prevents you from making mistakes of larger amounts in the future. Everybody makes mistakes, but a wise person will learn from them.

FAMILY FINANCE

Bob looked up from the television as Laura came through the front door. "Hi, honey," he said. "How was the meeting?"

Laura sat down on the couch and kicked off her shoes. "Great!" she said, smiling. "We're official! We have a name—the Parkside Women's Investment Club. We have 15 members, all of whom are from the Parkside Women's Club. We have a president, treasurer, and secretary. We've decided that each member will contribute $75 a month. And we're working on our group's guidelines for ethical investing."

"Really? What does that mean—that you won't invest in tobacco companies?"

"That's part of it," Laura said. "We discussed this for quite a while, actu-

ally. We agreed that we won't buy stock in a company whose primary business objective is related to tobacco or alcohol. That was pretty easy. But it was harder to find consensus on other aspects. Two women felt strongly that we shouldn't invest in any company that manufactures in China because of reports of poor working conditions and the concerns about unsafe products. Three other women are interested in investing in companies they consider environmentally responsible.

Bob raised his eyebrows. "It might be tough to find a company that fits everyone's qualifications."

"That's true. We'll try to respect everyone's point of view, but we'll also have to be somewhat flexible." She

How to avoid "investment amnesia"

Several years ago, I heard a friend had a "surefire" method to get rich quick. He invested in some gold and silver mine stocks listed on the Vancouver Exchange. He had become convinced that this little-known avenue of investment would give him a 60 to 70 percent return in one year based on then-current metal prices and the mine's proven ore reserves. As you can imagine, he wound up losing most of his money. Fortunately, the amount he invested was relatively small, and he didn't borrow to make the investment. He learned a lifelong lesson.

Our human nature usually leads us to rationalize after mistakes. "This time it will be different," we say, and we fail to learn from our past errors. In my years of counseling, I have been amazed at how people who have been burned significantly are still looking for that next good deal. I describe this as investment amnesia.

God knows human nature well. In the book of Deuteronomy, He exhorts the Israelites not to forget the covenant, their experiences, or God Himself. But how could they forget what they had just gone through? They had been delivered from slavery, seen tremendous miracles such as the parting of the Red Sea, and been totally dependent upon God for their food—the manna. Yet God continually had to remind them not to forget: "Only be careful, and watch yourselves closely so that you do not forget the things

shrugged. "The treasurer is going to bring a short list of possible stocks and mutual funds to the next meeting for us to discuss, and then we'll vote on which one to invest in first."

"I'll look forward to hearing what you learn," Bob said, nodding. "Maybe we'll be able to apply some of it to our own investing. We're so close to meeting a few of our long-term goals—like figuring out how to pay for Liz's college education. In three or four years we'll have more money available, and I'd like to put a lot of that into investments. We're pretty well diversified, so we could even afford to take a little more risk with some new investments."

"I agree," Laura said. "But you know,

even a little bit every month can add up to a significant amount. I wonder if the two of us could invest more now just by cutting back on a few services we don't really need anymore."

"Such as?" Bob asked.

"Such as the housecleaning service every other week. Now that Liz is practically out of the house, I think the two of us can handle that."

"And I suppose we could hold off on replacing this old recliner," Bob said ruefully, looking down at his worn chair.

"Yeah, so I guess that means you have to watch TV without a built-in cup holder for a while longer," Laura finished teasingly. "I think it's worth the sacrifice."

your eyes have seen or let them slip from your heart as long as you live" (Deuteronomy 4:9).

The Prudent Investor's Secret: Dollar Cost Averaging

Investors in the stock market or mutual funds have learned that the market can go in one of three directions: up, down, or sideways. But not even the experts can consistently choose the correct direction.

The future of the market is an unknown. It always has been and always will be. With that in mind, is there a method of investing that reduces risk for the individual amateur investor while producing consistent results? Good news, there is! The method is called dollar cost averaging.

> Dollar cost averaging: A method of purchasing securities at regular intervals with a fixed amount of dollars, regardless of the prevailing prices of the securities. Due to the market's fluctuations, this method enables the investor to improve the potential for a gain when he or she sells.

Dollar cost averaging is simply investing the same amount of money in a mutual fund or stock at regular intervals over a long period of time. Let's look at three simple illustrations. Suppose you have $1,500 to invest. You can choose either to put all of it in an investment at once or to make five equal installments.

DECLINING MARKET		
Regular Investment	**Share Price**	**Shares Acquired**
300	25	12
300	15	20
300	20	15
300	10	30
300	5	60
Total: 1,500	75	137

Average price per share over time period ($75 ÷ 5) = $15.00.
Dollar cost averaging price paid per share ($1,500 ÷ 137) = $10.95.

As you can see, the discipline of dollar cost averaging forces you to buy more shares when they are the cheapest. Any recovery above the dollar cost average price of $10.95 produces a profit. You are in an excellent position for a market recovery. If you had invested the entire $1,500 at $25 per share, the market would have to go above $25/share before you realize a profit. You could have a long wait!

STEADY MARKET

Regular Investment	Share Price	Shares Acquired
300	12	25
300	15	20
300	12	25
300	15	20
300	12	25
Total: 1,500	66	115

Average price per share over time period ($66 ÷ 5) = $13.20.
Dollar cost averaging price paid per share ($1,500 ÷ 115) = $13.04.

Not much difference exists here, but remember you have achieved slightly better results by taking less risk; you were not in the market from day one with $1,500 of your money.

RISING MARKET

Regular Investment	Share Price	Shares Acquired
300	5	60
300	15	20
300	10	30
300	15	20
300	25	12
Total: 1,500	70	142

Average price per share over time period ($70 ÷ 5) = $14.00.
Dollar cost averaging price paid per share ($1,500 ÷ 142) = $10.56.

In a rising market, dollar cost averaging provides a limit to market exposure. You buy fewer shares when they are expensive or overvalued.

Three conditions help dollar cost averaging to work:

1. The stock market fluctuates.

2. Over a long period of time the stock market will generally trend upward.

3. You have a disciplined approach and resist taking short-term gains or succumbing to panic selling in declining markets.

In a declining market, dollar cost averaging can position you for handsome gains because you own more shares at the lowest average cost. In a rising market, dollar cost averaging provides positive returns. In any of these markets—whether declining, steady, or rising—you have not exposed

100 percent of your principal to the market, but rather have been earning interest in money market funds on the uninvested balance.

The drawback to dollar cost averaging? It's so simple and structured that you can't brag to your friends about how shrewd you are! Dollar cost averaging doesn't tell you when to sell, but provides a systematic buying process.

A Case Study: After the Crash of 1987

At the time of the October 1987 stock market decline (still the biggest one-day decline of the Dow Jones average), I was immersed in growing a financial planning firm and working with many clients.

For many years an elderly couple had asked for my advice about where to put their life savings of approximately $30,000. This couple was living well within their pension and Social Security income and simply wanted to put their life savings away for the future and protect it against a loss of purchasing power from inflation. For years, I advised them to keep their money in money market funds or certificates of deposit, but they continually pressured me for my thoughts on mutual funds. Finally, in the spring of 1987, I began to feed them some information regarding different mutual funds. I suggested they put a portion of their life savings into three different mutual funds that had a consistent record of avoiding big losses and yet participating in most of the gains of the stock market. We talked about diversification and a long-term perspective, and I told them they should put that money there and forget about it for the long term.

In August 1987, they invested a portion of their savings into the three mutual funds. On October 19, when the stock market fell, theirs was one of the first telephone calls I received. The couple reached me directly because they were my parents. My counsel at that time was not to do anything, because no one really knew what to expect. This was neither the time to panic nor the time to sell.

As you remember, the stock market continued down through December 1987, when my parents finally decided they could wait no longer and liquidated out of all their mutual funds. By January 1988 when the market began to rise again, all of the mutual funds they had liquidated out had come back to their precrash levels. In the next few years, the market and their former mutual funds advanced many times beyond their original level. What happened to my parents was that they bought at the highest possible point and sold at the lowest—a classic case of what happens to most investors in the stock market.

The key issues, however, are not what has happened or where we are today, but rather where we are headed. We do not attempt to predict where we are headed economically, as that is too difficult to do with any degree of certainty. But we do know that regardless of the economic scenario one wishes to project, the four biblical principles explained in this book will always work:

1. Understand the biblical principles of stewardship.

2. Maintain good liquidity.

3. Have a low use of debt.

4. Maintain a nonconsumptive lifestyle.

What about Moral Considerations When Investing?

In recent decades, more investors have been concerned about investing surplus dollars in a way that reflects their values. Their main concern has been to avoid "ill-gotten gain" or profits from companies engaged in immoral activities.

Ethical or socially conscious investing can mean different things to different people. Generally it involves following one's moral principles in choosing specific investments. This trend began to be noticeable in the 1980s. For example, some sincere groups refused to invest in companies with ties to South Africa when the government enforced apartheid policies. Another equally sincere group didn't find South African investments objectionable. Other people wanted to invest only in companies that are environmentally responsible.

This trend became known as "socially responsible investing." Adherents to the socially responsible crowd tended to be focused on the more liberal political spectrum. They wanted to avoid defense contractors and chemical companies but favored companies that offered benefits to couples living together (homosexuals or heterosexuals).

More recently, Christians have expressed interest in investing according to their values. Traditionally, most Christians have not wanted any of their money invested directly in companies with operations in alcohol, tobacco, gambling, or pornography. Some have opposed investments in China, Sudan, or Iran. (To contrast with the term *socially responsible investing*, many began using the term *biblically responsible investing*. Others have referred to it as values-based investing or faith-based investing. The label is not particularly important.)

Does God care about how we invest His resources? I think so. How can you honor Him with your wealth? That's a legitimate question.

While the goal is the same—investing according to one's principles—no matter what it's called, the implementation varies greatly. Many Christians find owning stock in a distillery objectionable. But many would not be uncomfortable investing in a company that makes and sells bottles to various customers, one of which is a whiskey maker. The problem is that when one attempts to invest responsibly, it can drift toward legalism. The danger of legalism is that we begin to substitute outward behavior for inward faith and obedience.

Reality versus perfection

Is there a pure values-based, biblical investment? No, because we live in a fallen, imperfect world. Every time I think I have found the perfectly pure Christian investment, somebody bursts my balloon.

To avoid owning individual stocks that may be objectionable, I recommend mutual funds, which have a wide diversity of portfolios. A mutual fund may own several hundred different stocks. The mutual fund likely owns less than 0.5 percent (0.005) of the outstanding stock of any one company. Let's say the mutual fund owned some of Altria's stock. Altria, formerly Philip Morris, has interests in tobacco and beer, but also owns Kraft and aircraft leasing operations. If you own 0.001 percent (or 0.00001) of the mutual fund, you could own 0.000005 percent of an objectionable company. If you held $50,000 in this mutual fund, then you would have one-fourth of a penny (0.0025) invested in Altria. Is a quarter of a penny wrong? It's certainly different from investing $50,000 directly in Altria stock.

What about values-based real estate investing? Owning a shopping center without a liquor store or a massage parlor as tenants should be okay. But wait, the grocery store chain sells wine and beer, and the center contains a video store, which rents some objectionable DVDs.

Well, surely a CD in the local bank would be acceptable. But that bank could be comingling your CD with other funds to lend money to a doctor who wants to build an abortion clinic. We seem to be foiled at every turn.

A biblical perspective

What does the Bible say about ethical investing? First, we need to consider two types of investments: active and passive. Active investments are those in which we actively own or participate in the management of a business. If the purpose of that business is clearly not honoring to God, then we have a real problem. A second questionable situation to consider is being in partnership with an immoral non-Christian, and therefore be unequally yoked (2 Corinthians 6:14). Someone who is yoked can be controlled, and no one should be controlled by an investment or business partner who would force compromise.

God gives us obvious guidelines on how to allocate our resources in activities in which we are actively involved to make a profit. But what about passive investing—those investments I have no control over? I personally see nothing wrong in passive investment such as a mutual fund, real estate, or banks whose stated purpose does not disagree with any of God's principles and whose only "violations" are solely incidental to the operation of the investment.

Some people go further and look for investments that have the express purpose of avoiding all alcohol, tobacco, and gambling stocks. The objection I have found with many of those funds, however, is that their performance is not as good as a broadly diversified mutual fund.

A practical approach

In response to questions about this issue, I've responded, "Some friends whom I respect attempt to invest according to their values by positive and negative screening. I have other friends whom I respect who say that they do no screening and believe holding indirect investments is fine. I'm for my friends." While that

Q: I am considering being partners in a business with someone who is not a Christian. I am a Christian and I generally trust this person, but are we unequally yoked?

ANSWER: Second Corinthians 6:14 says, "Do not be yoked together with unbelievers. For what do righteousness and wickedness have in common? Or what fellowship can light have with darkness?" I've read this passage many times before and have thought a lot about it over the years. The principle is that whenever a relationship, be it personal or business, is such that my testimony of Christ's goodness and faithfulness could be harmed, damaged, or mitigated, then I need to avoid that relationship.

Let's apply this principle to marriage, for example. It's very clear that if I, as a Christian, marry a non-Christian—and I marry her for life and for better or for worse—my testimony for Christ is almost certainly going to be harmed or mitigated. In a business relationship, it's similar, but business relationships can be defined contractually. I advise those who are entering into a business relationship, be it with a Christian or a non-Christian, to make the terms very clear and determine ahead of time what circumstances would cause the relationship to end and what the terms would be should that happen. In the business world we call it an exit strategy.

For illustration, consider a Christian ob-gyn who does not believe in abortion entering into partnership with another ob-gyn who is not a Christian. If the non-Christian partner prohibits or inhibits in any way the testimony of the Christian, then it's a very unbiblical and unwise relationship to be in. It can be handled ahead of time by having a buy/sell agreement between the parties and a resultant exit strategy.

God has put me on earth to be a witness for the Lord Jesus Christ. If I am entering into a relationship, I must ask: What is the likelihood of my testimony for Christ being harmed? This question is important because harming Christ's reputation would be unacceptable.

sounds like I'm avoiding taking a position, I'm seeing that Christians may have different viewpoints. Romans 14 addresses these types of issues and encourages believers to not pass judgment on "disputable matters." Romans 14:5 says, "One man considers one day more sacred than another; another man considers every day alike. Each one should be fully convinced in his own mind."

How can we approach this subject practically? First, we should realize that we are *in* the world but not *of* it. God has given Christians a sound mind with which to deal with the world (2 Timothy 1:7). For instance, we should actively avoid business partnerships and investments in which the stated purposes are not acceptable to God. In passive investments, however, use common sense. Find a bank with a good reputation in the community. Ask a bank officer about the types of loans it makes. Find out if the bank has ever been involved in a scandal. When investing in a mutual fund, realize that you are insulated from the management decisions of that fund. Look for funds with a widely diversified portfolio that have dealt honestly and ethically with their shareholders over a long time. If you are investing in real estate, ask the general partner or manager what types of tenants he has in his office building, apartment complex, or shopping center. Consider raw land as an investment, since it has no tenants.

Above all, make a positive investment of your time. People (including myself) often worry about what not to do so much that they don't actively invest even an hour a week in an activity that can have a significant impact in their sphere of influence.

Finally, avoid legalism and tunnel vision. Recognize that we do live in an imperfect world. Your passive investments are merely a tool to provide you return that will ultimately go to fulfill the great commission.

As I mentioned in the previous chapter, there are competing investment objectives. It's impossible to achieve all of these objectives: (1) maximize growth; (2) maximize income; (3) maximize liquidity; (4) minimize risk; and (5) be morally responsible. Using my investments to make a statement of values is legitimate. It may or may not cost me something in the way of return, risk, or liquidity.

10 Biblical Principles for Successful Investing

Throughout these two chapters about investments and investing strategies, you've had a lot to absorb. From the advantages of a mutual fund to dollar cost averaging to diversification, I've covered a lot of territory. As we close these chapters, I encourage you to consider the biblical perspectives on investing, which are summarized in the chart below, one more time. Then determine whether you're satisfied with your own mind-set on this issue.

10 BIBLICAL PRINCIPLES OF SUCCESSFUL INVESTING	
1. Establish written financial goals	Proverbs 20:5; 21:5
2. Seek wise counsel	Proverbs 19:20
3. Cultivate a long-term perspective	Luke 14:28
4. Diversify your portfolio	Ecclesiastes 11:2
5. Strive for consistency; don't make haste to get rich quick	Proverbs 28:20, 22
6. Avoid risky investments if you can't afford the loss	Ecclesiastes 5:13-15
7. Avoid high leverage	Proverbs 22:7
8. Monitor your anxiety	Psalm 131:1
9. Establish limits on the amount you invest	Proverbs 15:16; 30:8
10. Share and discuss your decisions with your spouse	Genesis 2:24

CHAPTER 24

Taxes: Just Doing Your Duty

If there's one cash outflow that everyone is eager to reduce, it's taxes. From ancient Rome to modern civilizations, people have groused about taxes. At times, that grousing results in rather humorous lines. Perhaps you'd agree with actor Arthur Godfrey, who once quipped: "I'm proud to be paying taxes in the United States. The only thing is—I could be just as proud for half the money."

I've often asked myself, *Why is it that we detest paying taxes?* I believe the answer is multifaceted, but the primary reason is that we get no perceived benefit from paying taxes. Only in this area of our finances do we feel that once the money is gone, it is gone forever.

When I was a practicing CPA, I prepared hundreds of tax returns each year and was asked hundreds of times, "How can I reduce my taxes?" I had a facetious answer for that question: "It's easy to reduce your taxes—just reduce your income." It's a guaranteed way to reduce taxes, and there is no audit risk to it. The point is that if your taxes are going up, your income is also going up.

I'm not proposing that we should pay more than we rightfully owe in taxes. There is a big difference, however, between tax avoidance and tax evasion. Tax evasion results in a jail sentence; tax avoidance results in lower taxes, but it almost never results in zero taxes. Tax avoidance is planning wisely and prudently to pay a fair share of taxes, but no more than what is legally owed.

Taxes need to be put into proper perspective, and the proper perspective is that income taxes are levied only when there is income earned. Also, though we may see waste and inappropriate use of some tax dollars, many are spent for services we use. We are not "entitled" to those services for free. If we use them, we must pay for them. Entitlement is definitely an attitude bred by our have-it-all culture, not by God. Check your perspective and thank God for your government.

The typical perspective on taxes found in conversations at the water cooler or coffee shop consists of the following:

- Paying taxes is bad.
- Cheating by the other guy is normal, so a little "fudging" by me is acceptable.
- I shouldn't have to support an irresponsible government.
- I'm paying more than my fair share, but the rich aren't.

As I've considered taxes and worked with them for so many years in my professional life, I've come to these conclusions:

- Paying income taxes is not a "bad" thing.
- Integrated tax planning is critical to long-term financial success.
- A direct correlation exists between income and income taxes due.
- Tax reduction is a legitimate goal.
- Income taxes may be an indicator of God's blessings.
- Income tax planning requires highly specialized expertise.
- Tax reduction should never be the "tail that wags the dog."
- An inability to pay taxes due is symptomatic of poor planning.
- Taxes should never be a source of cash flow problems.
- Tax reduction and debt reduction are in direct conflict with one another.
- Getting a large refund check may be a sign of poor stewardship.

In addition to my facetious but true suggestion that the way to lower taxes is to lower income, I offer a second guaranteed way to reduce taxes: Spend all your money on deductible items, such as charitable contributions, medical bills, mortgage interest, and IRA/401(k) contributions. There is no such thing as a free tax deduction. If you are in the 15 percent tax bracket, then a dollar spent on a deductible item costs you 85 cents cash out of pocket. True, it reduces your taxes, but there has been a cost to it. I can state unequivocally that there is no free tax deduction anywhere, at any time, for anything! When you read or hear of persons who pay no taxes or who pay low taxes and have huge incomes, that may be true in the short term because of their high deductions, but those deductions have to be paid for at some time.

Integrated tax planning is critical to long-term financial success.

Here's a piece of advice for tax deductions: Don't ever expect to get a free tax deduction, and never make a financial decision on the basis of its tax deductibility.

My second piece of advice is to avoid getting a large refund check. It's a sign of poor stewardship. It's easy for a tax accountant to make a client happy by having him overpay on withholdings and quarterly tax estimates during the year so that he always gets a refund. I don't believe this is ethical, and it certainly does not make good economic sense.

A refund check means that the taxpayer has planned poorly. The United

States government does not require anyone to pay in tax withholding or quarterly estimates any more than what the taxpayer has determined the actual liability will be. I know that my perspective and advice so far in this chapter may be difficult to deal with if they go against the grain of everything you think and perhaps even the way you plan. For example, many people plan to have that refund check in order to make major purchases each year. What they are really doing is admitting they do not have the discipline to save for that major purchase. You will gain more in interest if you learn to save that money little by little each month from a more accurate withholding. Please remember that tax planning does not have to be a mystery or even very difficult, especially if you understand the above two pieces of advice.

> **A refund check means that the taxpayer has planned poorly.**

What Does the Bible Say about Taxes?

I'd like to think that God has shaped my thinking on this topic over the years. I admit that I had looked in the Bible for years for the verse that says, "Thou shalt not pay any taxes." Unfortunately, I haven't been able to find it; nor have I been able to find a verse that tells me exactly how much I should pay in income taxes. However, I do find a few passages that support the payment of taxes.

> Whoever can be trusted with very little can also be trusted with much, and whoever is dishonest with very little will also be dishonest with much. (Luke 16:10)

> Give everyone what you owe him: If you owe taxes, pay taxes; if revenue, then revenue; if respect, then respect; if honor, then honor. (Romans 13:7)

> "Is it lawful for us to pay taxes to Caesar or not?" [Jesus] . . . said to them, "Show me a denarius. Whose portrait and inscription are on it?" "Caesar's," they replied. He said to them, "Then give to Caesar what is Caesar's, and to God what is God's." (Luke 20:22-25)

Let me apply these verses to our present-day tax system:

• Your choice is fraud or faithfulness. You may reduce taxes by illegal or questionable means, but faithfulness requires you to use good planning and honesty to reduce taxes or to pay the full amount without begrudging where no deductions can be taken. Your objective is faithfulness—not tax reduction. It is God's money. Remember that He owns it all. If He doesn't resent that you have to use some of it for taxes, then why should you?

- Some taxes are certainly due, because our government has supplied services. Quite frankly, the freedoms and protection we enjoy in the United States are unparalleled anywhere in the world, and I believe that we all have a part in paying for these privileges.

- Be a planner—not a responder. It's especially important to plan in the tax area because of the many types of taxes you have.

Render cheerfully unto Caesar what is Caesar's, but no more than he requires.

I think these principles can be summed up by saying, "Render cheerfully unto Caesar what is Caesar's, but no more than he requires."

After considering this philosophical view of taxes, let's turn our attention toward how taxes work. Then, in the next chapter we'll look at some strategies for saving taxes.

Types of Taxes

You are taxed when you earn, when you spend, when you use your phone, when your investments do well, and when you die. As a matter of fact, you are taxed almost any time there is a money transaction.[1]

The complexity of the U.S. tax system is mind boggling. Consider this: The Bible contains 774,746 words. The Internal Revenue Code? More than 2,800,000.

Some of the many kinds of taxes that you pay are

- **Income taxes:** Federal, state, city, and county taxes on income earned.
- **Sales taxes:** Taxes imposed by state and local communities on sales of all types of goods and services sold.
- **Intangible taxes:** Taxes on various intangible properties owned, usually including stocks, bonds, and other investments. State governments generally impose this tax.
- **Use taxes:** Taxes for the use of goods and services provided by taxing authorities, such as gasoline taxes for the use of roads and airport taxes for the use of airports.
- **Estate taxes:** Taxes imposed by the federal government on the accumulation of material wealth when a person dies.
- **Inheritance taxes:** Taxes imposed by state and local governments, again, on estates accumulated.
- **Gift taxes:** Taxes imposed on the transfer of various kinds of property to another person. Gift taxes and estate taxes are typically referred to as transfer taxes. In other words, the transferring of property from one person to another may result in a tax.
- **Property taxes:** Taxes imposed by local authorities on property owned.

- **Social Security and Medicare taxes:** Taxes imposed by the federal government on wages, earnings, and self-employment income to pay for Social Security and Medicare benefits.

This list is not meant to be all-inclusive, but merely to illustrate that you do pay taxes at almost every turn of your financial life. In this chapter I will discuss tax planning in the area of income taxes at the state and federal levels only. It's income tax that's so confounding. I'm comforted by Albert Einstein's words, "The hardest thing in the world to understand is the income tax." In chapter 21, I dealt with estate taxes. None of the other taxes will be covered in this book, because they are difficult to control, except as they relate to other spending decisions.

Income Tax Rates

Two terms must be understood before we discuss tax planning: *marginal tax rates* and *effective tax rates* or, stated another way, *marginal tax brackets* and *effective tax brackets*. When people say they are in a 15 percent tax bracket, they mean that their next dollar of income is taxed at the 15 percent level or, conversely, that their next dollar of tax deduction reduces taxes by 15 cents.

The graduated income tax system in the United States means that various levels of income are taxed at different rates. As the income reaches a higher level, the rate goes up, but it is important to remember that *the rate does not go up on all of the previously earned and taxed income*. It only applies to that next dollar of income. For illustrative purposes I have constructed a hypothetical tax table as follows:

HYPOTHETICAL TAX TABLE

1. If Taxable Income Is at Least	2. Tax on Column 1	3. Tax on Excess (above amount in column 1)
10,000	1,000	12%
20,000	2,200	15%
30,000	3,700	20%
40,000	5,700	30%
50,000	8,700	40%
60,000	12,700	50%

The illustration is clearer when we define some terms.

Taxable income: The portion of your earned income that is ultimately taxed after taking into account all deductions, exemptions, and other reductions such as IRAs.

Tax bracket: The percentage applied to the *last* dollar of taxable income.

If the taxable income in this illustration is anyplace between $10,001 and $20,000, the tax bracket is 12 percent, the percent paid on the last dollar of income.

Marginal rate: This determines the amount that will be paid on the *next* dollar of income that cannot be offset with a deduction.

If a person currently has taxable income of $30,000 and he earns one more dollar of income, that dollar of income is taxed at 20 percent. In this case, his tax bracket and marginal rate are the same. Therefore, his marginal rate is 20 percent, and that stays 20 percent until his taxable income reaches $40,001, at which time the marginal rate to be paid goes to 30 percent. The marginal rate and the tax bracket could be the same but won't always be. The tax bracket is determined by the *last dollar* of taxable income, and the marginal rate is determined by the *next dollar* of taxable income.

The Historical Top Tax Rate chart illustrates how the maximum marginal tax rate has changed over time. Note how low the marginal rate is during the 2000s relative to other time periods. The first thing to realize is that the lower the marginal rate, the less tax motivated any financial decision should be. Second, be on guard, because marginal tax rates can be (and will be) changed at the whim of Congress. What's true today regarding wise tax planning may not be true next year.

Effective rate: The total amount paid in taxes divided by the total income earned.

Let's assume that a married couple earned $59,600 last year. However, they are allowed exemptions for themselves and their children, as well as itemized deductions for medical expenses, property taxes, state income taxes, and charitable contributions. All of these deductions and exemptions reduce the total income down to the taxable income. The income taxes are then computed on taxable income.

If we assume that their taxable income was $40,000, then the taxes that they would pay on the $40,000 are $5,700, which represents 9.5 percent of the total income of $59,600. Therefore, we can say that even though they are in the 20 percent tax bracket and will marginally pay 30 percent, they are effectively paying only 9.5 percent of their income in taxes. *The effective rate is the key number.* It is much more important than the tax bracket or marginal rate. The simple objective in tax planning is to reduce the effective tax rate in order to generate after-tax dollars for any goals that you have.

Living expenses and debt retirement are categories of cash flow require-

Historical Top Tax Rate in the United States

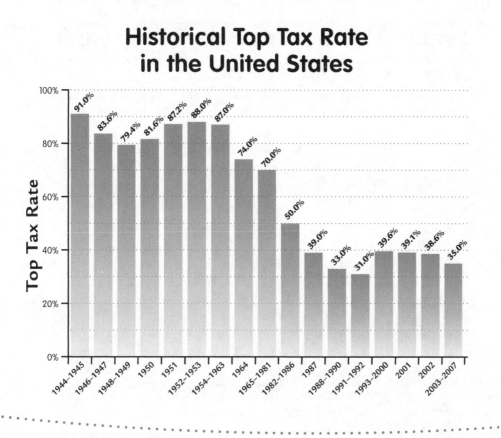

ments that in almost every case are paid with after-tax dollars. Therefore, if the objective is to pay zero taxes, all living expenses and debt retirement must either be paid with borrowed funds or not paid at all.

For example, if a couple decides to pay off their home mortgage of $150,000, that means over time they must generate, after taxes, $150,000 with which to pay that debt. There is no way they can pay the debt with pretax dollars. By the same token, if their objective is to have $30,000 of living expenses this year, then they must generate $30,000 after taxes, after giving, and after debt repayment. The lower the effective tax rate, the more easily this is accomplished. The question is, how can you reduce your effective tax rate? (Remember, the effective rate is far more important than the tax bracket or marginal rate.) In the next chapter, I discuss strategies for lowering your effective rate. First, let's continue exploring how income taxes work.

> **The simple objective in tax planning is to reduce the effective tax rate in order to generate after-tax dollars for any goals that you have.**

Simplifying Your Tax Return Preparation

When the first of the year rolls around and you begin receiving those W-2s and 1099s, here are some tips to help you in organizing that information.

First, obtain a multipocket expanding file folder from your local office supply store. Take some time to label the file pockets using the following headings:

Income:

> Wages (W-2)
> Dividends, interest (1099s)
> Capital gains (losses)
> Other

Expenses:

> Medical
> Taxes (property)
> Interest
> Charitable contributions
> Miscellaneous
> Child care expenses

Special items:

> Closing statements on residence
> Moving expense statements
> Copy of prior year's return
> Partnership K-1s
> IRA contributions
> Rental property statements

If you are self-employed, you will also need to set up a section on self-employment income and related expenses.

Throughout the year, you can use the folder to hold relevant tax information. During January and February you will receive a number of statements from your employer and other financial companies that should be filed in this folder under the appropriate headings. In mid-February you should be in a position where most, if not all, of your information is in hand.

By filing the documentation in the folder, you will be ready to total the numbers for your return. In addition to filing your receipts, you should also spend some time going through all your canceled checks and credit card statements (if any) for the year. Pull out or highlight those items that are tax deductible and file them in the appropriate folder.

By spending the time pulling your data together in an organized fashion, you will actually save yourself time in preparing your returns. Furthermore, if you are using a professional tax preparer, you will save yourself money,

Q: What should I do with old financial records?

ANSWER: Many of us tend to be "neatniks" about that bothersome stack of records we use to prepare our tax returns. But that tendency can sometimes be very costly.

One lawyer, for example, was required by the courts to pay taxes, interest, and late filing penalties merely because he was unable to produce his tax records for the prior year. The courts sustained a reconstruction of his return prepared by the IRS.

Therefore, it's wise to retain your financial records. But the next question is, for how long? In routine tax matters the statute of limitations is generally three years from the filing deadline. This is doubled if the IRS suspects that you have failed to report 25 percent or more of your income. If fraud is involved, or you did not file a return, there is no statute of limitations.

With those limitations in mind, here are some general guidelines on what to retain.

- Keep all canceled checks and supporting documents until you are at least under the protection of the statute of limitations listed above.
- Keep documents relating to the purchase of your home, investments, or other assets indefinitely. This is also true for any improvements you have made to your home. These are required to calculate your gains (or losses) when the assets are sold, which may be years in the future.
- Copies of your prior years' tax returns should be retained indefinitely. This also holds true for canceled checks used to pay the tax liability.

You need four prior years' returns, for example, just to determine if you are eligible for income averaging. Finally, the old returns can often be used to disprove an IRS "net worth" test if they claim your estate is larger than it should be, based on their estimates of your income.

Perhaps the best general guideline that can be given about data that supports your tax return is that it is better to be safe than sorry. It always seems that the one document you don't have is the one to which the IRS gives its greatest attention.

because these documents should significantly aid him or her in completing your return as quickly as possible.

Tips for Realistic Tax Planning

For many readers, complicated tax planning is not an urgent and relevant topic. It may be interesting information (well, perhaps not) but just not applicable. Most people receive annual salaries, which do not allow much flexibility in determining when taxable income can be received or deductible expenses incurred. So what kind of tax planning can you do?

Basic tax planning means avoiding unpleasant surprises. Perhaps the most common surprise involves an individual who unknowingly fills out his withholding form (W-4) so that too little is withheld from his paycheck. Most often this underwithholding condition is not discovered until the tax return is prepared, and then it's too late.

How do you avoid underwithholding? First, check your pay stub periodically for the withholding amounts for the current period and the year-to-date totals. If your payroll stub does not disclose this, ask your employer for the numbers. Then make a rough calculation of what the total withholdings will be for the year. Next, compare this total to your last year's tax return to see how your withholdings stack up against what you had to pay. If your circumstances have changed (your income or deductible expenses changed, or you added or dropped a dependent), you need to estimate whether your withholding is keeping pace with what you will owe in taxes. This simple exercise should help you determine whether your withholdings are close. If not, adjust them as soon as possible.

How do you determine the number of exemptions to claim on your W-4? You can complete the worksheet on Form W-4, but most people find it incomprehensible. Here some conservative guidelines. Take one exemption for yourself (unless you are claimed as a dependent on your parents' return) and one exemption for each of your dependents, including your spouse. If you own a house and pay interest on it, or if your giving is such that you can itemize deductions, add another exemption. If your spouse also works, then have the

FAMILY FINANCE

"That was delicious." Tanya's father, Kevin, set down his fork with a sigh and turned to their server. "I'm not sure I have room for dessert, but I might have some coffee. Anyone else want something?"

"I'll take some decaf," Tanya said.

As the waiter left the table, Tanya's mother, Louise, raised her eyebrows. "Decaf? At lunchtime? You're usually a caffeine junkie. What's going on?"

Tanya and Brian exchanged knowing glances.

"What?" Louise asked again.

"Well," Tanya said, "we were hoping to come up with a more dramatic way to tell you but—" she smiled at Brian— "we're expecting a baby! I'm due December 20."

"Our first grandchild!" Louise squealed. She got up from her chair to hug Tanya.

Kevin reached over the table to grab Tanya's and Brian's hands. "Congratulations, you two," he said huskily. "We're thrilled for you."

"It was a bit of a surprise," Brian admitted, "but we're excited. Tanya's 10 weeks along now, and she's been feeling great."

"We're getting over the shock, and now we're starting to plan ahead," Tanya added. "We're so grateful that we were able to buy the house, thanks to your gift. We have an extra bedroom for the baby, and having a yard will be wonderful when he or she is older. We'll have to decorate the room, of course, but we have some time."

spouse with the lower salary claim "Married but withhold at higher Single rate," and the other claim according to the above guidelines.

Another surprise is the self-employment shock. Wage earners who move from employment status to independent contractor status are basically treated as self-employed. Those who hire them do not withhold any income taxes from what they are paid. Rather, self-employed individuals are responsible to pay estimated tax payments quarterly in order to cover their taxes. However, self-employed people are taxed in two ways: They pay income tax plus self-employment tax (Social Security and Medicare taxes). The Social Security tax is 15.3 percent of their net self-employment (up to certain limits). Income tax on that same amount will be 15 percent, 25 percent, or higher depending on the total taxable income. That means 30.3 percent to 40.3 percent of your self-employment earnings may be paid out in tax. Ouch! Most individuals do not plan for that, spend all of the self-employment income, and end up with significant tax liabilities on April 15, which can include underpayment penalties and interest.

Ongoing planning and monitoring are essential to avoid these surprises. Self-employed individuals especially must keep track of their earnings and make sure their estimated payments keep pace. Any major change in income, marital status, and the number of dependents will affect their tax situation. If you are self-employed, a brief visit with a local CPA will usually help you determine quickly whether you are on or off track and provide you with potential remedies.

"We're also looking at our finances to figure out if we can manage on one income. Tanya would like to stay home, although she's open to working part-time too," Brian explained.

Kevin cleared his throat. "As you're working the numbers, keep in mind that your tax situation will change as well," he said. "You're in a house now, so you'll be able to deduct the interest you pay on your mortgage. That's a pretty significant deduction."

"And you'll be able to claim another dependent this year, which will also help," Louise added. "Assuming that the baby isn't born too much later than the due date."

Tanya groaned. "I hope not!"

"You might have deductible medical expenses too, depending on your insurance coverage," Kevin noted.

"I hadn't thought of those pieces of the puzzle," Brian admitted.

"All of those things will decrease your taxable income, but they will also make your tax return more complicated," Kevin said. "I really encourage you to consider talking with a CPA—now, not just next spring when you're ready to file your return. If you talk to him soon, he'll be able to make sure you're doing the right things so you can take the maximum allowed deductions."

"Good advice, Dad," Tanya agreed. "We'll look into it."

How to Avoid IRS Penalties

If paying taxes feels as painful as going to the dentist, paying penalties is like a root canal without local anesthetic. The IRS can assess various kinds of penalties if you're late, if you're way off, or even if you're not paying in enough soon enough. Let's review the different types of penalties assessed by the IRS:

Failure-to-pay-when-due penalty. A penalty is imposed for the failure to pay income or self-employment tax when due. Generally, this means the failure to pay your income taxes by April 15. This penalty equals 0.5 percent or (0.005) of the unpaid tax for each month or fraction thereof that the tax is unpaid. It's applied monthly against the unpaid balance. The maximum penalty is 25 percent.

Failure-to-file penalty. If you fail to file your return by April 15, you will be assessed a 5 percent penalty of the tax due each month you are late in filing. (The overall maximum penalty is 25 percent.) If the return with tax due is filed more than 60 days late, the minimum penalty is the lesser of $100 or the tax due. (Note: There is no failure-to-file penalty if you file a return late that has a refund.)

Underpayment/estimated-tax penalty. The Internal Revenue Service requires that taxpayers pay their tax liability on an "as-you-go" basis. The IRS does not look favorably on large payments (greater than $1,000) with your April 15 filing. They are as interested in the time value of money as you are (or as you should be). Therefore, they require your liability to be paid evenly on a withholding basis with each paycheck, or quarterly using estimated tax payments.

In most cases, the penalty assessed on an underpayment of estimated taxes is a result of the failure to make estimated payments (or have withheld) at least 90 percent of the current year tax liability, or 100 percent of the prior year's tax liability. (Note: People with higher incomes, defined as $150,000 for married taxpayers, $75,000 for single taxpayers, must pay in 110 percent of the prior year's tax if it is less than 90 percent of their current tax year liability.)

Once you have completed your April 15 tax forms and have calculated your refund or additional tax due, the next step—if tax greater than $1,000 is due—is to calculate the underpayment penalty (using Form 2210). The penalty is imposed on the amount of underpayment of estimated tax at a rate periodically published by the IRS (as of the date of this writing, 8 percent).

Therefore, potentially a person could face a tax penalty for failing to pay in enough during the year, for not paying the amount due by April 15, as well as for failing to file a return on time. In addition, if the return is filed late, these amounts are assessed an interest charge. For example, the interest rate for the third quarter of 2007 was 8 percent. It changes quarterly and is determined by the federal short-term rate plus 3 percentage points.[2]

Besides the above-mentioned penalties related to not paying or filing on time, the IRS can assess additional penalties on a taxpayer, including accuracy-related penalties, a fraud penalty, and a bad check penalty.

The accuracy-related penalty is assessed when there is negligence or failure to make a reasonable effort to comply with the tax law. If you substantially understate income tax (more than 10 percent of the correct tax and more than $5,000) or substantially misstate the value of an item, then accuracy-related penalties apply. The penalty is 20 percent of the underpayment attributed to the negligence or understatement.

The IRS can also assess fraud penalties when there is an intentional attempt to defraud the government in the underpayment of taxes. This penalty is 75 percent of the total underpayment due to fraud. Separate penalties for frivolous returns or frivolous court actions may also apply. The IRS considers the common tax protestor argument of taxes being unconstitutional as frivolous (and taxpayers lose these arguments every time in court).

It's important to understand that penalties accrue in addition to the interest charged on the unpaid taxes. Penalties and interest apply on past due tax. To make matters worse, penalties are not deductible.

If you have reasonable cause, it's possible to request penalties to be waived. Reasonable cause for late filing may include death or serious illness of the taxpayer or an immediate family member, destruction of your house or business, or unavoidable absence (you were held hostage, trapped in a mine, stranded on an island, etc.). You can't have the interest waived, but a waiver request for penalties should include a written statement of the facts and circumstances to the IRS.

Both the estimation of your income tax as well as the timely filing and correct preparation of the return are crucial if you want to avoid paying unnecessary penalties. The IRS has become increasingly severe in assessing penalties and is requiring more diligence by taxpayers to be sure their returns are completed properly.

Hopefully, you will never have to pay any penalties. If you feel you may be subject to a penalty or have been assessed a penalty from the IRS, consult a local tax professional for help in determining the reason for the penalty, any remedies available, and ways to avoid penalties in the future.

CHAPTER 25

Taxes: The Ways It Pays to Plan Ahead

The most popular time for tax planning by taxpayers is December; the second most popular month is April. However, it's too late to do any serious tax planning in either month. Once December 31 has passed, little can be done to reduce taxes for the previous year, except perhaps an IRA contribution. My general observation for tax planning is:

> The shorter the perspective on tax planning, the higher the risk that must be taken and/or the fewer the options that are available.

I believe that most income tax planning should be done at least one year in advance, with monitoring and necessary adjustments made at least quarterly during the year. This means that the tax planning you do on December 31 should not be for the current year but for the next year, so that you are always one year ahead. Tax planning is like a funnel—at the beginning of the year, the options are many, but as you go through the year, the funnel narrows and the options become fewer.

The Four Key Tax-Planning Strategies

Tax planning can be divided into four general strategies: timing, shifting, investing, and use of the tax law. You don't need to be an expert to understand these four general strategies; you merely need to ask yourself four questions:

1. **Timing.** Can I reduce my taxes by changing the year I am to receive income or to claim deductible expenses?

2. **Shifting.** Can I reduce my taxes by shifting my income to someone in my family who is in a lower tax bracket?

3. **Investing.** Can I reduce my taxes through the use of investments?

4. **Using tax laws.** Can I reduce my taxes through the wise use of any additional tax law provisions that I am not now using?[1]

1. Timing strategies

Timing strategies involve deciding when to recognize income and deduct expenses. The general rule is that you should always push income into a future year and pull expenses into the current year. Why? Because even if these actions do not change the tax bracket one way or the other, they do delay the payment of taxes.

Tax planning is like a funnel—at the beginning of the year, the options are many, but as you go through the year, the funnel narrows and the options become fewer.

Delaying income. If a taxpayer is in the 15 percent tax bracket and has the opportunity to delay $1,000 of income, it will reduce the current taxes by $150. But because that income is reported the next year, it increases the taxes paid next year by $150. That may not seem to make any difference; however, the taxpayer, not the government, has use of the $150 for one year and the time to earn interest on it. Previously, we saw how a little bit over a long time period can add up to a great deal through the magic of compounding. In other words, this strategy enables the taxpayer to control the $150 for a longer time.

However, before using this strategy, the tax law doctrine called constructive receipt must be understood. The doctrine of constructive receipt simply says that if you earn the income and have a right to receive it, you cannot postpone the taxes incurred on that amount by merely choosing not to receive it.

For example, a contractor offering his services receives checks near the end of the year, but in an effort to avoid taxable income, he sticks them in a bottom drawer and does not deposit them until after December 31. This violates the doctrine of constructive receipt. He is attempting to use a timing strategy to reduce his income; however, he's engaging in tax evasion, not tax avoidance. He must receive and report the income the year it was given.

There are many legal ways to defer income, such as postponing the work that would generate the income so that the payment received for it is not due until the following year. Also, money invested in a savings type of account, such as a money market fund, is taxed, as the interest is earned on a daily basis. Instead of leaving the money in such an account, you might invest it in a treasury bill that has a maturity date beyond the end of the year. Then the income generated by that investment will be taxed in the subsequent year rather than the current year.

Accelerating deductions. Accelerating or pulling deductions into the current year has the same effect. For example, if a taxpayer is in the 15 percent tax bracket and pulls $1,000 of deductions from next year into this year, the tax liability goes down $150 for the current year and up $150 for the next year.

One of the obvious ways to pull deductions into the current year is to make a charitable contribution in the current year rather than waiting until January. Other ways are to pay for all expenses incurred, but not yet due, prior to the end of the year—for example, interest on debt that has been incurred, medical expenses that have been incurred but not yet paid, property taxes, legal fees, state income taxes, and so on. You cannot, according to the law, prepay interest and medical expenses, but you can bring the payments up to date, thereby deducting them in the current year as opposed to the subsequent year.

My recommendation is that you review last year's tax return and ask yourself the question for each item of income, *Could it have been deferred into the subsequent year?* And for each deduction you took, ask yourself the question, *Could I have pulled more deductions in this area from the subsequent year?* Because of their nature, timing strategies are about the only tax strategies that work near the end of the year. Almost all of the other strategies must be implemented earlier in the year.

2. Shifting strategies

Understanding tax brackets is essential to understanding shifting strategies. The shifting strategies ask the question, "Can I shift what would be taxable income to me to a tax-paying entity in a lower tax bracket? For example, can I shift income from my wife and me, who are in a high tax bracket, to our children, who are in a very low tax bracket, and perhaps pay no taxes at all?" The assumption in using this type of strategy is that you can shift the income and either still retain control of that income or use it for an item that you would have paid for anyway.

Setting aside money for college. Probably the classic example of shifting income is in the area of providing for the college education of children. Often parents will have the opportunity to give their children income-producing assets so that the child can pay the income taxes earned on that income rather than the parent and use the income left over, after paying taxes, to pay for a college education.

> **Timing strategies are about the only tax strategies that work near the end of the year.**

For example, if college education costs are $9,000 per year and the parents are paying that cost, they must earn the $9,000 plus the taxes on that $9,000 in order to have $9,000 left over to pay for the college education. If their tax bracket is 30 percent, then they must earn approximately $12,857 to have $9,000 left over with which to pay education costs.

Recent tax law changes have brought better tax-advantaged ways of saving for education expenses than the classic shifting. The Coverdell Education

Savings Account (ESA) provides tax-free growth if the withdrawals are used to pay education expenses. Parents may contribute up to $2,000 each year for each child/student. The ESA may be invested in various mutual funds. Let's say that a parent contributes $2,000 for one year only. Over time, the investments in this ESA increase to $5,000. When the parent withdraws the $5,000 to help pay for education costs, there is no tax due! The growth is not simply tax deferred, but tax free. The parent, then, has paid for the college education for that year with substantially fewer dollars than had the parent paid the taxes on his or her earnings and then funded the college education with after-tax earnings.

If parents (or grandparents) want to contribute more than $2,000 per child per year, another alternative is the 529 plan. Named after the Internal Revenue Code Section 529, the 529 plans offer tax-free growth similar to the ESA. However, a maximum of $60,000 (under 2008 tax law) may be contributed at once. Contributions to 529 plans are removed from the donor's estate and are no longer taxed if the withdrawals are used for education. Mutual fund companies have teamed up with states to offer these plans. The 529 legal landscape has been changing regularly since their introduction; therefore, I would recommend working with a financial advisor who can guide you as to the best choice.

In addition, many states offer various prepaid tuition programs. Although the various options present more complexity, think of them as a blessing. When I was saving for and assisting my children with college costs, I didn't have these outstanding tax-advantaged plans available. (See chapter 17 and appendix B for more information on saving for college education.)

Gifting. The shifting strategy includes gifting income-producing assets, such as cash, real estate, stocks, bonds, closely held stock and notes, or mortgages receivable, to another family member. Frequently these items are gifted in the form of a trust. The parents and an independent person act as trustee for the child's benefit. The only problem is that the property must be legally transferred to the other person or trust. It cannot be loaned to them nor transferred under any type of facade. A gift must actually be made, and if the gift is large enough, a gift tax may have to be paid.

3. Investment strategies

The basis of every investment you make is to produce more value or more income over time. Income from investments is taxed in various ways and can, therefore, have a great impact on total taxes paid. Income investments are taxed in four ways:

Tax exempt/tax free. The income from some investments, such as municipal bonds, is tax exempt by law. As a result, this income is substantially lower than the fully taxable income earned on similar types of investments.

Roth IRAs, named after the senator who initially proposed the legislation authorizing them, provide tax-free returns. Any contribution to a Roth IRA is after-tax, but any appreciation, interest, or dividends is tax-free. Inside of your Roth IRA you can invest in mutual funds, individual stocks, or certificates of deposit. Roth IRAs are excellent vehicles for retirement and long-term savings. To be eligible, you must have earned income and total adjusted gross income less than $166,000 (2007 limit) for a married couple filing jointly.

Tax deferred. Some investments require that no tax be paid on the income earned until the future. Almost all retirement plans fall into this category, whether it is an employer-sponsored plan such as a 401(k) or 403(b), or one of your own retirement plans such as a traditional IRA, SEP, or another qualified retirement plan. In addition, tax-deferred annuities from insurance companies allow you to earn a return on a tax-deferred basis.

> **Income from investments is taxed in various ways and can, therefore, have a great impact on total taxes paid.**

The value of a tax-deferred investment is that compounding works for you not only on your portion of the income earned on the investment but also on the portion that would have gone to pay taxes, if it had not been deferred. Additionally, when it is time to pay taxes on the investment income that has been generated, presumably the investor is retired and in a lower tax bracket, so therefore, in real dollar terms, he or she will pay less in income taxes. These instruments are excellent ways to avoid taxes now and save for future long-term goals.

Tax favored. Tax-favored investments are investments having special income tax allowances and provisions, again merely as a matter of law and not because of the nature of the investment. For example, dividends from stocks or from stock mutual funds enjoy a favored status. Dividend income is taxed at a maximum of 15 percent—even if a person's marginal income tax bracket is 28 or 31 percent.

Fully taxable. The fourth type of investment is one that is fully taxable and includes almost all interest-bearing types of investments other than those described above.

Remember that anytime there is a favorable tax consequence to an investment, there is a corresponding cost somewhere. For example, in the tax-exempt investments, the cost is that the yield is not as high as in fully taxable investments. In the case of tax-deferred investments, the cost is that the investment is not accessible—unless you pay the penalties for early withdrawals.

4. Use of tax law provisions

The last strategy to use in tax planning is to review the tax law provisions that allow for deductions, deferrals, credits, and the like to make sure you are using

ANSWER: The passage about giving in secret is in the Sermon on the Mount in Matthew 6, where Jesus says, "Do not let your left hand know what your right hand is doing." Interestingly, in that same sermon, Jesus says, "Let your light shine before men that they may see your good deeds and praise your Father in heaven" (Matthew 5:16). I heard author Randy Alcorn explain the apparent conflict by pointing out the difference in motive. The idea of giving in secret or anonymously is very biblical, but at the same time, the world needs examples of Christians who give with the right motives. In other words, people need to see that there are many Christians who understand that God owns all of the financial resources that they have and that they are merely exercising stewardship over those resources. Good stewardship begins with generosity.

As far as taking a deduction on my tax return for charitable contributions, it seems to me that it is poor stewardship not to do so. It's not about giving in secret in this particular case but about wisely using God's resources. The tax return is private anyway. Most churches take great care in keeping donations confidential. To not take the deduction is to give up a legitimate benefit.

all that are applicable to your situation. These provisions are somewhat technical and fill thousands of pages of the Internal Revenue Code, so I will explain only the major categories, and then in each category list some of the tax law provisions that might apply. Review these and seek advice from a professional if you think they are applicable.

Adjustments to income. Adjustments to income are exactly that—certain expenditures that adjust the income reported on the tax form in order to compute what is called adjusted gross income. Adjusted gross income is an important number because some deductions on the tax return relate to that number. The most common adjustments allowable to income are traditional IRA contributions, retirement plan contributions of self-employed individuals, alimony paid (not child support), student loan interest, moving expenses, and teacher's unreimbursed expenses.

Itemized deductions. Some itemized deductions that are allowable are medical and dental expenses (when your expenses exceed a percentage of your adjusted gross income); state and local taxes, including property taxes, income taxes, and all personal property taxes; mortgage and investment interest paid; charitable contributions of either cash or property; and investment-related expenses. Let me point out here that many people overstate, in their minds, the value

Advantages of Charitable Giving

GIVE CASH	
25% ORDINARY INCOME TAX BRACKET	
Sale price	$ 20,000
Tax on gain (Capital gain = 15%)	- 1,500
Given to charities	18,500
TAX ON SAVINGS:	**$ 4,625**
COST TO GIVER	
Stock value	$ 20,000
Less tax savings	- 4,625
ACTUAL COST:	**$ 15,375**

GIVE PROPERTY	
25% ORDINARY INCOME TAX BRACKET	
Given to charities	$ 20,000
Tax savings	- 5,000
Actual cost	15,000
Savings to donor	375
INCREASED GIFT TO CHARITY:	**$ 1,500**

of deductions. For example, I've heard many people say, "I don't want to pay off my mortgage because of the tax benefits of deducting the interest." Unfortunately, many bankers, real estate agents, and accountants perpetuate this myth. On an after-tax cash flow basis, you're better off with no itemized deductions than with them. To get a $250 reduction in income taxes, you must pay $1,000. Your net cash outflow is $750.

I'm often asked whether contributions of time are deductible, and the answer is no. If you do not receive income for the time spent, you already have received, in effect, a deduction by not having the income to report as taxable income.

The most commonly overlooked itemized deductions are

- Expenses paid as a volunteer for charitable organizations
- Points paid on a purchase of a personal residence
- Personal property taxes

Tax credits. In addition to deductions and adjustments to income, the tax law provides for tax credits that reduce taxes dollar-for-dollar, whereas adjustments and deductions do not.

The principal tax credits include the child tax credits, child and dependent care credit for expenses paid by a working couple, adoption credit, college credit, and a contribution to a retirement plan credit.

Tax credits reduce taxes dollar-for-dollar; adjustments and deductions do not.

Special opportunity. The United States is one of the few countries in the world that allows charitable deductions for income tax purposes. One of the principal advantages that our government allows in this area is the deduction of the full fair market value of a gift of property. For example, let's say you purchased stock for $10,000 and it had appreciated in value to $20,000. If you sold that stock and paid the tax on it of, say, $1,500, you would have $18,500 left to give to a charitable organization. The $18,500 contribution would further reduce your taxes by (for illustration purposes) 25 percent or $4,625. The net cost to making the charitable contribution would be the $20,000 property less the $4,625 tax savings, or $15,375.

FAMILY FINANCE

"Thanks for meeting with me, Ms. Hedrick." The woman's voice was kind. "The hospital is thrilled that you're considering a gift. Would you like to tell me about your plans?"

For the past year, Nancy had been considering what would be an appropriate memorial in honor of her late husband, Joe. She had decided on an amount of $10,000 and then had begun considering various charitable organizations that Joe had supported. But none of them seemed right. They could certainly use the money, but it wouldn't be in a way that was specifically appropriate to Joe.

Joe's career had been in medical administration. For years he had worked at the hospital, eventually heading up their human resources department. He had reservoirs of compassion for the hospital's patients, and he worked hard to develop a staff that would be effective, competent, and caring. He

enjoyed his work—but his real passion had been gardening. Every Saturday from April to October found him out in their yard, pruning bushes, weeding beds, or planting annuals. In their backyard he had created what Nancy always thought of as an oasis—a small gazebo surrounded by plants in vibrant colors. It was a sheltered, quiet spot where Nancy loved to sit and think or pray. So as soon as she'd had the idea of giving the seed money for a courtyard garden at the hospital, she knew it was the right way to remember Joe.

Now she looked up at Julie Gordon, one of the hospital's financial officers. "Joe always felt strongly that patients and their families needed some quiet spaces at the hospital—spaces to pray, to be alone, to compose themselves. There are small chapels throughout the hospital, but to Joe, nothing was more peaceful than the outdoors. In his memory, I want to give $10,000 to be-

If, on the other hand, you contributed the appreciated stock directly to the charitable organization, you would receive a $20,000 contribution deduction with a tax savings of $5,000, for a lower net cost to you of $15,000. The charity, in turn, could sell the property for $20,000 and have $20,000 rather than $18,500, and it would have cost the taxpayer $375 less ($5,000 - $4,625) to give a charity $1,500 more ($20,000 - $18,500). Obviously, this is a win-win situation. The chart on page 385 illustrates this opportunity for taxpayers.

How to Estimate Your Tax Liability

As a taxpayer you can take three steps to pay only what you are obligated to pay. First, determine your projected tax liability for the following year as early in the year as possible; second, plan to reduce that liability through the many items discussed here; and third, set the withholding amount and tax estimate amount at the accurate projected liability amount.

To avoid an underpayment penalty, most taxpayers must pay in estimated tax or withholding an amount at least equal to their last year's tax liability or

gin work on a courtyard garden. I want it to be a beautiful place with benches, walking paths, and perhaps a fountain. Joe would have loved it to be colorful and serene."

Julie nodded. "That's a wonderful idea. I'd be willing to recommend that the hospital administration allocate some of the additional cost in next year's budget. Given Joe's reputation at the hospital and in the community, I don't anticipate any difficulty fund-raising the rest. We could call it the Joe Hedrick Memorial Garden—in honor of your gift, but more importantly, in honor of a man we all knew and respected."

Nancy blinked back tears and smiled. "Thank you," she said.

"When are you planning to give the money, and in what form?" Julie asked.

"Next month," Nancy replied. "I want to get it in this calendar year for tax purposes. But I'm not sure I understand what you mean by 'in what form.'

I have stock I'm planning to sell, so presumably I'd just give you a check after I cash it out."

"Well, you may want to talk to your financial advisor about that," Julie said. "Many people find that donating the stock itself, rather than the proceeds from the stock sale, is beneficial."

"Really? Why?" Nancy asked.

"For one thing, the recipient organization receives the full value of the stock, rather than the value minus the tax you pay upon selling it. Also, you can claim the stock's full value as a charitable contribution. Essentially, it often costs you less to give the organization more."

Nancy looked surprised. "I'll run it by my financial advisor and then call you to let you know for sure. But that certainly sounds like a better option." She smiled. "I'm happy to give the money, and I'll look forward to the ground breaking. Joe would be thrilled."

Income Tax Analysis

	LAST YEAR	ESTIMATED THIS YEAR
INCOME		
Salary		
Interest & dividends		
Net business income (Schedule C)		
State tax refund		
Capital gains income (Schedule D)		
Rental and S-Corp. income (Schedule C)		
Other		
GROSS INCOME:	$	$
LESS ADJUSTMENT TO INCOME		
Traditional IRA		
Other (moving, student loan, interest)		
ADJUSTED GROSS INCOME (AGI):	$	$
LESS ITEMIZED DEDUCTIONS		
Medical expenses over 7.5% of AGI		
Taxes		
Interest		
Contributions		
Miscellaneous over 2% of AGI		
TOTAL DEDUCTIONS:	$	$
LESS EXEMPTIONS:	$	$
TAXABLE INCOME:	$	$
FEDERAL INCOME TAX:	$	$
PLUS OTHER TAXES		
Self-employment tax		
Other		
LESS CREDITS		
Children		
Child care		
College		
Other		
TOTAL FEDERAL TAX:	$	$
TOTAL STATE TAX:	$	$
TOTAL TAX:	$	$
MARGINAL TAX RATE:		
EFFECTIVE TAX RATE:		

90 percent of their current year's liability, whichever one is less. (High-income taxpayers with joint incomes over $150,000 must pay in at least 110 percent of the past year's tax liability to avoid a penalty.) As I said earlier, to receive a tax refund is a sign of poor planning. I recommend that you determine your projected tax liability simply by taking last year's tax return and projecting to the best of your knowledge what the numbers will be this year. Use the Income Tax Analysis worksheet.

After doing this, determine if the withholding amounts paid year to date are on track to cover your expected tax liability. If needed, you can adjust the withholding to the newly determined amount. In the tax year of 2005, nearly 100 million taxpayers received refunds (three out of every four returns). The average refund was $2,287.[2] In effect, what they had done was make an interest-free loan to the government.

A Proper Perspective on Tax Planning

Tax planning must be integrated with all other types of financial planning. However, tax planning should not be the "tail that wags the dog"; it should remain the tail. Investment planning requires, first of all, that you make a good investment and then consider the tax consequences, rather than make the investment for tax consequences. That goes for charitable contributions, estate planning, and any other type of financial decision.

Tax planning is very important, but it is not a panacea for cash flow problems. Every decision that causes a reduction in taxes has a corresponding cost associated with it. Therefore, reducing taxes may increase cash flow in the short term, but the cost must be considered. Just remember, there is no free lunch, especially in the cafeteria of tax reductions.

Tax planning can and will change as Congress changes tax laws, as the IRS decides how to administer the law, and as the courts interpret the law. The principles contained in this chapter almost certainly *won't* change as long as we have a graduated income tax system, but the specific application may vary as laws are changed.

One constant in the tax system of the United States is that charitable contributions are deductible. But that's not the only reason to give. In the next two chapters, we'll explore further why to give and how much to give. You'll see how much more there is to giving than the tax deduction.

CHAPTER 26

Giving: A Foolproof Way to Enrich Your Life

Dave is a terrific pharmaceutical representative. He is also a Christian. For several years, he earned $60,000 and dutifully earmarked 10 percent—or $6,000—for tithing.

One year, though, Dave outdid himself at work. His company introduced a blockbuster drug, and he worked harder than ever. With bonuses, he earned nearly $200,000. Faced with a tax problem at the year's end, he sought the advice of a Christian financial planner.

"What do you want to do in terms of your year-end giving?" the planner asked.

Dave explained how he had already given his typical $6,000—which, he figured, pretty much covered him in terms of a tithe.

"No," countered the planner, "the tithe on $200,000 is $20,000. To meet that, you'd have to give $14,000 more."

Taken aback, Dave protested that there was no way he could write a check for $14,000. "God wouldn't expect that!" he reasoned. "He knows I've given already. This is just an unusual year."

The financial planner paused for a moment, then quietly asked a question. "Where," he said, "do you think the $200,000 came from?"

While most of us do not have $200,000 to tithe from, we do share Dave's reluctance to part with "our" hard-earned money. Yet that's exactly what God asks us to do. The Bible never applauds an accumulator. Over and over again, God's praise is reserved for the giver.

On one occasion, Jesus met a young man who wanted to know the secret to eternal life. The fellow had lived a good, clean life, keeping all of the commandments. Yet he knew he still lacked something.

Jesus advised the man to sell all that he had and give the proceeds to the poor. Disheartened, the fellow "went away sad, because he had great wealth" (Matthew 19:22).

Why was Christ so eager to separate the young man from his money? Was

Q: How can our church encourage its members to be better stewards?

ANSWER: If I knew the answer to that question, I'd be in great demand. Throughout the history of the church, the question of financing has always been of concern. My mentor, Dr. Howard Hendricks, used to say, "If there is mist in the pulpit, there is fog in the pews." I interpret that to mean that if a pastor is unclear as to what stewardship is and the benefits of stewardship, he's going to be very unclear when trying to communicate those principles to his congregation. The pastor bears the primary responsibility in his church for having a personal conviction about stewardship and then passing that conviction on to his church members.

My desire is that pastors would better understand what God's Word has to say about giving and the joy of giving. It is to each person's eternal benefit to give generously while he or she has a chance here on earth. Scripture is very clear that there are eternal rewards associated with giving. Jesus talked about it in the parable of the talents. Paul talks about it in 2 Corinthians 8 and 9 and in Philippians 4, where he says, "Not that I am looking for a gift, but I am looking for what may be credited to your account" (verse 17). Pastors need to understand that the people whom God has entrusted to them need to experience the joy and the freedom of a generous lifestyle.

He holding out the promise of heaven like a carrot, as the ultimate fund-raising gimmick?

No. Jesus knew the young man was wealthy—and that he had placed his trust in his own wallet. Until he could bring himself to part with that financial security blanket, the rich young man would never be free to place his trust in Christ. He would never know the true riches and security of eternal life.

Like the rich young man, you have a choice to make. Will you control your money, or will it control you? Our tendency, particularly during financially trying times, is to want to hang on to what we have. As we do that, though, we transfer our trust further and further away from God and deeper and deeper into our own inadequate resources.

Dave's story has a happy ending. The day after their meeting, the financial planner got a call from Dave's wife. "My husband was awake all night wrestling with your question, 'Where did the money come from?'" she said. "Eventually, he got out of bed and wrote a $14,000 check. Then, and only then, did he finally feel free and at peace."

Financial contentment and freedom begin with a willingness to give. Dave recognized this principle, and in making his resources available to God, he received a liberating reward. Giving should be an integral part of every maturing believer's life. Giving is commanded in Scripture for the benefit of both the giver and the recipient. This advantage is readily available to each one of us—whether you make more than Dave or less—once we discover exactly why, and how, we should give.

The money-management objectives we have considered so far—setting goals, following a spending plan, and avoiding debt—are logical supports in a well-built financial plan. Giving, however, is often relegated to a discretionary category. It becomes no more than a noble pursuit that can be postponed until later when funds "become available." Yet giving should not be merely a pillar in your financial plan; it should be a cornerstone.

> **Financial contentment and freedom begin with a willingness to give.**

Where Does Giving Fit in with Financial Planning?

As I've mentioned before, giving is one of the five uses of money. You may think that it's a nonproductive use of money because it doesn't build your net worth like saving does. To the contrary, I think that giving is one of the most productive uses of money.

I struggled early in my family life and early in my Christian life to give generously. I knew I was supposed to give, but I was trying to juggle the other uses of money. Then, because I was a new Christian, guilt would crop up as I wrestled with biblical commands to support the poor and needy—while I sent my own children off to expensive summer camps and signed them up for tennis and piano lessons. And the frustration mounted as, month after month, I struggled to get "control" of my money, wondering whether or not it was already too late to pursue and achieve my financial goals—goals like providing for my children's education and building a nest egg for retirement.

Almost everyone I met grappled with these same kinds of questions, regardless of how much money they had. Most people also struggled with the negative emotions—fear, guilt, and frustration—to some degree. But that didn't make the feelings any more right or desirable. There *had* to be a better way. Instead of fear, I wanted contentment. Instead of guilt, I wanted joy. And instead of a confused frustration, I wanted order, confidence, and peace. How could I make the move?

The answer came over time as I talked with, counseled, and observed my clients and the clients of the advisors in the organization I now serve, Kingdom Advisors. Over the years I have had the opportunity to work with a number of individuals, some middle class and some very wealthy. Many of these people are genuinely happy. Yet the key to their freedom, joy, and confidence is not their money. Having the cash to buy or do whatever they please does not guarantee contentment.

Likewise, the secret to financial contentment is not couched in wise investments, meticulous budgets, or debt-free living. All these things are valuable— yet even the highest investment return or the most carefully constructed budget affords very little in the way of real confidence and joy if one key ingredient is neglected. That one ingredient—and the ingredient that makes true freedom possible—is generosity: the willingness to give your time, talents, and material wealth to benefit others and impact eternity. I've learned and clearly observed that generosity and financial freedom are inextricably linked. The Bible supports this principle.

FAITH & FINANCE

> He who gives to the poor will lack nothing. (Proverbs 28:27)

> Whoever sows generously will also reap generously . . . for God loves a cheerful giver. (2 Corinthians 9:6-7)

The folks who enjoy genuine contentment and freedom are those who give the most, relative to their incomes. Giving is more than just a way to use your money. It is a lifestyle, a way of living that allows you to hold all that you own—including your time and your talents—with an open, generous hand.

Author and speaker Nancy Ortberg tells the story of someone who lived such a lifestyle. Larry was a volunteer with whom Nancy worked while heading Axis, the ministry for young adults at Willow Creek Community Church. After taking early retirement from IBM at about age forty, Larry began volunteering full-time for Axis. He lived on very little but enthusiastically began mentoring the young leaders around him. He once said, "I am an artist, and my canvas is people."

When he died unexpectedly in a bizarre accident while jogging, eight hundred people turned out for his visitation. While friends were cleaning out his apartment afterwards, they found a $50 check from Willow, given in appreciation for his service, on his desk. Attached to it was a Post-it note on which he'd written the name of someone he planned to give the money to. No wonder the Axis staff called their own memorial service for Larry "A Life Well Lived."

These chapters about giving are designed to get you to that place. I want to challenge you, philosophically, to evaluate your willingness and ability to give. I want to teach you how to make sense of all the requests for your money, time, and talents so you can maximize the effectiveness of your giving. I want to help you open your hands.

Five Good Reasons to Give

As I shared in chapter 1, my vision is to enable others, through wise financial planning, to free up more of their resources for giving. I want to encourage people to give generously—regardless of their income level.

I have spent a good deal of time thinking about why people do—and do not—give. What motivates a giver? Is it the strength of some heart-wrenching financial appeal? Is it genuine altruism—the desire to help someone or something? Is it the perceived need for a tax write-off? guilt?

People give for all sorts of reasons. For some people, giving meets an ego need—perhaps as they see their names on a plaque or as they acquire an impressive list of friends or benefactors. For others, giving—usually some token amount—is merely a way to avoid or lessen the nuisance of fund-raising appeals.

Generosity and financial freedom are inextricably linked.

Whatever the motivation, one fact is clear: Financially speaking, giving doesn't make sense. When you give your money away, you always have less of it for yourself. Even the much-ballyhooed tax breaks for charitable contributions do not keep pace with the size of the gifts themselves. If you give $1,000, your tax bill is reduced by $250 if you're in the 25 percent federal income tax bracket. Any donation—no matter how large or how small—reduces your total net worth.

So why do I want to make giving part of your financial plan? I can think of at least five good reasons, every one of which will contribute to your financial contentment.

1. Giving breaks the power of money

Let's say that you're in a time period of global uncertainty and fear. In times of economic uncertainty, the only people who seem to be free of financial worry are the naive, the uninformed, and the givers.

The naive simply do not have a clue as to the severity or urgency of their situation. "Don't confuse me with the facts," they seem to protest. Like Scarlett O'Hara in *Gone with the Wind*, they prefer not to concern themselves with potentially difficult circumstances, reasoning that they can "worry about that tomorrow."

The uninformed may be perceptive people, yet they simply do not have the necessary facts to come to any educated conclusions. Ignorant about matters such as government debt or the global economic effects of terrorism, they fail to grasp the total financial picture and thus operate from a false sense of security.

The givers, on the other hand, understand the economic causes of fear. Yet because they have a biblical perspective on money, they experience real security and contentment. They have learned, firsthand, the truth of Matthew 6:8, that "your Father knows what you need before you ask him." Their trust in God's provision allows them to give with an open hand.

The world's perspective—that accumulation should be our ultimate goal—creates a bondage to money. "Get all you can, can all you get, and save the cans" advise modern pundits. Any thought of giving money away is a threat to our overall security. So we simply can't give freely. We become slaves to our finances.

Givers, on the other hand, master their money. In giving their resources away, they relinquish worldly security and significance; they acknowledge their dependence on and service to God. Money no longer has any hold on them. David Robinson, a retired all-star basketball player who has given millions of dollars to the foundation he established to help underprivileged children, wisely said, "If I'm clutching on to my money with both hands, how can I be free to hug my wife and kids?"

The world's perspective— that accumulation should be our ultimate goal— creates a bondage to money.

Either we control our money, or it controls us. We cannot be accumulators first and still serve God. Luke 16:13 explains why this is so: "No servant can serve two masters. Either he will hate the one and love the other, or he will be devoted to the one and despise the other. You cannot serve both God and Money." God really wants our hearts, not our money.

FAMILY FINANCE

Laura and Liz sat at the kitchen table, Liz sorting mail and Laura paying some bills. "I can't believe the amount of junk mail we get, Mom!" Liz said. "Ads for home renovations. Coupons for restaurants we never go to and dry cleaners we never use."

"Credit card offers," Laura added, laughing. "Offers for extended warranties on products we no longer own."

"And all these fund-raising appeals!" Liz said.

"Do you consider those junk mail?" Laura asked, surprised. "I don't."

"That's because you actually have some money to give," Liz answered. "Seeing them just makes me depressed. All the problems of the world are laid on our doorstep, and I can't do anything about them. I'd rather not look at them at all."

Laura looked at her daughter curiously. "You're working part-time, Liz. You must have some money you can give. Are you tithing?"

"Are you kidding?" Liz looked frustrated. "I'm trying to save for college expenses for next year, and I'm paying for my gas and insurance. I'm just finally starting to see my checking account grow a little, and I can't stand the thought of reducing it even more by giving money away. Besides, tithing is really for wealthy people, not students like me."

Laura shook her head. "No, it's not," she said firmly. "Tithing is a discipline, no matter how much money you have."

"Maybe," Liz said grudgingly. "But how much could my measly tithe help anyway? I'm working 15 hours a week

2. Giving promises rewards

Again and again throughout Scripture, God's command to give goes hand-in-hand with a promise:

> Honor the LORD with your wealth . . . then your barns will be filled to overflowing. (Proverbs 3:9-10)

> Give, and it will be given to you. (Luke 6:38)

God is serious about giving. He knows—and He promises—that we will be better off for it. If pastors don't talk about money, their church members may miss out on the blessings associated with giving. Many people interpret these promises to mean that the more they give, the more they will get. Were this actually the case, giving would become the hottest investment strategy on Wall Street. It would make unquestionably good economic sense.

The truth, I believe, is that God's promised rewards are much more significant than financial blessing. Material reward *may*—and often does—follow a faithful giver, yet it should neither be promised nor expected.

Instead, as you give, expect God to bless you in ways you may never have imagined. Perhaps He will give you good health, favor with your boss, or

at minimum wage. I'm not going to save the world by giving $10 a week. But I might lose out on something I really need."

Laura tilted her head. "You know, that's a pretty common mind-set, Liz. I know that because I've had it myself. But it can backfire. When we grasp money tightly, it has power over us. We end up spending a lot of our time and energy trying to hold on to it. Letting go of it can be freeing—not to mention that giving is pleasing to God."

Liz looked skeptical. "I'm still not sure what God could do with my little bit of money."

Laura went to the file drawer, rummaged around, and pulled out a catalog from an international Christian relief organization. "Take a look at this, Liz. Twenty-five dollars can buy two chick-ens for a family in another country, providing them with food and income. Twenty dollars can provide mosquito nets to protect a family from malaria. Thirty-six dollars can provide Bibles for people who have never seen one in their own language. It doesn't take a lot to make a huge difference in someone's life." She handed the catalog to Liz.

After a few minutes, Liz looked up, somber. "Look at this, Mom! For $30 a month I could sponsor a child! I could pay for that just by not stopping at the coffee shop every Saturday morning and cutting out two movies every month. That's pretty humbling."

Laura smiled. "Generous giving pleases God—and it changes us, because it helps us look beyond ourselves. I'm proud of you for wanting to do something about that, Liz."

wisdom in your financial decision making. He may use your gift mainly to draw you closer to Himself. He may, in fact, choose to bless you with an eternal reward—one you will never see on this side of heaven. Whatever the case, give cheerfully. Your promised reward will surely come.

3. Giving provides an eternal perspective

I have a friend who says his net worth is not the sum total that appears on his bank or accounting statements. Instead, he says his net worth is based on his faithfulness and generosity in giving. Because of his convictions, this fellow gives away 70 percent of his income every year. His basic needs are met, he enjoys contentment and financial freedom, and he sees his giving as an eternal—rather than temporal—investment.

Those who give can expect God to bless them in ways they may never have imagined.

The apostle Paul would have loved my friend's attitude. In Philippians 4:17, Paul commends the church members for their generosity toward him—not because of his needs but because of the gifts that will be credited to their accounts. Paul is talking about the Philippians' eternal accounts—the place where, as Christ puts it, "neither moth nor rust destroys, and where thieves do not break in or steal" (Matthew 6:20, NASB).

Few people have articulated the importance of maintaining an eternal perspective better than the missionary Jim Elliot. Jim and his wife, Elisabeth, went to South America during the 1950s to work with the Waodani people. Jim and four other men took a small airplane into the jungle to meet the tribe. They landed and were immediately murdered by headhunters.

When Elisabeth received the word that her husband had been martyred, she resolved to stay in South America and live among the Waodani, sharing with them the message of Jesus Christ.

Today, years after Jim's death, many in the Waodani tribe have become Christians. (You may have seen the movie *End of the Spear*, which tells their story.) How did Elisabeth find the strength to see their mission through? How was she able to respond to the uncertain future with such courage and faith? A key to her resolve may be found in her husband's letters and journals: "He is no fool," Jim wrote, "who gives what he cannot keep to gain what he cannot lose."

If you apply Jim's message to your financial life and if you really believe in eternal rewards, why would you not want to give something you cannot keep to get something you cannot lose? Why would you hang on to your money when you could have an eternal reward instead? After all, as the saying goes, "You can't take it with you." If you are truly concerned about planning for the future and withstanding economic uncertainty, it only makes sense to pursue that which is both certain and secure. It only makes sense to give. As my friend Randy Alcorn says in his book *The Treasure Principle*, "You can't take it with you—but you can send it on ahead."[1]

4. Giving demonstrates God's ownership

God owns it all. If I could only proclaim one message, this would be it: Everything we have belongs to God. The Bible says, "The earth is the LORD's, and everything in it, the world, and all who live in it" (Psalm 24:1). When we give, all we are really doing is demonstrating this fact. I love David's declaration,

> Yours, O LORD, is the greatness and the power and the glory and the majesty and the splendor, for everything in heaven and earth is yours. Yours, O LORD, is the kingdom; you are exalted as head over all. Wealth and honor come from you; you are the ruler of all things. In your hands are strength and power to exalt and give strength to all. (1 Chronicles 29:11-12)

Recognizing God's ownership of our resources—actually of all resources—is probably the biggest key to financial freedom. Kathy is a young mother I know. Not long ago she lost $20—a bill she had hurriedly thrust into her pocketbook as she dashed out the door for a quick trip to the grocery store before she was due to pick up a car pool of five preschoolers. She discovered the loss when she started to pay for her groceries and realized the money was gone.

Looking for a sympathetic ear, Kathy later confided her trouble in the car pool. "Children," she said, sighing, "I just lost $20, and I'm feeling sad."

The questions and advice came with rapid fire:

"What did you need the money for?"

"Can't you just go to the bank and get some more?"

"Maybe, if you ask her, my mommy will give you some of her money."

Kathy could not help but smile at the youngsters' eagerness to help—and suddenly her spirits lifted.

"You know what?" she said to herself as much as to the children, "God owns everything. He can help me find that money, or He can provide for us in some other way. We don't need to even worry about it!"

Thus liberated, Kathy cheerfully finished her car pool rounds and drove home with a newfound peace and sense of security. She knew God would take care of her, and as she pulled into her driveway, she saw it. Tucked among the blanket of fall leaves that covered her drive was a $20 bill.

In acknowledging God's ownership of her resources, Kathy was able to mentally release the $20 and experience true freedom from worry. She learned a valuable lesson about financial security: Financial freedom does not come from having money in your wallet when you go through the grocery store checkout line. Financial freedom comes when you turn your resources fully over to God.

When you manage your money with the conviction that it is actually God's money, giving becomes a logical, natural part of your total financial plan. It confirms God's ownership of your resources, demonstrating again that He really does own it all.

5. Giving demonstrates obedience to God's commands

How do you show your love for God? There are many ways to answer this question, but Jesus summed it up for us in John 14:15. "If you love Me," He said, "keep My commandments" (NASB).

The secret to giving generously is deciding, in advance, how much money you really need to live on. In the next chapter, you'll meet a pediatrician and his wife who set their lifestyle goals early on. As they reached them, they were able to give away the extra. Because of this commitment, the couple will ultimately wind up giving away more than 10 times what they would have if they had toed the line on the 10 percent mark.

> **When you manage your money with the conviction that it is actually God's money, giving becomes a logical, natural part of your total financial plan.**

Plan to give. One of the biggest barriers to giving is that we wait until needs are presented to us and then we react to them. At that point, the money is rarely available—and no matter how much we may want to help, we are simply unable to do so.

Why We Don't Give More

The "why" question is one I have wrestled with for years. I am often asked to speak to ministry groups and their donors, and as I prepare for these talks, the "why" question always factors into my thinking. I figure if ministries understand why Christians don't give, they will be better equipped to help potential givers overcome the obstacles. And I like to think that my analysis will motivate donors to give more by addressing the specific issues that hinder their own generosity.

There are seven reasons why Christians don't give, which are illustrated on the next page.

The underlying root cause is ultimately a spiritual problem. Then our financial problems, such as carrying too much credit card debt, further limit our ability to give. Even if a person is spiritually mature and doesn't have financial problems, he or she may not give because of not knowing and not planning what can be done. Throughout this book, I've used the term *financial planning*, but what about *giving planning*?

Why Christians Don't Give

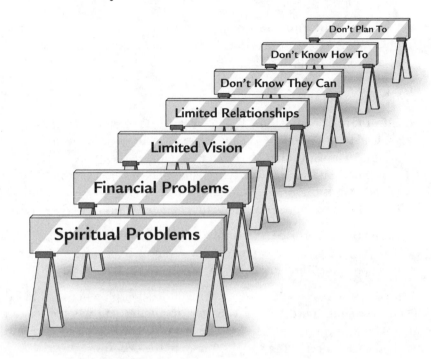

Don't Plan To

Don't Know How To

Don't Know They Can

Limited Relationships

Limited Vision

Financial Problems

Spiritual Problems

Getting Started: A Five-Step Plan

When you think about giving, don't just think of it as writing a check. While that's important, you can give so much more than money—including your time and abilities. Just as having a financial plan can help you free up more money for giving, so having a lifestyle strategy can help make generosity a reality in your life. In my book *Generous Living: Finding Contentment through Giving*, I presented these five action steps to help you identify and take advantage of the opportunities God gives you:

1. **Examine your priorities.** Do they reflect what God says has eternal value? Remember the high value He puts on people: "Do nothing out of selfish ambition or vain conceit, but in humility consider others better than yourselves" (Philippians 2:3). As you consider what matters most to God, be sure to put those things (or people) at the top of your list.

2. **Inventory your assets.** List all your resources: your time, your talents, and your possessions. All of us have different gifts or abilities, which we are to share with others. And just as financial resources must be managed

carefully, so the assets of time and talents must be used effectively to serve others.

3. **Ask the right questions.** If you are asked to give your time, skills, or possessions to a cause, ask the right questions before responding. Instead of asking yourself, *Is it convenient for me?* or *What do I get out of it?* consider whether or not God would want you to use your resources—*His* resources—in this way.

4. **Eliminate expectations.** When you give, do so without expecting anything in return. Don't be like the Pharisees, who gave so they could "walk around in flowing robes and be greeted in the marketplaces, and have the most important seats in the synagogues and the places of honor at banquets" (Mark 12:38-39). *Sacrificial* giving costs the giver something, and he or she may not be rewarded immediately for his or her generosity.

5. **Give your schedule to God.** Give your appointments and plans to God first thing each day. Ask Him to show you how He wants you to use your time, and give Him permission to interrupt your agenda.[2]

You can enrich your life by developing a lifestyle of generosity. It won't happen overnight, but the more you give, the better you will feel—and the more joyful and contented you are, the more you will want to give. In the next chapter, we'll cover the various phases in the generosity process. As you work your way through the cycle, you'll discover how generosity—in your finances and in your lifestyle—really is the key to freedom, satisfaction, and contentment.

CHAPTER 27

Giving until It Feels Good

Three men were discussing how to determine how much money to give to the Lord. The first man said he drew a circle on the ground, took all the money out of his pockets and threw it into the air; whatever landed inside the circle was the Lord's. He spent the rest.

The second man disagreed; he said whatever fell *outside* the circle belonged to the Lord, and he spent the money that fell inside the circle.

The third man, being more "spiritually mature," said he threw his money into the air. Whatever God wanted He kept, and whatever fell to the ground was the man's to spend!

Obviously, this is a facetious way to approach the giving decision. However, many people do not even go as far as those three men in their decision-making process regarding giving and tithing. There may be no more controversial issue in the Christian life—and I would venture to say, no greater issue of disobedience—than tithing and giving. How much to give can be one of the most difficult questions for the Christian to answer.

So just what does the Lord command when it comes to giving? In the Old Testament, a tithe was 10 percent—the first 10 percent—of any livestock, produce, or other sources of income. We have already discussed Malachi 3:8-10, in which God promises a curse for those who withhold the tithe and great blessings for those who give wholeheartedly. Likewise, the promise in Proverbs 3:9-10 is that if we honor our Lord with our wealth, with the "firstfruits" of all our crops, our "barns will be filled to overflowing" and our "vats will brim over with new wine."

Frequently I'm asked whether we are supposed to tithe off of our gross paycheck or wait until the taxes and other withholdings have been taken out and then tithe off of what we actually receive—the net. My answer is simple: Do you want God to bless the gross or the net? God gives us the gross; therefore, we should tithe on the gross.

This net-versus-gross question loses much of its relevance, however, when we examine the New Testament perspective on giving. In 1 Corinthians 16:2,

Paul admonishes the Christian to give "as he may prosper" (NASB). We are to give as God has prospered us.

Also, our gifts should be generous because, as Christ tells us, we get what we give: "Give, and it will be given to you. A good measure, pressed down, shaken together and running over, will be poured into your lap. For with the measure you use, it will be measured to you" (Luke 6:38).

One danger of sticking too closely to the Old Testament specifics is that our perspective may get skewed. If we give only 10 percent out of every paycheck, we may begin to feel that 10 percent is God's while the remaining 90 percent belongs to us. Remember: God owns it all.

A Portrait of Priorities

We may think the more money we make, the less trouble we will have tithing—but IRS statistics prove otherwise. As our salaries grow, our giving percentage does not keep pace. The average person making half a million dollars per year gives away only 2.5 percent—no more in percentage terms than the person whose annual income is only $25,000.

FAMILY FINANCE

"So Luis and I are both working extra hours this month and next month to pay down the credit card debt," Victoria told her friend Anna with a sigh.

Anna shook her head. "Financial stresses are the worst," she said. "Justin and I are going through a tough time right now too. Justin's company is downsizing, and he's worried about job security. His overtime has been cut off completely. Our refrigerator broke down, and we're in the middle of remodeling our bathroom! It just never ends."

Victoria looked concerned. "I'm sorry to hear about Justin's job. How are you handling everything?"

"Well, we've come up with a payment plan for the refrigerator. We just signed for a home equity loan for the bathroom. We've cut down on going out to eat." She paused. "And we've stopped tithing for now. Honestly, we just can't make ends meet on 90 percent of our income." She glanced at Victoria. "Do you think we're horrible?"

"Of course not!" Victoria said. "I can't say I've never thought about skipping the tithe check. But we feel pretty strongly about giving."

"We do too," Anna clarified. "But I think God understands that we're in a tough spot right now. Don't get me wrong. We haven't stopped giving altogether. We may not be able to give 10 percent this year, but we'll make it up in the future when we're more financially stable."

Victoria thought about her friend's words all afternoon. It was tempting not to give. How much faster their credit card debt would decrease if they added their tithe money to it each month! She could almost con-

An even more sobering indictment may be leveled at many American Christians. The organization called Empty Tomb, Inc. provides a very interesting analysis of giving and lifestyle research. They found the following:

> Protestant denominations have published data on an ongoing basis throughout the century. In 1916, Protestants were giving 2.9 percent of their incomes to their churches. In 1933, the depth of the Great Depression, it was 3.2 percent. In 1955, just after affluence began spreading through our culture, it was still 3.2 percent. By 2004, when Americans were over 554 percent richer, after taxes and inflation, than in the Great Depression, Protestants were giving 2.6 percent of their incomes to their churches.[1]

Recognizing how many Christians fall short of the 10 percent mark mandated in the Old Testament, one pastor I know challenged his congregation: "How many of you," the pastor asked, "drive stolen cars? Live in stolen houses? Wear stolen clothes?"

vince herself that it would be good stewardship.

That evening, she recounted the conversation to Luis as they were working on the bills. "Anna's arguments sound so good in some ways. I'm sure God does understand."

"Yeah, though I think it would be easy to get stuck in that kind of thinking. I mean, if we stop thithing until we feel caught up on all our bills, will we ever start thithing again? Something always seems to come up."

Luis took Victoria's hand. "God certainly "God certainly sees and understands our financial struggles. But the Bible also says that He loves generosity. Think about the story of the widow's mite. God was more pleased with her small offering than with wealthy people's large offerings because she gave the little she had."

"That's true," Victoria said thoughtfully. "Jesus could have told His disciples, 'Oh, she doesn't really need to give because she has so little.' But instead, He spoke highly of her because she gave sacrificially."

"When we give in the midst of our financial difficulties, I think we're acting on our faith," Luis added. "We're proclaiming that we believe in God's provision. We're stating that pleasing God is more important to us than holding on tightly to our money."

"That's an important message for us to remember, and it's important for Manuel and Cristina to see too," Victoria concluded. "If we wait to give until we're in great financial shape, we may never give."

She reached for the checkbook. "The next check I'll write out will be for church Sunday."

Some may balk or take offense at the implied accusations of such pointed questions. The pastor backed up his questions with the verses from Malachi 3:8-10:

> "Will a man rob God? Yet you rob me. But you ask, 'How do we rob you?' In tithes and offerings. You are under a curse—the whole nation of you—because you are robbing me. Bring the whole tithe into the storehouse, that there may be food in my house. Test me in this," says the LORD Almighty, "and see if I will not throw open the floodgates of heaven and pour out so much blessing that you will not have room enough for it."

This passage indicates that to tamper with or withhold even a portion of the tithe is to steal from God. Yet when you consider our total spending habits, a mild surprise over our charitable shortcomings gives way to astonishment or dismay.

Americans donate $216 billion annually to all charities—from education institutions to disaster relief. Narrowing this amount to all religious organizations, Americans give $93.2 billion.[2] This includes all churches and synagogues in the United States—Protestant, Catholic, Jewish, etc.

That sounds like a lot, doesn't it? Yet consider this: Americans spend about $705 billion on entertainment and recreation each year,[3] $135 billion on fast food,[4] and $101.6 billion on their lawns and gardens.[5]

As you can see, much of the discretionary lifestyle expenditures by Americans exceeds what is given to churches. Now, let's hone in a bit further. Those who give to churches sometimes benefit themselves, since the donations may go to constructing new buildings, gyms, and family outreach centers. Let's look, therefore, at missions giving to reach the world. Giving to overseas mission agencies (690 different denominational, interdenominational, and independent agencies and ministries) totals about $3.8 billion.[6] That compares to the $9.4 billion dollars in domestic box-office receipts in 2004.[7]

What Counts Most: Attitude or Amount?

How much we give in quantitative terms is not as important as our attitude toward giving. In 2 Corinthians 9:7 we read that our giving should be done "not reluctantly or under compulsion, for God loves a cheerful giver." In 2 Corinthians 8:9, Paul gives us the example of Christ to suggest the right attitude toward giving: "For you know the grace of our Lord Jesus Christ, that though he was rich, yet for your sakes he became poor, that you through his poverty might become rich." So as we give, we should strive to have an attitude of cheerfulness and grace. Freely we have received, freely we must give.

The question, *How much should I give?* is not a simple matter. We sometimes want a legalistic formula: Give 13.5 percent of gross income or 8.9 percent of net take-home pay. The Bible is not that rigid or dogmatic.

For I testify that they *gave as much as they were able, and even beyond their ability*. Entirely on their own, they urgently pleaded with us for the privilege of sharing in this service to the saints. And they did not do as we expected, but they gave themselves first to the Lord and then to us in keeping with God's will. (2 Corinthians 8:3-5, emphasis added)

Therefore how much we give should not be determined either by what we can see or according to our abilities, but by what God instructs us each to do. That will vary for each Christian family.

Have a Giving Plan

Like a preacher emphasizing his main points, I suggest you give based on a three-part, alliterative outline. Give based on the three *P*s: give *proportionately*, give on a *planned* basis, and give on a *precommitted* basis. These three *P*s work themselves out in three levels of giving—the "should give" level, the "could give" level, and the "would give" level.[8]

Proportionate giving. The "should give" level includes our proportionate giving. Each Christian should give in proportion to the amount that he or she has received. The Bible instructs that the starting point is 10 percent of our gross income.

Planned giving. The "could give" level is the amount that we could give if we were willing to give up something else. It may mean that we give up a vacation, a savings account, a lifestyle desire, or something else. Giving at this level is the closest any American Christian can come to sacrificial giving as described in Luke 21:4: "All these people gave their gifts out of their wealth; but she out of her poverty put in all she had to live on."

> Give based on the three *P*s: give proportionately, give on a planned basis, and give on a precommitted basis.

Sacrificial giving is giving up something in order to give to the Lord. I recommend that after a financial plan is put together, a family should regularly choose to give up something in order to give at the "could give" level. This level requires little faith, so it is not a faith pledge. There is no faith required because you can see the amount, and faith, by definition, requires seeing the unseen. It is simply a sacrificial love gift, an exercise to tangibly show God your love, your willingness to trust Him, and your loose hold on the things and desires of earth.

Precommitted giving. The third level of giving more clearly approximates faith giving, and I call it precommitted giving (committed in advance), or

Giving Plan

CAUSE	MY CITY	MY STATE	MY COUNTRY	WORLD	HOW MUCH*
Evangelism					$
Discipleship					$
Poor					$
Widows					$
Orphans					$
				TOTAL:	$

*How much:
    Proportionate—should: $ _____
    Planned—could: $ _____
    Precommitted—would: $ _____
    TOTAL: $ _____

When:
    Preemptively—as received
    Periodically

the "would give" level. We commit ourselves to giving if God provides a certain amount supernaturally. God can do this only if there is a financial plan in place that allows us to see His providing an additional cash flow margin through either additional income or decreased expenses. Unless we are precommitted to give the surplus, we will not give it, and we may miss out on having the incredible blessing of seeing His hand at work to provide in unique ways.

In summary, how much we can give is dependent upon three levels: I should give an amount proportionate to my income; I could give an additional amount by giving up something; and I would give more if God increased my cash flow margin. The how much is not dependent upon a set formula, and it gives us the opportunity to see God at work in our financial lives.

To help you commit, I encourage you to complete the Faith Giving Pledge form on the next page.

A Model of Giving: The Woman Who Couldn't Afford to Give

As you reviewed the earlier list of how much we spend relative to giving to missions organizations, you may have thought, *But I have to have money to eat and live in this world!* Of course, you have to purchase food, clothing, and other things your family needs. But remember: From a strictly logical and economic standpoint, giving will never make sense.

First, it's easy to assume your giving will accomplish very little—in fact, it may seem pointless. After all, you will never be able to meet all the world's

Faith Giving Pledge

Recognizing that God wants us to be good stewards of His resources and use them for His purposes, we make the following giving pledge for the coming year:

	AMOUNT
What we **should** give	$
What we **could** give by making a sacrifice in the following area	$
What we **would** give if God blesses us with	$
WE WILL GIVE:	$

_____   _____
Sign Name   Date

_____   _____
Sign Name   Date

- -

needs. Your $20 (or even $2,000) will hardly make a dent in the overwhelming needs.

Second, when asked to support a new cause, you may question where the money will come from. Rarely will you feel financially able to give generously toward a newly recognized need while continuing to fund the people or projects you already support.

Finally, no matter how much money you have or what your tax bracket is, you can never gain financial ground by giving. Even when you factor in the deductions for charitable contributions, giving will never put you ahead financially, because it always costs money to give.

Of course, that's the point. When Jesus talked about giving, He applauded those who gave what they could not logically afford to give. He reserved His praise for those who gave extravagantly—regardless of how much they could give. Perhaps the best-known example in Scripture is the poor widow whose offering the Lord commended in Mark 12:41-44.

Mark tells us that Jesus was sitting across from the Temple treasury, watching people make their contributions. Many rich people dressed in fine clothes approached the offering box with an air of religious pomp and ceremony. The

Bible says they "threw" their money in—probably feeling smug satisfaction as they heard the clink of their coins falling into the box.

Into this crowded scene came a poor widow. She probably went almost unnoticed in the hustle and bustle of the Temple courtyard. Unlike her wealthy neighbors, she could not afford to make a hefty donation. In fact, she could not really afford to give at all. But still she came, hoping (I imagine) to slip unobtrusively alongside the money box and quietly drop in her offering—two small coins with very little value.

Jesus, not wanting to embarrass the woman, did not make a scene. And yet whom did He use as an example to His disciples? He called them over to point out her gift, not those of the wealthy Pharisees: "The truth is that this poor widow gave more to the collection than all the others put together. All the others gave what they'll never miss; she gave extravagantly what she couldn't afford—she gave her all" (Mark 12:43-44, *The Message*).

In fact, this woman's story is the only direct reference Jesus gave as to the manner in which Christians should give. The Lord singled her out—both from the Temple crowd and from all the other examples in Scripture. That widow gave God all that she had, so while it amounted to almost nothing in financial terms, the Lord valued it far more than the outwardly more "impressive" gifts of those who lived lavishly.

A Modern Example of Giving: The Couple with a Cap on Their Lifestyle

When Jack and Lisa bought their first home about 20 years ago, the real estate agent who sold it to them figured it wouldn't be long before the $71,000 house would be on the market again. Jack was a doctor who'd recently finished medical school, so the agent reasoned he and his wife would want to upgrade to a larger home in a fancier neighborhood within two or three years. Most young professionals, after all, moved out of their starter homes as quickly as possible. But then, she didn't really know Jack and Lisa.

Throughout his training, Jack had watched other doctors pursue wealth and prestige, usually at the expense of their families. Jack wanted to be sure his own wife and children didn't suffer as a result of his concentrating on building his practice and getting ahead. Instead, he wanted something more. Luke 6:38, in particular, stayed with him: "Give, and it will be given to you. For with the measure you use, it will be measured to you." Without realizing it, he was at the start of the generosity process, the preparation phase.

"Maybe," he suggested to Lisa as his practice grew, "the extra money I'm making is not meant for us. Maybe God is increasing my income so we'll have more money to give away."

Jack and Lisa, convinced of the basic truth that God owns it all, asked themselves, *How much is enough?* They then set a cap on the lifestyle they wanted to attain. They resolved not to move the markers as their income rose; instead, they planned to use the extra—their cash margin—for strategic "investing." They wanted to give to God's Kingdom.

Lest you assume Jack and Lisa were starry-eyed idealists, I can assure you they recognized the financial implications their decision would have. They knew they could not, for example, always follow their friends as they moved into larger homes. Instead, their family remained in their first three-bedroom house for seven years—despite the increasingly crowded conditions as the first four of their five children were born. While admitting that the home felt cramped at times, the couple were pleased that their children learned how to share space.

Because every large purchase had to be made in light of their decision to commit their cash margin to God's Kingdom, they made other choices that struck their friends and colleagues as odd. Why did Jack continue to drive the older sedan he had bought from his mother during medical school? He was a doctor, after all. Why didn't Jack and Lisa take many vacations or live in a fancier home?

I later asked Jack, "What have you learned from choosing to live in this way?"

He responded, "I've learned how to receive."

Making his rounds at the hospital, Jack was on his feet almost constantly. He had to wear costly orthopedic shoes—and he knew that to replace them when they began to wear out would leave that much less for him and Lisa to give away. One day, as Jack knelt at the bedside of a young patient, the boy's father noticed the holes in the doctor's shoes. "Please," the man asked, "allow me the privilege of putting new soles on your shoes. It's my business—and I want to thank you for the care you have given my son."

Jack saw this man's offer as God's way of providing for his material needs in order to free up more money for giving. He accepted the man's proposition—and from that day on he took his worn-out shoes to this man whenever they needed repairing.

Jack is right—learning to receive is an important lesson. It then frees you up to give. It changes your paradigm.

He and Lisa saw many other examples of God's provision over the years. Once when Lisa's parents invited their family to visit them on the West Coast, Jack and Lisa felt they had to decline. While they wanted to see her parents, the only way they could afford to fly all seven family members across the country was to increase their lifestyle spending, which would mean cutting into their giving budget. It was a difficult decision, but Jack hoped his in-laws would understand why they couldn't accept the invitation.

They did. Even so, they wanted to see their grandchildren, so they sent Jack a check to help cover the cost of the tickets. Again, Jack saw God's hand at work, and they made the trip.

Jack and Lisa have many other stories of the way God provided for their expenses—from family vacations to the kids' education (which Jack's father unexpectedly offered to help fund).

By maintaining their lifestyle boundaries, Jack and Lisa were able to steadily increase their giving and eventually give away about half of everything they earned. It wasn't always easy. Many times, Jack says, they felt—and still feel—the pinch of sacrifice. Sometimes they battled self-pity or the temptation to increase their living expenses and upgrade their lifestyle. Even so, their commitment to giving has provided them with firsthand exposure to God's promise in Luke 6:37-38: "Give away your life; you'll find life given back, but not merely given back—given back with bonus and blessing" (*The Message*).

In effect, what Jack and Lisa did was to set a "finish line" on their lives. This concept is a biblical one. In Hebrews 12, for example, Paul admonishes us to do the following:

> Strip down, start running—and never quit! No extra spiritual
> fat, no parasitic sins. Keep your eyes on Jesus, who both began
> and finished this race we're in. Study how he did it. Because he
> never lost sight of where he was headed—that exhilarating finish
> in and with God—he could put up with anything along the way.
> (verses 1-2, *The Message*)

If you choose to run life's race with an eternal perspective, your decision will be evidenced by your lifestyle—specifically, how you choose to use the money you have.

What about you? Is your focus on eternity? Are you keeping your eyes on Jesus? It's so easy in our culture to allow the "fat" and "sin" of materialism, covetousness, and self-centeredness to drag us down.

Naming Your Treasure

Am I suggesting that the examples of the poor widow and Jack and Lisa mean God commends only those who hand over their life savings and literally give away *all* they have?

I believe the answer is no and yes. While God does command us to give, it is not because He needs our money. What He really wants is our hearts.

One of the most significant verses in the Bible to me is Matthew 6:21: "For where your treasure is, there your heart will be also." What's your treasure? It's whatever is most important to you. Maybe it's a job promotion, a new house, or a new car. Maybe you long to get married or have a child. Maybe you just need a vacation, and you dream about soft white beaches and vibrant sunsets. Your treasure is what you think about, what you go after, what you want to attain. It's where your heart is.

Early in my career, my treasure consisted in the recognition and success

Q: We are currently between churches and looking for one to join. Should we give our tithe to the churches we are visiting?

ANSWER: God's Word says in Galatians 6:6, "Anyone who receives instruction in the word must share all good things with his instructor." To me that would mean that if I'm being ministered to by a church and God has given me financial resources, then I should give to that church. Therefore, while visiting churches I would think giving to those churches would be the biblical thing to do.

Second, I believe the tithe is recognition of God's ownership as opposed to a payment to God. So, if the tithe is in recognition of God's ownership, then the local church is merely the vehicle to receive the tithe. Which local church you give to is not of significance. The bottom line is that everyone should tithe.

My wife and I belong to a church, and we tithe to that church on a weekly basis. I believe that giving weekly reminds me that I am merely a steward of God's resources and not an owner. Therefore, I personally like to write a check every week. When I am visiting another church, I write what would be my tithe check to that church.

I have been asked many times over the years what my position is on "storehouse giving," which means giving your tithe to your local church. This term comes from Malachi 3:8-10:

> "Will a man rob God? Yet you rob me. But you ask, 'How do we rob you?' In tithes and offerings. You are under a curse—the whole nation of you—because you are robbing me. Bring the whole tithe into the storehouse, that there may be food in my house. Test me in this," says the LORD Almighty, "and see if I will not throw open the floodgates of heaven and pour out so much blessing that you will not have room enough for it."

I personally believe that any giving to evangelical causes would qualify as a part of my tithe amount, whether it's the local church or a parachurch organization. However, many pastors believe and preach that the tithe should all come into the storehouse. My counsel is that if you belong to a church that preaches "storehouse giving" then, in obedience to the leadership of that church, you should practice "storehouse giving" as well. If you can't come to that personal conviction, then the question is whether you should remain in that particular church.

I achieved in business. When I became a Christian, though, those priorities began to change. My heart turned toward my family, and I began to think more about their eternal destiny than about our material needs and desires. My treasure was no longer bound up in outward success.

As I discovered, God knows our hearts can't be devoted both to Him and to wealth or material pursuits. As Matthew 6:24 tells us, we cannot serve both God and money. God does not say it's *difficult* to serve both. He does not say we should try *really hard* to serve both. He says it's *impossible* to serve both. You must decide which is more important to you.

Setting Your Own Finish Lines

If you make God your treasure, you will need to put a finish line on your lifestyle, just as Jack and Lisa did. With such a cap in place, you can free up more of your cash flow margin for things that will have lasting value—such as charitable giving and investments in your family's spiritual growth and development. Financial decisions that might otherwise seem difficult or confusing become natural and easy choices.

You can begin determining your own finish lines by asking yourself some basic questions. What kind of home do you want for your family, and how much will it cost? How much money do you need to meet your living expenses? How much do you need to save for college, retirement, or some other long-term goal? What will you spend on vacations and other leisure activities?

On an athletic track, the finish line serves two purposes. First, it serves as a goal for the runners; second, it tells them when they have completed the race. Likewise, financial finish lines keep you focused on your goals and prevent you from racing past them in pursuit of something else. For example, if your goal is to be out of debt within five years, you might adopt a lifestyle finish line that will help you avoid additional borrowing. Once your debt is paid off, your finish line will confirm that accomplishment and give you the freedom to divert the funds you had been using for debt repayment to more satisfying use.

Financial finish lines keep you focused on your goals and prevent you from racing past them in pursuit of something else.

As we wrap up our discussion on financial finish lines, I do not want to leave you with the impression that this process creates a legalistic barrier that cannot be moved. Instead, let me remind you that it is designed to help you make lifestyle choices. A couple with two children may, for example, assume they'll stay in a house that costs $100,000. Six years and two more children later, they may actually buy a more expensive home to get the additional space they need. Their living expenses may go up, but their finish line—the type of lifestyle they have chosen for their family—remains constant.

Unless you've set your own financial finish line, decisions related to living expenses may seem to be strictly economic, the kind of choices you could easily make with the help of a good financial or estate planning book. However, the answers to these questions should not primarily be driven by what you can *afford* to purchase but by what you think you *ought* to buy.

Many years ago, a friend asked me whether or not I thought it was all right for him to send his teenage son to a week of soccer camp that cost $1,000. He could afford to pay for the camp, but he wasn't sure if such an expense was appropriate.

There was no "right" answer to my friend's question. Instead of looking for a formula or rule to dictate his spending decision, I asked him to consider, *What ultimate purpose will this expense fulfill?* If God owns it all, then every spending decision—including a $1,000-a-week soccer camp or a $5,000 piano for a gifted daughter—becomes a spiritual decision. We are always using God's resources. The question we must ask is not *Can I afford this?* but *Would God want me to use His money this way?*

Surely Jack and Lisa would view an expensive soccer camp as a frivolous expense, right? Not necessarily. Just as having an eternal perspective can turn your focus toward giving, it will also open your eyes to the things you can do to develop godly characteristics in your family. Soccer camps may hone athletic skills, but they may also encourage traits such as responsibility, discipline, integrity, and a strong work ethic. Chances are that Jack and Lisa might see this soccer camp or a new piano as a valuable, worthwhile, and economically sound investment in their children's future.

In other words, you will always be able to find a "better way" to use your money. After all, there will always be needy people and causes. When you come up against soccer camp questions and other spending decisions, don't fall into the guilt-laden trap of thinking you always have to give your money to the impoverished. Instead, go back to the beginning of the generosity process. Read the Bible and listen to what God is saying. He might want you to give away every cent you have. Or He might want you to send your son to camp. You won't know unless you ask.

When I ask, "How much is enough?" most people immediately start thinking about how much money they need to live on or to achieve their long-term goals. Obviously those are important issues to consider—especially as you set your lifestyle finish lines—but I want to challenge you to look at the question in another way. How much is enough to *give?* Rather than asking yourself how much money you need and then trying to figure out how much you can give out of whatever's left over, flip-flop your perspective. Start by asking yourself how generous you want to be. Your life will become richer as a result!

Use a "Target" for Giving

George Dayton founded Dayton's department store, the beginning of a very successful retail empire. The Dayton grandsons created a discount store concept in 1962, called Target, which became the company's most profitable store. In 2000 the company renamed itself the Target Corporation.[9]

The founding Dayton had instructed his children and grandchildren to be generous givers. In 1946, the company became only the second company to institute a policy of giving 5 percent (the maximum amount deductible for corporations under the tax code then) of the company's pretax profits to charity.

Kenneth Dayton, one of George Dayton's grandsons, became a public advocate for giving. He identified nine stages of giving and encouraged others to progress through these stages. (When he wrote about these nine stages a few years before his death, he acknowledged he was in the seventh stage and trying for the final ones.)

What I find useful about Mr. Dayton's list of the stages of giving is its planned nature, its challenge beyond taxes, its "finish line" aspect, and its plan of giving after death. I challenge you to determine what stage you are currently in and how you can move up on his suggested "ladder of giving":

1. **Minimal response**—Giving because we were asked and only because we were asked.

2. **Involvement and interest**—As soon as one becomes involved . . . giving becomes more meaningful.

3. **As much as possible**—Giving this amount requires a plan and a budget.

4. **Maximum allowable**—Giving the most that IRS allows as deductible.

5. **Beyond the max**—No longer would we let the IRS tell us how much (or how little) we could give . . . [however], we no longer had a benchmark . . . we, therefore, needed to invent one.

6. **Percentage of wealth**—Until we started to measure our giving against our wealth, we did not fully realize how much we could give away and still live very comfortably.

7. **Capping wealth**—Giving each year a percent of one's wealth forces one to start thinking about the relative importance of increasing giving versus increasing wealth.

8. **Reducing the cap**—We can visualize the possibility of doing so . . . we cannot say whether we will ever have the courage.

9. **Bequests**—Having given our heirs enough assets, we are able to leave almost all our remaining assets [to charities].[10]

We generally want a set of rules to guide our giving, but that's just the attitude the Pharisees had. God wants it all—all of our hearts, that is. My experience is that very generous givers exhibit humility. They're usually joyful as well. Which came first: the generosity or joy? I suspect joy is a result of a generous life. I encourage you to be a cheerful giver too.

CHAPTER 28

Life Insurance: Don't Let It Take the Life Out of You

The basic purpose of insurance is to transfer the risk that one is not willing to take (or is unable to take) to a company willing to take the risk in return for compensation. In the case of life insurance the objective is, first, to protect the family income and net worth growth in the event of the death of the breadwinner. A second objective is to provide protection to maintain the estate in order that it might pass on to heirs, allowing the continuation of capital from one generation to the other.[1]

Why Insurance?

Using the Financial Planning Diagram (see page 44), life insurance could be depicted by putting an umbrella over the "Growth in Net Worth" box as illustrated in the diagram on the following page. (This is similar to the one in chapter 3, page 42, but shows the protective umbrella that insurance provides for net worth.) Thus, the risk of loss of income or the erosion of the estate through estate taxes is passed to the insurance company. The same idea applies to the protection of houses, automobiles, and other property. Few individuals could afford to replace a house in the event of loss, so they purchase insurance for it.

The key theme expounded in insurance sales is protection. While this is certainly the purpose of insurance, emphasizing it unfortunately induces an attitude of fear. Most insurance is purchased on an emotional rather than a factual basis. This attitude may lead to attempts to provide enough insurance to protect against any unknown. For the Christian, this may lead to a shifting of trust from God to insurance and to an imbalance between the amount of coverage being provided and amounts one can afford.

The perspective on insurance changes somewhat if the word *provision* is used instead of *protection*. God's purpose for the breadwinner, according to the Bible, is to provide for his family:

> If anyone does not provide for his relatives, and especially for his immediate family, he has denied the faith and is worse than an unbeliever. (1 Timothy 5:8)

In-Depth Financial Strat

The Role of Insurance

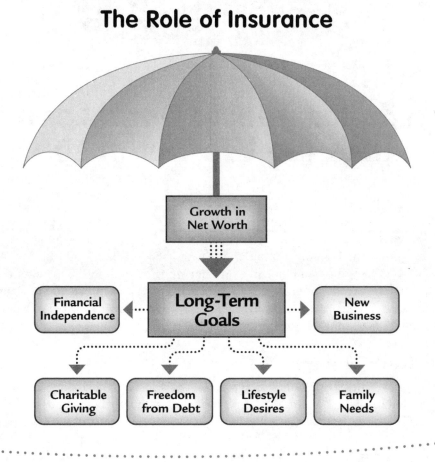

In the biblical system, when the father died, the oldest son took the bread-winner's responsibility. If a man had no son, then his brother undertook the care of the family through the laws God had established for widows and orphans (Deuteronomy 14:28-29; James 1:27). Ideally, these caring functions today would be provided by the body of Christ, the church. Unfortunately, they usually are not. So a vital part of family financial planning today includes providing continued provision through the use of life insurance.

You may say that purchasing insurance shows a lack of trust in God to provide. Rather, this is the sound-mind principle being put to use. If you did not purchase life insurance and you are married with children, it's possible that your spouse would have to go on welfare (becoming dependent on the government) should you die prematurely. As a result, your family's spiritual and physical needs could go unmet.

Life insurance, on the other hand, could give your family the opportunity to continue to live in an environment to which they're accustomed. Insurance is not a lack of trust in God's provision; it may be a form of His provision when wisely secured. Insurance is acknowledgment of the certainty of death. It's consistent with the whole counsel of Scripture.

How Much Life Insurance Do You Need?

You can determine how much you need through the Insurance Needs Analysis on page 421. First determine the insurance necessary to meet income goals, and then add to it the amount needed for long-term liquidity needs such as major expenses and estate taxes. This will facilitate the transfer of your assets from one generation to the next without tax erosion.

A key distinction in the Insurance Needs Analysis is determining whether your primary need is to provide for your

> **Insurance is not a lack of trust in God's provision; it may be a form of His provision when wisely secured.**

family's needs now if something were to happen to you or if you have longer-term needs to provide for. A clear delineation can help you decide between the various types of insurance, which are defined on pages 420–427.

I'm frequently asked whether a spouse who is not in the workforce needs insurance. My answer: Yes, if the family can afford it. Consider the cost of replacing the service this spouse provides (example: child care, home-cooked meals, laundry, house cleaning). The Web site Salary.com calculated what a mother's salary should be based on the tasks completed and the number of hours worked. If you combine the roles of housekeeper, van driver, cook, facilities manager, psychologist, and janitor, her contributions annually are worth $138,095 (including overtime pay).[2] If these tasks cannot be provided by the remaining spouse, how will they be paid for?

If funds to spend on insurance are limited, they belong on the breadwinner of the family, but don't ever leave a spouse uninsured for life insurance if at all possible. Funeral expenses alone may cost up to $10,000. If the family is dependent on both spouses' income, then it's likely both need insurance. The least expensive way to do this is to include coverage for both as a part of the insurance coverage for the spouse earning the greatest income.

In addition to covering both parents, some families buy coverage for their kids. Since the purpose of insurance is provision, however, insurance should always be provided for the breadwinner first.

That said, there are four basic reasons to consider having insurance on a child:

1. To provide guaranteed insurability. This is a major point used in selling insurance for children. The idea is that the child needs insurance in case he or she becomes disabled prior to becoming an adult and can no longer qualify for insurance. The probability of this happening is very small.

2. To accumulate cash that can be used in purchasing other insurance policies at a later time.

3. To secure low rates at an early age.

4. To provide for unexpected funeral expenses.

I bought a relatively small whole life policy on each of my children. My intention was to provide them with some life insurance in case they had health problems and would not be insurable. The policy offered the option to buy additional insurance at various intervals as they grew. When they kids were on their own, I gave them these policies and let them decide whether to keep them or not. Consider your budget and priorities when determining how much, if any, insurance should be purchased.

I don't recommend using insurance as a primary way to save for education. Other tax-advantaged ways exist to save for higher education.

If your funds are extremely limited, I advise you to get all the insurance you can for the dollars available. Also, to assist your family in the event of your death, be sure your family has a written plan that recommends how the insurance funds should be used and identifies where the additional dollars needed would come from (spouse working, family help, where to get counsel, etc.).

At some stage in life, you may determine that insurance coverage is no longer necessary. At retirement, for instance, you're no longer responsible for dependents and your income should be set. It may come from Social Security, pension plans, annuities, or investments. If your spouse's needs can be met after your death—and you anticipate no estate taxes or need for additional liquid assets—there is no need for insurance to supply additional provision. Until that time, insurance offers an umbrella of protection to provide the needed resources in the event that you die before meeting your financial goals.

At the other extreme, young single persons with no family or support responsibilities have no great need for insurance—though they may wish to have a limited amount of insurance so that burial costs or debt repayment would not present a burden to anyone.

What Type of Insurance Product Do You Need?

Although insurance comes in hundreds of "wrappers," there are basically four different types of insurance policies. These are term (such as annual renewable term and guaranteed level premium 5-, 10-, 15-, 20-, and 30-year products), traditional whole life, universal life, and variable life.

Term life insurance

Annual renewable term life insurance provides the maximum insurance coverage for the lowest initial premiums, with premiums increasing annually. The

Insurance Needs Analysis

INCOME GOALS FOR THE FAMILY

Living expenses *Use 80% of present annual living expense*	
Taxes	
Giving	
TOTAL INCOME NEEDED	$ **A**

SOURCES OF INCOME *Income anticipated on a regular basis*

Social Security	
Pension or retirement plans	
Annuities or trusts	
Income from investments not liquidated	
Spouse working	
Other	
TOTAL INCOME AVAILABLE	$ **B**
ADDITIONAL INCOME NEEDED PER YEAR [1]	$ **A–B=C**
INSURANCE REQUIRED TO PROVIDE INCOME [2]	$ **C×10=D**

ADDITIONAL FUNDS NEEDED

Funeral costs	
Debt repayment (current need)	
Estate tax and settlement expense (long-term need)	
Educational costs (current need)	
Major purchases	
TOTAL ADDITIONAL FUNDS NEEDED	$ **E**
SUBTOTAL INSURANCE NEEDED [3]	$ **E+D=F**

OTHER ASSETS AVAILABLE

Real estate available for sale	
Stocks and bonds available for sale	
Savings available *To meet needs (E); not including family living needs (A)*	
TOTAL FROM OTHER ASSETS AVAILABLE:	$ **G**
TOTAL INSURANCE NEEDED [4]:	$ **F–G=H**
INSURANCE AVAILABLE NOW:	$ **I**
ADDITIONAL INSURANCE NEEDED:	$ **H–I=J**

(1) Total income needed less the total income available

(2) Assumes the life insurance proceeds could be invested at 10% and provide the needed amounts. The investment percentage may be contingent on economic conditions or investment knowlege. The multiplication factor is 1 divided by the percentage return on insurance proceeds.

Examples: 10% = 1/.10 = 10; 8% = 1/.08 = 12.5; 12% = 1/.12 = 8.33

(3) Insurance required to provide income plus total additional funds needed

(4) Subtotal insurance needed less the amount available from the sale of assets

Note: No adjustment has been made in these calculations for inflation. If you feel you can earn 10% but that will be eroded by 3-4% inflation, then you should use 6-7% in equation and not 10%. This will increase the amount of insurance needed. You can use any investment or inflation assumption you would like.

In-Depth Financial Strategies | 28

obvious advantage of this type of coverage is the low initial cost. Typically, when you are young and in the accumulation stage, you have a growing family and a lot of current needs (debt, education, and living expenses). You have a need for a large amount of insurance coverage but usually limited funds with which to buy the insurance. This usually requires a purchase of term insurance.

Annual renewable term life insurance provides the maximum insurance coverage for the lowest initial premiums, with premiums increasing annually.

Level-premium term policies provide the benefit of locking in a premium for a certain period of time, say 20 years. In general, young families should provide the majority of their insurance needs with term insurance. I recommend locking in your term insurance with a guaranteed level premium for 15 to 20 years when you need the maximum life insurance protection (when your children are young).

The not-so-obvious disadvantage of term life insurance is the high cost during the later years. The premium costs at older ages (age 60 to life expectancy) are prohibitive and make it difficult to maintain this type of policy until death. This product does not allow any flexibility in premium payments to meet changing circumstances.

Another downside to buying term insurance is that policyholders must reevaluate their company every few years to determine if it's still the cheapest term possible. If you buy annual renewable term life insurance (not locked in for 15–20 years), then the annual premium may rise rapidly after the first few years—a perceived negative to many.

As the return rates and dividends on permanent policies like whole life insurance have increased in recent years, they have become a reasonable way to build up equity. Yet many people favor term insurance anyway, noting that they can invest the extra money they would have paid to whole-life premiums into their own investments. However, we have found that very few of our clients actually take the difference and invest it systematically—missing the whole purpose.

The best way to invest the difference is to set up a systematic withdrawal from your bank account and invest it into a no-load mutual fund. Each month the bank drafts a check against your savings account or money market fund and invests in the mutual fund. This not only gives you the advantage of a disciplined periodic investment, but automatically allows you to practice dollar cost averaging through the mutual fund.

Traditional whole life insurance

Whole life insurance provides permanent coverage, assuming premiums are paid, and includes both a death benefit and a cash value element. Advantages of whole life are its level premium cost and the savings generated through the cash accumulations. Disadvantages are its much higher cost over term insurance in the early years and the fact that at death only the face value of the policy is paid, not the accumulated cash value.

This product is more expensive initially than a term policy because of the level premiums, the cash value buildup, and the higher commission costs to the agent. In a sense, the insurance owner overpays in the early years in order to underpay (or not pay) in later years.

In essence, this type of policy results in forced savings for the policyholder, and since most people do a poor job of saving for the future, this aspect of a whole life policy may be helpful.

In other words, a whole life policy may discipline the insured to save money he or she might not otherwise have saved. After being held five years, such a product generally begins to have more of a buildup of cash value.

For people who find it difficult to save regularly, the mere fact that they get a bill from their life insurance company each month causes them to save more than they normally would. Furthermore, if they purchase a contract with a good mutual company, they have made a decision they do not have to rethink every few years.

Insurance companies have become much more competitive in increasing the amount of dividends they credit to their policyholders. *Consumer Reports* uses the "Linton Yield" to calculate the rate of return on whole-life policies. In 1980, the yields were in the neighborhood of 2 to 6 percent. Now, a 4 to 7 percent return is possible on policies held for more than 20 years.

This is an adequate return, considering that the risk on this return is much lower than in the stock market and that the return grows on a tax-favored basis within the life insurance policy.

Even though the policy contract may require premiums to be paid for a certain length of time (that is, one's lifetime), the policy may be paid up much sooner with the use of dividends. The primary disadvantage of a whole life policy is the high outlay of premiums required in the early years. Although term life insurance is more cost effective and should be used for most of your life insurance needs, I think that some of your insurance protection may be met through whole life.

For that reason, I advise holders of whole life insurance policies to deliberate carefully before converting a policy with a high cash value to term insurance. Simply put, I have never seen any widow or family member complain that the deceased had too much life insurance! If you have had your whole life insurance policy for many years with a good company, you are probably earning a relatively good yield for the low level of risk. You may be better off to keep it.

Perhaps you have an old policy that you haven't given much thought to in years. Again, don't automatically assume you should cancel it. Go to the library to obtain a copy of the *Best's Insurance Reports* 10- and 20-year dividend comparisons and see how your company compares to other life insurance companies. (For more information on these reports, see http://www.ambest.com.) Is it among the leaders in paying dividends to its policy owners? Has your company offered you the chance to update your policy and receive higher dividends by amending your contracts? If so, you may own a good policy. The longer you own the policy the better the investment it becomes, since the front-end load and commission are spread over a longer period of time.

I would recommend that you work through the specific facts and circumstances with a financial advisor. Your advisor can help you see how much life insurance you need and help hold you accountable to invest the cash value wisely (rather than spend it) if you decide to cancel the policy.

Universal life insurance

This type of insurance is a blend of permanent and term insurance. Its primary advantage is flexibility with regard to the death benefit, premiums paid, and the ability to withdraw cash from the policy. The insured makes premium payments

FAMILY FINANCE

Brian settled back in his recliner. Tanya was working late tonight, so he'd decided to start reading through a recent gift from his older brother, Reid—a "survival guide" for first-time dads. Reid had two little kids of his own, and he shared Brian's excitement about the coming baby. Four days after Brian had called Reid to tell him the news of Tanya's pregnancy, the book had arrived in the mail.

Brian flipped to the table of contents and found chapters on the physical and emotional aspects of pregnancy, childbirth, and infant care. *Hmm, I'm not sure I need that quite yet.* What else did the book cover? Financial preparations seemed like a good place to start. He turned to the right page and started reading the opening checklist.

· Develop an emergency fund. Check. He and Tanya had been saving a little money every month in a money market mutual fund,

and they now had a few months of living expenses accumulated.

· Consider tax ramifications of a new dependent. Check. Thanks to their conversation with Tanya's parents, Brian and Tanya were talking this through with their CPA.

· Consider whether your wife will go back to work after the baby is born, and what the financial implications will be. Check—kind of. They were starting to consider their options.

· Find out if your employer has paternity leave or if you will need to use vacation or take unpaid time off when the baby is born. Check. He had one week of paternity leave.

· Look into term life insurance.

Brian looked up abruptly. Life insurance? He and Tanya had never talked about that before, but it made perfect sense. It wasn't fun to think about, but if something happened to him, he

to the contract. These paid-in premiums are credited with an interest rate on a monthly basis. Certain charges are taken out from the fund on a monthly basis. These include the cost of the insurance and other administrative expenses.

A word of caution about universal life: The same feature that could be an advantage of this contract may become a disadvantage. The ability to vary the premium payments may put the insured in a position of having underfunded the contract in later years and seeing his coverage expire. This is particularly true when an agent or company has projected a high rate of return through the life of the policy, when in fact the economic environment dictates that a lower interest rate is actually credited to his account during many of these years. Certain minimum premium payments must be made, which are computed by the insurance company, to keep the policy in force.

Variable life insurance

As if insurance were not confusing enough, a product known as variable life has been marketed to the consumer with increasing frequency. Variable life

would want Tanya to have a significant financial cushion so she wouldn't have to go back to work full-time until their child was older. But how much coverage was necessary?

By the time Tanya got home an hour later, Brian had found an online program that calculated how much life insurance he might need to cover funeral expenses, pay off the mortgage, fund some college savings for their child, and provide living expenses for 20 years.

"Now I just have to fill out this application from our insurance company and then go get a physical," he told her. "We can easily have this taken care of before the baby is born."

"I'm impressed!" Tanya said, smiling. "But what about me? Do I need life insurance too? I probably won't be providing the majority of our family's income, but if something happened to me, you would have to pay for child care for the baby."

"That's true," Brian agreed. "Not to mention all the stuff you do around the house. At least I do some of the cleaning, but you usually take care of the laundry, cooking, and grocery shopping. Wow, I guess that would be worth a lot of money."

Tanya laughed. "It's nice to feel appreciated!" She suddenly got serious. "Our lives are going to change when this baby is born, aren't they? It's a little scary to think about being totally responsible for someone else."

Brian nodded and took her hand. "The good news is that probably every other first-time parent feels the same way! We can't know the future, but we can prepare ourselves as best as we can to be parents, financially and spiritually."

"And then we can ask God to give us wisdom," Tanya added, "which we'll probably do many, many times over the next 18 years!"

Q: Should I borrow from my life insurance?

ANSWER: Money borrowed from whole-life (sometimes called permanent) insurance polices is called a life insurance loan. (Note that you cannot borrow from a term life insurance policy.) However, they're not really debt. You have accumulated these funds in a life insurance product, and they are yours any time that you choose to cancel the life insurance.

When you borrow from a life insurance policy, you're required to pay interest on the money borrowed at a rate specified in the insurance contract. This rate can be very low for older policies but fairly high and variable for new policies.

In essence, then, you're borrowing from yourself, and there is a guaranteed way of repayment. One guaranteed way of repayment is when you die (a guaranteed event). At that time, the amount borrowed will be repaid from the proceeds of the life insurance policy. Another guaranteed method of repayment is canceling or giving up the life insurance. The loan amount would be deducted from any cash value proceeds sent to you.

A related question I'm frequently asked regarding life insurance loans is whether or not they should be repaid, since repayment is not required. The answer is not an easy one because the biggest variable as to whether or not they should be repaid involves the insurance company itself. If your policy is with a good quality insurance company with a history of increasing dividends (which are really returns of excess premiums) to policyholders, then repaying the loan makes sense. First, repaying will reduce your interest cost each year, and second, it will allow for a good tax-deferred buildup of cash within the insurance policy.

In summary, if you have whole life insurance and need to borrow money for whatever purpose, then that is typically a good source. It's certainly better than a credit card loan or an installment loan with high interest costs. If you have borrowed money from a life insurance policy, then it may make good sense to repay the loan if it will increase your dividends within the policy.

insurance is similar to whole life in that the premium payments are level, and there is generally a minimum guaranteed death benefit. Unlike whole life policies, however, variable life policies permit the policyholder to allocate a portion of each premium payment to one or more investment options after a deduction for expense and mortality charges. The investment options are typically mutual funds inside the whole life product.

Traditional whole life and universal life policies typically have a fixed dividend or interest rate credited to their accounts on an annual basis. In the last decade, as interest rates declined, the interest rates credited to these products also decreased. This resulted in the current cash values being significantly less than the projections that were made when they were sold when interest rates were higher. At the same time that interest rates declined, the stock market achieved double-digit returns. During this period, variable life appeared attractive because the cash value buildup inside these policies, if projected at the historical earning rates of the stock market, could outperform other insurance products.

Should you purchase a variable life insurance product? In most cases, no. Variable life is often sold as an investment product. I feel strongly that you shouldn't mix investments with insurance. Life insurance has traditionally been associated with protection.

If you are a knowledgeable investor and understand the downside risk of the stock market, then you know the cash value of such a contract may decline. Second, a policyholder needs to have an extremely long-term perspective, since the near-term volatility of the stock market would give most people false hopes or false fears about their policy. Be sure that you fully understand the risks and rewards before purchasing a variable life product.

Deciding between Short-Term and Long-Term Life Insurance

In order for you to determine what kind of insurance you need, it's important for you to step back and look at these insurance products in light of your financial goals. This means asking the questions *How much do I need?* (see the Insurance Needs Analysis table on page 421), *How long will I need it?* and *How much can I afford?* Once you answer these questions, the appropriate product should become obvious.

Some consumer groups claim that buying term is always the only way to go. However, the idea of buying term and "investing the difference" is based on a short-term perspective. Although it may be sufficient to meet current needs and is much less expensive than whole life, universal, or variable life insurance, term insurance does get more expensive over time.

You have a long-term need for insurance if you will be counting on it after age 65. First, you may need to have insurance available in your sixties or seventies in order to pay funeral expenses or estate taxes that will be due on a nonliquid estate. You may have a closely held business or some significant nonliquid assets that you want to pass on to your heirs along with insurance proceeds to cover the estate taxes. In this case, whole life insurance, with its level premiums and lower costs (assuming it was purchased at a much younger age), would be the preferable product so that it lasts your entire life.

Long-term insurance offers flexibility. In your thirties and forties you do not know what your situation will be when you are in your sixties. Having a cornerstone of permanent insurance available at that stage in your life is simply wise planning—one example of looking down the road and counting the cost.

The issue of how long you need insurance is difficult to resolve because no one knows what the future holds. But if the need is strictly short term or intermediate term and will never be any longer than that, then the obvious solution is term insurance. However, if there is an outside chance that estate taxes must be paid or if you want to build in some flexibility for long-term planning, you should consider some type of permanent insurance for part of your coverage as soon as you can afford it.

For long-term needs, I recommend that you go with a financially strong insurance company with a good agent who will be around to service the product 10 or 20 years down the road. The product type will depend on available cash, but traditional whole life insurance may be the best choice, although the other products mentioned certainly merit consideration.

> **The issue of how long you need insurance is difficult to resolve because no one knows what the future holds.**

Short-term and intermediate-term needs can be met through term insurance, but here again I would recommend a higher-quality company over the lowest-cost term. This is because of convertibility, not insurability. (This is a key factor because a significant portion of term insurance is converted to whole life insurance, and being with a quality company is a plus at the time of conversion.)

Insurance is a wise cornerstone of a complete financial plan, and it's necessary for a family's peace of mind. Although the marketplace can be confusing, thinking through the issues raised in this chapter should help you arrive at a sound decision. However, certain questions about insurance are common, and you may need the help of a professional advisor to determine the best product for you.

Comparing premiums

To help you understand the difference in premiums and the amount of coverage, I've compared several top-rated insurance companies. I assumed that a 30-year-old male and female were looking for life insurance coverage of $500,000. Here is the lowest premium available for various types of insurance:[3]

ANNUAL INSURANCE PREMIUMS FOR 15-YEAR, $500,000 POLICY

Insured	Term	Whole	Universal
Male, 30, nonsmoker, good health	$260	$4,560	$2,031
Female, 30, nonsmoker, good health	$240	$3,945	$1,677

To see the difference that age makes, let's assume the couple is now 50 years old. The premiums cost more because the policyholders are more likely to die while still covered by the policy.

ANNUAL INSURANCE PREMIUMS FOR 15-YEAR, $500,000 POLICY

Insured	Term	Whole	Universal
Male, 50, nonsmoker, good health	$954	$11,565	$4,920
Female, 50, nonsmoker, good health	$680	$8,925	$3,996

As you can see from the next chart, the entire 15 years of premium for term life insurance for the young couple is less than one year of whole life coverage. This is why I've been saying term insurance is the most economical for purchasing pure life insurance coverage.

TOTAL PREMIUMS PAID AFTER 15 YEARS FOR $500,000 POLICY

Insured	Term	Whole	Universal
Male, 30, nonsmoker, good health	$3,900	$68,400	$30,465
Female, 30, nonsmoker, good health	$3,600	$59,175	$25,155

The drivers of the premium amount are health status, age, tobacco use, and gender. The premium, however, is only part of the picture. You must also look at the cash value available at the end of the coverage period.

CASH VALUE AVAILABLE FOR $500,000 POLICY AFTER 15 YEARS

Insured	Term	Whole	Universal
Male, 30, nonsmoker, good health	$0	$64,560	$15,362

Although you won't pay much for term, there's nothing left at the end. You simply receive life insurance coverage for the period insured. With other types of insurance, you build up some cash that will be available at some future date (15 years later in this example). You would receive $64,560 from the whole life policy. For the whole life, you would have ended up paying a total of $3,840 ($68,400 in total premiums less the cash value received at the end). The term cost $3,900. Ignoring any tax impact, the term and whole life cost about the same in absolute dollars.

But you must consider the time value of money and the opportunity cost. In other words, what could you have done with the extra money if you had bought term instead of whole life insurance? If you had been disciplined enough to save the difference between the term life insurance and the whole life of $4,300 per year for the 30-year-old male, then buying term is a wiser choice. Investing the $4,300 each year, or $358 per month, and earning an annual return of 7 percent would result in $112,005. This is where the mantra of "buy term and invest the difference" comes from.

Reviewing Your Insurance Coverage

Insurance needs change, which is why you should perform a periodic review of your insurance with respect to your overall financial position and provision requirements. For example, when a man marries, he is responsible to provide for his wife. This may precipitate an insurance need. When children come along, the need for insurance may increase because of the need to assure that they are educated and then given an opportunity to make a living. Also, adequate capital is needed so the wife would not have to go to work to support their children if her husband died. As children gain independence, the provision needs may decrease.

> **Insurance needs change, which is why you should perform a periodic review of your insurance.**

Other factors may also prompt an insurance reevaluation: (1) a significant rise in inflation; (2) increased income or lifestyle costs; (3) heavy personal or business debt obligations; (4) a change in estate liquidity needs; and (5) long-term flexibility.

If you're interested in considering insurance as an investment vehicle, be prepared to do some careful research. Unfortunately, there is more misinformation available than hard facts on which to make wise decisions. Insurance policies are extremely difficult to compare on an "apples-to-apples" basis. Look at cash value policies carefully before you decide whether to purchase more or to cancel existing policies.

We suggest you seek out a financial advisor in your community whom you can trust to give you some sound counsel on your insurance decision. (You may be able to find a Christian financial advisor in your area by going to http://www.kingdomadvisors.org.)

Many outstanding Christian insurance specialists with pure motives can lead you to the most economical life insurance for you. Our counsel is never to view life insurance as an investment, but strictly as good stewardship to protect your family in the event of your death. Therefore, *always* make sure you are adequately covered.

CHAPTER 29

Other Insurance You Can't Do Without

Having three daughters is a joyful privilege—but it brings an accompanying challenge. It's the event that causes grown men to shudder: the wedding. To help me cope, I didn't have another of the insurance industry's creative products—a wedding insurance policy—available to me. No kidding, you can insure against "cold feet."

Imagine what an evacuation of a coastal town from a threatening hurricane or a flu outbreak among the bride and her family could do to the big matrimonial day. A postponement might cause the bride's parents to lose some of those non-refundable cash deposits for halls, caterers, bands, and the whole range of wedding vendors. Holders of wedding insurance policies may recoup those costs.

As is common with other types of insurance policies, wedding insurance products have evolved. Fireman's Fund Insurance Company was the first insurer to offer "change of heart" coverage in its policies. If the bride or groom gets cold feet, the insurance company still pays. With the average cost of weddings approaching $27,000, the insurance company thinks the bride's father is a good prospect. But read the fine print: The change of heart must occur at least four months before the wedding date.[1]

As I mentioned in the previous chapter, the basic purpose of insurance is to transfer a risk that you're not willing or able to take to someone (usually a company) willing to take the risk in return for compensation. You can find insurance for just about anything. Lloyd's of London is essentially a market for trading insurance risks of all kinds. Investors and companies there will insure a football player's knee, a pop singer's voice, or a special event. Of course, they do it for a price, called a premium.

While relatively few people are in the market for wedding insurance, in the

> **The basic purpose of insurance is to transfer a risk you're not willing or able to take to someone (usually a company) willing to take the risk in return for compensation.**

Q: Are those special insurance plans I receive in the mail a good deal?

ANSWER: Let the buyer beware! Your mail undoubtedly brings many offers for special insurance plans from your bank, credit card company, or an insert in the newspaper. Are they wise investments? Let's consider some of them.

I remember reading an offer from a credit card company for a special insurance program. I read it over several times to make sure I was reading it correctly. For the "low cost" of $.59 per $100 of the outstanding monthly balance, I could have life insurance that would pay my unpaid credit card balance if I died prior to age 66. At first glance, this does not appear to cost too much (only $.59 per $100 of insurance). But once you start to multiply the numbers you soon find that, on an average balance of $1,000, a person would be paying $70.80 over the course of a year for that $1,000 of life insurance!

To put this in perspective, the average cost of term insurance today in the first year will run between $1 and $1.50 per $1,000. Consider the $70.80 that a person would pay for $1,000 of coverage with this credit card company. If you spent the $70.80 to buy term life insurance, you could potentially buy $70,000 of life insurance instead of $1,000 from the credit card company.

As I thought about the insurance proposal for credit card debt, I asked myself if there were any other types of insurance the consumer may be tempted to buy at an outlandish cost. One that came to mind was mortgage life insurance. I was curious to do some research and find the cost for this type of insurance.

Mortgage life insurance is marketed as a way to pay off the house debt when the homeowner (borrower) dies. It's actually a decreasing term type of insurance because, as the debt is decreased, the insurance company's liability is decreased. These policies are almost always more expensive than yearly renewable term products after the first several years. Most mortgage insurance is very expensive when reduced to the dollar cost per $1,000 of insurance base. This is especially the case if it is purchased through a mortgage company or bank.

Usually, a better alternative is to increase your existing life insurance to provide this coverage (if it is not already provided through a previous needs analysis) or to purchase a separate decreasing term life insurance policy for this purchase and cancel it when the mortgage is paid.

This reminds us again of the importance of our stewardship responsibility. We must make sure that our overall insurance program is in order, thus eliminating the need for these types of special insurance coverage. If a person has a life insurance program calculated and funded correctly, then he or she will be less apt to make the mistake of signing up for coverage of this type.

Your Insurance Needs Analysis (see page 421) includes provision for debt payoff. Since debt varies, you may want to make a provision for an average amount of debt. Of course, the simplest way to deal with this area is to live debt-free as a part of your financial plan.

last chapter you read about why you need to consider buying life insurance. In this chapter, we'll consider a few other important forms of insurance.

Disability Insurance

How dependent is your family on earned income? If you're like most people, you're very dependent! Most people would indeed encounter serious financial difficulties if their regular stream of earned income were to cease. The fact is, you have one chance in three that you'll suffer a long-term disability sometime between the ages of 35 and 65—a higher probability than your dying. Even so, disability income protection is often overlooked in financial planning.

> **There's one chance in three that you'll suffer a long-term disability sometime between the ages of 35 and 65.**

But certain questions naturally arise. How much coverage do you need? And what kind of policy should you obtain? To determine how much disability insurance you need, complete the worksheet shown below.

NEEDS ANALYSIS

Income Goals for Your Family (monthly)

Living expenses	$
Taxes	$
Giving	$
Miscellaneous	$
Education expenses	$
Debt repayment	$
Total uses	$

Income Sources (monthly)

Social Security	$
Retirement assets	$
Interest and dividends	$
Earned income	$
Unearned income	$
Disability	$
Total sources	$

Most insurers won't allow the amount of disability coverage to exceed approximately 60 percent of your earned income. Be certain to ask your agent how the coverage you are considering would integrate with any existing group or other personal disability insurance.

Perhaps the single most important question in evaluating disability income coverage is the definition of disability. Is it the inability to perform the main duties of *your* occupation or *any* occupation, or does it relate to some loss of earnings that you experience? You need to determine the answers to these questions before proceeding.

The main drivers in the cost of the disability premium are your occupation and your health. The premium for a construction worker is much higher than for a banker. If you have experienced previous back problems or arthritis, then your premium will be much higher than someone without these medical issues. If a person's occupation is too dangerous or his or her health too poor, the insurance company may not insure that person at all.

Notice also these important aspects of the coverage:

Renewal protection. An individual policy should be noncancelable and guaranteed renewable. This means the insurer can never cancel the policy as long as you continue to make the premium payments. Your future health will not be a factor in your ability to continue the coverage or the amount of premiums you pay.

Benefit period. The benefit period stated in the policy dictates how long you will receive the monthly benefit once payments have begun. The longest duration commonly available is to age 65. Normally this would be the appropriate benefit period to choose because one is really trying to protect his or her family in the event of a long-term catastrophic disability. Naturally, the amount of investment assets that can generate income will play a part in determining not only the *amount* of monthly benefit, but also the *duration* of the benefit necessary.

Waiting period. The elimination or waiting period is the length of time after you become disabled before benefits begin. Very short elimination period coverage is available, but it may not be wise. For example, the premium for a 30-day elimination period is much more expensive than one for 90 days. Perhaps your emergency savings can cover you for a short-term period rather than paying a higher premium. Waiting periods of 30, 60, 90, and 180 days are the usual options. Most people choose the 90-day elimination period.

In addition, some policies also offer a cost-of-living rider or coverage for partial disability.

I encourage you to evaluate your needs objectively by using the Needs Analysis worksheet on page 433 to determine the appropriate amount of disability income coverage. Once you have determined the appropriate amount, be certain to shop the market, as there are significant differences both in premiums and contractual provisions. Disability income coverage is a specialty; many insurance agents are not as knowledgeable in this area as they are about property and casualty and life insurance. In light of this, you may want to ask your agent to involve another more qualified agent to help you determine your policy needs.

Homeowners' Insurance

Imagine a muggy summer evening. You're finishing dinner when a thunderstorm rolls through your town. A bolt of lightning knocks out the electricity to your home. When the power is restored, you find that your television, computer, garage door opener, and stereo have been damaged. If you have home insurance coverage, you may be able to get those items replaced or repaired. The insurance company may also pay to remove the 80-year-old tree that was hit by the lightning.

If you're like most people, your home and its contents represent some of your most expensive purchases. You likely paid dearly for your belongings and may still be paying on the mortgage. Therefore, you need to be sure that all of it is properly insured.

If you rent rather than own a home, you need to insure your belongings, though not the physical building you live in. It's estimated that very few renters have insurance to protect their possessions.

Homeowners' insurance covers obvious destruction such as damage from fire and storm and loss through theft or lawsuit. Some situations you wish would be covered, like flood or earthquake coverage, often aren't. If you live in an area that is often affected by those problems, it's possible to purchase separate coverage.

As with any insurance, the primary issue is to be sure you are adequately insured. Therefore, in the event of a partial or complete loss, your insurance would provide adequate money to get you where you were before the calamity. For instance, if your home was totally destroyed by fire and insured for its full replacement costs, it would be up to the insurance carrier to rebuild the house, refurnish it, purchase new clothes—even stock your refrigerator and cupboards.

> **Your home and its contents represent some of your most expensive purchases, so you need to be sure that all of it is properly insured.**

Homeowners' insurance covers several risk areas. The first is *property protection*. This reimburses you for loss or damage to your house and its contents. The amount of coverage is based on the cost of replacing the entire structure.

Usually the amount of personal property coverage is figured as a percentage of the value of the house—often 50 percent. There are, however, monetary limits for specific types of possessions within the home, such as currency, jewelry, furs, and silver. You want to be sure you understand these limits. If the value of your possessions in those areas are above those limits, you should purchase additional insurance for them.

The second type of risk coverage is *liability protection*. This pays for injury or damage to others caused on or by your property or family members. It includes accidents that happen around your home. For instance, if a neighborhood kid was playing in your yard and tripped over a rake you left on the ground, suffering a broken bone, your property insurance would pay for his medical expenses. In the event that his parents filed a lawsuit, your insurance would pay any settlement costs and legal costs up to the amount of your coverage.

Additionally, homeowner's policies cover such things as temporary housing and meal reimbursement in the event you are unable to live in your house for a while.

There are various kinds of insurance protection; they vary from minimal coverage (which basically is the house at cost) to the cost of the house plus 5 to 10 percent more for personal possessions, to full coverage of the house and all possessions. There are specific policies for renters and for condominium or co-op owners; some carriers even offer policies designed specifically for older homes.

The drivers of home insurance premiums are the cost of your home and furnishings, the availability of fire protection, the liability coverage limits, and the proximity to special risk areas (ocean, for example). The key factor in knowing how much insurance you need is knowing the value of your house. Your real estate property tax is probably based on your home value. This figure may or may not be accurate, but it certainly is a benchmark you can compare to. The purchase price is not necessarily a good guide, particularly if you bought the house some time ago.

You would be most protected by an insurance policy that covers 100 percent of repair and replacement costs. This shifts the responsibility for rebuilding to the insurance company. This type of coverage ensures that the insurance company would bear the full cost of rebuilding your home, even if your home was valued at $100,000 but cost $115,000 to rebuild.

Some homeowners' policies reimburse for the contents of your home based on actual cash value, which is what it would cost to buy the item today minus depreciation. That means if your 10-year-old stereo is damaged in a lightning storm, you would get only what your stereo would have brought at a garage sale. You are much better off to have your property covered with replacement cost coverage. It will probably add 10 to 15 percent to the cost of the insurance, but in the event of a claim it will be well worth it.

Your insurance carrier will require you to document all your possessions in the event of a major claim. It's virtually impossible for you to remember the contents of one room of your house, much less the entire house. However, a very easy and cost-effective way of doing this is to record the inventory of your house on a video camera (which you can rent or borrow if necessary) or a still camera. Spend a few hours walking from room to room in your house to record every piece of furniture, every knick-knack, and the inside of every cupboard and closet so it is very obvious what you have in your home. The videocassette, DVD, CD, or photos should be stored safely, preferably in a safety deposit box away from your home or at a relative's house so they will not be destroyed if your home sustains heavy damage.

You should evaluate your insurance regularly, particularly if you undergo any major changes in your home (such as remodeling, relocation, new furniture). In addition to the video inventory, you should record serial numbers, model numbers, and purchase dates, and retain sales receipts for significant items for proof of ownership in the event of a major claim. A copy of this listing of items should be kept off-site at a safety deposit box or at a relative's house.

As with all insurance, it pays to shop the market. Insurance is very competitive. Deal with a reputable agent and a quality insurance carrier. Don't be underinsured; in the event you have a claim, you'll go through enough trauma without having to lower your lifestyle or do without some of the things you consider necessities because you didn't pay the additional small premium dollars to properly insure your valuables up front.

Health Insurance: A Diagnosis

In the United States, Americans enjoy relatively high-quality, accessible health care. But we certainly pay for it. Health care costs have increased dramatically in the last generation. Even a minor outpatient surgery can result in expensive bills from many different sources. Treating a child's broken arm could easily cost $5,000.

Health insurance is the most important insurance policy to purchase.

With little reservation, I suggest that health insurance is the most important insurance policy to purchase. The likelihood of you or a family member needing care is almost certain. The cost of that care is very high. Is it worth transferring that risk to an insurance company? Yes. Another reason health insurance is almost a necessity is that insurers have arranged for discounts from healthcare providers. So the actual cost of a procedure, after applying the contractual adjustment with the insurance carrier, is less than the cost to someone without insurance.

As an employee, you probably consider health insurance a standard benefit of working for your company. However, if you're self-employed, unemployed, or retired, you no doubt realize that your insurance choices are complex, broad, and perhaps frustrating.

The highest escalating operating expense for most businesses over the last several years has been providing health insurance for employees. Cost increases of 25 to 40 percent per year or more have not been unusual. Therefore, many businesses have been forced to alter their health insurance package of benefits.

Until the last couple of decades, an employer often paid the full cost of health insurance for employees and their families. Typically the deductible was $100, and employees paid 20 percent of the next $1,000, with the insurance carrier paying the rest. Therefore the employees' maximum expense may have been $300 per year per family member.

Now the deductible is usually $500 or perhaps $1,000. Coinsurance and copayment maximums have increased. Employees' out-of-pocket expenses may be as much as $2,500 (for the deductible, copayments, and share of medical costs). Also, employees are often expected to pay part of their personal coverage; family coverage generally costs thousands of dollars more. So individuals are looking now at premium costs ranging from $1,000 to $2,000 per year with the possibility of insurance claims costing up to $2,500 for each family member with major claims in a year.

Ordinarily, three kinds of health insurance packages are available. The most typical plan allows employees to select their own doctors and hospitals, processing their claims through the insurance company.

A second type of coverage is called a health maintenance organization (HMO). Large corporations often offer these. They save money for the employer but offer very structured benefits for the employee, who is required to go to specific doctors. However, the insured may not have to pay anything toward the health costs. If someone goes to work for a corporation that offers an HMO, he or she may go through culture shock leaving the longtime family doctor. But if that is the only option, obviously the employee has no choice.

The third type of health package is a preferred provider organization (PPO). Many smaller companies are moving this way. In this plan, some doctors and hospitals in a given area have prenegotiated rates with the PPO. Since their rates have been capped, the insurance company can offer a lower premium cost. Typically, it's possible for an employee to use his or her own doctor or a different hospital, but he or she may pay a higher deductible or surcharge.

Most people are still covered through the typical health insurance plan that allows them to choose their own doctor and hospital and pay a deductible on a calendar-year basis. The coinsurance amounts and the out-of-pocket maximum depend on what has been negotiated by the employer with the health insurance provider.

What can be done to control these expenses? How can you keep your personal insurance claims down? Here are several suggestions:

Hold on to the claims for each family member, submitting them to the insurance company only when each has met the deductible. This is likely to lead to more accurate processing on the part of the insurance company. It also benefits the employer, because each time the insurance company has to process a claim—even if that claim is not paid because the deductible has not yet been met—it goes on record as a claim against that company, and their rating has the potential to go up.

Become a careful consumer of health insurance. Don't go to an emergency room unless it's absolutely necessary. Likewise, visit a doctor rather than a 24-hour emergency medical clinic. Use outpatient rather than inpatient surgery if at all possible. Do preadmission testing as an outpatient.

Take steps for preventive medical maintenance. Do things to stay healthy. Get proper exercise, follow a sensible diet, and have an annual physical.

Keep accurate records of your medical expenses and double-check statements when they come back from the insurance processor. Nobody is infallible, and it's possible they have made a mistake in your favor.

Opt for a higher deductible on your health insurance package if your family has been generally healthy. The cost of your premiums will be less for the higher deductible insurance.

Use insurance wisely. Health insurance costs increase partly because of overuse on the part of the insured. Certainly malpractice rates have had an impact on health insurance costs. But overuse certainly has increased the expense also.

Understand the coordination of benefits if you and your spouse are covered by separate insurance policies.

Finally, become familiar with the details of your company's health insurance package. This will help you maximize the benefits.

Long-Term Care Insurance

No one likes the thought of needing long-term care. No one likes to imagine battling Alzheimer's disease for five to eight years, having a stroke that results in partial paralysis, or not being able to get around because of severe arthritis or osteoporosis. In a recent survey, more people thought going to a nursing home was worse than dying or becoming bankrupt.[2] But the fear of long-term care should not keep you from wise planning. Denial is not an appropriate solution.

What's your potential financial exposure from a long-term care event? Potentially unlimited. The average annual cost of one year in a nursing home is $74,806, or $204.95 a day.[3] Stay a few years and your IRA will take quite a dent. Assisted living facilities have an annual cost of $32,572 for a one-bedroom unit.[4]

How will you pay for long-term care? You have four basic options.

- **Self-insure.** You could pay for the care from your current income (pensions, Social Security) and saved assets. The downside of this option, however, is that the significant cost of care could eliminate a lifetime of saving.

- **Rely on the government.** You may use Medicaid if you're poor enough. If you spend all your assets, Medicaid will pay for your nursing home coverage. Few, if any, middle-class Americans will qualify for Medicaid initially. Contrary to the perception of many, Medicare does not cover long-term care costs.

- **Rely upon family members.** Are they nearby? Do they have the time and expertise to care for you? Is there enough room to live together? Can you (or they) stand it?

- **Purchase long-term care insurance.** Such insurance provides coverage for nursing home stays, home health care, assisted living, and/or other types of care. By paying these costs, long-term care insurance protects your assets. The drawback of obtaining this insurance is its cost.

FAMILY FINANCE

"Bye, Mom," Bob said as he hung up the phone. He leaned back in his chair.

"How is your dad today?" Laura asked.

"Not good. Mom said he's been confused all morning, and there was one point where he didn't seem to know who she was." Bob sighed. His father had been diagnosed with Alzheimer's a month ago. "She's starting to worry about the future. She's not sure how long she can take care of him without other help, but she's also concerned about how much that help will cost."

Laura frowned. "I know it's difficult for her."

Bob turned toward her abruptly. "You know, my dad is the third of five siblings to be diagnosed with Alzheim-er's. As much as I hate to admit it, that means I'm at pretty high risk too."

Laura glanced up at him. "I have to admit I've thought about that too, and it is scary. But what can we do about it—besides pray?"

"I want to make sure I learn from my parents' experience. My mom's decisions about care are that much harder because of her financial stresses and uncertainties. If we ever face this situation, I want to be prepared." He swallowed hard. "We're here for my parents, but in 15 or 20 years Liz might be living halfway across the country. I'm sure she would help, but we can't count on her to be our primary support."

Laura took Bob's hand. "Our last meeting with the financial planner was

How much will you pay for this coverage? That depends on your age when you initially obtain the insurance, your health, and the benefits you select. Couples applying together receive discounts. A couple in their early sixties may pay anywhere from $250 to $500 a month. A good time to begin considering this type of insurance is when you are in your fifties or sixties.

These policies can be fairly complex with many added features. Generally, most policies begin coverage either when you show mental impairment, such as Alzheimer's disease, or when you can no longer perform by yourself any two of the six activities of daily living, which include bathing, eating, dressing, toileting, continence, and walking/transferring.

Joe spent a lifetime saving and doing all the right things in planning for retirement and older age. He had a big IRA balance, a small pension, and no debt by the time he retired. After he was diagnosed with Parkinson's disease, he started to need some help. His wife, herself suffering from bad knees and a bad back, was limited in how much she could help. First they needed in-home health care regularly. After suffering a mild stroke, Joe needed to be placed in a nursing home. In bad shape, but several years from dying, Joe's cost of care was significant. He had neglected to address the potential risk to his family's financial wealth that long-term care costs pose. His IRA account was used almost entirely for his care, leaving very little for his wife. If you have some assets and income, then you are a suitable candidate for long-term care insurance.

so positive. We're doing well and saving quite a bit of money. Don't you think we'll be stable enough to finance nursing care if we need it?"

Bob shook his head. "We do have quite a bit saved, and I'm grateful for that. But I don't want to see all of our assets wiped out because of a medical crisis for one of us. If something happens to me and I end up in long-term care, I want to make sure that you still have enough to live on."

"What about long-term care insurance?" Laura suggested. "I know my parents have looked into that. It might allow us to protect our assets and retain some independence."

"I don't know how much it would cost," Bob said. "Especially for some-one with my family's medical history. I might be considered high risk."

"That's possible," Laura admitted. "But if a relatively moderate monthly expenditure would give us peace of mind and protection for the future, it might be worth it. I can do some calling next week and get a few quotes," she offered.

"Okay. That sounds like a good idea." Bob let out a deep breath and put his arm around Laura. "I guess I just need to remember that no matter how much I plan, I can't control the future."

"That's true. We can only trust that God will be with us," Laura added. "And I know he has good plans for our family, no matter what the future holds."

At times, the insurance industry has used fear and emotional appeals to induce people into buying their product. Some have done this with long-term care insurance. The National Association of Insurance Commissioners, an organization of all the state insurance commissioners, makes the following recommendations to help consumers determine whether or not they should consider buying long-term care insurance.

They suggest you should consider buying this insurance if

- You have substantial assets and income that you want to protect
- You want to pay for your own care
- You don't want to depend on others for support

On the other hand, they recommend you not buy such insurance if

- You can't afford the premiums
- Your assets are limited
- Social Security or Supplemental Security Income is your only source of income
- You struggle paying for basic needs like utilities, food, and medicine[5]

If you think that long-term care insurance makes sense for you, speak with your financial advisor or insurance agent. Obtain quotes from at least three insurance companies that are rated highly for financial strength and have a long history of not raising premiums on existing policies.

CHAPTER 30

Can't Buy Me Love: Communicating with Your Spouse about Money

Divorced couples have revealed that money is one of the main reasons for their breakups. It's not just a lack of money, because many affluent couples have struggles and tension about money. I'm reminded of an interview:

> Reporter: "So you are 100 years old. How did you manage to live so long?"
>
> Old man: "Well, son, I got married when I was 21. The wife and I decided that if we had arguments, the loser would take a long walk to get over being mad. I suppose I have been benefited most by 79 years of fresh air and exercise."[1]

Arguments about money—not sex or household chores—are what couples between the ages of 18 and 40 fight over the most, according to a recent survey. In fact, money is such a troublesome issue that 82 percent of survey respondents say they have hidden shopping bags and various purchases from their spouse.[2] So much for marital oneness and unity, huh?

When my wife, Judy, became a Christian in 1972, I was busy building a business, growing our income, and providing for our family. She asked me about giving money to the church by tithing. Not being a believer at that time, I wouldn't hear of it. I didn't think it made financial sense. Judy showed patience and a winsome, submissive spirit. We didn't begin giving significantly until I became a Christian.

> **Arguments about money—not sex or household chores—are what couples between the ages of 18 and 40 fight over most.**

Should Judy have begun tithing, or nagging me to do so, even when I wasn't in agreement? I don't think so. God is more interested in a couple's relationship than the "correct" answer. God doesn't need our money. He owns it all. In a marriage, it's not a matter of who's right, but submitting to one another in love.

The Bible on Communication

As with most issues of importance in our daily lives, the Bible has a lot to say about the marriage relationship. Marriage was God's idea from the beginning. He knows what works best for us. In His creativity—or perhaps it was His sense of humor—He made men and women unique. He intended them to complement each other. As Larry Burkett often said, "If both of you are the same, then one of you is unnecessary."

Bookstore shelves are full of how-to books from popular psychologists and other communication gurus. While they may have some good advice to offer, nothing beats the Bible when it comes to providing wisdom for daily living.

Tonight, before you go to bed, get out a Bible and look up one of the following verses in context. Each passage reveals God's design for marriage or provides wisdom on the workings of a good relationship. Copy the verse or commit it to memory, asking God to make it real in your life. Then, when conflict arises in your marriage because of your different backgrounds, your different perspectives, or something else, use your verse to help you respond wisely to the situation.

> The LORD God said, "It is not good for the man to be alone. I will make a helper suitable for him." (Genesis 2:18)

> So the LORD God caused the man to fall into a deep sleep; and while he was sleeping, he took one of the man's ribs and closed up the place with flesh. Then the LORD God made a woman from the rib he had taken out of the man, and he brought her to the man. The man said, "This is now bone of my bones and flesh of my flesh; she shall be called 'woman,' for she was taken out of man." For this reason a man will leave his father and mother and be united to his wife, and they will become one flesh. (Genesis 2:21-24)

> May your fountain be blessed, and may you rejoice in the wife of your youth. (Proverbs 5:18)

> Better a dry crust with peace and quiet than a house full of feasting, with strife. (Proverbs 17:1)

> Starting a quarrel is like breaching a dam; so drop the matter before a dispute breaks out. (Proverbs 17:14)

> Enjoy life with your wife, whom you love, all the days of this meaningless life that God has given you under the sun—all your

FAITH & FINANCE

meaningless days. For this is your lot in life and in your toilsome labor under the sun. (Ecclesiastes 9:9)

"I hate divorce," says the LORD God of Israel, "and I hate a man's covering himself with violence as well as with his garment," says the LORD Almighty. (Malachi 2:16)

Some Pharisees came to him to test him. They asked, "Is it lawful for a man to divorce his wife for any and every reason?"

"Haven't you read," he replied, "that at the beginning the Creator 'made them male and female,' and said, 'For this reason a man will leave his father and mother and be united to his wife, and the two will become one flesh'? So they are no longer two, but one. Therefore what God has joined together, let man not separate."

"Why then," they asked, "did Moses command that a man give his wife a certificate of divorce and send her away?"

Jesus replied, "Moses permitted you to divorce your wives because your hearts were hard. But it was not this way from the beginning. I tell you that anyone who divorces his wife, except for marital unfaithfulness, and marries another woman commits adultery." (Matthew 19:3-9)

Love is patient, love is kind. It does not envy, it does not boast, it is not proud. It is not rude, it is not self-seeking, it is not easily angered, it keeps no record of wrongs. Love does not delight in evil but rejoices with the truth. It always protects, always trusts, always hopes, always perseveres. (1 Corinthians 13:4-7)

But now you must rid yourselves of all such things as these: anger, rage, malice, slander, and filthy language from your lips. Do not lie to each other, since you have taken off your old self with its practices. (Colossians 3:8-9)

Let your conversation be always full of grace, seasoned with salt, so that you may know how to answer everyone. (Colossians 4:6)

[An overseer] must manage his own family well and see that his children obey him with proper respect. (If anyone does not know how to manage his own family, how can he take care of God's church?) (1 Timothy 3:4-5)

An elder must be blameless, the husband of but one wife, a man whose children believe and are not open to the charge of being wild and disobedient. (Titus 1:6)

My dear brothers, take note of this: Everyone should be quick to listen, slow to speak and slow to become angry, for man's anger does not bring about the righteous life that God desires. (James 1:19-20)

Such truth, such wisdom. If we practice what James says about being quick to listen, slow to speak, and slow to anger, then we'll do pretty well when communicating about money. There's not much more I can add. But I don't think my publisher will accept a reference book about money that just says, "Read the Bible, knucklehead, and do what it says."

So, knowing that I can't improve on the truth in the Bible, allow me to comment on a few of the vexing areas of managing money for couples. I think it will be particularly helpful to consider the different perspective and approach of husbands and wives when it comes to debt, spending and budgets, and investing.

Working through Key Financial Issues

Debt

As a young businessman drove home from the jewelry store shortly before Christmas, he was beside himself with excitement. It had been a tough year at his business, so he'd had to borrow to purchase the diamond necklace. But he knew the thrill on his wife's face would be worth the cost. Once home, he carefully placed the box under the Christmas tree. He watched with delight as his wife looked at the box and shook it, wondering what it might be.

Finally the big day arrived! Christmas morning, as the wife opened the box, the look on her face changed from curiosity . . . to shock. She began to cry, because she knew he had taken on more debt to obtain the necklace.

Surprised at her response? You shouldn't be. I've counseled with hundreds of couples over the years and have noted specific differences in the ways men and women react to debt. In this section we'll compare those responses. I realize that the following generalizations may not apply to every couple; some husbands are much more sensitive about taking on debt than their wives. However, overall I have found some fairly standard reactions to debt among men and women.

Let's begin by examining the typical husband's response. First, the husband will tend to become a workaholic in order to handle the debt. Even though more work and longer hours are not the answer, they are typically the husband's first response when faced with debt. But it's a response that the wife normally does not want. She wants him to be home more. And thus conflict builds.

A husband's first response to debt typically is to work longer hours.

Second, the husband will stop telling his wife what he is doing regarding debt. He won't even let her know when he takes on more debt or why. Many times as I work through the assets and liabilities with a couple, the wife will exclaim, "I didn't know we owed that!" The husband stops communicating with his wife regarding debt because he is concerned about her reaction. He knows her response will normally be negative. So rather than try to explain why, he says nothing.

Third, the husband may exhibit ups and downs in his spiritual life. I've noticed in counseling with couples that if things are going well (income, job, promotions), then debt is not a big issue and their spiritual life is strong. However, if there is a glitch in their income or the debt load becomes too great, then the couple tends to go into a spiritual tailspin. This is to be expected, because they must work harder and therefore have less time to spend with God. They can't get ahead because they must put all their energy into paying debt, which adds to their stress. This should not be surprising because when we're in debt we feel anxious that our income not go down. Proverbs 22:7 is true—"The borrower is servant to the lender." Therefore, debt can put the spiritual leader on a spiritual roller coaster.

A fourth way the husband may respond to debt is to blame his wife and take no personal responsibility for it. He concludes that he has been driven to assume an inordinate amount of debt in order to satisfy his wife's desires for "things." As a result, he may feel little personal responsibility and even develop an attitude of apathy toward paying back the debt. He takes on more debt yet works less. Eventually he doesn't care if the debt is even paid back. His wife's security is of very little concern to him.

The wife should understand these responses of the husband to debt. Likewise, the husband should expect the following responses from his wife.

Debt causes most wives to become very anxious. This is because she has a basic God-given need for security. Because of the woman's basic nurturing instincts, she desires to have a secure environment. Debt threatens this.

I've known of husbands who have suggested to their wives that they go into debt to finance a business opportunity, an investment, or the purchase of a new "toy." The husband is generally surprised by his wife's strong response. Her anxiety and fears may surface with a simple comment that includes the word *debt*.

She may say, "Why do we need the debt? What if our income goes down?

> **Debt causes most wives to become very anxious.**

What about our home?" Often a wife's response to debt is much different than her husband's. What a husband may see as a wise business move, the wife may see as a threat to her security.

At this point—just before the blowup or the tears, depending on the wife's modus operandi—it is the husband's responsibility to help his wife understand his reasoning. If she is not comfortable, then perhaps the husband should not take out the debt. After all, is money more important than your marriage?

Out of anxiety comes the wife's second response: nagging. She may continually push her husband on the debt issue. "Why don't you reduce the debt?

Why do we have so much debt?" It's my observation, however, that this nagging is simply a plea for communication, a request by the wife for her husband to let her in on what he is doing. She needs to hear his thinking on debt—and how it will be paid for.

A third response of the wife to debt is apathy. She may feel there is no reason for her to watch what she spends if he is going into large amounts of debt. What does her little bit for clothes really matter if the husband is going to spend huge amounts on houses, boats, and other "investments"? Basically, this attitude results if the husband does not help the wife understand why and where debt fits into the overall provision plan.

The final response the wife may have to debt is disrespect for the husband. She does not feel he really cares about her, since he is willing to threaten her basic security by taking on debt. So she begins to belittle him and tear him down. If he really cared for her, she concludes, he wouldn't take on so much debt.

Obviously, debt exists in most marriages. Therefore, husbands and wives must prepare for it. The husband's basic drive to provide may conflict with the wife's basic need for security. To avoid problems in marriage caused by debt, each partner should strive to communicate with the other—before debt is assumed. Husbands especially should make sure their wives understand why

FAMILY FINANCE

The minute Brian walked through the door, he knew Tanya was upset. She was sitting in the dining room, looking straight ahead, her fingers drumming on the table.

"Hi," he said tentatively. "Is something wrong?"

Apparently that was just the opening she'd been waiting for. "Wrong? Why would you think that?" she asked sarcastically. "Nothing's wrong—except that I found a printout of an e-mail exchange you had with Dwayne. The one where you talked about taking out a loan with him so the two of you could start an online business."

"Aha." Brian suddenly understood. "I was going to mention it. It's a great idea—buying and selling comic books online. I've told you before how Dwayne and I have loved trading baseball cards and comic books since we were kids. Dwayne found some good suppliers, and he's sure we can turn a profit within a year. . . ." His voice trailed off as he saw the look on Tanya's face.

"I cannot believe you would consider taking on debt without talking to me about it! Why would you do that?"

Brian sat down across from her. "Tanya, I'm sorry that I didn't discuss it with you. But I'm worried about how tight finances might be after the baby is born and you're not working full-time anymore. I think we're going to need more income. Dwayne and I started talking, and this new business seemed like a great possibility."

Tanya took a deep breath and let it out. "Brian, I'm worried about our finances too. But the idea of taking on more debt right as we're going to have

a debt is needed and how it will be covered. Couples should have a financial strategy in place to avoid the use of debt. Don't let debt become a cause of discontent in your marriage.

Spending plans: Five good reasons you and your spouse should start one

Reduce conflict. The number one reason for couples to develop a spending plan—a budget—is to reduce conflict in their marriage.

"What's that?" you say. "Budgeting can *reduce* marital conflict?" I can just see all you "My-spouse-and-I-can-talk-about-anything-but-money" people scratching your heads—but hear me out. Budgeting reduces conflict for the simple reason that it provides built-in accountability and an objective standard for all of your spending decisions.

You might be surprised at the number of financial transactions you make. If you add up all the checks you write, all the credit card purchases you make, and everything you pay cash for, you could easily make 1,500 or 2,000 transactions a year. With or without a budget, you are going to spend money, whether it's to buy groceries, pay the rent, or take a family vacation. If you don't have a budget—a spending plan that allocates your income to reflect

a child to support makes me incredibly anxious. And I can't believe you would talk to your friend about our finances instead of talking to me. Aren't we supposed to be on the same team here?" She blinked back tears.

"We are on the same team!" Brian protested.

"Then don't hide things from me," Tanya said firmly. "Going into debt is enough to make me anxious. But if I find out about it after the fact, it also makes me feel insecure. I want to trust you—I do trust you. But something like this shakes me up."

Brian took her hand. "I really am sorry, Tanya," he said slowly. "I wasn't thinking about how it would make you feel. I guess with the baby coming I feel so strongly that I need to provide for you. I got caught up in that and forgot

that you have to be comfortable with the financial choices we make too."

"I know you're feeling some pressure," Tanya admitted. "But I also know that you're dependable and hard working. You are a great provider and you'll be a great father. I'm not worried about that side of things."

"Thanks for the vote of confidence," Brian said, smiling.

"We need to talk about our budget, and we may need to do some tightening—but overall, we're going to be okay," Tanya continued.

"You know," Brian said thoughtfully, "we have a lot of major changes coming up, both personal and financial. We each have our own anxieties. But I guess we need to talk about them openly—so we face them as a team."

"Agreed," Tanya said.

CAN'T BUY ME LOVE: COMMUNICATING WITH YOUR SPOUSE ABOUT MONEY

In-Depth Financial Strategies | 30

449

your priorities—any of these expenditures could touch off an argument. In fact, if you disagree on only about one out of every 100 purchases, you will wind up at odds with your spouse at least once a month. Statistically speaking, money fights or frustrations are a virtual certainty!

Judy and I use a computer software program to track our purchases. According to the computer, we make anywhere from 2,000 to 3,000 transactions each year. But since most of our spending decisions are made ahead of time in our family budget, there is very little disagreement about where our money should go. As a result, we have the freedom and flexibility to enjoy our purchases without fear, guilt, or conflict. Our budget works to eliminate potential problems before they arise.

Create focus. The second reason why a spending plan makes sense is that it allows you to create and maintain a vision for the future. A budget gives you the guidelines you need to successfully spend less than you earn—which, as any financial analyst can tell you, is the key to long-term financial security. Whether you want to buy a home, start your own business, fund your children's college education, or set yourself up for a comfortable retirement, a spending plan can keep you focused on your goals.

Balance spouses' input on spending. Third, a spending plan means that nobody has to be the bad guy. As I mentioned earlier, most marriages usually have a spending spouse and a saving spouse. Any time the spender buys something, he or she becomes a potential target: *Why did you buy that? It costs too much! And we don't really need it. Couldn't you have found something less expensive?* Likewise, when the saver refuses to spend money, he or she may invite criticism: *Why can't we buy that? It's not that expensive—and besides, it's on sale. You worry about money too much. Don't be such a killjoy.*

> **A spending plan can keep you focused on your goals.**

A budget can help eliminate such tension. Objective and impartial, the spending plan draws a line between the affordable and the out-of-reach, the wise purchase and the foolish. Because a budget is drafted with input from both spouses, the spending/saving decisions are not "mine" or "yours," but "ours." You're on the same side of the fence.

Aid communication. A fourth reason for a spending plan is that it forces couples to communicate. You can't establish budget categories and allocate income without talking about priorities, needs, dreams, and goals. Fears and insecurities can also be part of the process. By providing a forum for discussion, the budgeting process enables you to define and address philosophical differences—everything from how much to spend on food and clothing to how, where, or when you want to give money to your children, your church, or your charity.

Q: My husband thinks I spend all the money on household expenses and clothes for the children, but in reality I think he spends too much on his hobbies, sports, and workshop. What's the answer?

ANSWER: Budgeting and communication. It's easy for married couples to jump to conclusions about each other's spending habits. You're probably both good at spending money on what you think is important. The question is how to allocate your limited resources between what's important for both of you. Agree on that. The first step is a budget so that each person has the freedom to spend the amounts allocated in the budget categories over which he or she is responsible. The second step is a simple monthly review of expenses and whether more money needs to be allocated into any category. Bottom line: Communicate about your finances.

Set an example. Finally, by establishing and using a budget you set a great example for your kids. As Judy and I often remind ourselves, "More is caught than taught." When your children see you exercising financial discipline and making progress toward your goals, they will learn a valuable lesson about how to handle their own money.

Reducing conflict, creating vision, eliminating the bad guy, fostering communication, and demonstrating wise money management are all good reasons to develop a spending plan. But I'm not pretending that the process will be easy. At times it might even be a struggle. It's like going for a swim in the ocean: You have to get through a few rough spots before you get past the breakers. But I can promise you that once you get beyond the turbulence and out to where the water is gentle and clear, you will never want to go back.

Investing

It can be difficult for couples to maintain an atmosphere of trust and open communication about investing. Many husbands and wives simply do not discuss their investments. I am constantly amazed by the number of people I meet who approach investing with the idea that there is no point in talking with the other person because their spouses wouldn't understand the proposals, or are not interested in financial matters, or would automatically nix any investment opportunity.

Usually, though not always, men are the ones with this attitude. If you think I am making this up, I wish you could stand at the podium with me during some of my speaking engagements. If the audience is strictly male, generalizations such as those I've just made elicit guilty laughter, knowing looks, and nods of understanding. But if the audience includes women, the men sit rigidly in their chairs, wearing poker faces and even getting defensive. Men know how they think; they just don't want to admit it in front of their wives.

Although I didn't acknowledge it at the time, the way I handled our finances during the early years of our marriage generated major problems in my relationship with my wife. Simply put, Judy didn't trust me. She had no idea what I did with our money or what my actions might mean for our future.

While the children were at home, Judy was focused on raising our children. At first, the money or what I did with it didn't matter; Judy was just glad that I put food on the table. But when I started an accounting firm in Indiana, things began to change. As she tells it, the steady stream of papers I asked her to cosign for the business began to make her uncomfortable. She didn't understand exactly what she was signing, and I never took the time to explain things.

All Judy knew was what she saw: We were making payments on the two new cars I had purchased, we still had my college loans to pay off, and we took on a significant amount of debt when I started the business. From a financial standpoint, Judy was scared—but what was even worse was her fear that if she questioned any of my decisions, I might leave her. Remember, neither of us knew the Lord then. The way Judy saw it, I loved the business more than I loved her.

Even after we became Christians, I failed to bring Judy into the financial loop. In 1977, I sold my Indiana accounting firm so we could go into full-time ministry. At the end of the year, I realized I had an unexpected tax problem: The proceeds from the business sale had boosted my income, and I hadn't planned for the tax consequences this increase would create. On the advice of a Christian financial planner, I invested in some apartment buildings and a gold mine—two of the myriad tax shelters that everyone seemed to be jumping into at the time.

When I mentioned the investments to Judy, she instantly spotted a problem. Designed to shelter income and provide tax-reduction benefits, the apartments and the gold mine had no real economic promise. As investments, the chances that either asset would grow in value or generate income were slim. To Judy (and eventually to the bulk of the financial community), investments like these didn't make much sense. Even so, she did nothing to try to change my mind. "I was past the point where I wanted to protest—much less fight—about money," she says.

I knew, of course, that investing in the apartments and the gold mine carried a measure of risk; every investment is "risky," to some degree. But in my mind, the risk was secondary to our perceived need for a tax shelter. Heedless of Judy's perspective or the risk the investments carried, I rationalized my decision. (As things turned out, we did not lose any money and we did reap some tax benefits. But, as Judy predicted, the investments themselves turned out to be economically worthless.)

Any investment can be rationalized—especially if you are a man. Men seem uniquely capable of attaching a "no risk" or "low risk" label to any financial move they want to make. Not long ago, I met with a couple who had a large amount of money to invest. They wanted to know where they could get a 30 to 50 percent return, saying they had heard of something called a market neutral investment.

Never having heard that term before, I was intrigued. "What is a market neutral investment?" I finally asked.

"One where there is no risk," the fellow answered—with a completely straight face. "If the market drops, market neutral investments are not affected."

I wanted to laugh, but I looked at his wife. She was as concerned as any investor I have ever seen. From what I could tell, her husband was the financial "expert" of the family, but he had missed a truth that she intuitively understood: There is no such thing as a "risk-free" investment.

Strategies for Effective Conflict Resolution

Call them debates, conflicts, arguments, or vehement fiscal discussions—every couple will have disagreements. When a man faces a confrontation with his wife, he typically responds in one of three ways. Husbands, which one of these statements best describes the way you react?[3]

1. I give in. I'd rather give up than fight.

2. I flee the scene, hoping the problem will take care of itself.

3. I assert my authority to gain control of the situation and get my way.

Unfortunately, when you give in, flee, or fight over your differences, you will never experience the satisfaction that comes with effective conflict resolution. Instead, you could find yourself sleeping on the couch.

Wives, when you disagree with your husband about something, which one of these responses best describes your approach to the situation?

1. I try to get the upper hand through manipulation or hiding the facts.

2. I challenge my husband—especially when I think I know better.

3. I pretty much do as he says; things seem to go more smoothly that way.

Of course, women aren't the only ones who manipulate and challenge their spouses, just as men aren't the only ones who fight or flee. But none of these options will promote long-term satisfaction or peace in a relationship. Instead, God intends for spouses to practice effective communication and conflict resolution in marriage.

First, let's reflect on the biblical principles. When husbands and wives commit to one another, we see the outworkings of Christ's relationship with the church, as described in Ephesians 5:28-29: "He who loves his wife loves himself. After all, no one ever hated his own body, but he feeds and cares for it, just as Christ does the church."

Scripture commands husbands to selflessly love their wives and wives to respect their husbands. It's not difficult to see how, in a perfect world in which these commandments were never broken, marriages would be peaceful, satisfying, and uplifting. But we don't live in a perfect world. We live in a fallen world, and our natural tendencies are to focus on ourselves and attempt to impose our will on others. Any of my selfish attempts to get Judy to do something "my" way causes communication breakdowns. Those breakdowns often leave ugly scars. Wounded relationships, broken families, and a discouraging lack of peace and satisfaction are just a few of the consequences that can mar a marriage.

In order to maintain our commitment to love, cherish, and honor our spouses, we need to yield ourselves and our rights, first to God and then to one another. Over the years, Judy and I have used several strategies to help prevent communication stalemates, blowouts, and breakdowns. If you and your spouse have a difference of opinion, try approaching conflict with one or more of these guidelines in mind:

> **Husbands and wives need to yield themselves and their rights, first to God and then to one another.**

Stick to the problem at hand. Focus on the current conflict, and don't accuse your spouse of "always" or "never" behaving a certain way. Putting your spouse on the defensive is never wise.

Get on the same side of the fence. Rather than attempting to resolve an issue "my way" or "your way," work toward a solution that represents "our way."

Try to identify the core issue. Arguments often arise because of events or issues that disguise the real problem. Consider what attitudes or beliefs are motivating your behavior for clues as to what the core issue in any conflict is.

Don't be a mind reader. Discuss your beliefs and expectations openly. Don't try to interpret your spouse's thoughts or motives from his or her behavior; instead, ask direct questions. Likewise, don't expect your spouse to know what you are thinking.

Don't let the sun go down on your anger. Settling disputes takes hard work and can also take time. If you haven't reached an agreement by bedtime, put the matter aside with the understanding that you will resume discussion the next day. Nursing anger overnight gives the devil a foothold (see Ephesians 4:26-27). Don't leave yourself (or your marriage) vulnerable.

Avoid character assassination. As you work to resolve conflict, it's okay to talk about circumstances and behavior. However, attacking your spouse's personality or character is never acceptable.

Never forget that your relationship with your spouse is far more important than "winning" an argument or "being right."

Remember that love keeps no record of wrongs. Be quick to forgive, quick to admit your own mistakes, and quick to move on from the conflict.

CHAPTER 31

The Working Woman: At Home or in the Workplace

In-Depth Financial Strategies | 31

I'm taking a big risk here. Part of this chapter covers a subject that's particularly controversial and affects women more directly than men. Let me start with a qualification. My wife actually wrote the section on moms working outside the home. No, just kidding. But I will be adapting some materials from the book Judy and I wrote together called *Money Talks and So Can We*.[1]

After a brief look at the value of work and the reasons women enter the marketplace, we'll discuss what couples with young children should consider when deciding if both spouses should work outside the home. Finally, we'll look at some special financial considerations that single career women without children need to make.

The generalizations and information included in this chapter may not apply to single mothers. Raising a family without a husband's income (and, in some cases, without any form of child support), a single mother faces her own set of unique challenges, restrictions, and economic trade-offs. (I cover some of the single-parenting financial issues in chapter 32.)

Work: A God-Given Gift

If you were to conduct a "person on the street" interview asking people what they thought about work, you'd probably hear comments like this:

- The factory worker punching in for the next shift: "I owe, I owe, it's off to work I go."
- The executive waiting for a client in an upscale restaurant: "My career is very important—it's who I am."
- The stay-at-home mom pouring cereal for her babbling toddler: "My work is never finished. When I get up tomorrow, I know I'll start this whole morning routine all over again."
- The middle-aged manager boarding a plane to make yet another sales presentation: "I work hard now so someday I won't have to."

The world's perspective on work ranges from the extremes of a daily drudgery all the way to viewing one's career as life's central purpose.

So let's take a moment to consider what work really is. Work is the physical and mental energy exerted to provide for oneself and one's family (1 Timothy 5:8), as well as for the needs of others (Exodus 16:18; 2 Corinthians 8:14-15) when we are able.

All people have an innate, God-given drive to work (Genesis 2:5,15). Work is good, since it was given to man and woman before the Fall. Work became harder to accomplish after the Fall, but it remains worthwhile. The frustration we experience as we toil is balanced by the joy of accomplishment and provision our work produces.

Work also provides an environment for living the Christian life—sharing our faith in Christ or growing with other believers. Christianity should not be just a segment of one's life; it should overflow into every aspect of life—especially in our work.

The significance of our work is found in its focus on others; therefore, it's not necessarily the *product* of our labor that brings fulfillment, but the *purpose* for which we work. If you're a stay-at-home mother, your work clearly has a purpose and a focus on others, but no monetary paycheck.

This is why we must understand the purpose of our labor. God wants us to focus on *people* rather than product in our work. He is not concerned about the amount of product produced but the degree of faithfulness to the opportunities we have been given.

If we view work merely as a means to generate income and meet our needs, we will become competitive, anxious, unsatisfied, self-centered wealth-seekers, always measuring what we do by the fruit of our work. On the other hand, if we accept the philosophy that work is simply an environment in which to live and share the Christian life, confident that God will meet our needs, we will experience freedom and a balanced lifestyle that includes hard work and leisure. God may use our jobs to provide our needs, but that is not the same as saying we look to our jobs for our provision.

As Charles Spurgeon once said, "All men must work, but no man should work beyond his physical and intellectual ability nor beyond the hours which nature allots. No net result of good to the individual or to the race comes of any artificial prolonging of the day at either end. Work while it is day. When night comes, rest."

Spurgeon encourages us to work diligently during our allotted time. But what is your "allotted time"? That comes by figuring out your priorities—if you're married or a parent, that will include time nurturing your spouse and/ or children; if you've always been single, you may devote time to caring for your parents, nieces and nephews, and friends. Other priorities women must consider are service to church and the community, as well as self-care and development. When you've figured the time needed to care for these priorities properly, you can allot time for work. During work time, labor diligently and heartily, trusting God for the income. Certainly you can make more money by working harder and longer, but there will be more problems in the long run (Proverbs 10:22).

One key to putting work in proper perspective is to take a long-range perspective, which will force you to look to the end of your life and see that one day you will distribute what you have worked so hard to earn. You have an entire lifetime to accumulate, so do everything possible to keep work from stealing time from family, friends, and church. If you can sleep, relax, enjoy what you are doing, and keep a good self-image apart from your job, you probably have a proper understanding of the purpose of work.

Why Women Go to Work

Women work because they're able and capable

Someone my wife and I respected greatly was Judy's aunt Avis. She was close to 90 years old when she died. She became a teacher in the 1930s and never married. She taught in only two school districts, and when she retired in 1975, she owned her home and was caring for an aged mother and younger sister at her own expense.

Women like Avis were once quite extraordinary. However, the number of professional women has been growing for several decades. Today, 60 percent of all women 16 and older are either in the workforce or looking for work. The largest percentage of employed women—38 percent—work in professional or managerial positions. Most other women work in sales or office positions (34 percent) or service occupations (20 percent).[2]

> **If you can sleep, relax, enjoy what you are doing, and have a good self-image apart from your job, you probably have a proper understanding of the purpose of work.**

Obviously, women have abilities and skills of great value, and many derive great purpose from serving others in the marketplace.

Women work because society tells them to

Women have made great contributions in the workplace, and expanding professional opportunities for women have brought many benefits. However, while a century ago a mother with young children was often prohibited from holding a job, today women often feel looked down upon if they're *not* in the marketplace. Popular culture has lumped mothers into two categories: those who work outside the home and those who are "just moms." A young mom, therefore, may wonder if staying home to raise a family is a second-rate job, one that will lead her to "waste her education" or prevent her from "pulling her own weight" financially. For a stay-at-home mother who doesn't get a paycheck, who lacks adult companionship, and who gets little or no recognition for her job, accusations like these can devastate her sense of self-worth or purpose.

A wife who stays at home needs the following from her husband: (1) verbal praise and affirmation for the job she does as a wife and mother, (2) tangible at-home support to help her cope with the physical and emotional demands of mothering, and (3) a long-term perspective on why you've decided together for her to be a stay-at-home mom.

Judy has led women's Bible studies for many years, and several of her groups have been made up of young mothers. As we discussed the content of this chapter, she reminded me of a true story she told one of these groups years ago. A man came home from work to find his wife close to tears, exhausted from a trying day at home with their two preschool-aged boys. "I feel like all I did today was break up fights and enforce discipline," she said. She told how

FAMILY FINANCE

"Thanks, Monica. I'll get back to you tomorrow, okay?" Victoria hung up the phone and turned to Luis with a bemused look on her face. "That's the fourth phone call this week from a mom asking if I'll watch her kids. I don't know why so many people are interested."

"I do," Luis said with a smile. "You've been taking care of Sylvia's daughters every Monday and Wednesday after school for three months. Word has obviously gotten out that you do a great job with the kids."

Victoria shrugged. "It's fun," she said. "I really don't do a lot."

"That's not true," Luis said. He pointed to the kitchen table, which was covered with craft supplies. A bag full of library books was leaning against the wall, and clear plastic containers of toys were stacked neatly in the corner. "You always have projects for them to do or books for them to read. You get them involved in cooking snacks. You're patient and fun. You help with homework.

And the parents love that you never turn on the TV."

"Well, when you put it like that . . . ," Victoria said, laughing. "I'm really happy to be taking care of Bethany and Janna. They're great girls, and they enjoy Cristina and Manuel. I feel like I have a chance to share the love of Christ with them. And to be honest, I'm glad to be making some extra money, too."

"It's certainly helping us pay down our debt," Luis agreed.

"So these extra babysitting jobs provide a great opportunity to make even more money," Victoria said. "If I accepted every assignment I've been offered this week, I could triple what I'm making now. But I'm not sure that's the best approach. I'm worried about getting too busy."

"What kinds of things are you being offered?" Luis asked.

"Well, Monica asked if I would watch her son after school on Mondays. Kristin asked if I would pick up her son from

the boys had repeatedly disobeyed her by climbing on furniture, calling each other names, and throwing food. "I must have spanked Tommy and Jimmy three or four times each!" she said.

The husband thought a moment and then took his wife into his arms. "Do you mean to tell me," he said, "that you have spent the entire day *building character* into our sons?" As any mother will tell you, this kind of support and perspective—looking down the road to see future rewards for current efforts—can provide valuable motivation in a relatively thankless job.

Closely related to the woman who works because society tells her to is the mother who keeps her job or reenters the workforce in order to maintain her competitive edge. I once heard about a mother who returned to the workplace after a six-year absence because, as she put it, "I am about to turn 40, and if I wait any longer no one will want to hire me. Companies would rather have someone younger, whose skills are fresh and who has a longer work life ahead of them."

school on Tuesdays and keep him here until six—but that would mean I might have to wake up Cristina from her nap so I could get to the school on time. Nora wants to know if I would take care of her three-year-old daughter every weekday afternoon. And Selma asked about adding her daughter to Wednesday afternoons."

"That's a lot of options," Luis said. "What are you most concerned about missing if you get too busy?"

Victoria frowned. "Well, I like to have the freedom to help at Manuel's preschool occasionally, especially when they have field trips. I love seeing him with his classmates and sharing that experience with him. Cristina thrives on a routine, so I don't want to shake it up too much. And I also want to make sure I'm giving her enough one-on-one time."

"How do you feel about adding more kids to the Monday or Wednesday groups you already have?" Luis asked. "Would that be too much?"

"I don't think so," Victoria answered thoughtfully. "All of those kids are already in elementary school, so they don't require intense supervision. Having one more doing a craft or helping make cookies isn't a big deal." She paused to think. "Maybe what makes sense right now is to take on one more child on Mondays and another on Wednesdays. I'm already in a routine with those days, so that should work well. I'll turn down the other offers for now, since those conflict with preschool and Cristina's nap schedule."

"Sounds like a good plan," Luis agreed. "You'll make more money but won't add any more time commitments to your weekly schedule."

Victoria let out a deep breath. "It's a challenge to balance family needs with financial needs," she said. "But I think this will work. I feel better already."

If you're concerned about losing market skills or your competitive edge, ask yourself several questions: (1) Are there courses I can take or certifications I should pursue to keep my skills or degrees current? (2) Are there career paths other than the one I am trained for that interest me? (3) What's the worst that could happen if I do not return to the workplace right now? and, most importantly, (4) Why do I really want to work?

Women work because they want a creative outlet

When Michael, our youngest, left home for college, Judy really struggled with the transition. She did not work outside the home while the children were growing up. Instead, she spent 31 years taking care of five children—an effort that, I belatedly realized, took an incredible amount of creative and physical energy. When the kids were gone, Judy found herself wondering what she should do next. What was her purpose in life?

Had Judy worked while our children were at home, the transition from mothering to empty-nesting would have been easier. As it was, she felt unprepared for a change that she knew would be difficult. All the energy she once channeled toward our children needed a new outlet. Gradually, she discovered several new outlets.

In addition to leading Bible studies and adapting to her new role as a grandmother, Judy recently stepped into a home-based business, selling a nutritional product we started using some time ago. Judy did not set out to get a job, but when she began to recommend and sell this particular product, she discovered that it was a wonderful outlet for her talents and abilities. She welcomed a fresh direction for her creative energy.

As God's children, we are commanded to work, to "do something useful with our hands" (see Ephesians 4:28). For many women, caring for a family taps just a part of their usefulness. Some mothers take great delight in exercising their God-given talents by volunteering at schools or in community organizations, leading or participating in Bible studies, or pursuing various hobbies and interests. Sometimes these pursuits come with a paycheck attached. The woman in Proverbs 31, for example, cooks, sews, and gardens to provide for her family. She also trades and sells in the marketplace, burning the midnight oil to ensure that her work is profitable. She watches over her household, cares for the poor, and makes money in the marketplace—no wonder she wins lavish praise from her children, her husband, and the community leaders.

If the image of the Proverbs 31 woman leaves you feeling exhausted or depressed by the thought of trying to measure up, take heart: Many Bible scholars believe that she was not a real woman, but a composite of many noble and virtuous qualities. Even so, her endeavors at home and in the marketplace open the door for contemporary women to prayerfully consider where they should direct their energies and talents. For some, it will be as a full-time, stay-at-home mother. For others, creative energy may find an outlet in the workplace.

As you make your decision, think about your overall purpose. Will you be more apt to meet your goals by focusing your creative energy at home or in an outside job? If you are looking for a way to use your talents and abilities, is there a home-based business or ministry opportunity you should consider? Would your family be better served if you postponed a career move for a year or two, or perhaps much longer? If you opt to work outside your home, can you use some of the money you earn to hire domestic help to free up more of your nonworking hours? Don't limit yourself to the one-dimensional question of whether or not you should work; instead, open your eyes to all of the alternatives.

Women work to make money

Just over half of all adult American women are not married. For them, deciding to hold down a job outside the home is relatively straightforward—most have no one else to rely on for their income.

Yet the desire for additional income is often what drives married mothers into the workforce as well. Their family may want to fulfill some material desires or to obtain employee benefits like health insurance. In some cases, our current financial system—including higher tax rates, inflated prices for homes and cars, company layoffs, and skyrocketing college costs—makes it difficult to survive on just one income.

> Don't limit yourself to the one-dimensional question of whether or not you should work; instead, open your eyes to all of the alternatives.

Husbands and wives, if you think you both *need* to work—that is, if your family requires both salaries for its very survival—you might be right. Then again, you might be wrong. Have you ever stopped to consider just how much of a financial contribution the second income is actually making to your family's lifestyle?

In the following section, you'll find some tools to help you decide what working arrangement is best for your family. On page 472, we'll look at the financial considerations unique to single career women.

All Moms Are Working Women

It's become something of a cliché, but it's true: Whether a mom chooses outside employment or not, she is a working woman. Some women capably manage a full-time career and their family's needs. Many other women work part-time, often around the hours their kids are in school; others have built thriving home-based businesses. Still others have decided to focus all their energies on their home and family. The challenge is determining, along with your spouse, what the best situation for your family is.

One woman was as sincere as she could be when she told me how concerned she was that she would be quitting her bank teller job. I asked how much she was making at her part-time job to determine how seriously quitting her job would impact their family situation. She told me she was making over $400 a month and that the $5,000 a year was crucial in their family situation. I was saddened as I realized that she really did not know how little she was contributing to the bottom line of her family finances.

Few mothers working outside the home actually understand the true financial ramification of their working efforts. Their husbands usually don't understand either. As a financial advisor, the story I frequently heard was that the spouse had to work or wanted to work in order to provide the family with a few extras. However, they fail to realize that a working mother can actually *cost* more money than is made.

Larry Burkett once told me that the unfortunate truth is that most working mothers sacrifice time with their families with little or nothing to show for it. Most of the average working mother's wages are consumed by taxes, transportation, child care costs, and clothing. Even when a working mother's income substantially adds to her family's budget, the surplus is often consumed by an expanded lifestyle.

To make an informed, objective decision about the relative worth of a wife's paycheck, you need to accurately evaluate the size and impact of the second income as it pertains to the family budget. If you have not already done so, take a few moments to assess your situation:

1. Write down your gross (pretax) income.

2. Deduct the amount you normally tithe.

3. Deduct the amount you pay in federal, state, local, Social Security, and Medicare taxes. (Typically, taxes eat up anywhere from 25 to 40 percent of your income, with self-employed people at the higher end of the scale. If you are unsure how much to figure in this exercise, check last year's tax return or assume an average rate of about 30 percent.)

4. The amount you have left over is your net income. Now deduct the cost of all your work-related expenses. Remember to list things like transportation costs, day care expenses (less whatever tax credit you receive, if any), and other items such as career clothing and accessories, domestic help, restaurant lunches or take-out meals, gifts for coworkers, eating out more at night—those things that you would not spend money on if you did not work.

5. The remaining amount—after you account for taxes, tithe, and expenses—is your contribution to your family's income. Is it worth it? Here is what your personal economic analysis might look like:

WHAT IS YOUR PAYCHECK REALLY WORTH?

Second Salary	$15,000	$30,000	$45,000	You*
1. Giving	1,500	3,000	4,500	
2. Federal Tax	4,200	8,400	12,600	
3. State Tax	750	1,500	2,250	
4. FICA Tax	1,148	2,295	3,443	
5. Child Care	9,600	9,600	9,600	
6. Transportation	1,200	1,200	1,200	
7. Meals	1,000	1,000	1,000	
8. Extra Clothes/Dry Cleaning	600	600	600	
9. Miscellaneous	600	600	600	
Work-Related Expenses	20,598	28,195	35,793	
Salary Minus Expenses	-5,598	1,805	9,207	
10. Plus Child Care Credit	2,592	1,920	1,920	
Net Additional Family Income	-3,006	3,725	11,127	
Net Hourly Rate (Net additional family income divided by annual hours)	None	1.79	5.35	

*Use the last column to figure out what a second income is really worth in your family. If you don't have actual figures, you can estimate with the information in the chart below.

Expense	Suggested or Average Amount
1. Giving	10 percent of income
2. Federal Tax	28 percent tax rate
3. State Tax	5 percent tax rate
4. FICA Tax	7.65 percent tax rate (15.3 percent if self-employed)
5. Child Care	Two children at an average cost of $400 per child per month
6. Transportation	$100 a month (additional gas, maintenance, and repairs)
7. Meals	$20 a week for 50 weeks
8. Extra Clothes and Dry Cleaning	$50 per month

continued on page 466

Expense	Suggested or Average Amount
9. Miscellaneous	$50 per month (personal grooming, convenience foods, etc.)
10. Plus Child Care Credit	Between 20 and 30 percent of child care expenses depending on income. Per U.S. tax law, the value of the child care credit diminishes as a family's income increases.

If, after completing this exercise, you and your spouse realize that the second income is not contributing as much to the bottom line as you thought, you might go back to chapter 8 ("How to Spend Less Than You Make") to consider ways to make up some of the shortfall in your financial plan. If you determine that both spouses should work outside the home, recognize that your situation will bring both rewards and challenges to your family. It's critical that you learn to talk openly and work together to find solutions when problems or frustrations arise.

Weighing the Trade-Offs

Whether you choose to work in the marketplace or stay home, there will be trade-offs and sacrifices to consider. Working mothers may find themselves missing a toddler's first step, a second-grader's school performance, or a teenager's soccer tournament. They may wrestle with frustration as they return home at night to prepare dinner and cram a day's worth of household chores and family communication into a few precious hours. In juggling the polarized demands of their jobs and families, they may—as one mother we talked to put it—experience "stress times ten." And while it's true that some women work so their families can afford extras like vacations or private schools, the high cost of living means that these things are out of reach for many families where both parents work.

On the other hand, stay-at-home moms may feel isolated in a world dominated mainly by children or bored with a household routine that varies little from day to day. Confronted with other full-time mothers who seem to thrive on everything from dirty diapers to PTA meetings, some stay-at-homers may struggle with their own sense of inadequacy. And the financial sacrifices associated with one-income living—from dining out less to giving up things like household help, family vacations, or private schools—can lead to discouragement and doubt.

When her sons were young, Erica worked part-time as a legal secretary while her mother cared for the children two or three days per week. Erica enjoyed her career and assumed that, as her children grew and went off to school, she would be able to return to work full-time. But when her younger son, Timmy, was diagnosed with a mild learning disability, everything changed. In addition to driving him to and from classes at a special school located 40 minutes from their home, Erica wanted to be available to help Timmy with his schoolwork in the afternoons. She realized that she simply could not work full-time and meet her son's special needs; in fact, she and her husband decided that the best option, at least for the time being, would be for her to stop working entirely.

Although Erica felt she had made the right choice, she was not prepared for the sense of loneliness and isolation that engulfed her when she quit her job. She did not have any close friends who were full-time mothers, and as she drove the long trip to and from Timmy's school, she brooded over her current lack of intellectual stimulation and adult companionship. She missed the office camaraderie—not to mention her paycheck. How, she wondered, did other stay-at-home moms do it?

Unity, Unity, Unity

I'm not a marriage counselor, but I've seen how important unity between a husband and a wife is for these decisions. Working in the home or outside of it is difficult; each spouse needs support. Whether a wife wants to pursue a career or devote herself to full-time mothering, she needs the full and unqualified support of her husband. Likewise, if a husband wants his wife to work (or if he asks her to stay home), they need to talk and act as a team.

We know of one couple—Lucy and Bill—whose daughter was struggling in school, primarily due to a personality conflict with her teacher. As they considered the situation, Lucy and Bill felt that their best option was for Lucy to accept a teaching position in a local private school, since her employee tuition discount would make it financially possible for them to enroll their daughter. But as Lucy reflected on their decision, she grew increasingly concerned about the ramifications it would have on their lifestyle. "I knew that if I started teaching," she said, "it would throw off the whole balance of our family life. Financially, we could afford to send our daughter to private school—but the noneconomic cost would be too much to bear."

An implicit assumption in decision making is that the choice you ultimately make will satisfy various personal objectives and priorities. For Lucy, the ability to maintain balance in her family life was a high priority—one she was not willing to sacrifice. Fortunately, she and Bill were wise enough to realize that a teaching job for Lucy (and the private school option it afforded) was not their only alternative. They continued to pray about the situation, and ultimately, the problem was resolved when school administrators offered to transfer their daughter to another class.

When you have to make an important decision, one of the best ways to objectively review your alternatives is to map them out in a decision matrix. I covered this tool in chapter 6, but let's review another instance in which it can apply. As we review the steps, we'll consider how Callie, a writer who is married and has three young children, used this process to determine the best use of her time, energy, and skills. (See her matrix on page 470.)

A decision matrix is based on a six-step process:

1. **Write out or verbalize the actual decision you need to make.** For a wife who is considering a career or part-time job, the decision might be worded this way: "I must choose the best way to spend my time, my talents, and my energy." That's how Callie worded the decision she faced.

2. **List all your objectives that relate to this decision, both quantitative and qualitative.** Think about the things you want to maximize and minimize. For example, in deciding whether or not Callie should return to work, she listed her objectives this way:

   > Maximize time with husband and children
   > Maximize use of skills and talents
   > Maximize income
   > Maximize character development in children
   > Maximize time for kids' friends, school functions, activities, etc.
   > Minimize boredom
   > Minimize commute time
   > Minimize costs (child care, transportation, etc.)
   > Minimize stress

3. **Rank your objectives in order of their importance.** Since you can't have everything, there will always be some degree of conflict in your priorities. Give each objective a number value from 1 to 5, with 5 being a nonnegotiable priority and 1 being an objective you could live without. Obviously, the objectives and their relative rankings will be different for each individual or couple, since any given goal or priority will matter more to one person than it does to someone else.

   For Callie, spending time with her family matters more, relatively speaking, than earning additional income. When Callie ranked her objectives, her priorities looked like this:

   > 5 Maximize time with husband and children
   > 5 Maximize use of skills and talents
   > 2 Maximize income
   > 5 Maximize character development in children
   > 4 Maximize time for kids' friends, functions, etc.
   > 1 Minimize boredom
   > 1 Minimize commute time
   > 3 Minimize costs (child care, transportation, etc.)
   > 4 Minimize stress

4. **List all possible alternatives.** Write down all of your options, no matter how unappealing or unattractive they may initially appear. As the late author and management consultant Peter Drucker used to say, "A decision is a judgment . . . a choice among alternatives. Rarely is the choice between right or wrong, but rather the best choice between almost right and probably wrong." And since your decision can never be better than your best known alternative, the more alternatives you can come up with, the better your chances will be of settling on the choice that is "almost right."

    Callie initially decided she had three alternatives: staying home with her children, working in a full-time career (as she had before her children were born), and working part-time outside her home. You might have additional options or possibilities to consider.

5. **Evaluate each alternative based on how it fulfills your objectives and priorities.** If an alternative meets a particular objective, give it "points" based on the numerical ranking you assigned to that objective in step 3. If the alternative allows you to fully maximize (or minimize) an objective, give it the full value of its rank. If it contributes toward the objective but does not entirely fulfill it, assign it a partial score. The idea is to begin thinking in terms of *objectives* rather than *alternatives*.

6. **Choose the alternative that best meets your objectives and priorities.** Add up the "points" under each alternative based on the evaluation you did in step 5. In Callie's case, staying at home received the highest score (23). Even so, Callie was not entirely comfortable with that alternative. She welcomed the additional income that would come with working, but even more than that, the stay-at-home alternative ran counter to her deep conviction that God wanted her to use her professional skills and talents for some specific jobs and projects, both paid and unpaid. Given the importance of the "skills and talents" objective, Callie began to wonder if there might be another option she had not originally considered.

> **Your decision can never be better than your best known alternative; the more alternatives you can come up with, the better your chances will be of settling on the choice that is "almost right."**

Two weeks later, Callie got her answer. A home security company for which she had once designed a brochure called to see if she would write a few articles for their quarterly newsletter on a freelance basis. As she considered the company's offer, a new idea began to take shape in Callie's mind: If there was a market for freelance writing (and she felt sure that there was), she might be able to network with her former business contacts and develop a writing career from her home! Intrigued by the prospect, Callie updated her matrix by adding the freelancing alternative. The results then looked like this:

CALLIE'S DECISION MATRIX

Rank	Objective	Stay Home/ Not in the Workforce	Part-Time Job	Full-Time Career	Freelance/ Home-Based Business
5	Maximize time with husband and children	5	2	0	4
5	Maximize use of skills and talents	0	3	5	5
2	Maximize income	0	1	2	1
5	Maximize character development in children	5	2	0	4
4	Maximize time for kids' friends' functions, etc.	4	2	0	3
1	Minimize boredom	1	1	1	1
1	Minimize commute time	1	0	0	1
3	Minimize costs (child care, transportation, etc.)	3	0	0	3
4	Minimize stress	0	0	0	0
	Total points	23	11	8	22

Again, staying at home fulfilled more of Callie's objectives, but only by the slimmest margin over the freelancing option. And the difference between freelancing and working in a full- or part-time position left Callie wondering why she hadn't thought of freelancing right from the start! But that is exactly the point: Sometimes the best alternative does not present itself until you have already considered—and discarded—the obvious. If you lack an alternative that meets or fulfills most of your objectives, don't get discouraged. Ask God to open your eyes and your mind to alternatives you might not have considered before, and then weigh these new possibilities in light of your objectives.

In my experience, the "either/or" options we tend to consider at the outset of any decision usually transform themselves into another solution that is often more creative—and almost always more appealing—than anything we had thought of at first.

Q: Before having my two kids, who are now in elementary school, I worked as a reporter for the local paper. My former boss just called to encourage me to apply for an opening in the news division. I get excited at the prospect of writing stories again—until I try to imagine myself juggling a full-time job and my family's busy schedule. How do I decide whether or not to apply for this job?

ANSWER: First, don't assume that your only two choices are staying home or working full-time. In today's world, many other options are available—particularly to someone who is valued by her employer, past or present.

I suggest you work through the decision-making matrix outlined in this chapter to determine your priorities. If such factors as using your professional skills and supplementing your family's income are important to you, don't assume you must take a full-time position at an employer's office. Many employees today are opting for alternatives that give them greater flexibility, including freelancing, job sharing, telecommuting, or working flexible hours. You might investigate whether your former employer offers such opportunities or even approach your former boss to see if management might be open to the idea, even on a trial basis. Finally, I recommend you and your husband talk about this opportunity together. If you do return to work, your family will face some new challenges and rewards, and all family members should be prepared to take a more active role in household chores and responsibilities.

Once you have worked your way through the decision matrix, evaluate the risk associated with your decision. Ask yourself two questions: (1) What's the worst thing that could happen if I pursued this alternative? and (2) How likely is that worst-case scenario to occur? The answer to these questions will help you assess the level of risk associated with your top choice. If the risk factor is too high, eliminate that alternative and focus on the option with the next highest score.

Put another way, *are you comfortable with the decision?* If Callie had chosen the alternative with the highest score (23), she would have stayed home and not worked at all. But by moving on to her second alternative, freelancing, she discovered that it was actually a better choice, in terms of the objectives it fulfilled. Again, when you begin to see a decision in terms of the objectives or priorities that it meets (rather than looking at the alternatives themselves), the best option often becomes obvious.

These are some of the questions a husband and wife must consider together as they decide whether a wife should seek outside employment: Would the additional income or creative outlet provided by a wife's job enhance her overall objectives, or would it take her focus off of her ultimate goals? Would a part-time or home-based business contribute to the fulfillment of her purpose in marriage, or would it open the door to stress or confusion in the home? How would a commitment to full-time mothering affect a couple's lives—and their children's lives—5, 10, or 20 years down the road?

Only you can answer questions like these. My goal throughout this book is not to tell you what to do with your money, your talents, or your life. Rather, my aim is to give you the principles and tools you need to make wise decisions.

The Financially Savvy Single

Earlier in the chapter, I introduced you to my wife's aunt Avis. She worked hard all her adult life and managed her money wisely. Not only was she able to help support family later in life, but her financial nest egg continued to grow until her death. Avis did things many things right: She spent less than she earned, saved for the future, never borrowed except for a home mortgage, and always took a long-term perspective in her financial decision making.

Aunt Avis's story isn't unusual. I don't have statistics, but I would guess that single career women do a better job of managing their finances than any other group in America today. They have no one else to depend on, so they tend to seek good counsel and make sound decisions. Additionally, they don't have the major cash needs of a family.

Career singles often have more opportunity for financial success than their married contemporaries. They may also have greater opportunity to funnel the resources God has entrusted to them into the work of His Kingdom.

A career single woman needs to begin by learning and applying the financial basics discussed previously. Then, after age 30, a few commonly asked financial questions will come up; the balance of this chapter deals with them.

Renting or buying your home

The basis of this question is the common belief that renting will leave you behind financially. The four assumptions that have made buying a home seem like the most attractive alternative are: (1) expectations of rising home values; (2) low fixed interest rates; (3) deductibility of mortgage interest and property taxes; and (4) high income tax rates. Purchasing a home on the expectation that it will appreciate in value assumes inflation. But home values don't always go up. In many areas of the country, they've gone down dramatically in recent years. Also, fixed interest rates often fluctuate. Lenders have built into mortgage rates an inflation expectation that makes you, the borrower, pay for inflation.

The deductibility of mortgage interest and property taxes has been chipped away by Congress. High-income taxpayers have already lost a portion of that deductibility. There's certainly no guarantee that home mortgage interest and property taxes will be deductible forever.

Additionally, marginal income tax rates are lower today than they've been in the past 50 years. That means the tax benefit associated with mortgage interest and property taxes is less attractive today than in recent history.

Career singles, then, shouldn't feel pressured to buy a home or condominium to provide financial security. Renting means you'll spend a lot less for maintenance, repairs, insurance, property taxes, and so on. Investing those savings will give you the same financial security provided by appreciation in home value. In fact, you'll be more secure, because your savings will grow, whereas the owner's home may not appreciate in value. All this put together says that buying a home isn't required to provide financial security for anyone, let alone a career single.

Thus, if you're going to buy a home, it should be for reasons other than the economic benefits. Perhaps it provides some stability and roots you desire. In that case, it's a wise purchase rather than a good investment. It may turn out to be a good investment, but you shouldn't buy it with that expectation.

> **Singles shouldn't feel pressured to buy a home or condominium to provide financial security.**

If you purchase a home, I offer the following suggestions regarding the financing. First, make a down payment of at least 20 percent. Second, choose a fixed rate mortgage rather than an adjustable rate mortgage. You can then plan for the future with certainty. Third, if you can afford to make the payments on a 15-year loan as opposed to the standard 30-year loan, you'll have the mortgage paid off in half the time and with an enormous savings in interest expense.

Those aren't rules that will break you if you break them, but they're guidelines that will provide you with greater financial security sooner.

Life insurance

Life insurance is usually bought to meet the needs of a surviving family. As a career single, you have no such needs to worry about. If you leave behind any debt, it can normally be repaid from the sale of assets you've also left.

Why, then, might you want to buy life insurance? Possible reasons include providing for the care of a parent or sibling; covering estate taxes; paying for your funeral expenses; and benefiting family, friends, and charities. Here again, however, property in your estate could be sold to meet some of the needs, so life insurance may not be needed.

ANSWER: Obviously, if you are the mother of dependent children, it is critical that you have a will. In fact, drafting (or updating) your will should be one of the first steps you take.

If you are single with no dependents, a will may still be important. For instance, if you own property of any kind, you need to have a will prepared to ensure it will be distributed as you wish. The more assets you accumulate over the years, the greater the need for a will. Many times a career single, because she doesn't have the responsibilities of children, can do significant charitable giving through her estate plan. I strongly encourage such an approach.

When you don't have a will prepared, you place the burden of distributing your property on someone else who may not understand your desires. So having a will prepared is not only good stewardship, it's also a thoughtful act toward the person who will be your executor.

Your decisions about life insurance will depend on your desires and your estate size. All in all, life insurance needs for a career single are minimal. They should be considered carefully, however, before a decision is made.

Saving for retirement

Chapters 22 and 23 cover the basics of investing for retirement and sequential investing, and these principles are the same regardless of your marital status. Investment objectives in every case are income, appreciation, minimizing risk, and maintaining some level of liquidity. It's impossible to find an investment that has no risk, total liquidity, and continues to grow in value and generate a high yield. There are always trade-offs.

The only way to meet long-term goals with some degree of certainty is to diversify your investments among various classes of investment such as cash equivalents (like money market accounts), bonds, stocks, and mutual funds. And the diversification needs to be strategic. A professional advisor can assist you in specific investment selection. Chapter 33 explains how to pick a financial advisor, along with other types of advisors.

Becoming a generous giver

One great benefit of not having a family to provide for is the opportunity to give at a higher level than someone else earning the same income. It may very well be that God has allowed you to remain single in part to be able to maximize your giving.

One of the great barriers to giving, however, is fear of the future when you're the sole source of your financial security in retirement. For that reason, regardless of your income level, you should prepare a financial plan as outlined in chapter 8. It will help you determine whether you're on track to meet your long-term needs. If you are, maybe you can increase your giving merely by planning to do so rather than waiting until you reach retirement age.

You should consider the three levels of giving, which are discussed in chapter 27. The "should give" level is your tithe. At the "could give" level, you choose to give money set aside for other purposes. The "would give" level comes from having prepared a financial plan and seeing God provide money in unexpected ways through either increased income or reduced expenses.

> **One great benefit of not having a family to support is the opportunity to give at a higher level than someone else earning the same income.**

When you're operating from a financial plan, those unexpected increases in cash are obvious and can be precommitted to giving. As a career single, you may have more opportunities to give than a married woman who, in many cases, has little control over the family finances.

Buying a car

Buying cars is covered in chapter 14, and I recommend you read that section for a fuller treatment of the subject. But in summary, remember that the cheapest car you will ever own is the car you're presently driving. The longer you drive a car, the cheaper it becomes to operate. Whenever you buy a car, you should pay cash. If you can't afford to save for it, you can't afford to borrow for it. The time to purchase a different car is when the car has become unsafe, or the cost or inconvenience of repairs makes it uneconomical to continue repairing your current car.

Women tend to make very good automobile decisions. In fact, they make better decisions than men because women are usually looking primarily for transportation, whereas men often let their egos get in the way.

Caring for aging parents

Whether it's equitable or not, the chore of caring for aging parents usually ends up with a single woman rather than her married sister or her brother. It seems that siblings assume that because she is single and female, her life can more easily be arranged around the needs of Mom and Dad. Even if the others agree to help with their parents' care, the single woman spends more than her fair share on groceries, pharmacy trips, and incidentals that the parents mention they need. If she is an only child, the economic burden may be especially significant.

Of course, some professional single women were once married. In the next chapter, we'll examine the financial steps women must take if they are widowed or divorced.

CHAPTER 32

Single Again: Managing the Financial Fallout

A group of men spent three days together at a beautiful retreat setting in Montana. They planned, prayed, and dreamed together about the future. One of the men was a pilot, and he invited three of the others to fly back to Dallas with him. One of the four was an entrepreneur with a young wife and two boys below the age of five. Another was a banker who had three boys, one of whom was in high school and two of whom were in college. The third was a surgeon with three grown children, and the fourth was a pastor who also had three children.

The small plane took off all right, but en route to Dallas it disappeared. Several days later, when the wreckage was found, there were no survivors. In an instant, four women had become widows, and 11 children were left without a father.

I visited with one of the widows many months later, and she said her husband had always told her that in the event of his death, she needn't worry because his best friend knew all about their financial situation. The friend was well prepared to help her cope financially with her husband's death. Unfortunately, however, that friend had been one of the four men on the plane.

Death is rarely expected, so people rarely plan for it adequately. Yet when it occurs, it changes forever the lives—including the financial situations—of those left behind. Even couples who have discussed the financial implications of losing the other may discover their plans are no longer relevant because of those changing circumstances.

Karen Loritts, a regular speaker at Campus Crusade's Family Life conferences, tells the story of a different kind of loss—one that devastated another family. Karen was jarred awake one night by the ringing telephone. A friend of hers was calling in anguish over her marital breakup, which had shocked those who knew the couple. This woman and her husband were both hard workers, and the entire family was active in their church. As Karen listened to her friend pour out her feelings of grief, she silently prayed for words to comfort her friend—and shed some tears herself. "I felt her pain and cried at the prospect of having my friend struggle with this 'death,'" said Karen.

The loss of a husband or wife—whether through death or divorce—affects more than his or her spouse. Children pay a particularly high cost when they lose a parent. According to the U.S. Census Bureau and the National Center for Health Statistics, the percentage of children within the total population has decreased. Yet the number of children being raised by single parents has skyrocketed. In 1960, 5 million children were being raised by mothers who were widowed, divorced, separated, or never married. By 2002, the number had risen to 16.4 million.[1]

This chapter is directed at women because far more women than men must navigate the road of widowhood or single parenthood. Seventy percent of all married women will be widowed, and marriages formed today have about a 41 to 43 percent change of ending in divorce.[2] In the vast majority of cases, the mothers are granted primary custody of their children.

Having said that, men who are widowed or divorced often must deal with financial fallout as well. If you are a man in either situation, this chapter certainly applies to you as well.

Widowhood and Divorce: Alike but Different

Losing a spouse through widowhood or divorce tends to hit women especially hard. Often they must assume most of the responsibility for their children's care with little time to prepare financially for the adjustment.

Newly divorced and widowed individuals face two of the same big questions:

1. What do I need to do when?

2. Will I be able to meet my needs and my children's needs?

After losing a spouse, a person is left as the primary decision maker in all areas of family life. Whether to replace the air conditioner, change the insurance deductible, or invest in mutual funds—the newly single individual must make all the financial decisions. That burden is very real.

Yet there are also significant differences between divorce and widowhood. For one, divorce will almost certainly be more difficult financially. Not only does a divorced individual lose most or all of his or her spouse's income to help support the family, but he or she also doesn't receive the life insurance proceeds or Social Security benefits a widowed person does.

Again, this hits women particularly hard. Statistics show that a divorced mother has only 40 percent of the income that used to come into the household. Obviously, that kind of income drop makes paying the bills very difficult. Additionally, child-rearing expenses are just as great—maybe even higher if the woman was a homemaker and now has to get a job and pay for child care. Some single moms, desperate to avoid the cost of child care, go off to work and leave their children home alone.

Q: You mention two vital questions that every newly single adult must ask: (1) What do I need to do when? and (2) Will I be able to meet my needs and my children's needs? Are there any other questions that both widowed and divorced individuals must face?

ANSWER: Certainly. In terms of financial issues, I think another critical question is this: Whom can I trust as an advisor? Whether a person loses a spouse through divorce or death, the feelings of grief can be overwhelming. Unfortunately, insecurity over their financial situation often leads newly single adults to make major financial changes much too quickly—often at the urging of someone who doesn't have their best interests at heart.

For example, a reader of one of my books once sent me the following question: "I am a widow with a teenage son. Several years ago I switched the life insurance settlement due to my husband's death from certificates of deposit in my local bank to a brokerage firm managed by a friend in our church. Now that friend has left the firm, the business is in trouble with lawsuits against it, and we have lost over $40,000. What advice can you give me?"

Though it was too late for her to recoup the money she had lost, perhaps her story can help other singles choose a well-qualified financial planner. Chapter 33 deals with the actual process of choosing a financial advisor. But for now I want to offer four thoughts regarding such a choice.

First, if you are widowed or divorced, I recommend you choose a personal advisor, not necessarily a financial advisor. What you need at this point is not technical advice but wisdom and judgment. You can find an advisor to help with money management later. Just because someone is a CPA, attorney, banker, broker, life insurance agent, or financial planner doesn't make that person knowledgeable in all the emotional and spiritual areas where you may need advice.

Second, don't choose advisors just because they're Christians or family members or friends. Those may be important factors to consider, but again, what you need are wisdom, judgment, and perhaps experience. If you're taking an airplane trip, you want a pilot who has the skills, training, experience, and wisdom to make the right decisions. You wouldn't choose a pilot merely because the person is a Christian or a family member or friend. In the same way, it may be that another widowed individual would be your best personal advisor or could at least direct you to other helpers. You might also ask your pastor for recommendations.

Third, you may want more than one personal advisor. It's biblical to seek the advice of more than one counselor.

Fourth, always remember that you're still the decision maker. You can't abdicate that responsibility, even if you receive bad advice. Seek the best counsel you can find; then rely on the wisdom, comfort, and encouragement of the Holy Spirit to guide you during this difficult period of time.

Divorced mothers typically face limited income and carry debts from the failed marriage. They're often in a far less secure financial position than when the marriage began. In addition, simply securing a divorce is often costly.

Some have observed that the feminist movement may have contributed to some of divorcées' financial woes, since courts are far less lenient in granting benefits to a divorced woman than they were prior to the movement's advent. The courts now consider women equal to men in earning ability. The reality, however, is that most women don't have the same earning potential as their ex-husbands.

These differences mean that a divorced mother generally has different financial issues than a widow does. A divorced woman is usually dealing with day-to-day cash flow concerns, while widows are more likely to have investment and planning questions.

With this in mind, let's consider what each should consider as they answer the same basic questions. We'll begin by considering the person who is widowed.

Widowed: What to Do When

Mental-health experts estimate it takes about two years for a widow or widower to absorb what has happened and be capable of making major decisions again. The initial shock and numbness give way to a deep sense of loss and then a realization that those tasks that were once shared—including financial ones like tax preparation and insurance decisions—now must be done alone.

Because of that two-year period of psychological adjustment, I advised all my clients who were widowed not to make any major financial decisions during that time. However, the fear of being unable to maintain their standard of living often drives people to make major financial decisions too soon. In many cases, they make the wrong decisions.

One client's husband was killed in an accident, and she received a fairly large wrongful-death settlement that should have made her financially independent for the rest of her life. She had no knowledge of money matters, however, and turned to a friend for investment counsel. She was advised to make some specific investments, including the purchase of a seven-bedroom house, even though she only had two children left at home. When she came to me for counsel, she was living alone in that huge house and had no cash reserves.

You must make some decisions, of course, but be careful about making any big choices immediately. Here are the steps I recommend you follow.

Immediately

First, look for funeral directions left by your spouse. They may be found in a will or in a separate letter.

Second, order (either from the funeral director or the county clerk's office) 10 to 20 certified copies of the death certificate. This needs to be done right after the funeral in order to claim the benefits due you from company pension plans, Social Security, life insurance proceeds, annuities, and so on. You'll also need the documentary proof of your spouse's death to change titles on cars and your home.

Third, arrange for someone to stay at your house during the funeral to protect your property. Unfortunately, unscrupulous people prey upon those who've been widowed, and a favorite ploy is to burglarize a home during a funeral.

> **I advise those who are widowed not to make any major financial decisions during the first two years.**

Within the first two weeks

Have your attorney review your spouse's will and file it in probate court if necessary. Collect any documents needed to claim death benefits (bank and brokerage statements, marriage certificate, and birth certificate). Contact your insurance agent, investment advisor, spouse's employer and former employers, and the Social Security office to start the process of claiming benefits due to you.

Within one month

Keep a record of your cash flow so you can determine where you stand financially and what your living expenses are likely to be.

As money from insurance or employers begins to come in, deposit it in a bank in short-term certificates of deposit (CDs) or money market funds. One strategy is to put the money equally into 6-, 12-, and 18-month CDs so that you'll have money coming available to you every six months. At this point it's not necessary to worry about missing out on "better" investment opportunities. Your primary focus now should be to ensure you can pay your bills as they arise.

Within the first six months

Update any of *your* insurance policies that name your deceased spouse as beneficiary. Change any joint billing and credit card accounts that have his or her name on them. If you are the executor of your spouse's estate, notify your creditors and satisfy the debts as they come due. If there are likely to be estate taxes, get professional advice to determine how much they'll be and when they'll be due.

Review all insurance coverage, especially medical insurance, to make sure you and your family are adequately protected. Have your will revised to reflect your changed circumstances. If you don't have a will, then get one. It's more important for a widowed or single parent to have a will than it is for a married couple. You may need to appoint a guardian for your young children or change the executor or trustee, since your spouse was most likely named as executor and trustee in your will.

Review your checking account or spouse's checkbook and files to determine if you may be due benefits from sources you didn't know about. Look for automatic checking account deductions for life insurance. Look for other possible benefits, such as a union policy, fraternal organization, credit life insurance, military benefits, or other life insurance policies.

By the second year

By the second year, you should develop short- and long-term financial plans. Major investment decisions still do not need to be made, but it's time to do the following:

1. List all the assets you now have.

2. List all debts.

3. List all the life insurance covering you.

4. List all sources of income.

5. List all expenses, categorized by major area.

6. List all insurance policies.

7. Begin thinking about listing some long-term, major needs such as college education, lifestyle needs, debt payoff, giving, and so on.

In the second year and beyond, implement your financial plan, making decisions about housing, investments, insurance, and lifestyle.

> **By the second year, widows should develop short- and long-term financial plans.**

While this is the approach I recommend, it's not written in concrete. Depending on your personality, training, age, and income level, the sequence and time frame you follow may differ. I do strongly encourage you, however, to delay making major lifestyle and investment decisions to allow some time for grieving and adjustment. It may be nine months, a year, or two years. You need that time to adjust to the death of a significant part of your life.

Widowed: Will You Be Able to Live as Well in the Future?

Doubt about the future strikes every new widow and widower at a time when their security has been greatly shaken. Many fears and questions arise. If you've had no experience in managing money, even $1 million of life insurance may feel inadequate.

I would encourage you to go back and reread the first two parts of this book to help you understand the basics of money management. Realizing that

God owns it all and provides all the resources you will need should help you overcome some of the fear.

Whether or not you'll be able to live as well in the future is determined by three things: your income, expenses, and long-term needs. I know that when you prepare a financial plan, peace of mind results. It results from knowing either what steps you have to take to get your house in order or that you really are okay financially.

Here are three rules for preparing a financial plan: Keep it simple, keep it flexible, and make it yours and not someone else's. These are the elements of a good financial plan: determine what you owe, what you own, what your income is, what your expenses are, what your long-term needs are, and the medical and liability insurance your circumstances dictate.

When preparing a financial plan keep it simple, keep it flexible, and make it yours and not someone else's.

Your income may come from several sources. Life insurance proceeds can be taken either in a lump sum, which I generally recommend, or as a monthly income for the rest of your life. You may remember that in chapter 28 I suggested that taking a pension payout is often better than taking a lump sum. That generally is true when a retiree has a spouse to consider, since a pension payout can provide income during the lives of both spouses. As a widow(er), however, the life insurance payout is needed to provide income for you only. If you choose a lifetime payout and then die earlier than expected, little to none will be available for your heirs. The lump sum is also preferable because life insurance proceeds are often needed right away to pay for the funeral or final medical bills, or to pay off debt. Furthermore, life insurance proceeds taken in a lump sum are tax free, while monthly payouts are partially taxable. By taking the money all at once and investing it yourself, you have more control over the results—and can provide a greater inheritance should you die relatively soon.

The second source of income is salaries and wages from either salary continuation plans your spouse may have had or, more likely, your own ability to work.

Your spouse's former employers may have 401(k) plans or pension plans that will provide you either regular income or lump sum payments. Your age, the amount in the plan, and your needs will determine the best method to take those payments. Again, the lump sum option is generally preferable for the reasons given above.

Social Security may provide some benefits for the widow(er) who has children under the age of 18, as well as the surviving spouse over the age of 60. Your local Social Security office can answer questions about the benefits to which you're entitled. How much you receive will depend on how much you and your spouse paid into the Social Security system.

Some of the less-obvious sources of income mentioned earlier in the chapter—fraternal organizations, unions, and perhaps the military—may also provide certain benefits.

Once you add up all the sources of income, you've completed the first significant step in determining whether you'll be able to meet your needs and your children's needs.

The second major step is to calculate what your expenses will be. That will take some time, as many things will be changing. Most couples assume that if they have an income of $40,000 and are saving no money, the spouse would continue to need $40,000 to maintain his or her lifestyle. That's not the case. Expenses such as food, clothing, and transportation will likely go down. Other expenses, such as bills for home repair, lawn care, housekeeping, cooking, and other tasks done by your spouse may go up.

If you weren't doing it before, you'll now need to reconcile your monthly bank statements. (See page 116 in chapter 8 for more details.) In the process, you'll be reviewing how you're spending money, and you'll have a greater

FAMILY FINANCE

"And so we are proud to open the Joe Hedrick Memorial Garden of St. John Hospital, in honor of a man we worked with, respected, and loved." Thomas Vogl, the hospital's president, turned to Nancy. "We are grateful to Joe's widow, Nancy, who gave the seed money for this garden."

To applause, Nancy stepped forward and faced the small group of people gathered in the gazebo. "This garden is everything I hoped for. Joe would be proud to see this wonderful place that will provide peace and refreshment for patients and their families. Thank you for making this dream come true."

Fifteen minutes later, Nancy stared at the small fountain, blinking back tears. She had maintained her poise through the ceremony and the beginning of the reception, shaking hands with everyone and speaking cheerfully about the garden's breathtaking design. But now that the adrenaline had run down, her emotions were churning.

"Want to take a break?" Nancy glanced up to see her friend Helen coming toward her, looking concerned.

Once they were settled in a nearby empty waiting room, Nancy let go. Helen waited patiently while Nancy cried, patting her on the back occasionally and offering her Kleenex. Finally, Nancy was able to speak.

"I've been thinking so much about the garden that I pushed away thoughts about Joe," she said. "Then today it suddenly hit me again. Here I am spending time and effort on a garden for him—but he'll never be here to see it." She wiped her eyes. "I miss him so much."

Helen nodded sympathetically. "Of course you do," she said. "You were married for more than 30 years."

"I just don't understand why I'm feeling this way. It's been two years. Shouldn't I be over this by now?"

sense of control over your financial situation. At first you may feel *less* secure because you understand better how much money is being spent, perhaps without the provision of regular income from your spouse. Over time, however, you should begin to feel more control and security.

The third major factor determining your standard of living is your long-term major needs. Make a list of those needs, the dates when they're needed, and the estimated amount that will be needed. Typical needs include college education for your kids, debt payoff, and lifestyle needs such as replacement of cars and home repairs. Committing the needs to paper will begin to give you a sense of control and security because you eliminate the anxiety of the unknown.

Life insurance also becomes a key consideration. If you're a single parent and don't have enough financial resources, it's vital that you provide for your kids through insurance on your life. Life insurance may also be appropriate to meet estate tax needs. A competent financial advisor can help you determine whether you need it and, if so, how much coverage you should obtain.

The last issue affecting how well you'll be able to live is the whole area of

"Grief has no timetable," Helen said. "Besides, Joe's death was so sudden that you weren't able to prepare. And afterward, it seems to me that you've kept so busy that maybe you haven't taken time to process your grief."

Nancy nodded. "I think that's true. After he died, I did what I had to do, like contacting Social Security and our insurance company. But I did the bare minimum. Then I tried to get back to normal—at least as normal as life could be. I went back to work. I stayed in the house and kept my same schedule. I didn't even go through Joe's clothes until I was getting ready for Alysha and the kids to move in."

"Maybe the ceremony today reminded you of what you've been trying to ignore: the finality of it all," Helen suggested.

"Yes. In the back of my mind I've been wishing that this would all go away. I don't want to make major decisions on my own without Joe, so I've been avoid-ing big decisions." She sighed. "That's not the way to live."

Helen paused. "You know, I don't think you ever get over the death of a spouse, just like you would never expect someone to get over the death of a child or another major loss. But you do eventually find a way to move on."

"One tangible way I need to move on is to look at my finances," Nancy said. "I can get by on just my income, so I haven't even touched our other accounts. But I know that our retirement investments should be reexamined now that I'm only saving for one person. Basically, I need to sit down with my financial advisor and answer the questions he's been trying to ask me for the past two years."

Helen put an arm around Nancy's shoulders as they headed back to the reception. "I admire you for facing your grief. Just remember that I'm here for you, okay?"

investments. Life insurance proceeds or investments your spouse left you may be your primary source of income. How much money is available to invest is extremely important to your long-term financial security. Always remember that *every investment carries some risk*. Generally speaking, the higher the rate of return you're seeking, the greater risk you're taking. You can minimize the risk in two ways. First, take a long-term perspective on your investing. Don't try to get in and out of investments as markets change. Second, make sure your investments are well diversified so that when one goes down, as it most certainly will, others will provide stability.

Divorced: What to Do When

Please understand that I'm *not* advocating divorce. God hates divorce (see Malachi 2:16), and so should we. Marriage vows are taken far too lightly today; when couples say "Till death do us part," they often mean "Till we don't *feel* in love anymore." We need to take more seriously the warning of Deuteronomy 23:23: "Whatever your lips utter you must be sure to do, because you made your vow freely to the LORD your God with your own mouth." The commitment to love in spite of feelings and circumstances is essential to upholding a marriage through thick and thin, and reconciliation should always be our goal if it's at all possible.

I have to acknowledge, however, that couples do divorce—even Christians— and say that if it appears to be a definite possibility in your case, you need to make some appropriate plans. Like a widowed person, a divorced man or woman faces enormous psychological, emotional, and financial adjustments. Therefore, if you go through divorce, *you should give yourself some time before making any major investment or financial planning decisions.* Obviously, day-to-day concerns have to be taken care of, but choices like when and where to move, estate plans, and investment decisions (if any) should be delayed. You might delay those decisions anywhere from six months to two years.

I know a couple with teenage children who went through a divorce several years ago. The woman has been a teacher for many years. Unlike many other single parents, she has a profession she can rely on. The divorce was prompted largely by the husband's inability to maintain a steady job. He never could support the family adequately, which is why she always worked. Together they struggled with debt and inadequate income for the needs of a growing family.

I've received many letters over the years from women who tell of the stresses brought about by the poor financial decisions of their husbands. One lady wrote that her husband's attitude toward debt was so stressful to her that she "has to legally cut [her] ties." Her fear was that she was going to lose all financial security.

Those letters and the story of our friend demonstrate that financial problems often contribute to divorce. In fact, more than 50 percent of the people who divorce indicate that financial problems fostered the breakup. Those problems may be only symptomatic of others, but they clearly add to the strain the family is under.

As we've already acknowledged, women are often more vulnerable financially in a divorce, so I now want to focus on the steps a woman needs to take to protect herself during a divorce.

Before the divorce becomes final

The first step is to pick a competent and trusted advisor. You may want to choose a personal advisor as opposed to a financial advisor first. A friend, another woman who has gone through a similar situation, or the elders at your church may be able to guide you through the process of selecting an attorney to handle your side of the divorce. Your goal should not be to "get" your husband or take him for all he's worth, but to be sure you and your children are provided for.

The financial cost of divorce may be significant. Even a simple, uncontested divorce can cost from several hundred to several thousand dollars in legal and filing fees, depending on how much property is involved.

More than 50 percent of the people who divorce indicate that financial problems fostered the breakup.

It's possible to avoid attorneys entirely by using a do-it-yourself divorce kit found in many bookstores. I don't recommend that approach, however, because you could easily overlook crucial details. Your situation may not be as simple as you think. Anytime property or children are involved, the situation is complex. Also, each state's divorce and property laws are different. The divorce can be further complicated if you've lived in more than one state or acquired property in more than one state. For the same reasons, you should never attempt to be your own divorce attorney.

The primary way to reduce the cost of divorce is to avoid contentiousness. The more contentious your split, the more expensive it will be. If your husband agrees, you might want to approach a service such as Christian Conciliation Service[3] or some other mediating body that could help reduce costs and still provide competent advice.

In addition to choosing trusted advisors and legal counsel, you need to do the following during the divorce process:

1. **Establish credit in your own name.** It's almost impossible to function in our culture without a credit rating. If credit cards, bank accounts, and other accounts are in your husband's name alone, you may have difficulty establishing your own credit. It's therefore advisable to apply for credit in your own name at your bank.

2. **List all assets you can find, along with how those assets are titled.** This includes cars, timeshare units, furniture, bank accounts, valuable jewelry, boats, life insurance policies, savings bonds, retirement plans, and brokerage accounts.

3. **Notify banks and brokerage firms—wherever you have joint accounts—of your intention to divorce.** Ask both the banker and the broker to allow no transactions in your accounts without written approval by both you and your spouse.

4. **Close out all joint charge accounts.** If you don't complete this step—and your husband makes charges—you are jointly as well as individually liable for that debt. Notify the creditors in writing that you're no longer responsible for your spouse's purchases. Creditors may agree to let you keep accounts open in joint names but only be liable for your own purchases.

5. **Consider setting up a savings account in your own name.** This will serve as a place to keep cash if your husband stops contributing to the payment of household bills. You'll probably be liable for all utilities and household expenses if your husband decides to stop making those payments.

6. **Make sure you understand the true costs of operating the household.** The budget worksheets in chapter 8 will help you identify many of the costs. Go through the check registers from the past two or three years and list your expenses by major category. This will help you negotiate the terms of divorce, such as child support and alimony payments. And it will be far less expensive for you to gather the information than to hire an accountant or your attorney to do it.

   In addition, you can review prior years' tax returns to get some indication of money spent, investments made, and sources of income you may not have known about. The more information you have, the more you're able to assist your attorney in negotiating a fair and reasonable settlement.

The negotiation process

The last financial step in divorce, one that could take a long time, is the negotiation process. In that process, all assets will be divided; the responsibility for debts will be determined; child support amounts will be set; alimony amount and duration will be decided; and last and very important, visitation rights will be established. How well the negotiation is done will depend not only on the information you provide your attorney, but also on his or her skill as an advocate for you.

How well the settlement is negotiated will largely determine the tax consequences of the divorce too. What appears valuable *before* taxes may be far less valuable *after* taxes. For example, any alimony paid to you will be deductible to your husband on his tax return and taxable to you as income. On the other hand, child support payments are neither taxable as income to you nor deductible by him.

To illustrate, suppose your ex-husband pays you alimony of $35,000 the first year, $20,000 the second year, and $5,000 the third year. He will be able to deduct $60,000 from his tax returns over those three years, and you'll have to report taxable income of $60,000. Thus, your attorney should attempt to increase the amount of alimony paid to take into account the tax benefit your former husband is getting and the tax liability you are assuming. If you were to receive $60,000 of child support over a period of years, you would pay no income tax. Child support is better for you than alimony from a tax perspective, but is less attractive to him financially.

Another issue relative to child support is who gets to claim exemptions for the children on tax returns. The parent who pays more than 50 percent of the child's support gets the exemption unless the other spouse signs a waiver. So even if your ex-husband provides more than half your child's support, you can still claim the exemption if your former spouse will agree to it.

If your spouse is extremely well paid, he should be especially amenable to signing a waiver, because dependent exemptions are phased out anyway for single taxpayers with higher incomes. If your former husband fits that category, he'll get no benefit from the exemption, so it should be used by you if you're in a lower tax bracket.

> **The parent who pays more than 50 percent of the child's support gets the tax exemption unless the other spouse signs a waiver.**

This is all a moot issue, of course, if you provide more than half the support of your child, which can be determined by the family budget you've already prepared. In that case, you can just take the exemption on your return and reduce your tax liability accordingly.

Property settlements can also have tax consequences. Generally, property transferred as part of a divorce settlement is treated as a gift between spouses, so no taxes are paid on the transfer. But certain assets, such as an IRA or 401(k), will have future tax consequences. Many women recognize too late that $20,000 in a savings account (not taxable) is much more desirable than $20,000 of their husband's 401(k) (taxable upon withdrawal and not accessible until age 59½).

Although the transfer of most property without taxation sounds good, keep the following in mind. If property (stock, real estate, etc.) that originally cost $1,000 but is now worth $50,000 is transferred, you don't have $50,000 available to you. When the property is sold, you will have a taxable gain of $49,000. The income tax on the gain will reduce substantially the amount of money available to you. If, on the other hand, property that cost $50,000 is transferred to you and you sell it for $50,000, you have no tax on that gain, so you really do have $50,000. Thus, the specific property transferred in the divorce settlement can change your cash flow significantly.

Another issue in the property settlement is the family home. If that's transferred to you, you get the tax benefit of avoiding most or all of the income tax on the gain from a sale. Current tax laws allow you to exclude from income any gain up to $250,000 ($500,000 for a married couple) from the sale of your principal residence.

Finally, while the divorce is being negotiated, you need to review the medical insurance coverage you and your children will have. If you need to provide the insurance yourself, chapter 29 will help you make good decisions.

After the divorce is final

By the time the divorce becomes final and all property transactions are completed, you should have your own bank and brokerage accounts and credit cards. Now, besides living in accordance with a financial plan, you need to rewrite your will, change the beneficiary for life insurance policies on your life, and review your children's medical insurance coverage, which may have been provided by your spouse.

Those protections become more critical now than ever because you may be your kids' sole support. Chapters 28 and 29 can help with your insurance questions, and an attorney can assist you with the will revision. These steps are too important to delay beyond the first few weeks after the divorce is final.

Divorced: Will You Be Able to Live as Well in the Future?

The financial consequences of divorce on single mothers are often devastating. In my experience in counseling those who have gone through a divorce, I've concluded that couples rarely do as well separately as they did together. It's important from a biblical perspective, however, not to be resentful, bitter, or fearful. Rather, you need to be realistic about where you are financially and what your alternatives are, as well as remain dependent upon a faithful and all-powerful God.

You can begin to determine whether lifestyle changes will be needed by developing a financial plan as outlined in chapter 8. You'll confront the same questions, problems, and challenges during the various seasons of life that a married couple will face. The primary difference will be that you don't have the financial resources you had as a couple, and therefore you may be forced to choose different alternatives.

While your children are young, for example, you'll be concerned with living on a budget, avoiding debt, maintaining the right life insurance, having a will, deciding how to school your kids, training your children to manage money, and choosing whether to buy a house (if that's possible for you) or rent—just like a married couple.

During your children's teen and college years, you'll be concerned with providing a secondary education for them. It may be more likely that they'll have to work to pay part of the cost, attend a less expensive school, or rely on financial aid now that household income is reduced. That wouldn't hurt them, of course, and may be God's best way of supplying their college education. What you spend on their cars and weddings will also be affected.

Those are just a few examples. The underlying reality is that you'll almost certainly have to take a more conservative approach to planning and managing your financial life than you did when you were married.

One other financial challenge you may face is caring for your aging parents. Studies show that women provide most of the care for their parents. Furthermore, nearly 40 percent of those caring for the elderly are still raising children of their own.

A U.S. House of Representatives report showed that the average American woman will spend 17 years raising children and 18 years helping aged parents. As people live longer and chronic disabling conditions become more common, the likelihood increases that your parents will need extra care.

> **Nearly 40 percent of adults caring for the elderly are still raising children of their own.**

The topic of caring for aging parents is broad and difficult and is only partially answered in chapter 17. When your parents move in with you or you're financially responsible for them, you have to revise the family budget to reflect the increased expenses. There are no easy answers. The only thing you can do is discuss that possibility ahead of time with your parents and make provisions when everyone is fully competent to do so. Such decisions are always best made ahead of time rather than in the heat of the need.

As a single-again woman, you need to remember that the keys to financial success are very simple regardless of your financial situation: Understand that God owns it all, spend less than you earn, avoid the use of debt, build an emergency savings fund, and set some long-term goals. Those may prove difficult to follow, I know, but God is faithful.

Approaching Remarriage

I'm hesitant to tread very far into all the relational and spiritual aspects of remarriage. Let me just comment on the unfortunate possibility of a widowed or divorced individual—particularly one with sizeable financial assets—being preyed upon by someone of the opposite sex. I've observed how vulnerable the newly single may be to remarrying too quickly or remarrying those primarily interested in their money. The stories are sad but true.

Certainly, remarriage should be considered carefully and only after a couple has sought premarital counseling. Here are a few pointers specifically related to finances that may be helpful:

- Obtain premarital counseling together. (Warning sign alert: He or she is not willing to do so.)
- Consider your dependent children's financial future. You may want to fund college, set money aside in a trust, or otherwise reserve funds for your children. (Warning sign alert: He or she wants you to use your money to buy jointly owned assets or is resistant about setting some aside for your children.)
- Be discreet and guarded about financial details early in your dating or courting relationship. (Warning sign alert: He or she seems too interested in financial details too early.)
- Meet together with a financial advisor you can trust. (Warning sign alert: He or she refuses to consider the advisor's recommendations.)
- Have an accountability partner to act as a sounding board for anything that sounds unusual—a wise uncle, a parent, a friend who's been in the same position. (Warning sign alert: He or she doesn't want you to confide in anyone else.)

Forging a New Identity

My wife and I were visiting one of the widows described at the start of this chapter. It had been more than two years since her husband died in the plane crash. She has had a significant ministry around the country sharing some of her challenges as a widow. Her life has been no easier than that of other widows, but she turned the tragedy into an outreach to others in similar circumstances.

As we talked with her she raised an interesting point. "After these last several years," she said, "I have reached an identity crisis. Who am I? Am I to be forever my husband's widow, or am I a unique person? I do not want to make a career out of widowhood."

In saying that, she expressed considerable insight into one of the keys to building a new life after widowhood or divorce, and that's determining who you are and what you want to be. God has given you experiences that build wisdom if interpreted and used correctly. And that wisdom can be a tremendous benefit to others who will go through the same dark valley.

CHAPTER 33

Choosing a Financial Advisor: When and Where to Get Professional Advice

My former firm once developed a survey asking what questions a person would like to put to a prospective financial advisor. One woman responding to our survey said, "Do you realize you hold my future in your hands?" That response reminded me of the importance and sacred trust of my role.

Indeed, much depends on the quality of professional advice you receive. I remember reading an article years ago in the *Atlanta Journal-Constitution* portraying what can happen when that advice is bad. The newspaper report explained how an Illinois woman lost her life savings when the savings-and-loan company in which she invested her money was taken over by the federal government and stopped paying interest on its notes. Even though she considered herself a cautious investor, she had put all her money into the unsecured debt offering after being convinced by an official at the savings and loan to do so. Ms. Dixon wept as she told her story to a U.S. Senate committee in Chicago.

This modern horror story raises the question, If you can't trust your banker, then whom can you trust? Choosing a professional advisor, someone defined and perhaps licensed as an expert, can be extremely intimidating. You must face language barriers, fee barriers, and confusion about where to seek advice for your particular situation. For example, do you need a CPA, CFP, RIA, or a CFA? One woman raised a couple of common concerns when she told us, "All counselors seem to have their pet investments, and you never know how competent they really are." She concluded, "How do you know when you're getting good advice?"

That's a good question, because choosing the wrong advisor can be extremely costly. The fee paid is just one expense associated with professional advisors. Bad advice can be far more costly. I worked with a person who was getting ready to declare bankruptcy. This man had been advising many couples in his church about investments and had lost more than $2.5 million of their money through poor decisions.

In-Depth Financial Strategies | 33

We've all heard sad stories about people who trusted advisors and got burned. But choosing qualified professionals should bring positive results for you. Good advisors can provide thorough legal documents, reduced taxes, prudent insurance plans, and sound investment strategies.

Full disclosure, right up front: I think most people need a financial advisor. You can try to be a do-it-yourselfer to save a few dollars, but I wouldn't recommend it. I've owned a small financial advice firm and a big one. You may be surprised to learn that I have a financial advisor. As president of Kingdom Advisors, a not-for-profit entity designed to equip professional financial advisors to use biblical principles in their work with clients, I've trained financial advisors to use another financial advisor.

I'm convinced that we benefit from the perspective of another. We don't see our own tendencies. We can't be experts in everything. We need accountability. The Bible seems to agree with me on this point: "Plans fail for lack of counsel, but with many advisors they succeed" (Proverbs 15:22).

> **Good advisors can provide thorough legal documents, reduced taxes, prudent insurance plans, and sound investment strategies.**

As part of Kingdom Advisors, I've had the privilege of working with hundreds of Christian financial advisors from all over the country in both a speaking and training capacity. Most typically when I call my wife, Judy, after one of these events I find myself saying, "What an outstanding group of people I have just had the privilege of interacting with." She has responded on more than one occasion, "You say that every time."

I do say it every time, because I have had the privilege of being with so many financial advisors who are extraordinarily professionally competent and spiritually passionate. I am seeing men and women who are very serious about making their lives count for Christ and who are attempting to integrate their faith into their practices and into the advice and counsel that they are privileged to give.

Professional Christian advisors are uniquely positioned to have one of the greatest Kingdom impacts anywhere. Through the application of biblical wisdom, professional Christian advisors are able to lead clients through financial decision making that results in confidence, peace of mind, an eternal perspective, and a clear focus on God's agenda. Biblical wisdom is timeless, accurate, universal, and completely practical. As we search the counsel of Scripture and allow the Holy Spirit to guide us in truth, and as we are encouraged and challenged by other believers, we will be able to effectively apply biblical wisdom to every area of our lives, including our financial practices.

The secular advisor can't deliver peace of mind. There's also a difference

Q: Is the decision to send our kids to a private Christian school or to homeschool them mainly an economic decision?

ANSWER: I once counseled a young professional couple whose income was nearly $100,000. Their problem was that they did not have enough money to tithe, pay off their debt, maintain their chosen lifestyle, and send their children to a private Christian school. They came to ask me what to do with their financial situation to move from a negative cash flow to a positive one.

While reviewing their budget together, I asked them if they were willing to move their children out of private school into the public school system. They indicated strongly that that was not an option as far as they were concerned. In reflecting upon that answer before our next time together, I realized that the private school decision they had made was not an economic decision; it was rather a priority decision. They were telling me that, because acceptable public education was not available to their children, one of their highest priorities was to be able to send their children to private schools.

I told them that their finances indicated that their priorities were, in order of importance, (1) to maintain a particular lifestyle, (2) to pay their taxes, (3) to send their children to private school, (4) to pay off their debt, (5) to tithe, and (6) to provide for the future through savings programs. Because they were running a negative cash flow, they were unable to accomplish the last three priorities at all. Rather than reducing debt, they were in fact increasing it. I pointed out to them that private school education was therefore a priority decision rather than an economic decision.

By this I meant that if they chose to make private school a high priority and still desired to tithe, pay off debt, pay their taxes, and save for the future, then their only option was to reduce their lifestyle. They could continue to live in the same home and neighborhood, take the same vacations, spend as much on entertainment and clothes, but have to take their children out of private school. Or, they could keep them in the private school and reduce their lifestyle. This couple realized that, in fact, it was a priority decision for them. They chose to reduce their lifestyle in order to maintain the priorities they felt God would have them follow.

So often the decisions we make seem to be strictly financial decisions, when in reality they are priority decisions. Once the priorities of life are set, then money becomes nothing more than a tool to be used to accomplish those priorities. Unless you have unlimited resources (and no one does), you will never be able to spend on an unlimited basis. As God makes available more and more financial resources to a family, then they have the opportunity to accomplish more of their priorities.

But what we need to recognize is that when money is spent to accomplish one objective or priority, it is not available for other objectives or priorities. Therefore, we should be certain we are making spending decisions that are in line with the priorities we have set.

between a financial advisor who's a Christian but operates based on secular financial principles and one who provides his or her advice from a Christian worldview and perspective.

A trusted financial advisor is someone who

- Facilitates the decision-making process of the clients, using his or her professional expertise while integrating appropriate biblical principles

- Leads his or her clients, encouraging them to implement the decisions that they have made

- Contributes to the peace of mind of his or her clients because *their* goals are being accomplished

- Helps clients overcome their economic uncertainties (fear of the economy or government, security in their bank accounts or investments) because of the wisdom of God's truths

- Sees the Holy Spirit working in the lives of clients to contribute to the fulfillment of the great commission

If you need help locating a qualified Christian financial professional in your area, visit http://www.kingdomadvisors.org. There you can see whether one of our financial planners, investment professionals, attorneys, accountants, or insurance professionals is practicing in or near your community. (You can also contact Kingdom Advisors at 404-497-7680.)

The Alphabet Soup of Credentials

As you choose an advisor, it's helpful to understand the variety of credentials that are offered by financial planners and tax advisors. The most respected designations—those that require the most preparation and knowledge and the highest ethical standards—are the CPA, CFP, ChFC, CFA, and PFS. Here's a bit of explanation (just a bit because so many new initials and credentials have been developed for marketing purposes) for the alphabet soup of credentials in the financial advisory world:

ATA or ATP. Accredited tax advisors or accredited tax preparers have completed the College for Financial Planning's Accredited Tax Preparer Program and passed an exam administered by the Accreditation Council for Accountancy on Taxation.

CFA. Chartered financial analysts must pass a rigorous, three-level test on investment analysis, economics, portfolio theory, accounting, corporate finance, and other topics, that is administered by the Financial Analysts Federation. CFAs also must demonstrate expertise in a specialized area of investments.

CFP. Certified financial planners must meet experience and education requirements and pass a 10-hour exam.

CFS. Certified fund specialists have completed a 60-hour self-study course and passed an examination on mutual fund investing administered by the Institute of Business & Finance in La Jolla, California.

ChFC. Chartered financial consultants are typically insurance agents who have passed college-level courses in financial planning.

CLU. Chartered life underwriters have the highest professional designation for life insurance agents and must meet extensive experience and education requirements in the life insurance industry.

CMFC. Chartered mutual fund consultants have completed a 72-hour self-study course on mutual funds. The program is administered by the College for Financial Planning and the Investment Company Institute.

CPA. Certified public accountants have completed college and often post-graduate education in accounting and have passed a rigourous certification test. CPAs are often tax specialists and keep current on changes in tax law. They may also audit businesses, appraise businesses, and serve as consultants.

EA. Enrolled agents are tax preparers who either worked for the IRS for at least five years or passed a two-day test on federal tax law.

PFS. Personal financial specialists are CPAs who have met education and experience requirements and passed a comprehensive exam on financial planning.

RIA. Registered investment advisors. This designation simply means they have registered with the Securities and Exchange Commission and paid a registration fee.

Besides the abbreviations and initials following a name on a business card, there are many other types of professional advisors. The most common are lawyers, accountants, investment advisors, financial planners, insurance agents, real estate experts, and bankers. Rarely will anyone need all of them. At times, however, you might need more than one.

Legal advisors

We could write a full book on choosing a legal advisor, because there are so many specialty areas within the practice of law. At a minimum, you should seek legal advice anytime you're dealing with lawsuits, divorce, estate documents, contracts, or real estate transactions. Never practice do-it-yourself law; it may be less expensive in the short run but extremely costly in the long run. If you follow the process of choosing an advisor outlined in this chapter, you can avoid the pitfalls of picking poor legal advisors.

Accountants

Generally, two situations warrant help with your tax returns. One is if you've had any significant change in your financial situation during the tax year—for example, widowhood, divorce, a move, or a capital gain transaction. The second is if your situation is complex because of owning a business, buying or selling investments, caring for aging parents, large charitable contributions, or other unusual itemized deductions. Occasionally Judy and I seek advice for particularly difficult questions. Because the tax laws are so complex and ever changing, even CPAs have trouble keeping up with them.

Investment advisors (or financial advisors)

When do you need an investment advisor? After you reach level 4 of the investment hierarchy (see chapter 23) and have some money to invest, you may need an investment advisor. Prior to that, you can get most answers from your own reading and research.[1]

I've used the following chart with the Kingdom Advisors organization. It divides the population into segments of wealth.

If you're in the crisis or month-to-month levels, then you're not ready for an investment advisor. As you become more affluent, then you have a greater need for advisors. You also have more tools and products available.

> **Not everyone needs a financial planner—but everyone needs a financial plan.**

Be aware that there is little regulation over who can and can't call themselves professional investment advisors. Virtually anyone can use the label. Because some people find the word *investment* mysterious or intriguing, many salespeople try to take advantage of potential clients by calling themselves investment advisors. Even ordinary car purchases are sometimes called investments, which they are not.

Financial planners

Sometimes the terms *financial advisors* and *financial planners* are used synonymously. But I'm using *financial planner* to mean a person who is paid a fee specifically to help you come up with your financial plan. Having worked in the financial planning business for almost all of my professional career, I believe that not everyone needs a financial planner. What they need is a financial plan.

As with investing, the financial planning industry is largely unregulated, and anyone can claim to be a professional advisor. Most so-called financial planners have no real training or expertise; they're really salespeople.

If your income reaches $100,000 or you have more than $50,000 in investments, you may need an investment or financial advisor. Until then, however,

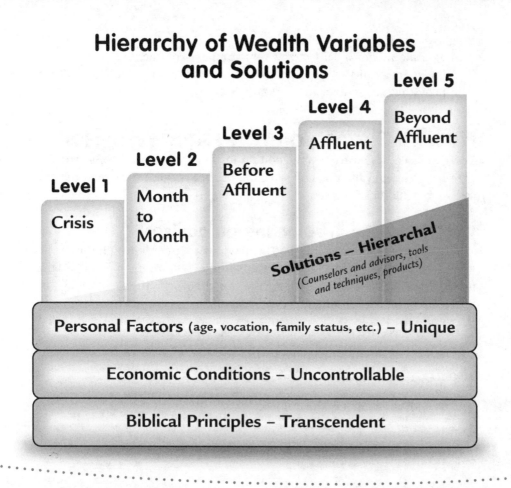

Hierarchy of Wealth Variables and Solutions

Level 1 — Crisis

Level 2 — Month to Month

Level 3 — Before Affluent

Level 4 — Affluent

Level 5 — Beyond Affluent

Solutions – Hierarchal
(Counselors and advisors, tools and techniques, products)

Personal Factors (age, vocation, family status, etc.) – Unique

Economic Conditions – Uncontrollable

Biblical Principles – Transcendent

you really just need a financial plan. If you require help preparing a budget or financial plan, read books on the subject and do it yourself, or contact your church to see if anyone in the congregation is qualified to help you.

Insurance agents

It's wise to seek insurance counsel early in life. Choosing the right products for your life, health, car, and home is extremely important; it's also essential to being a good steward. Buying insurance does not demonstrate a lack of faith but is prudent in today's litigious society.

Bankers

When America was more community centered, having a personal banker was a fact of life. Today, having a banker you can rely on is far less certain. Most banks are large, and branch managers are transferred regularly. You only need a relationship with a banker, however, if you require services other than checking, savings, credit cards, consumer loans, and a safe deposit box.

If you're going to invest using a bank (i.e., in CDs, money market accounts, etc.), you should find a banker in whom you have confidence—someone recommended by a satisfied customer whose judgment you trust, and someone who takes the time to explain everything clearly.

How to Choose a Professional Advisor

There are two keys to choosing good professional advisors. First, learn what criteria to use in evaluating and selecting them. Second, understand the process of making those choices.

Criteria to use in selecting an advisor

There are seven important criteria. The first four are must-haves. If the advisor you're interviewing doesn't meet any one of these, you should eliminate that person from consideration. The last three are important criteria, but they may not be essential. The criteria are as follows:

1. Technical expertise

2. Experience with similar clients

3. Wisdom and judgment

4. Worldview and like-mindedness

5. Fees

6. Service

7. Location

The selection process

Three steps make up the selection process. Step 1 is to interview prospective advisors. Step 2 is to check their referrals. Step 3 is to have them send you an engagement letter or investment policy statement. These summarize the services provided, define the objectives, outline responsibilities, describe how changes in objectives are made, and disclose fee arrangements.

During the initial interview, your goal is to see how well each advisor meets the seven criteria listed above by asking a series of questions.

To determine technical expertise, ask questions such as "What degrees have you earned?" "What type of training have you had relative to my particular situation?" and "Have you ever been sued? If so, tell me the circumstances."

Those questions are not presumptuous. After all, you're going to pay for the person's services. The question about being sued may indicate whether others have encountered any problems. You may also search the regulatory Web site at http://www.nasdr.com/ for any complaints or proceedings against the advisor. You could also ask if he or she has ever been used as an expert witness in a legal proceeding.

To check work experience, begin by asking, "Who are some other clients similar to me? What are some of the facts involved? What were the results in those situations?" You might also inquire about previous positions they have held.

In discerning whether an advisor has wisdom and judgment, it would be good to know whom he or she relies on for advice. That would tell you whether he or she feels self-sufficient or understands that gathering wisdom is a continuous process.

You might also ask, "Can you tell me about your family?" to determine whether family is a priority. Professionals who spend a lot of time working and little time with family cut themselves off from the opportunity to gain wisdom from family, and that should concern you. Technical expertise is important, but judgment and wisdom are just as critical.

As I discussed in chapter 2, your worldview is important in shaping how you approach handling your money. It follows, then, that when choosing your financial advisor, you should dis-
cern his or her worldview. You should have a like-mindedness—your values and convictions should mesh as closely as possible with your advisor's. You should feel confident and trusting after your first meeting. Ask questions such as "What's the biblical teaching on the issues we're discussing?" Ask about personal goals and why he or she chose to work in this field. You are attempting to match the advisor's philosophies with your specific needs.

> **Technical expertise is important, but judgment and wisdom are just as critical.**

The first four criteria above are most critical. Yet everybody is concerned about fees charged by a professional advisor. Fees shouldn't be overemphasized, however.

The greatest barrier to a satisfactory working relationship with an advisor is unrealistic expectations regarding fees. A professional who operates with integrity is never concerned about discussing fees. Charges should reflect the value of the service given and received. When a working relationship begins with improper expectations on either side, problems can occur.

A balance needs to be struck regarding fees. Many times, paying too little results in receiving lesser-quality service. On the other hand, paying too much is poor stewardship. But it's difficult for advisors to work with you if you continually balk at their normal fees; you might find your work being lowered in priority. You want your advisors to receive a fair and clearly understood fee for services rendered.

I was recently involved in a minor accident in which a bicyclist was riding down the wrong side of the street and hit my car when he pulled away from a stop sign. There was no damage to the car, and the cyclist was only bruised. The father of the cyclist decided, however, to contact my insurance company about a possible settlement.

Because it was in another state and I was uncertain of my own rights, I engaged an attorney in that state to assist me. When I asked about fees, he indicated they would be minimal. When I received his first bill for more than $1,000 and the process wasn't even half completed, I was extremely agitated. I hadn't pinned the lawyer down precisely enough on a fee quote. Of all people, I should have known better, but even I find it difficult to ask about fees.

You need to ask three questions concerning fees: "How do you charge for your services? When do you bill? And what is either the range or the maximum fee for the services you'll perform for me?" Never enter into a professional relationship without knowing the answers to those questions.

FAMILY FINANCE

Laura, Bob, and Bob's parents, Chet and Alice, settled into their seats along the third-base line. "Looks like we're just in time for the first pitch, Dad," Bob commented.

"Great seats, too," Chet concurred.

Watching baseball together was something Bob and Chet had done since Bob was in grade school. Through countless games they'd seen in person and on TV, Chet had instructed Bob on batting stances, fielding fundamentals, and pitching strategies. They had followed their local major league team for years, but these days Chet got tired so easily that they usually skipped the big trip to the stadium and instead attended the minor-league games 10 minutes from home.

Fortunately, Chet's Alzheimer's did not seem to be progressing quickly. Aside from periodic moments of confusion, he was functioning okay. And baseball always cheered him up.

Midway through the third inning, Bob bought hot dogs for everyone. Handing one to his dad, he unwrapped his. "So how's it going, Dad?" he asked before he took a bite.

"Okay," Chet said. "But Alice and I have been talking about finances a lot recently. She's concerned about having enough money readily available if we suddenly have to pay a down payment for an apartment in an assisted-living facility. I told her I'd talk to Jim about cashing out a CD early."

Bob nodded. "Dad, I know you trust Jim a lot. You two have been friends for years, and he certainly knows the banking business. But have you and Mom considered talking with another financial planner?"

"Why would we do that?" Chet asked. "I've always talked to Jim about financial decisions."

"I know," Bob agreed. "And I'm sure he's been very helpful." He hesitated, then glanced at his mother, who was listening. "Your finances may become

It's also important to know how advisors will work with you. Creating realistic expectations is vital for a harmonious relationship. Ask potential advisors questions such as these:

- How soon can I expect my telephone calls or e-mails to be answered?
- What is the projected turnaround time on this project?
- How can I make your job easier and help you reduce the turnaround time?
- How do you choose the staff assigned to my case?
- Who will be doing the work specifically?
- What are your goals in servicing clients? Do you always meet them?
- When is the last time you lost a client? Why?
- Do I really need you?

Another factor to consider is the location of your advisor. If frequent face-to-face meetings are needed, proximity is important. On the other hand, if

a lot more complicated in the next few years. I just think it might be wise to work with a professional who's being paid to look out for you."

Alice nodded. "I have thought about that, but I don't know where to start. How do we find the right person?"

"Well, we'd be happy to recommend our financial planner," Laura interjected. "We've used Bill Oliver for the past five years, and we've been very happy with him."

"Last time I talked with him, I asked if he had experience working with seniors," Bob added. "He said he has a number of senior clients, and he gave me some names of people you can call for references if you'd like."

Chet still looked skeptical. "But Jim is my friend. Why should I trust someone else?"

"I understand your hesitation, Dad," Bob said. "Friends can give valuable advice—but sometimes their expertise is limited. Jim knows the bank's prod-ucts really well, but he may not have a clear idea of other financial services that are available. Also, off-the-cuff advice can be different from professional advice. If you're paying someone, he's accountable for his counsel. And he's also guaranteeing that he will put in time and effort on your behalf."

"Well, it's true that Jim is sometimes too busy to talk with me right when I need advice," Chet admitted.

Alice cleared her throat. "Another thing to consider is that while I like Jim, he's really *your* friend. I don't know him very well. If sometime in the future I need to make more of the financial decisions, I need to be comfortable with whoever is advising us."

Chet sighed. "Okay. You've all come up with good reasons. We'll at least call a few of the references and make an initial appointment with this Bill Oliver."

"Thanks for listening, Dad," Bob said, gripping his father's shoulder. "I don't think you'll regret it."

most of your business can be conducted over the phone or with e-mail, even an out-of-town advisor can provide good service. Any concerns you have about proximity should be dealt with on the front end of the relationship.

After the interview process is completed, you're ready to check the references of those advisors in whom you're still interested. Talking to other clients about their experience with the advisors will give you peace of mind, knowing you've left no stone unturned.

When you've picked your advisors, you should ask them to send you an engagement letter you can sign and return spelling out several things: how your account will be serviced, the fees agreed upon, and the length of the engagement. An ending point should be specified so you're not committing yourself to work with a given advisor perpetually, and the term should be no longer than one year. (At the end of that time, you can renew the agreement or not as you choose.) With this information on paper, you and the advisor are clear about expectations.

Last, a procedure for handling disputes needs to be outlined. Perhaps you'll agree to use mediation or a Christian conciliation service. Whatever the specifics, just realize that disputes may come up, and you need to have predetermined how they will be resolved.

The process of choosing advisors may seem overwhelming, but remember the cost of picking the wrong ones. Time spent on the front end making good selections will save you dollars, frustration, and time in the long run. Remember, too, that you're the employer; you're the one spending money for services. You're also the one who lives with the consequences of the advice taken. If the advisors you're evaluating don't have the patience to answer your questions now, they probably won't have the patience to service you properly later.

The good news is that you generally have more choices than time available to evaluate them all. Although there are lots of bad advisors out there, there are also many competent, trustworthy ones available to you.

In many ways, selecting a professional advisor is like choosing a marriage partner. There needs to be give and take, because not all aspects of the relationship will be smooth sailing. The more that's defined ahead of time, however, the greater the chances for a satisfactory partnership.

How Is a Christian Financial Professional Similar to a Counselor?

A Christian financial professional is often called upon to fill several roles in order to help clients. He or she provides professional financial advice and leadership in setting goals for clients' finances. But there are times when clients cannot or will not follow the advisor's financial advice until some of their root issues are addressed. They may find themselves receiving bits of emotional, marital, or spiritual counseling from their advisor in order to help them achieve financial contentment. In those cases, Christian financial professionals counsel their clients from Scripture to get their clients' thinking in the right place.

Here are the three roles that I see the financial advisor filling at certain times:

- Professional financial advisor, who provides technical advice
- Leader, who provides motivation and direction
- Counselor, who provides insight and support

When I met with clients, I knew it was important to understand what role I was serving when giving financial advice. Was it purely technical advice, as in the financial advisor role? Was it a leadership role, where I wanted to inspire a client to make the changes that we had identified as necessary? Many of the recommendations that I made, such as getting out of debt or increasing giving, were the result of my role as a professional financial advisor; however, that advice made no difference in the lives of my clients unless they also followed my direction as a leader and made the changes and took the risks necessary to implement the professional advice.

In many cases, I was also in a counseling role. My clients encountered emotional or psychological barriers to taking my advice and making necessary changes. I had to learn how to tailor my message to the individual personalities I encountered. For example, I discovered that in almost every case husbands and wives thought differently about finances. I had to find a way to communicate so both could respond to my counsel. But there were many cases when it was just better to encourage couples to seek professional marital counseling because the problems were beyond the scope of my skill and experience.

Identifying Root Causes of Financial Decisions

In my experience of providing financial advice—speaking, being interviewed, and interacting with Christians over the last few decades—I have found several things. First of all, almost all financial problems and issues are only symptomatic of the real issues, which tend to be spiritual and/or emotional in nature. Some issues that create financial problems and issues—such as the loss of a job, a major medical emergency, or widowhood—occur outside of one's control. All of the other issues are driven for the most part by poor thinking and poor decision making. When a husband and wife have conflict over money or debt, it's really symptomatic of poor communication skills, bad belief systems, or poor training.

> **Almost all financial problems and issues are only symptomatic of the real issues, which tend to be spiritual or emotional in nature.**

Many times the symptom that presents itself is debt. Over the years, I have been asked thousands of times, "How can I get out of debt?" However, the questions that first must be addressed are "How did I get here? What belief drove me to make the decisions that resulted in debt?" Fear of rejection, fear of failure, poor self-image, and lack of self-control pave the road to debt, and these are often the issues a financial advisor faces in advising his or her clients.

The advisor who recognizes that a financial issue—whether debt or something else—is symptomatic of an underlying issue can be better able to meet the real needs of his or her clients. Sometimes that means referring them to a Christian counselor before advising them financially.

Referrals to professional counselors should take place within the context of the local church. Christian believers are God's strategy in terms of achieving His plans and purposes on earth, and believers are networked together most effectively in a local church that is fulfilling its role.

In his book *Telling Yourself the Truth*, professional counselor William Backus says, "The words you tell yourself have power over your life."[2] Likewise, Neil Anderson says in his book *The Bondage Breaker*, "All behavior is a product of what we choose to think or believe. . . . Trying to change behavior without changing what we believe and therefore think will never produce any lasting results."[3]

In other words, if I want my clients to make good financial decisions, I need to help them believe and think correctly so that they will behave correctly. The financial problems in which people find themselves in most cases are the function of a bad belief system. The Christian financial professional can have a dramatic impact in people's financial lives just by helping them to think biblically.

PART 4

Bringing It Home: Final Thoughts and Additional Resources

The Whole Conclusion of the Matter

can't kid myself. I know the last chapter of a financial reference book doesn't have quite the climax of a Frank Peretti or John Grisham novel. But I would like to share some final thoughts about what I've been learning recently.

I've written this book out of my vision to communicate hope, encouragement, and freedom to those who will follow the biblical principles of planning and money management. I have a passion to see husbands and wives communicate about money and money management. I have a passion to make order out of what appears to be confusion. I know it's possible to achieve order in a world that appears to be confused because our God is not confused, nor does He author confusion.

Making money is a lot easier than managing money. We tend to earn our money in a professional setting where we have been adequately trained and equipped. When it comes to handling our own money, though, we are in unfamiliar territory. Few of us have been schooled in financial management. As a result, we can make mistakes, become fearful, or find it very difficult to make good decisions.

Over the years, I've observed that in many cases more money equals less freedom, not more. That's because the more money you have, the more options you have. Consequently, the more time and energy you must spend making decisions and managing your resources. Yet no matter how great or small your financial assets, God will use those resources powerfully if you keep your focus on bringing Him glory and look beyond the here and now.

Glorifying God

During the past year or so, I've been rethinking my life purpose and evaluating it to make sure I am still on track. I know that it's my desire to glorify God in all that I do and to know Him more intimately every day.

As I meditate on how to glorify God, the obvious channels come to mind: quiet times, prayer, witnessing, Bible study, giving, going to church, and maintaining

Bringing It Home

my body as a temple of the Holy Spirit. As I think about these behaviors, I realize it's not the *behaviors* that bring glory to God, but rather the source behind my motivation to carry them out.

It is God who is at work in me to will and to work for His good pleasure. A more radical thought is that it's not I who brings glory to God but it's God who brings glory to Himself. I'm merely an instrument by which He can glorify Himself.

The question then becomes whether or not my life allows God to glorify Himself. There is no way I can glorify God in my humanness. I can, however, be a tool in the hands of God for Him to glorify Himself. I believe He desires to glorify Himself because He is the only answer to any question humanity can raise. He is the light of the world. He is the hope of the world, in Him is joy, and at His right hand are pleasures forevermore.

In His mercy and grace He must glorify Himself. He is the awesome, incomprehensible, sovereign creator, God of the universe. My heart responds, "Oh Lord, glorify Yourself through me in whatever way You see fit."

Hall of Fame of Faith

As fallen human beings, seeking to exalt God doesn't come naturally, of course. Too often, we seek to exalt ourselves. After all, the payoff is much more immediate. Yet two thoughts struck me recently as I was spending my quiet time in Hebrews 11. First, the men and women mentioned in this "hall of fame" of faith lived as "aliens and strangers" here on earth; secondly, "they did not receive the things promised."

> Now faith is being sure of what we hope for and certain of what we do not see. This is what the ancients were commended for. . . . All these people were still living by faith when they died. They did not receive the things promised; they only saw them and welcomed them from a distance. And they admitted that they were aliens and strangers on earth. . . . They were longing for a better country—a heavenly one. (Hebrews 11:1-2, 13, 16)

I have had to ask myself, "Am I living as an alien and stranger here on earth?" I think of the many times I travel, spending nights in other people's homes or a hotel room. When I do, in no way do I set down roots. I may make my presence known briefly, but when I walk out of that room, nothing of mine is left behind—I hope—because it is not my home. I do not change the pictures on the walls, I do not have a phone installed, I do not do anything that would tie me to that particular location because I do not intend to stay there very long. The question is, Is this the way I spend my *whole life on earth*—because I am here only temporarily as well?

I believe one can only live as an alien and stranger if he or she has an eternal perspective. That is why it is said of those in Hebrews 11, "All these people were still living by faith when they died. They did not receive the things promised." They did not look for their promises *here*—they had an eternal mind-set.

Let's relate this eternal perspective to our finances. Obviously, we brought nothing into the world, and we will take nothing out if it—we are here only temporarily. Our real home is in heaven, and our life here should testify to the world that we consider our sojourn temporary. Nowhere are we tested as severely as in the area of finances, because they represent so much to us in the way of security, power, prestige, and position.

The challenge to each of us is to establish no roots here, especially with our finances. Hold on to them loosely, even as you strive to be a faithful steward of all that God has entrusted to you.

Important Consumer Protections

To be a smart money manager, you should know about a few important laws designed to protect you as a consumer. Rather than provide the precise statutory language and lengthy code, I'll summarize the key elements of these acts:

Consumer Credit Protection Act. This legislation launched "Truth in Lending" regulations that provide a uniform and consistent manner of disclosing interest rates for loans. How does this act protect *you*?

Fair Credit Reporting Act. What credit and personal information do credit reporting agencies have about you? How can you get a free credit report?

Fair Credit Billing Act. What rights do you have to dispute an incorrect charge on your credit card bill?

Bankruptcy Acts. What do the various "chapters" of bankruptcy cover? What debts are not eliminated through bankruptcy proceedings?

These questions will be answered below. As is true in any area of life, the better you understand your rights under the law, the better off you'll be.

CONSUMER CREDIT PROTECTION ACT

The Truth in Lending disclosures originated from the Consumer Credit Protection Act of 1968, which was landmark legislation. For the first time, creditors had to state the cost of borrowing in easy-to-understand language so that the consumer could understand the charges, compare costs, and shop for the best credit deal. Congress has also made various other amendments and new legislation to strengthen consumer rights.[1]

Shopping on credit

Credit is a convenience that allows you to make purchases, large and small, when you don't have the cash available. With it, you charge a meal on your credit card, pay for an appliance on the installment plan, or get a mortgage. Credit can be appealing, since it enables you to enjoy your purchase while you are still paying for it.

Of course, you must pay back what you've borrowed. In addition, credit almost always costs something. Whenever you are considering borrowing or opening a credit account, you should first figure out how much it will cost you and whether you can afford it. Then you should shop for the best terms.

Two regulations can help you compare costs: Truth in Lending requires creditors to disclose basic information about the cost of buying on credit or taking out a loan. Consumer Leasing disclosures enable you to compare the cost and terms of one lease with another and with the cost and terms of buying for cash or on credit. As you look at the cost of credit from different sources, you'll want to pay special attention to two numbers: the finance charge and annual percentage rate (APR).

Understanding the finance charge and annual percentage rate

Truth in Lending requires creditors to tell you—in writing and before you sign any agreement—what the finance charge and APR will be.

The finance charge is the total dollar amount you pay to use credit. It includes interest costs and other fees, such as service charges and some credit-related insurance premiums. The Federal Reserve Board's "Consumer Handbook to Credit Protection Laws" explains it this way:

> Suppose you borrow $100 for one year, and the interest is $10. If there is a service charge of $1, the finance charge will be $11.
>
> The annual percentage rate is the percentage cost (or relative cost) of credit on a yearly basis, which is your key to comparing costs, regardless of the amount of credit or how long you have to repay it.
>
> Again, suppose you borrow $100 for one year and pay a finance charge of $10. If you can keep the entire $100 for the whole year and then repay $110 at year's end, you are paying an APR of 10 percent. But if you repay the $100 and finance charge (a total of $110) in twelve equal monthly installments, you don't really get to use $100 for the whole year. In fact, you get to use less and less of that $100 each month. In this case, the $10 finance charge amounts to an APR of 18 percent.
>
> All . . . creditors must state the cost of their credit in terms of the finance charge and the APR. Federal law does not set interest rates or other credit charges, but it does require creditors to reveal these figures so you can compare credit costs.[2]

The Federal Reserve Board's consumer booklet contains another helpful example, which illustrates how easy it is to underestimate the difference in dollars that different terms can make:

> Suppose you're buying a $7,500 car. You put $1,500 down and need to borrow $6,000. Compare the three credit arrangements in the chart [below]. How do these choices compare? The answer depends partly on what you need. The lowest cost loan, in terms of total finance charges and total of payments, is available from Creditor A.

	APR	Length of Loan	Monthly Payment	Total Finance Charge	Total of Payments
Creditor A	14%	3 years	$205.07	$1,382.52	$7,382.52
Creditor B	14%	4 years	$163.96	$1,870.08	$7,870.08
Creditor C	15%	4 years	$166.98	$2,015.04	$8,015.04

> If you were looking for lower monthly payments, you could get them by repaying the loan over a longer period. However, you would have to pay more in total costs. A loan from Creditor B, also at a 14 percent APR, but for four years, will add about $488 to your finance charge.
>
> If that four-year loan were available only from Creditor C, the APR of 15 percent would add another $145 or so to your finance charges, compared with Creditor B.
>
> Other factors, such as the size of the down payment, will also make a difference. Be sure to look at all the loan terms before you choose.[3]

What about open-end credit?

Open-end credit generally allows consumers to continue borrowing, generally until they reach their prearranged borrowing limit. Examples include bank and department store credit cards, home equity lines of credit, and check-overdraft accounts. Truth in Lending requires that open-end creditors tell you the terms of the credit plan so that you can shop and compare costs.

The APR, figured on a yearly basis, is only the periodic rate that you will be charged on an open-end plan. (For instance, a creditor that charges 12 percent interest each month would quote you an APR of 18 percent.) Annual membership fees, transaction charges, and points are not included in the APR. Be sure to consider both the APR and these other fees when comparing credit plans.

What else must creditors reveal?

They must indicate when finance charges begin on your account, so you know how much time you have to pay your bill before a finance charge is added. Creditors may give you a 25-day grace period, for example, to pay your purchase balance in full before you must pay a finance charge.

Creditors must also reveal the method they use to figure the balance on which you pay a finance charge; the interest rate they charge is applied to this balance to compute the finance charge. Creditors use a number of different methods to arrive at the balance. Since they can significantly affect your finance charge, consider them carefully.

Leasing costs and terms

Leasing has become a popular alternative to buying in some situations. For instance, businesspeople sometimes need to relocate to another city for a year-long assignment. They might consider leasing, rather than buying, furniture for the apartment where they'll live such a short time.

The Consumer Lending Act is designed to protect those who enter into a consumer lease. This is defined as a contract between a lessor (property owner) and lessee (property user) for the use of personal property primarily for personal, family, or household purposes for a period of more than four months and with a total contractual obligation of no more than $25,000. That means long-term leases of cars, furniture, and appliances are covered; daily car rentals or apartment leases are not.

This act requires lessors to group together (but separately from other information in the lease documents) certain information on costs and terms. This information provides a snapshot of what you will pay

- At the beginning of the lease—either at lease signing or delivery
- During the lease—that is, the monthly or periodic payments
- In other charges
- In total over the lease term

The disclosures for vehicle leases require lessors to itemize the amount due at lease signing and how that amount will be paid. The disclosures also explain how the monthly payment was determined. The final section of the segregated disclosures includes information on early termination, excess wear and use, mileage limits and excess mileage charges, and any purchase option at the end of the lease, and directs you to other disclosures and lease terms.

What Creditors Look For

As you apply for credit, remember that it is not offered to every consumer. According to the Federal Reserve Board, creditors look for the "three Cs"—capacity, character, and collateral—when deciding whether to extend credit.

- **Capacity.** Can you repay the debt? To determine this, creditors will check your employment and income information, as well as your total expenses.

- **Character.** Will you repay the debt? Creditors will look at your credit history, including the amount of debt you have and whether you pay your bills on time. They also look for signs of stability: the length of time you've lived at your present address and worked for your current employer, for instance.
- **Collateral.** Is the creditor fully protected if you fail to repay? Creditors want to know what could be used to back up or secure your loan. They're also interested in other resources you have to repay debt other than income, such as savings, investments, or property.

Creditors use these three factors in different ways. Many use a statistical credit-scoring system to determine whether you're a good credit risk. Others may rely on their own instincts and experience. Because of this, creditors may reach different conclusions based on the same set of facts. One creditor may determine that you are an acceptable risk, even though another lender has denied you a similar loan.

Information the creditor can't use

The Equal Credit Opportunity Act does not guarantee that you will get credit. It does, however, require creditors to be fair and impartial. The act bars discrimination based on age, gender, marital status, race, color, religion, and national origin. The act also bars discrimination because an applicant receives public income, such as veterans benefits, welfare, or Social Security, or because a person has exercised his or her rights under federal credit laws, such as filing a billing error notice with a creditor. This protection means that a creditor may not use any of these grounds as a reason to (1) discourage a person from applying for a loan; (2) refuse the applicant a loan if he or she qualifies; (3) lend money on terms different from those granted another person with similar income, expenses, credit history, and collateral; or (4) close an existing account.

If you're denied credit

Under the Equal Credit Opportunity Act, you must be notified within 30 days of your completed application whether your loan has been approved or not. If credit is denied, this notice must be in writing, and it must explain the specific reasons that credit was denied or explain the consumers' right to ask for an explanation. You have the same rights if an account you have had is closed.

If you are denied credit, be sure to find out why. Remember, you may have to ask the creditor for this explanation. It may be that the creditor thinks you have requested more money than you can repay on your income. It may be that you have not been employed or lived long enough in the community. You can discuss terms with the creditor and ways to improve your creditworthiness. If you think you have been discriminated against, tell the creditor that you know your rights under the Equal Credit Opportunity Act.

FAIR CREDIT REPORTING ACT

Have you ever applied for a credit card, personal loan, insurance, or job? If so, there are files about you that contain information on where you work and live, how you pay your bills, and whether you've been sued or arrested or have filed for bankruptcy.

Companies that gather and sell this information are called consumer reporting agencies (CRAs). The most common type of CRA is the credit bureau. The information CRAs sell about you to creditors, employers, insurers, and other businesses is called a consumer report. In addition to your employment and payment history, your credit report includes a list of all creditors who have asked for your credit history within the past year and those businesses that have asked for your credit history for employment purposes within the past two years. If applicable, information from the public record, such as bankruptcies, lawsuits, or criminal convictions, is generally included as well.[4] Finally, your report includes an overall credit score, designed to help lenders determine what type of credit risk you are.

The three major U.S. credit reporting bureaus are Equifax, Experian, and TransUnion, and each maintains a separate file on consumers. (Each may have slightly different information on you, so your credit score may be different at each of the main credit reporting agencies.)[5]

The Fair Credit Reporting Act (FCRA), enforced by the Federal Trade Commission, is designed to promote accuracy and ensure the privacy of the information used in consumer reports.[6]

While the FTC is interested in protecting consumer information, you need to play an active role in ensuring your credit report's accuracy. Creditors will review your credit report when you seek to buy insurance or make a major purchase like a house or car. For that reason, it's important to be sure your report is accurate, complete, and current before applying for a major loan.

In addition, periodically reviewing your credit report will help you guard against identity theft, which occurs when someone uses your name, Social Security number, or credit card number to commit fraud. Identity thieves may use this information to open a charge account in your name without your knowledge. When they don't pay the bills, the delinquent account will show up on your credit report.

Fortunately, the FCRA requires each of the nationwide consumer reporting companies—Equifax, Experian, and TransUnion—to provide you with a free copy of your credit report, at your request, once every 12 months. The Federal Trade Commission (FTC), the nation's consumer protection agency, has prepared a brochure, *Your Access to Free Credit Reports*, explaining your rights under the FCRA and how to order a free annual credit report.

Requesting a free credit report

The three nationwide consumer reporting companies, Equifax, Experian, and TransUnion, have set up a central Web site, a toll-free telephone number, and a mailing address through which you can order your free annual report. For your *free* copy, do not contact one of the companies individually; instead, make your request through one of the following channels:

- Visit http://annualcreditreport.com
- Call 877-322-8228
- Mail a completed request form (available at http://ftc.gov/bcp/conline/include/requestformfinal.pdf) to Annual Credit Report Request Service, PO Box 105281, Atlanta, GA 30348-5281

You can request a report from any or all of the three nationwide consumer reporting companies at the same time, or you can order your report from each of the companies one at a time. (Some financial advisors suggest staggering your requests during a 12-month period so you're more likely to catch and resolve errors or suspicious listings quickly.)

Beware of other Web sites offering free credit reports, scores, or monitoring. Such sites often sign you up for a supposedly free service that converts to one you have to pay for after a trial period. Also, be aware that neither annualcreditreport.com nor the nationwide consumer reporting companies will send you an e-mail asking for personal information. If you receive such an e-mail, do not respond; instead, consider forwarding the e-mail to the FTC at spam@uce.gov.

You may be entitled to a free credit report at other times as well. Under federal law, you're authorized to receive a free report if a company takes adverse action against you, such as denying your application for credit, insurance, or employment. You must ask for your report within 60 days of receiving notice of the action. The notice will give you the name, address, and phone number of the consumer reporting company. You may also be eligible to receive a free report if you've been out of work within 60 days; if you're on welfare; or if your report is inaccurate because of fraud, including identity theft.

Otherwise, a consumer reporting company may charge you up to $9.50 for another copy of your report within a 12-month period. To contact the reporting companies directly:

- Equifax: 800-685-1111; www.equifax.com
- Experian: 888-EXPERIAN (888-397-3742); www.experian.com
- TransUnion: 800-888-4213; www.transunion.com

Dealing with errors in your credit report

If you find an error, such as an inaccuracy or incomplete information, on your report, you should notify the consumer reporting company and the information provider (the person, company, or organization that provided the information to the consumer reporting company). Under the FCRA, they are responsible for correcting errors in your report.

First, tell the consumer reporting company, in writing, what information you think is inaccurate. Consumer reporting companies must investigate the items in question—usually within 30 days—unless they consider your dispute frivolous. They also must forward all the relevant data you provide about the inaccuracy to the organization that provided the information. After the information provider receives notice of a dispute from the consumer reporting company, it must investigate, review the relevant information, and report the results back to the consumer reporting company. If the information provider finds the disputed information is inaccurate, it must notify all three nationwide consumer reporting companies so they can correct the information in your file.

When the investigation is complete, the consumer reporting company must give you the written results and a free copy of your report if the dispute results in a change. (This free report does not count as your annual free report.)

If an investigation doesn't resolve your dispute with the consumer reporting company, you can ask that a statement of the dispute be included in your file and in future reports. You also can ask the consumer reporting company to provide your statement to anyone who received a copy of your report in the recent past, though you'll pay a fee for this service. In addition, if you tell the information provider that you dispute an item, a notice of your dispute must be included anytime the information provider reports the item to a consumer reporting company.

FAIR CREDIT BILLING ACT

Have you ever spotted an error on your credit card bill? Perhaps you were charged twice for the same item or billed for an order you returned, or perhaps you weren't credited for a payment you made. Getting such a mistake corrected may be aggravating—but the Fair Credit Billing Act (FCBA) does outline dispute settlement procedures to assist you.[7]

These settlement procedures apply only to disputes about "billing errors," such as unauthorized charges (federal law limits your responsibility for unauthorized charges to $50); charges that list a wrong date or amount; charges for goods and services you that didn't accept or weren't delivered as agreed; payments or credits for returns that haven't been posted; and math errors. You may also dispute a bill if the creditor did not send it to a new current address, as long you sent a change of address, in writing, at least 20 days before the billing period ended, or if you've asked for an explanation for a charge or sent proof of purchase, along with an explanation of a perceived error or request for clarification.

(Because a dispute about the quality of goods and services is not a billing error, the dispute procedures explained below do not apply. However, if you have made an effort to resolve such a dispute with the seller first, you can take the same legal actions against the card issuer as you could against the seller under your state's law, provided the charge was more than $50 and you purchased it within your state or 100 miles of your current billing address. If the seller is also the card issuer, the dollar and distance limitations don't apply.)

If you wish to dispute anything on your bill, you must send your query to the address given by the creditor for "billing inquiries" (which may not be the same as the address to which you send your payments). Be sure to include your account number and an explanation of the billing error, along with any documents that support your position, such as a photocopy (not the original) of a sales slip. The letter must reach the creditor no more than 60 days after the first bill with the error was mailed to you.

So you have proof the creditor received your letter, send it by certified mail with return receipt requested. Keep a copy of your letter and any attachments as well.

While your claims are being investigated, you may withhold payment on the disputed amount and any related charges. However, you must continue making payments on any part of the bill not in question. Also, the disputed amount may be applied against your credit limit, though your account may not be closed or restricted.

In addition, the creditor cannot threaten your credit rating or report you as delinquent, though it can report that you have issued a challenge. The Equal Credit Opportunity Act prohibits creditors from discriminating against credit applicants who make a dispute, in good faith, under the FCBA, so you cannot be turned down for credit simply because you're disputing a bill.

If the creditor determines that you were improperly billed, it must explain to you in writing what corrections will be made to your account. It must also remove all charges (such as finance charges or late fees) to the item or service related to the error. If the creditor determines you owe a portion of the disputed amount, it must provide a written explanation. You may ask for copies of documents validating its decision.

If the creditor decides the bill is correct, the creditor must tell you that promptly, in writing. It must explain how much you owe and why and, if you request them, provide copies of supporting documents. If you disagree with the decision, you must contact the creditor within 10 days to say you refuse to pay the disputed amount. The creditor may begin collection procedures; however, if the creditor reports you as delinquent to a credit bureau, it must explain that you don't think you owe the money, and it must let you know who gets these reports.

If a creditor does not follow the settlement procedures, it may not collect the disputed amount or any related finance charges, up to $50, even if the bill is eventually determined to be correct.

Other Billing Rights

According to the Federal Trade Commission, a business that offers open-end credit must also

- Give you a written notice when you open a new account—and periodically thereafter—explaining your right to dispute billing errors.
- Send you a statement for each billing period in which you owe—or they owe you—more than one dollar.
- Send your bill at least 14 days before the payment is due if you have a period when you can pay the bill without incurring additional charges.
- Credit all payments to your account on the date they're received, unless no extra charges would result if they failed to do so. (They may, however, set a reasonable time by which a payment must be received to be credited that same day.)
- Promptly credit or refund overpayments and other amounts owed to your account.

What I Hope You'll Never Need— Bankruptcy Information

While dealing with errors on a credit report can be annoying and time consuming, some consumers face a far more serious problem: They frequently receive calls from collectors demanding payment for debts they know they owe but cannot pay. Seeking relief from what feels like a hopeless financial situation, they wonder, *Could bankruptcy be the answer?*

If the thought of declaring bankruptcy has crossed your mind, I hope you've already begun implementing many of the steps on dealing with debt outlined earlier in this book.

Generally, bankruptcy should be considered only after every other debt-busting option has been explored. While bankruptcy may seem to promise immediate relief, the effects are long-lasting, since this incident will remain on your credit report for 10 years.[8]

In addition, Congress made sweeping changes to the bankruptcy laws in 2005, which can make it more difficult to file. For instance, consumers must now seek credit counseling from a government-approved organization at least six months before filing for bankruptcy. (If you're considering bankruptcy as a last resort, the Federal Trade Commission offers a helpful resource called

"Knee Deep in Debt," available at http://www.ftc.gov/bcp/conline/pubs/credit/kneedeep.shtm.)

There are four different types of bankruptcy designed to meet the different needs and profiles of debtors:

Chapter 7. This type of protection enables individuals to liquidate all debt. A trustee is appointed to take over a person's property, which may be sold to pay creditors. Debtors may be able to keep some personal items and possibly real estate, depending on the law of the state where they live and applicable federal laws. Not everyone qualifies for chapter 7. Those earning less than the median income for a family of their size in their state can automatically file for this form of bankruptcy. Those whose income is greater must file for chapter 13 instead.

Chapter 13. People seeking this type of protection usually are allowed to keep their property, but they must earn wages or have some other source of regular income. They also must agree to pay part of their income to their creditors. The court must approve the repayment plan and budget. A trustee is appointed and will collect the payments, pay the creditors, and make sure the terms of the repayment plan are followed.

Chapter 12. This form is like chapter 13 but is an option only for family farmers and family fishermen.

Chapter 11. Businesses typically file under this type of bankruptcy. They may continue to operate as their creditors and the courts work out a plan to repay their debts. No trustee is appointed unless the judge decides that one is necessary; if a trustee is appointed, the trustee takes control of the business and property.

What is a bankruptcy discharge?

One of the reasons people file bankruptcy is to get a discharge, a court order that releases them from repaying most of their debts. Some debts, such as most taxes, child support, alimony, most student loans, court fines, and criminal restitution, cannot be discharged.

The discharge applies only to debts that arose before bankruptcy was filed. If the judge finds that the person filing received money or property by fraud (for instance, if someone lied on an application to secure a loan), that debt may not be discharged.

It is important that all property and debts are listed in bankruptcy schedules. Otherwise, it is possible the debt will not be discharged. The same is true if the person filing is caught destroying or hiding property, falsifying records, or disobeying a court order.

You can only receive a chapter 7 discharge once every eight years. Other rules may apply if you previously received a discharge in a chapter 13 case. No one can make you pay a debt that has been discharged, but you can voluntarily pay any debt you wish to pay. You do not have to sign a reaffirmation agreement (see below) or any other kind of document to do this.

Some creditors hold a secured claim (for example, the bank that holds the mortgage on your house or the loan company that has a lien on your car). You do not have to pay a secured claim if the debt is discharged, but the creditor can still take the property.

What is a reaffirmation agreement?

Even if a debt can be discharged, a person may wish to promise to pay it. For example, you might work out a plan with the bank to keep your car. To promise to pay that debt, a reaffirmation agreement must be filed with the court. Such agreements are not required by bankruptcy law or by any other law. Reaffirmation agreements must be voluntary; must not place too heavy a burden on you or your family; must be in your best interest; and can be canceled anytime before the court issues your discharge or within 60 days after the agreement is filed with the court, whichever is longer. The agreement will not be legally binding until the court approves it.

If a reaffirmation agreement is in place, however, the debt cannot be discharged and the creditor can take action to recover any property on which it has a lien or mortgage.

Saving for College

When Americans are polled about their top financial concerns, saving for their children's college education is always near the top. And it's no wonder: College expenses have been increasing faster than the rate of inflation for many years—4.1 percent in 2007 alone.[1] Fortunately, several beneficial and tax-advantaged strategies to fund children's education expenses are available. Each method has advantages and disadvantages, and not all are appropriate for every individual. In addition, a few alternatives require legal and professional guidance; therefore, proper counsel should be obtained before any method is implemented. This appendix describes each strategy and discusses some of the implications and tax considerations. It then offers some background and resources on financial aid.

QUALIFIED STATE TUITION PROGRAMS

A section 529 qualified state tuition plan is a tax-advantaged savings tool used to pay for higher education expenses. Each 529 plan is either a savings plan or a pre-paid tuition plan that provides tax incentives for individuals at any income level to plan for future college expenses. (A prepaid tuition plan allows an individual to "buy" future college credits at today's prices. Prepaid tuition plans are generally less flexible than 529 savings plans and are not discussed in this appendix.) At the present time, most of these savings plans are sponsored by individual states, although section 529 does allow private institutions (like colleges) to administer these as well. Currently, all fifty states have at least one type of 529 plan.

A 529 savings plan allows individuals to invest money in a taxed-advantaged savings vehicle to help pay for all or part of future anticipated college costs.

Advantages of a 529 savings plan
- A 529 plan allows any individual, not just the child's parents, to invest funds in a tax-deferred account with a major mutual fund company or brokerage account (as determined by each state).

- Distributions from these accounts are tax free if they are used to pay for qualifying higher education expenses.
- These plans allow for flexibility if the child receives a scholarship, does not attend college, dies, or becomes disabled. Generous provisions exist for transferring the assets to other relatives of the child, or the assets may be withdrawn by the adult. Withdrawals not used for qualifying education costs or that do not meet certain other exceptions may be subject to a 10 percent penalty (on the earnings).
- A critical element of 529 plans is that although current year contributions are considered a gift to the child, the parent (or other contributor) maintains ownership over the assets at all times.
- An individual may contribute up to $12,000 per year per child without filing a gift tax return. A unique provision of 529 plan contributions allows the contributor to roll the maximum annual contribution for five years into one $60,000 gift. This reduces the donor's estate immediately (which helps the donor) and puts more assets in a tax-free account more quickly (which helps the student). A gift of this size to a 529 plan requires that an informational gift tax return be filed in the year of the gift. Contributors do *not* need to file an informational return in the four succeeding years unless they make additional gifts during those years.

Disadvantages of a 529 savings plan

- Many state plans do not allow the donor to choose the investment allocation, which is based on the age of the intended student and automatically adjusts as they grow older.
- Distributions for nonqualifying education expenses are taxed to the individual (the donor, not the child) at ordinary income rates and a 10 percent penalty does apply.
- Code section 529 provides great flexibility, but each state may place certain limitations on the maintenance of the accounts in that state. You can learn more at the Web site http://www.savingforcollege.com.
- Contributions to 529 plans are considered gifts; therefore, contributions may be limited or may require a gift tax return.

COVERDELL EDUCATION SAVINGS ACCOUNTS

A Coverdell Education Savings Account (ESA) is a trust or custodial account created or organized in the United States for the sole purpose of paying the qualified education expenses of the designated beneficiary of the account. When the account is established, the designated beneficiary must be a child under age 18. To be treated as a Coverdell ESA, the account must be designated as a Coverdell ESA when it is established.

Advantages of Coverdell Education Savings Accounts

- Coverdell ESAs allow tax-free distributions for qualifying private primary and secondary school expenses, as well as higher education costs, and, in some cases, the purchase of home computer equipment.
- Assets can be rolled over from one Coverdell ESA to another. The designated beneficiary can be changed, and the beneficiary's interest can be transferred to a spouse or former spouse because of a divorce.
- The Coverdell ESA is generally just as advantageous as a 529 plan from a financial aid perspective because a Coverdell ESA is also considered an asset of the account custodian (usually the parent).
- Because a Coverdell ESA is a self-directed account, the contributor has many investment options.

Disadvantages of Coverdell Education Savings Accounts

- The annual contribution limit is $2,000 per child.
- To be eligible to establish a Coverdell ESA, married taxpayers who file jointly can have a maximum adjusted gross income of $190,000 to $220,000. The maximum adjusted gross income for all other filers is $95,000 to $110,000.
- Contributions are not tax deductible.
- Distributions for nonqualifying education expenses are taxed at ordinary income rates and a 10 percent penalty applies.

CUSTODIAL ACCOUNTS

A custodial account is an arrangement in which a donor transfers property irrevocably to a minor, but rather than giving it outright, transfers it to a custodian (usually the donor parent) who is to use it on behalf of the minor until he or she becomes an adult. This technique allows the shifting of assets to the child and the resulting income tax liability of the investment earnings.

Advantages of custodial accounts

- The assets can be used for any purpose for the child; they are not limited to education. Funds can be used to pay for a honeymoon, start a business, go on a mission trip, or buy a car.
- Income-producing assets can be shifted to the custodial account and result in tax savings on investment earnings, which are taxed to the children.
- An individual is allowed to give $12,000 per year per donee without any gift tax consequences. In addition, the amount gifted to the account is removed from the donor's estate if the parent is not the custodian.

- The custodian of the account has control of the funds until the child reaches the age of majority for his or her state of residence.
- The simplicity of the custodial account allows the donor to begin making contributions early in the child's life.
- A custodial account is an excellent tool for gifting appreciated assets because the donor avoids paying the capital gains tax on the difference between the basis of the property transferred and its fair market value. This tax burden is shifted to the child.

Disadvantages of custodial accounts
- It's an irrevocable gift to that child. Assets cannot to be transferred to other children.
- Control of assets is given up by the donor permanently. There is a potential gift tax liability on transfers to the account for gifts over $12,000. If the donor or spouse is the custodian of the account and the child dies before the age of majority, the property will be included in the custodian's estate.
- Taxes will be due on any gains when sold.
- The "kiddie tax" is imposed on unearned income in excess of $1,700. The kiddie tax rate is equal to the parents' marginal tax bracket. So the income shifting benefit to a child is limited. In other words, if a parent tries to shift a $50,000 CD earning 4 percent to his five-year-old daughter, the $2,000 of income will be taxed at the parent's rate. So there is no income tax benefit in shifting significant assets that produce income.

IRREVOCABLE EDUCATIONAL TRUST

The educational trust is useful for those who may be subject to estate taxes and want to remove assets from their estates, especially assets likely to appreciate further. The maker (or "grantor") of the trust can retain control of how money is used (even after his or her death) by specifying the criteria and conditions for trust disbursements to be made. At the termination of the trust, any funds left after paying educational expenses are distributed to the trust beneficiaries at intervals specified by the grantor.

Advantages of irrevocable educational trusts
- The grantor saves money on income tax, since income is taxed to the trust or to its beneficiaries.
- Trust assets and resulting appreciation are removed from the grantor's estate unless the grantor dies within three years of transfer.
- The provisions of the trust ensure that funds will be used for educational purposes.

- Distributions of the trust corpus can be made at any age designated by the grantor.
- Professional investment and property management is available for the creator if a professional or corporate trustee is named.

Disadvantages of irrevocable educational trusts
- Setting up a trust can be complex and costly (in terms of legal fees, annual tax returns, etc.).
- The assets placed in the trust will not revert back to the grantor.
- There is a potential gift tax liability on transfers greater than $12,000 per donee.

Loans and Scholarships

Most colleges, along with federal and state governments, provide loans, grants, scholarships, and work-study programs to help students pay for their education. Some are need based; others are merit based. This aid often provides at least partial financial assistance for students entering college. Parents should make every effort to determine whether their children qualify for merit or other types of scholarship assistance. A college's financial aid office is the best source for financial aid for that particular institution. Generally, most of the funds received in the form of scholarships are income tax free to the recipient. Most states also have special grants (which do not have to be repaid) for fields of study in which there may be an occupational shortage in that state.

As a last resort, student loans are another source of paying for a college education. As we discussed in the chapters on debt, student loans are "good debt"—or at least not as bad of a form of debt as credit cards or other consumer loans. Theoretically, the loans are an investment to increase the future earning potential of the student. Unfortunately, loans are often overused as a source of easy money for students. Then, upon graduating, young adults may feel overwhelmed at starting off with such debt. Incredibly I find that with many students and parents who take out loans, the student earns no income during the school year and very little during the summer. I prefer to see students earn some income by working and use loans as a final, fill-in-the-gap option. Many students would be wise—from both a maturity and financial standpoint—to work a year after high school to save more money before going to college.

If your business situation permits, consider putting your children on the corporate payroll. Office work such as filing, cleaning, and phone answering could be compensated by a salary or wage. This would be a means of moving taxable income out of the corporation and allowing your children to begin accumulating funds for college. Experience in a business environment will also be helpful in securing future part-time college employment, if required.

If your student will soon be enrolling in college, you should also explore state- or government-subsidized loans. Interest rates are usually lower than current market rates, and loan repayments do not usually begin until several months after the borrower has graduated from college.

It is never too early to start exploring sources of college loans and scholarships. Since each state has its own state-assisted loan program, contact the admissions and/or financial aid office of all potential colleges your children are considering attending.

In general the types of aid available fall into two categories:

1. Individual College or University Awards
   ➤ Regular scholarships (usually based upon need)
   ➤ Honors and merit scholarships
   ➤ Loans financed by the school
   ➤ Other scholarships available through local individuals, businesses, civic organizations, churches, foundations, etc.

2. Federal and State Programs
   ➤ Basic educational opportunity grants
   ➤ National direct student loan program
   ➤ Guaranteed student loan program
   ➤ Veteran administration awards
   ➤ State scholarships
   ➤ State and federal occupational grants

One organization that assists parents and students in obtaining and guaranteeing loans is the Higher Education Assistance Foundation. Each state has its own separate Higher Education Assistance Foundation; you can do an Internet search to find the contact information for the organization in your state.[2]

To find out more about U.S. federal student aid programs, see http://www .fafsa.ed.gov.

The Bigger Picture

A great deal of thought and prayer should be given to deciding how to fund education. The above recommendations focus primarily on economic benefits. Just as much thought (if not more) should be given to the total needs of the child at the time he or she enters college. For example, having the child help earn his or her way through school as a means of teaching responsibility may be a more important consideration than transferring assets for educational needs. Loaning the child a large sum interest-free may encourage responsibility, but it could also have the opposite effect by putting more responsibility on the child than he or she is spiritually or emotionally able to handle.

Equally important is the temperament of the person funding the education. A risk is always involved in lending assets to a minor, so the one providing the funds should be comfortable with the arrangement.

Finally, remember the primary objective is to provide your children with an education that they will appreciate and use for a lifetime. Potential tax savings or other economic opportunities should not interfere with this very important investment.

Recommended Resources and Ministries

This book is meant to be a comprehensive resource on the most pertinent financial topics you and your family will face. As you read various chapters, you may identify some issues of particular concern for your family. For that reason, I want to recommend some other resources you may wish to consult when you face financial decisions or questions.

There's always a danger in providing such a list; namely, that some worthwhile resources or ministries will be left out, either inadvertently or because of space restrictions. Nonetheless, if you want to delve deeper into a specific area of finances, these books and Web sites are excellent places to begin.

Church Giving

Becoming a Firstfruits Congregation: A Stewardship Guide for Church Leaders
Robert C. Heerspink

(Grand Rapids, MI: Faith Alive Christian Resources/CRC Publications, 1996)

Pastors and congregants often dread discussing the topic of stewardship. Robert Heerspink, pastor of Faith Community Christian Reformed Church in Wyoming, Michigan, has written a book to help other church leaders discover how to motivate their church to catch a stewardship vision. It outlines the biblical principles of stewardship, offers practical steps to help church leaders teach on stewardship effectively, and includes study guides at the end of each chapter.

Appendices include suggested sermon topics and worship songs, as well as sample budgets and giving cards.

Debt

Financial Peace University

Dave Ramsey

(The Lampo Group, Inc., http://www.daveramsey.com)

A 13-week CD/DVD series with workbooks designed to teach families to get out of debt and stay out of debt. Classes are facilitated in churches, military bases, workplaces, and community centers. A home study version is also available.

Help! I'm Drowning in Debt

Ron Blue

(Colorado Springs: Focus on the Family, 2007)

A concise, easy-to-use guide to help you become debt free and secure your family's financial future.

Estate Planning

Splitting Heirs: Giving Money and Things to Your Children without Ruining Their Lives

Ron Blue with Jeremy White

(Chicago: Northfield Publishing, 2004)

You can't take it with you. But the wealth you leave behind could be the best thing that ever happened to your loved ones—or the worst. Learn why it's so important to make these decisions now—instead of forcing your heirs to do it later. With practical tips, tools, charts, and worksheets, this book will help you (1) leave an inheritance that helps your heirs without spoiling them, (2) communicate your desires the right way, at the right time, (3) navigate the legal and tax issues surrounding your estate, and (4) decide which charities or ministries to support.

Financial Planning

Biblical Financial Study

Crown Financial Ministries

(Gainesville, GA: Crown Financial Ministries, 2003)

One of Crown's most widely used resources, this adult small-group study helps answer financial questions and difficulties from a biblical perspective. This study is designed to train individuals over a 10-week period to use money in eternally significant ways that benefit not only the individual but also his or her church. Topics include planning financial goals, getting out of debt, budgeting, saving, spending, earning money, investing, giving, and organizing one's estate. It is accompanied by a practical application workbook with CD and by Howard Dayton's book *Your Money Counts: The Biblical Guide to Earning, Spending, Saving, Investing, Giving, and Getting Out of Debt*. A leader's training kit is also available.

Biblical Financial Study Special Edition
Crown Financial Ministries
> (Gainesville, GA: Crown Financial Ministries, 2002)

> This six-week special edition of *Crown's Biblical Financial Study* is designed for those entrusted with wealth or significant income. For most people, making financial decisions can be compared to taking a trip by car. Just as road signs provide direction to motorists, most people's cash and credit limitations serve as clear boundaries. However, for those with wealth, the boundaries are not so clearly defined. Making financial decisions is more like navigating a ship on the open seas in the 1800s, when there were no roads to follow or signs warning of danger ahead. With fewer financial limitations to serve as boundaries, those with significant resources face unusual challenges. This book, however, unpacks the Bible's specific instructions intended to help the wealthy navigate the ocean of almost unlimited choices. A leader's guide is available.

The New Master Your Money: A Step-by-Step Plan for Gaining and Enjoying Financial Freedom (Fourth Edition)
Ron Blue with Jeremy White
> (Chicago: Moody Publishers, 2004)

> The original edition of this book was the first—and most popular—book I've written. Designed to apply to general audiences interested in wise financial planning from a biblical perspective, it covers the basics of budgeting, debt management, and investing. It offers practical help to those desiring to practice faithful money management.

Giving

Fields of Gold
Andy Stanley
> (Carol Stream, IL: Tyndale House Publishers, 2004)

> This inspirational book focuses on the principle of sowing and reaping. If we sow fear, what will be our harvest? And conversely, if we sow faith, what will we grow? This book moves the reader beyond fear and guilt about money and into confidence, security, and excitement. Andy Stanley unpacks our irrational fears about money, helping us discover

that generous giving is actually an invitation for our heavenly Father to get involved in our finances and resupply us with enough seed to sow generously throughout our lifetime.

The Genius of Generosity
Chip Ingram
(Atlanta: Living on the Edge)

What's so genius about generosity? After all, our world celebrates people who have learned how to have it all . . . not those who have learned to give it all away! This five-CD series explores where and why the Bible teaches that the wisest thing we can do with our resources is to learn to invest them in Christ's Kingdom; and why becoming a generous person is the smartest way to prepare for an eternal future. Message titles are "What's the Genius of Generosity?" "Generosity: The Gateway to Intimacy with God," "Why God Prospers Generous People," "How Does God Measure Generosity?" and "How to Become Winsomely Generous All the Days of Your Life."

Treasure Principle Bible Study: Unlocking the Secret of Joyful Giving
Brian Smith and Randy Alcorn
(Sisters, OR: Multnomah Publishers, 2005)

This companion Bible study to *The Treasure Principle: Unlocking the Secret of Joyful Giving* probes deeper into the big message of Alcorn's best-selling small book, which challenges and motivates readers to embrace material freedom and radical generosity. Whether as individuals or in small groups, this study guide will help Christians to explore and embrace the joy of giving. Managing God's earthly trust will become a new delight as readers learn to use it for eternal purposes. This resource includes practical quotations from the book, thought-provoking study questions, group discussion starters, and short Scripture passages for meditation and memorization. Alternatively, consider a shorter study of this book using Generous Giving's "Study Questions for *The Treasure Principle*, by Randy Alcorn," available at http://www.generousgiving.org.

Kids and Money

Your Kids Can Master Their Money: Fun Ways to Help Them Learn How
Ron and Judy Blue and Jeremy White
(Carol Stream, IL: Tyndale House Publishers, 2006)

Are you ever frustrated by your kids begging you for the latest gizmo advertised on TV? Or the way they seem to squander their allowance and then ask for more money? Since a kid's perspective on money often doesn't go beyond what it can buy now in the candy aisle of the store, such demands are natural—but not unalterable. This book will help you teach your kids how creatively using and saving money can be fun and rewarding. It includes detailed instructions on over 50 activities parents can do with their children (ages 4 to 22) to teach them how to be generous givers, savvy savers, sharp shoppers, prudent planners, intelligent investors, and willing workers. Investing in your children's outlook on finances now will result in great payoffs when they're adults.

Retirement

Your Money after the Big 5-0: Wealth for the Second Half of Life
Larry Burkett and Ron Blue with Jeremy White
    (Nashville, TN: Broadman and Holman Publishers, 2007)

Targeting the retired or nearly retired age bracket, we worked with teacher Larry Burkett to produce a book outlining biblical principles for financial planning. Each chapter contains several easy-to-follow points, ending with questions for practical application answered with illustrative examples from the authors' own lives. The focus of the book is not on budgets or getting out of debt but on common issues among the baby boomers: long-term care, pension selection, Social Security, insurance, retirement, giving to adult children, and widowhood. (Originally published as *The Burkett and Blue Definitive Guide to Securing Wealth to Last: Money Essentials for the Second Half of Life*.)

Financial Software

Crown Money Map Financial Software
Howard Dayton
    (Gainesville, GA: Crown Financial Ministries, 2006)

This software package is designed to help you simplify your family's money management and achieve specific financial goals such as creating reasonable spending and saving plans, eliminating debt, creating a balanced budget, and managing investment. The automated Envelope Budgeting System will enable you to spend only what you earn. Using the software, you can also generate reports to help you stay on top of your finances.

Other Resources

Crown Financial Ministries

PO Box 100
Gainesville, GA 30503-0100
770-534-1000
800-722-1976
http://www.crown.org

This ministry offers biblically based financial advice and study materials for all ages on the biblical approach to stewardship and money management.

Focus on the Family

(Street address not required)
Colorado Springs, CO 80995
719-531-5181
800-A-FAMILY (800-232-6459)
http://www.focusonthefamily.com

Focus on the Family offers some articles on family finance in the "Life Challenges" section of their Web site: http://www.family.org/lifechallenges/ManagingMoney/.

Generous Giving

820 Broad St., Suite 300
Chattanooga, TN 37402
http://www.generousgiving.org

This privately funded ministry offers practical advice and helpful resources to people of all income levels who long to experience the joy of giving and live a lifestyle of generosity.

Kingdom Advisors

5605 Glenridge Dr., Suite 550
Atlanta, GA 30342
Phone: 404-497-7680
Fax: 404-497-7685
http://www.kingdomadvisors.org

This organization equips Christian financial advisors to communicate biblical wisdom to their clients, apply professional principles in their practices, and live out their faith in the marketplace. Kingdom Advisors may also be able to provide you with the names and contact information of Christian financial advisors in your area. Visit their Web site for more information.

Notes

Introduction

1. See http://www.campuscrusade.com/fourlawseng.htm.

Chapter 1

1. *Merriam-Webster's Collegiate Dictionary*, 11th ed., s.v. "steward."

2. The four principles of stewardship are adapted from Blue, *The New Master Your Money* (Chicago: Moody, 2004) 22–26.

3. *The American Heritage Dictionary of the English Language*, 4th ed., s.v. "worldview," http://dictionary.reference.com/browse/worldview (accessed December 27, 2006).

4. Barna's research was based on, in my opinion, a very accurate description of a biblical worldview: First, absolute moral truth exists, and this truth is defined in the Bible. This truth leads to six specific religious views: (1) Jesus lived a sinless life; (2) God is the all-knowing and all-powerful creator of the universe; (3) salvation is a gift of God and cannot be earned; (4) Satan is real; (5) Christians have a responsibility to share their faith in Christ; and (6) the Bible is accurate in all its teachings. These results come from a national random survey of 2,033 adults from September through November 2003. The Barna Research Group, "A Biblical Worldview Has a Radical Effect on a Person's Life," The Barna Update, The Barna Group, Ltd., December 1, 2003, http://www.barna.org/FlexPage.aspx?Page=BarnaUpdate&BarnaUpdateID=154.

5. Recognizing that Christians as a whole are not impacting the culture or living eternally significant lives, Focus on the Family has founded the Truth Project. This DVD-based small group curriculum includes 12 one-hour lessons designed to help Christians understand the relevance, importance, and practicalities of living out the Christian worldview in daily life.

Chapter 2

1. W. Ian Thomas, *The Mystery of Godliness* (Grand Rapids, MI: Zondervan, 1964).

Chapter 3

1. Spend less than you earn (see Proverbs 13:11); avoid the use of debt (see Proverbs 22:7); build liquidity (see Proverbs 6:6-8); set long-term goals (see Philippians 3:14); and believe that God owns it all (Psalm 24:1).

Chapter 4

1. Oseola McCarty, *Simple Wisdom for Rich Living* (Atlanta: Longstreet Press, 1996), 17.

2. Robert T. Grimm Jr., ed., *Notable American Philanthropists: Biographies of Giving and Volunteering* (Westport, CT: Greenwood Press, 2002), 205.

3. McCarty, *Simple Wisdom*, 75.

Chapter 5

1. Mark H. McCormack, *What They Don't Teach You at Harvard Business School: Notes from a Street-Smart Executive* (New York: Bantam Books, 1984).

2. Thomas Lifson, "GWB: HBS MBA," *American Thinker*, February 3, 2004, http://www.americanthinker.com/2004/02/gwb_hbs_mba.html (accessed January 13, 2007).

Chapter 6

1. Peter F. Drucker, *The Effective Executive: The Definitive Guide to Getting the Right Things Done* (New York: HarperCollins, 2002), 143.

Chapter 7

1. The inflation myths are adapted from Ron Blue, *The New Master Your Money* (Chicago: Moody, 2004), 55–59.

Chapter 9

1. "Priced out of the American Dream," *Marketplace*, American Public Media, November 13, 2007, http://marketplace.publicradio.org/display/web/2007/11/13/consumed4_mmr_2 (accessed November 17, 2007).

2. American Fact Finder, U.S. Census Bureau, http://factfinder.census.gov/servlet/GRTTable?_bm=y&-geo_id=01000US&-_box_head_nbr=R2304&-ds_name=ACS_2006_EST_G00_&-format=US-30.

3. Federal Reserve Board, "Household Debt Service and Financial Obligations Ratios," second quarter, 2007, http://www.federalreserve.gov/Releases/housedebt/ (accessed November 13, 2007).

4. Survey by the American Enterprise Institute for Public Policy Research, *Investment News*, February 26, 2007, 1.

Chapter 10

1. Much of this chapter has been adapted from chapters 2 and 5 of Ron Blue, *Taming the Money Monster* (Colorado Springs: Focus on the Family, 1993), which outlines five steps to getting out of debt.

Chapter 11

1. Jeremy Simon, "Credit Card Debt a Big Concern on College Campuses," CreditCards.com, August 25, 2006, http://www.creditcards.com/ credit-card-debt-a-big-concern-on-college-campuses.php (accessed December 10, 2007).

2. Much of this chapter has been adapted from Ron Blue, *Taming the Money Monster* (Colorado Springs: Focus on the Family, 1993), chapters 8–13.

3. Ben Woolsey, "Credit Card Industry Facts and Personal Debt Statistics," CreditCards.com, http://www.creditcards.com/statistics/credit-card-industry-facts-and-personal-debt-statistics.php (accessed January 27, 2007).

4. These questions are based on an article by Sian Ballen that appeared in *Money* magazine, April 1987, 96.

5. Russell D. Crosson, *Money and Your Marriage* (Atlanta: Ronald Blue and Company, 1989), 152.

Chapter 12

1. Some material in this chapter has been adapted from Ron Blue, *Taming the Money Monster* (Colorado Springs: Focus on the Family, 1993), chapter 7.

Chapter 13

1. U.S. Department of Housing and Urban Development, Office of Policy Development and Research, "U.S. Housing Market Conditions," data for second quarter 2006, August 2006, 3.

2. Much of this chapter has been adapted from Ron Blue, *Taming the Money Monster* (Colorado Springs: Focus on the Family, 1993), chapter 12.

3. "How Much Can You Afford to Spend on a Home?" Freddie Mac, http://www .freddiemac.com/corporate/buyown/english/preparing/right_for_you/afford.html.

Chapter 14

1. Much of this chapter has been adapted from Ron Blue, *Taming the Money Monster* (Colorado Springs: Focus on the Family, 1993), chapter 11.

2. PRNewsWire, "R. C. Polk & Co. Reports U.S. Motor Vehicle Longevity Increases in 2006," news release, February 15, 2007.

3. *Money*, March 1989, 165–66.

4. Jonathan Welsh, "When a $38,000 Car Costs $44,000," *Wall Street Journal*, May 22, 2007.

5. This illustration ignores the tax impact of both interest deductions and interest income, but the point is still valid. It also assumes your interest would be compounded annually; if compounded more often, as is usually the case, your earnings would be a lot higher—e.g., $566,143 with quarterly compounding.

Chapter 15

1. Department of Labor, Bureau of Labor Statistics, "Report on the American Workforce 2001," 87.

Chapter 16

1. "Change Your Students' Lives," Money Savvy Generation, http://www.msgen.com/assembled/change_lives.html.

2. Jean Chatzky, "7 Rules for Raising Money Smart Kids," *Money*, September 2004, http://money.cnn.com/magazines/moneymag/moneymag_archive/2004/09/01/379419/index.htm.

3. National Council on Economic Education, "Survey of the States: Economic and Personal Finance Education in Our Nation's Schools in 2004: A Report Card," March 2005, 3.

4. Harvard University, Kaiser Family Foundation, and National Public Radio, "Sex Education in America: Principals Survey," January 2004.

5. National Consumers League, "Teens and Finances," *NCL Bulletin*, March/April 2002, http://www.nclnet.org/finances/teens.htm.

6. Each activity includes teaching goals, method, and age range (plus a "sweet spot" pinpointing the very best age-group for that activity). A step-by-step description shows you what to do, and the background information tells you why the activity is important.

Chapter 17

1. For more detailed information on estate planning, see Ron Blue, *Splitting Heirs: Giving Money and Things to Your Children without Ruining Their Lives* (Chicago: Northfield Publishing, 2004).

Chapter 18

1. Pruneville.com, "Jokes and Quotes," http://www.pruneville.com/jokesandquotes/cleanjokes/ (accessed May 22, 2007).

2. Because of the high infant mortality at that time, these life expectancy figures were misleading. Many people who reached adulthood lived beyond age 65.

3. Sara Arber, "Midlife Attitudes to Retirement: International Comparison of Changes," Economic & Social Research Council, as reported in J. Ginn and S. Arber, "Longer Working: Imposition or Opportunity?" *Quality in Ageing* 6, no. 2 (2005): 26–35.

4. Peter Drucker, quoted in Bob Buford, *Halftime*, (Grand Rapids, MI: Zondervan Publishing House, 1994), 13.

5. United Nations, "United Nations Releases New Statistics on Population Ageing," press release, February 28, 2002, http://www.un.org/swaa2002/.

6. *The American Heritage Dictionary of the English Language*, 4th ed., s.v. "retirement," http://dictionary.reference.com/browse/retirement (accessed December 4, 2007).

7. Billy Graham, interview by Katie Couric, *Today*, msnbc.com, June 23, 2005 (transcript accessed at http://www.msnbc.msn.com/id/8326362, May 25, 2007).

8. "One in 10 Americans Fear Losing Their Job," *Investment News*, February 26, 2007, 1.

Chapter 19

1. Kathie O'Donnell, "Advisers Bolster Retirement Income, Report Shows," *Investment News*, April 9, 2007, 16.

2. Social Security Administration, "Social Security: A Brief History," October 2007, http://www.ssa.gov/history/pdf/2007historybooklet.pdf.

3. Institute of Certified Public Accountants, *Understanding Social Security Reform: The Issues and Alternatives*, 2nd ed., March 2005.

4. Stephen Ohlemacher, "First Boomer Applies for Social Security," Associated Press, October 16, 2007.

5. Jo Anne B. Barnhart, "Your Social Security Statement."

6. Social Security Administration, http://www.socialsecurity.gov/cola/colafacts2008 .htm. The amounts shown are the statutory amounts for 2008. These amounts are indexed to inflation and change annually.

7. Social Security Administration, http://www.socialsecurity.gov/OACT/COLA/ examplemax.html.

8. For more details on applying for benefits, see http://www.ssa.gov/retirement.html.

9. Ellen Schultz, "Workers May Get Help on Pension Choices," *The Wall Street Journal*, October 17, 2002.

10. Philip Cooley, Carl Hubbard, and Daniel Walz, "Retirement Savings: Choosing a Withdrawal Rate That Is Sustainable," *AAII Journal*, February 1998.

11. American Funds, "The 'New Math' of the Distribution Phase," *Insights* newsletter, Winter 2007.

12. The amount per month was obtained by averaging three leading insurance companies' annuity quotations. The amount varies by each insurer.

Chapter 20

1. John Havens and Paul Schervish, "Why the $41 Trillion Wealth Transfer Estimate is Still Valid: A Review of Challenges and Questions," *The Journal of Gift Planning* 7, no. 1 (2003): 11–15, 47–50.

2. Much of this chapter has been adapted from Ron Blue, *Splitting Heirs: Giving Money and Things to Your Children without Ruining Their Lives* (Chicago: Northfield Publishing, 2004).

3. Randy Alcorn, *The Treasure Principle: Discovering the Secret of Joyful Giving* (Sisters, OR: Multnomah Publishers, 2001), 19.

4. Ibid., 42, 45.

Chapter 21

1. For more on estate planning, see Ron Blue, *Splitting Heirs: Giving Money and Things to Your Children without Ruining Their Lives* (Chicago: Northfield Publishing, 2004).

Chapter 22

1. Andrew J. Donohue, "Testimony Concerning Improving Disclosure for Workers Investing for Retirement," testimony before the Ways and Means Committee, U.S. House of Representatives, October 30, 2007, http://www.sec.gov/news/testimony/2007/ts103007ajd.htm.

2. Luisa Kroll and Allison Fass, eds., "The World's Billionaires," *Forbes*, March 8, 2007, http://www.forbes.com/2007/03/07/billionaires-worlds-richest_07billionaires_cz_lk_af_0308billie_land.html.

Chapter 23

1. I introduced this concept in my first book, which has been revised and updated: Ron Blue, *The New Master Your Money* (Chicago: Moody, 2004).

Chapter 24

1. Some of the material on tax types and rates first appeared in Ron Blue, *The New Master Your Money* (Chicago: Moody, 2004).

2. Internal Revenue Service, "No Change in the Interest Rates for the Third Quarter of 2007," June 21, 2007, http://www.irs.gov/newsroom/article/0,,id=171504,00.html (accessed July 26, 2007).

Chapter 25

1. Some of the material in this chapter has been adapted from Ron Blue, *The New Master Your Money* (Chicago: Moody, 2004).

2. Internal Revenue Service, "Tax Stats at a Glance," July 9, 2007, http://www.irs.gov/taxstats/article/0,,id=102886,00.html.

Chapter 26

1. Randy Alcorn, *The Treasure Principle: Discovering the Secret of Successful Giving* (Sisters, OR: Multnomah Publishers, 2001), 18.

2. For more details, see *Generous Living: Finding Contentment through Giving* (Grand Rapids: Zondervan, 1997).

Chapter 27

1. Empty Tomb, Inc., "Giving Research," http://www.emptytomb.org/fig1_05.html.

2. Based on giving recorded in 2006. Holly Hall, "Donations to Charity Rose by 2.7% Last Year, Study Finds," *The Chronicle of Philanthropy*, June 18, 2006, http://philanthropy.com/free/update/2006/06/2006061901.htm.

3. Spending amount for 2004. "Self-Actualization Drives Spending on Entertainment and Recreation," Unity Marketing, January 1, 2005, http://www.unitymarketingonline.com/reports2/entertainment/pr2.html.

4. 1999 figures adjusted for annual inflation of 3 percent. Kirby Pringle, "Fast Food: How America (and the World) Traded Genteel Dining for a Good, Fast Meal," *Champaign-Urbana News Gazette*, January 23, 2000.

5. Based on $85 billion spent in 2000 and adjusted for 3 percent annual inflation

and growth. "Accessories Keep Lawn and Garden Industry Growing," *Champaign-Urbana News Gazette*, August 19, 2001.

6. Dotsey Welliver and Minnette Northcutt, eds., *Mission Handbook 2004–2006* (Wheaton, IL: Evangelism and Missions Informational Service, 2004), 13.

7. Empty Tomb, Inc., "Lifestyle Spending Table," http://www.emptytomb.org/lifestylestat.html.

8. For more information on creating your own giving plan, see *Generous Living: Finding Contentment through Giving* (Grand Rapids: Zondervan, 2007).

9. Robert T. Grimm, Jr., ed., *Notable American Philanthropists: Biographies of Giving and Volunteering* (Westport, CT: Greenwood Press, 2002), 73–76.

10. Kenneth N. Dayton, *The Stages of Giving* (Washington, DC: Independent Sector, 1999).

Chapter 28

1. Some of the material in this chapter first appeared in Ron Blue, *The New Master Your Money* (Chicago: Moody, 2004).

2. Salary calculated for 2007. Jared Jost, "Mom Deserves a Raise in 2007," Salary.com, May 2, 2007, http://salary.com/sitesearch/layoutscripts/sisl_display.asp?filename=&path=/destinationsearch/par639_body.html.

3. Per review of 15 insurance companies from their quoted premiums in November 2006.

Chapter 29

1. Gary Mogel, "Dump the Bum—and Collect the Insurance," *Investment News*, May 14, 2007.

2. John Hancock Insurance Company, 2006 Long Term Care Survey.

3. 2007 Cost of Care Survey, commissioned by Genworth Financial.

4. Ibid.

5. National Association of Insurance Commissioners, *A Shopper's Guide to Long-Term Care Insurance* (1999).

Chapter 30

1. Pruneville.com, "Jokes and Quotes," http://www.pruneville.com/jokesandquotes/cleanjokes/ (accessed May 22, 2007).

2. Charles Paikert, "Money Battles Top List of Fights," *Investment News*, February 12, 2007, 6.

3. The following information is adapted from Ron Blue and Judy Blue, *Money Talks and So Can We* (Grand Rapids: Zondervan, 1999), 28, 34–35.

Chapter 31

1. Ron Blue and Judy Blue, *Money Talks and So Can We* (Grand Rapids: Zondervan, 1999).

2. U.S. Department of Labor, Women's Bureau, "Quick Stats 2006," http://www.dol.gov/wb/stats/main.htm.

Chapter 32

1. U.S. Census Bureau, "Children's Living Arrangements and Characteristics: March 2002," June 2003.

2. Glenn T. Stanton, "Do Half of All American Marriages Really End in Divorce?" Focus on the Family, http://www.family.org/socialissues/A000000596.cfm (accessed 26 July 2007).

3. See http://www.peacemaker.net.

Chapter 33

1. I wrote *The New Master Your Money* (Chicago: Moody, 2004) to help people prepare their own financial plan without incurring the costs of a professional advisor.

2. William Backus and Marie Chapian, *Telling Yourself the Truth* (Bloomington, MN: Bethany House, 2000).

3. Neil T. Anderson, *The Bondage Breaker* (Eugene, OR: Harvest House, 2006).

Appendix A

1. The Federal Reserve Board, "Consumer Handbook to Credit Protection Laws," August 16, 2007, http://www.federalreserve.gov/pubs/consumerhdbk/.

2. Ibid.

3. Ibid.

4. The consumer reporting companies can keep most accurate negative information on a report for seven years. Information about a lawsuit or an unpaid judgment against you can be reported for seven years or until the statute of limitations runs out, whichever is longer. Bankruptcy information remains for 10 years. No time limit exists for reporting information about criminal convictions.

5. For more information on credit reports, see http://www.ftc.gov/bcp/menus/consumer/credit/reports.shtm.

6. The complete text of the Fair Credit Reporting Act is available at the Federal Trade Commission's Web site; see http://www.ftc.gov/os/statutes/fcradoc.pdf.

7. For more details, see www3.ftc.gov/bcp/conline/pubs/credit/feb.shtm.

8. Much of this information has been adapted from U.S. Trustee Program, "Bankruptcy Information Sheet," Department of Justice, June 15, 2007, http://www.usdoj.gov/ust/eo/ust_org/bky-info/.

Appendix B

1. Kim Clark, "College Tuition Prices Continue to Rise," *U.S. News and World Report*, October 23, 2007, http://www.usnews.com/articles/business/paying-for-college/2007/10/23/college-tuition-prices-continue-to-rise.html.

2. Much of this material on saving for college has been adapted from "Education Funding," (Atlanta: Ronald Blue & Co., 2002–2006). Used with permission.

Glossary

After-tax return: The yield of an investment after taxes have been taken out.

Annual percentage rate (APR): The cost of credit expressed as a yearly rate.

Annuity (immediate): An individual pays an insurance company a specified amount of money in exchange for a promise that the insurer will, at some time in the future, begin to make a series of periodic payments to the individual for as long as he or she lives, or for some other specified period of time.

Appreciation: An increase in fair market value.

Assets: Everything a person owns, including cash, investments, property, or vehicles. It includes physical, tangible assets (land, jewelry, cash) as well as intangible assets (patents, mineral rights, intellectual property).

Automated teller machines (ATMs): Electronic terminals located on bank premises or elsewhere, through which customers of financial institutions may make deposits, withdrawals, or other transactions as they would through a bank teller.

Balance sheet: A condensed financial statement showing the amount and nature of an individual's assets and liabilities at a given time. A "snapshot" of what a person owns and what he or she owes. Sometimes referred to as net worth statement.

Bankruptcy: The inability, for whatever reason, to repay debt.

Basis: The price paid for an asset. Used to figure capital gains tax.

Beneficiary: One who is designated to receive a benefit; for example, the person who would receive the proceeds of a life insurance settlement.

Bid and asked: The "bid" is the highest price a buyer is willing to pay for a security at a given time; the "asked" is the lowest price a seller will take at that time. Stocks are usually purchased at "bid" and sold at "asked."

Bond: A promise of a corporation, municipality, government, church, etc., to pay interest at a stated rate and repay the face value of the bond. It is a loan from you to the organization that will mature at a specified date.

Borrow: To enter into a contract to rent money for a specified time period, with the rent being called *interest*.

Budget: A plan or guideline for spending.

Capital gain or loss: Profit or loss from the sale of a capital asset such as real estate, stock, commercial property, land, or equipment. Any capital asset held at least one year is classified as long term and receives favorable income tax treatment.

Capital needs: In personal financial planning, the amount of capital (assets or cash) needed in a lump sum to enable one to meet income needs and expenses should death or disability occur.

Cash flow: The process of money coming in from various sources (income) and being spent on various uses (expenses). A cash flow statement is a look at both the income and the expenses over any period of time, usually for at least a month and/or a year.

Cash received in primary mortgage refinance: An owner can receive cash from a mortgage lender by refinancing the primary mortgage. This increases the outstanding balance of the loan.

Cash surrender value: The actual value of your whole or permanent life insurance policy. It is the amount of cash you would receive if you voluntarily terminated your whole life policy before it matured. It is also the amount that can be borrowed from your policy while still keeping the policy in force. This value can be found in the policy contract. It may be more than the contract value, as it can be increased by dividends and interest on dividends that are left to accumulate (dividend deposits). (Term life insurance has no cash value.)

Collateral: Property, such as stocks, bonds, or a car, offered to support a loan and then subject to seizure if you default.

Common stock: Securities that represent an ownership interest in a corporation. These generally have dividend and appreciation potential.

Cosigner: Another person who signs your loan and assumes equal responsibility for it.

Cost per thousand: Refers to the cost of each thousand dollars of life insurance protection.

Credit: The right to borrow. More formally, the right granted by a creditor to pay in the future to buy or borrow in the present; a deduction from an amount that had been owed.

Credit bureau: An agency that keeps your credit record; also called a consumer reporting agency (CRA).

Credit card: Any card used periodically or repeatedly to borrow money or buy goods or services on credit.

Credit history: The record of how you've borrowed and repaid debts.

Credit insurance: Health, life, accident, or disruption of income insurance designed to pay the outstanding balance on a debt.

Creditor: A person or business from whom you borrow or to whom you owe money.

Credit-scoring system: A statistical system used to rate credit applicants according to various characteristics relevant to creditworthiness.

Creditworthiness: Past, present, and future ability to repay debts.

Current assets: Those assets that can be converted easily into cash or sold in a short period of time. Examples include stocks, certificates of deposit, cash value of life insurance, and money market funds. Also known as liquid assets.

Debit card (EFT card): A plastic card, which looks similar to a credit card, that consumers may use at an ATM or to make purchases, withdrawals, or other types of electronic fund transfers from their checking or savings account.

Debt: A sum owed to someone else, either a financial or personal obligation; a state of owing.

Debtor: One who owes money.

Diversification: Spreading money among different types of investments.

Dividends: The payment designated by a corporation to be distributed proportionally among outstanding shares of stock. Corporations usually declare dividends from their profits, and the amount is in relation to the amount of the profit.

Dividend election: The method you choose to receive your dividends; most often refers to life insurance. You may elect that dividends be paid in cash or accumulate at interest, or you may request they be used to reduce premiums or buy paid-up additions.

Dollar cost averaging: A method of purchasing securities at regular intervals with a fixed amount of money, regardless of the prevailing prices of the securities. Payments buy more shares when the price is low and fewer shares when it rises. Because of the fluctuations of the market, this method enables an investor who consistently buys in both good and bad times to be able to improve his potential for a gain when he sells. It is an effective method for a single investor to strategically invest his money.

Effective rate: The amount of each dollar earned that goes to pay taxes. The ratio of total taxes paid to gross income.

Face value: The amount an insurance company promises to pay upon the death of the insured.

Fiduciary: One who acts for another in financial matters.

Fixed: Refers to an asset in which principal does not grow in value. You will never get back more or less than you invested if held to maturity. For instance, certificates of deposit, cash value, and bonds are assets that are fixed yield in nature.

Home equity line of credit: A revolving home equity loan that allows the property owner to borrow against the equity up to a fixed limit set by the lender without reapplying for a loan.

Home equity loan: A loan against the value of your residence. It is usually a second mortgage.

Home equity lump-sum loan: A home equity loan that is paid out in a one-time lump-sum amount and must be repaid over a set period of time.

Individual retirement account (IRA): A retirement provision established by law that allows an individual to set aside funds for future retirement and receive tax advantages. A traditional IRA provides an immediate tax deduction and grows tax deferred. Taxes are paid when the traditional IRA is distributed. A Roth IRA provides no immediate tax deduction, but all the growth in value is tax free. There are no taxes when the Roth IRA is distributed.

Inflation: An increase in the volume of money and credit relative to available goods resulting in a substantial and continuing rise in the general price level.

Inflationary spiral: A continuous rise in prices that is sustained by the interaction of usage increases and cost increases.

Investment: The use of money for the purpose of making more money: to gain income, increase capital, save taxes, or a combination of the three.

Land contract: An arrangement for the sale of real estate whereby the buyer may use and occupy land, but in which no deed is given by (and no title passes from) the seller until all of the sale price has been paid.

Lessee: The party to whom an item is leased. In a consumer lease, the lessee is you, the consumer. The lessee is required to make payments and to meet other obligations specified in the lease agreement.

Lessor: The person or organization who leases, offers to lease, or arranges for the lease of an item.

Leverage: The use of a small amount of equity or assets to control or purchase an asset worth substantially more. The value to the investor is that you receive appreciation on the total worth of the asset, not just your equity. Although leveraging increases your earnings potential, you are at risk for the amount leveraged (the loan). For example, if you put $10,000 down and borrow $70,000 to buy an $80,000 home, you have leveraged.

Liabilities: All the claims against you; the obligations you owe. Some may be current (owed within the year), such as credit card loans; others may be long term, such as a home mortgage.

Liquidity (liquid): Describes assets that can readily be converted to cash at their current fair market value.

Long-term assets (nonliquid): Those assets that cannot be converted easily to cash or sold or consumed in a short period of time. Examples include home, real estate, and land assets.

Margin: In this book, margin means the cash sources less the cash uses, or the amount you have left to spend as you desire after all living expenses, mandatory commitments, and taxes are met. (Margin has another meaning in the context of stock brokerage accounts: borrowing funds from your broker to purchase financial securities.)

Marginal rate: The tax bracket percentage from which your income tax is calculated. For example, in the case of a person in the 28 percent tax bracket, 28 cents of each additional dollar earned would go to the government in taxes.

Marital deduction: In calculating estate tax, a deduction allowed by law against the estate of the first spouse to die. The amount of the qualifying property or deduction is the entire estate of the first to die.

Money market fund: A mutual fund that invests in money market instruments such as treasury bills, U.S. government agency issues, commercial bank certificates of deposit, and commercial paper. The interest rate on a money market fund fluctuates with the prime interest rate.

Mortgage: Usually refers to the balance of the loan on a home. The amount of money borrowed to purchase a home. It refers to all forms of debt for which the property is pledged as security for payment of the debt. It includes such debt instruments as deeds of trust, trust deeds, mortgage bonds, home equity lines of credit, home equity lump-sum loans, and vendors' liens. Also included as a mortgage or similar debt are contracts to purchase, land contracts, and lease-purchase agreements where the title to the property remains with the seller until the agreed-upon payments have been made by the buyer.

> **Adjustable rate mortgage:** The interest rate on the loan could be changed during the life of the mortgage, altering the amount of the payments required.

> **Adjustable term mortgage:** The amount of the payment stays constant, but the number of payments required to pay off the loan can change over time as interest rates change.

> **Balloon mortgage:** Only part or none of the principal is paid off during the term of the loan (which commonly is about five years). At the end of the term, the principal is paid off in one lump sum, refinanced with a new loan, or extended by renewal of the loan.

Fixed payment, self-amortizing mortgage: Payments do not change during the term of the loan, with the principal payments sufficient to pay off the loan completely within the stated term.

Graduated payment mortgage: Allows monthly payments to change during the term of the mortgage by means other than a change in interest rate. This mortgage begins with lower payments that rise later in the life of the mortgage.

Reverse mortgage: Involves borrowing against home equity for retirement or income; sometimes doesn't need to be repaid until after the owner's death.

Nonliquid: Investments not easily converted to cash at their current fair market value. Examples include land, home, or private business.

Overdraft checking: A line of credit that allows you to write checks or draw funds for more than your actual balance, with an interest charge on the overdraft.

Point of sale (POS): A method by which consumers can pay for purchases by having their deposit accounts debited electronically without the use of checks.

Points and origination fees: Fees paid to the lender for a loan. One point equals one percent of the loan amount. Points are usually paid in cash at closing. In some cases, the money needed to pay points can be borrowed, but doing so will increase the loan amount and the total costs. An origination fee covers the lender's work in preparing your mortgage loan.

Preferred stock: Similar to common stock. Generally less dividend and appreciation potential but receives a higher priority or preference over common stock in dividend payments or in the event of liquidation.

Premium: The payment an insurance policy holder agrees to make for coverage.

Present value: The value of a sum of money to be received in the future in today's dollars, taking into account either interest rates, inflation, or both. (Example: $10,000 received ten years from now may have a present value of $6,830.)

Prime rate: The interest rate charged by large U.S. money center commercial banks to their best business borrowers.

Principal: The amount owed on a loan. It may be the original amount of loan or the remaining balance. It does not include any interest.

Private mortgage insurance: Insurance that a lender generally requires a home buyer to obtain if the down payment made by the home buyer is below a certain percentage (often 20 percent down payment for conventional loans). Mortgage insurance is a promise to pay the lender's losses in case the borrower fails to keep up the required mortgage payments and defaults on the loan.

Property insurance: Refers to insurance on a home's structure and/or its contents (such as furniture, appliances, or clothing) and usually contains some liability insurance.

Prospectus: A circular that describes securities or investments being offered for sale to the public.

Purchasing power: The ability of a dollar to buy a product or service. As prices increase, purchasing power decreases. Today's dollar will not buy as much today as it would have in 1980.

Real estate tax: A tax charged to the owner of land and buildings. Usually assessed by a state or local government, it includes special assessments, school taxes, county taxes, and other property taxes.

Savings: Money or other financial assets not spent and reserved for future use. Savings include savings in a bank, other financial institution, or a money market account. Other investments that may be considered as savings include stocks, bonds, properties, certificates of deposit, and IRA or employer retirement accounts. Savings usually exclude the primary residence, its furnishings, and vehicles.

Small business retirement or Keogh plan: Similar to an IRA but designed for small businesses or self-employed individuals. These small business plans (sometimes called SIMPLE Profit Sharing, or Simplified Employee Pension [SEP] plans) permit the setting aside of a specified part of current earnings for use as a retirement fund in the future. The amount deductible for these plans may be much greater than the limits on IRAs or 401(k)s. *Keogh plan* is an outdated term after tax acts in the 1980s effectively eliminated their use. Some people still refer to retirement plans for the self-employed as Keogh plans.

Surety: Guaranteeing the payment of someone else's debt; to become a cosigner on a debt.

Time-sharing: A form of ownership in which a single property is owned by multiple owners. Each is entitled to occupy that unit for a limited period of time each year. The number of years of ownership may vary depending on the terms of the contract. Participants in time-sharing ownership usually, but not always, receive a deed of ownership. The property is usually a condominium or townhouse structure.

Unified credit: A credit, established by law, applied to tentative federal estate taxes owed upon the death of an individual (like an exemption amount for estate taxes).

Variable: Refers to assets, such as an annuity invested in stocks or mutual funds, that have the potential to grow, primarily through appreciation. These may be sold for more or less than you invested.

Will: The directions of a testator (the person who makes a will) regarding the final disposition of his or her estate.

Withholding: Refers to the amount of tax withheld from a paycheck.

Withholding allowances: Used by an employer to calculate the amount withheld monthly from your check for federal and state taxes.

Yield: Dividends or interest paid by a company, expressed as a percentage of the current selling price.

Index

Index

Index

RON BLUE has been a financial planner and consultant for more than 30 years. Early in his career he founded an Indianapolis-based CPA firm that is now one of the 50 largest such firms in the United States. He then spent two years with Leadership Dynamics, developing and teaching biblically based leadership and management seminars in the United States and Africa. In 1979, he founded a financial planning firm because of his conviction that Christians would handle their personal finances better if they were counseled objectively with the highest technical expertise from a biblical perspective. That firm grew to manage over $2 billion in assets for more than 5,000 clients nationwide.

Ron retired from his financial planning firm in 2003 in order to serve as president of Kingdom Advisors. This organization is an international effort to equip and motivate Christian financial professionals to serve the body of Christ by implementing biblical wisdom in their lives and practices, resulting in financial freedom and increased giving to Christian ministries around the world.

Ron is the author of 16 books on personal finances from a biblical perspective, including the best seller *Master Your Money*. This book, which was first published in 1986, was revised and released as *The New Master Your Money* in 2004. His other books include *Generous Living*, *Wealth to Last* (coauthored with Larry Burkett), *Splitting Heirs*, and *Your Kids Can Master Their Money*.

JEREMY WHITE has been a certified public accountant since 1988, with financial experience in public accounting and industry. He is a partner with Blythe, White & Associates, a certified public accounting and consulting firm in Paducah, Kentucky. He is a Kingdom Advisors Qualified Member. Jeremy has coauthored or assisted with four other best-selling financial books. These include *The New Master Your Money*, *Splitting Heirs*, and *Your Kids Can Master Their Money*. Along with Ron Blue and the late Larry Burkett, he also wrote *Your Money after the Big 5-0*.

Faced with Financial Pressures? Want to be a More Faithful Steward? Need Help with a Financial Decision?

The Ron Blue Library
BIBLICAL FINANCIAL DECISION MAKING

Extensive resources from Ron Blue for biblical financial
decision-making are available **free** on the Internet

- Watch Q & A video of Ron as he answers 80 frequently asked questions about your finances
- Learn what the Bible says about faithful stewardship
- Discover the key principles for successful biblical decision making
- Explore the financial areas that you need the most help with now
- Access biblically-based advice developed over 40 years in the financial services industry

www.RonBlueLibrary.org

Your core values

are not one size fits all

Now you can find an advisor who shares your faith

KINGDOM ⦚ ADVISORS
Qualified

visit www.kingdomadvisors.org to start your search

Kingdom Advisors, led by Ron Blue and founded by Larry Burkett, exists to engage, equip, and empower Christian financial advisors to communicate biblical wisdom to their clients, apply professional principles in their practices, and live out their faith in their marketplace for Kingdom impact.

Your financial advisor's worldview is of critical importance because ultimately, all good financial advice has its root in biblical wisdom. Only a Christian financial advisor equipped to deliver biblical wisdom can offer advice and counsel consistent with the values and priorities of a believer. Our goal at Kingdom Advisors is two-fold: both to equip Christian financial advisors to integrate that biblical wisdom with their financial counsel and to provide you with confidence in your search for such a financial advisor by designating those advisors who have met our criteria and completed our training as Qualified Kingdom Advisors[TM].

Kingdom Advisors | 5605 Glenridge Dr., Suite 450 | Atlanta, GA 30342
404-497-7680 | www.kingdomadvisors.org

FOCUS ON THE FAMILY®

Welcome to the family!

Whether you purchased this book, borrowed it, or received it as a gift, we're glad you're reading it. It's just one of the many helpful, encouraging, and biblically based resources produced by Focus on the Family for people in all stages of life.

Focus began in 1977 with the vision of one man, Dr. James Dobson, a licensed psychologist and author of numerous best-selling books on marriage, parenting, and family. Alarmed by the societal, political, and economic pressures that were threatening the existence of the American family, Dr. Dobson founded Focus on the Family with one employee and a once-a-week radio broadcast aired on 36 stations.

Now an international organization reaching millions of people daily, Focus on the Family is dedicated to preserving values and strengthening and encouraging families through the life-changing message of Jesus Christ.

Focus on the Family Magazines

These faith-building, character-developing publications address the interests, issues, concerns, and challenges faced by every member of your family from preschool through the senior years.

Focus on the Family
Citizen®
U.S. news issues

Focus on the Family
Clubhouse Jr.™
Ages 4 to 8

Focus on the Family
Clubhouse™
Ages 8 to 12

Breakaway®
Teen guys

Brio®
Teen girls
12 to 16

Brio & Beyond®
Teen girls
16 to 19

Plugged In®
Reviews movies,
music, TV

FOR MORE INFORMATION

Online:
Log on to www.family.org
In Canada, log on to
www.focusonthefamily.ca

Phone:
Call toll free: (800) A-FAMILY
In Canada, call toll free:
(800) 661-9800

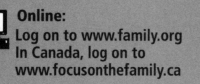